Tolley's
Tax Guide
1996–97

Tolley's Tax Guide 1996–97

by

Arnold Homer

Rita Burrows

Tolley Publishing Company Ltd

un A United News & Media publication

Fourteenth Edition May 1996

Published by
Tolley Publishing Co Ltd
Tolley House
2 Addiscombe Road
Croydon Surrey CR9 5AF
England
0181-686 9141

Typeset by
Letterpart Limited, Reigate, Surrey

Printed in Great Britain
by The Bath Press, Somerset

About this book

This is the fourteenth edition of Tolley's Tax Guide, which is one of the range of Tolley annuals on all aspects of taxation.

The Guide is updated annually to incorporate the changes in law and practice that occur each year, and is published soon after the passing of the Finance Act.

The aim of the book is to provide clear and concise guidance on all aspects of taxation that are likely to be encountered from day-to-day by businessmen, practitioners, professional advisers and private individuals. It deals with income tax (including self-assessment), corporation tax, capital gains tax, inheritance tax, value added tax and stamp duty. There are also chapters on council tax and business rates, national insurance contributions and statutory sick pay and statutory maternity pay. There are numerous examples to demonstrate how the provisions work in practice.

The authors use their wide practical experience to bring out the tax planning opportunities in the various areas, and these are highlighted as 'tax points' at the end of most chapters.

This edition gives the position for the tax year 1996/97 and covers all legislation, statements of practice and other relevant sources of information including the provisions of the Finance Act 1996. Where appropriate the position for earlier years is also explained.

All chapters have been revised to incorporate the many changes that have taken place since the previous edition, and there is a useful summary of the main changes.

The general law, as opposed to tax law, is not always the same in Scotland and in Northern Ireland as in England and Wales. Except where otherwise stated, this book is concerned with the law in England and Wales. Readers in Scotland and Northern Ireland should take advice if in any doubt.

The assistance of professional colleagues is gratefully acknowledged by the authors.

Any comments on this publication will as always be welcomed by the publishers.

TOLLEY PUBLISHING COMPANY LIMITED

Stop Press

A number of references are made in the text to the date of Royal Assent to the Finance Act 1996. The Act received Royal Assent on 29 April 1996.

Contents

CONTENTS

Employment

CONTENTS

Pensions

Trades, professions and vocations

CONTENTS

CONTENTS

CONTENTS

Tax and the family

CONTENTS

Miscellaneous

CONTENTS

Abbreviations

ACT	=	Advance Corporation Tax
BES	=	Business Expansion Scheme
Board	=	Board of Inland Revenue
CAA 1990	=	Capital Allowances Act 1990
CGT	=	Capital Gains Tax
CTT	=	Capital Transfer Tax
DSS	=	Department of Social Security
EEA	=	European Economic Area
EIS	=	Enterprise Investment Scheme
ESC	=	Extra-Statutory Concession
EU	=	European Union
FA	=	Finance Act
FID	=	Foreign Income Dividend
FYA	=	First-year allowance
F(No 2)A	=	Finance (No 2) Act
IHT	=	Inheritance Tax
IHTA 1984	=	Inheritance Tax Act 1984
MIRAS	=	Mortgage Interest Relief At Source
NIC	=	National Insurance Contributions
PAYE	=	Pay As You Earn
PEP	=	Personal Equity Plan
PPC	=	Personal Pension Contribution
RAP	=	Retirement Annuity Premium
reg	=	regulation
s	=	section
SA 1891	=	Stamp Act 1891
SAYE	=	Save As You Earn
Sch	=	Schedule
SI	=	Statutory Instrument
SMP	=	Statutory Maternity Pay
SP	=	Inland Revenue Statement of Practice
SSCBA 1992	=	Social Security Contributions and Benefits Act 1992
SSP	=	Statutory Sick Pay
TA 1988	=	Income and Corporation Taxes Act 1988
TCGA 1992	=	Taxation of Chargeable Gains Act 1992
TMA 1970	=	Taxes Management Act 1970
VAT	=	Value Added Tax
VATA 1994	=	Value Added Tax Act 1994
VCT	=	Venture Capital Trust
WDA	=	Writing-down Allowance
WDV	=	Written-down Value

Table of rates and allowances

(Correct to 1 May 1996)

Income and corporation tax

Personal allowances (see chapter 2 for full description)

	1994/95 £	1995/96 £	1996/97 £
Personal allowance—under 65	3,445	3,525	3,765
—65 to 74	4,200	4,630	4,910
—75 and over	4,370	4,800	5,090
Married couple's allowance—under 65	1,720*	1,720*	1,790*
—65 to 74	2,665*	2,995*	3,115*
—75 and over	2,705*	3,035*	3,155*
Income limit for age-related allowances	14,200	14,600	15,200
Additional personal allowance for single parents etc.	1,720*	1,720*	1,790*
Widow's bereavement allowance	1,720*	1,720*	1,790*
Blind person's allowance	1,200	1,200	1,250

* These allowances attract tax relief at only 20% for 1994/95 and 15% for 1995/96 and 1996/97.

Income tax rates on taxable income (see chapter 2)

Rate	1994/95 Band £	Tax £	1995/96 Band £	Tax £	1996/97 Band £	Tax £
Lower (20%)	0–3,000	600	0–3,200	640	0–3,900	780
Basic (*)	3,001–23,700	5,175	3,201–24,300	5,275	3,901–25,500	5,184
Higher (40%)	Over 23,700		Over 24,300		Over 25,500	

* The basic rate is 25% for 1994/95 and 1995/96 and 24% for 1996/97.

See page 16 for the rate of tax on savings income (before 1996/97, dividend income).

Car benefit scale rates (see chapter 10)

1994/95 and subsequent years

The taxable benefit is 35% of the list price of the car plus certain accessories, or 35% of £80,000 if lower. The benefit is reduced by one-third where business mileage is at least 2,500 and by two-thirds where business mileage is at least 18,000. The resulting figure is further reduced by one-third for cars at least four years old at the end of the tax year. There are special rules for 'classic cars' and for contributions by the employee. See chapter 10 for the full details.

Car fuel scale rates (see chapter 10)

1994/95

	Petrol £	Fuel benefit £	Diesel £
(a) with a cylinder capacity of:			
up to 1,400 cc	640		580
1,401 cc to 2,000 cc	810		580
2,001 cc or more	1,200		750
(b) without a cylinder capacity		1,200	

1995/96

	Petrol £	Fuel benefit £	Diesel £
(a) with a cylinder capacity of:			
up to 1,400 cc	670		605
1,401 cc to 2,000 cc	850		605
2,001 cc or more	1,260		780
(b) without a cylinder capacity		1,260	

1996/97

	Petrol £	Fuel benefit £	Diesel £
(a) with a cylinder capacity of:			
up to 1,400 cc	710		640
1,401 cc to 2,000 cc	890		640
2,001 cc or more	1,320		820
(b) without a cylinder capacity		1,320	

Fixed profit car scheme (FPCS) (see chapter 10)

1994/95

cc	First 4,000 business miles	Additional business miles
Up to 1,000	27p	15p
1,001 to 1,500	33p	19p
1,501 to 2,000	41p	23p
Over 2,000	56p	31p

1995/96

cc	First 4,000 business miles	Additional business miles
Up to 1,000	27p	15p
1,001 to 1,500	34p	19p
1,501 to 2,000	43p	23p
Over 2,000	60p	32p

1996/97

cc	First 4,000 business miles	Additional business miles
Up to 1,000	27p	16p
1,001 to 1,500	34p	19p
1,501 to 2,000	43p	23p
Over 2,000	61p	33p

Official rate of interest—beneficial loans (see chapter 10)

From 6 February 1996	7.25% p.a.
From 6 October 1995 to 5 February 1996	7.75% p.a.
From 6 November 1994 to 5 October 1995	8% p.a.
From 6 January 1994 to 5 November 1994	7.5% p.a.
From 6 March 1993 to 5 January 1994	7.75% p.a.
From 6 January 1993 to 5 March 1993	8.25% p.a.
From 6 December 1992 to 5 January 1993	9% p.a.
From 6 November 1992 to 5 December 1992	9.75% p.a.
From 6 June 1992 to 5 November 1992	10.5% p.a.
From 6 March 1992 to 5 June 1992	10.75% p.a.
From 6 October 1991 to 5 March 1992	11.25% p.a.
From 6 August 1991 to 5 October 1991	11.75% p.a.
From 6 July 1991 to 5 August 1991	12.25% p.a.
From 6 May 1991 to 5 July 1991	12.75% p.a.
From 6 April 1991 to 5 May 1991	13.5% p.a.
From 6 March 1991 to 5 April 1991	14.5% p.a.
From 6 November 1990 to 5 March 1991	15.5% p.a.
From 6 November 1989 to 5 November 1990	16.5% p.a.
From 6 July 1989 to 5 November 1989	15.5% p.a.

Interest on overdue tax/Repayment Supplement (pre-self-assessment) (see chapters 2 and 3)

From 6 February 1996	6.25% p.a.
From 6 March 1995 to 5 February 1996	7% p.a.
From 6 October 1994 to 5 March 1995	6.25% p.a.
From 6 January 1994 to 5 October 1994	5.5% p.a.
From 6 March 1993 to 5 January 1994	6.25% p.a.
From 6 December 1992 to 5 March 1993	7% p.a.
From 6 November 1992 to 5 December 1992	7.75% p.a.
From 6 October 1991 to 5 November 1992	9.25% p.a.
From 6 July 1991 to 5 October 1991	10% p.a.
From 6 May 1991 to 5 July 1991	10.75% p.a.
From 6 March 1991 to 5 May 1991	11.5% p.a.
From 6 November 1990 to 5 March 1991	12.25% p.a.
From 6 November 1989 to 5 November 1990	13% p.a.
From 6 July 1989 to 5 November 1989	12.25% p.a.

Interest on overpaid tax for company accounting periods ending after 30 September 1993 (Pay and File) (see chapter 3)

From 6 February 1996	3.25% p.a.
From 6 March 1995 to 5 February 1996	4% p.a.
From 6 October 1994 to 5 March 1995	3.25% p.a.
From 6 January 1994 to 5 October 1994	2.5% p.a.
From 1 October 1993 to 5 January 1994	3.25% p.a.

Corporation tax rates (see chapter 3)

Year beginning	Full rate	Small companies				
		rate	upper profit limit	marginal relief		
				upper profit limit	relief fraction	effective marginal rate
1 April 1991	33%	25%	£250,000	£1,250,000	1/50	35%
1 April 1992	33%	25%	£250,000	£1,250,000	1/50	35%
1 April 1993	33%	25%	£250,000	£1,250,000	1/50	35%
1 April 1994	33%	25%	£300,000	£1,500,000	1/50	35%
1 April 1995	33%	25%	£300,000	£1,500,000	1/50	35%
1 April 1996	33%	24%	£300,000	£1,500,000	9/400	35.25%

Capital gains are included in profits and therefore chargeable at the corporation tax rate applicable.

The advance corporation tax (ACT) rate is 1/4 with effect from 6 April 1994. It was previously 9/31 for 1993/94 and 1/3 for 1988/89 to 1992/93.

Capital gains tax (see chapter 4)

Rate: Gains are chargeable to capital gains tax for individuals at the rates that would apply if they were the top slice of income.

Annual exemption (Individuals)	1991/92	£5,500
	1992/93, 1993/94 and 1994/95	£5,800
	1995/96	£6,000
	1996/97	£6,300

See pages 66, 67 for the positions for personal representatives and trustees.

TABLE OF RATES AND ALLOWANCES

Retail prices index (for indexation allowance)

	1982	1983	1984	1985	1986	1987	1988
January		82.61	86.84	91.20	96.25	100.0	103.3
February		82.97	87.20	91.94	96.60	100.4	103.7
March	79.44	83.12	87.48	92.80	96.73	100.6	104.1
April	81.04	84.28	88.64	94.78	97.67	101.8	105.8
May	81.62	84.64	88.97	95.21	97.85	101.9	106.2
June	81.85	84.84	89.20	95.41	97.79	101.9	106.6
July	81.88	85.30	89.10	95.23	97.52	101.8	106.7
August	81.90	85.68	89.94	95.49	97.82	102.1	107.9
September	81.85	86.06	90.11	95.44	98.30	102.4	108.4
October	82.26	86.36	90.67	95.59	98.45	102.9	109.5
November	82.66	86.67	90.95	95.92	99.29	103.4	110.0
December	82.51	86.89	90.87	96.05	99.62	103.3	110.3

	1989	1990	1991	1992	1993	1994	1995
January	111.0	119.5	130.2	135.6	137.9	141.3	146.0
February	111.8	120.2	130.9	136.3	138.8	142.1	146.9
March	112.3	121.4	131.4	136.7	139.3	142.5	147.5
April	114.3	125.1	133.1	138.8	140.6	144.2	149.0
May	115.0	126.2	133.5	139.3	141.1	144.7	149.6
June	115.4	126.7	134.1	139.3	141.0	144.7	149.8
July	115.5	126.8	133.8	138.8	140.7	144.0	149.1
August	115.8	128.1	134.1	138.9	141.3	144.7	149.9
September	116.6	129.3	134.6	139.4	141.9	145.0	150.6
October	117.5	130.3	135.1	139.9	141.8	145.2	149.8
November	118.5	130.0	135.6	139.7	141.6	145.3	149.8
December	118.8	129.9	135.7	139.2	141.9	146.0	150.7

	1996
January	150.2
February	150.9
March	151.5
April	
May	
June	
July	
August	
September	
October	
November	
December	

The index was re-referenced in January 1987 from 394.5 to 100. The figures above which relate to months before January 1987 have been worked back from the new base and are not, therefore, those produced at the time by the Department of Employment.

See page 49 for how to use the Retail prices index to calculate capital gains tax indexation allowance.

National insurance contribution rates

Employers and employees (see chapter 13)

	6/4/95 -5/4/96	6/4/96 -5/4/97
Lower earnings limit per week (LEL)	£58.00	£61.00
Upper earnings limit per week (UEL)	£440.00	£455.00

Employees pay no contributions if their weekly earnings are below LEL. Otherwise, they are liable as below.

Not contracted out

Employee		
— earnings up to LEL	2.0%	2.0%
— balance of earnings up to UEL	10.0%	10.0%
Employer (% payable on **all** earnings)		
— earnings up to LEL	—	—
— earnings LEL to £109.99 pw (1995/96 LEL to £104.99 pw)	3.0%	3.0%
— earnings £110 to £154.99 pw (1995/96 £109.00 to £149.99 pw)	5.0%	5.0%
— earnings £155.00 to £209.99 pw (1995/96 £150.00 to £204.99 pw)	7.0%	7.0%
— earnings £210.00 pw and above (1995/96 £205.00 pw and above)	10.2%	10.2%

Contracted out

Reduction in 'not contracted out' contributions (but applied only to part of earnings falling between LEL and UEL)		
— employee	1.8%	1.8%
— employer	3.0%	3.0%

Reduced rate for certain married women and widows

% payable on **all** earnings up to UEL providing earnings exceed LEL	3.85%	3.85%

Self-employed (see chapter 24)

	1995/96	1996/97
Class 2 contributions per week	£5.75	£6.05
Class 4 contributions		
rate	7.3%	6.0%
on profits between	£6,640 and £22,880	£6,860 and £23,660

Voluntary (see chapters 13 and 24)

	1995/96	1996/97
Class 3 contributions per week	£5.65	£5.95

TABLE OF RATES AND ALLOWANCES

Employers' national insurance contributions on company cars and fuel (see chapter 13)

1995/96 (annual contributions due)

Cars

10.2% of the taxable car benefit (see page xxi)

Fuel

	Petrol	Diesel
Up to 1,400 cc	£68.34	£61.71
1,401 cc to 2,000 cc	£86.70	£61.71
Over 2,000 cc	£128.52	£79.56

1996/97 (annual contributions due)

Cars

10.2% of the taxable car benefit (see page xxi)

Fuel

	Petrol	Diesel
Up to 1,400 cc	£72.42	£65.28
1,401 cc to 2,000 cc	£90.78	£65.28
Over 2,000 cc	£134.64	£83.64

Statutory sick pay from 6 April 1996 (see chapter 14)

Average weekly earnings   £61.00 and over
SSP flat weekly rate   £54.55

Statutory maternity pay from 6 April 1996 (see chapter 14)

Higher rate   9/10ths of employee's average weekly earnings
Lower rate   £54.55 per week

Main state benefits (see chapter 10)

Taxable (weekly rates)	1994/95 £	1995/96 £	1996/97 £
Retirement pension*			
—single	57.60	58.85	61.15
—wife non-contributor	34.50	35.25	36.60
Old person's pension*			
—higher rate	34.50	35.25	36.60
Widow's benefits			
—widowed mother's allowance	57.60	58.85	61.15
—widow's pension (standard rate)	57.60	58.85	61.15
Incapacity benefit			
short-term (weeks 29 to 52)			
—under pension age	—	52.50	54.55
—adult dependant	—	27.50	28.55
—over pension age	—	56.45	58.65
—adult dependant	—	33.85	35.15
long-term (after 52 weeks)			
—standard rate	—	58.85	61.15
—adult dependant	—	35.25	36.60
Industrial death benefit***			
widow's pension			
—higher permanent rate	57.60	58.85	61.15
—lower permanent rate	17.28	17.66	18.35
Invalidity allowance**			
—higher rate	12.15	12.40	12.90
—middle rate	7.60	7.80	8.10
—lower rate	3.80	3.90	4.05
Invalid care allowance*			
—single	34.50	35.25	36.60
—adult dependant	20.65	21.10	21.90
Unemployment benefit****			
under pension age			
—single	45.45	46.45	48.25
—adult dependant	28.05	28.65	29.75
over pension age			
—single	57.60	58.85	61.15
—adult dependant	34.50	35.25	36.60

Main state benefits (see chapter 10) (continued)

	1994/95	1995/96	1996/97
Non-taxable (weekly rates)			
(excluding income-related benefits)	£	£	£
Child benefit			
—eldest child	10.20	10.40	10.80
—other children	8.25	8.45	8.80
Maternity allowance			
—higher rate	52.50†	52.50	54.55
—lower rate	44.55	45.55	47.35
One parent benefit	6.15	6.30	6.30
Child addition to benefits	11.00	11.05	11.15
Sickness benefit			
under pension age			
—single	43.45	—	—
—adult dependant	26.90	—	—
over pension age			
—single	55.25	—	—
—adult dependant	33.10	—	—
Incapacity benefit (first 28 weeks)			
under pension age			
—single	—	44.40	46.15
—adult dependant	—	27.50	28.55
over pension age			
—single	—	56.45	58.65
—adult dependant	—	33.85	35.15
Disability living allowance			
care component			
—higher rate	45.70	46.70	48.50
—middle rate	30.55	31.20	32.40
—lower rate	12.15	12.40	12.90
mobility component			
—higher rate	31.95	32.65	33.90
—lower rate	12.15	12.40	12.90
Attendance allowance			
—higher rate	45.70	46.70	48.50
—lower rate	30.55	31.20	32.40
Invalidity pension			
—single	57.60	—	—
—adult dependant	34.50	—	—
Severe disablement allowance*			
—single (standard rate)	34.80	35.55	36.95
—adult dependant	20.70	21.15	21.95

 * A taxable age addition of 25p per week is payable to persons aged 80 or over with any one of these benefits.

 ** Taxable only if paid with retirement pension.

 *** For deaths before 11 April 1988 only.

 **** To be replaced from October 1996 by jobseeker's allowance.

 † Higher rate applies to certain women expecting a baby after 15 October 1994.

Value added tax (see chapter 7)

Standard rate (from 1/4/91)   17.5%

	from 30/11/94	from 29/11/95
Registration threshold taxable supplies		
—in last four quarters	More than £46,000	More than £47,000
—in next 30 days	More than £46,000	More than £47,000
Deregistration limits taxable supplies	from 30/11/94	from 29/11/95
—in the next year	£44,000 or less	£45,000 or less

VAT—fuel scale rates—private motoring (from 6/4/96)

Return period	Car's cc	Scale benefit (VAT inclusive) £	Vat @ 17.5% £
Petrol			
Quarterly	to 1,400	177	26.36
	1,401–2,000	222	33.06
	over 2,000	330	49.14
Monthly	to 1,400	59	8.78
	1,401–2,000	74	11.02
	over 2,000	110	16.38
Diesel			
Quarterly	to 2,000	160	23.82
	over 2,000	205	30.53
Monthly	to 2,000	53	7.89
	over 2,000	68	10.12

Inheritance tax (see chapter 5)

Tables of rates (from 18/3/86)

Transfers on and after 18/3/86 and before 17/3/87

Cumulative chargeable transfers (gross)	On death		*Tax payable* Lifetime transfers	
	Rate %	Cumulative total tax	Rate %	Cumulative total tax
0– £71,000	Nil	Nil	Nil	Nil
£71,000– £95,000	30	£7,200	15	£3,600
£95,000–£129,000	35	£19,100	17.5	£9,550
£129,000–£164,000	40	£33,100	20	£16,550
£164,000–£206,000	45	£52,000	22.5	£26,000
£206,000–£257,000	50	£77,500	25	£38,750
£257,000–£317,000	55	£110,500	27.5	£55,250
£317,000 and above	60		30	

Transfers on and after 17/3/87 and before 15/3/88

Cumulative chargeable transfers (gross)	On death		*Tax payable* Lifetime transfers	
	Rate %	Cumulative total tax	Rate %	Cumulative total tax
0– £90,000	Nil	Nil	Nil	Nil
£90,000–£140,000	30	£15,000	15	£7,500
£140,000–£220,000	40	£47,000	20	£23,500
£220,000–£330,000	50	£102,000	25	£51,000
£330,000 and above	60		30	

From 15 March 1988, there has been a single rate of inheritance tax of 40% (20% for lifetime transfers), applicable to the excess of gross cumulative chargeable transfers over a 'nil rate' threshold. The thresholds since that date have been as follows:

Transfers on and after 15/3/88 and before 6/4/89	£110,000
Transfers on and after 6/4/89 and before 6/4/90	£118,000
Transfers on and after 6/4/90 and before 6/4/91	£128,000
Transfers on and after 6/4/91 and before 10/3/92	£140,000
Transfers on and after 10/3/92 and before 6/4/95	£150,000
Transfers on and after 6/4/95 and before 6/4/96	£154,000
Transfers on and after 6/4/96	£200,000

Main Tax Changes

The most far-reaching change as far as income tax and capital gains tax are concerned is the introduction of self-assessment. This is accompanied by a radical change in the way business profits and some other sources of income are calculated for tax purposes. 1996/97 is a transitional year, and thereafter income tax will be charged according to the income of the current rather than the previous tax year. Another important change is the reduction in the rate of tax on virtually all savings income to 20% (except for higher rate taxpayers, who will still be taxed at 40%).

New rules apply for companies in relation to interest paid or received and gains or losses on the disposal of loan stock and other debts.

The main changes are outlined below. The changes are operative from 6 April 1996 unless otherwise stated. General points for each tax are shown separately, and points that relate to specific chapters bear the same chapter heading.

Income tax

For income other than savings income (which includes dividends), the 20% lower rate band is increased to £3,900 and the basic rate band to £21,600, thus raising the threshold for the 40% higher rate tax to £25,500. The basic rate is reduced from 25% to 24%. Savings income is chargeable at 20% to the extent that taxable income does not exceed £25,500 and 40% thereafter. Where tax is deducted from savings income at source, it is deducted at the lower rate. The tax rate for discretionary trusts is reduced from 35% to 34%.

The basic personal allowance has been increased to £3,765, and personal allowances for those over 65 have been increased by £280 for those under 75 and £290 for those over 75. Married couple's allowance for the under 65s and linked allowances (i.e. widow's bereavement allowance and additional personal allowance for single parents etc.) have been increased from £1,720 to £1,790, so that with tax relief at 15% the allowance saves tax in 1996/97 of £268.50. Married couple's allowances for the over 65s have been increased by £120. The income limit for the age allowances has been increased from £14,600 to £15,200. Blind person's relief has been increased from £1,200 to £1,250.

Self-employed people will no longer be entitled to a deduction against their income for half their Class 4 contributions, but the rate of contributions has been reduced from 7.3% to 6% to compensate.

Corporation tax

The small companies rate is reduced from 25% to 24% from 1 April 1996, which increases the marginal rate of tax on income lying in the marginal small companies rate band from 35% to 35.25%.

With effect from 1 April 1996 (subject to transitional provisions), a company will include both interest paid or received and gains or losses on disposing of loan stock and other debts in calculating its income.

Capital gains tax

The annual exemption is increased to £6,300, with corresponding increases in the exemptions for trustees. The age limit for retirement relief has been reduced from 55 to 50 for disposals on or after 28 November 1995.

Inheritance tax

The inheritance tax nil threshold has been increased to £200,000. Business property relief has been increased from 50% to 100% for transfers of unquoted shareholdings of 25% or less (larger holdings already qualifying for relief at the 100% rate).

Value added tax

From 29 November 1995, the VAT registration limit is increased to £47,000, and the deregistration limit to £45,000. Changes have been made to the annual accounting scheme and to the scheme for monthly payments on account by large VAT payers. The anti-avoidance provisions in relation to groups of companies have been strengthened.

Dealing with the Revenue (chapter 9)

From 1996/97, individuals need to retain records relating to their tax affairs in order to complete their tax returns and, if they wish, to self-assess their income tax and capital gains tax. The first self-assessment returns will be sent out in April 1997. Interest will be charged on underpaid tax or allowed on overpaid tax from the payment dates.

Employment — income chargeable and allowable deductions (chapter 10)

From 1996/97, employers must provide employees with copies of year-end forms P11D showing the cash equivalent of benefits provided.

Share options, share incentives, and profit-related pay (chapter 11)

The Chancellor's intention to remove the tax advantages from non-savings related share option schemes has not been put into effect, but for options granted on or after 17 July 1995, their value (together with any non-savings related options already held) must not exceed £30,000. The period that must elapse before options may be exercised under SAYE schemes, and for which shares need to be retained by trustees under profit sharing schemes, is reduced from five years to three years from 29 April 1996.

National insurance contributions — employees and employers (chapter 13)

The various earnings levels have been increased, but there is no change in the rate of contributions for 1996/97. Under the 'NIC holiday' provisions, employers may claim back their contributions if they take on someone who has been out of work for two years or more.

From 6 April 1997 the rate of employers' contributions is to be reduced from 10.2% to 10% and age-related rebates of contributions are to be introduced where employees contract out of the State Earnings Related Pension Scheme.

Statutory sick pay and statutory maternity pay (chapter 14)

There has been a relaxation in the record-keeping rules from 6 April 1996. Provisions may be introduced from April 1997 enabling employers to opt out of the statutory sick pay scheme if they pay equivalent sick pay. For small employers, the recovery rate over and above the amounts paid for statutory maternity pay has been increased from 5% to 5.5%.

Occupational pension schemes (chapter 16)

The pension scheme earnings cap is increased from £78,600 to £82,200.

Providing your own pension (chapter 17)

The limit of net relevant earnings for personal pension contributions is increased from £78,600 to £82,200. Under self-assessment, the treatment of backdating of pension premiums has changed.

Compensation received for mis-sold personal pensions is tax-exempt.

How are business profits charged to tax? (chapter 21)

1996/97 is the transitional year for the changeover from taxing profits according to the previous year's results to the new current year basis. For businesses in existence at 5 April 1994, the taxable profits for 1996/97 are normally arrived at by averaging the profits of the two years to the accounting date in 1996/97. Anti-avoidance provisions apply to prevent the transitional rules being manipulated.

Partnerships (chapter 23)

Under the current year basis provisions, partners are taxed separately on their profits as well as any other partnership income. For partnerships in existence at 5 April 1994, this will not apply until *1997/98*. Partnership tax returns under self-assessment must, however, be sent in from *1996/97*.

Losses of sole traders and partners (chapter 25)

The transitional provisions that apply on the introduction of the current year basis of assessment affect the calculation and treatment of losses and the way in which capital allowances may be included in loss claims.

From 1996/97, where losses are carried back to earlier years, the backdating will only affect the way in which the tax saving is calculated. The tax saving from backdating will reduce the tax bill for the tax year of loss.

Company losses (chapter 26)

New rules apply for dealing with a company's losses in relation to loans.

Husband, wife and children (chapter 33)

Relief is no longer available for maintenance under pre-15 March 1988 court orders to children over the age of 21.

Investing in stocks and shares (chapter 38)

The new treatment of a company's loan stock and other debts means that companies may now have taxable profits and allowable losses on disposals of government stocks and qualifying corporate bonds, since these are brought into account in calculating a company's income. The capital gains exemption still applies for individuals. The accrued income scheme and deep discount/deep gains provisions no longer apply to companies, and the rules for dealing with discounted securities for individuals have been streamlined.

The overseas element (chapter 41)

For companies, foreign securities and other debts are dealt with under the same rules as for UK loans from 1 April 1996, and Schedule D, Case IV no longer applies. For individuals, there are transitional provisions for the changeover to the current year basis for sources of foreign income that have been previously charged on the previous year's income. Special rules have been introduced in relation to the rental income of non-resident landlords.

Charities and charitable trusts (chapter 43)

The amount that can be deducted from pay under the 'Give As You Earn' scheme is increased from £900 to £1,200 per tax year.

Subcontractors in the construction industry (chapter 44)

The rate of tax deduction under the subcontractors' scheme is reduced to 24% from 1 July 1996.

1
Introduction

The tax year 1996/97 (the year running from 6 April 1996 to 5 April 1997) sees the introduction of one of the biggest ever changes in the personal tax system — self-assessment. Although only applicable to individuals at present, self-assessment will be introduced for companies in the near future. It will not actually make much difference as far as companies are concerned, because they already work out their own tax, but this is then followed by a technical 'assessment' by the Revenue. Nor will it make much difference to the majority of individual taxpayers, because out of around 26 million taxpayers, only 9 million get tax returns to fill in and it is those 9 million who will be affected by the change (and even they will be able to get the Revenue to work out the tax for them if they wish). Everyone who pays all their tax through the PAYE system will wonder what all the fuss is about.

One of the problems is that the Government has chosen to introduce two major reforms (and a host of minor ones) at the same time. Not only are we faced with self-assessment, but the long-standing way of charging tax on business profits and some other sources of income has been changed as well. The changes to the law imply that the two are inextricably linked, with the heading 'Changes for facilitating self-assessment' attached to the new rules for working out profits. But there is no reason why the new rules for calculating taxable profits should not have been introduced and the transitional period completed before requiring taxpayers to self-assess — in fact it would have been infinitely preferable. Indeed, it is questionable whether self-assessment is a sensible idea at all given the complexities of the UK system. The Government has recently called for a report on tax simplification, which has just been produced. The main suggestion is a rewrite of the tax law in plain English over a five-year period. That in itself would bring its own problems, with the law then being an uneasy mix of the old and the new. It therefore seems likely that the tax system will be in a somewhat chaotic state for some time to come. As always, the aim of this book is to present the basic rules in as straightforward a way as possible.

Efforts have been made to make the system more 'user-friendly'. We have a 'taxpayer's charter' setting out your rights to fair and even-handed treatment from the tax authorities. On the other hand, you are required to deal with your tax affairs honestly and accurately and to pay your tax on time. So although you are entitled to receive prompt and efficient service from the tax authorities, they have extensive powers to impose sanctions on wrongdoers.

If your main source of income is from your employment, you may not need to know very much about tax, because it will be handled by your employer. Even so, you may have questions about what expenses you can claim, and how various benefits are taxed, what your national insurance and pension position is and so on.

Those who are self-employed are in a much more difficult position, because the rules for working out their profits, and the deductions they can claim are very complicated indeed. And if you run your business through a company your tax affairs are even more complex, since you are both employer and employee. You have to think about PAYE, national insurance, sick pay, maternity pay, VAT, pensions, as well as how much tax you will pay on your profits.

Knowing how the UK system works, what taxes can be charged in particular circumstances, what deductions and allowances are available, and what the tax effect is of alternative courses of action, will help you to use the tax system to your best advantage. The first part of this book contains a brief outline of all the various taxes, including the council tax. The following sections deal with specific subject areas, such as 'Employment', 'Pensions', 'Tax and the family', 'Choosing your investment' and 'Trades, professions and vocations'. Any special tax saving opportunities or possible problems are highlighted in the form of 'Tax points' at the end of each chapter.

Avoiding tax is not the same as illegally evading tax. If you break the law, you can not only be required to pay the tax you should have paid plus interest and penalties, but you could be facing a criminal prosecution. You must therefore make sure that you seek professional advice where appropriate.

For those who need to look at a topic in more depth, there are statutory references to help track down the relevant legislation. The main statutes are the Income and Corporation Taxes Act 1988, the Capital Allowances Act 1990, the Taxation of Chargeable Gains Act 1992, the Value Added Tax Act 1994 and the Inheritance Tax Act 1984. In addition there are annual Finance Acts (sometimes two in a year) which alter some of the existing provisions and bring in new ones, and various statutory instruments. A major source of information is the explanatory booklets put out by the various Government Departments. And there are also published Statements of Practice and Extra-statutory Concessions, which explain the Revenue's views on particular aspects and sometimes allow matters to be treated more sympathetically than the strict letter of the law allows.

Despite the vast array of tax statutes and supplementary material, it is not always clear what the law means. Alternatively, the meaning of the law may not be in doubt, but the facts of the case may be. You may therefore take a different view from the Revenue either on the interpretation of the law, or on the facts, or a mixture of the two.

You may for example produce accounts which show a much lower rate of profit than that customary in your type of business. The Revenue may take the view that you have made more profit than you have declared. You have no disagreement with them about whether your profit should be taxed or not, only on the amount of profit that has actually been made. This is a dispute on a question of fact. On the other hand, you may contend that someone who does some work for you is self-employed whereas the Revenue say he is an employee. The dispute is not about how much has been earned, but about the categorisation of the person concerned and therefore whether PAYE has to be deducted from the earnings and national insurance applied. This is a question of law, and it has led to many cases going before the Courts, some won by the Revenue and some by the taxpayer.

If a dispute cannot be resolved by negotiation, then for tax years before 1996/97 the Revenue will issue an assessment based on their view, but you have the right to appeal against the assessment to a tribunal of Appeal Commissioners. Although income tax and capital gains tax are 'self-assessed' from 1996/97, the Revenue will have the right to make amendments if they disagree with your figures, and if you do not accept their amendments you will still have the right to appeal to the Commissioners. There are two types of Commissioners, the General Commissioners, who are usually local business people acting in a voluntary unpaid capacity, and the Special Commissioners, who are full-time civil servants who travel on circuit to the different parts of the country. Most appeals are heard by the General Commissioners, but some specialised appeals have to go to the Special Commissioners. You cannot make a non-specialised appeal to the Special Commissioners unless there are points in dispute. The General Commissioners hear appeals in private and their decisions are not reported. The Special Commissioners may hear appeals in public and may publish reports of their decisions. They may also award costs if either the taxpayer or the Revenue has acted unreasonably.

The distinction between questions of law and fact is important, because what an appeal tribunal decides on questions of fact is generally binding on both the taxpayer and the Revenue. The tribunal's decisions on points of law, however, can be referred by the losing party to the High Court, then to the Court of Appeal (or the equivalent Scottish or Irish Courts) and finally, if leave is granted, to the House of Lords. You should, however, think very carefully before taking an appeal on a question of law to the appeal tribunal, because it may take a very long time before it is settled, it will cost you a lot of time and money, and at the end of the day you may find yourself on the losing side. In that event you may be required to pay the Revenue's costs, although they will not always ask for them, and may sometimes agree in advance not to do so if the case deals with a point of principle that is of widespread importance. But that could still leave the taxpayer with his own costs to bear. In addition, many taxpayer victories are short-lived, because the law is then changed to what the Revenue think it ought to be.

The Revenue have yet another weapon in their armoury, in that they can challenge 'a series of transactions with a tax avoidance motive' so that any intermediate steps are ignored and only the end result is taken into account. This has not only blocked some complicated tax avoidance schemes, but has also led to the need for caution to be exercised even when considering modest tax-saving plans. Advance planning by way of a series of transactions is still possible providing they are not so pre-planned and interlinked that they can only really be regarded as a single transaction.

Your tax dispute may be with Customs and Excise instead of with the Revenue. Appeals about VAT matters are dealt with in the first place by VAT tribunals, but there is the same possibility of taking the dispute to the Courts if you do not agree with the tribunal's decision. And with VAT there is the further possibility of going to the European Court if you think UK law is not in accordance with European Union rules.

Despite all the difficulties and the very high cost, a surprising number of people take their cases to the Courts, with varying degrees of success. Most people will not want to go to those lengths and will simply wish to ensure that the taxman's share of their cake is the smallest possible slice. The chapters of this book explain in detail how tax liabilities are calculated and highlight some of the ways in which they may be minimised.

2
Income tax: general principles

Basis of charge

The word 'income' is not defined in the tax legislation. Instead, the legislation classifies amounts received under various headings, called Schedules (sometimes subdivided into 'Cases'), and an item must come within one of these headings to be charged as income. Sometimes the tax law requires capital items to be treated as income. For example, when a landlord charges a tenant a lump sum for granting him a lease for up to fifty years, part of the lump sum is taxed as income. But unless there is a specific provision like that, an amount cannot be charged to income tax unless it has the quality of income rather than capital. There is a separate heading, Schedule D, Case VI, which deals with items of an income nature that are not covered elsewhere, and also certain capital items that the legislation regards as income.

The distinction between income and capital used to be very important because the top income tax rate was twice as much as the capital gains tax rate. Since 6 April 1988, gains have been charged at the same rates as income, after an exemption for the first slice, currently £6,300 (see chapter 4).

Exempt income

Certain types of income are specifically exempt from tax, notably the following, which are dealt with in the chapter indicated:

	Chapter
The first £70 interest (husband and wife £70 each) from national savings bank ordinary accounts.	37
Interest on Tax Exempt Special Savings Accounts (TESSAs)	37
Income within Personal Equity Plans (PEPs)	38
Increase in value of national savings certificates.	36
Premium bond prizes.	36
Other prizes and betting winnings	4
Bonuses and profits on life assurance policies (subject to detailed anti-avoidance rules).	40

The capital part of the yearly amount received from
a purchased life annuity.   34
Local authority home improvement grants.
Housing benefit.
Some social security benefits (but others are taxable).   10
Sickness and unemployment insurance payments
(including mortgage protection insurance payments)
Damages and compensation for personal injury
(whether received as a lump sum or by periodic
payments)
Save As You Earn account bonuses.   36
Shares allocated to you by your employer under an
approved profit sharing scheme.   11
Profit-related pay, up to a maximum of £4,000.   12
Educational grants and scholarships.
Statutory redundancy pay, pay in lieu of notice and
certain larger amounts received from your employer on
termination of your employment.   15
Maintenance payments under arrangements made after
14 March 1988, and the first £1,790 (for 1996/97)
of maintenance payments under earlier arrangements.   33

Persons chargeable

Each individual, whether man, woman or child, is responsible for tax on
his/her own income, although a child's income may be treated as the
parent's if it or the capital which produces it comes from the parent (see page
440). Before 6 April 1990 the income of a married woman was normally
treated as her husband's income. Personal representatives and trustees pay
tax on estate and trust income. Companies pay corporation tax instead of
income tax (see chapter 3).

Income tax is charged broadly on the income of UK residents, whether it
arises in the UK or abroad, subject to certain deductions for earnings abroad
and for individuals who are not ordinarily resident or not domiciled in the
UK. Non-residents are liable to income tax only on income that arises in the
UK. Double tax relief is available where income is taxed both in the UK and
abroad. For detailed provisions on the overseas aspect, see chapter 41.

Calculating your taxable income

The tax year runs from 6 April in one year to 5 April in the next, the current
year from 6 April 1996 to 5 April 1997 being known as 1996/97. You are
charged to tax on your income at the rates in the table on page xx, the current
rates being the lower rate of 20%, the basic rate of 24% and the higher rate of
40%. Special rules apply, however, to dividends and, from 6 April 1996,
income from savings. These are dealt with on page 16.

Taxable income is broadly worked out by adding together the amounts under the Schedules and Cases referred to on page 5, then deducting certain payments known as charges on income and also deducting your personal allowance and blind person's relief if relevant. Those deductions and allowances save tax at your highest rate. Certain other deductions and allowances save you a specified amount of tax. The detailed provisions are dealt with later in the chapter.

The following table outlines the income charged under each of the Schedules and Cases and how that income is measured (the basis of assessment). The rules for measuring income have been changed from 6 April 1996. Subject to some transitional provisions, the income charged to tax is now always that of the current tax year. Under the rules that applied up to 1995/96, the income of the previous year was usually treated as the taxable income of the current year for the first five Cases of Schedule D (covering business profits, certain interest received and income from abroad). The rules for measuring income had already changed for new sources acquired on or after 6 April 1994. The changes are dealt with in detail in chapter 21 for business profits and in the other relevant chapters for other types of income. There was a change in the income tax rules for taxing rental income from 1995/96. Special transitional provisions apply to deal with the change (see chapter 32). (The old rules still apply for dealing with rental income for companies.)

Note that there is no Schedule B or Schedule C. Schedule B was a charge on the occupation of woodlands, but it was abolished from 6 April 1988 (see chapter 31). Income from UK and foreign government stocks, paid through a UK paying agent such as a bank, was previously charged under Schedule C but that income has now been brought within Schedule D, Case III or Case IV from 6 April 1996.

Schedule and Case	Type of income	Basis of assessment
Schedule A	Rents from UK land and buildings	Rent for tax year less allowable expenses
Schedule D Case I	Profits of trade	Normally net profits of accounting year ended in current tax year, with special rules for opening and closing years and on change of accounting date, and subject to transitional provisions for 1996/97
Case II	Profits of profession or vocation	
Case III	Interest, annuities or other annual amounts received, including, from 6 April 1996, income from government stocks	Income received in tax year (subject to transitional provisions for 1996/97 for certain income from which tax was not deducted by the payer). There is no relief for expenses

Schedule and Case	Type of income	Basis of assessment
Case IV	Income from foreign securities	Normally the amount arising in current tax year subject to transitional provisions for 1996/97, and reduced by a percentage deduction where the income is from a pension. Based on amount remitted to UK if taxpayer resident but not ordinarily resident and/or not domiciled in UK
Case V	Income from foreign possessions	
Case VI	Income not assessable under any other Schedule or Case	Profits or gains arising in the tax year, less appropriate expenses
Schedule E		
Case I	Earnings of employee resident and ordinarily resident in UK, other than 'foreign emoluments' earned wholly abroad. (Foreign emoluments are earnings of non-UK-domiciled employee from non-UK-resident employer)	All earnings in the tax year whether duties are performed in the UK or abroad, but special rules apply to earnings during long absences abroad
Case II	Earnings of employee not resident or resident but not ordinarily resident in UK	Earnings for UK duties
Case III	'Foreign emoluments' earned wholly abroad by person resident and ordinarily resident in UK	Remittances to UK in tax year. No charge if not remitted
	Earnings abroad of person resident but not ordinarily resident in UK	
Schedule F	Dividends and distributions of UK-resident company	Dividends and distributions in the tax year plus accompanying tax credits

How is tax collected?

Both before and after the introduction of self-assessment, tax is collected from most individuals without any direct contact with the taxman. The most common sources of income are earnings from employment and interest from banks and building societies. Tax on bank and building society interest (except most interest from the National Savings Bank) is deducted by the bank or building society, and there is nothing more to pay unless you are liable to tax at the higher rate. (Tax is not deducted if you have certified that you are entitled to receive the interest in full because you are not liable to pay *any* tax on your income — see chapter 37.) Tax on your earnings is collected through the Pay As You Earn (PAYE) scheme, whether the earnings are taxable at the lower, basic or higher rate. Tax on occupational pensions is collected in the same way. If you have some small items of other income that you have received in full (such as interest on a national savings bank account) this is adjusted through your PAYE coding.

A minority of employees and pensioners, and all self-employed people, have to fill in tax returns and pay some or all of their income tax directly to the Revenue. Those with capital gains above the exempt limit are also required to fill in tax returns and pay the tax directly. Under the rules that applied before self-assessment, tax that was payable directly was due on different dates according to the type of income (two equal instalments on 1 January and 1 July for business profits, 1 January in the tax year for rents, 1 December following the tax year for collecting any extra tax on investment income from higher rate taxpayers and for collecting capital gains tax, and so on). If the Revenue had not issued the tax bill in time, the due date became 30 days after the issue of the assessment, although this did not necessarily stop interest being charged on the overdue amount from the normal due date. Sometimes the system allowed the Revenue to charge tax provisionally and adjust it when the true figures were known.

Following the introduction of self-assessment from 1996/97, tax that is due to be paid direct to the Revenue will be collected by means of two provisional half-yearly payments on 31 January and 31 July, based on the total income tax payable directly for the previous tax year, with a balancing payment (plus the first provisional payment for the following year) on the next 31 January. Any capital gains tax due will be included in the balancing payment. The present system of collecting tax through PAYE and by deduction from interest, etc. will continue. This is dealt with in more detail on page 120. See also page 20.

Charges on income and other deductions

Certain payments you have made, known as charges on income, are allowable as deductions in arriving at your taxable income, thus saving tax at your top rate. The main items are:

Allowable interest payments other than home loan interest (see page 11).

Covenanted payments to charity, and gifts to charity of at least £250 each, net of 24% tax.

Payments by individuals for their own vocational training (see chapter 10).

Payments under the first heading are made in full, and you get relief at your top tax rate by having your tax code adjusted or in working out your self-assessment. Tax at 24% is deducted from payments under the second two headings and there is normally no further effect on your tax position unless you are liable to tax at the 40% rate, in which case you will get the extra relief to which you are entitled by an adjustment in your coding or self-assessment. The end result is that the amount of tax you suffer is the same whether charges are paid net or gross. See example 1.

Example 1

In 1996/97, self-employed higher rate taxpayer pays two payments of £500 gross each, being:

(a) allowable interest on car loan (after excluding private use proportion)

and

(b) covenanted donation to charity, tax of £120 being deducted, reducing his net payment to £380.

Tax relief due for each type of payment is 40% of £500, i.e. £200. In working out his self-assessment, the taxpayer would deduct both amounts of £500 from his taxable income, giving him relief of £200 × 2 = £400, but in respect of the covenanted payment he would have to increase the amount of tax payable in his self-assessment by the £120 tax relief he had already had by deducting it from the payment, so that he did not get that amount of relief twice.

If the taxpayer had been an employee who paid all of his tax through the PAYE system, relief at 40% on the amount of the car loan interest and at 16% on the charity covenant would be given by a coding adjustment.

If the taxpayer had been a basic rate taxpayer, the relief on each payment @ 24% would be £120. If he was self-employed, he would deduct both the loan interest and the charity covenant from his income in his self-assessment, giving him relief of £240, but he would then have to increase the tax payable by the £120 tax relief he had already had on the covenant (so effectively the entries on his tax return relating to the covenant would cancel each other out). If he was an employee, he would still need a coding adjustment to give him 24% relief on the car loan interest, but he would have already had the 24% relief on the charity covenant, so no further adjustment would be required.

If the taxpayer's income was too low to cover the payments, so that no tax was payable, the tax deducted from the covenanted payment should still strictly be handed over to the Revenue. They will not usually enforce this, but if a tax repayment was being claimed, the amount repayable would be reduced by the tax deducted and retained by the payee out of the covenanted payment.

Before 1996/97, you could also deduct as a charge on your income one half of your Class 4 national insurance contributions if you were self-employed. It has been decided that this is an unnecessary complication for self-assessment, and the deduction is no longer available. The rate of Class 4 contributions has been reduced from 7.3% to 6% to compensate.

Other payments entitle you to a tax saving at a specified rate, as follows:

Interest on the first £30,000 of home loans (for the detailed provisions see page 412) 15%

Up to £1,790 maintenance payments to former or separated spouse (special rules apply to maintenance arrangements made before 15 March 1988 — see chapter 33) 15%

Private medical insurance premiums paid by or on behalf of those aged 60 and over and their spouses (see page 480) 24%

The tax saving on mortgage interest under the MIRAS (Mortgage Interest Relief At Source) scheme and on medical insurance premiums is obtained by deducting it before making the payment (so that, for example, if gross MIRAS interest is £1,000 you will pay £850 net; if your gross medical insurance premium is £1,000 you will pay £750 in 1995/96 and £760 in 1996/97). Non-MIRAS interest on home loans and maintenance are paid in full and the tax saving is given by an adjustment in your coding or self-assessment.

If you are self-employed, or are not in your employer's pension scheme, you may pay premiums under a personal pension policy. Such premiums are deductible from your earnings and are not a charge on your general income. Self-employed people pay the premiums gross and obtain a deduction in their self-assessment. But if you are an employee, the premiums are paid after deducting tax at 24%, and any higher rate relief you are entitled to is given by coding adjustment. For the detailed provisions, see chapter 17.

Allowable interest (TA 1988, ss 353–379; FA 1994, s 81; FA 1996, s 76)

Not all interest payments are deductible in calculating taxable income. Mortgage interest on the first £30,000 of a home loan now saves tax at a specified rate, as indicated above. This is dealt with in detail on page 412. You are usually entitled to relief at your top tax rate on interest relating to let property (see pages 444 and 445). You are also entitled to relief at your top tax rate on the following interest payments, most of which are dealt with in context in the appropriate chapter.

(a) On a loan for the purchase of a partnership share, for introducing capital to a partnership or for lending money to it, providing that you are not a limited partner and providing you are still a partner when the interest is paid (see pages 272 and 333).

(b) On a loan to buy shares in or lend money to a trading company controlled by its directors or by five or fewer people, so long as, at the time the interest is paid, either you own more than 5% of the issued ordinary share capital or you own any part of the ordinary share capital, however small, and work for the greater part of your time in the management or conduct of the company or an associated company. (But if you or your spouse have claimed relief under the Business Expansion Scheme in respect of shares acquired on or after 14 March 1989 or under the Enterprise Investment Scheme, you cannot also claim interest relief on a loan to buy the shares.)

(c) On a loan to buy plant or machinery (for example a car) for use in your partnership or employment. Relief is available for interest paid in the tax year of purchase and the next three tax years. Where there is part private use, only the business proportion qualifies (see chapter 10).

(d) On a loan to personal representatives of a deceased person to pay inheritance tax (see chapter 35).

(e) On a loan to acquire shares in an employee-controlled trading company.

(f) On a loan to acquire a share or shares in a co-operative.

Where you are 65 years of age or over, you are entitled to relief for interest paid on a loan of up to £30,000 secured on your home to purchase an income for life (called a life annuity) (see page 478). Relief is given at the basic rate of tax and not the lower rate applicable to home loans. Relief for such interest continues for one year (or longer if the Revenue allow) if you move out and put the property up for sale (whether or not you buy a new property).

Interest is allowable on loans which replace existing qualifying loans.

Relief is only available as the interest is paid. It is not spread over the period of accrual and will not be allowed if it is never paid.

Bank overdraft interest is never allowed as a deduction from *total* income. Relief is only available where the overdraft is part of the funding of a trade and therefore allowable as an expense in arriving at trading profits.

Personal allowances (TA 1988, ss 256–265; FA 1994, s 77; FA 1996, ss 74, 75)

In addition to relief for charges, you may claim certain allowances, as detailed below, the amounts stated relating to the tax year 1996/97. For the rates of allowance for earlier years, see page xx. The personal allowance and blind person's relief are deducted from your income and save tax at your highest tax rate. Married couple's allowance, additional personal allowance and widow's bereavement allowance save tax at only 15% and are given by reducing the amount of tax payable. The basic allowance of £1,790 saves tax of £268.50 in 1996/97. (For the way relief is given under PAYE, see page 166.)

Personal allowance

Every individual who is a UK resident (and some non-residents — see page 563) is entitled to a personal allowance, whether he or she is single or married.

The allowance depends on your age, and is increased in and after the tax years in which you reach age 65 and age 75, as follows:

Under 65	Age 65 to 74	Age 75 and over
£3,765	£4,910	£5,090

The higher allowances for those aged 65 and over are, however, subject to an income limit (see page 14).

Married couple's allowance

A married man is entitled to a married couple's allowance (subject to any claim by his wife — see below). The allowance is increased in and after the tax years in which the older spouse reaches age 65 and age 75, as follows:

Elder under 65	Elder aged 65 to 74	Elder aged 75 and over
£1,790	£3,115	£3,155

Again, an income limit applies to the higher allowances for those aged 65 and over (see page 14).

The married couple's allowance starts in the year of marriage, but in that year it is reduced by one-twelfth (£149.17 for 1996/97 if both are under 65) for each complete tax month (ending on the 5th) before the wedding date. If in the year of marriage a man is entitled to the additional allowance as a single parent (see below), he can claim that allowance instead of the reduced married couple's allowance. The married couple's allowance is given in full in the year of divorce, separation or death of either spouse. A widow will get the benefit of any unused married couple's allowance in the year of her husband's death (as well as the widow's bereavement allowance — see below).

A married woman is entitled as of right to half the basic married couple's allowance (not any extra married couple's allowance given to the over 65s), if she makes a claim to that effect. Alternatively the couple may jointly claim for the *whole* of the basic allowance to be given to the wife. In either case, the claim must be made *before* the beginning of the relevant tax year, e.g. before 6 April 1996 for 1996/97 (except in the year of marriage, when the claim may be made within that tax year). Claims must be made on form 18, available from the Revenue. The allowance will then be allocated in the chosen way until the claim is withdrawn, or, where a joint claim has been made for the whole allowance to go to the wife, until the husband makes a fresh claim for half of the allowance. The withdrawal or the husband's claim must also be made before the beginning of the tax year for which the revised allocation is to take effect. Choosing to allocate all or part of the allowance to a wife does not reduce the tax bill, but there may be a cash flow benefit if, say, a wife pays tax under PAYE and a husband is self-employed, because the wife will start to get the benefit of the allowance at the beginning of the tax year, whereas the husband's first tax payment is due much later. If no claim to allocate half or all the allowance to the wife is made, it is given to the husband.

If either husband or wife pays insufficient tax to use the married couple's allowance to which they are entitled (including any additional allowance available to the husband because one of them is over 65), that spouse may notify the Revenue (not later than five years after the 31 January next following the relevant tax year) that the unused amount is to be transferred to the other. The unused amount is *not* transferred automatically.

Income limit for age allowances

Your increased personal allowance because of age is reduced by £1 for every £2 by which your net total income (after deducting charges) exceeds £15,200, but the allowance cannot fall below £3,765.

The married couple's age allowance is similarly reduced by half of the excess of the husband's total income over £15,200 which has not already been taken into account to reduce his personal allowance, but again it cannot fall below £1,790. The wife's income is not taken into account at all, even if the allowance is given because of her age rather than the husband's, or if the tax saving is transferred to the wife because the husband's income is too low to use it.

A single person or married woman will lose the benefit of age allowance if income is higher than the following:

Age 65 to 74	£17,490
Age 75 and over	£17,850

A married man will lose the benefit of married couple's age allowance, and his own age allowance if relevant, if his own income is higher than the following:

Husband under 65, wife 65 to 74	£17,850
Husband under 65, wife 75 or over	£17,930
Husband 65 to 74, wife under 75	£20,140
Husband 65 to 74, wife 75 or over	£20,220
Husband 75 or over	£20,580

Transitional provisions

Special transitional provisions were introduced from 6 April 1990 to ensure that a married couple's combined allowances did not fall when wives started to be taxed independently from their husbands. Very few people are now affected by these rules. Further transitional provisions enabled a married man under 65 whose wife was 75 or over in 1989/90 to claim a personal allowance of £3,540 instead of the normal personal allowance (subject to the age allowance income limit). For 1996/97, the normal personal allowance is £3,765 so these transitional provisions are no longer of any benefit. The transitional provisions are dealt with in detail in earlier editions of this book.

Additional personal allowance for single parents, etc.

An additional personal allowance of £1,790 is available for a claimant who is single, widowed, divorced or separated if he or she has one or more qualifying children resident with him or her for all or part of the year. If the child is your own child (including a stepchild or an adopted child who was under 18 when adopted), the child must either be under 16 at the beginning of the tax year or be in full-time education (or undergoing a minimum two-year full-time training for a trade, profession or vocation). If the child is not your own child, then in addition to the requirement for the child to be under 16 or in full-time education or training, you must maintain the child for all or part of the year, and the allowance for a child who is not your own is not available in any event if the child is over 18 at the beginning of the tax year. The relief is apportioned where there are two or more claimants in respect of the same child, but if, say, separated parents each claim for a different child, the full relief is available to each if the conditions are satisfied (except that the husband cannot claim the allowance in the tax year of separation). If, however, an unmarried couple live together as man and wife, they are entitled to only one allowance between them, no matter how many qualifying children there are.

A man entitled to the married couple's allowance cannot claim the additional allowance as well, unless his wife has throughout the year been totally incapacitated by physical or mental infirmity.

Widow's bereavement allowance

In the tax year in which her husband dies and in the following tax year (unless she marries before the beginning of it) a widow is entitled to a bereavement allowance of £1,790.

Blind person's relief

Relief of £1,250 is available to a blind person. A married couple who are both blind may each claim the allowance. A married blind person may transfer unused blind person's relief to the spouse (whether or not the spouse is blind).

Life assurance relief (TA 1988, ss 266–274 and Schs 14 and 15)

Life assurance relief is no longer available for contracts made after 13 March 1984 but it continues for policies made on or before that date. The relief is currently at the rate of 12½% of qualifying premiums, subject to a limit on allowable premiums of either one-sixth of total income or £1,500, whichever is greater.

The relief is deducted when the premium is paid, and may be retained whether you are a taxpayer or not.

There were many restrictions on what policies qualified for relief, and there are anti-avoidance rules under which the Revenue recover excess relief. The provisions are dealt with in detail in chapter 40.

Life cover for a limited period (term assurance) is available with tax relief on the premium at the highest rate you pay, under the 'personal pension scheme' provisions (see chapter 17).

Special treatment of savings income, including dividends (TA 1988, s 1A; FA 1996, s 73)

Since 6 April 1993, the tax credit that accompanies dividends has amounted to only the lower rate tax of 20%. You have, however, only had to pay further tax on the dividends if your taxable income exceeded the basic rate threshold. From 6 April 1996, the same treatment applies to most savings income, so that not only dividends but also bank and building society interest, interest on government stocks and the income element of a purchased life annuity will all be taxed at only 20% providing your taxable income does not exceed the basic rate limit, £25,500 for 1996/97. Tax deducted by the banks, etc. and dividend tax credits will be at the 20% rate. (Tax will be deducted from most savings income, but some of it may be received in full — see page 9.) The full lower rate band, currently £3,900, is available to set against other income, and allowances and reliefs are regarded as reducing the other income in priority to the savings income. The effect for 1996/97 is that if your income after deducting any charges and allowances as indicated earlier does not exceed £25,500, the slice of income taxed at only 20% is £3,900 plus the whole of your savings income. Where tax at 20% is deducted by the payer (or covered by a dividend tax credit), basic rate taxpayers have no further tax to pay, higher rate taxpayers have to pay a further 20% and those entitled to a refund will recover tax at the lower rate of 20%.

The 20% rate also applies to savings income from abroad, unless you are charged to tax on foreign income only when it is brought into the UK, called the remittances basis (see chapter 41).

Example 2

Illustration of tax calculation for 1996/97 for married man claiming full married couple's allowance and paying MIRAS interest of £850 (i.e. £1,000 net of £150 tax relief) and charitable covenant of £380 (i.e. £500 net of 24% tax relief)

		£
Earnings from self-employment		28,765
Savings income:		
National Savings Bank interest		
(investment account opened		
many years ago)	100	
Other bank interest (from which		
20% tax deducted) 320 + 80	400	
Dividends 800 + 200 tax credits	1,000	
		1,500
		30,265
Less: Charitable covenant (gross amount)		500
		29,765
Less: Personal allowance		3,765
Taxable income		26,000

Tax thereon:

	£
Non-savings income (26,000 – 1,500)	
3,900 @ 20%	780.00
20,600 @ 24%	4,944.00
24,500	
Savings income	
1,000 @ 20% (up to basic rate limit)	200.00
25,500	
500 @ 40%	200.00
26,000	
	6,124.00
Less: Married couple's allowance 1,790 @ 15%	268.50
	5,855.50
Add: Tax relief already retained on covenant	
500 @ 24%	120.00
Total tax payable	5,975.50

This will be reduced by the tax already deducted on the savings income (£80 + £200) and by provisional payments of tax made on 31 January 1997 and 31 July 1997. The balance will be payable by 31 January 1998 (see page 120).

The MIRAS relief of £150 has been retained out of the mortgage interest payments to the building society and does not affect the tax payable.

Example 3

Individual with available personal allowances of £3,765 has savings and other income as shown in 1996/97. His tax position is:

	£	£	£
Income other than from savings	19,265	19,265	19,365
Savings income (gross amounts)	10,000	10,100	10,000
	29,265	29,365	29,365
Personal allowances	(3,765)	(3,765)	(3,765)
	25,500	25,600	25,600

Tax payable:
Non-savings

	£	£	£
income 3,900/ 3,900/ 3,900 @ 20%	780	780	780
11,600/11,600/11,700 @ 24%	2,784	2,784	2,808

Savings

	£	£	£
income 10,000/10,000/ 9,900 @ 20%	2,000	2,000	1,980

25,500 25,500 25,500

	£	£	£
— / 100/ 100 @ 40%		40	40

25,500 25,600 25,600

	£	£	£
	5,564	5,604	5,608

In the second column, an extra £100 of savings income results in extra tax of £40 because the extra savings income is in the higher rate band. In the third column, where the extra £100 is non-savings income, the extra tax is £44. This is because savings income is always treated as the top slice of income, so basic rate tax of £24 is payable on the extra non-savings income, but it causes £100 of the savings income to be in the higher rate band, so that a further 20% is payable on that savings income. Tax will have been deducted or credited at source on most savings income, so that only the extra 20% will remain payable.

Since 1 July 1994 companies have been able to pay 'foreign income dividends' (FIDs). Such dividends carry a notional rather than an actual tax credit. The national credit is treated in the same way as an actual credit for those liable at basic and higher rate tax, but non-taxpayers cannot claim a refund. Some companies give shareholders the opportunity of taking shares instead of dividends (scrip dividends). No tax is payable by or repayable to those liable at or below the basic rate, but higher rate taxpayers have to pay extra tax (see page 512).

Postponement applications and interest on overdue tax (TMA 1970, ss 55, 86, 88; FA 1995, s 110; FA 1996, s 131 and Sch 18 paras 3 and 4)

Years up to 1995/96

For years up to 1995/96, tax was due for payment either on the normal due date, which varied according to the source of income (see page 9), or 30 days after the issue of the assessment if later. The due date of payment could sometimes be delayed if you appealed against an assessment and applied for postponement of all or part of the tax charged. If postponement was not applied for, tax was due on the normal due date despite the appeal.

If the outcome of the appeal was that all or part of the tax postponed was in fact payable, it was due for payment 30 days after the appeal was settled (or the normal due date, if later).

Interest is charged when tax bills (and Class 4 national insurance contributions) are not paid on the due date. The interest is frequently added into later demands when full payment is not made on time, rather than being demanded separately. The interest is not deductible in calculating tax liabilities. The interest rate is adjusted frequently in line with commercial interest rates. Recent rates are as follows.

6.25% p.a. from 6 February 1996
7% p.a. from 6 March 1995 to 5 February 1996
6.25% p.a. from 6 October 1994 to 5 March 1995
5.5% p.a. from 6 January 1994 to 5 October 1994
6.25% p.a. from 6 March 1993 to 5 January 1994
7% p.a. from 6 December 1992 to 5 March 1993
7.75% p.a. from 6 November 1992 to 5 December 1992
9.25% p.a. from 6 October 1991 to 5 November 1992

The Revenue publishes tables of interest rate factors to help with the necessary calculations, and these are updated when rates change.

Interest is charged from the 'reckonable date', which normally means the date when the tax was actually due for payment. Where any of the tax was postponed, however, interest may run from an earlier date than that on which the tax itself was payable. Interest runs from either 30 days after the issue of the original assessment or, if later:

For Schedules A and D	1 July after the tax year (e.g. 1 July 1996 for 1995/96).
For higher rates on taxed income	1 June in next but one tax year (e.g. 1 June 1997 for 1995/96).

Interest will, however, run from the normal due date, as distinct from the reckonable date if that is later, where the reason for an assessment being made late is the fraudulent or negligent conduct of the taxpayer. (See chapter 9.)

Detailed calculations of interest are not usually shown on tax demands. Since mistakes do occur, the amount charged should be carefully checked.

1996/97 onwards

Under the self-assessment system that applies from 1996/97, you may work out your own tax or ask the Revenue to work it out for you and in either case this counts as self-assessment. Assessments by the Revenue and applications for postponement of tax will be rare. The Revenue will be able to 'determine' the tax you owe if you do not send in your return, but their tax figure will be replaced by your self-assessment when it is received, so that appeals are not relevant. If the Revenue enquire into your return (see page 123), you will have the right to appeal against any amendments they make to your figures, and also to apply to postpone payment of any disputed amount until the appeal is settled. The Revenue will also continue to be able to issue assessments if they discover that tax has been underpaid through a tax-payer's fraudulent or negligent conduct, or because of inadequate disclosure of information (see page 141), and the appeal/postponement procedures will still apply to such assessments.

The payment dates under self-assessment are outlined on page 10. You will make provisional payments on 31 January and 31 July based on half the total net income tax and self-employed Class 4 national insurance contributions payable for the previous tax year, even if the current year's tax turns out to be lower. A balancing payment (or refund) will be made on the following 31 January (which will include any capital gains tax due). At any time before that date you may claim to reduce the provisional payments (or get a refund if already paid) if you think your current year's tax will be lower (subject to penalties if you do so fraudulently or negligently). Interest will be charged on underpayments or allowed on overpayments, but the interest rate on overpaid tax will be lower. (Interest on overpaid tax is called repayment supplement.) The interest will be based on the correct amount of tax after all amendments. If the final amount of total income tax due for the year exceeds the provisional payments based on half the previous year's tax, interest is charged on the balance only from the 31 January due date for the return. If the provisional payments exceed the final tax bill, it is understood that interest will be payable on half the excess from the half-yearly due dates for the provisional payments, or from the payment date if later. This will not apply to the extent that all or part of the provisional payments has already been repaid, plus the appropriate interest, following a claim to reduce them before the 31 January filing date for the return. If, following such a claim, the reduced amounts prove to be lower than half of the final tax figure (excluding capital gains tax), interest will then be charged on the shortfall.

See example 4.

Example 4

Assume all tax payments are made on due dates. Total income tax payable directly to the Revenue for 1996/97 is £15,000, so that the provisional payments for 1997/98 should be £7,500 on each of 31.1.98 and 31.7.98. The due date for the final payment/repayment is 31 January 1999. If no claim is made to adjust provisional payments, no interest will be charged if final tax exceeds £15,000; if final tax is less than £15,000, interest will be allowed on half of the shortfall from each of the 31.1.98 and 31.7.98 payment dates.

Say taxpayer, having made first provisional payment of £7,500 on 31.1.98, applies to reduce the payments to £6,000 each because he thinks the 1997/98 tax will be around £12,000. The overpayment of £1,500 on the first instalment will be refunded with interest from the payment date to the date the repayment order is issued. If the final figure for 1997/98 (excluding any capital gains tax) turns out to be:

£16,000

A balancing payment of £4,000 will be due on 31.1.99.

Interest will be charged on the difference between the provisional amounts that should (with hindsight) have been paid, i.e. £7,500 each, and the £6,000 actually paid. The interest will therefore be:

On £1,500 re 1st instalment from 31.1.98 to 30.1.99
On £1,500 re 2nd instalment from 31.7.98 to 30.1.99

£14,000

The balancing payment due on 31.1.99 will be £2,000, and the interest charges will be based on £1,000 re each provisional payment (since the payments should only have been reduced to £7,000 each).

£10,000

The taxpayer would be entitled to a refund of £2,000, with interest on £1,000 from 31.1.98 and £1,000 from 31.7.98 to the date the repayment order is issued.

The Revenue will issue statements to keep you up to date with all payments made and all liabilities outstanding.

Repayment claims

Before 6 April 1996, one of the main reasons for tax being overpaid was that pensioners had received income net of basic rate tax and had not obtained the benefit of the full amount of their personal allowances and lower rate band. Those who paid tax on pensions through PAYE might have avoided such overpayments because they would have been given an adjustment known as 'taxed income relief' in their codings. But millions more did not, in fact, claim the refunds to which they were entitled. From 6 April 1996, such repayments will rarely be necessary, because the tax rate on savings income has been reduced to the lower rate (unless income exceeds the basic rate limit), and most people will have been given the benefit of their personal allowance against their earnings or pensions. There will still be those for whom this is not the case (see example 5), and there are other instances where the tax deducted from savings income may exceed the tax due, for example where a self-employed person makes a trading loss.

Example 5

Income of widow aged 67 in 1996/97 is £3,200 widow's pension, £1,500 occupational pension and £800 net building society interest. The age allowance available against the occupational pension was (4,910 − 3,200 widow's pension) = £1,710, so no tax was charged under PAYE.

Tax can be reclaimed as follows:

			Tax paid
	£	£	£
Widow's pension		3,200	—
Occupational pension		1,500	—
Building society interest (net)	800		
Tax thereon	200	1,000	200
		5,700	200
Age allowance		4,910	
Taxable income		790	
Tax thereon @ 20%			158
Repayment due			£42

Note that the widow could not have applied to receive her building society interest in full, because this is only possible for someone who expects to pay *no tax at all*. Had she received the interest in full she would have owed tax of £158.

It is understood that the Revenue will continue to deal with repayment claims such as that shown in example 5 by issuing a repayment claim form outside the self-assessment system.

From 1996/97, repayments will also arise if your provisional payments exceed the final tax liability shown in your self-assessment. The claim will usually be made in your tax return, but you may claim earlier if you believe an overpayment will occur (see example 4).

Repayment supplement (TA 1988, s 824; FA 1994, Sch 19 para 41)

For years up to 1995/96, a tax-free repayment supplement is paid to UK resident individuals receiving a repayment of tax and Class 4 national insurance contributions more than one year after the end of the tax year to which the repayment relates. Recent rates are the same as those for interest on overdue tax as shown on page 19.

The supplement runs from the end of the tax year following the year for which the repayment is made (or from the end of the tax year in which the tax was paid if later) to the next 5th of the month after the repayment date. See example 6. The Revenue publishes tables of interest rate factors to help with the necessary calculations, and these are updated when rates change. Where the tax or any part of it has been paid late, repayments will be treated as relating to tax paid later rather than earlier.

The Revenue's calculations of supplement should be checked carefully to make sure supplement has been paid up to the end of the tax month *after* the repayment date (hence, in example 6, up to 5 *June* 1996 for a repayment on 10 May 1996), and also that the calculation starts from the correct 6 April.

Example 6

Self-employed person paid tax for 1993/94 on due dates, 1 January and 1 July 1994, totalling £5,000. A repayment of £1,000 is subsequently made on 10 May 1996. The repayment supplement added to the repayment is reckoned from 6 April 1995 and amounts to:

£1,000 × 7% × 10 mths to 5.2.96	58.33
£1,000 × 6.25% × 4 mths to 5.6.96	20.83
	£79.16

If the second instalment of tax for 1993/94 had not been paid until May 1995, that is in 1995/96, the supplement would have been calculated from 6 April 1996 and would have been:

£1,000 × 6.25% × 2 mths to 5.6.96	£10.42

Repayment supplement is also due on overpaid Class 4 national insurance contributions.

Example 7

Higher rate tax for 1995/96 due on 1 December 1996 was paid two months after the due date, i.e. on 1 February 1997. Interest will be charged from 1 December 1996 to 31 January 1997. If any of the tax is subsequently repaid, supplement will be due from 6 April 1997.

Under the self-assessment system from 1996/97, repayment supplement will apply from the date of any overpayment of tax to the date the repayment order is issued, but at a lower rate than the interest charged on underpaid tax (see page 20 and example 4). It will not be restricted to UK residents.

An important point that needs to be recognised is that under the previous rules, where the tax liability of an earlier year was revised (say because of a claim to carry back a trading loss in a new business — see chapter 25), supplement then became payable from one year after the end of the earlier tax year, as in example 6. Under self-assessment, any claim that results in relief being given in relation to an earlier tax year will be *given effect* by an adjustment to the tax of the year of claim, so that supplement will be payable only by reference to the payment date for the later year.

3
Corporation tax: general principles

Basis of charge (TA 1988, s 6)

Corporation tax is charged on the profits of companies and of unincorporated bodies that are not partnerships, for example members' clubs (see page 41). The term profits includes all sources of income (other than dividends from UK companies) and also capital gains.

Corporation tax is charged on the world profits of UK-resident companies. Non-resident companies carrying on a trade, profession or vocation in the UK through a branch or agency are charged on the income arising from the branch or agency and on capital gains on the disposal of assets in the UK used for the purposes of the trade, profession or vocation or otherwise for the branch or agency. The overseas aspect is dealt with in chapter 41.

Pay and File (TMA 1970, ss 11, 11AA, 11AB, 29, 87A, 91, 94; F(No 2)A 1987, ss 82–86; TA 1988, s 826; FA 1994, ss 182, 183, 191)

For accounting periods ending after 30 September 1993, the 'Pay and File' system applies. Under Pay and File, companies have to estimate and pay their corporation tax not later than 9 months after the end of the accounting period, and file a statutory return with supporting accounts and computations within 12 months after the end of the accounting period. Interest is payable on unpaid tax from the 9 months date (and overpayments attract interest from the payment date). Automatic penalties apply if returns are filed late (although by concession a penalty will not be charged if the return is received on or before the last business day within seven days after the due date). The provisions for returns and assessments under Pay and File are dealt with in chapter 9, and the interest provisions on page 38.

Under Pay and File, the provisions for making various claims, and for amending claims that have been made, are formalised and most claims will be incorporated in the statutory return or in an amended return.

For accounts ending on or after a date to be fixed, not earlier than 1 April 1996 nor later than 31 March 1998, companies will be required to 'self-assess' their corporation tax. Although companies are already working out the tax under Pay and File, the Revenue still issue formal assessments and also estimated assessments if they disagree with a company's figures. Under self-assessment, the responsibility for assessment will become that of the company. The provisions will be broadly the same as those that apply for income tax, except that companies will not have the option of asking the Revenue to work out the tax. The Revenue will be able to correct obvious errors in the corporation tax return within 9 months, and the company will be able to notify amendments within 12 months after the filing date. The Revenue will broadly have 12 months to select returns for audit. If the return is not selected, the self-assessment will stand unless an underpayment of tax is subsequently discovered that arises because the company gave inadequate information or because of its fraudulent or negligent conduct.

Calculation of profits (TA 1988, ss 9, 401; TCGA 1992, s 8)

A company's taxable income is computed broadly using income tax rules. The income tax rules do not apply to the calculation of a company's rental income (see page 446), nor, for accounting periods ending after 31 March 1996, to the treatment of interest paid and received by companies (see page 27).

The only source of income that escapes corporation tax is dividends or other distributions from UK-resident companies. Such dividends, with their related tax credits, are called franked investment income and their tax treatment is dealt with below. Special rules apply to certain dividends from authorised unit trusts (see page 527).

In computing the company's trading profits, capital allowances are deducted as trading expenses, and balancing charges treated as trading income (see chapter 22). Pre-trading expenditure of a revenue nature incurred not more than seven years before commencement of trading is treated as incurred on the day the trade commences.

A company's chargeable gains are normally computed using capital gains tax principles (see chapter 4). Companies are not, however, entitled to any annual capital gains exemption. Furthermore, since 23 March 1995 (subject to transitional provisions), profits and losses on a company's capital transactions relating to foreign exchange and certain financial instruments have been brought into account in calculating income (see page 575). The same now applies from 1 April 1996 to a company's capital transactions relating to loans (see page 27).

Charges on income (TA 1988, ss 338, 339, 349, 350)

Having arrived at the company's total profits (both income and capital), charges on income are deducted to arrive at the profits chargeable to corporation tax. Until 1 April 1996, charges have usually comprised the payments from which the company has deducted income tax at source, and the main category for most companies has been interest payments (other than bank interest). New provisions dealing with 'loan relationships' now apply to *all* interest paid and received (see below), and interest paid on or after 1 April 1996 is no longer classed as a charge on income. The main examples of charges on income are now patent royalties and covenanted payments to charity. One-off donations to charity are also sometimes treated as a charge (see page 596). (Holding companies and their 51% subsidiaries may elect to pay charges from one group company to another without deducting tax — see page 40).

The full amount of the charges paid in the accounting period (that is, before the income tax deduction at source) is deducted from profits, and the company has to account to the Revenue for the income tax it has deducted (subject to a set-off for any income tax suffered on its income) (see under 'Accounting for income tax deducted' on page 36).

If the charges exceed profits, the excess may be carried forward as a trading loss to set against later profits from the same trade provided that the charges are wholly and exclusively for the purposes of the trade. No carry-forward is available for non-trade charges which exceed profits, such as charitable covenants and one-off charitable donations. The treatment of excess charges is dealt with in chapter 26 on company losses.

Treatment of interest paid and received and profits and losses on loans (FA 1996, ss 80–105 and Schs 8–12, 14, 15)

Before 1 April 1996, the treatment of interest paid by trading companies was that if paid to a bank it was paid in full and deducted as a trading expense, and if paid other than to a bank it was paid net of basic rate tax and was deducted from *total* profits as a charge on income. Interest received was dealt with under three separate headings, Schedule C for interest on government stocks, Schedule D, Case III for most other interest and Schedule D, Case IV for interest on foreign securities. Bank and building society interest was received in full, and other interest was received net of basic rate tax, although companies in the same group could elect to pay interest between group companies without deducting tax. This treatment of inter-group payments will continue (see page 40). For capital gains purposes, the loss of money lent has rarely been allowable against gains (see page 46).

New treatment applies from 1 April 1996 to a company's 'loan relationships', which covers all loans made both by and to the company. Loans to the company include bank overdrafts and loans by the company include holdings of gilt-edged securities, corporate bonds and building society permanent interest bearing shares. For accounting periods ending after 31 March 1996 (subject to transitional provisions to deal with the period that straddles that date and also subject to special provisions concerning particular types of security), all interest paid and received by companies is brought into account normally on an accruals basis (i.e. taking into account amounts in arrear and advance), and profits or losses made on loans (whether as borrower or lender) are treated as income or expenses, either on an accruals basis or on a 'mark to market' basis, which means that the profit or loss is worked out year by year according to market value. Any costs incurred will also be taken into account. The accrued income scheme no longer applies to companies after 31 March 1996.

As far as non-trading profits, losses, interest paid and interest received are concerned, they will all be aggregated and will be merged with any foreign exchange or financial instruments gain or loss (see page 575). An overall profit is chargeable under Schedule D, Case III. If there is an overall loss (a 'non-trading deficit'), relief will be available similar to that available for trading losses. Amounts that relate to the trade will be taken into account in arriving at the Schedule D, Case I trading profit or loss. (Interest receivable and profits/losses on loans will not normally relate to the trade, except for financial businesses.) Schedule C has been abolished altogether and Schedule D, Case IV now applies only for income tax and not for corporation tax. For the treatment of losses in relation to money borrowed or lent, see chapter 26.

Interest paid by building societies and paid by or to banks will be paid in full, as will short interest (on loans for a fixed period of less than a year). Apart from special arrangements available to companies in respect of interest on government stocks (see page 497), tax will be deducted at source from other interest (although groups may make inter-group payments gross — see page 40). Where tax is deducted, it will be the lower rate of 20% from 6 April 1996. For the way in which tax is accounted for, see page 36.

Periods of account and chargeable accounting periods (TA 1988, s 12)

A company's taxable profits are computed for a chargeable accounting period, which normally means the period for which the company's accounts are made up, no matter how short it is. If, however, a company makes up an account for a period greater than 12 months, it is split into one or more chargeable accounting periods of 12 months plus a chargeable accounting period covering the remainder of the period of account.

In arriving at the split of profits for an account exceeding twelve months, the trading profit is usually split on a time basis. Capital allowances are calculated for each chargeable accounting period, so that if for example an account was made up for the fifteen months from 1 January 1996 to 31 March 1997 and plant was bought in February 1997, the first writing-down allowance would be given against the profit of the three months to 31 March 1997.

Interest received or paid used to be allocated to chargeable accounting periods according to the date of receipt or payment. Following the change in the treatment of interest from 1 April 1996, interest relating to the trade will be taken into account in arriving at the trading profit of the period of account, and will normally be time apportioned in the same way as the trading profit. Time apportionment will also apply to non-trading interest if dealt with on an accruals basis. If the 'mark to market' basis is used, the relevant amounts to be included will need to be established for each chargeable accounting period. Other sources of income, such as rents, are allocated to the chargeable accounting period in which they arise (with no apportionment over the period during which they accrue). There are, however, some anti-avoidance provisions where rent is received from an associated company — see page 446. Chargeable gains are allocated to the chargeable accounting period in which the disposal occurs, and charges on income (i.e. patent royalties and charitable covenants/donations) to the chargeable accounting period in which they are paid.

If a company ceases to trade, the date of cessation marks the end of a chargeable accounting period even if the period of account continues to the normal accounting date. The commencement of winding-up also marks the end of a chargeable accounting period, accounting periods then running for successive periods of 12 months until the winding-up is completed.

Losses (TA 1988, ss 393, 393A, 396; FA 1996, s 83 and Sch 8)

When a company incurs a trading loss, it may set the loss against any other profits of the same accounting period, both income and capital, and then, if it wishes, carry any balance back against the total profits of accounting periods ended within the previous three years, latest first, proportionately restricted to exclude profits of an accounting period falling partly outside those three years. Any balance of loss remaining (or the whole loss if the company does not wish to claim the current set-off and carry-back) is carried forward to set against later profits of the same trade. The detailed provisions are in chapter 26, which also deals with the transfer of trading losses within groups.

Where a loss arises under Schedule D, Case III (a non-trading deficit — see page 28), the relief available is similar to that for trading losses.

If a company sustains losses on other sources of income, for example on rented property, the set-off is confined to the same source of income (and in the case of rented property, depends on the type of lease — see chapter 32).

Capital losses are set against capital gains of the same chargeable accounting period, any excess being carried forward to set against future gains. Capital losses cannot be carried back.

Rate of tax (TA 1988, s 8; FA 1996, s 77)

Corporation tax rates are fixed for financial years ending 31 March. Financial years are identified by the calendar year in which they commence, so the financial year 1996 is the year to 31 March 1997. The rate for the financial year 1996 is 33%. A lower small companies rate applies where profits are below a stipulated threshold (see below). For details of the rates in recent years, see page xxiv.

Where the tax rate changes during a company's chargeable accounting period, the total profits are apportioned on a time basis (in days) and charged at the respective rates in calculating the corporation tax payable for the period.

Small companies rate (TA 1988, s 13; FA 1996, s 78)

Where a company's profits are below a stipulated amount, a lower rate of tax is charged. The small companies rate has been 25% since 1 April 1988, but it has now been reduced to 24% from 1 April 1996. There is a special definition of profits for the small companies rate. It includes not only the profits chargeable to corporation tax (which are called the 'basic profits') but also dividends received from other UK companies plus their related tax credits (the dividends plus the credits being called 'franked investment income'). The tax credit is at the rate of ¼ of the cash dividend, so that a cash dividend of £800 carries a tax credit of £200 and thus represents franked investment income of £1,000. The inclusion of franked investment income in the calculations means that it is not possible for a company with a large amount of income in that form to obtain the benefit of the small companies rate on only a small amount of profits chargeable to corporation tax.

Where the profits as defined lie between the stipulated level for small companies rate and an upper maximum, marginal relief is available. The marginal relief is given by calculating tax on the basic profits at the full corporation tax rate and reducing it by an amount arrived at by the following formula:

$$(M - P) \times \frac{I}{P} \times F$$

where M = Upper maximum
P = Profits as defined for small companies rate purposes (see above)
I = Basic profits, i.e. the income and gains chargeable to corporation tax
F = Small companies marginal relief fraction

The upper and lower limits for the years to 31 March 1992, 1993 and 1994 are £1,250,000 and £250,000 and for the years to 31 March 1995, 1996 and 1997 they are £1,500,000 and £300,000. The marginal relief fraction is ¹⁄₅₀ for the five years to 31 March 1996 and ⁹⁄₄₀₀ for the year to 31 March 1997 (see page xxiv).

The marginal relief ensures that the corporation tax rate on the profits is gradually increased to the full level, but the effect is that profits lying between the lower and upper limits suffer a tax rate in excess of the full rate. This marginal rate was 35% for the five years to 31 March 1996 and is 35.25% for the year to 31 March 1997 where there is no franked investment income. (Where there is franked investment income the marginal rate is less.) See example 1.

> **Example 1**
>
> Year to 31 March 1997
>
> Company with no franked investment income has the following profits chargeable to corporation tax:
>
> | | | £ |
> |---|---|---:|
> | (i) £300,000 @ 24% | | 72,000 |
> | or | | |
> | (ii) £310,000 @ 33% | | 102,300 |
>
> Marginal relief $(1,500,000 - 310,000) \times \dfrac{310,000}{310,000} \times \dfrac{9}{400}$ 26,775   75,525
>
> Additional corporation tax on extra £10,000 profits (35.25%)   £3,525

To the extent that a company is able to reduce its profits within the marginal tranche, it can thus save tax at the marginal rate.

The lower and upper limits are annual limits and they are scaled down proportionately if an accounting period is less than 12 months. They are also scaled down where for any part of a chargeable accounting period a company has associated companies. Associated companies include both companies associated through being members of the same group and companies controlled by the same persons. If, for example, the same persons control five companies, the limits for each company for the year to 31 March 1997 are £60,000 and £300,000. If four have profits of £70,000 and one £20,000 the small companies rate will only apply to the last one, and the others will have profits subject to the marginal relief. On the other hand if, say, there were two companies associated with each other and one's profits were £1,800,000 and the other's £150,000, the company with £150,000 profits would qualify for small companies rate even though the combined profits greatly exceeded the upper maximum.

If a company's accounting period does not end on 31 March and there is a change either in the marginal relief fraction (as in the year to 31 March 1997) or in the marginal relief limits or both, the profit figures have to be apportioned to apply the respective figures for the different financial years.

The small companies rate or marginal relief must be specifically claimed, by a statement in the company's return, computation or accompanying correspondence and, except for unincorporated associations such as members' clubs, the statement should indicate how many associated companies there are. If there are none, this should be stated. The claim is incorporated in the Pay and File return CT 200 (see page 136).

Franked investment income (TA 1988, s 238)

Dividends and other distributions of company profits are not allowable deductions in calculating the profits chargeable to corporation tax. Where dividends from UK-resident companies are received by a company, they do not have to be included in that company's profits chargeable to corporation tax because the underlying profits of the paying company have already suffered corporation tax before the dividend was paid. In the hands of the receiving company the dividends plus their related tax credits are termed 'franked investment income'. Such income may be passed on as dividends to the receiving company's own shareholders without tax consequences for the receiving company. The tax credit attached to a dividend is equal to the amount of corporation tax accounted for in advance (ACT) by the paying company (see below).

Dividend payments and other distributions (TA 1988, ss 14, 20, 231, 238, 239, 241, 246 and Sch 13)

When a company pays dividends or makes other qualifying distributions (see page 35), such as distributions in kind instead of cash, it has to pay over in advance some of the corporation tax on the profits of the period in which the dividend is paid. The dividend plus the ACT is called a franked payment.

Where a company has *received* dividends, it only has to pay ACT to the extent that its franked payments (i.e. dividends paid plus ACT) exceed its franked investment income.

From 1 April 1994, the ACT rate and tax credit rate are equivalent to the lower rate of income tax (currently 20%).

Example 2

Company received a dividend of £100,000 with a tax credit of £25,000 on 1 May 1996. It paid a dividend of £160,000 to its own shareholders on 1 November 1996, passing on tax credits of £40,000. The company has franked investment income of £125,000 to set against its franked payment of £200,000. It therefore pays ACT on £75,000 at 20%, i.e. £15,000.

From 1 July 1994, companies may pay and receive 'foreign income dividends' (FIDs), i.e. dividends paid out of foreign source profits. These are dealt with separately from other dividends paid and received, although ACT on the FIDs is calculated in the same way as on other dividends and is entered in a separate section of the quarterly return form CT 61 (see below). For details, see page 571.

Within fourteen days after the end of each calendar quarter ended 31 March, 30 June, 30 September and 31 December the company has to account to the Revenue (on form CT 61) for the ACT on dividends paid during the quarter. If the company's accounting period does not end on one of those dates, there are five return periods, the fifth ending at the end of the accounting period, with the ACT due within fourteen days thereafter.

Where there is a change in the rate of advance corporation tax, the previous rate is used for a dividend paid between 1 and 5 April inclusive. If the change occurs during an accounting period in which a dividend has been paid before 6 April and a dividend has been paid or received on or after that date, the parts before and after the change are treated as separate accounting periods for ACT purposes (but the dates of the return periods are not affected).

If a company's franked investment income exceeds its franked payments, the excess, known as surplus franked investment income, may be carried forward and a later dividend payment made out of it. It may alternatively be used to obtain a repayment of tax credit where a company has made a trading loss. This is dealt with in chapter 26.

As the name indicates, advance corporation tax is an advance payment of the company's liability to pay corporation tax, and, subject to a maximum set-off limit, it reduces the corporation tax on the profits of the accounting period in which the dividend is paid. For the five years ended 31 March 1993, the set-off limit was 25% of the company's profits chargeable to corporation tax, reduced to 22½% for the year to 31 March 1994 and 20% thereafter.

Example 3

Company had following profits in year to 28 February 1995:

	£
Income from trading, etc.	1,400,000
Capital gains	100,000
Profits chargeable to corporation tax	£1,500,000
Corporation tax payable @ 33%	£495,000
Maximum ACT set-off:	
1/12 × £1,500,000 × 22½%	28,125
11/12 × £1,500,000 × 20%	275,000
	£303,125

The limit for the year of £303,125 is compared with the ACT on dividends paid in the year, no matter whether they are paid before or after 31 March 1994 when the rate changed.

Where the ACT rate changes during the accounting period, the set-off limit is arrived at by applying the different rates to a proportionate part of the profits, as shown in example 3.

Surplus ACT (TA 1988, s 239)

If the amount of ACT paid exceeds the permitted set-off, the excess — called surplus ACT — may be carried back and set against the corporation tax liability of accounting periods commencing in the previous six years, latest first, but again subject to the maximum relief limit for those years. The carry-back claim must be made within two years after the end of the accounting period in which the surplus ACT arises. Any balance of ACT remaining unrelieved may be carried forward without time limit. See example 4.

A company may find itself with surplus ACT for an earlier year as a result of carrying back a trading loss, but be unable to claim to carry back the surplus because the time limit has expired. When such ACT is carried forward to a later year, it may then be included in a carry-back claim for that later year. See example 5.

Where ACT is carried back, the tax for the earlier period will usually already have been paid, so that a tax repayment will result. For the calculation of interest on such a repayment, see page 38.

The balance of corporation tax payable after the set-off of ACT is popularly called mainstream corporation tax.

Example 4

	Year to 31 March			
	1993 £	1994 £	1995 £	1996 £
Profits chargeable to corporation tax	80,000	100,000	95,000	120,000
Maximum ACT set-off:				
(25% of profits)	20,000			
(22½% of profits)		22,500		
(20% of profits)			19,000	24,000
Corporation tax payable at small companies rate of 25%	20,000	25,000	23,750	30,000
Less ACT paid in year, say	(10,000)	(19,900)	(18,000)	(36,075)
Surplus ACT carried back	(8,475)	(2,600)	(1,000)	12,075
Mainstream corporation tax payable	£1,525	£2,500	£4,750	£6,000

Example 5

A company claims to carry back a loss of the year to 31 December 1995, and as a result ACT that was originally within the permitted set-off limit becomes surplus ACT in the year to 31 December 1992. A claim to set the surplus ACT off against corporation tax payable for the six years back to 1986 cannot be made for 1992, but a claim to carry back surplus ACT for, say, 1994, made within the two-year time limit, i.e. by 31 December 1996, could include the 1992 surplus ACT that had been carried forward into 1994, so that the surplus could then be carried back to 1988.

When the small companies rate was the same as the ACT set-off rate, a company chargeable at small companies rate had no mainstream tax charge where the maximum ACT set-off was made. The reduction in the ACT rate from 25% to 22½% for the year to 31 March 1994, and then to 20% thereafter, means that even with the maximum set-off, there will still be some mainstream corporation tax to pay (see example 4).

Foreign income dividends

In the normal way, ACT may only be used to reduce a corporation tax bill. Although carrying back surplus ACT may generate a tax refund, the refund represents mainstream tax no longer due because of the ACT set-off. The ACT itself is not repaid. From 1 July 1994 companies with overseas profits may pay 'foreign income dividends' on which any surplus ACT will be repaid to them. For details see page 571.

Qualifying and non-qualifying distributions (TA 1988, ss 14, 233, 234, 238)

The legislation distinguishes between 'qualifying distributions' and 'non-qualifying distributions'. Qualifying distributions attract an ACT liability as indicated above. Non-qualifying distributions are broadly those that confer a future rather than a current claim on the company's assets, such as a bonus issue of redeemable shares. The company has no tax liability on such a distribution, but the shareholder is liable where appropriate to the excess of higher rate over lower rate income tax. The company is required to notify the Revenue within fourteen days after the end of the quarter in which the non-qualifying distribution is made.

When the shares are redeemed, the redemption is a qualifying distribution liable to ACT, but any tax paid by the shareholder on the non-qualifying distribution may be set against higher rate tax due from him on the later qualifying distribution.

Where a company supplies goods or services to a shareholder for more than cost but at a price concession, a distribution does not arise because there is no cost to the company, as distinct from a reduction in profit margins, so that no part of the company profits has been distributed.

Accounting for income tax deducted

Where companies deduct income tax from payments made, they have to account to the Revenue for the tax deducted. Before April 1996 the rate of tax deducted was always the basic rate of income tax. For payments made on or after 6 April 1996, payments of interest will be made net of 20% tax. Other payments from which tax is deducted, such as patent royalties and charitable covenants/donations, will still be paid net of basic rate tax. The basic rate has been reduced from 25% to 24% from 6 April 1996.

In the same way, income *received* by a company in the form of interest may have had tax deducted at 20% (see page 28), whereas patent royalties received would be net of 24% tax. Any income tax deducted from a company's income may be retained out of income tax to be accounted for on the company's payments. If any income tax suffered cannot be recovered in this way, it will be set against the company's corporation tax liability, or if that is insufficient it will be repaid.

Tax payable is accounted for at the appropriate rate of either 20% or 24% on the same form CT 61 as that used for advance corporation tax. Returns are made to 31 March, 30 June, 30 September and 31 December, the tax being due within fourteen days after the quarter ends. Where a company's accounting year does not end on one of the four calendar quarter days the company has five return periods, the first running from the first day of the account to the next calendar quarter day and the last ending at the end of the accounting period.

Date of payment of mainstream corporation tax (TA 1988, s 10)

Since the introduction of the Pay and File system for accounting periods ending on or after 1 October 1993, the due date of payment of mainstream corporation tax is nine months and one day after the end of the accounting period in all cases, even though the tax return is not due until twelve months after the end of the accounting period. Assessments will not normally be issued until the corporation tax liability has been agreed (and will not normally be issued at all once self-assessment applies — see pages 25, 26). Where, as will often be the case, the amount calculated at the nine-month date is estimated, further amounts should be paid, or repayments may be claimed, as the company revises its estimate of the amount due, or following the submission of the tax return, or following the settlement of queries raised by the inspector and (before self-assessment) the issue of the corporation tax assessment. The Revenue has stated that

Example 6

Company's results for the year to 31 March 1997 are:	£
Trading profits, net of allowable expenses	
other than interest (see below)	311,000
Rents receivable, net of allowable expenses	16,000
Interest received net of tax June 1996 (gross amount)	30,000
Chargeable gains	104,000
Patent royalties paid net of tax May 1996 (gross amount)	48,000
Loan interest relating to the trade, paid net of tax	
November 1996 (gross amount)	10,000

Interest received and interest receivable are the same amounts. The interest payable for the year exceeds the interest paid during the year by £3,000.

The company paid a dividend of £100,000 in October 1996. There were no amounts brought forward from earlier years.

Corporation tax computation	£
Trading profits net of £13,000 interest *payable*	298,000
Interest received	30,000
Rents	16,000
Chargeable gains	104,000
Total profits	448,000
Less charges on income — patent royalties	48,000
Profits chargeable to corporation tax	400,000

(Maximum ACT set-off 20% × 400,000 = £80,000)

Corporation tax thereon @ 33%	132,000
Less marginal relief for small companies rate	
(1,500,000 − 400,000) × $\frac{9}{400}$	24,750
Corporation tax payable	107,250

How tax accounted for

CT 61 return for quarter to 30 June 1996	
Income tax deducted from patent royalties paid	
May 1996 48,000 @ 24%	11,520
Less income tax deducted from interest received	
June 1996 30,000 @ 20%	6,000
Income tax payable by 14 July 1996	5,520

CT 61 return for quarter to 31 December 1996	
Income tax deducted from loan interest paid	
November 1996 10,000 @ 20%	2,000
ACT on October 1996 dividend ¼ × 100,000	25,000
Payable by 14 January 1997	27,000

Pay and File payment	
Corporation tax as shown above	107,250
Less ACT paid (within permitted ACT set-off of £80,000)	25,000
Mainstream tax payable 1 January 1998	82,250

claims for repayment may be made before the due date for the return if a repayment is considered to be due, but repayment claims after the return due date should be supported by the completed return. Once the liability is finally agreed, the tax under- or overpaid will be adjusted, together with interest (see below).

Interest on overdue and overpaid tax (TMA 1970, s 87A; TA 1988, s 826)

Interest is charged on overdue corporation tax and the interest is not allowable in calculating taxable profits. If tax is overpaid, interest is added to the repayment, and such interest is free of tax. Before Pay and File, the rate of interest on under- or overpaid tax was the same, but there was a year's delay before interest started to run on an overpayment (such interest being called 'repayment supplement'). Under Pay and File, which applies to accounting periods ending after 30 September 1993, the one-year delay no longer applies, but the rate of interest on overpaid tax is lower than the rate on underpayments. The latest rates of interest available are shown on page xxiii.

As indicated on page 25, the due date for payment of corporation tax is nine months after the end of the accounting period, despite the fact that the actual liability may not be agreed for some considerable time after that date. Interest is charged from the nine-month date on any underpayments, and interest is paid on any overpayments from the date the overpayment was made until the date the repayment order is issued. The estimate of the amount of tax due may be amended several times before the liability is finally established. Companies will therefore pay or receive interest on a provisional basis, until the time that the corporation tax liability is finally agreed, when the interest charge will be finally adjusted.

Interest on tax underpaid or overpaid and surplus ACT

Where surplus ACT is carried back, the carry-back usually affects interest calculations only from the normal due date of payment for the period in which the surplus ACT arose.

Where, however, surplus ACT arises in an accounting period ended after 30 September 1993 *and* as a result of carrying back a loss *further* than twelve months, interest calculations are affected only from the normal due date of payment for the period in which the loss arose. This will be much later than the accounting period in which the ACT arose, and can substantially affect the amount of interest on overpaid tax that the company receives.

Company liquidations (TA 1988, ss 12, 342)

When a company goes into liquidation this is usually preceded by a cessation of trade. The cessation of trade triggers the end of a chargeable accounting period, and a chargeable accounting period also ends at the commencement of winding-up (and at twelve-monthly intervals until the winding-up is completed).

Problems can arise when a company that has been making trading losses realises chargeable gains on the sale of its assets, because if the gains are realised after the trade ceases there will be no current trading losses to offset them, but it is not possible to part with the assets until the trade has ceased. This problem can be avoided if the contract for sale of the assets takes place before ceasing to trade, with completion taking place subsequently. The contract date is the relevant disposal date for capital gains purposes, and any trading losses occurring in the accounting period in which the trade ceases will then be available to reduce the gains. The gains cannot, however, be reduced by trading losses brought forward (see chapter 26 for the detailed provisions on company losses).

Close companies (TA 1988, ss 13A, 414–422; FA 1989, ss 103–107 and Sch 12)

A close company is a company under the control of five or fewer participators (which broadly means shareholders, although it is defined more widely), or under the control of its directors. In considering what rights an individual has in a company, the rights of his 'associates' are included, which covers close family, partners and the trustees of any family settlements.

As well as being subject to the normal corporation tax rules, close companies are subject to additional requirements.

Benefits in kind to participators are treated as distributions (except where already treated as earnings under the Schedule E benefits rules, see chapter 10) and loans to participators attract a tax liability. These provisions are dealt with in chapter 12.

If the company is a 'close investment-holding company', tax is charged at the full rate of corporation tax (currently 33%) rather than at the lower small companies rate, whatever the level of the company's profits. A company is not a close investment-holding company if it is a trading company (including companies that deal in land, shares or securities) or a member of a trading group, or if it carries on the business of property investment on a commercial basis.

Close company liquidations

Where a close trading company ceases to trade and goes into liquidation, it will not be treated as a close investment-holding company for the accounting period beginning at the commencement of winding-up, providing it was within the definition of a close trading company for the previous accounting period. This provision will be of little benefit to most companies, since there will almost always be a gap between ceasing to trade and commencing winding-up, and that gap is treated as a separate accounting period (see page 39). The 33% rate will thus apply to the period in which the winding-up commences as well as to later chargeable accounting periods until the winding-up is completed.

Groups of companies (TA 1988, ss 240, 247, 248, 402–413; TCGA 1992, ss 170–175, 178–181, 190; FA 1996, s 83, Sch 8 para 2 and Sch 14 para 13)

The Taxes Acts do not treat a group of companies as a taxable entity. The corporation tax position of each company in the group is computed independently (small companies rate and various other limits being scaled down according to the number of associated companies). There are, however, various provisions that recognise the group structure and give special treatment in the appropriate circumstances.

Holding company and its 51% subsidiaries

(a) ACT paid by the holding company on dividends (not other distributions) may be surrendered to one or more subsidiaries for use against the subsidiary's corporation tax liability for the corresponding or future accounting periods. It cannot be carried back by a subsidiary.

(b) A subsidiary cannot surrender ACT to its holding company, but it can avoid paying ACT in the first place, because an election may be made for a subsidiary to pay a dividend to its holding company (or to a fellow subsidiary) without accounting for ACT. Such a dividend is termed 'group income'. The receiving company will thus have no tax credit passed to it and will pay ACT in the normal way as and when it passes the dividend on to its own shareholders. These provisions also apply to dividends paid by a trading company to a consortium of UK resident companies who own 75% or more of its issued ordinary share capital.

(c) Charges on income and interest may be paid gross by any group company to another, providing they make an election to do so.

Holding company and its 75% subsidiaries

(a) Trading losses (and charges in excess of other profits) can be surrendered to other group members for use against total profits (including capital gains) of the corresponding accounting period. The same applies from 1 April 1996 to an excess of non-trading losses/payments on loans over non-trading income on loans. (Trading interest paid and losses on trade loans will be a trading expense from that date and will thus form part of a trading loss.) These provisions — called group relief — are dealt with in chapter 26.

(b) Chargeable assets for capital gains purposes are transferred to another group company without a chargeable gain arising, the transferee company assuming the base cost and acquisition date of the transferor company. In this way assets to be sold outside the group can first be centralised in one company for setting off losses against profits. Otherwise there is no facility for chargeable gains of one group company to be relieved by capital losses of another.

(c) A chargeable gain made by one group company on a business asset qualifying for rollover relief may be rolled over or held over against an acquisition by another group company. Rollover relief is dealt with in chapter 4.

The group provisions have frequently been manipulated in order to make tax savings over and above what the provisions are intended to allow, and there are numerous anti-avoidance provisions. These include provisions charging gains where a company leaves a group within six years after acquiring an asset inter-group on a no gain/no loss basis, denying group relief for losses where there are 'arrangements' under which some or all of a company's shares could be disposed of to another party and preventing groups using the acquisition of companies with capital losses to avoid tax on current gains, or acquiring companies that have not used their available ACT set-off in earlier years in order to reduce surplus ACT within the group by means of inter-group dividends.

Members' clubs

As stated on page 25, the profits of members' clubs are chargeable to corporation tax. This applies to profits from transactions other than between the club members themselves, so it covers such items as interest received on deposits of the club's funds, and any trading profits on transactions with non-members, no matter how small such income may be. Clubs with taxable profits should complete corporation tax return forms CT 200. Sometimes the Revenue have been prepared to treat a club as 'dormant', so that returns have not been required, and this has particularly been so where the only income is interest from which basic rate tax has been deducted, since the club's corporation tax liability would be at the same rate. Now that the income tax rate on interest has been reduced to 20% it would appear that 'dormant' status will no longer be available to any clubs if there is any investment income at all.

Encouraging business efficiency

Various measures are available to enable companies to operate in a
tax-efficient manner and to stimulate investment in new and expanding
ventures:

>Enterprise investment scheme.
>Purchase of own shares by company.
>Demergers.

These are dealt with separately in chapter 29.

4
Capital gains tax: general principles

Introduction

Capital gains tax was introduced with effect from 6 April 1965. The law was consolidated in the Taxation of Chargeable Gains Act 1992 but has been substantially amended since then. All references in this chapter are to that Act unless otherwise stated.

Basis of charge (ss 1–6, 16(2A), 35 and Sch 3; FA 1995, s 113)

Capital gains tax applies when chargeable assets are disposed of. Gains and losses are calculated on each asset. In general, the cost of an asset acquired before 31 March 1982 is taken to be its value on that date, although there are provisions to use original cost in some circumstances. An allowance, called indexation allowance, is made to adjust for inflation, and the gains and losses are then aggregated to give the net chargeable gains or allowable losses for the year. If losses exceed gains, the losses are carried forward without time limit, to set against later gains to the extent that they are not covered by the annual exemption (see page 54). Details of losses used to be required by the Revenue only at the time when they were used to reduce gains. Following the introduction of self-assessment in 1996/97, relief for losses will usually be claimed in tax returns, with an overall time limit to make the claim of 5 years 10 months from the end of the tax year in which the loss occurred (without, however, restricting the time for which the losses may be carried forward).

The first £6,300 of an individual's gains in 1996/97 is exempt and the balance is charged at income tax rates as if it were the top slice of the taxpayer's income (although personal allowances, charges on income, etc. cannot be offset against chargeable gains) — see example 1.

If an individual's income includes dividends and/or other income from savings, and his taxable income from other sources (after deducting available allowances) is less than the lower rate band of £3,900, the balance of the lower rate band is available against gains. The basic rate threshold for income tax is then reduced by the amount of gains charged at the lower rate. See example 2.

Example 1

Net gains in 1996/97 £17,300 less annual exemption £6,300 = £11,000.

If taxpayer's taxable income is	Capital gains tax payable is		£
Nil, because income is equal to or less than available allowances	3,900 @ 20%	780	
	7,100 @ 24%	1,704	2,484
£6,000	11,000 @ 24%		2,640
£15,000	10,500 @ 24%	2,520	
	500 @ 40%	200	2,720
£26,000	11,000 @ 40%		4,400

The annual exemption and tax rates for personal representatives and trustees are dealt with on pages 66 and 67.

Trading losses

Sole traders and partners may set off unrelieved trading losses against their capital gains in certain circumstances — see chapter 25 for the detailed provisions.

Persons liable (ss 2, 9–12)

Individuals who are resident or ordinarily resident in the UK are liable on all gains wherever they arise, if UK domiciled, and on gains arising in, or remitted to, the UK if domiciled elsewhere. Non-residents carrying on a trade, profession or vocation in the UK are liable on gains arising on the disposal of business assets in the UK. The overseas aspect is dealt with in chapter 41.

For the position of personal representatives and trustees, see page 66.

Husband and wife (ss 2, 58)

Gains of husband and wife are calculated and charged separately, each being entitled to the annual exemption (£6,300 for 1996/97). Losses of one may not be set against the other's gains. Disposals between husband and wife in a tax year when they are living together are, however, not chargeable. The acquiring spouse is treated as having acquired the asset when the other

Example 2

Fact as in example 1, i.e. gains net of annual exemption are £11,000, but taxable income includes savings income comprising dividends (inclusive of tax credits) as shown below (the capital gains tax payable where all income was covered by allowances remains the same):

Dividends £	Other income £	Total taxable income £
5,000	1,000	6,000
14,000	1,000	15,000
25,000	1,000	26,000

Since in each case there is £2,900 of the lower rate band available to use against capital gains, the basic rate threshold available for income tax is reduced to (25,500 – 2,900) = £22,600.

Income and tax thereon		£	£	Capital gains and tax thereon		£	£
Other	1,000	@ 20%	200	2,900	@ 20%		580
Divs	5,000	@ 20%	1,000	8,100	@ 24%		1,944
	6,000		1,200	11,000			2,524
Other	1,000	@ 20%	200	2,900	@ 20%		580
Divs	14,000	@ 20%	2,800	7,600	@ 24%		1,824
				500	@ 40%		200
	15,000		3,000	11,000			2,604
Other	1,000	@ 20%	200	2,900	@ 20%		580
Divs	21,600	@ 20%	4,320	8,100	@ 40%		3,240
	22,600						
Divs	3,400	@ 40%	1,360				
	26,000		5,880	11,000			3,820

In the first two instances, the capital gains tax payable is £116 less than in example 1, representing £2,900 @ (24 – 20)%. In the third instance, there is no overall benefit, since the reduction in capital gains tax (£2,900 @ (40 – 20)% = £580) is matched by the increase in income tax, a further £2,900 of dividends being charged at 40% instead of 20%.

spouse acquired it, at its original cost plus indexation allowance to the date of transfer (subject to rules to ensure that the indexation allowance does not create or increase a loss when the other spouse disposes of the asset — see page 65). It should therefore be possible through advance planning and transfers of assets between them to ensure that one spouse is not left with unrelieved losses while the other has gains in excess of the exemption.

Companies (s 8 and TA 1988, s 6)

Gains are computed on capital gains tax principles but are charged to corporation tax and not capital gains tax. The rate of corporation tax payable is the same as that charged on the company's other profits. The annual exemption is not available. Recent corporation tax rates are shown on page xxiv.

Chargeable assets and exempt assets (ss 21–27, 51, 251–255)

All forms of property are chargeable unless specifically exempt and disposal of a chargeable asset may give rise to a chargeable gain or allowable loss. A chargeable gain or allowable loss may also arise when a capital sum is realised without any disposal taking place (for example if compensation is received for damage to an asset, although if the compensation is used to restore the asset no gain arises).

As far as the treatment of money lent is concerned, the rules are different for companies and for other taxpayers. Capital gains and losses on money lent by or to companies are brought into the company's computation of income from 1 April 1996 (see page 27). The rules for other taxpayers are dealt with below.

Where an asset is exempt no chargeable gain or allowable loss can normally arise, although there are some special rules about losses on chattels. See the table on page 47 for exempt assets and for the chapter in this book which deals with them.

If you win a lottery prize it is exempt from capital gains tax, as indicated in the table. If you play as a member of a group, the group should draw up an agreement setting out how the group will operate, who will buy tickets and claim prizes, and how any prize money is to be shared. Otherwise a group claimant passing on shares of prize money to other group members could be regarded as making gifts for inheritance tax purposes. The same would apply to similar group arrangements, such as for football pools. There would not, however, be any inheritance tax to pay unless the person who passed on the shares of prize money died within seven years, and even then there may be exemptions available to cover the gifts.

Treatment of loans

For companies, capital transactions relating to loans are brought into account for income purposes (see page 27). For individuals, trustees and personal representatives, a debt is not within the capital gains provisions unless it is a 'debt on a security' (which broadly means marketable loan stock). Even then, most loan stock is within the definition of a 'qualifying corporate bond' (see page 532), and is exempt from capital gains tax. The effect is that if capital losses arise on simple debts, or capital losses or gains arise on qualifying

Exempt assets

	TCGA 1992 reference	See chapter
An individual's only or main residence (providing various conditions are satisfied, otherwise part or all of the gain may be chargeable)	222, 223	30
Chattels which are wasting assets, unless used in a business	45	39
Non-wasting and business chattels where disposal proceeds do not exceed £6,000	262	39
Government securities and qualifying company loan stock	115	38
SAYE contracts, savings certificates and premium bonds	121	36
Prizes and betting winnings	51	See page 46
Private motor cars, including veteran and vintage cars	263	
Sterling currency, and foreign currency for an individual's own spending and maintenance of assets abroad	21, 269	39
Decorations for valour if disposed of by the original holder or legatees but not by a purchaser	268	
Compensation or damages for personal or professional wrong or injury (and by concession, certain compensation from foreign governments for property lost or confiscated)	51	
Life assurance policies but only in the hands of the original owner or beneficiaries	210	40
Gifts of assets that are considered by the Treasury to be of national, historic or scientific interest, but breach of any conditions imposed will nullify the CGT exemption	258	
Gifts to charities	257	43

corporate bonds, no relief is available for the losses (subject to some special rules for loans to UK traders — see pages 63 and 532), and gains are exempt. For the treatment of loan stock that is outside the definition of qualifying corporate bonds see page 532. Where a simple debt has been assigned other than to someone with whom the creditor is 'connected' (see page 60), the debt is a chargeable asset for the assignee, thus giving rise to a chargeable gain or allowable loss on a disposal by the assignee.

Computation of gains and losses (ss 2, 15–17, 35–57 and Schs 2–4)

Gains and losses are worked out by deducting from the sale proceeds or, in some instances, from the market value at the time of disposal (see page 60) the following amounts:

> Original cost and incidental costs of acquisition
> Expenditure that has increased the value of the asset
> Incidental costs of disposal

An indexation allowance (see below) is then given to reduce or eliminate a gain, but for disposals on or after 30 November 1993 the allowance cannot create or increase a loss (subject to certain transitional provisions for 1993/94 and 1994/95).

Effect of capital allowances (s 41)

Gains on some assets that qualify for capital allowances are exempt from capital gains tax, such as on items of movable plant and machinery bought and sold for less than £6,000 (see page 541). Where an asset is not exempt, capital allowances are not deducted from the cost in computing a gain, so that there will be a gain before indexation allowance only if the asset is sold for more than original cost. Capital allowances are, however, taken into account in computing a loss, so that losses cannot normally arise, since the capital allowance system covers any drop in value. For disposals before 30 November 1993 a loss usually arose because of the indexation allowance, but this is no longer possible.

For an example, see page 310.

Indexation allowance (ss 53, 54; FA 1994, s 93)

The indexation allowance is calculated by applying to each item of expenditure the increase in the retail prices index between the month when the expenditure was incurred, or March 1982 if later, and the month of disposal of the asset. The index increase is expressed as a decimal and rounded (up or down) to three decimal places. The movement in the index is published monthly and the figure for each month since March 1982 is tabled on page xxvi. The formula for working out the increase is:

$$\frac{RD - RI}{RI} \text{ or put more simply } \frac{RD}{RI} - 1$$

RD is the index for the month of disposal and RI the index for the month in which the expenditure was incurred. Using the figures in the table on page xxvi, the increase from November 1982 to February 1996 is

$$\frac{150.9}{82.66} - 1 = .826 \text{ (or as a percentage, 82.6\%)}$$

For disposals on or after 30 November 1993, the indexation allowance can only reduce or eliminate a gain and cannot create or increase a loss (except to the extent that transitional relief was available in 1993/94 and/or 1994/95).

Where the expenditure was incurred before 31 March 1982, the indexation calculation is made by reference to the value of the asset at 31 March 1982 if the taxpayer has elected to be treated as if he had acquired all the assets he owned on 31 March 1982 at their market value on that day (see below). If the election has not been made, the 31 March 1982 value will still be used to calculate the indexation allowance unless using original cost would give a higher figure, in which case the higher figure is taken.

Assets held on 31 March 1982 (ss 35, 36 and Schs 3, 4; FA 1996, Sch 21 para 35)

Originally, capital gains tax applied to gains or losses made on or after 6 April 1965, and there were special rules relating to assets already owned on that date to ensure that when they were disposed of, pre-6 April 1965 gains and losses were excluded. As from 6 April 1988, only gains or losses on or after 31 March 1982 are to be taken into account. Taxpayers may make an irrevocable election (a rebasing election) to regard all assets owned on 31 March 1982 (except plant and machinery on which capital allowances have been, or could have been, claimed) as having been acquired at their market value on that day. The election could have been made by 5 April 1990, whether or not any disposals were made before then. Otherwise, it must be made within two years after the end of the tax year or company accounting period in which the first disposal is made after 5 April 1988 (reduced for individuals from 1996/97 to one year from 31 January following the relevant tax year). For many people the time limit will have already expired because of earlier disposals, so that if the election has not already been made it is no longer available. Most disposals that normally result in no chargeable gain or allowable loss are not, however, treated as triggering the time limit (see Revenue Statement of Practice SP 4/92).

If the election is not made, the 31 March 1982 value is still used to calculate gains and losses, unless using original cost would show a lower gain or lower loss, in which case the lower figure is taken. If one method shows a gain and the other a loss the result is treated as neither a gain nor a loss. In making these calculations indexation allowance is always based on the higher of cost and 31 March 1982 value (see above).

For many assets it may be costly to find out their value at 31 March 1982, but this has to be done whether the election to use 31 March 1982 value is made or not. Examples 3 and 4 show the effect of making or not making the rebasing election.

Example 3

Chargeable asset was bought for £20,000 in 1980 and was worth £24,000 on 31 March 1982. It was sold in December 1996. Taxpayer had made no other disposals since 5 April 1988.

Assume the retail prices index for December 1996 to be 154.9. This gives an index increase from March 1982 of:

$$\frac{154.9}{79.44} - 1 = .95, \text{ i.e. } 95\%$$

Indexation allowance (based on 31 March 1982 value since higher than cost) is therefore £22,800.

If general rebasing election is not made

	(a) £	(b) £	(c) £
Sale proceeds, say	50,000	19,000	22,000
31.3.82 value (giving lower gain)	(24,000)		
Cost (giving lower loss)		(20,000)	
Unindexed gain (loss)	26,000	(1,000)	
Indexation allowance	(22,800)	—	
Chargeable gain (allowable loss)	3,200	(1,000)	No gain, no loss

If rebasing election is made

	(a) £	(b) £	(c) £
Sale proceeds as above	50,000	19,000	22,000
31.3.82 value	(24,000)	(24,000)	(24,000)
Unindexed gain (loss)	26,000	(5,000)	(2,000)
Indexation allowance	(22,800)	—	—
Chargeable gain (allowable loss)	3,200	(5,000)	(2,000)

Rebasing election is either neutral or favourable, depending on sale proceeds.

Example 4

Using the same figures as in example 3, but assuming that cost price was £24,000 and 31.3.82 value was £20,000, i.e. figures are reversed.

If general rebasing election is not made

The outcome will be the same as in example 3, since the lower gain or loss is always taken, and there is no gain or loss where one computation shows a gain and the other a loss.

If general rebasing election is made

Cost of £24,000 becomes irrelevant. Indexation allowance on 31.3.82 value of £20,000 is £19,000.

	(a) £	(b) £	(c) £
Sale proceeds as above	50,000	19,000	22,000
31.3.82 value	(20,000)	(20,000)	(20,000)
Inindexed gain (loss)	30,000	(1,000)	2,000
Indexation allowance	(19,000)	—	(2,000)
Chargeable gain (allowable loss)	11,000	(1,000)	—

Rebasing election is unfavourable or neutral depending on sale proceeds.

Where the right to make a rebasing election is still available, you cannot be selective about making it. If it is made at all, it applies to all chargeable assets you owned on 31 March 1982 (except plant and machinery) and it cannot be revoked. The election does simplify the calculations and it makes it unnecessary to maintain pre-31 March 1982 records.

There are many instances in the capital gains legislation where tax on gains may be deferred to a later time, either by treating the gains as reducing other expenditure, or by treating them as arising at a later time. Where gains were deferred before 31 March 1982, the effect of using 31 March 1982 value to calculate later gains is that these deferred gains will escape tax altogether, since the cost from which the deferred gain was deducted is no longer used. Where an asset acquired after 31 March 1982 but before 6 April 1988 is disposed of after 5 April 1988, and the gain relates wholly or partly, directly or indirectly, to an asset acquired before 31 March 1982 (in other words, where a claim for deferral was made between 31 March 1982 and 5 April 1988 that related to an asset acquired before 31 March 1982), a claim may be made for one-half of the gain to be exempt from tax (see example 5).

The main occasions when this relief applies are:

Rollover and holdover relief on replacement of business assets or compulsorily acquired land (see page 55).

Example 5

1979 Taxpayer acquires business asset No. 1 for £5,000.

1984 Asset No. 1 is sold at a gain of £2,000 and asset No. 2 is acquired for £8,000. The gain is rolled over.

1986 Asset No. 2 is sold at a gain of £5,000 (after taking into account gain rolled over on asset No. 1) and asset No. 3 is acquired for £20,000. The gain is rolled over.

1996 Asset No. 3 is sold for £33,000. Available indexation allowance is, say, 55%.

Gain on sale of asset No. 3 is as follows:

	£	£
Sale proceeds 1996		33,000
Cost 1986	20,000	
Less half of rolled over gain of £5,000 (other half being exempt)	2,500	
	17,500	
Indexation allowance 55%	9,625	27,125
Chargeable gain		£5,875

This gain could be rolled over if another qualifying business asset was acquired within three years.

Holdover of gains where assets were acquired by gift, including the charge when the donee emigrates (see pages 60, 61).

Rollover of gains on the transfer of a business to a company (see page 383).

Assets held on 6 April 1965 (s 35 and Sch 2)

Assets already owned on 6 April 1965, the original start date for capital gains tax, will be treated as acquired at market value on 31 March 1982 if the rebasing election is made (see above). If it is not, the position is more complicated, because the old special rules for those assets must be considered in conjunction with the new. The old rules for calculating the position on assets owned on 6 April 1965 contained separate provisions for land with development value, for quoted securities and for all other assets.

The gain or loss on land with development value was calculated by comparing the proceeds either with the original cost or with the value at 6 April 1965, whichever showed the lower gain or loss. If one method showed a gain and the other a loss there was neither gain nor loss. The same rules applied to quoted securities, except that it was possible to elect for quoted securities to be treated as having been acquired on 6 April 1965 at their value on that date and pooled with later acquisitions of shares of the same class in the same company. The detailed provisions are in chapter 38.

Where an asset other than quoted securities or land with development value was acquired before 6 April 1965, only the time proportion of the gain falling after 6 April 1965 was chargeable, although the earliest date that could be used in a time apportionment calculation was 6 April 1945. You could elect to work out the gain by using the 6 April 1965 value as the cost instead of using time apportionment, but once made this election was irrevocable, even if it resulted in more tax being payable.

Following the 1988 changes in the legislation, if the rebasing election has not been made, the above rules are modified to bring the 31 March 1982 value into the calculation. The calculation is first made using the old rules for assets owned on 6 April 1965 but with indexation allowance based on 31 March 1982 value if higher. When making the time apportionment calculation for assets other than quoted securities and land with development value, indexation allowance is deducted before the gain is time apportioned. The resulting gain or loss is compared with the result using 31 March 1982 value. The lower gain or loss is then taken and if one calculation shows a gain and the other a loss, the result is neither gain nor loss. If, however, the old 6 April 1965 rules have already resulted in a no gain/no loss result, that position is not disturbed. See example 6.

Part disposals (ss 42, 242)

Where part only of an asset is disposed of, the cost of the part disposed of is worked out by taking the proportion of the overall cost that the sale proceeds bear to the sum of the sale proceeds plus the market value of what remains unsold. The indexation allowance is calculated on the apportioned part of the cost and not on the total.

Where part of a holding of land is sold for £20,000 or less, and the proceeds represent not more than 20% of the value of the land, the taxpayer may claim not to be treated as having made a disposal, but the amount received reduces the allowable cost of the remaining land for a future disposal. The indexation allowance on a subsequent disposal is calculated on the full cost in the usual way, but is then reduced to take account of the previous part disposal. This claim may not be made if other disposals of land are made in the same year, and the total proceeds for all disposals of land exceed £20,000.

Leases (s 240 and Sch 8)

The grant of a lease at a premium gives rise to a capital gains tax liability, and also an income tax liability if the term is 50 years or less. The calculation of the income and capital elements is shown in chapter 32. Where a tenant assigns a lease at a premium to another tenant, the premium is charged to tax in the normal way if the lease has more than 50 years to run at the time of the assignment. If, however, it has 50 years or less to run, it is a wasting asset and the cost has to be depreciated over that 50 years according to a table in Sch 8 which ensures that the cost is depreciated more slowly during the early part of the 50-year period than during the later years.

Example 6

Cost of antique 6.4.57	£4,000
Value at 6.4.65	£4,500
Value at 31.3.82	£15,000
Sale proceeds 6.4.96	£31,500

Indexation allowance March 1982 to April 1996, say 90%

If no election to use 31.3.82 value for all assets

Calculation using old rules

	£	£
Sale proceeds	31,500	31,500
Cost	(4,000)	
6.4.65 value		(4,500)
Indexation allowance @ 90% on		
31.3.82 value of £15,000	(13,500)	(13,500)
Overall gain	£14,000	

Time proportion since 6.4.65 $\frac{31}{39} \times 14{,}000 =$ 11,128

Gain	£11,128	or	£13,500

Therefore no election would be made to use 6.4.65 value and gain under old rules is £11,128.

Calculation using new rules

	£
Sale proceeds	31,500
31.3.82 value	(15,000)
Indexation allowance 90%	(13,500)
Gain under new rules	£3,000

Chargeable gain is the lower of £11,128 and £3,000, i.e. £3,000.

If election made to use 31.3.82 value for all assets

Chargeable gain is not affected, since the 31 March 1982 value is used in any event.

Annual exemption (s 3 and Sch 1)

The annual exemption is £6,300 for 1996/97, available to each of husband and wife. Provision is made for the exempt amount to be increased each year in line with increases in the retail prices index unless Parliament decides otherwise. Although your gains and losses in the same year must be netted off, brought-forward losses need not be set against gains covered by the exemption. So if, say, you have net gains in the current year of £5,600 and brought forward losses of £4,000, the £4,000 losses are carried forward intact.

If the gains are £7,000, only £700 of the brought-forward losses is used to reduce the gains to the exempt £6,300, leaving £3,300 to be carried forward.

For the annual exemption available to personal representatives and trustees, see pages 66 and 67.

Reliefs

Specific reliefs are available for:

(a) replacement of business assets;
(b) retirement of a sole trader or partner and certain full-time directors and employees;
(c) gifts of certain assets;
(d) transfer of a business to a company;
(e) reinvesting gains into qualifying shares;
(f) assets of negligible value; and
(g) losses on certain loans.

These are dealt with in the following paragraphs, except for (d) which is dealt with in chapter 27.

Replacement of business assets and compulsorily purchased land (ss 152–160, 247; FA 1993, s 86; FA 1995, s 48; FA 1996, s 141)

Where there is a chargeable gain on the disposal of a qualifying business asset and the proceeds (or deemed proceeds if the asset is given away) are matched by the acquisition of another qualifying business asset within the period commencing one year before and ending three years after the disposal, a claim may be made for the gain to be deferred. The Revenue has discretion to extend the time limit. The replacement asset need not be used in the same trade where one person carries on two or more trades either successively or at the same time. For holding companies and their 75% subsidiaries, the disposal and acquisition need not be made by the same group company. But an asset acquired inter-group on a no loss/no gain basis cannot be treated as a qualifying acquisition.

The relief applies to land and buildings, fixed plant and machinery, ships, aircraft, hovercraft, satellites, space stations and spacecraft including launch vehicles, goodwill, milk and potato quotas and ewe and suckler cow premium quotas. The replacement asset does not have to be in the same category as the asset disposed of, providing both are qualifying assets, and the proceeds of a single disposal could be applied in acquiring several qualifying assets or vice versa.

If only part of the sale proceeds is used to acquire replacement assets within the rollover period, the remaining part of the gain is chargeable immediately, treating the gain as the last part of the proceeds to be used.

If the replacement asset has a life of more than 60 years (e.g. freehold land or goodwill) the gain is rolled over and treated as reducing the cost of the replacement asset (see example 7). Indexation allowance on the replacement asset is calculated on the cost less the rolled over gain.

If, however, a gain has been rolled over in this way against a replacement asset acquired before 31 March 1982, the effect of using 31 March 1982 value as the cost of such an asset is that the rolled over gain escapes tax altogether.

If the replacement is a depreciating asset with a life of 60 years or less (which in fact applies to most of the business assets qualifying for relief) the gain does not reduce the tax cost of the replacement (so the calculation of the indexation allowance is not affected) but it is held over for a maximum of ten years. It becomes chargeable when the replacement asset is sold or ceases to be used in a business carried on by the taxpayer, or, at latest, ten years after acquisition of the replacement asset (see example 7). The gain will not crystallise at that point, however, if at or before that time a non-depreciating asset has been acquired against which a claim is made for the gain to be rolled over instead. The held-over gain will escape tax altogether if the disposal to which it relates was made on or before 31 March 1982.

Example 7

Qualifying asset that cost £100,000 sold for £150,000, giving rise to a gain of £20,000 after indexation allowance. Qualifying replacement asset (freehold land) acquired within rollover period for:

£180,000   Full gain reinvested, therefore CGT cost of replacement reduced to £160,000

£145,000   Only £15,000 of gain reinvested, therefore CGT cost of replacement reduced to £130,000 and remaining gain of £5,000 chargeable immediately (unless other qualifying assets acquired within rollover period)

£129,000   No part of gain reinvested therefore full £20,000 chargeable (unless other qualifying assets acquired within rollover period)

If the replacement had been a depreciating asset, there would be no change in the gains immediately chargeable. The CGT cost of the replacement asset would, however, not be reduced. Instead the reinvested gain would be deferred for not more than 10 years.

Both rolled over and held-over gains escape tax completely on the taxpayer's death.

Rollover relief claims must give full details of assets disposed of and acquired, including dates and amounts (and where two group companies are involved, they must make a joint claim). For companies, the time limit for the original rollover or holdover claim is six years from the end of the accounting period to which the claim relates. Following the introduction of self-assessment, the time limit for individuals from 1996/97 is five years from the 31 January following the tax year to which the claim relates. The claim will normally be made in the tax return. Where the replacement asset(s) have not been acquired by the due date for the return, a provisional claim may be made in the return for the tax year in which the disposal took place, and the relief is then given as for an actual claim. The provisional claim will either be superseded by an actual claim, or will cease to have effect three years from the due date for the return for the period of disposal (e.g. for a disposal in 1997/98, the return for which is due by 31 January 1999, the provisional relief would no longer apply after 31 January 2002). All necessary adjustments to assessments and tax bills, including interest on underpaid tax if appropriate, will then be made. Where a holdover claim is being replaced by a rollover claim as a result of the later acquisition of a non-depreciating asset (which could in fact be up to thirteen years after the disposal giving rise to the gain that had been held over), it is thought that the claim to switch from holdover to rollover relief would need to be made in the return for the year in which the non-depreciating asset was acquired.

Rollover relief is also available where an asset owned personally and used in the owner's partnership or personal trading company (see below under 'Retirement relief') is disposed of and replaced. The payment of rent does not affect the availability of the relief.

Rollover relief is only available on investment property in two instances. If the property is the subject of compulsory purchase (or compulsory acquisition by a lessee), the relief is available provided that the replacement is not a capital gains tax exempt dwelling-house — see page 452. (Companies in a 75% group can claim this relief if one company makes a disposal under a compulsory purchase order and another acquires the replacement.) The relief is also available on property let as furnished holiday accommodation (see chapter 32).

See page 51 for the treatment of disposals after 5 April 1988 that are affected by deferred gains on assets acquired before 31 March 1982. See chapter 41 for the overseas aspect of rollover relief.

Retirement relief (ss 163, 164 and Sch 6; FA 1993, s 87 and Sch 7; FA 1994, s 92; FA 1996, s 176 and Sch 39 para 7)

Retirement relief is available to an individual aged 50 or over (55 or over for disposals before 28 November 1995). It is also available to someone who retires at an earlier age because of ill health. To qualify for the relief, the individual must dispose of all or part of his business or partnership share, or of shares in his personal trading company in which he is a director or employee working full-time in a managerial or technical capacity. The relief is available in respect of aggregate gains (net of losses) on the disposal of 'chargeable business assets', which means assets (including goodwill, but not including shares and other assets held as investments) that are used for the purposes of a trade, profession, vocation, office or employment, other than an asset on which no chargeable gain or loss would be made if it was disposed of. Plant or machinery is a chargeable business asset unless it is movable plant or machinery with a cost and value of £6,000 or less (when it would be an exempt chattel). Private type cars are excluded since they are exempt. You are not entitled to the relief just because you sell a qualifying asset. You must dispose of 'part of a business'.

Where the disposal qualifies for relief, all or part of the gains arising on the business assets are exempt up to a maximum of £250,000 and all or part of gains between £250,000 and £1,000,000 are reduced by 50%. A husband and wife can each get relief on gains of up to £1,000,000 providing each satisfies the necessary conditions. 'Personal company' means one in which the individual owns at least 5% of the voting rights.

Where the capital gains cost of a qualifying asset has been reduced by rollover relief (see page 55), the full gain qualifies for retirement relief. But if a gain has been held over because the asset is a depreciating asset (see page 56), retirement relief is not available in respect of the heldover gain.

The available relief is reduced proportionately where the business has not been owned for the whole of the previous ten years, or, in the case of personal companies, where the director or employee has not been working full-time for that period. Where, however, a director or employee ceases full-time working some time before he disposes of his shares, then providing he works for at least ten hours a week on average in the period before disposal, the relief will be given by reference to the length of time for which he was working full-time. The full-time working condition is satisfied if a director or employee spreads his full-time working over several group or associated companies.

The minimum period of ownership or full-time working to enable relief to be claimed is one year (called the qualifying period). In working out how long the business has been owned, the date of disposal is strictly the contract date, but by concession the completion date may be taken instead where business activities have continued up to completion. Where someone has been in business for two or more separate periods, with an intervening gap not exceeding two years, the periods are added together to determine the qualifying period (but if they overlap, the overlap is counted only once). Any part of the resulting period that goes back earlier than ten years is disregarded. It does not affect the relief if part of the qualifying period relates to a self-employed business and part to full-time working in a personal company. Note that it is the length of time the *interest in the business* has been owned that determines the available relief, not the time for which the assets themselves have been owned.

Where the disposal is of shares in a personal company, the gain on the shares is reduced in the proportion of the company's chargeable business assets (i.e. excluding assets held as investments) to the total chargeable assets to arrive at the gain qualifying for relief. Chargeable assets are all assets on which a chargeable gain or allowable loss would arise if the company disposed of

Example 8

In June 1996, Mr C has gains of £850,000 on disposal of business assets on retirement at age 63 from a business he has owned throughout the previous seven years.

In business seven years out of ten, therefore upper limit for relief is 7/10 × £1,000,000 = £700,000

		£
Gains are		850,000
Relief: Fully exempt 7/10 × 250,000	175,000	
50% × (700,000 – 175,000)	262,500	437,500
Chargeable gains		£412,500
If gains had been		400,000
Relief would be: Fully exempt 7/10 × 250,000	175,000	
50% × (400,000 – 175,000)	112,500	287,500
Leaving chargeable gains of		£112,500

which would be further reduced by the annual exemption if not otherwise used.

them (or which would be treated as disposed of for neither gain nor loss). Current assets are therefore excluded. On a disposal of shares in a family holding company of a trading group, it is the group's assets that are taken into account, and inter-group shareholdings are ignored. There is no restriction in the relief if the company or group has no chargeable assets at all.

Property let commercially as furnished holiday accommodation (see chapter 32) qualifies as a business asset for this relief.

The relief may also be given where a director, partner or employee disposes of assets owned by him which have been used for the purposes of the business or employment, or where trustees dispose of settled property consisting of assets qualifying for relief in which a beneficiary has an interest in possession. The relief is, however, restricted if rent is paid, and charging a full market rent during any part of the ten-year qualifying period would deny the relief altogether for that part of the period, except for that fraction of premises let to a partnership that corresponds to the owner's share in the partnership, since he cannot let to himself.

For the interaction of retirement relief and reinvestment relief, see page 62.

Gifts and transactions with connected persons (ss 17–19, 67, 165–169, 258–261, 281, 286 and Sch 7; FA 1993, Sch 7)

For capital gains tax, a gift of a chargeable asset is regarded as a disposal at open market value (except for husband/wife transfers), and the chargeable gain or allowable loss is computed in the usual way, with indexation allowance being taken into account to reduce or eliminate gains. There are, however, some special rules for both gains and losses.

Not only gifts but all transactions between connected persons, or not at arm's length, are regarded as at open market value except for husband/wife transactions, which are not normally chargeable (see page 44). Broadly, a person is connected with his or his wife's close relatives and their spouses, with business partners and their spouses and relatives (except in relation to normal commercial transactions), and, if he is the trustee of a settlement, with the settlor (if an individual) and with any person connected with the settlor. The relatives that are taken into account are parents and 'remoter forebears' (i.e. grandparents, etc.), children and 'remoter issue' (i.e. grand-children, etc.), and brothers and sisters. Companies under the same control are connected with each other and with the persons controlling them.

Where an asset is disposed of to a connected person (other than the individual's husband or wife) and a loss arises, the loss may not be set against general gains but only against a later gain on a transaction with the same connected person. Where someone disposes of assets on different occasions within a period of six years to one or more persons connected with him, and their value taken together is higher than their separate values, then the disposal value for each of the transactions is a proportionate part of the aggregate value, and all necessary adjustments will be made to earlier tax charges.

Where a gain arises on the gift of an asset by an individual or trustees, it may be deferred if the asset qualifies for gifts relief. Gifts relief used to be available on virtually any asset, but the gifts that now qualify for relief are as follows:

(a) Business assets, which comprise
   (i) Assets used in the donor's business or in his personal trading company (i.e. one in which he owns at least 5% of the voting rights);
   (ii) Farm land and buildings that would qualify for inheritance tax agricultural property relief — see page 80; note that this enables relief to be claimed on agricultural land held as an investment, providing the appropriate conditions are satisfied;
   (iii) Shares or securities in trading companies that are neither quoted on the Stock Exchange nor dealt in on the Unlisted Securities Market;
   (iv) Shares or securities in the donor's personal trading company (relief being restricted proportionately if not all the company's assets are business assets);
(b) Gifts of heritage property (works of art, historic buildings, etc.);
(c) Gifts to funds for the maintenance of heritage property;
(d) Gifts to political parties;
(e) Gifts that are *immediately* chargeable to inheritance tax or would be had they not been covered by the inheritance tax annual exemption. This mainly covers gifts into and out of discretionary trusts but also covers any other gifts that are within the inheritance tax annual exemption (see page 70).

Gifts relief is available, where appropriate, on transfers into and out of trust, the relief under heading (a)(i) applying where the business is carried on by trustees or by a beneficiary with a life interest in the trust. For the detailed provisions, see chapter 42.

Where gifts relief is claimed, the donor is not charged to tax on the gain and the value at which the donee is treated as having acquired the asset is reduced by the gain, so that the donee will make a correspondingly larger gain (or smaller loss) when he disposes of the asset. The Revenue have stated that in most circumstances it will not be necessary to agree market values at the time of the gifts relief claim. Establishing the market value at the date of the gift can normally be deferred until the donee disposes of the asset (Revenue Statement of Practice SP 8/92). There are provisions to ensure that the gifts relief is not used to avoid tax altogether, for example where the donee is not resident in the UK. If a donee who is an individual is resident at the time of the gift but becomes not resident and not ordinarily resident in the UK before disposing of the asset and within six years after the end of the tax year in which the gift was made, the gain is then charged to tax. This provision does not apply to trustees, because separate rules impose a tax charge on all trust assets when a trust becomes non-resident — see page 576.

Gifts relief is also available where assets are not given outright but are disposed of for less than their value. If, however, the amount received exceeds the original cost, the gain that may be deferred does not include the excess of the proceeds over cost.

Claims for gifts relief to apply must be made by the donor and donee jointly except where the donees are trustees, in which case only the donor need make the claim. Under self-assessment from 1996/97, claims will usually be made in tax returns. The overall time limit for claims is five years from the 31 January following the tax year to which the claim relates.

Where part of a gain on a gift is covered by retirement relief, gifts relief may be claimed on the balance. Where a gift on which the gifts holdover relief is claimed attracts inheritance tax, either immediately or as a result of the donor's death within seven years, the donee's base cost for capital gains tax is increased by the inheritance tax (but not so as to create a loss on future disposal). If, however, a lifetime gift does not qualify for holdover relief and capital gains tax is paid, there is no inheritance tax relief for the capital gains tax paid if the gift becomes chargeable for inheritance tax because of the donor's death within seven years.

Where gifts relief is not available, tax may be paid by ten annual instalments on gifts of land, a controlling shareholding in a company, or minority holdings of shares or securities in a company that are neither quoted on the Stock Exchange nor dealt in on the Unlisted Securities Market. Interest will, however, be charged on the full amount outstanding and not just on any instalment which is paid late.

See page 51 for the treatment of disposals that are affected by deferred gains on assets acquired before 31 March 1982.

Reinvestment relief (ss 164A–164N; FA 1993, s 87 and Sch 7; FA 1994, s 91 and Sch 11; FA 1995, ss 46, 47; FA 1996, s 177)

A claim may be made for gains on disposals on or after 30 November 1993 of *any* chargeable assets to be rolled over and treated as reducing the capital gains tax cost of ordinary shares in a qualifying unquoted trading company acquired within one year before or three years after the disposal. The relief is only available to those who are resident or ordinarily resident in the UK. This applies to disposals by individuals, and by trustees if the beneficiaries of the trust are individuals or charities. The relief may be claimed for the full amount of reinvested gains or for whatever lower amount is required. If the disposal qualifies for retirement relief, you may claim either retirement relief, or reinvestment relief, or any combination of the two.

Shares on the Unlisted Securities Market (USM) do not count as unquoted shares, but shares on the new Alternative Investment Market (AIM) will be treated as unquoted, so reinvestment relief will be available providing the AIM company carries on a qualifying trade.

Reinvestment relief was introduced on 16 March 1993, but it was originally restricted to gains made by full-time directors or employees disposing of all or part of a holding of 5% or more of the voting rights in a qualifying unquoted trading company. The relief was further restricted to an acquisition of at least 5% of the voting shares in the new company. These restrictions were removed from 30 November 1993.

The trades that do not qualify are broadly finance, leasing, holding commodities as investments (e.g. fine wines and antiques) and legal and accountancy services. Farming and property development were originally excluded, but became qualifying trades from 29 November 1994. Dealing in land is still, however, not a qualifying trade.

The relief may be claimed on a subsequent disposal of the new shares where the gain on that disposal is itself reinvested in a qualifying holding, but the deferred gain will become chargeable if you sell without reinvesting or if, within three years of the reinvestment, you emigrate or the company ceases to qualify. In the latter case, the deferred gain may itself be reinvested, and further relief claimed.

Separate rules give relief for reinvestment of gains on disposal of any assets by *subscribing for* qualifying shares under the Enterprise Investment Scheme (see page 403) and/or shares in Venture Capital Trusts (see page 528). For both of those reliefs, there is the added advantage of 20% income tax relief on up to £100,000 invested, so they are more attractive from a tax point of view if the conditions are satisfied.

Assets of negligible value (s 24; FA 1996, Sch 39 para 4)

If an asset is lost, destroyed or extinguished, you are treated as disposing of it at that time, even if no compensation is received. This means, for example, that if you own shares in a company that goes into liquidation, you will be regarded as disposing of the shares when the liquidation is completed, and relief may be claimed for the loss.

It is, however, possible to get relief before the asset is lost or destroyed if its value has sunk to a negligible level. You may make a claim for the asset to be treated as sold and reacquired at that negligible value, establishing an allowable loss accordingly. You are treated as having disposed of the asset either on the date of the claim or, if you wish, on an earlier date indicated in the claim. The earlier date must fall within the two years before the tax year or company accounting period in which the claim is made, and the asset must have been of negligible value on that earlier date (whether or not it was of negligible value before then). Now that indexation allowance is no longer available to increase losses (see page 48), backdating cannot have the effect of making indexation allowance available, even if it would have been available at the earlier date. Backdating used to be available only by Revenue concession (D28) but it has been made statutory for claims made on or after 6 April 1996. You do not need to make a negligible value claim unless and until you wish to, so that for example a claim should not be made if it would mean wasting the annual exemption.

Relief for losses on loans (ss 251–255; FA 1996, Sch 39 para 8)

For accounting periods of companies ending after 31 March 1996, special rules apply to the loss of money lent (see page 27). For other taxpayers, the normal rules for working out allowable capital losses do not apply to ordinary debts (unless the debt has been assigned to someone with whom the creditor is not 'connected' — see page 60 — in which case the assignee may claim relief by reference to the amount he has paid for the assigned debt). The normal rules do, however, apply to the loss of money lent if the loan is marketable loan stock or a similar security *other than* a qualifying corporate bond (see page 532). The loans qualifying for relief under the normal rules will therefore mainly be non-sterling loan stock, loan stock that is convertible into shares, and loan stock acquired before 14 March 1984.

Qualifying corporate bonds are exempt from capital gains tax, and if a loss arises it will not normally be an allowable loss. There are, however, special rules to allow the relief described below in certain circumstances — see page 532.

Relief is available to the lender or guarantor for losses on loans or guarantees that do not qualify under the normal rules outlined above if the borrower is a UK resident and uses the money lent wholly for the purposes of a trade carried on by him. Upon an appropriate claim by the lender or guarantor, an irrecoverable loan or payment under guarantee gives rise to an allowable loss for CGT, provided that the debt or the rights acquired by the guarantor following the guarantee payment are not assigned. If any amount is subsequently recovered (whether from the borrower or from any co-guarantor) it will be treated as a capital gain. The loss under these provisions is treated as a loss at the date of the claim, unless the claim stipulates an earlier time falling not more than two years before the beginning of the tax year of claim, and providing the amount was irrecoverable at the earlier date.

Relief is not available if the loss arises because of something the lender, or guarantor, has done or failed to do, or where the amount has become irrecoverable in consequence of the terms of the loan, nor is it available where the claimant and borrower are husband and wife.

Due date of payment, interest on overdue tax and repayment supplement (ss 7, 283; TMA 1970, ss 59B, 86, 88; FA 1994, s 193, Sch 19 para 46; FA 1995, s 110)

Years up to 1995/96

For years up to 1995/96, capital gains tax is due for payment on 1 December after the end of the tax year, or 30 days after the issue of the assessment if later, unless tax has been postponed following an appeal. When the amount of tax that may be postponed on an appeal has been agreed, the due date for the non-postponed balance is 30 days after the date of that agreement, unless the normal due date is later. If, when the appeal is settled, any of the postponed tax becomes payable, it is due 30 days after the issue of the revised assessment (or the normal due date, if later).

Interest on overdue tax is charged from the due date of payment except in relation to tax postponed following an appeal, on which the date from which interest runs will never be later than 1 June in the next but one tax year after that to which the tax relates (unless the original assessment was issued very late, in which case interest would run from 30 days after that assessment if it was later than the 1 June date). Where there is substantial delay in submitting a return, interest runs from the date the tax ought to have been paid (see chapter 9). The Revenue will usually regard a delay as substantial if a return has not been made by 31 October in the tax year following that in which the gain arose and they were not otherwise made aware of the gain or given sufficient information to enable an assessment to be raised. (Revenue Statement of Practice SP 6/89). The rates of interest in recent years are given on page xxiii.

Where capital gains tax has been overpaid, a UK or EU resident is entitled to repayment supplement, from the end of the tax year following the year for which the repayment is made (or from the end of the tax year in which the tax was paid if later) to the next 5th of the month after the repayment date. The supplement is at the same rate as the rate of interest on overdue tax.

1996/97 onwards

Following the introduction of self-assessment from 1996/97, the same rules will apply for both income tax and capital gains tax (see page 20), except that capital gains tax will not be included in provisional payments and will be payable on 31 January following the end of the tax year (two months later than under the previous provisions). Interest on underpaid tax will be charged from the due date and repayment supplement on overpaid tax will apply from the date of overpayment to the date the repayment order is issued. Repayment supplement will not be restricted to UK and EU residents.

Payment by instalments (s 280; FA 1996, Sch 20 para 65)

Capital gains tax may at the taxpayer's option be paid by instalments where the proceeds are being received by instalments over 18 months or more. The instalments run over eight years, or until the last instalment of the price is received if sooner, with relief for bad debts being available if part of the amount due proves irrecoverable. Interest is charged on any instalments paid late (but only on the instalment and not on the full amount outstanding).

Capital gains tax is also payable by instalments on certain gifts, but interest is then payable on the full amount outstanding, not just on overdue instalments — see page 61.

Quoted and unquoted securities

Special rules apply to the treatment of both quoted and unquoted securities. These are dealt with in detail in chapter 38.

No gain/no loss disposals

Special provisions apply to certain disposals, the main ones being:

(a)   Transfers on company reconstructions (s 139).
(b)   Transfers within a 75% group of companies (s 171).
(c)   Husband/wife transfers (s 58).

The disposal is effectively treated as giving rise to neither gain nor loss, and the transferee's acquisition cost is the original cost plus indexation allowance to date. Any indexation allowance added to cost *after* the last no gain/no loss transfer made before 30 November 1993 will, however, not be able to create or increase a loss on ultimate disposal (unless the transitional relief applies — see page 48). But indexation allowance that had been added to cost up to the time of the last no gain/no loss transfer made before 30 November 1993 may still create or increase losses. See example 9.

Example 9

Asset that cost £10,000 was transferred from husband to wife in September 1993 at an indexed cost of £13,000. The wife disposed of it in June 1996 for £11,000. The position is as follows:

	£	£
Sale proceeds June 1996		11,000
Cost	10,000	
Indexation allowance to September 1993	3,000	13,000
Allowable loss		£2,000

No further indexation allowance can be added to the indexed figure of £13,000 for the period September 1993 to June 1996, since the disposal already shows a loss.

Death (ss 3(7), 62; FA 1996, Sch 17 para 2)

No capital gains tax charge arises on death. If losses arise in the year of death these may be carried back and set against gains assessable in the three previous tax years, latest first (with the set-off being made only against any gains not covered by the annual exemption in those years). Tax will be refunded accordingly, with repayment supplement where appropriate. For repayments for years before 1996/97, repayment supplement dates from one year after the end of the tax year in which the losses were set off (see page 64). Under self-assessment for repayments for 1996/97 onwards, repayment supplement will run from the payment date for the tax year of death (see page 119).

The personal representatives or legatees are treated as acquiring the assets at the market value at the date of death. When personal representatives dispose of assets at values in excess of the values at death, gains arising will be charged to tax (and exemptions the deceased could have claimed may not be available, for example on a private residence) but they may claim the annual exemption, currently £6,300, in respect of disposals by them in the tax year of death and in each of the following two tax years, any balance of gains being taxed at 24% (25% before 6 April 1996).

Where within two years after a death the persons entitled to the estate vary the way in which it is distributed, and notify the Revenue within six months after the variation, the variation is not regarded as a disposal by those originally entitled but as having been made by the deceased at the date of death so that no CGT charge arises on any increase in value since death.

Trusts (ss 3, 68–98 and Schs 1, 5)

Trustees are chargeable persons for capital gains tax. If, however, the settlor retains an interest in the trust, any gains are taxed as the settlor's gains (see page 583). Where that does not apply, the trustees are entitled to an annual exemption of £3,150 for 1996/97, this being divided where there are several trusts created by the same settlor, but with each trust getting a minimum exemption of £630. The exemption is usually increased each year in line with the retail prices index.

When assets are placed in trust, and when they are transferred to beneficiaries other than on the death of a life tenant, a disposal at market value is treated as taking place, but gains may sometimes be rolled over under the gifts relief provisions dealt with on page 60. When a life interest ends other than on the death of a life tenant, but the property remains in trust, this has no effect for capital gains tax. When a life tenant dies and someone else becomes entitled to the life interest, or a beneficiary becomes absolutely entitled to trust assets following a life tenant's death, the trustees are not treated as making either chargeable gains or allowable losses (except to the extent of any gains held over under the gifts relief provisions when the assets were put into trust), but the market value of the trust property at that time becomes the future base value for capital gains tax, either in the hands of the trustees or of the beneficiary.

The detailed provisions on the capital gains position of trusts are dealt with in chapter 42, except for the overseas element, which is dealt with in chapter 41.

Options (ss 114, 143–148; FA 1994, s 96)

There are special rules concerning options connected with employment (see chapter 11). For companies, currency options and interest rate options are taken into account in calculating income under the rules for transactions in foreign exchange and financial instruments and are not subject to the capital gains provisions indicated below (see page 575). Apart from these exceptions, the treatment of options depends on the type of option.

The following options are not treated as wasting assets.

> Quoted options to subscribe for new shares
> Traded options to buy or sell shares or other financial instruments quoted on a recognised stock exchange or futures exchange (such as the London International Financial Futures and Options Exchange — LIFFE) and 'over the counter' financial options
> Options to acquire assets for use by the option holder in his business.

This means that when they are disposed of or abandoned, an allowable loss or chargeable gain may arise.

Other options are treated as wasting assets, so that their cost wastes away over their life, restricting loss relief accordingly if they lapse or become valueless. If such options are abandoned, no allowable loss can arise. The forfeiture of a deposit is treated as the abandonment of an option.

Whether an option is treated as a wasting asset or not, it is generally treated as a separate chargeable asset, so that the full amount of the consideration for the option is chargeable as a gain. This separate treatment does not apply if the option is exercised. In that case the price paid for the option is incorporated with the cost of the asset to form a single transaction both as regards the seller and the buyer. Where a call option is exercised and settled in cash, rather than by delivery of the asset, the grantor of the option is treated as having disposal proceeds equal to the price paid by the grantee for the option, less the cash payment made by the grantor, and the grantee is treated as having disposal proceeds equal to the cash received less the indexed cost of the option (but with indexation restricted so as not to create or increase a loss).

In relation to shares, the above provisions are modified to bring options within the share pooling provisions. Purchased options of the same series will therefore be pooled if an acquisition is not matched with a disposal on the same day or within the next nine days, and indexation allowance will then be available. If an option is exercised, the shares acquired will merge with any existing pool of shares of the same class in the same company, and the indexed cost of the option will form part of the pool cost. The disposal of an option to buy or sell gilt-edged securities or qualifying corporate bonds is exempt.

Deferred consideration

An increasing number of transactions are being structured along lines where only part of the consideration is received at the time of the sale, with further amounts depending upon later events, for example profit performance in the case of the sale of a family company. This aspect is dealt with briefly in chapter 28.

5
Inheritance tax: general principles

Introduction

Inheritance tax may be charged on certain lifetime gifts, on wealth at death and on certain transfers into and out of trusts. It used to be called capital transfer tax, and it was introduced in 1975 to replace estate duty. The law is contained in the Inheritance Tax Act 1984 (abbreviated in this book to IHTA 1984) and subsequent Finance Acts. All references in this chapter are to the Inheritance Tax Act 1984 unless otherwise stated.

Persons liable (ss 6, 48, 158, 159, 267)

UK domiciled individuals are chargeable to inheritance tax in respect of property anywhere in the world and non-UK domiciled individuals in respect of property in the UK. Husband and wife are separate chargeable persons, so any available exemptions apply separately to each of them and each can make transfers free of tax up to the nil threshold (see below).

Domicile is a legal term that is not easy to define but essentially it means the country you regard as 'home'. The term has an extended meaning for inheritance tax, and you are treated as UK domiciled if:

(a) you were UK domiciled on or after 10 December 1974 and within the three years preceding the transfer; or
(b) you were resident in the UK on or after 10 December 1974 and in at least 17 of the 20 tax years up to and including the year of transfer.

Double taxation relief is given where the transfer of assets attracts tax overseas as well as in the UK.

Exempt transfers

Many gifts are completely exempt from tax. Others are exempt only if they are made in lifetime. The exempt lifetime gifts are as follows.

Small gifts to same person (s 20)

Any outright lifetime gifts to any one person in any one tax year if the total gifts to that person do not exceed £250 in that year.

Gifts in consideration of marriage (s 22)

Gifts of up to £5,000 by a parent, £2,500 by a grandparent, £2,500 by one party to the marriage to the other, or £1,000 by anyone else.

Normal expenditure out of income (s 21)

To obtain exemption the gift must be part of the donor's normal expenditure, and must not, taking one year with another, reduce the donor's available net income (after all other transfers) below that required to maintain his usual standard of living. The exemption will often apply to life assurance policy premiums paid for the benefit of another.

Waivers of remuneration and dividends (ss 14, 15)

A waiver or repayment of remuneration does not attract inheritance tax. Nor does a waiver of dividends made within twelve months before any right to the dividend arises.

Capital transfers for family maintenance (ss 11, 51)

It may sometimes be necessary to make transfers of capital in order to provide for your family, for example following divorce when the usual exemption for transfer between husband and wife (see below) no longer applies, or to make reasonable provision for a dependent relative. Such transfers may be made without attracting liability.

Annual transfers not exceeding £3,000 (s 19)

The first £3,000 of lifetime transfers in any tax year are exempt. Any unused portion of the exemption may be carried forward for one year only for use in the following tax year after the exemption for that following tax year has been used.

Other exemptions are available whether the transfer is made in lifetime or on death, as follows.

Transfers between husband and wife (s 18)

These are exempt, except where a husband or wife domiciled in the UK transfers to a foreign domiciled spouse, when transfers are only exempt up to £55,000.

Gifts to charities (s 23)

Gifts to charities, either outright or to be held on trust for charitable purposes.

Gifts to political parties (s 24)

Gifts to qualifying political parties, i.e. parties that either have at least two MPs in the House of Commons, or one MP and at least 150,000 votes in their favour at the last general election.

Gifts of land to registered housing associations (s 24A)

Gifts for national purposes (s 25)

Conditional exemption for heritage property (s 26)

Providing various undertakings are given, for example public access, conditional exemption applies to the lifetime or death transfer of property which is designated by the Treasury as of national, scientific, historic, artistic, architectural or scenic interest (e.g. works of art and historic buildings). If there is any breach of an undertaking, inheritance tax becomes payable by the donee.

Maintenance funds for heritage property (s 27)

Transfers into a settlement established for the maintenance, repair or preservation of heritage property are exempt providing a Treasury direction is made.

Mutual transfers

Where a potentially exempt transfer (see below) or a chargeable transfer is made and the donee then makes a gift back to the donor, there are provisions to avoid a double charge to tax if the donor dies within seven years.

Basis of charge (ss 1–8, Sch 1; FA 1996, s 183)

A running total is kept of chargeable lifetime transfers and no tax is payable either on the lifetime gifts or on your wealth at death until a threshold is reached. The threshold has been increased to £200,000 for transfers on and after 6 April 1996. The full rate of tax on transfers above the threshold is 40% (unchanged since 15 March 1988) but to encourage lifetime giving, chargeable lifetime transfers above the nil threshold are charged at only half rate, i.e. at 20% (but see page 75). The scales of rates for earlier years are shown on page xxxii. Transfers are excluded from the running total seven years after they are made.

The threshold is increased annually, at least in line with increases in the retail prices index, unless Parliament decides otherwise. Any annual increases do not enable tax paid on earlier transfers to be recovered.

Potentially exempt transfers (s 3A)

Most of the transfers you are likely to make in your lifetime are either wholly exempt from tax (see page 69) or are 'potentially exempt', and will only be subject to tax if you die within seven years after making them. Even then, there will be no tax to pay on them unless the total of such potentially exempt transfers (and any transfers in the seven years before death that were chargeable in lifetime — see pages 73, 74) exceeds the nil threshold. They will, however, be taken into account to decide how much, if any, of the nil band is available to set against the value of your estate at death.

Example 1

The only lifetime transfer made by a widower is a gift of £60,000 on 10 June 1995 to his daughter towards the cost of buying a house. He dies in March 1997, leaving an estate at death of £160,000.

After deducting two years' annual exemptions totalling £6,000 (see page 70), there is a potentially exempt transfer of £54,000, which becomes chargeable because of the widower's death within seven years. No tax is payable on that gift because it falls within the £200,000 nil threshold. There is then, however, only £146,000 of the nil threshold remaining, so that £14,000 of the death estate of £160,000 is chargeable to tax at the rate of 40%.

If the widower had survived until 10 June 2002 the lifetime gift would have been completely exempt, and tax would only be payable if the estate at death exceeded the nil threshold at that time.

Transfers into and out of trusts in which someone is entitled to the income (called interest in possession trusts) are also potentially exempt. Trusts are dealt with in chapter 42.

A potentially exempt transfer which becomes a chargeable transfer because of your death within seven years is brought into account at the value of the gift when you made it, and tax is calculated taking into account any chargeable transfers (including potentially exempt transfers that have become chargeable) within the seven years before that transfer. The nil rate threshold and rate of tax used are, however, those in force at the date of your death.

It is therefore possible to fix the value of the transfer by giving in lifetime and this may be particularly useful where there are appreciating assets, since any later growth in value is in the hands of the donee. The capital gains tax effect must also be considered, however, because a lifetime gift of a chargeable asset will be liable to capital gains tax unless the gain can be deferred using the gifts relief provisions (see page 60), whereas if the asset is held until death the increase in value up to that time escapes capital gains tax. Any capital gains tax paid on a gift that is a potentially exempt transfer cannot be offset if that same gift becomes liable to inheritance tax.

If the capital gains tax gifts relief *is* available, and the potentially exempt transfer becomes liable to inheritance tax, any inheritance tax payable is deducted in computing the donee's gain when he eventually disposes of the asset.

See page 75 for the treatment of a gift that has fallen in value by the time of the donor's death.

Retaining a benefit (FA 1986, s 102 and Sch 20)

Property you give away is still treated as belonging to you if you continue to enjoy any benefit from the gifted property. If you still retain a benefit at the time of your death, the property is treated as remaining in your estate and is taxed accordingly. See example 2.

These rules can result in a double tax charge and there are special rules to eliminate any double charges that occur.

Example 2

A donor gives away his house but continues to live in it. He will be treated as making a second gift at the time when he ceases to occupy the house or pays a proper rent for his occupation so that inheritance tax may be payable if he does not then survive for a further seven years.

The same applies where a donor gives away £50,000, but continues to receive the interest on it. He will be treated as making a second gift when he ceases to receive the interest.

Chargeable lifetime transfers (ss 2, 3, 5)

The main category of transfers which are immediately chargeable in lifetime is transfers to a discretionary trust (i.e. a trust in which no-one has a right to the income, and it is up to the trustees how much of the income, if any, they distribute). The nil threshold of £200,000 is available providing it has not already been used against earlier chargeable transfers, and also the annual exemption. As with potentially exempt transfers, chargeable lifetime transfers are taken into account in the running total at death if the donor dies within seven years of making them and tax is recalculated on them at the full rate, taking into account any chargeable transfers (including potentially exempt transfers that have become chargeable) within the seven years before the transfer.

If the gifted asset was a chargeable asset for capital gains tax, and the gain had been deferred under the gifts relief provisions, any inheritance tax paid immediately or on the donor's death within seven years is deducted in computing the donee's gain when he eventually disposes of the asset.

The tax on a chargeable lifetime gift is usually paid by the recipient, but it may be paid by the donor. In that event, the amount chargeable to tax is found by grossing up the amount of the gift to allow for the tax which the donor has to pay.

Example 3

Donor makes a chargeable lifetime transfer of £8,000 when the nil threshold had already been used, so that the rate of tax is 20%. He pays the tax.

The value for inheritance tax is £8,000 × 100/80 = £10,000.

Being: The chargeable transfer	10,000
Tax payable @ 20%	2,000
Leaving for the donee	£8,000

If the donor fails to pay the capital gains tax on a gift, it may be collected from the recipient, and in that event it is deducted from the value of the gift in calculating the value for inheritance tax.

Position on death (s 4)

When you die, you are treated as making a final transfer of the whole of your estate and the tax charged on the estate depends on the total of chargeable lifetime transfers and potentially exempt transfers within the previous seven years.

Your estate is the total of all the property to which you are beneficially entitled. As well as your own property, it includes:

(i) an interest as a joint tenant. Such an interest is automatically transferred to the other joint tenant(s) on your death, but it still forms part of your estate for tax purposes (this differs from a share as a tenant in common, which means each person has a separate share which he may dispose of as he wishes, and which therefore counts as his own property for all purposes); and

(ii) the capital value of a trust fund where you are entitled to the trust income (called an interest in possession).

The inclusion of the capital in a trust fund in your estate means that on your death, you are treated as making a chargeable transfer of the capital in the fund, although the tax on that amount is paid by the trustees.

On the other hand, there is no charge to tax when someone entitled to the income from a trust fund is allocated part of the supporting capital, because the capital is treated as being part of his estate already.

Where assets in your estate at death are left to your spouse, no tax is payable (unless the spouse is not domiciled in the UK, in which case the exempt amount is limited to £55,000). The same applies to other exempt transfers (see page 70). For more detailed points relating to the death estate, see chapter 35.

Transfers made within the seven years before death (s 7)

Where you have made a chargeable lifetime transfer, all or part of which has been charged at the 20% rate, and you die within seven years of making it, additional tax may be payable, because the tax is recomputed at the full scale rate applicable at the date of death, taking into account other chargeable transfers (including potentially exempt transfers that have become chargeable — see below) within the seven years before the transfer (and using the nil rate threshold applicable at the date of death).

If you have made any potentially exempt transfers in the seven years before your death, they become chargeable, and are taken into account in the running total, along with any chargeable lifetime transfers, according to the date each transfer was made. This may mean that the nil threshold is no longer available against a chargeable lifetime transfer, causing tax, or more tax, to be payable. See example 4.

If the value of a gifted asset has fallen between the time of the gift and death, the lower value may be used to calculate the tax, unless the asset was tangible movable property with a predictable life of 50 years or less (for example, a car). The sale proceeds, if lower than the value when given away, may also be used where the donee has sold the asset before the donor's death in an arm's length, freely negotiated sale, to an unconnected person.

Tapering relief

When working out the tax, or additional tax, payable on gifts within the seven years before your death, the tax is reduced if you have survived the gift by more than three years. The percentage of the full scale rate payable following the reduction is as follows (see example 5 on page 77).

Time between chargeable gift and death	*% payable*
Up to 3 years	100
More than 3 but less than 4 years	80
More than 4 but less than 5 years	60
More than 5 but less than 6 years	40
More than 6 but less than 7 years	20

The donee has to pay the amount by which the tax at the appropriate percentage of the full scale rate exceeds any tax paid on the gift in lifetime. If, however, the lifetime tax exceeds the death tax, no repayment is available.

Example 4

Donor who died on 25 May 1996 made the following gifts in lifetime (after taking annual and other exemptions into account):

9 April 1989	To brother	£20,000
26 July 1989	To son	£70,000
15 September 1990	To daughter	£60,000
1 April 1994	To discretionary trust (tax paid by trustees)	£160,000
30 June 1994	To sister	£20,000

The only chargeable lifetime gift was the gift to the discretionary trust, on which the tax was

(£160,000 – £150,000 nil band) = £10,000 @ 20%	£2,000

On death:

Gift on 9 April 1989 is not taken into account, since it was more than seven years before donor's death. Gifts to son, daughter and sister become chargeable, but no tax is payable on gifts to son and daughter, since they are below nil threshold. Threshold remaining is, however, (£200,000 – £130,000) = £70,000.

Tax on gift to trust	
(£160,000 – £70,000) = £90,000 @ 40%	36,000
Less paid in lifetime	2,000
	£34,000
Tax on gift to sister £20,000 @ 40%	£8,000

Tax @ 40% will also be paid on estate at death.

Had the gift on 9 April 1989 been to a discretionary trust, it would have been taken into account in calculating the tax on the other lifetime transfers, since it was made within the seven years before each of them, but it would have been excluded from the running total at 9 April 1996 and would not therefore have been taken into account in calculating tax on the death estate.

Example 5

The only chargeable transfer made by a taxpayer is a transfer to a discretionary trust of £210,000 (after exemptions) on 30 September 1996. The tax payable by the trustees is (£210,000 − £200,000 nil band = £10,000 @ 20%), i.e. £2,000.

Assuming that the tax rate and threshold remain unchanged, so that £4,000 is in fact the amount of tax at the full scale rate, the effect of the tapering relief is as follows.

If taxpayer dies on	Time between gift and death	% of £4,000 payable	Amounting to
			£
10.10.97	Less than 3 yrs	100	4,000
31.12.99	3 to 4 yrs	80	3,200
31.1.2002	5 to 6 yrs	40	1,600

Extra tax if death occurs on 10.10.97 will be £2,000.

Extra tax if death occurs on 31.12.99 will be £1,200.

No extra tax will be due if death occurs on 31.1.2002 because the reduced tax of £1,600 is less than the tax already paid of £2,000.

The tax on death may not be double the earlier lifetime tax as in this example, because of the indexation of the threshold.

If the lifetime gift had been to an individual, or an 'interest in possession' trust, it would have been potentially exempt, and no tax would have been paid on it in lifetime, but the calculation of the tax at death would be the same.

Valuation of property (ss 160–198; FA 1993, ss 198, 199)

The value of property for inheritance tax is the amount it might reasonably be expected to fetch if sold in the open market. The price is not, however, to be reduced on the grounds that the whole property is placed on the market at one time.

If the asset to be transferred will give rise to a capital gains tax liability, and the donee agrees to pay that tax, then the value transferred is reduced by the capital gains tax paid. However, capital gains tax may sometimes not arise on gifts because of the availability of gifts holdover relief. See page 60.

Valuation on death

The way in which the death estate is valued, and the reliefs which are available, are dealt with below. The exemptions available are dealt with on pages 70, 71.

Transfers of 'excluded property' are ignored in valuing the death estate (ss 3, 5, 6, 48). The most common forms of excluded property are:

(i) property situated overseas where the owner is not domiciled in the UK; and

(ii) reversionary interests in trust funds (which means the right to the capital when the present beneficiary's right to the income comes to an end).

Apart from life assurance policies (see below) the value of property to be included in the estate at death is that immediately prior to death. Changes in the value of the estate as a result of the death are taken into account, for example the increased value of life assurance policies and the reduction in the value of goodwill which depends upon the personal qualities of the deceased. Allowance is made for reasonable funeral expenses. In the case of overseas property, allowance is also made for additional expenses incurred because of its situation, subject to a limit of 5% of the value of the property.

Quoted securities and land transferred on death

Where an estate on death includes quoted securities, and they are sold by the personal representatives within twelve months after death for less than their value at death, then the total sales proceeds before expenses may be substituted for the death value. A revised value may also be included for quoted securities that are cancelled, or in which dealings are suspended, within the twelve months after death. If the estate includes land which is sold by the personal representatives within four years after death, relief is available for the reduction in value by comparing the total sale proceeds before expenses with the value at death.

Related property

If you own part of an asset, and part is owned by your husband or wife, or you have made an exempt transfer of part of an asset to a charity, political party or national heritage body and it is still owned by that body or has been so owned at any time within the previous five years, the related property provisions apply. The related property provisions are mainly relevant to valuing transfers of unquoted shares and where freehold or leasehold property is owned jointly.

If it produces a higher value than its unrelated value, the value of a part of related property is taken as an appropriate portion of the total value of all the property. See example 6.

If related property is sold within three years after death to an unconnected person, a claim may be made for the tax at death to be recomputed using its unrelated value (not its sale value).

Example 6

The shareholders of Related Ltd, an unquoted company, are Mr R 40%, Mrs R 25%, others 35%. Shareholdings are valued as follows:

65%	£58,500
40%	£24,000
25%	£15,000

Inheritance tax values are:

Mr R 40/65 × £58,500 £36,000 (being greater than £24,000)
Mrs R 25/65 × £58,500 £22,500 (being greater than £15,000)

Life assurance policies

The valuation of life assurance policies depends on whether the transfer is during the lifetime or on the death of the donor. Policies transferred in lifetime are valued at the greater of the surrender value and the premiums paid. Sometimes it is the policy premiums, rather than the policy itself, which are transfers of value (e.g. where a policy is written in trust for another person and the premiums are paid by the person whose life is assured) and in such cases each premium payment will be a potentially exempt transfer unless it is already exempt as a gift out of income or as a small gift or because of the annual exemption.

On death the maturity value of a policy taken out by a person on his own life will be included in his estate unless it has been assigned to someone else in lifetime, or it has been written in trust for the benefit of someone else.

Associated operations (s 268)

There are rules to enable the Revenue to treat a series of connected operations as a single transfer of assets made at the time of the last of them.

Business property relief (ss 103–114; FA 1987, s 58 and Sch 8; FA 1994, s 247; FA 1996, s 184) and agricultural property relief (ss 115–124B; FA 1987, s 58 and Sch 8; FA 1994, s 247; FA 1995, s 155; FA 1996, s 185)

Business property relief is available on valuing transfers of business property, providing certain conditions as to the length of ownership and type of business are satisfied. For transfers on and after 10 March 1992, and any recalculation of tax on earlier transfers following a death on or after that date, the relief is given at the following rates:

A business or interest in a business (including a partnership share)	100%
Transfers out of unquoted shareholdings	100%*

Transfers out of a controlling shareholding in a quoted company
(including control through 'related property' holdings)   50%
Land or buildings, machinery or plant used for a business
carried on by:
    a company of which the donor has control; or a partner-
    ship in which the donor was a partner; or the donor, being
    settled property in which he had an interest in possession   50%

* The rate of relief for transfers out of unquoted shareholdings of 25% or
less was previously 50%, but has been increased to 100% for transfers
on or after 6 April 1996, and for recalculating tax on earlier transfers
where death occurs on or after 6 April 1996.

Shares on the Unlisted Securities Market and on the new Alternative Investment Market (AIM) are treated as unquoted shares. Relief is not available on
quoted or unquoted shares if the company's business falls within those listed
in the following paragraph.

The property transferred must normally have been owned by the donor
throughout the previous two years. For transfers out of unquoted shareholdings before 6 April 1996, the donor needed to have owned more than 25% of
the voting power *throughout* the two years before the transfer in order to get
the 100% rate of relief. Business property relief is not available where the
business consists of dealing in stocks and shares (except market makers on
the Stock Exchange and discount houses), dealing in land and buildings or
holding investments (including land which is let).

The relief is applied automatically without a claim and is given after
agricultural property relief (see below) but before available exemptions.

Agricultural property relief is available on the transfer of agricultural property so long as various conditions are met. Agricultural property is agricultural land or pasture (including short rotation coppice land), woodland and
buildings used for rearing livestock or fish where the occupation of the
woodland and buildings is ancillary to that of the agricultural land, and
cottages, farm buildings and farmhouses occupied with the agricultural
land. As with business property relief, the rates of relief have been increased
to 100% or 50% for transfers on and after 10 March 1992, and for any
recalculation of tax on earlier transfers following a death on or after that
date. The relief only applies to the agricultural value of the property, and in
arriving at that value any loan secured on the agricultural property must be
deducted.

The agricultural property must at the time of the transfer have been either
occupied by the donor for agriculture throughout the two years ending with
the date of transfer or owned by the donor throughout the previous seven
years and occupied for agriculture by him or someone else throughout that
period. Note that this enables relief to be given on agricultural investment
property. In certain circumstances these rules are modified if the property
transferred was acquired as a replacement for other agricultural property.

Relief is available both on the transfer of agricultural property itself, and on the transfer of shares out of a controlling holding in a farming company to the extent of the underlying agricultural value.

Relief is given at the rate of 100% where the donor had the right to vacant possession immediately before the transfer, or the right to obtain vacant possession within the next twenty-four months, or where the property is valued broadly at vacant possession value despite the tenancy. For other tenanted agricultural property the relief is 100% for transfers of property where the letting commences on or after 1 September 1995 (including successions to tenancies following the death of the previous tenant on or after that date) and 50% for transfers of property let before that date. Special provisions enable relief to be claimed at the 100% rate on tenanted agricultural property where the donor had been beneficially entitled to his interest in the property since before 10 March 1981 and would have been entitled to the higher rate of relief (then 50%) under the former provisions for agricultural relief which operated before that date.

Where agricultural property satisfies the conditions for business property relief, agricultural property relief is given first and business property relief is given on the non-agricultural value. As with business property relief, agricultural property relief is given without the need for a claim.

Binding contract for sale (ss 113, 124)

Property does not qualify for business or agricultural relief if it is subject to a binding contract for sale (except a contract relating to the conversion of an unincorporated business to a company, or a company reconstruction). A 'buy and sell' agreement made by partners or company directors to take effect on their death is considered by the Revenue to constitute such a contract, but it is understood that a double option agreement whereby the deceased's personal representatives have an option to sell and the surviving partners or directors an option to buy would not be so treated.

Calculation of tax on lifetime transfers following death within seven years (ss 113A, 113B, 124A, 124B; FA 1987, s 58 and Sch 8; FA 1994, s 247)

Many lifetime gifts of agricultural and/or business property will be potentially exempt when they are made. The gift will later become chargeable if the donor dies within seven years.

There will also be occasions where the transfer was chargeable at the time (such as a transfer into a discretionary trust), but because the donor dies within seven years, the charge has to be recomputed at the full scale rates (allowing for tapering relief).

In computing the tax payable as a result of the death, business and agricultural property relief is applicable so long as:

(i) the original property (or qualifying property which has replaced it) was owned by the donee throughout the period beginning with the date of the transfer and ending with the death of the donor; this condition will be regarded as satisfied if there is a period of up to three years between the sale of one qualifying property and the acquisition of another; and

(ii) immediately before the death of the donor, the property (or any replacement property) is qualifying business or agricultural property (this may not apply because, for example, there might have been a change of use, or at the time of death there might be a binding contract for sale). In order for unquoted shares to be qualifying business property they must still be unquoted when the donor dies.

If the donee died before the donor, the periods at (i) and (ii) are from the date of the gift to the date of death of the donee.

Proportionate relief is available where only part of the property continues to qualify, for example, where part of the property has been sold.

Since any increase in the value of assets up to the date of death is also exempt from capital gains tax (see page 66), the availability of the 100% business or agricultural property relief is an important influence in estate planning, because where it applies there will be no tax benefit from making potentially exempt transfers in lifetime. On the other hand, it cannot be certain that the tax regime will remain as favourable as it now is.

Growing timber (ss 125–130)

Where an estate on death includes growing timber, an election may be made to leave the timber (but not the land on which it stands) out of account in valuing the estate at death. The relief is dealt with in chapter 31.

Quick succession relief (s 141)

Where a donee dies shortly after receiving a chargeable transfer, the transfer has increased his estate at death and therefore attracts tax in his estate as well as possibly having been taxed at the time of the earlier transfer. Relief is given where the death occurs within five years after the earlier transfer. There is no requirement to retain the actual asset obtained by that transfer.

The total tax on the chargeable estate is calculated in the normal way and reduced by the quick succession relief. The relief is arrived at by first making the following calculation:

$$\frac{\text{Previous transfer net of tax}}{\text{Previous gross transfer}} \times \text{Tax paid on previous transfer}$$

The relief is the following percentage of the calculated amount:

Period between transfer and death	Percentage relief
Less than 1 year	100%
1–2 years	80%
2–3 years	60%
3–4 years	40%
4–5 years	20%

Example 7

Thomas, who died on 28 June 1996 leaving an estate of £250,000, had received a gift of £50,000 from his father on 30 October 1993, on which he had paid tax of £20,000 following his father's death on 26 May 1995.

Tax on Thomas's estate will be reduced by quick succession relief as follows (Thomas died 2–3 years after gift):

$$\frac{\text{Net transfer } 30,000}{\text{Gross transfer } 50,000} \times \text{Tax £20,000} \times 60\% = \underline{£7,200}$$

Quick succession relief is also available where there are successive charges within five years on trust property in which there is an interest in possession. The rates of relief are the same as those quoted above, with the percentage relief depending on the period between the successive charges.

It may be that at the time the donee dies, the transfer to him is still classed as a potentially exempt transfer because the donor is still alive, but the donor may then die, after the donee but within the seven-year period, so that the potentially exempt transfer becomes chargeable in the donor's estate, with the personal representatives of the donee being liable to pay any tax. Quick succession relief will then be available in the donee's estate by reference to that tax.

Survivorship clauses (s 92)

Although the tax on successive transfers may be reduced by quick succession relief where death occurs within five years after the first transfer, this is not so beneficial as the value not being included at all. It is possible to include a survivorship clause in a will stipulating that assets do not pass to the intended beneficiary unless he/she survives the deceased by a prescribed period, limited to a maximum of six months (see page 486). This avoids the double charge to tax.

Varying the distribution of the estate (ss 17, 142)

The way in which the estate liable to inheritance tax at death is distributed may be varied by those entitled to it, and legacies may be disclaimed wholly or in part. Where this happens within two years after the death, the variation or disclaimer is not a separate transfer of value provided that written notice is given to the Revenue within six months after the variation or disclaimer. This must be signed by those making it, and by the personal representatives if it results in additional tax being paid by them. Inheritance tax will then be payable as if the revised distribution had operated at death. A claim may be made for the variation to apply for capital gains tax as well (see page 66), or for it to apply only for capital gains tax and not for inheritance tax. For further details, see chapter 35.

Interest-free loans

Where a loan is made free of interest there is no transfer of capital and it is usually possible to regard the interest forgone as being normal expenditure out of income and thus exempt. If, however, a loan is made for a fixed period, or is not repayable on demand, it may be treated as a transfer of value equal to the difference between the amount lent and the present value of the future right to repayment.

Date of payment and interest on overdue or overpaid tax (ss 226–236)

The normal due dates of payment are as follows.

Chargeable lifetime transfers between 6 April and 30 September	Chargeable lifetime transfers between 1 October and 5 April	Death — including additional tax on chargeable lifetime transfers and tax on potentially exempt transfers which become chargeable
30 April in following year	6 months after end of month in which transfer was made	6 months after end of month in which death occurs

The personal representatives must, however, pay any tax for which they are liable at the time they apply for probate, even if this is before the due date as shown above.

Interest is payable on overdue tax (or repayable on overpaid tax), recent rates being as follows.

5% p.a. from 6 October 1994
4% p.a. from 6 January 1994 to 5 October 1994
5% p.a. from 6 December 1992 to 5 January 1994
6% p.a. from 6 November 1992 to 5 December 1992
8% p.a. from 6 July 1991 to 5 November 1992

9% p.a. from 6 May 1991 to 5 July 1991
10% p.a. from 6 March 1991 to 5 May 1991
11% p.a. from 6 July 1989 to 5 March 1991

Interest on overdue tax is not deductible in arriving at income tax payable by the personal representatives and interest on overpaid tax is tax-free. Overpayments carry interest from the date of payment.

Where tax has not been paid because a transfer was conditionally exempt, the due date is six months after the end of the month in which the event by reason of which it is chargeable occurs (e.g. breach of an undertaking in respect of heritage property).

Payment by instalments

Tax may be paid by equal yearly instalments over ten years on qualifying assets. This applies where the assets are transferred on death, and also to chargeable lifetime transfers if the *donee* pays the tax. The option to pay by instalments also applies to a potentially exempt transfer of qualifying property which becomes a chargeable transfer on the death of the donor within seven years after the gift, so long as the donee still owns the gifted property (or, for transfers of property qualifying for business or agricultural relief, replacement property) at the time of the donor's death. The first instalment is due on chargeable lifetime transfers on the normal due date and in the case of tax payable in consequence of death, six months after the end of the month in which the death occurred.

The instalment option applies to land wherever situated, to a business or interest in a business, to timber when it becomes chargeable after being left out of account on a previous death, to controlling shareholdings, and to unquoted shares if certain conditions are met. For unquoted shares, the instalment option is not available for tax payable as a result of the donor's death, unless the shares are still unquoted when the donor dies (or, if earlier, when the donee dies).

Interest normally runs only from the date the instalment falls due and not on the full amount of the deferred tax. This does not apply in the case of land, other than land included in a business or partnership interest and agricultural land, nor in the case of shares in an investment company. Interest in those two cases is charged on the total amount remaining unpaid after the normal due date, the interest being added to each instalment as it falls due.

If the property is sold, the outstanding tax becomes payable immediately.

Liability for tax (ss 199–214, 237)

On lifetime transfers of property which are immediately chargeable, other than transfers of property in a trust fund, primary liability for payment rests with the donor. The donor and donee may, however, agree between them who is to pay, the transfer having to be grossed up if the donor pays (see example 3 on page 74).

In the case of lifetime transfers of property which is within a discretionary trust, the primary liability is that of the trustees.

On death, the personal representatives are liable to pay the tax on the assets coming into their hands, while the liability for tax on trust property which becomes chargeable at death rests with the trustees. See the example on page 585.

Where, as a result of the death of the donor within seven years, additional tax becomes payable on a lifetime transfer, or a potentially exempt transfer becomes liable to tax, the primary responsibility for paying the tax is that of the donee. The personal representatives are only liable if the tax remains unpaid twelve months after the end of the month in which the donor died, or to the extent that the tax payable exceeds the value of the gifted property held by the donee.

In addition to the persons mentioned, certain other people may be liable to pay inheritance tax, but usually only where tax remains unpaid after the due date. Where tax is unpaid the Inland Revenue are usually able to take a legal charge on the property concerned.

The person who is liable to pay inheritance tax is not necessarily the person who ultimately bears the tax. The trustees of a settlement are liable to pay any tax arising on the transfer of trust funds, but the next person to enjoy the income or to receive the capital bears the tax because the trust funds are correspondingly lower. Personal representatives are liable to pay the tax on the assets of the deceased at death, but the residuary legatees (those who receive the balance of the estate after all other legacies) will suffer the tax by a reduction in the amount available for them, the other legatees receiving their legacies in full unless the will specifies that any particular legacy should bear its own tax.

Use of insurance

There are many instances in the inheritance tax provisions where the potential liability to tax is not known at the time of the transfer, notably when potentially exempt transfers are made, but also when chargeable transfers are made, because if the donor dies within seven years additional tax may be payable. Temporary insurance cover may be taken out on the life of the donor to provide for the possible tax liability, with the policies being tailored to take account of the reduction in potential liability once the donor has survived the gift by three years.

6
Stamp duty

Background

Stamp duty is a fixed or ad valorem charge on documents. It has been charged since the seventeenth century, and present legislation is based on the Stamp Act 1891 as amended by numerous subsequent Finance and other Acts. It is administered by the Commissioners of Inland Revenue through the Office of the Controller of Stamps. A separate tax — stamp duty reserve tax — was introduced by Finance Act 1986 to charge certain share transactions which otherwise escape stamp duty.

It was announced by the then Chancellor in his 1991 Budget that stamp duty was to be charged only on land and buildings. All other stamp duties, including stamp duty reserve tax, were to be abolished. The legislation to put this into effect has been passed, but the abolition was to be timed to coincide with the introduction of the TAURUS system of paperless share dealing on the Stock Exchange. The TAURUS proposals were abandoned and a new system of paperless share dealing — CREST — is being introduced. The Government has not, however, announced a date for the stamp duty abolitions that were supposed to coincide with the state of paperless share dealing, and has in fact introduced various changes to the stamp duty legislation from 1 July 1996 in order to adapt the rules to the paperless system.

Stamp duty

'Heads' and basis of charge (mainly in SA 1891, Sch 1)

Stamp duty is charged on certain documents completed in the UK or relating to UK property or transactions. No duty arises on transactions carried out orally.

Generally, documents should be stamped before they take effect, although in practice the Commissioners permit stamping within 30 days without charging any penalty.

Duty is either fixed or based on value depending on the head of charge under which the transaction falls. Some of the main heads of charge and rates of duty (some of which are on a sliding scale) are given in the table on page 88.

There are many other heads, a number of which attract only a fixed duty of 50p. There are numerous exemptions and reliefs from each head. There will be no 50p charge when shares are converted from certificated to paperless form on being deposited into CREST (FA 1996, s 186). The fixed duties enable the Stamp Office to scrutinise documents that may be liable to ad valorem duty.

Head of charge	Rate of duty
Bearer instruments	
Inland bearer instruments (other than deposit certificates for overseas stock)	1½%
Overseas bearer instruments (other than deposit certificates for overseas stock or bearer instruments by usage)	1½%
Bearer instruments excluded above	10p per £50 or part
Conveyances or transfers on sale	
Stock and marketable securities	½%
Other transfers (including house purchase)	1%
Duty on 'certified transactions': not exceeding £60,000	Nil
Various share transactions	
Such as takeovers, mergers, demergers, schemes of reconstruction and amalgamation (except where there is no real change in ownership), purchase by a company of its own shares	½%
Shares converted into depositary receipts or put into duty free clearance systems	1½%*
* But see page 92	
Leases	
For definite term less than 1 year of furnished dwelling house at rent in excess of £500 per annum	£1
For any other definite or indefinite term (rent)	Ad valorem duty from 0 to 24% on sliding scale by reference to average rent
For any other definite or indefinite term (premium)	As for conveyances or transfers on sale

Adjudication and valuation (SA 1891, s 12)

Adjudication is the assessment by the Commissioners of the amount of duty, if any, payable on a document. Adjudication may be voluntary or compulsory. Any person may ask the Commissioners to state whether a document is chargeable, and if so, the amount of duty payable. Sometimes, adjudication is compulsory, for example where exemption from duty is claimed on a company reconstruction without change in ownership.

Having considered the document the Commissioners will either stamp it 'adjudged not chargeable with any stamp duty' or they will assess the duty and when it is paid, they will stamp the document 'adjudged duly stamped'. An adjudication stamp is normally conclusive evidence of due stamping.

Letters of allotment

Sales of renounceable letters of allotment are chargeable to stamp duty reserve tax at ½% (see page 92).

Conveyances and transfers on sale (FA 1963, s 55 and Sch 11; FA 1958, s 34; FA 1987, ss 50, 55; FA 1990, ss 107–109, 111; FA 1993, s 201)

Documents relating to sales of all types of property are currently covered under this heading, including house sales and transactions such as the release of an interest in property or the surrender of a lease. It also includes shared ownership schemes run by local authorities and housing associations under which those who cannot afford the full amount needed to buy their house are able partly to buy and partly to rent the property. But no duty is payable where property can be handed over without a document of title, for example ordinary trading stock or plant and equipment.

'Certified' transactions up to £60,000 are exempt from duty. A certificate cannot be given for the transfer of stock or marketable securities, or units in a unit trust. Nor can it be given for a lease where the rent exceeds £600 per annum. An instrument is certified at a particular amount if it contains a statement that the transaction contained therein does not form part of a larger transaction or series of transactions whose value exceeds the certified amount. Where land is purchased for less than £60,000 and a house is subsequently built on it, no stamp duty is payable. But if the purchase of the land and the erection of the house are really a single transaction, stamp duty must be paid on the combined amount.

Certificates are also required for the following transactions (see below):

(a) Exchanges of interests in land.
(b) Premiums paid under leases.

No duty is payable in connection with British Government stock, including gilt warrants, nor in respect of a conveyance, transfer or lease to the Crown.

Value added tax

The value on which stamp duty is charged includes any value added tax on the transaction. Share transactions are generally exempt from VAT, so this is mainly relevant to transactions in land and buildings. Where a landlord has the option to charge VAT, but has not chosen to do so, stamp duty will still be charged on the VAT inclusive amount unless there is a binding agreement that the option will not be exercised. For further details on the VAT position on property, see chapter 32.

Exchanges of interests in land (FA 1994, s 241)

In view of the depressed housing market, many house builders have been prepared to accept a purchaser's existing house on a trade-in basis. Where they did so, considerable savings on stamp duty could previously be made, as duty only became payable if the cash difference exceeded £60,000.

The 1% duty is now charged on the full sale price of the new house (unless it is below £60,000), although providing the transaction is structured as a sale with part payment in kind there is still only 50p duty on the house tendered in part payment. Professional advice is essential on property exchanges to ensure that stamp duty is minimised.

Premiums on leases of land and buildings

Where a premium is paid on a lease for a definite term exceeding one year or for an indefinite term, the premium is treated as the consideration on a conveyance or transfer on sale and chargeable accordingly. The exemption for certified transactions up to £60,000 only applies to the premium, however, if the rent payable under the lease does not exceed £600 per annum.

Surrenders of leases

Where a lease is surrendered, duty is payable on any consideration paid by the landlord as for a conveyance on sale. If there is no consideration, a fixed duty of 50p is charged. Where the provisions of a lease can only be altered by surrender and re-grant, for example the alteration of the term, the re-granted lease will bear the appropriate duty but no duty will be paid on the surrender of the old lease.

Rents to mortgages scheme (FA 1993, s 202)

Where council house tenants buy their homes under a 'rents to mortgages scheme', stamp duty will apply at the time they enter the scheme, on the then market value of the property, less any discount under the 'right to buy' provisions. If that amount is less than £60,000, no stamp duty will be payable. 'Rents to mortgages' schemes enable tenants to buy their homes for an initial payment, which may be financed by a mortgage and repaid in place of rent, plus a balance provided by way of interest-free loan. The amount payable when the purchaser is ready to repay the loan depends on the market value of the property at that time.

Gifts (SA 1891, s 57)

There is no stamp duty on gifts unless the gift is of mortgaged property, in which case stamp duty is charged on the amount of the mortgage, as if it were a sale.

Trusts

No stamp duty is charged on the creation of a trust by will.

There will be a 50p stamp on any written declaration of trust in lifetime. Property that is vested in the trustees by way of conveyance or transfer will usually be exempt from duty as a gift. Property that can be vested in some other way, for example cash, does not require a document and will not attract duty. If the trust is declared in writing prior to the transfer, there will be a 50p declaration of trust stamp.

Once a trust has been created, the trustees are subject to stamp duty in the same way as any other person. Thus, if they purchase land, they will pay the stamp duty on the conveyance.

If a new trustee is subsequently appointed, the deed of appointment does not attract duty.

There is no duty on a transfer of trust property to a beneficiary.

Deeds of family arrangement
Transfers of property on break-up of marriage (FA 1985, ss 83, 84)

All qualifying deeds of family arrangement (see chapter 35) and deeds conveying property under a divorce order or on separation are exempt from duty.

Company takeovers (FA 1986, ss 75–77)

Transactions currently attract duty at ½%.

Foreign exchange currency rules (FA 1985, s 88)

All foreign currency amounts on which duty is payable are converted to sterling at the rate applying on the date of the document.

Interest and penalties (SA 1891, s 15)

Where documents are submitted late for stamping, the maximum penalty is £10 plus interest plus an amount equal to the duty payable. Providing the document is not two years late or more, the penalty will usually be mitigated so that the total penalty does not exceed the equivalent of interest at around 10% per annum for a delay of up to three months, gradually increasing to around 20% per annum for delays between 3 and 24 months. Detailed information on penalties is in Stamp Office leaflet SO 10.

Stamp duty reserve tax (FA 1986, ss 86–99; FA 1987, s 56 and Sch 7; FA 1990, ss 110, 111; FA 1996, ss 187–196)

Stamp duty reserve tax (SDRT) at the rate of ½% has previously applied to share transactions which escape duty, for example, sales of renounceable letters of allotment and transactions within the same Stock Exchange account. On the introduction of the CREST system of paperless share dealing on the Stock Exchange, CREST transactions that would have attracted stamp duty at ½% will attract ½% SDRT instead. SDRT does not apply to gilt-edged stocks, traded options and futures, non-convertible loan stocks, foreign securities not on a UK register, purchases by a charity, transfers of units to unit trust managers and of units in foreign unit trusts, and the issue of new securities. There are also special exemptions for Stock Exchange market makers, for broker-dealers who buy and sell shares within seven days and for principal traders on the London International Financial Futures and Options Exchange (LIFFE). Liability to stamp duty reserve tax had previously arisen two months after the date of the transaction, unless stamp duty had become payable in the meantime. From 1 July 1996, liability to SDRT will arise at the date of the agreement (or if the agreement is conditional, at the date the condition is satisfied). The tax is payable by the end of the next following month. If duty is paid after reserve tax has been paid, the reserve tax is refunded (plus income tax-free interest on refunds over £25). The tax is collected by market makers, brokers and dealers.

Stamp duty reserve tax also applies to shares converted into depositary receipts or put into a duty free clearing system, and the rate of tax on these transactions is 1½%. The tax is only payable, however, to the extent that it exceeds any ad valorem stamp duty on the transaction, and where the ad valorem duty exceeds the amount of reserve tax, no reserve tax is payable. From 1 July 1996, clearing systems will be able to elect to pay stamp duty or

SDRT in the normal way on their transactions, and in that event the 1½% charge when shares are put into the system will not apply.

Interest and penalties (SI 1986/1711 Parts IX and X)

Interest is charged on overdue reserve tax, and there are various penalties for defaults, including a mitigable penalty of £50, plus £10 a day following a declaration by the Commissioners, where the appropriate notice of liability has not been given and the tax has not been paid.

7
Value added tax: general principles

Basis of charge (VATA 1994, ss 1, 4)

Value added tax (VAT) is charged on the supply of goods and services in the UK and on the import of goods and certain services into the UK. It applies where the supplies are taxable supplies made in the course of business by a taxable person. Significant changes were made to the UK system as a result of the introduction by the European Union of the Single Market on 1 January 1993. These are outlined on page 105.

References in this chapter are to Value Added Tax Act 1994 unless otherwise stated, but many of the detailed regulations are by statutory instrument. The main VAT regulations have been brought together in a single statutory instrument.

Taxable supplies (s 5 and Schs 4 and 6; FA 1996, s 33)

All supplies of goods and services to UK or overseas customers (including goods taken for own use) are taxable supplies, apart from items which are specifically exempt (see below). Goods for own use are taxable supplies valued at cost. Business gifts are taxable supplies except where the gift is valued at £15 or less (£10 for gifts before 29 November 1995) and does not form part of a series of gifts to the same person. They are valued at cost. There is not usually any VAT on gifts of services.

Exempt supplies (s 31 and Sch 9)

Exempt supplies are broadly supplies of:

Land
Insurance
Postal services (but not telephones)
Education
Finance services

Betting, lotteries and gaming
(except takings from gaming and
amusement machines)
Health services
Burial and cremation

Who is a taxable person? (Sch 1)

From 29 November 1995, you are liable to be registered for VAT at the end of any month if the taxable turnover of all your business activities in the year ended on the last day of that month has exceeded £47,000 (unless you can satisfy Customs and Excise that your taxable turnover in the next twelve months will not exceed £45,000). You are required to notify Customs and Excise within 30 days of the end of the month in which the yearly limit was exceeded and will be registered from the beginning of the next month or such earlier date as is agreed with Customs and Excise.

Liability to register also arises at any time if your taxable supplies in the next 30 days are expected to exceed £47,000. You must notify Customs and Excise within the 30 days and you will be registered from the beginning of the 30 days.

Example 1

Your turnover for the twelve months ended 30 June 1996 was £48,000, having been below the yearly limit at the end of previous months. You must notify liability to register by 30 July 1996 and will be registered from 1 August 1996 unless you can show that your turnover in the year to 30 June 1997 will not exceed £45,000.

Example 2

On 15 June 1996 you start trading and expect your first month's turnover to be £48,000. You must notify liability to register by 15 July 1996 and will be registered from 15 June 1996.

There is a penalty of up to 15% of the net tax due for failure to register, with a minimum penalty of £50.

Farmers are able to avoid VAT registration if they opt to become 'flat rate farmers' — for details, see page 433.

See also below as regards voluntary registration and selling a business as a going concern.

Notification is made on form VAT 1 and a certificate of registration VAT 4 is then issued showing the VAT registration number.

There are provisions for groups of companies to have group registration if they wish (see page 105).

Customs and Excise have discretion to exempt you from registration if you make only zero-rated supplies (see below), and do not wish to be registered. In that event you must notify Customs and Excise within 30 days of a material change in the nature of supplies made, or within 30 days after the end of the quarter in which the change occurred if it is not more precisely identifiable.

There are provisions to prevent the splitting of businesses in order to stay below the VAT registration threshold. Customs and Excise have the power to direct that where two or more persons are carrying on separate business activities which are effectively parts of the same business, they are to be treated for VAT purposes as the same business, e.g. where one spouse is a publican and the other runs the catering within the public house. Such a direction only affects future supplies and is not retrospective.

Cancellation of registration

From 29 November 1995, you will no longer be liable to be registered if your tax-exclusive turnover in the next twelve months will be £45,000 or less, unless the reason for turnover not exceeding £45,000 is that you will cease making taxable supplies in that year, or will suspend making them for 30 days or more.

You must notify Customs and Excise within 30 days of ceasing to make taxable supplies, upon which your registration will be cancelled from that date or a later date agreed with Customs and Excise. VAT will be payable on the business assets at their value at the time of deregistration, unless no input tax was recovered on their purchase, or the business is transferred as a going concern (see page 101), or the total VAT does not exceed £250.

Rates of tax (s 2 and Sch A1)

There are three rates of VAT, a standard rate of 17½%, the zero rate and a special rate of 8% on fuel and power for domestic or charitable use. (See also page 99 re imported antiques, etc.).

The VAT fraction on tax-inclusive supplies at the standard rate is 7/47 and on tax-inclusive supplies at the 8% rate is 2/27.

Zero rate (s 30 and Sch 8)

The main zero-rated items are:

Food, except where supplied in the course of catering, or where it is pet food, or a 'non-essential' item such as chocolate, ice cream, alcoholic and fruit drinks or crisps

Construction of buildings for residential or charitable use

Children's clothing and footwear

Transport (but not taxis or hire cars)

Water and sewerage services, except where supplied for industrial purposes

Books (but not stationery)

Drugs and medicines on prescription

Exports and international services (but see page 105 re the European Union)

These are only broad categories and there are extremely detailed rules relating to what items fall under each of the headings, giving rise to many disputes between Customs and Excise and the taxpayer, a large number of which have to be settled by VAT tribunals or the courts.

How the system works (ss 24–26)

Each person in the chain between the first supplier and the final consumer is charged VAT on taxable supplies to him (input tax) and charges VAT on taxable supplies made by him (output tax). He pays over to Customs and Excise the excess of output tax over input tax, or recovers the excess of input tax over output tax. The broad effect of the scheme is that businesses are not affected by VAT except in so far as they are required to administer it, and the burden of the tax falls on the consumer. All businesses will, however, pay some VAT that they cannot recover from Customs. Non-VAT registered businesses cannot recover any VAT at all, partially exempt businesses cannot recover all their VAT and there is some VAT that cannot be recovered by fully taxable businesses, as indicated below.

VAT repayments are likely to arise where most supplies are zero-rated. The effect of the zero rate is that the person is making taxable supplies, albeit charged at a nil rate, and can therefore recover input tax suffered. If you make exempt supplies you are outside the scheme and cannot recover input tax (except under the partial exemption rules — see below).

If you offer a cash discount you charge VAT only on the discounted amount whether the discount is taken or not.

You can recover input tax not only on goods purchased for resale but also on expenses such as telephones and stationery and on capital items. You cannot, however, recover input tax on business entertaining (subject to what is said on page 271) or on cars (other than for resale, or use in a car hire or driving school business, or bought after 31 July 1995 exclusively for business purposes, for example leasing). Businesses paying car leasing charges for cars on which input tax has been recovered by the lessor can recover only 50% of the input tax on the leasing charges if there is any private use of the cars. Companies cannot recover input tax on repairs, refurbishments and other expenses relating to domestic accommodation provided for directors or their families.

Output tax must be charged on all taxable supplies, including, for example, sales of fixed assets like plant and machinery. (Special rules apply to second-hand goods — see page 98.) Where business cars on which input VAT was not recovered are sold, VAT is only payable to the extent that the selling price exceeds the cost (i.e. the second-hand margin scheme out-lined below applies). If any input VAT was recovered, VAT is payable on the full selling price.

If your business petrol bills include petrol for private use by you or your employees, an adjustment must be made in respect of the non-business proportion unless, in the case of employees, they have paid for it in full, including VAT, in which case the output VAT has to be accounted for. For commercial vehicles, the adjustment is made by disallowing the private proportion of the input tax. For cars, a private use scale charge applies, based on the income tax fuel benefit for directors and employees (see page xxxi). It applies whether the car is provided by the employer or owned by the employee. The VAT charged on car fuel bills is fully recoverable, but a tax-inclusive supply equal to the car fuel scale charge is regarded as made in each return period for the appropriate number of cars. By concession, the scale charges do not apply if you notify Customs that you are not going to claim an input tax deduction for *any* fuel (including fuel used in commercial vehicles). The scale charges also do not apply if the input tax claimed relates only to business mileage (this being supported by detailed records) and the cost of private mileage is not included in the business accounts.

Where input VAT has not been recovered from Customs, it can be included as part of the business expenditure for income tax or corporation tax, subject to any disallowance under the rules for measuring profit (so that for example business entertainment expenses cannot be included at all, and proprietors' car fuel expenses must be restricted by any private use — see chapter 20). Disallowed VAT on cars will form part of the cost for capital allowances (see chapter 22).

Second-hand goods (s 50A)

Many second-hand goods sold in the course of business have been obtained from the general public rather than from VAT registered traders, and if there were no special rules, the dealer buying the second-hand goods would have to charge VAT on the selling price without having any input tax to recover. Various special schemes used to be available in the UK for particular types of goods, but from 1 January 1995 a single Margin Scheme has been adopted by EU countries which may be used for the sale of all second-hand goods, works of art, antiques and collectors' items except precious metals and gemstones. Where goods are sold under the Margin Scheme, VAT is charged on each item only on the excess of the selling price over cost (i.e. the dealer's margin). VAT is not shown separately on the invoice, and no input tax is recoverable by the purchaser. Where individual items cost £500 or less and are purchased in bulk, businesses may also adopt 'global accounting', under which they work out the margin on the difference between total purchases and sales rather than item by item. Global accounting cannot be used for aircraft, boats and outboard motors, caravans, horses and ponies and motor vehicles, including motorcycles. The Margin Scheme does not have to be used for all second-hand sales, so that VAT may be charged in full under a normal VAT invoice on sales to VAT-registered businesses.

EU margin scheme sales are charged to VAT in the country of origin rather than the country of destination. This means that UK margin scheme sales to someone from a country within the EU will be taxed only in the UK (exports outside the EU are zero-rated). Acquisitions from countries in the EU are dealt with in the same way as purchases in the UK. VAT will not be charged on acquisitions from private EU individuals, and the margin scheme may be used when the goods are sold in the UK. Acquisitions from EU VAT registered businesses may either be made through the scheme, so that the scheme may be used on resale, or outside the scheme, in which case VAT will be recoverable but the scheme cannot be used for the resale.

Imports of second-hand goods from outside the EU are subject to import VAT in the normal way (see below), except that from 1 June 1995, imports of certain works of art, antiques and collectors' items, which were previously relieved from VAT, are charged at an effective import VAT rate of 2½% (compared with a rate of 5% in the rest of the EU).

Imports (s 37)

VAT is chargeable on imports when they are entered for home use. The importer has to pay VAT on the goods on importation, and then gets a credit for the input tax on his next return (subject to any restriction for partial exemption, etc.). If the goods are for resale, output tax will be accounted for in the normal way when they are sold. No VAT is payable on goods temporarily imported for repair, processing or modification, then re-exported. Goods which have been temporarily exported and are re-imported by the same person after repair, process, or modification will bear VAT only on the value of the repair, etc. plus freight and insurance.

Separate rules apply to the European Union — see page 105.

Voluntary registration

Customs and Excise will allow you to register voluntarily if your business makes taxable supplies even though your turnover is below the statutory limits. Once you are registered, you will then charge VAT on your supplies and recover input tax suffered. This may be beneficial if your customers are mainly taxable persons, but not where they are the general public. Registration will bring the burden of complying with the administrative requirements of the scheme, so may not be thought worthwhile even though a price advantage may arise. See example 3.

Example 3

You are in business as a handyman and pay input tax of £750 on phone, stationery, etc. Your turnover is £15,000, including £750 to cover the tax suffered.

If you register voluntarily for VAT, you need only charge £14,250 for the same supplies and your turnover will then be:

£14,250 + 17½% VAT £2,494 = £16,744.

You will pay to Customs and Excise £2,494 less £750 = £1,744, leaving you with £15,000 as before. If your customers are the general public your prices to them will be £1,744 higher, but if they are taxable persons they will recover £2,494, so that their net price will be £14,250.

Intending trader registration

If you are in business and are not currently making taxable supplies, but intend to do so in the future, you may apply for registration and Customs and Excise are required to register you. This enables you to recover any input tax suffered even though no taxable supplies are being made.

Exemption and partial exemption (SI 1995/2518 Pt XIV)

If you make only exempt supplies you do not charge VAT but you cannot recover input tax charged to you, so your prices must include an element to recover the VAT suffered. Some businesses make both taxable and exempt supplies and are thus partially exempt.

In these circumstances, there are rules to determine how much of your input tax can be recovered. You can recover all the input tax directly attributable to your taxable supplies, and none of the input tax directly attributable to exempt supplies. As to the remainder of the input tax that relates to overheads, input tax is deductible in the proportion that taxable supplies bear to total supplies. The proportion is expressed as a percentage, rounded up to the nearest whole number. Alternatively, a 'special method' can be agreed with Customs and Excise. Certain exempt supplies can be ignored in these calculations, but only where they are supplies of capital goods used for the business or are 'incidental' to the business activities. Input tax relating to certain other exempt supplies can be treated as relating to taxable supplies. There is a right of appeal against the proportion of input tax which is recoverable.

If you are partially exempt you can recover all input tax suffered despite the exempt supplies if your input tax on exempt supplies does not exceed 50% of total input tax and does not exceed £625 a month on average.

Capital goods scheme (SI 1995/2518 Pt XV)

Input tax recovery on certain capital items acquired on or after 1 April 1990 does not depend just on the initial use of the asset but must be adjusted over a longer period where use changes between exempt and taxable supplies.

The assets concerned are computer hardware of a tax-exclusive value of £50,000 or more per item, and land and buildings of a tax-exclusive value of £250,000 or more. The adjustment period is ten years except for computers and leases for less than ten years, where the adjustment period is five years. The adjustments will be reflected in the business capital allowances computations for the calculation of tax on your profits (see page 313).

Changes in circumstances

Where your circumstances change, you are required to notify Customs and Excise within 30 days of the change. Some changes require cancellation of your registration, others merely an amendment.

Your registration will require cancellation when you cease business, or take in a partner, or revert from a partnership to a sole proprietor, or incorporate or disincorporate your business, or cease to make taxable supplies. In some circumstances it is possible to transfer your registration number to the new business.

Many changes require amendment to your registration, such as changes in the composition of a partnership, change of business name, changes in a group of companies, change of address and so on.

Selling a business as a going concern

If a VAT registered trader sells all or part of a business as a going concern, the seller does not normally have to account for VAT on the sale consideration, and the purchaser does not have any input tax to reclaim where the sale is to another taxable person or to someone who becomes a taxable person immediately after the sale. This does not apply to the transfer of land and buildings on which the option to charge VAT has been exercised or to commercial buildings and civil engineering works that are unfinished or less than three years old unless the purchaser has also opted to charge VAT and has so notified Customs by the date of the transfer. (For details of the option to charge VAT, see page 454.) If the purchaser is not already registered, the rules for deciding whether he is liable are the same as those outlined on page 95, except that the seller's supplies in the previous twelve months are treated as made by the purchaser. The purchaser must notify his liability within 30 days of the transfer, and will be registered from the date of the transfer. If the seller was not VAT registered, his turnover would not have to be taken into account by the purchaser in deciding when registration was necessary.

These rules do not apply when you merely sell assets, rather than an identifiable part of the business which is capable of separate operation. The sale of a family company is dealt with in chapter 28.

Anti-avoidance provisions have been introduced in relation to transfers to partially exempt groups (see page 105).

Records and returns (Sch 11)

VAT registered businesses must supply tax invoices in respect of taxable supplies, keep a VAT account showing the calculations of the VAT liability for each tax period, and make returns to Customs and Excise showing the VAT payable or repayable.

Tax invoices (SI 1995/2518 Pt III)

Where you make standard-rated supplies to another taxable person, you must provide and keep a copy of a tax invoice showing the following:

Identifying number
Tax point (see below)
Date of issue of the invoice
Your name, address and VAT registration number
Customer's name and address
Type of supply (e.g. sale, hire-purchase, rental)
Description of goods or services supplied, and for each type of
goods, the quantity, rate of tax and tax-exclusive amount payable
Total amount payable excluding VAT
Rate of cash discount offered
Total tax chargeable

Retailers may provide a less detailed invoice omitting the customer's name and address and the amount (but not the rate) of VAT, if the tax-inclusive price is £100 or less. Copies of these less detailed invoices need not be kept.

There is a penalty of up to 15% of the amount charged as VAT for unauthorised issue of a VAT invoice, with a minimum penalty of £50.

Tax point (time of supply) (s 6)

The basic tax point is normally when goods are made available or services are performed, unless they are invoiced and/or paid for earlier, in which case the earlier date is the tax point. Where goods or services are invoiced within 14 days after supply, the later date is the tax point, and if you invoice monthly you can adopt a monthly tax point, but in either case the tax point will be the date payment is received if earlier.

Special schemes for retailers

The normal VAT procedure requires records to be kept of every separate transaction. Retailers would find it virtually impossible to keep such detailed records, so there are a number of special schemes which enable retailers to calculate output tax in a way that suits their particular circumstances.

Lost goods (s 73) and bad debts (s 36)

If goods are lost or destroyed before being sold, output tax is not chargeable.

But once a supply has been made, VAT is chargeable. If a customer fails to pay, VAT may be reclaimed on any debt which is more than six months old and has been written off in your accounts. VAT must be accounted for on any part of the debt that is later recovered. If the debtor is declared insolvent, the claim in the insolvency will be the VAT-inclusive amount, because you have to account for VAT on any debt recoveries.

Cash accounting

Businesses with a tax-exclusive turnover of not more than £350,000 can avoid the problems and delay in recovering VAT on bad debts by using the cash accounting system, providing they are up-to-date with their VAT returns and have either paid over all VAT due or have arranged to pay any overdue amount by instalments. Once a business has started using the scheme, it must normally stay in it for at least two years unless annual turnover exceeds £437,500. Tax invoices still have to be issued but output tax will not have to be accounted for until cash is received. On the other hand, input tax will not be recoverable until suppliers are paid.

VAT account, tax periods and tax returns (ss 59, 79; SI 1995/2518 Pt V)

The results for each tax period must be summarised in a VAT account. Returns are made to Customs and Excise on form VAT 100 for each tax period, showing the VAT payable or repayable and certain statistical information (including specific entries for European Union sales and purchases). The return is due within one month after the end of the tax period. Customs will usually extend this period by seven days where payment is made by credit transfer.

A 'default surcharge' is payable if two or more returns within a year are not made on time. When a return is late, a 'surcharge liability notice' is issued. The notice remains in force for a period of one year, unless a further return is made late, in which case the surcharge liability period is extended for a year from the last day of the period covered by that return and so on. The surcharge is 2% of the tax due for the first late return in the surcharge liability period, then 5%, 10% and a maximum 15% for subsequent late returns. The 2% and 5% surcharges will not be collected if they are less than £200. The minimum surcharge at 10% or 15% is £30. If no VAT is due, or the VAT is paid on time even though the return is late, then although the late return affects the surcharge liability period, the surcharge does not apply and the rate for subsequent late returns is not increased.

Where there is an unreasonable delay on the part of Customs in making a VAT repayment, a repayment supplement amounting to an extra 5% (or £50 if more) will be added to the repayment, providing the return claiming the repayment was made on time.

A tax period is normally three months, but if you regularly claim VAT repayments (for example because you make mainly zero-rated supplies) you may have a one-month period if you wish. The advantage of earlier repayments in those circumstances must be weighed against the disadvantage of having to complete twelve returns annually.

Quarterly return dates are staggered over the year depending on your business classification. You can ask for the dates to be changed to coincide with your accounting period.

Annual accounting (SI 1995/2518 Pt VII)

Businesses with an annual tax-exclusive turnover of not more than £300,000 that have been registered for at least one year may apply (on form VAT 600) to join the annual accounting scheme. They then agree a provisional VAT liability with Customs and Excise based on the position for the previous year. The agreed figure is divided by ten. Nine equal monthly payments are then made by direct debit starting four months after the beginning of the year. The annual return and balancing payment have to be made within two months after the end of the year.

From 1 April 1996, businesses with a turnover of less than £100,000 will be able to make quarterly instead of monthly interim payments, the quarterly payments being 20% of the previous year's VAT liability (unless it was below £2,000, in which case no interim payments will be required).

Monthly payments on account for large VAT payers (s 28; SI 1993/2001; SI 1995/291; SI 1995/2518 Pt VI)

Traders who pay more than £2m VAT a year have to make payments on account in the first two months of each quarter, based on 1/24th (1/12th before 1 June 1996) of their total liability for the twelve months to the previous 31 March, 30 April or 31 May, depending on their VAT return periods. The payments are calculated and notified to the trader by Customs, and the trader makes any necessary adjustment on his quarterly return. From 1 June 1996, traders may elect to pay their actual monthly VAT liability instead of the notified amount (which may be preferable where there are seasonal variations). Payments on account *must* be made by electronic means and there will be no seven-day period of grace. Default surcharge (see page 103) will apply if payments are not made on time.

Group registration (ss 43, 44 and Sch 9A; FA 1995, s 25; FA 1996, s 31 and Sch 4)

Two or more resident UK companies, and non-resident companies with an established place of business in the UK, may apply to be treated as a group if one of them controls each of the others, or if an individual, partnership or company controls all of them. Only one VAT return is then required.

Where there is no group registration, VAT has to be added to charges for supplies from one company to the other, such as management charges, and care must be taken to ensure that this is not overlooked. There are provisions to ensure that unfair advantages are not obtained by group treatment, and the powers of Customs and Excise to counter VAT avoidance involving the transfer of companies or assets into or out of groups have been increased from 29 November 1995.

An EU decision has been made that basic activities of holding companies, such as holding shares and acquiring subsidiaries, are not business activities and any associated input tax cannot be recovered. This only applies, however, to holding companies that neither trade themselves, nor have active trading subsidiaries making taxable supplies outside the VAT group, nor provide genuine management services to separate trading subsidiaries.

Where a business is transferred as a going concern to a partially exempt group, the transfer is treated as a supply to and by the group. The group will therefore have to account for output tax, and will only be able to recover its allowable proportion of input tax according to the partial exemption rules (see page 100). This does not apply if the person who transferred the assets to the group acquired them more than three years previously. Nor does it apply to items covered by the capital goods scheme (see page 101).

European Union Single Market

Supplies of goods between European Union countries are not regarded as imports and exports, but as 'acquisitions' and 'supplies'. The registration and deregistration threshold for acquisitions from other EU countries is £47,000 (from 1 January 1996). When goods are acquired in the UK from an EU supplier, output tax must be accounted for on the next VAT return, but with an equivalent amount being deducted as input tax in the same return (subject to any partial exemption restriction). Supplies by a UK supplier to VAT registered EU customers are zero-rated, but VAT is accounted for by the customer at his country's VAT rate, i.e. the country of destination. (At a later stage, not before 1 January 1997, it is intended to move to a charge based on the country of origin.) Special rules apply to new motor vehicles, motor cycles, boats and aircraft, under which VAT is charged at the rate of the purchaser's country. Other supplies to non-VAT registered EU individuals are at the rate applicable in the UK, although if sales to an EU country exceed that country's stipulated threshold the seller must register for VAT in that country (or appoint a tax representative to act for him) and that country will then become the place of supply. There are special rules where there is an intermediate supplier between the original supplier and the customer.

For supplies to VAT registered EU customers, a UK seller must state both his own and the customer's VAT number on VAT invoices. In addition to making his normal VAT returns, he also has to submit a return of all supplies to VAT registered customers in the EU for each calendar quarter (known as aggregate sales lists). Larger businesses (acquisitions or supplies above £160,000 from 1 January 1996) have to submit monthly returns known as Intrastat returns.

See page 99 for the EU treatment of second-hand goods.

Assessments (ss 73, 76, 77)

If a taxpayer fails to make returns, or the Commissioners feel returns are incomplete or incorrect, they may issue assessments of the amount of VAT due. Such assessments must normally be issued before the expiry of two years from the end of the return period, or, if later, one year after the facts come to light. Assessments cannot be made later than six years after the end of the return period, except in cases of fraudulent or negligent conduct, when the period is increased to 20 years. Where the taxpayer has died, no assessment can be made later than three years after death, or relate to a period more than six years before death. If a taxpayer does not submit a return and instead pays the VAT shown on an estimated assessment, the Commissioners may fix an estimated assessment for a later period at a higher figure than they otherwise would have done. Penalties for late submission may also arise.

Interest, penalties and surcharge (ss 59–72, 74)

In addition to their right to take criminal proceedings (for other than regulatory offences) which could lead to a fine or imprisonment or both, Customs and Excise have the power to charge interest on overdue tax in certain circumstances, and there are severe penalties, for late, incorrect or incomplete returns, or for failure to notify liability to be registered for VAT or unauthorised issue of VAT invoices, or for failure to keep proper records (which have to be retained for six years). As indicated on page 103, there is also a default surcharge for repeated late submission of VAT returns.

Where there are errors in a VAT return, they will not normally be penalised if they are discovered and corrected in the next following return (even if the error was discovered by Customs). Nor will errors that are corrected by a compensating error in the next following return, such as input VAT claimed in the return before the correct return, or output VAT accounted for in the return following the correct return. Subject to these relaxations, the system works as follows.

If a taxpayer finds he has made mistakes in earlier returns causing tax to be overpaid or underpaid and the total net errors discovered are £2,000 or less, he may correct them by adjusting the amount of VAT payable or repayable in the current return or by notifying Customs. Providing this is done voluntarily, no penalty will apply and no interest will be charged on any overdue amount. If net errors totalling more than £2,000 are discovered, they cannot be adjusted in the current return and must be separately notified (on form 652) and if tax has been underpaid, interest will be charged on the overdue amount, but again no penalty will be charged if the errors are disclosed voluntarily.

Unless covered by this errors procedure, or the taxpayer can show a reasonable excuse, a penalty for serious or repeated misdeclaration may apply. The serious misdeclaration penalty of 15% will only apply where the underpaid or over-reclaimed VAT amounts to at least 30% of the total of the input and output tax figures that should have been stated on the return (or £1m if less), and it is possible for the penalty to be mitigated in appropriate circumstances. Smaller misdeclarations will be subject to a (mitigable) 15% repeated misdeclaration penalty where Customs and Excise have served a penalty liability notice following a material error and there are at least two further material errors within two years. A material error is one where the understated VAT is at least 10% of the combined input/output tax that should have been shown on the return (or £500,000 if less). If the error has been penalised as a serious misdeclaration (see above), it will not be double penalised but it will count in calculating whether repeated errors have occurred.

With such a wide range of possible penalties, you need to be careful that your VAT accounting procedures will enable you to account for VAT correctly and on time.

Interest to taxpayer following Customs error (s 78)

Taxpayers are entitled to interest on repayments where tax has been overpaid or underclaimed as a result of error by Customs.

Administration and appeals (Sch 12)

VAT is under the control of the Commissioners of Customs and Excise, operating through the VAT Central Unit and through local VAT offices under Collectors of Customs and Excise. If you disagree with a decision of Customs and Excise as to the VAT payable or various other matters, such as registration or cancellation of registration, use of a retailer's scheme, calculation of output tax, etc., you may appeal to an independent VAT and duties tribunal within 30 days of the decision. Normally, any tax in dispute must be paid before the tribunal hearing, but this requirement may be waived to avoid hardship. VAT tribunals normally hear appeals in public. If you are dissatisfied with the tribunal decision, further appeal is possible to the High Court, the Court of Appeal, and, where leave is granted, to the House of Lords. Taking an appeal to the courts may, however, result in costs being awarded against you if the appeal fails.

Insurance premium tax (IPT) (FA 1994, ss 48–74 and Sch 7; FA 1995, Sch 5)

From 1 October 1994 insurance premiums are subject to tax at 2.5%. This does not apply to long-term insurance such as life insurance, pension premiums or permanent health insurance, nor to general insurance of international air and sea transport and trade, nor to reinsurance. There were provisions to prevent tax being avoided by making abnormal arrangements to pay in advance for policies commencing on or after 1 October 1994, or to pay several years' premiums at once.

Customs and Excise intend to operate the tax on the basis of co-operation rather than confrontation, and have issued various concessions to smooth the workings of the system. Insurers must, however, register (on form IPT 1) within 30 days if they intend to receive taxable premiums, and they must maintain appropriate records. They will add the tax to premiums charged and pay over 1/41 of the tax-inclusive amount to Customs and Excise quarterly. If a premium covers taxable and exempt items it is apportioned. Late or incorrect returns are subject to penalties. Non-UK insurers have to appoint a UK representative to account for the tax. Although collected by Customs and similar in nature to a value added tax, the tax is an entirely separate tax and does not have any interaction with VAT.

8
Council tax and business rates

Introduction

This chapter gives an outline of council tax and business rates. Additional points of detail relating to specific areas are dealt with in the appropriate chapters, in particular employment aspects in chapter 10 and let property in chapter 32.

The council tax replaced the poll tax from 1 April 1993 in England, Wales and Scotland. Domestic rates are still payable in Northern Ireland. There are some differences in the system in Wales and Scotland and this chapter deals mainly with the system for England. There is a brief comment on the differences in Wales and Scotland on page 115.

Many people suffered large increases in their bills under the poll tax compared with what they had paid in rates. These were cushioned by a reduction scheme. There is now a similar scheme to give transitional relief to households whose council tax bills are significantly more than their combined poll tax.

Business rates are paid by businesses all over the country at a uniform level fixed by central government except for businesses served by the City of London Corporation. The introduction of this system was preceded by a property revaluation and revaluations are to be made every five years, the first of which affected assessments from 1 April 1995. Annual increases in the business rate will not exceed the increase in the Retail Prices Index, but the overall bill will be affected by valuation changes. There are transitional provisions to limit gains and losses for individual businesses over the first few years.

Council tax — the general rules

Council tax is payable on a 'dwelling', i.e. a house, flat, mobile home or houseboat, and there is a single bill for each dwelling. Some properties will be mixed private/business properties, and any part of a property that is wholly used for business purposes will be subject to the business rate, with the council tax applying to the 'dwelling' part. Some dwellings are exempt (see below at page 111).

Council tax bills may be reduced by one or more of the following:

The disability reduction scheme (see page 113).
Discounts where there are less than two occupiers (see page 112).
The transitional reduction scheme mentioned above (see page 114).
Council tax benefit for those on low incomes (see page 114).

Where more than one of these reductions is relevant, they are applied in the order stated.

The amount of the bill before any available deductions depends on the estimated value of the property at 1 April 1991, but taking into account any significant alteration to the property before 1 April 1993, such as an extension, and assuming that the property is in reasonable repair. Newly built property will similarly be valued back to what it would have been worth at 1 April 1991. The bill is calculated according to which of the following valuation bands the property falls in:

Band	England	Scotland	Wales
A	Up to £40,000	Up to £27,000	Up to £30,000
B	£40,001–£52,000	£27,001–£35,000	£30,001–£39,000
C	£52,001–£68,000	£35,001–£45,000	£39,001–£51,000
D	£68,001–£88,000	£45,001–£58,000	£51,001–£66,000
E	£88,001–£120,000	£58,001–£80,000	£66,001–£90,000
F	£120,001–£160,000	£80,001–£106,000	£90,001–£120,000
G	£160,001–£320,000	£106,001–£212,000	£120,001–£240,000
H	Over £320,000	Over £212,000	Over £240,000

The council tax bills for the various bands vary according to proportions laid down by law. The full bill for a band H dwelling is twice that for a band D dwelling and three times that for a band A dwelling.

Properties will normally only be revalued when they are sold, even if they have been substantially improved or extended. There is, however, provision for adjusting values downwards at any time if there is a major change in the area, such as a motorway being built nearby, or if part of the property is demolished, or if the property is adapted for someone who is disabled. If, because of inaccuracies in the original list, a valuation is wrong, it can be corrected. Increases in bandings only take effect from the day the valuation list is altered.

You can appeal against the valuation in certain circumstances (see page 114).

Council tax is calculated on a daily basis and is adjusted appropriately when a change of circumstances affects the bill, such as the property becoming or ceasing to be eligible for exemption or discount, and when you move from one house to another (the day you move in being a chargeable day but not the day you move out). This means that householders need to notify their councils of changes affecting their liability.

Council tax is normally paid by ten monthly instalments, but other payment methods may be offered. If you fail to pay on time, you may lose the right to pay by instalments and action may be taken against you for recovery. Collection may then be enforced in various ways, including an attachment of earnings order requiring your employer to deduct the outstanding tax from your salary and account for it to the council. If you do not pay at all, you may be sent to prison (except in Scotland).

Exempt dwellings

Exemption may be claimed in the following circumstances. The council must be notified if the exemption ceases to apply, otherwise penalties may be imposed.

A   Newly built or structurally altered or repaired property that is unfurnished and unoccupied. Exemption applies for up to six months after the work is substantially completed.

B   Empty property owned and last used by a charity, exemption applying for up to six months.

C   Empty, unfurnished property, for up to six months (ignoring any period of reoccupation for less than six weeks).

D   Dwellings left empty by someone in prison (other than for not paying fines or council tax).

E   Dwellings left empty by someone now living in hospital or in residential care.

F   Property empty following a death, for up to six months after granting of probate or administration.

G   An empty dwelling in which occupation is prohibited by law, e.g. after compulsory purchase (but there would be no exemption for squatters occupying such a building).

H   Property left vacant for a minister of religion.

I   Property that is empty because the occupier is now living elsewhere to receive care because of old age, disablement, illness, alcohol/drug dependence or mental disorder.

J   Property empty because the occupier is resident elsewhere to look after someone needing care as indicated in I above.

K   Empty property last occupied by a student whose main residence it was but who now lives elsewhere to be near to his place of education.

L   Unoccupied mortgaged property that has been repossessed by the lender.

M   Students' halls of residence.

N   Property wholly occupied by students as their full-time or term-time residence.

O   Dwellings owned by the Secretary of State for Defence and used as accommodation for members of the Armed Forces (other than Visiting Forces).

P   Accommodation for Visiting Forces.

Q   Unoccupied property for which someone is liable only as a Trustee in Bankruptcy.

R   A pitch not occupied by a caravan or a mooring not occupied by a boat.

S   Properties occupied solely by people under 18 years of age.
T   Unoccupied annexes.
U   Properties occupied solely by severely mentally impaired people.

The exemption under the last three categories applies from 1 April 1995.

Who is liable to pay?

There is only one council tax bill for each dwelling. The person liable is whichever resident (or residents) comes first on the following list.

(a)   An owner-occupier.
(b)   A resident leaseholder (including assured tenants under the Housing Act 1988).
(c)   A resident statutory or secure tenant.
(d)   A resident who has a contractual licence to occupy the property, such as someone living in a tied cottage.
(e)   A resident with no legal interest in the property, such as a squatter.

A resident is someone over 18 who lives in the property as his only or main home.

Where more than one person falls into the first category to apply, such as where there are several joint owners, they are jointly liable for the tax. Where only one of a married or cohabiting heterosexual couple owns or leases a property, the partner is also jointly liable. Homosexual couples are only jointly liable if they both fall into the first category to apply, for example where they are joint owners/tenants. Where people are jointly liable, councils may choose to send the bill to just one or all of them. Unlike the position with the poll tax, those who are jointly liable are liable from the outset and not just where someone else has failed to pay the bill. But the council must name them on the original demand, or under a separate notice, in order to be able to take enforcement action against them.

Where there are no residents, the owner is liable. The owner is also liable instead of the residents in the case of the following dwellings.

 (i)   Multi-occupied properties such as bed-sits where rent is paid separately for different parts of the property.
 (ii) Residential care homes, nursing homes, and some hostels providing a high level of care.
(iii) Dwellings occasionally occupied by the owner whose domestic staff are resident there.
(iv) Monasteries, convents, and dwellings occupied by ministers of religion.

Discounts

Unlike the old rates, a council tax bill is regarded as having a 50% property element and a 50% personal element. The bill is reduced by 25% if there is only one householder and by 50% if the property is no-one's main home (except in Wales — see page 115).

The following are not counted in deciding how many residents there are, providing certain conditions are met.

A   People in prison, except for non-payment of fines or council tax, and those detained in hospital under the Mental Health Act 1983.
B   Those who are severely mentally impaired.
C   Full-time students, student nurses, apprentices and those undergoing Youth Training.
D   Long-term hospital patients and people being looked after in residential care homes, nursing homes, and hostels providing a high level of care.
E   Low-paid care workers employed by charities, such as Community Service Volunteers.
F   Members of international headquarters and defence organisations and their families.
G   Monks and nuns.
H   Those for whom child benefit is payable, and 18 and 19 year-olds whose course of education ended between 30 April and 1 November (who are counted only from 1 November).
I   Those staying in certain hostels or night shelters, such as Salvation Army Hostels.
J   People caring for someone with a disability who is not a spouse, partner or child under 18.

Not being counted as a resident does not alter your responsibility for payment if you are the person liable to pay the tax (for example a student owner sharing with another adult). But where, after ignoring those who are not counted, the dwelling is no-one's main home, the person liable to pay the tax would get a 50% discount.

You must notify the council if you are no longer eligible for a discount, or are only eligible for a smaller discount. Penalties apply if you do not.

Reduction for disabilities

Homes that provide one of the following special features for a substantially and permanently disabled adult or child who lives in the property will qualify for a one-band reduction in the bill. Any discounts, transitional relief and benefits will then apply to the reduced amount. If the home is already in band A no reduction is available. The special features are:

(a)   A room other than a bathroom, kitchen or toilet, that is mainly for the use of the disabled person (such as a ground floor bedroom in a two-storey property),
(b)   An extra bathroom or kitchen for the disabled person's use,
(c)   Extra floor space for a wheelchair.

To qualify for the reduction, the additional feature need not be specially built, but it must be shown that the disabled person would be severely adversely affected if the feature was not available. A claim should be made each year to your council, who may require additional evidence that the conditions for the reduction are satisfied.

Transitional reduction scheme

The transitional reduction scheme applies in England and Scotland (not Wales) to limit increases for certain households whose council tax is higher than their combined poll tax. The relief is being phased out, so that some households that qualified in earlier years are no longer eligible. Transitional relief is worked out automatically by councils and does not have to be claimed. You can appeal to a local review board if you disagree with the council's calculation.

There is no transitional relief for properties that were no-one's main residence at 31 March 1993. Although the transitional relief is based on whoever was living in the property at 31 March 1993, it will be available, where appropriate, to any person who moves into the property after that date. The relief is calculated on a daily basis and will be suspended for any period during which the property is no-one's main residence, but will reapply once a new resident moves in.

Council tax benefit

Those on low incomes may claim benefit of up to 100% of the bill. People with savings of more than £16,000 are not entitled to benefit. Where the income of the person liable to pay the bill is too high for benefit, it may be possible to claim a 'second adult rebate' of up to 25% for someone on a low income sharing the home (but not for a spouse, partner or lodger). Anyone who disagrees with the amount of benefit allocated to them may appeal to a local review board if they cannot resolve the dispute with the council.

Appeals

Valuation

You may appeal on the grounds that your home should or should not be shown on the valuation list. You may also appeal about your council tax banding if the value of the property has materially increased or decreased, or if the value has been affected by starting, stopping or changing business use. An upward revaluation because of extensions or improvements will only be made at the time of sale, so an appeal on those grounds will not be relevant until that time.

Valuation appeals are made initially to the Listing Officer at the local Valuation Office. If you cannot agree the appeal with him, it will be heard by a Valuation Tribunal.

Other grounds for appeal

Appeals may also be made where

(a) you consider your home should not be liable to tax; or
(b) you dispute your liability, either because you do not consider you are the liable person, or because of the calculation of available reductions; or
(c) you disagree with a penalty imposed on you; or
(d) you disagree with a completion notice identifying the date from which a new building becomes a dwelling, or when structural alterations are completed.

Appeal procedures differ depending on the nature of the appeal. Most disputes will be settled between the taxpayer and the council, but where agreement cannot be reached they will go to the Valuation Tribunal.

Wales and Scotland

Wales

Normally a dwelling that is no-one's main home qualifies for a 50% discount (see page 113). Because of the high proportion of Welsh holiday homes, councils in Wales will be able to restrict the discount for furnished dwellings that are no-one's main home to 25%, or even to give no discount at all. There is no transitional reduction scheme in Wales.

Scotland

In Scotland there are various differences in the way the council tax is administered and enforced. Scotland also has a separate council water charge, and those entitled to 100% relief from council tax still have to pay the water charge. Unlike taxpayers in England and Wales, Scottish taxpayers cannot be imprisoned for failing to pay the council tax.

Business rates

From 1 April 1990, businesses pay a uniform business rate (also called the national non-domestic rate) on their rateable values. (This does not apply to those served by the City of London Corporation, for whom there are special arrangements.) A revaluation was made as at 1 April 1988, prior to the start of the new system and this is to be updated every five years. A revaluation was accordingly made as at 1 April 1993, which came into effect from 1 April 1995. The level of the rate for 1996/97 has been fixed at 44.9 pence in the pound (compared to 43.2 pence for 1995/96). Annual increases cannot be more than the increase in the retail prices index.

Transitional arrangements were introduced at the outset for those facing large increases or decreases. The 1995 revaluation again resulted in some people facing large increases and others large decreases, and the transitional arrangements have been extended. For 1996/97, real annual increases will be restricted to a maximum of 7½%; the real increase will be only 5% for properties with revised rateable values of less than £10,000 (£15,000 in London) and only 2½% for small shops with living accommodation (rateable values below £10,000). Reductions in liability will be limited to a real rate of 10% for small properties and 5% for larger ones.

If a property changes hands, the new owner is entitled to take over the previous owner's entitlement to transitional relief.

Empty property attracts only half the normal rates bill, and then only after it has been empty for three months. And no rates are payable on empty factories and warehouses, or on empty properties with a rateable value of less than £1,000.

Self-catering holiday accommodation is normally subject to the business rate if available for short-term letting for 140 days or more in a year.

If you offer bed and breakfast, you will not be liable to business rates if you intend to offer such accommodation for not more than six people, you intend to live in the property at the same time and the property's main use is still as your home.

Those in mixed business and private accommodation pay the business rate on the non-domestic part and council tax on the private part.

The business rate is collected by individual local councils but it is paid into a national pool and is then distributed on a formula basis to county and district councils.

9
Dealing with the Revenue

Revenue officials

Income tax, corporation tax and capital gains tax are administered by the Commissioners of Inland Revenue (also called the Board of Inland Revenue). The Board operates through its appointed officers. The administrative structure was previously split between inspectors, who were responsible for raising tax assessments, and collectors, who collected the amount due as notified by inspectors. This is gradually being replaced by a new unified structure, under which there will be taxpayer service offices, taxpayer district offices and taxpayer assistance offices, each dealing with particular aspects of tax administration. Inheritance tax is administered by the Board of Inland Revenue through the Capital Taxes Office. Stamp duties are administered by the Board through the Office of the Controller of Stamps.

Responsibility to provide information to the Revenue

The Revenue send out tax returns to individuals, trusts and companies when they are aware that tax may be due. As far as individuals are concerned, most people have their tax dealt with through the PAYE system, and only about 9 million out of 26 million taxpayers receive tax returns. Nevertheless, if you do not receive a return and you have taxable profits or gains on which tax has not been paid and of which the Revenue are unaware, the onus is on you to tell the Revenue. Penalties apply if you do not, based on the tax unpaid at the normal payment date (see page 144, which also shows the time limits for notification). There is no obligation for employees or pensioners to notify if all their income will be taken into account under PAYE.

For individuals, the time limit for notification from 6 April 1995 is 5 October following the end of the tax year, e.g. by 5 October 1996 for 1995/96. That date will usually be before employees receive their annual PAYE coding notices, so they will not at that time know whether the Revenue have been informed by their employer of benefits arising for the first time. If, however, the employees have a copy P11D from their employers, they may assume that the Revenue know about its contents unless they have reason to believe otherwise.

Apart from returns made by employers in respect of earnings of their employees, there are various reporting requirements, such as by banks and building societies as to interest paid, payers of commissions and royalties, and those who receive profits and income belonging to other people (for example, interest or rent collected by solicitors or other agents).

Self-assessment from 1996/97 (FA 1994, ss 178–199 and Sch 19; FA 1995, ss 103–116 and Schs 20, 21; FA 1996, ss 121–136 and Schs 17–22)

Under the new self-assessment system from 1996/97 you will be able to work out your own tax if you want to. The existing rules apply to tax returns and assessments for 1995/96 and they are dealt with later in this chapter.

Self-assessment will apply to tax returns sent to you in April 1997 onwards and you will have until 31 January 1998 (the filing date) to send in the return for the year ended 5 April 1997. (If you do not get a return until after 31 October following the tax year, the due date for the return is 3 months from the date it is issued.) There will be automatic penalties for late returns. If you want the Revenue to work out the tax you will have to get the return in by 30 September 1997. You will also have to get the return in by 30 September if you are an employee and want to have a tax underpayment of up to £1,000 collected in a later year through the PAYE scheme rather than having to pay it by the 31 January filing date. When working out your own tax, you will need your coding notices to know the amounts of underpayments dealt with by coding adjustment (see page 121).

You will not be able to leave any entries in the return blank, or to put 'to be agreed', but if you cannot establish the correct figure in time, you will have to include a 'best estimate' and indicate that you have done so. The correct figure should then be notified as soon as possible, together with an amended self-assessment.

The Revenue will have 9 months from the date they receive your return to correct obvious errors, and you will have a year from the filing date to make amendments yourself.

Amendments cannot be made either to a return or to a claim (see below) if the return or claim is being enquired into by the Revenue (see page 123).

Claims for allowances, reliefs, etc.

Where a claim is made for capital allowances, the claim must normally be in the return or an amended return. Most other claims for reliefs and allowances will be made in the same way. For claims that are not included in a return or amended return, a separate claims procedure is laid down, under which the Revenue has the same 9-month period after the claim to correct obvious errors and the taxpayer has 12 months from the date of the claim to amend it. Unless another time limit is stipulated in the legislation, the time limit for claims is 5 years from the 31 January filing date for the return (i.e. 5 years 10 months after the end of the tax year).

Where capital losses are incurred, relief may be claimed either in the return or in a separate claim within the 5 years 10 months period (see page 43). There is, however, no time limit for carrying forward unused losses (see below re retaining records).

Backdated claims

Where relief is claimed for a loss incurred or payment made in one tax year to be set against the income of an earlier year, then although the tax saving from the claim is calculated by reference to the tax position of the earlier year, the claim is treated as relating to the later year and affects the tax payable for that later year. Repayment supplement will therefore be paid only from the payment date for the later year. This also applies to claims for averaging farming profits (see page 426) and carrying back post-cessation receipts (see page 295). See page 243 for the treatment of backdated personal pension premiums.

Keeping records

The Revenue may ask you to send accounts and supporting documents with your return, but this will not always be the case. You must, however, keep all records relevant to your return for 22 months from the end of the tax year, unless you are in business or you let property, in which case you must keep the records for 5 years 10 months from the end of the tax year. Even after the expiry of the time limit, if the Revenue enquire into a return (see page 123), the records must be kept until the enquiry is completed.

Where a claim is made other than in a return (see page 118), records relating to the claim must be kept until the day on which any Revenue enquiry into the claim (or amendment to a claim) is completed, or if there is no such enquiry, until the Revenue are no longer able to open such an enquiry (see page 123). (As far as claims for relief for capital losses are concerned (see above), this means that the time limit for retaining the records relating to the claim may have expired before the time when the loss is used to reduce a gain.)

A penalty of up to £3,000 could be charged for any tax year in respect of which you failed to comply with the record-keeping requirements.

Payment of tax

There is no change in the PAYE system or in the deduction of tax at source from bank interest, etc., but other tax payment dates have been standardised.

Provisional payments are due half-yearly on 31 January in the tax year and 31 July following. The provisional payments will normally be equal to half of the net *income tax* liability (and, for the self-employed, Class 4 national insurance contributions) of the previous tax year. You will work out the provisional payments yourself, except for 1996/97, where they will be calculated slightly differently and will be notified to you by the Revenue. Broadly the 1996/97 provisional payment due on 31 January 1997 will be an amount equal to all the 1995/96 tax due for direct payment on 1 January 1996 (first instalment on business profits plus all the tax on rent, gross interest and overseas income). The provisional payment on 31 July 1997 will equal the 1995/96 second instalment on business profits. The balancing payment for 1996/97 due on 31 January 1998 will include the *whole* of the higher rate tax on taxed income, as well as any capital gains tax. The first provisional payment for 1997/98 will be due at the same time and will include an amount equal to half of the 1996/97 higher rate tax, so that 1½ times the 1996/97 higher rate tax will be included in the payment due on 31 January 1998. For later years, the provisional payments will include the higher rate tax on continuing sources of income, so to that extent tax will be paid earlier than before. Provisional payments will not be required where most of the income is taxed at source (for example under PAYE) or the amount due is below a stipulated threshold which has not yet been announced. See page 243 for the treatment of personal pension premiums paid in 1996/97 and carried back to 1995/96.

Example 1

The self-assessment timetable will be as follows:

31 January 1997	1996/97 1st instalment due
April 1997	1996/97 return issued
31 July 1997	1996/97 2nd instalment due
30 September 1997	1996/97 return filed if Revenue to calculate tax
31 January 1998	1996/97 return filed if tax self-assessed. Final payment/repayment for 1996/97, including capital gains tax, plus 1st interim payment for 1997/98 (based on half 1996/97 tax paid directly on *all* income)
April 1998	1997/98 return issued
31 July 1998	2nd interim payment for 1997/98
30 September 1998	1997/98 return filed if Revenue to calculate tax
31 January 1999	1997/98 return filed if tax self-assessed. Final payment for 1997/98, plus 1st interim payment for 1998/99

Where income has fallen, you may make a claim to reduce or eliminate the provisional payments at any time before the 31 January filing date for your tax return (and if one or more of the payments has already been paid the appropriate amount will be refunded with interest from the payment date).

The total income tax, Class 4 national insurance and capital gains tax for the year will be shown in the tax return due on the 31 January after the end of the tax year (or worked out by the Revenue and notified to you if not self-assessed) and will be compared with the tax deducted at source and the provisional payments. Any underpayment will be due on that day and any overpayment will be repayable. The first provisional payment for the next tax year will be due at the same time.

If you or the Revenue make an amendment to your return resulting in extra tax payable, the tax is due 30 days after the amendment (although interest on overdue tax runs from the original due date for the return).

Tax return forms

The Revenue have been consulting people about the design of self-assessment returns and the format has not yet been finalised. Unlike the present returns (see page 124), the return for each tax year will deal with the income, gains and allowances of that year. The latest draft contains an 8-page tax return, with various supplementary pages depending on your circumstances. There will also be 'Help Sheets' giving more detailed guidance. It is intended that a free-of-charge floppy disk will be provided for those wishing to complete returns using a personal computer. Whatever form the final documents take, the self-assessment procedure can only be described as somewhat daunting. This is inevitable because despite all the changes aimed at simplifying the system, the UK tax provisions remain complex and confusing.

The Revenue are considering introducing a system of 'post-transaction rulings' under which you would be able to get a ruling from them on the tax effect of transactions you have undertaken, before you send in your return, and also a system of 'pre-transaction rulings', which would enable you to establish the tax effect of a transaction before it is carried out. The proposals have not yet been implemented.

Information from employers

Your employer should provide you with details of your pay and tax for the year (form P60) by 31 May and also the taxable amounts for benefits such as cars, cheap loans, etc. (form P11D) by 6 July. Under PAYE, coding adjustments are often made to collect underpaid tax from the previous year. If you have to fill in a tax return, the amount of PAYE tax that you take into account in calculating your tax position for the year will exclude any amount for a previous year's underpayment but will include any amount for the current year that is to be collected by a later coding adjustment. The tax return will provide information on how these adjustments are to be made.

Example 2

Total PAYE tax for 1997/98 shown on year end P60   £2,576
PAYE tax underpaid per coding notices: 1996/97   £50
                                                           1997/98   £80

£50 of the £2,576 is for the previous year, reducing the tax paid for 1997/98 to £2,526. But £80 for 1997/98 will be collected through PAYE in 1998/99, so the PAYE tax to take into account for 1997/98 is increased to £2,606.

Interest, repayment supplement, surcharges and penalties

Interest will be charged or repayment supplement allowed from the payment dates on tax (and Class 4 national insurance contributions) underpaid or overpaid. For further details and an illustration see pages 20, 21. Where an amendment is made to a return, interest is due on any additional tax payable from the original due date for the return, even though the tax itself is payable 30 days after the amendment. Unpaid surcharges and penalties (see below) will also attract interest.

If your balancing payment for a year is more than 28 days late, then unless you can show a reasonable excuse you will pay a surcharge on the late payment of:

> 5% of any tax not paid by 28 February.
> A further 5% of any tax still not paid by 31 July.

If additional tax becomes due following an amendment to your return, you have 30 days to pay the additional tax. Surcharges will only arise if the tax is paid more than 28 days after the 30-day period, and the further surcharge only if the payment is not made within a further 5 months.

The surcharge is in addition to interest on the overdue tax. There is no surcharge, however, if you have incurred a penalty based on the same tax.

The following automatic penalties will be charged for late returns:

> £100 if return is not made by 31 January (or filing date for return, if later), plus a further £60 a day if Revenue have applied for and received a direction from General or Special Commissioners to charge the daily penalty.

> Further £100 if Commissioners have not imposed the daily penalty and return not made by 31 July (or six months from filing date, if later).

Further penalty if return is not made by next 31 January (or one year from filing date, if later) of an amount equal to the tax that would have been payable under the return (not applicable to partnership returns).

A penalty (not exceeding the amount of the shortfall in the payment) plus interest may also apply if you fraudulently or negligently reduce your provisional payments.

Revenue enquiries (audits)

The Revenue will normally have a year from the filing date for the return to notify you that they intend to enquire into it (see page 578 in relation to personal representatives and trustees). If you file the return late, or notify an amendment to it, the enquiry period extends for a year from the date the return or amendment is filed plus the period to the next quarter day, i.e. 31 January, 30 April, 31 July or 31 October as the case may be. When the enquiry is completed, the Revenue will notify you of any amendments required to your return. You have 30 days from the date of the notification to appeal against the amendments, and the normal appeal and postponement procedures apply (see page 140). You may also within that period make amendments to the return yourself (for example, to revise a claim) providing the original return was made not later than 12 months from the 31 January filing date, but the Revenue would then have a further right to amend the self-assessment, against which you would have a further right of appeal.

The Revenue have similar powers to enquire into claims made separately from the return (see page 118). The time limit for opening an enquiry into a claim made outside the return is the same as that for an enquiry into an amendment to a return, and the same procedures apply for appealing against Revenue amendments and making amendments to the claim yourself when the enquiry is completed.

If the Revenue do not start an enquiry within the time limit, the tax as calculated will normally stand unless there has been inadequate disclosure or fraudulent or negligent conduct on your part. Although the implication is that the innocent taxpayer may regard the year as closed after the 12-month period, this does not sit easily with the fact that in most cases the Revenue will not require business accounts and other documents to be sent to them. In order to be sure of finality, it seems that you will need to make sure that the Revenue have in their hands as much detail concerning your tax affairs as they had under the old system, and furthermore that their attention is drawn to any contentious points.

Returns by individuals of income and capital gains for 1995/96 and earlier years (TMA 1970, ss 7, 8, 113)

Tax returns are strictly required to be sent in within 30 days from their issue, but the unofficial deadline is 31 October, e.g. 31 October 1996 for 1995/96 (see page 135). The Revenue will accept approved computer-produced returns and photocopies of returns and other tax forms (Revenue Statement of Practice SP 5/87). It is sensible to keep a photocopy of your return so that you have a full record of the information you have provided. See page 117 re notifying the Revenue if tax is payable and you do not receive a return. There are different return forms for self-employed and employed people, and a simplified form for employees with uncomplicated tax affairs. Each return requires details of income, allowable deductions and capital gains of the previous tax year and allowances claimed for the current tax year.

The 1996 return issued shortly after 5 April 1996 thus requires details of:

> Your income and deductions for 1995/96
> Capital gains — details of chargeable assets disposed of during 1995/96
> Claim for allowances for 1996/97

Husband and wife each get their own return to fill in.

You should attach explanatory schedules to your return where necessary. Some special points you need to be aware of when completing your return are as follows.

Income from self-employment

It is often appropriate, particularly so that your return is not delayed, to use the expressions 'As agreed', or 'To be agreed', or, if you are a partner, 'See partnership returns and accounts'. You should not, however, delay sending in supporting accounts and tax computations, since the return is strictly incomplete until these have been supplied to the Revenue, and interest and penalties may arise.

If, however, your turnover is less than £15,000, you do not have to send in your accounts (although you must still keep proper records in case the Revenue asks to see them) and you can just show your turnover, purchases and expenses, with the resulting net profit, in the spaces provided on the return.

Because of the transition to the current year basis for taxing income, accounts may not need to be sent with your 1996 return. The taxable profit for 1995/96 will usually be based on the accounts you have already sent in with your 1995 return. The profits of accounts ending in the tax year 1995/96 will normally be averaged with those of accounts ending in 1996/97 to arrive at the taxable profit for 1996/97, so that two sets of accounts will normally be relevant for the 1997 return. Accounts will be required with the 1996 return for new businesses, or businesses that have ceased, or where there are losses. For the detailed provisions on how taxable profits are worked out during the transitional period, see chapter 21.

Employments, etc.

This section of the return covers income as an office holder as well as that from a conventional employment. Thus an honorarium, or any excess of a general expenses allowance over the expenses incurred, should be declared.

Show each employment separately, and attach a schedule if need be. Enter the gross pay from the certificate of pay and tax given to you by your employer (P60). This information will also be sent to the Revenue by your employer, but you are still required to show it, and it will help you to check any assessment or summary of your tax position you receive from the Revenue.

If you left your job during the year and received a lump sum or pay in lieu of notice, this should be shown. The sum may not be taxable, or only partly so (see chapter 15), but it needs to be declared.

Tips and income from activities associated with the employment should be shown, whether they are paid by the employer or by someone else.

The form asks you to tick appropriate boxes if you get private use of a car, and if you are provided with fuel for private travel. You are also asked for details of any other benefits and expenses allowances (other than any amounts for which the Revenue have given a dispensation — see page 153). It is presently usually sufficient, even though not strictly correct, to say 'See employer's return', since the employer will have to make a detailed return on form P11D. You should, however, ask the employer for a copy of the P11D, since you are responsible for declaring the detailed items, and you should query any items with which you disagree, and ensure that the return has been submitted if you are relying on it to supply the Revenue with the full details required.

It will not be possible to leave out the figures when the new self-assessment rules come in, but they should have been supplied to you by your employer (see page 121).

Under the heading 'Expenses for which you wish to claim a deduction', as well as making specific claims, such as for professional subscriptions and items which either you or a trade association have agreed with the Revenue, insert a general heading 'Reimbursed expenses per employer's return', since this effectively cancels the payment to you by the employer of expenses properly incurred in the performance of your duties. The Revenue may, however, require a detailed claim setting out each item. Again, when self-assessment is introduced the claim will have to be quantified.

If you are entitled to a deduction for work abroad (see chapter 41), the periods of absence should be shown (on a separate schedule if necessary), clearly stating days of departure and return.

State pensions

Wives are entitled to a personal allowance in their own right, which can be used against any pensions or other income they have, whether the pensions are earned by their own contributions or by their husbands'. But where a husband gets an addition to his State pension because he has a non-working wife under 60, that counts as his income. It is not counted as the wife's income until it is paid to her, i.e. when she is 60.

National Insurance and Social Security benefits

You must show unemployment benefit or income support claimed when you were out of work, the taxable part of incapacity benefit (as notified to you by your Benefit Office — see page 201), widowed mother's allowance, invalid care allowance and industrial death benefit. Other benefits are not taxable and need not be shown.

Income from property

From 1995/96 (affecting the entries in your 1996 return), the calculation of rental income is very much simplified, and broadly you need to show total rents from both furnished and unfurnished property for the year ended 5 April less total allowable expenses (see chapter 32 for details). Interest is an allowable expense, restricted if necessary for any private use of the property (and this also applies to foreign property). Properties are dealt with separately rather than being included in the total figure if the 'rent a room' scheme applies, or if they are furnished holiday lettings, or if the property is abroad. Premiums on leases are also stated separately.

If you are claiming the 'rent a room' relief for rooms let in your own home (see page 410), fill in the appropriate boxes on the form.

Furnished holiday lettings in the UK are treated as trades even though the income is declared under this section, providing the relevant conditions are satisfied. This affects the tax treatment. For details, see page 451.

If you are the landlord and you pay your wife an amount for her assistance in rent collecting and administration which has been agreed with the Revenue as a proper deduction, this payment should be shown as her income in the employments section of her return.

If your total gross letting income before expenses is below £15,000 you do not need to provide a detailed statement showing how the total allowable expenses stated in the return were arrived at, although you must still retain detailed records in case any query is raised.

National Savings

Show the interest received or credited on National Savings Bank accounts and on deposit or income bonds and capital bonds in the year to 5 April. On a National Savings Bank account, take care to show whether the interest is on an ordinary account or an investment account. It is only the first £70 of *ordinary* account interest that is exempt from tax (for each of husband and wife). The full interest should be shown whether exempt or not. The Revenue will deduct the exempt amount when assessing you or including the amount in a summary of your tax position. If you have income from First Option Bonds you need to show the amount of tax deducted from the gross interest.

Income from other UK banks, building societies and deposit takers

This heading covers interest from local authorities as well as banks and building societies. Tick the appropriate box if you have registered to have interest paid gross (see chapter 37). Some other interest is also paid gross (see page 502).

Other interest you received in the UK

Other interest received is shown under this heading. This will include interest received in full, such as on War Loan, other government stocks bought through the National Savings Stock Register, certificates of tax deposit and loans to private individuals. It will also include interest from which tax has been deducted, such as on company loan stock and government stocks acquired through the Stock Exchange.

Accrued income, charges and allowances

Under the accrued income scheme (see page 497), you are required to show, in the return for the tax year in which the next interest payment on the stock fell due, the amount of any accrued income charges or accrued income allowances on your purchases or sales of stock. The amounts will usually be shown on the contract notes. Do not show the accrued income amounts if you are exempt from the charge because the nominal value of all your stock does not exceed £5,000 in the tax year or years concerned. Accrued income charges and accrued income allowances should both be shown under this heading.

Dividends from shares in UK companies

The amount to show is the dividend received in the year to 5 April and the tax credit, which is shown on the dividend counterfoil. The total of the two will be included in the summary of your tax position to see whether you are liable to higher rate tax or entitled to a refund. From 1 July 1994 you may have received a 'foreign income dividend' (FID) from a UK company, which is entered under a separate heading. The treatment of FIDs is the same as for stock dividends (see below). You need to show the cash dividend and the notional tax credit. The credit counts toward higher rate tax but is never repayable.

Stock dividends

If you took any stock dividends (also called scrip dividends — see page 512) instead of cash dividends, enter the appropriate amount notified to you by the company in the dividend column and an amount equal to ¼ of the dividend in the notional tax credit column. The credit will count as tax paid when working out whether you are liable to higher rate tax, but it cannot be repaid if you are not liable to pay that much tax.

Income from UK unit trusts

Unit trust income distributions will be included here. If you have acquired new units, you will usually have received with your income an amount called 'equalisation'. This is not income and should not be included. It should be deducted from the acquisition cost of the units for capital gains tax purposes, since it represents a reduction in the cost of your units to cancel the accrued income included in your purchase price when you bought them.

For 1994/95 and 1995/96, if you invest in interest-based funds or mixed funds, the part of your distribution that represents interest is net of 25% tax and the part that represents dividends has a 20% tax credit. These should be shown separately on your return. From 6 April 1996, the rate of tax deducted from interest has been reduced to 20%, which is the same as the dividend credits.

Income from savings and investments abroad

If tax has been paid abroad, you will need to make a claim for relief to be given for it in arriving at how much UK tax you will have to pay. Show the amounts of foreign tax deducted, and any UK tax deducted, for example by the Bank of England when acting as paying agent.

Other income from savings and investments

This heading covers miscellaneous items detailed in the notes accompanying the return. If you have purchased an annuity from a life assurance company, the income will include a non-taxable element to compensate you for having parted with capital in order to receive an income. This capital element should not be included in the amount entered on your return. The life assurance company and the Revenue will have agreed its amount and it will be clearly shown on the counterfoil accompanying your income. If you have entered into a life assurance contract in order in due course to replace the capital you have spent in purchasing the annuity, the life assurance company will only pay you the difference between the amount due to you under the annuity and the life assurance premium. This net amount is not the amount to show as income. The income is the income element of the annuity *before adding* the capital element and *before deducting* the life assurance premium.

Your life assurance company will issue a certificate of taxable gains which arise from your drawing a sum from a policy (partial surrender) or cashing it (maturity or complete surrender). The gains should be shown in the return of income for the year ended 5 April in which the policy year ends (see chapter 40).

Trust income

Include any income to which you are entitled in the year ended 5 April. The trustees should give you a certificate showing the amount, which will either have been paid to you or will be available for you to draw from the trust. You also have to give details of income received by some trust funds you have established yourself, for example where you have settled assets on your infant unmarried children, perhaps by making bank or building society investments in their name. Any such income remains yours for tax purposes and must be shown in your return, unless it amounts in total to £100 or less per child.

If you have established a trust for your children under which the income is either to be accumulated or used for their maintenance, any payments from the trust for their maintenance while they are under 18 and unmarried count as your income and must be shown on your return. The amount to be treated as your taxable income in this instance is 100/65ths of the maintenance paid (100/66ths from 6 April 1996).

Income from estates (in the course of administration)

If you are entitled to a share of the capital from an estate, the amounts you receive will be a combination of that capital and the income which it has generated. The personal representatives, who will themselves have paid income tax on the income, will give you either a certificate of the income, or estate accounts showing your income share. The amount before tax should be shown. For further details, see chapter 42.

You may sometimes be entitled to income under a trust created by will rather than a share of the capital, in which case the personal representatives will first of all complete the administration of the estate then transfer the residue to a trust fund. You should show the gross amount of any income you receive during the administration period. Any income you receive from the trustees after the residue has been transferred to them will be entered under the heading 'Income from trusts funded by others'.

Maintenance and alimony you receive

Maintenance or alimony is not chargeable to tax unless it is received under arrangements first made before 15 March 1988, and even then the first £1,720 (£1,790 from 1996/97) of maintenance from your divorced or separated spouse is exempt.

If you receive taxable maintenance, show the amount received in the year to 5 April and tick the box to claim the £1,720 (or £1,790) exemption.

All other income or profits

This section relates to any other income or profits you may have. Examples are given in the notes sent with the return. If in doubt as to whether an item should be included you should either seek appropriate professional advice or clear the point in writing with the Revenue.

If you have ceased to trade in an earlier year but have received some late income which was not included in your accounts, the amount should be included here.

Income from personal activities, for example from writing the occasional article or from an occasional commission, where the extent is insufficient to be regarded as from a profession or vocation, should be included in this section.

Where occasional profit items are included, relief may be available for losses on the same or other occasional activities. Include details and ask the Revenue to calculate and give relief for the losses against the profit items. If not obvious from other entries in the return, it is advisable to tell the Revenue about substantial gifts received or made, thus explaining movements in capital and consequent variation in income and perhaps later saving you a lot of trouble in answering time-consuming queries from the Revenue. An election for gifts holdover relief for capital gains tax might also need to be made — see chapter 4.

Mortgage or loan for main home

This section of the return covers interest relating to your only or main home (including caravans and houseboats). It also covers interest on loans taken out before 6 April 1988 if they are for home improvement, or to buy or improve the main home of your divorced or separated spouse, or to buy or improve a property occupied rent-free by a dependent relative. Married couples may choose to have tax relief allocated in a different way from the way in which they actually pay the interest (see chapter 30), in which case they should tick the appropriate box.

Tax relief may also be due on interest which you have paid on a bridging loan while you had two houses, or interest on borrowing to buy a property that you are not currently living in because you live in job-related accommodation (for example as a minister of religion, public house tenant or tenant farmer). Give full details of any such loans and the interest paid, if necessary in a schedule or covering letter.

The return also asks for information about loans paid off during the year.

Building society interest paid:

The society will advise the Revenue of the interest paid, and will usually have deducted the tax relief due under MIRAS (Mortgage Interest Relief At Source) in charging the interest to your account. If you did not get tax relief in this way, it is usually because the loan exceeded £30,000 and MIRAS relief was not given on the first £30,000. You will still get the relief by a deduction from the tax you owe or by repayment of any tax overpaid.

All other lenders:

Some banks are in the MIRAS scheme and again you may have had tax relief by deduction from the interest charged to your account. If you did not get relief in this way, the lender should be asked for a certificate of the interest paid and this should be sent with the return so that the relief can be given to you.

The return asks you to tick a box for non-MIRAS loans.

Other qualifying loans

You can claim a deduction for interest paid for the purposes listed on pages 11, 12. The interest must be on a loan. Overdraft interest does not qualify for relief except as a business expense. A certificate of the interest paid in the year ended 5 April must be attached.

Pension contributions and retirement annuity payments

These are dealt with in chapter 17. Payments under pre-1 July 1988 contracts are called retirement annuity premiums and payments under later contracts personal pension contributions. Two years' premiums have to be stated, those for the year to the previous 5 April so that the Revenue can see if further relief for that year is due because of payments in the year, and the anticipated payments for the year to 5 April next so that provisional relief can be given in assessments or codings. *Employees* paying new personal pension contributions or free-standing additional voluntary contributions get basic rate tax relief when they pay their contributions, so the payments are shown net. If the employee pays tax at higher rates, further relief is due, which should be claimed on form PP120. Contributions paid by an employer to an employee's own scheme are also shown. All pension payments by the self-employed, and retirement annuity payments under the old rules by employees, are paid in full and are shown gross. It is best to attach a schedule unless there are only one or two payments. You should tick the appropriate box if you want to treat all or part of a personal pension or retirement annuity payment as paid in the previous year, and the Revenue will then send you a claim form. (See page 243 for the treatment of 1996/97 payments backdated to 1995/96.) The supporting personal pension contribution certificate (PPCC) should be attached for the first of regular premiums and for isolated premiums. A certificate VCC should be attached for your first free-standing additional voluntary contribution (FSAVC) claim. If payments change in a later year, you should send in the payment receipts.

Other deductions

Private medical insurance for people aged 60 and over:

Where the insurance is with a UK insurer no entry is required on the return, because the premiums qualify for relief only at the basic rate of tax, and this is given by deducting it when paying the premium.

Relief is also available if the contract is with an insurer outside the UK but within the European Economic Area (i.e. the European Union plus Iceland, Liechtenstein and Norway). In this case an entry is required, and you need to provide the Revenue with a certificate of premiums paid from the insurer.

The premiums can be paid, and relief obtained, by the insured person or by a relative, so long as the insured person (or one of an insured married couple) is over 60 — see page 480. The premium on which relief is given is the gross amount payable inclusive of the new 2.5% insurance premium tax.

Maintenance or alimony payments:

Enter here those payments which are enforceable against you because of an order of a court in the UK or European Economic Area (i.e. the European Union plus Iceland, Liechtenstein and Norway), or under a written agree-ment, and maintenance assessed by the Child Support Agency. Maintenance paid to the DSS for a spouse who receives income support qualifies as if it had been paid to the spouse. Show the amount paid and tick the appropriate box on the form. If the maintenance arrangements were made after 15 March 1988, you will usually only get tax relief on maintenance to your spouse, not to children, and only on the first £1,720 (£1,790 from 1996/97). The rate of relief is restricted to 15%, giving a tax saving of £258 for 1995/96 and £268.50 thereafter. Relief at the 15% rate also applies to the first £1,720 (or £1,790 from 1996/97) of maintenance under agreements made before 15 March 1988, both to a spouse and by court order to children. The balance qualifies for relief in full at your top tax rate. Virtually all maintenance is now paid without tax being deducted at source (see page 466).

Gift aid donations and covenanted payments to charities:

All such payments should be shown net of tax. Donations under Gift Aid of a minimum of £250 net each qualify for tax relief. For details, see chapter 43.

Other covenants, etc. made for business reasons:

Since 6 April 1995, non-charitable covenants only qualify for relief if they were made for business reasons in connection with your trade or profession. Any such payments are shown net of tax.

Venture capital trust subscriptions:

This is a new heading covering shares subscribed for in a venture capital trust. For details of the relief available, see page 528.

Vocational training:

Enter the name of the training organisation and the net amount paid for qualifying vocational training (see page 162).

Capital gains

Chargeable assets disposed of:

If your total proceeds from all disposals did not exceed twice the exempt limit (£12,000 for 1995/96, £12,600 for 1996/97) and the chargeable gains were less than the exempt limit (£6,000 for 1995/96, £6,300 for 1996/97), there is a box to be ticked and no further details need be given.

In the case of quoted securities it is helpful to include a schedule showing the movements through purchases, sales, bonus and rights issues, etc., thus reconciling opening and closing holdings. The calculation of the chargeable gains on these and other assets is dealt with in the appropriate chapters, the date of disposal being the contract date in all cases.

Other information required:

You are also required to supply details of payments made or benefits provided to you by trustees of non-resident or dual-resident settlements, and of chargeable gains of settlements by reference to which you are chargeable as settlor (see pages 576 and 583).

Chargeable assets acquired:

Details of chargeable assets acquired are not now requested on returns. It is still, however, important to retain precise records of acquisitions and additional expenditure on chargeable assets, so that the capital gains tax on a future disposal can be accurately calculated.

The indexation allowance depends upon dates of purchase and sale, so make sure you record them accurately.

Claims for allowances

Some particular points are noted below.

Special personal allowance

An increased personal allowance is available to some married men with older wives, but it is only beneficial to men under 65 whose wives were over 75 on 5 April 1990. It enables a husband to claim an allowance of up to £3,540 instead of £3,525 for 1995/96 (see page 15).

Married couple's allowance

If you have married since the beginning of the previous tax year, give the date of marriage. This will enable the Revenue to work out your married couple's allowance. Married couple's allowance is not available for years after the year in which you separate. If you separated before 6 April 1990, however, but are still wholly maintaining your wife by unenforceable contributions, the married couple's allowance is still available while you remain married, although the Revenue will usually require proof that you are maintaining her.

All or half of the basic married couple's allowance (not the increase for those over 65) may be transferred to the wife (see page 13) but you need to make a claim *before the beginning of the tax year*. The tax office will send you a claim form (form 18) if you tick the box on the return. The only year when this could have saved tax was 1993/94, since the saving was reduced to a fixed rate of 20% for 1994/95 and 15% thereafter, whoever claims the allowance. But wives may still wish to make the claim, to get the benefit of a reduction in their own income rather than their husband's. No matter who has claimed the allowance, a claim may be made for any unused amount to be transferred to the other spouse where income is too low to use it.

Additional personal allowance

The question asking whether any other person is claiming the allowance is a reminder that the allowance may be split if two people claim it for the *same child*, and in these circumstances you should agree the split with the other claimant. But if, say, a couple with two qualifying children separate, each may claim the allowance for a different child providing the child is resident with that parent for all or part of the tax year. It is not, however, possible for an unmarried couple who are living together to claim two additional personal allowances (see page 466), so the name of a partner has to be shown also.

The allowance is not available to a wife in the year of separation if the full married couple's allowance has been transferred to her in that year (see page 465, which also deals with the position of the husband in those circumstances).

Surplus allowances

If your income may be too low to use your married couple's allowance (or blind person's allowance), you have to notify the Revenue in order to be able to transfer the surplus to your spouse. Put a tick in the box asking for a transfer notice form.

Personal details

You are required to give your date of birth if you are over 59, or if you are paying self-employed pension contributions (because you might qualify for a higher rate of relief than the minimum 17½% — see chapter 17), or if you are claiming relief for venture capital trust subscriptions (because you need to be over 18 to qualify).

Inheritance tax

Most lifetime transfers are 'potentially exempt' but a return to the Capital Taxes Office must be made by either transferor or transferee of those which remain chargeable, unless they do not exceed £10,000 and do not bring the cumulative total to more than £40,000. Returns are strictly not required until twelve months after the end of the month in which the transfer takes place, but interest on overdue tax runs from earlier dates, so returns should be lodged accordingly (see chapter 5).

In the case of death, the return is made in conjunction with the application for a grant of probate (where there is a will) or of administration (where there is no will or where the named executors cannot or will not act). Again, a twelve-month return period is allowed, but interest runs from six months after the end of the month of death, and the need to obtain a grant in order to deal with the affairs of the deceased ensures an earlier return in most cases.

The return at death has to include details of earlier transfers, whether chargeable or potentially exempt at the time, which are required for the calculation of the tax payable (see chapter 5). It is therefore essential that full records of lifetime gifts are kept.

An account need not be submitted for a deceased's estate not exceeding £145,000 (£125,000 before 1 July 1995) provided that no trust is involved, that not more than £15,000 is situated outside the UK, and that there have been no transfers within the seven years before death or gifts by the deceased where he retained a benefit. The Revenue reserve the right to call for an account later.

Late submission of returns

For years up to 1996/97, sending in your return after the officially allowed 30 days will not usually attract a penalty. If, however, your return is received by the Revenue later than 31 October after the end of the tax year, they cannot issue an assessment in time for tax to be paid on the normal due date. Unless you have given them enough information by that date for them to issue an adequate estimated assessment, you will be charged interest from the date the tax would have been due if the return had been made on time (Revenue Statement of Practice SP 6/89). This is particularly relevant for capital gains and new sources of income, which the Revenue are less likely to be aware of in the absence of a return, than continuing sources of income where an estimated assessment can be raised.

From 1996/97 late returns will be subject to automatic penalties, plus interest and surcharges where tax is underpaid (see page 122). Estimated assessments will not be issued. The Revenue will instead issue a 'determination' of the amount of tax due, which will be treated as the taxpayer's self-assessment until replaced by his actual self-assessment. Interest charges will run from the original payment dates and will relate to the amount of tax finally found to be due. The time limit for a Revenue determination is 5 years from the filing date for the return, and the taxpayer's superseding self-assessment can only be made within that time or, if later, within 12 months after the date of the determination.

Corporation tax returns (TMA 1970, ss 11, 11AA; F(No 2)A 1987, s 82; FA 1990, s 91; FA 1994, s 182)

The 'Pay and File' system (see page 25) applies to accounting periods ending after 30 September 1993. It is to be extended to include a formal self-assessment by the company of its own tax bill from a date not earlier than 1 April 1996 nor later than 31 March 1998 (see page 25).

Under 'Pay and File', companies are required to pay tax (estimated if necessary) nine months and one day after the year end, or suffer interest on the underpayment from that date, and file a statutory return (form CT 200), together with accounts and computations, twelve months after the year end, or three months after receiving a 'Notice to deliver a Corporation Tax Return' (form CT 203) if later. Form CT 200 must be completed by all companies, but trading companies that have no overseas income and are not members of groups are usually able to complete the short return in Section 2 of the form rather than the more detailed return in Section 3.

Claims for capital allowances and group relief for losses must be made in the CT 200 return or in an amended return (which need not, however, be on the official form CT 201). Claims for current set-off and carry-back of losses, and to carry back or surrender ACT, may also be made in the return, providing the return or accompanying computations identify the periods in which the amounts claimed arose and, for surrendered ACT, the company to which the ACT is being surrendered. The provisions for making and amending loss claims are dealt with in chapter 26.

If the return is not sent in by the due date, automatic fixed penalties are payable (although by concession a penalty will not be charged if the return is received on or before the last business day within seven days after the due date), and also tax-related penalties if the return is more than six months late (see page 144). Where, because of exceptional circumstances, a company cannot produce final figures within the time limit, 'best estimates' may be used without attracting late filing penalties, or penalties for fraudulent or negligent conduct (see page 143), but the figures must be adjusted as soon as the company is aware that they no longer represent the best estimate, and any late payment of tax will attract interest.

The Revenue have issued Statements of Practice SP 9/93, 10/93 and 11/93 dealing with various aspects of the Pay and File system.

Under company law, public companies must file accounts with the Registrar of Companies not later than seven months after the end of the accounting period, the time limit for private limited companies being ten months. Automatic late filing penalties apply for public companies, ranging from £500 if accounts are up to three months late to £5,000 if accounts are more than twelve months late, the figures for private companies being £100 to £1,000.

Assessments and additional assessments; error or mistake claims

Income tax and capital gains tax for years up to 1995/96; corporation tax (TMA 1970, ss 29–41)

Assessments to income tax, corporation tax and capital gains tax are based on returns of income and gains made to the inspector of taxes, or are estimated where a return has either not been made or the Revenue doubts its accuracy.

Estimated assessments are not normally necessary for companies under 'Pay and File', because companies have to pay interest from nine months after the end of the accounting period on any tax finally found to be due, so delaying the agreement of final figures is not to their advantage. Estimated assessments are still needed in some circumstances, for example where the company fails to file a return, or where there is a matter that is to be argued before the Appeal Commissioners. Where estimated assessments are issued, the normal appeal and postponement procedures apply.

If the Revenue discover that any profits or gains chargeable to tax have not been assessed, or have been insufficiently assessed, they may make an additional assessment. They will, however, not normally reopen an already agreed assessment, even if tax has been undercharged, unless the taxpayer failed to supply them with full information in reaching that agreement.

137

The normal time limit for making an assessment or additional assessment is six years from the end of the tax year to which it relates. If a taxpayer dies, new or additional assessments cannot be made later than three years after the tax year of his death.

Special rules apply in cases of fraudulent or negligent conduct. These are dealt with on page 142.

If an individual or company makes an error or mistake in a return causing an overpayment of tax, relief may be claimed at any time up to six years after the end of the tax year (or company accounting period) in which the assessment was made. Such a claim is not possible where no return has been submitted.

Position for income tax and capital gains tax under self-assessment (FA 1994, ss 190, 191 and Sch 19 paras 7, 8, 17, 18)

The self-assessment provisions apply to individuals from 1996/97 and to companies from a date to be fixed, between 1 April 1996 and 31 March 1998.

Under self-assessment, taxpayers will work out their own tax or (for individuals, not companies) ask the Revenue to work it out for them and in either case it counts as a self-assessment. The Revenue are able to make a 'determination' of the tax due in the absence of a return, but this will not be open to appeal, because it will be replaced by the taxpayer's self-assessment when it is received (see page 136). If the Revenue enquire into a return or into a claim made separately from the return (see pages 118 and 123), taxpayers are able to appeal against any amendments required by the Revenue, and the appeal and postponement provisions on page 140 onwards will apply. The Revenue will only issue assessments if they discover that tax has been underpaid through a taxpayer's fraudulent or negligent conduct, or because of inadequate disclosure of information (see page 141) and the appeal/ postponement procedures on page 140 apply to such assessments. Unless there is fraudulent or negligent conduct, the time limit for a discovery assessment under self-assessment is 5 years from the 31 January filing date for the return.

The 'error or mistake' provisions above apply in relation to returns and to claims made separately, but the time limit for a claim by individuals is 5 years from the 31 January filing date for the return.

Inheritance Tax (IHTA 1984, ss 221, 240, 241)

Notification of the amount of inheritance tax due is contained in a notice of determination issued by the Revenue. Adjustments for tax underpaid or overpaid, plus interest, may be made subsequently but not later than the end of six years from the date of payment, or if later, from the date payment was due. In cases of fraudulent or negligent conduct, the period of six years starts at the time the fraud, etc. became known to the Revenue.

Stamp duty (Stamp Act 1891, s 12)

The Revenue may be required to state whether an instrument is liable to stamp duty and if so how much duty is payable. There is a right of appeal to the High Court.

Repayment and remission of tax because of official error (Extra-statutory concession A19)

Unless a specific time limit is stated, the normal time limit for claiming reliefs is 6 years from the end of the relevant tax year (reduced to 5 years 10 months under self-assessment). Repayments will, however, be made on claims made outside the time limit where the overpayment was caused by an error by the Revenue or another Government department, providing the facts are not in dispute.

Where the Revenue discover that they have undercharged income tax or capital gains tax, although they have been given full information at the proper time either by the taxpayer, or by his employer, or (in relation to pensions) by the DSS, they may, by concession, not collect the underpayment. This will apply only if the taxpayer could reasonably have believed his affairs to be in order. The concession used to be given on a scale basis according to the taxpayer's income, but the income scale no longer applies from 11 March 1996.

Out-of-time tax adjustments in favour of taxpayer

The time limits for appealing against assessments, and for substituting a taxpayer's own self-assessment for a Revenue determination under the new self-assessment provisions, are indicated on pages 140 and 136 respectively. If action is not taken within the time limits, the tax assessed or determined becomes payable. Where tax has legally become due that is higher than it would have been if all the relevant information had been submitted at the proper time, the Revenue may be prepared to accept an amount equal to what the correct liability would have been, providing the taxpayer's affairs are brought fully up to date. This practice is known as 'equitable liability'.

Due dates of payment and interest on overdue and overpaid tax (TMA 1970, s 91)

Due dates of payment and interest provisions vary for the different taxes and before and after self-assessment, and are dealt with in chapters 2 to 7 and in this chapter. There are, however, special rules for interest where the taxpayer has been at fault — see page 143.

In general, you will get an appropriate refund of interest charged on overdue tax if your total tax bill is later reduced, but for years up to and including

1995/96, interest on a Schedule A or D assessment will not be adjusted as a result of a reduction in the tax due on other income. The same applies to an assessment to higher rate tax on interest and dividends, and interest on overdue income tax cannot be affected by a reduction in capital gains tax. These restrictions will not apply once self-assessment is introduced from 1996/97.

Certificates of tax deposit

Certificates of tax deposit may be purchased by individuals, partnerships, personal representatives or trustees, subject to an initial deposit of £2,000, with minimum additions of £500. The certificates may be used to pay any tax except PAYE, VAT and tax deducted from payments to subcontractors. Interest accrues daily for a maximum of six years, and provision is made for varying interest rates during the term of the deposit. A lower rate of interest applies if the deposit is withdrawn for cash rather than used to settle tax liabilities. The interest is charged to tax under Schedule D, Case III. Tax deposit certificates are a way of ensuring that liquid resources are earmarked for the payment of tax when due.

Companies used to be able to make use of certificates of tax deposit, but from 1 October 1993 they can no longer buy them. Certificates bought before that date may still be used to cover corporation tax bills until 1 October 1999.

Appeals (Income tax, corporation tax, capital gains tax — TMA 1970, s 31; FA 1994, Sch 19 para 7; Inheritance tax — IHTA 1984, s 222; Stamp duty — Stamp Act 1891, s 13)

Normally appeals must be made within 30 days after the date of issue of the assessment (or Revenue amendment to a self-assessment), except in relation to stamp duty where the prescribed period is 21 days. The appeal must state the grounds on which it is made (for example that the tax is estimated and not in accordance with information supplied or to be supplied or, under self-assessment, that a Revenue amendment to a taxpayer's self-assessment is incorrect). Late appeals may be allowed if the Revenue is satisfied that there was a good reason for the delay.

Postponement of payment of tax

Tax still has to be paid on the normal due dates even though an appeal has been lodged, except that in relation to income tax, corporation tax and capital gains tax an application may be made to postpone payment of all or part of the tax. The postponement application is separate from the appeal itself and must state the amount of tax which it is considered has been overcharged and the grounds for that belief. The amount to be postponed will then be agreed with the inspector or decided by the Appeal Commissioners (see below). Any tax not postponed will be due 30 days after the date of the decision as to how much tax may be postponed, or on the normal due date if later.

The appeal itself may be settled by negotiation with the inspector or, failing that, by following the appeal procedure to the Commissioners and thence if necessary to the courts. Once the appeal has been finally settled, any underpaid tax will be payable within 30 days after the inspector issues a notice of the amount payable. Any overpaid tax will be repaid. Although a postponement application may successfully delay payment of tax, it will not stop interest being charged against the taxpayer on any postponed tax which later proves to be payable (see the due date and interest provisions in chapters 2 to 4).

Appeal procedures

If an appeal is not settled between the taxpayer and the inspector, it is listed for hearing by the Appeal Commissioners. There are two types of Appeal Commissioners, General Commissioners and Special Commissioners. Appeals before the General Commissioners are heard in private. Appeals before the Special Commissioners are heard in public unless the taxpayer (or the Revenue with the Commissioners' consent) asks for a private hearing. Selected decisions of the Special Commissioners may be reported. Certain specialised appeals are heard by the Special Commissioners and other appeals normally by the General Commissioners. There are provisions for the transfer of proceedings between the two bodies of commissioners.

The decisions of the Commissioners on matters of fact are normally binding on both parties. If either the taxpayer or the Revenue are dissatisfied with a decision on a point of law, further appeal is possible to the High Court, the Court of Appeal and, where leave is granted, the House of Lords. It should be noted, however, that the decision to take an appeal to the Commissioners on a point of law must be weighed very carefully because of the likely heavy costs involved, particularly if the taxpayer should be successful at the earlier stages and lose before a higher court. Costs may be awarded against the unsuccessful party, not only by the courts, but also (if the party has acted unreasonably) by the Special Commissioners (not the General Commissioners).

Additional and extended time-limit assessments to income tax, corporation tax and capital gains tax (TMA 1970, ss 29, 34–36; FA 1994, s 191 and Sch 19 paras 10, 11)

The Revenue are able to issue an additional assessment for a year within the normal six-year time limit (5 years 10 months for individuals under self-assessment) without alleging that the taxpayer is at fault. They may 'discover' that an assessment is inadequate through considering facts already in their hands, such as by comparing gross profit rates from year to year, or through new facts, or even because they change their minds on how something should be interpreted. They have, however, stated that they will not normally reopen an assessment they later find to be incorrect if they had been given full and accurate information and either the point was specifically agreed or the view implicit in the computation submitted was a tenable one. Under self-assessment, the taxpayer is protected from further assessment after the Revenue period of enquiry expires (see pages 26 and 123) unless there has been fraudulent or negligent conduct, or the Revenue have not been supplied with full and accurate information. To reopen years outside the normal time limit, the Revenue have to show fraudulent or negligent conduct. In that event, assessments may be made at any time up to 20 years after the tax year/company accounting period concerned. Under self-assessment the time limit will be 20 years from the 31 January filing date for the return for individuals and 21 years from the end of the accounting period for companies. If the Revenue consider a case to be one of fraudulent or negligent conduct, then, unless they are considering a prosecution, they will usually invite the taxpayer to co-operate in establishing the understated income or gains. If he does so, they will then not normally have to resort to their statutory powers to call for documents and to enter and search premises.

Establishing the tax lost

The Revenue investigation will include some or all of the following for the appropriate period, the effect of one on another being considered:

(a) A full review of the business accounts, often including verification of transactions by third parties such as suppliers.

(b) A detailed reconstruction of the private affairs, establishing whether increases in private wealth can be substantiated; or a less time-consuming review ensuring that lodgements into bank and building society accounts can be explained.

(c) A business model based on a sample period, adapted for changing circumstances and compared with the results shown by the business accounts.

(d) A living expenses review and comparison with available funds to establish the extent to which personal and private expenditure could not have been met without additional income.

At the conclusion of the review, if the need for a revision of profits, income or gains has been established, the calculation of tax underpaid follows automatically.

Interest and penalties (TMA 1970, ss 86, 88, 88A, 95, 95A, 96, 98, 98A; FA 1989, ss 157, 158, 165; FA 1994, Sch 19 paras 27, 28; FA 1995, s 100; FA 1996, Sch 18 para 4)

Under self-assessment for individuals (applicable from 1996/97) and Pay and File for companies (applicable to accounting periods ending after 30 September 1993), interest on overdue tax (and Class 4 national insurance contributions where relevant) runs from the normal due date, whether the taxpayer has been at fault or not. For earlier years, whereas the assessment rules may sometimes have provided for interest to run from a later date than the normal date, this does not apply where the taxpayer has failed to supply the Revenue with appropriate information, whether or not this was done deliberately. In such cases, interest runs from the date the tax ought to have been paid. Where assessments to income tax or capital gains tax for years before 1996/97 are made after 5 April 1988, interest will run from 31 January following the relevant tax year.

In addition to the payment of tax and interest, the Revenue have statutory powers to impose penalties when it has been established that tax has been lost through a taxpayer's fraudulent or negligent conduct, and the provisions also cover unpaid Class 4 national insurance contributions. These powers are quite separate from their powers to take criminal proceedings for an offence against the Crown. The maximum penalties are shown in the table on page 144.

The Revenue have power to reduce both interest and penalties. They will rarely reduce interest, but will usually accept a smaller penalty where a settlement is made with a taxpayer without formal proceedings being taken.

Alternative to interest and penalty proceedings

Instead of formal proceedings being taken for interest and penalties, the taxpayer will usually be invited to make an offer to the Revenue in consideration of their not taking such proceedings.

The amount of the offer will in fact be negotiated between the Revenue and the taxpayer and will comprise the calculated tax (including any Class 4 national insurance contributions) and interest plus a penalty loading, the penalty being reduced principally on three counts:

(a) Whether the initial disclosure was voluntarily made by the taxpayer or induced or partly induced by communication from the Revenue.
(b) The size and gravity of the offence.
(c) The degree of co-operation by the taxpayer.

The acceptance of a taxpayer's offer by the Revenue creates a binding contract, and if the taxpayer fails to pay, the Revenue are able to proceed for the amount due under the contract itself without any reference to the taxation position, although the terms of the contract allow them to repudiate it if they wish in the case of non- or late payment (the Revenue then recommencing negotiations or taking proceedings), and further interest will be charged if payments due under the contract are delayed. This established procedure is used in the vast majority of cases, and has points both in the taxpayer's and in the Revenue's favour, in that the taxpayer may be treated less harshly than if proceedings were taken, and the Revenue are spared the trouble of taking those proceedings.

Non-compliance	Maximum penalty
Failure to notify liability within six months after end of tax year for income tax and capital gains tax, or twelve months after end of accounting period for corporation tax (TMA 1970, ss 7, 10; FA 1994, Sch 19.1)	The equivalent of the tax payable
Failure to submit income tax or capital gains tax returns within required period (TMA 1970, s 93)	For years up to 1995/96, £300, and £60 a day for every day failure continues after the £300 penalty has been imposed, plus an amount equal to the tax charged if failure continues beyond the end of the tax year following that in which the notice to submit the return was served (see page 122 for position from 1996/97)
Failure to submit corporation tax return (TMA 1970, s 94)	*Accounts ended on or before 30.9.93* £50, and £10 a day for every day failure continues after Commissioners or a Court have made an order for delivery of the return, plus an amount equal to the tax charged if the failure continues beyond the end of the period of 2 years from the date the notice to submit the return was served *Pay and File (accounts ended after 30.9.93) — automatic, non-mitigable penalties* £100 if return up to 3 months late (£500 for 3rd consecutive late return) £200 if return over 3 months late (£1,000 for 3rd consecutive late return) Plus following % of tax unpaid 18 months after end of accounting period: Return submitted 18 to 24 months after end of accounting period 10% Return submitted more than 24 months after end of accounting period 20%
Negligence or fraud in any return or accounts (TMA 1970, ss 95, 95A, 96)	An amount equal to the tax lost
Negligence or fraud in relation to a certificate of non-liability to tax, or failure to comply with any undertaking in such a certificate (TMA 1970, s 99A)	£3,000

Special situations

Death of a taxpayer limits the Revenue's right to reopen earlier tax years to the six years before that in which he died, and moreover restricts their right to raise new or additional assessments to the three years after the end of the tax year in which the death occurs, whatever the reason for the unpaid tax (TMA 1970, s 40). The time limit from 1996/97 under self-assessment is three years from the 31 January following the tax year of death (e.g. by 31 January 2001 for a death in 1996/97).

Partnerships in existence at 6 April 1994 have a joint income tax liability on trading profits (but not on other income or chargeable gains) until the partnership is brought within the new rules for the assessment of the self-employed (see page 322). No partner is able to settle separately with the Revenue in respect of his share of the partnership assessment on trading profits. Where a partner has died, the principle of joint liability will cause his share of profits to remain subject to review while the liability of his estate is limited to the six earlier years, putting an added burden on the surviving partners for the years before the normal six years.

Companies and company directors. While the liabilities of a company and its directors are entirely separate, their financial affairs will be looked at together if they are suspected of being at fault. Unexplained wealth increases or funding of living expenses will generally be regarded as extractions from the company, and, under his duty to preserve the company's assets, the director must account to the company for the extracted funds. The director does not have to pay income tax on the extracted funds, but is required to account to the company for the extractions, the company's accounts having to be rewritten accordingly and the extractions being subject to tax at corporation tax rates where they represent additional company profits. The company is also accountable for tax at the advance corporation tax rate on the grossed-up equivalent of the extractions unless they are repaid or covered by an amount already standing to the credit of the director. The tax liability attracts interest and is reckoned in the tax due to the Revenue when calculating penalties. Where the extractions do not represent additional taxed profits, but simply untaxed sums taken from the company, income tax will be payable by the director on the calculated benefit which he has enjoyed from the interest-free use of the company's money.

Tax points

- The married couple's allowance will save the same amount of tax whoever claims it. If, however, the wife is an employee taxed under Schedule E and the husband is self-employed, switching the allowance to the wife will reduce her tax from the beginning of the tax year, compared with reducing the husband's later payments of tax on his profits (see page 134).

- The Pay and File system requires a company to pay its tax and file its tax returns promptly. If you don't meet the deadlines, you will incur automatic interest and penalties. You should also be aware of the company law penalties for late filing of accounts.

- Self-assessment of income tax and capital gains tax has similar provisions for automatic penalties and interest, so you need to make sure you comply with the time limits.

- Under self-assessment, you need to retain records relating to your tax affairs for a stipulated period — see page 119. The Revenue give useful advice on the records to be kept in their booklet SA/BK4 Self Assessment — A general guide to keeping records. An additional booklet SA/BK3 is available for the self-employed and those who let property.

- Under self-assessment, interest is charged on underpayments from the original due date (and allowed on overpayments from that date, or the payment date if later), no matter how long it is before the tax position is settled. Where, however, a claim is made to backdate a loss incurred or payment made to an earlier year, the resulting tax adjustment is made for the tax year of loss or payment, so there is no extra benefit in terms of interest on tax overpaid.

- On 31 January 1998, you will be due to pay *all* the higher rate tax owing on taxed investment income for 1996/97 (as part of the balancing payment for that year) plus a further *half* of that amount (as part of the first provisional payment for 1997/98).

- If you are self-employed and your turnover is less than £15,000, you need only show your turnover, allowable expenses and net profit on your tax return. You must still have detailed records in case the tax office want to see them.

- If you delay sending in a return for 1995/96 or earlier which will trigger a tax liability of which the Revenue are otherwise unaware, this will invariably cause the Revenue to seek interest and perhaps penalties. Neither the interest nor the penalties are allowable in calculating your tax liability. To avoid an interest charge for years before 1996/97, your tax return must be received by the Revenue not later than the last business day in October. If the return is posted close to the deadline, obtain a certificate of posting to prove when the return was sent.

- If, in the case of a new business, the submission of accounts to the Revenue is delayed, not only will interest on overdue tax and sometimes penalties apply, but the Revenue may seek to review the accounts in depth, also looking at your personal financial affairs to confirm the accuracy of the business accounts.

- If you are guilty of known irregularities, a payment on account of the tax eventually to be accounted for will reduce the interest charge and also help to demonstrate your co-operation.

- If you are aware of irregularities in your affairs, you should disclose them fully to the Revenue before they make a challenge. You will thereby obtain the maximum penalty reduction when an offer in settlement is eventually made.

- Whilst the Revenue will usually settle for a cash sum comprising tax, interest and penalties, they may also take criminal proceedings in cases which they believe amount to provable fraud. They may still seek a civil money penalty on those aspects not brought before the court or where the taxpayer has been acquitted of fraud and they feel able to prove negligence (Revenue Statement of Practice SP 2/88).

- The Revenue and Customs and Excise have jointly issued a 'Taxpayer's Charter' setting out what standards they expect from a taxpayer, those which the taxpayer should expect from them, and the taxpayer's rights.

- If your business accounts or taxation affairs generally are under Revenue investigation, the Revenue will issue you with pamphlets IR72 and IR73 and their Code of Practice. These are no substitute for appropriate professional representation but they do explain your rights and are helpful in explaining Revenue procedures.

- The rates of interest on overdue tax vary frequently. Details are given at page xxiii, and the Revenue produce a table showing the interest factor to use in calculating interest on tax due for earlier years.

- Where a tax payment is made through the GIRO system, the date stamped by the branch bank on the payslip is treated as the payment date.

- You can register to receive bank and building society interest gross if you are not liable to tax. But you must not certify that you are entitled to this treatment unless you expect to have *no tax liability at all*. Merely being entitled to a repayment of some of the tax paid for the year is not enough. There is a penalty of up to £3,000 for false declarations.

If, having registered, you find you are no longer eligible, notify the bank or building society straight away, and let your tax office know if you think you may have some tax to pay.

10
Employments — income chargeable and allowable deductions

Basis of charge (TA 1988, ss 19, 134)

Employees and directors are charged to tax under Schedule E, tax normally being collected through the PAYE scheme. It is often hard to decide whether someone is employed or self-employed. See chapter 19 for further details. If an employer wrongly treats an employee as self-employed, he will be liable for the PAYE and national insurance contributions that should have been deducted, with only limited rights of recovery from the employee. The worker who is classed as employed rather than self-employed will find significant differences in his allowable expenses, the timing of tax payments and the liability for national insurance contributions. Most agency workers are required to be treated as employees. The agency is usually responsible for the operation of PAYE but the client is responsible if he pays the worker direct. Sub-contractors in the construction industry are treated as self-employed but are subject to special rules (see chapter 44).

Pensions and social security benefits (TA 1988, ss 150, 617; FA 1996, s 151)

Tax is also charged under Schedule E on pensions, whether from your employer or from the state, and on many other social security benefits, but certain benefits are exempt. From 1996/97, the legislation has been amended to enable the tax treatment of work incentive payments under various short-term pilot schemes (usually of up to three years' duration) to be stipulated by Treasury Order instead of by Act of Parliament. A Revenue concession published in May 1995 (A90) exempts payments under the Jobmatch pilot scheme (and national insurance contributions are not charged on such payments). A summary of the main taxable and exempt state benefits is given in the table on page 149. See pages xxix and xxx for the current amounts payable and page 475 for further comments.

Where incapacity benefit is taxable, the tax will be collected by a coding adjustment where the claimant is paying tax under PAYE on an occupational pension. If that does not apply, the DSS Benefits Agency will deduct tax from the benefit directly, under a modified version of the PAYE scheme.

SUMMARY OF MAIN STATE BENEFITS	
TAXABLE	EXEMPT
Retirement pensions	Wounds or disability pensions
Widow's pension and widowed	War widow's pension
mother's allowance	Disability living allowance
Statutory sick pay	Maternity allowance
Statutory maternity pay	Widow's payment
Industrial death benefit paid as	Child benefit and allowances
pension	Attendance allowance
Income support to unemployed	Incapacity benefit to those who
(replaced from October 1996 by	were receiving the former
jobseeker's allowance)	invalidity benefit at 12.4.95
Income support to	for the same incapacity
strikers	Severe disablement allowance
Unemployment benefit (replaced	Disability working allowance
from October 1996 by jobseeker's	Family credit
allowance)	Housing benefit
Invalid care allowance	Income support (other than as
Incapacity benefit (except for first	listed as taxable)
28 weeks and except as	Jobfinder's grant ('back to work'
opposite)	bonus)
	Christmas bonus for pensioners
	Industrial injury benefits

Persons liable (TA 1988, s 19)

Your liability to tax on earnings depends on your country of residence, ordinary residence and domicile. Broadly, residence normally requires you to be in the country at some time in the tax year, ordinary residence means habitual residence and domicile is the country you regard as your permanent home.

If you are resident, ordinarily resident and domiciled in the UK, you are normally charged to tax on your world-wide earnings, although earnings during 'long' absences abroad may escape tax.

If you are a visitor to the UK, you are liable to tax on the amount you earn in the UK. If you are not in the UK long enough to be classed as resident, you are not normally entitled to personal allowances, but certain categories of non-resident qualify (see page 563), and your liability to UK tax may be varied by double taxation agreements.

The detailed treatment of earnings abroad for both UK citizens and visitors is dealt with in chapter 41, which also explains residence, ordinary residence and domicile more fully and deals with the question of double taxation.

Assessable earnings (TA 1988, ss 131, 169–184, 200A, 202A, 202B; FA 1989, ss 37–40; FA 1995, s 93)

Pay for national insurance purposes is broadly the same as pay for income tax, but pay for national insurance includes profit-related pay even though such pay is tax-exempt, and it is not reduced by charitable payments under the payroll deduction scheme (see page 596), nor by occupational or personal pension scheme contributions paid by the employee. Contributions by the employer to approved company pension schemes or to an employee's approved pension plan do not count as earnings either for tax or national insurance. Some benefits in kind (in particular non-cash vouchers except for certain specified items) do not attract national insurance contributions. For further details on the national insurance position, see chapter 13, and on company and personal pensions, chapters 16 and 17.

Pay for income tax covers wages, salaries, commissions, bonuses, tips and certain benefits in kind. The earnings must be 'in the nature of a reward for services rendered, past, present or future'. (See chapter 11 for profit-related pay, up to £4,000 of which is exempt from tax, and chapter 15 for lump sum payments received on ceasing employment or taking up employment.)

If your employer pays a bill that you are legally liable to pay, this counts as the equivalent of a payment of salary. This point needs particular care, otherwise something that was thought to be a benefit in kind provided by the employer may in fact be the settlement by the employer of the debt under a contract entered into by the employee. PAYE tax should be deducted at the time of payment, and national insurance contributions are also payable. If the payment was overlooked, it must be reported at the year end on P9D or P11D (see page 169).

Employers must deduct and account for tax and national insurance contributions under PAYE when they provide pay in certain non-cash forms — see page 154.

Tax is charged on the earnings received in the tax year, no matter what period the earnings relate to. Certain expenses incurred may be deducted in arriving at the taxable earnings, as indicated later in this chapter.

Employees earning £8,500 per annum or more and directors — P11D employees (TA 1988, s 167)

If you are a P11D employee, you are taxed not only on cash pay but also on the cash equivalent of benefits in kind. All directors and employees earning £8,500 a year or more are P11D employees. Full-time directors earning less than £8,500 are not P11D employees unless they own more than 5% of the ordinary share capital. All part-time directors are P11D employees unless they work for a charity or non-profit making organisation and earn less than £8,500. (Form P11D is the form employers complete for such employees at the year end.)

Other employees

If you are not a P11D employee, you are not normally taxed on benefits unless they can be turned into cash, and the amount treated as pay is the cash which could be obtained. For example, if you are given a suit which cost your employer £180 but which is valued second-hand at only £20, you are taxed only on £20. You escape tax on the benefit of use of a car, unless you have the choice of giving up the car for extra wages. In that event the car could be turned into cash at any time by taking up the offer, so you would be treated as having extra wages accordingly. Some benefits are chargeable on all employees.

Benefits are dealt with in more detail later in this chapter.

Allowable expenses and deductions (TA 1988, ss 197B–197F, 198, 201, 201AA, 202, 577, 590–612; CAA 1990, s 27; FA 1995, ss 91, 92; FA 1996, s 109)

In arriving at taxable pay, you can deduct expenses that are incurred wholly, exclusively and necessarily in the performance of the duties of your employment and for travelling in the performance of those duties. Relatively few expenses satisfy this stringent rule. Some expenses which would not are specifically allowable by statute or by concession.

Travelling expenses from home to work are not allowed since they are not incurred in performing your duties. Travelling expenses on business journeys are allowed, and if you travel directly from home on a business journey away from your normal place of work, the allowable expense is the lower of the cost of the journey from home and what it would have cost to travel from your workplace. You can normally claim the full cost of subsistence when away from home, because it is recognised that you have continuing financial commitments at home. The Revenue are not strictly obliged to allow anything, since subsistence by its very nature can never satisfy the 'wholly, exclusively and necessarily' condition. If you are working at a temporary location for up to 12 months before returning to your normal workplace, travelling, accommodation and subsistence expenses are allowable. For longer moves to a different location, such expenses do not currently qualify for relief. This may change in 1997, because the treatment of travelling and subsistence expenses is currently under review, with the intention of clarifying and simplifying the rules.

Where you use your own car for business, you can claim the business proportion of the running expenses (calculated on a mileage basis) and also capital allowances, and relief for interest on a loan to buy the car (see pages 152, 153). If your employer pays you a mileage allowance, this will be taxable, but your employer may obtain a dispensation from the Revenue to enable the mileage allowance to be ignored, and you will not then need to make an expenses claim. If there is a profit element in the mileage allowance this may be adjusted through your tax coding. Some employers have used a scheme known as the 'Fixed Profit Car Scheme' (FPCS) by arrangement with the Revenue, under which the profit element in a business mileage allowance is identified according to bands of business mileage and agreed 'tax-free' rates fixed by reference to engine size. The rates are shown on page xxii. From 1996/97, the use by employees of the tax-free FPCS rates to calculate any taxable part of mileage allowances, or to claim a deduction for business motoring, is not dependent on their employers having entered into the FPCS arrangements. You can always calculate your expenses on the strict statutory basis if you wish. The FPCS does not cover interest on money borrowed to buy the car — relief for interest must be claimed separately. From 6 April 1996, national insurance contributions are not charged on mileage allowances that do not exceed the FPCS higher rates, i.e. for up to 4,000 miles, regardless of the miles travelled (the previous limits were the AA rates for 10,000 miles). As far as VAT is concerned, if you are provided with private petrol for your own car at below cost, your employer has to account for VAT based on the income tax scale charges (see page 98). The employer can reclaim the input tax on your fuel purchases if you are reimbursed, and input tax can be claimed on the fuel element of a mileage allowance, but not on the part of the allowance that is for repairs, etc.

For most manual workers, flat rate expenses allowances have been negotiated for the upkeep of tools and special clothing, although this does not preclude a higher claim being made. The cost of normal clothing is not allowed even if it costs more than you would normally pay and you would not wear the clothes outside work.

If it is *necessary* for you to work at home you will be able to claim a proportion of the cost of light, heat, phone calls, etc. The allowable proportion of such expenses is generally the subject of negotiation with the inspector. If you use a room *exclusively* for work, a proportion of your council tax is allowable as well.

Other allowable expenses include contributions to an approved pension scheme, charitable donations up to £1,200 a year (£900 a year before 6 April 1996) under the payroll giving scheme, and most professional subscriptions that are relevant to your job. The cost of business entertaining is not allowed, but the disallowance may fall on you or on your employer depending on how payment is made. You cannot claim a deduction for entertaining expenses paid out of your salary or out of a round sum allowance. If you receive a specific entertaining allowance from your employer or are specifically reimbursed for entertaining expenses, you are not taxed on the amount received, but no deduction for it can be claimed by your employer.

You can claim a deduction against your earnings for:

> Contributions to a personal pension plan (see chapter 17).
> Capital allowances if you buy equipment that is necessarily provided for use in your job, restricted by any private use proportion (CAA 1990, ss 27, 79). (If it is a car, there is no 'necessarily'

requirement and you can claim an allowance for the business use
anyway.)
Interest on money borrowed to finance the purchase of such equipment (restricted by any private use proportion) — for the tax
year of purchase and the three following tax years (TA 1988,
s 359(3)).

From 6 April 1995, the cost of directors' liability insurance, professional
indemnity insurance and work-related uninsured liabilities is not a taxable
benefit if paid by your employer and is an allowable expense if paid by you
(at any time up to six years after the end of the tax year in which the
employment ends). National insurance contributions are not payable on such
benefits.

Expenses payments and reimbursed expenses

The strict application of the rule for allowable expenses would require all
expenses payments to employees to be treated as wages, leaving the
employee to claim relief for the allowable part. To avoid a lot of unnecessary
work, expenses payments that do no more than cover expenses that are
'wholly, exclusively and necessarily incurred in the performance of the
duties of the employment' are not treated as pay under the PAYE scheme so
long as the employer obtains from the Revenue a dispensation enabling them
to be excluded. From 6 April 1995, dispensations are effective for national
insurance contribution purposes. The most common expenses for which a
dispensation is granted are travelling and subsistence allowances on an
agreed scale. Dispensations are never given for round sum expenses allowances, and may be denied in respect of directors of family companies.

From 6 April 1995 an employee away from home overnight on business is
exempt from tax and national insurance on payment or reimbursement by
his employer of personal expenses such as newspapers and 'phone calls up
to a VAT inclusive amount of £5 a night (£10 if outside the UK) (TA 1988,
s 200A; FA 1995, s 93).

For both P11D employees and other employees, there are special rules for
payments connected with relocation, as follows.

Removal and relocation expenses (TA 1988, s 191A and Sch 11A; FA 1993, s 76 and Sch 5)

From 6 April 1993 qualifying removal expenses and benefits are exempt
up to a maximum of £8,000 per move, providing they are incurred during
the period from the date of the job change to the end of the next following
tax year. Allowable expenses include expenses of disposing of the old
property and buying another, removal expenses, providing replacement
domestic goods, travelling and subsistence, and bridging loan expenses
(see page 421).

Employers do not have to operate PAYE on such payments, even if they exceed £8,000, but payments in excess of £8,000 must be reported on year-end returns.

Sale of home to relocation company or to employer (Revenue concession D37)

Where an employee sells his home to a relocation company or to his employer and has a right to share in any later profits when the home is sold, the value of that right is a taxable benefit if the amount paid to the employee initially is equal to the open market value of the property. As and when any additional amount is paid to him, the employee will be exempt from capital gains tax on it to the same extent as he was exempt on the original sale, providing the later sale occurs within three years. (Part of the original gain may have been chargeable because the home had not always been the main residence, or had been let, etc., in which case the same proportion of the later amount will be chargeable.)

Where an employer makes a payment to an employee to compensate him for a fall in value when he sells his home, the payment is fully taxable as earnings. It does not qualify for relief as a relocation expense.

Benefits in kind for all employees — specific charges

All employees and directors, no matter how much they earn, pay tax on the provision of living accommodation and vouchers (see below). There is also a tax charge if a loan made to you by reason of your employment is written off. For P11D employees, this applies even if the employment has ceased — see page 195.

If employers pay employees in marketable assets such as gold bullion or commodities, or assets which the employer has arranged for the employees to exchange for cash, they must account for tax under PAYE (see page 167). The same will apply if vouchers and credit tokens are used to provide the assets. These benefits would have been taxable in any event, but charging tax under PAYE accelerates the payment date for the tax. Such arrangements also attract national insurance contributions (see page 202).

Living accommodation (TA 1988, ss 145, 146, 146A, 163; FA 1996, s 106)

If your employer provides you with living accommodation, you are charged to tax on its annual value (i.e. letting value) less any rent you pay. (Annual values were based on gross rating values, and have continued on the same basis, even though domestic rates have been abolished. Employers are to estimate annual values where no rateable value is available, for example on new property.) There is no charge, however, if

(a)   you are a representative occupier, for example a caretaker, or
(b)   it is customary in your employment to be provided with living accommodation, or
(c)   the accommodation is provided for security reasons.

Except where the accommodation provided by a company falls within (c) above, a director cannot qualify for exemption from the charge unless he does not own more than 5% of the ordinary share capital and either he works full-time for the company or the company is a charity or an organisation which does not have a profit-making objective.

If you are exempt under one of the above headings, you are also exempt from both tax and national insurance on the payment of council tax by your employer. If you are not exempt, council tax paid on your behalf by your employer counts as pay for both tax and national insurance.

Employees who are not P11D employees escape tax on the provision of other benefits such as heating, lighting and the use of furniture, because they cannot be converted into cash.

If you are a P11D employee, you are chargeable on the value of other benefits relating to the accommodation whether or not you are chargeable on the letting value, but if you are exempt from the charge on letting value the charge for other benefits cannot exceed 10% of your taxable earnings excluding those benefits.

The charge for living accommodation is increased where the accommodation cost more than £75,000. The extra charge over and above the letting value is calculated as follows:

((Cost less £75,000) × appropriate %) less amount by which any rent paid exceeds the letting value.

The appropriate percentage is the official rate of interest chargeable on beneficial loans, as at the beginning of the tax year (for the latest rates, see page xxiii).

Vouchers (TA 1988, ss 141–144)

The vouchers rules apply to all employees and are wide-ranging.

Cash vouchers are treated as pay under the PAYE scheme for both tax and national insurance at the time the voucher is provided. Non-cash vouchers are taxable (with the exceptions noted below), although not through the PAYE scheme. National insurance contributions are not payable on non-cash vouchers, apart from the exceptions on page 202. Vouchers exchangeable partly for cash and partly for goods are fully liable to national insurance contributions.

Your employer has to provide details to the Revenue at the year end of the cost of providing transport vouchers (for example season tickets), vouchers for childcare and other vouchers (including cheques) and the cost of goods or services obtained through the provision of employer's credit cards. Tax on the value of the vouchers will usually be collected from you by a coding adjustment. Employees of passenger transport undertakings like British Rail who are not P11D employees are exempt from tax on transport vouchers.

There is still, by Revenue concession A2, a derisory exemption of 15p per day for luncheon vouchers, providing they are available to all employees, non-transferable and used for meals only. Any excess over 15p is taxable, details being notified to the Revenue by your employer at the year end. National insurance contributions are not, however, payable (see above). No tax arises on free canteen meals that are provided to staff generally so the luncheon voucher rules discriminate against employers who are too small to have their own canteen.

You are not taxed on non-cash vouchers and credit tokens used to obtain a car parking space at or near your place of work.

Benefits in kind for P11D employees (TA 1988, ss 153–168, 197A and Schs 6, 6A, 7)

If you are a P11D employee, you are charged to tax on all expenses payments received (unless covered by a dispensation, see page 153) and on the cash equivalent of virtually all benefits provided either direct to you or to your family or household. This includes benefits provided by someone other than your employer, except for corporate hospitality (providing it is not arranged by your employer and is not in return for services rendered by you) and, by Revenue concession A70, gifts costing not more than £150 in total from the same donor.

The main benefits that are not chargeable to tax are:

Meals in a staff canteen providing they are available to staff generally;

Employer's contributions to an approved occupational or personal pension scheme;

Directors' liability insurance, etc. (see page 153);

Free car-parking facilities at or near your workplace;

In-house sports facilities;

Counselling services to redundant employees;

Childcare for children under 18 (other than on domestic premises) provided by the employer alone or with other employers, local authorities, etc., but with each employer being partly responsible for finance and management. The exemption does *not* cover cash allowances, vouchers, or payment by the employer of the employee's childcare bills, which are taxable for all employees no matter what they earn.

By concession A70, you are not charged on the benefit of one or more annual staff dinners, providing the cost to the employer for each person attending is not more than £75 a year (VAT-inclusive). If, say, there were three annual functions at £30 each, the exemption would cover two of them and you would be taxed on £30.

You are taxed on the provision of medical treatment or insurance unless it relates to treatment outside the UK when on a business trip.

The cash equivalent of a benefit is normally the extra cost to your employer of providing the benefit (including VAT where appropriate, whether recovered or not, except for a gift that costs £15 or less, which does not attract VAT — see page 94) less any contribution from you.

Scholarships to employees' children are caught unless they are fortuitous awards paid from a trust fund or scheme under which not more than 25% of the total payments relate to employees.

Special rules apply to share option and incentive schemes (see chapter 11), the provision of cheap loans and the use of cars, vans and mobile phones (see below).

Where you are allowed the use of any asset that belongs to your employer, other than living accommodation (see page 154) or a car or van, you are charged to tax annually on the private use proportion of 20% of its cost. If the asset is later given to you, you are charged to tax on the higher of its market value at the date of the gift and the original market value less the intervening benefits assessments, whether charged on you or on other directors/ employees. See example 1.

Example 1

Television set cost employer £500. Used by director for two years, then given to him or any other P11D employee when market value is £50.

Tax will be charged on the following amounts:
For use of asset, 20% × £500 =   £100 per annum

On gift of asset, higher of £50 and
£500 − (2 × £100)
= £300, i.e.   £300

If, as well as allowing you to use an asset, your employer meets expenses on it, for example pays the running expenses of a boat or aeroplane, you are taxed on the private element of those expenses as well.

There is no charge for private use of a commercial vehicle of more than 3.5 tonnes gross weight (including the provision of private fuel), unless it is mainly used privately. The provision of a telephone in such a vehicle is, however, taxed (see page 159).

Motor cars (TA 1988, ss 157–159, 168A–168G, 197A and Sch 6; FA 1993, ss 70–72 and Sch 3; FA 1995, ss 43, 44)

From 6 April 1994, the benefit of private use of a car belonging to or leased by your employer is charged according to the value of the car. An additional charge is made, based on engine size, if, in addition to the provision of the car, you are also provided with car fuel for private use. There is a lower fuel charge for diesel cars. Details are on page xxi.

The tax charge for private use of a car is based on the list price (or £80,000 if lower). The list price is inclusive of VAT and includes delivery charges (but not road tax), extras supplied with the car and any accessory costing £100 or more that is added later (excluding mobile phones, which are charged separately, and excluding accessories designed only for use by the disabled). Cars valued at more than £15,000 and at least fifteen years old at the end of the tax year are taxed according to their open market value if more than the list price. Where an employee pays towards the initial cost of a car, a contribution of up to £5,000 reduces the cost on which the tax charge is based. The taxable benefit for those who do less than 2,500 business miles is 35% of the cost, reduced by one-third for those who do at least 2,500 but less than 18,000 business miles, and by two-thirds for those with business mileage of 18,000 miles or more. In each case, the taxable amount is reduced by one-third for cars four or more years old at the end of the tax year.

Any contribution you make to your employer for the use of the car is deducted from the car benefit charge, but there is no reduction in the car fuel charge for a contribution to the cost of fuel for private journeys. To escape the fuel charge you must reimburse the whole cost of private fuel to the employer, or pay for it yourself in the first place.

If you are provided with more than one car (for example a car for your spouse) the second and subsequent cars are charged at 35% of list price unless, exceptionally, you do 18,000 business miles or more in an additional car, in which case the 35% charge is reduced by one-third.

The car benefit charges cover the whole benefit obtained from the use of a car, except the expense of providing a chauffeur, which is charged in addition, and the provision of a car phone (see page 159). If a car is provided for only part of the year (for example in the year when you start or cease employment) the charge is proportionately reduced. It is also proportionately reduced if the car is incapable of being used for a period of 30 consecutive days or more. Where a car is replaced during the year, the appropriate proportion of each benefit figure is charged, and the 18,000 and 2,500 mile limits referred to above are also reduced proportionately and considered in relation to the use of each car.

See page 170 for the requirements for employers to notify the Revenue about new or changed arrangements for car provision.

The provision of a car for private use and of private fuel for the car also attracts employers' (but not employees') national insurance contributions — see page 203. Your employer will also have to account for value added tax on private fuel whether the car is provided by the employer or owned by you — see page 98. VAT does not apply to the provision of the car itself, even if the employee makes a payment for private use (unless the employer recovered input tax on the car — see page 97 — in which case a payment by the employee would attract VAT).

It is possible to escape tax on the benefit of use of a car if it is a pool car as defined, but the conditions are restrictive. A pool car is one where the private use is merely incidental to the business use, the car is not normally kept overnight at an employee's home, and the car is not ordinarily used by only one employee to the exclusion of other employees.

The increasing cost of providing employees with cars and private fuel has led some employers to consider offering employees extra salary instead. Some schemes for cash or car alternatives have enabled national insurance contributions and tax savings to be made. From 6 April 1995, the tax and national insurance contributions are based on what the employee actually gets, either salary or use of a car.

Vans (TA 1988, ss 159AA, 159AB, 168 and Sch 6A; FA 1993, s 73 and Sch 4)

There is a fixed taxable benefit of £500 per annum for private use of a van with a laden weight of 3.5 tonnes or less (including the provision of private fuel), reduced to £350 if the van is four years old or more at the end of the tax year. The taxable benefit is reduced proportionately if the van is not provided for the whole year, or is unavailable for 30 consecutive days or more. The taxable amount is also reduced by any payment by the employee for private use.

Where vans are shared between several employees, the total fixed charges are calculated and split evenly between those employees, regardless of variations in private use, but with no employee being taxed on more than £500. Alternatively, an employee can claim to be taxed on £5 for each day of private use.

National insurance contributions are not payable on private use of vans and private fuel for them, but contributions would be payable if an employer paid his employee's fuel bills.

Mobile telephones (TA 1988, s 159A) and home telephones

Mobile phones, including car phones, are subject to a fixed benefits charge of £200 per annum. The benefit is reduced proportionately if the telephone is not available for the whole of the year. The benefits charge is not made if there is no private use of the phone or if the employee is required to and does make good the full cost of any private use. This will require payment both for the calls and a proper proportion of other costs, but not including line rental, so long as the phone was provided for business use.

If your employer pays your home telephone bills, you will be taxed on the payments, but will be able to claim a deduction for the proportion relating to the business calls (but not any part of the line rental). The same applies for national insurance unless the employer made the contract for the telephone service, in which case no contributions are payable.

Cheap loans (TA 1988, ss 160, 161 and Sch 7; FA 1994, s 88; FA 1996, s 107)

If your employer lends you money interest-free or at a rate of interest below the official rate, you are charged to tax on an amount equal to interest at the official rate less any interest paid. If the loan is for a qualifying purpose for interest relief (see pages 11, 12), you are entitled to deduct from the amount of tax chargeable the appropriate tax saving on both the beneficial loan interest and any interest actually paid (see example 2). The tax charge and the compensating tax saving will normally be dealt with by a coding adjustment. The official rate of interest is varied by Treasury Order and is kept in line with typical mortgage rates (see page xxiii).

There is no tax charge on loans made to employees on commercial terms by employers who lend to the general public. Nor is there any charge if the total of all beneficial loans, including loans that would qualify for tax relief, does not exceed £5,000 at any time in the tax year. If there are qualifying loans (e.g. mortgage interest) and non-qualifying loans, there is no charge on the non-qualifying loans if they do not exceed £5,000 in total at any time in the tax year.

If the loan is written off, you are charged to tax on the amount written off whether you are still employed or not (see page 195).

Training and education

Scholarship and apprentice schemes

Employees on full-time and sandwich courses at universities and colleges lasting one year or more may receive pay of up to £7,000 a year tax-free while they are on the course (Revenue Statement of Practice SP 4/86).

External training courses

By concession A63, an employee is not taxed on payments by his employer

Example 2

Employer provides employee who pays tax at 24% with a loan of £3,000 to buy a season ticket and a home loan of £30,000, both interest-free, for the whole of the tax year 1996/97. Assume the official rate is 7¼% throughout. The tax position is as follows.

No tax on season ticket loan since it does not exceed £5,000.

Tax on notional interest on home loan:
(£30,000 @ 7¼%) = £2,175 @ 24%   522
Less tax relief on notional interest:
                £2,175 @ 15%   326

Net tax payable (9% of £2,175)   £196

If loan had been £40,000, the tax position would have been:

Tax on notional interest:
(£40,000 @ 7¼%) = £2,900 @ 24%   696

Less tax relief on (£2,900 × $\dfrac{30,000}{40,000}$) @ 15%   326

Net tax payable   £370

If employee's tax rate were 40%, the tax on the notional interest would increase, but the tax relief would remain the same.

for external training courses, either of general education where the employee is under 21 when the course starts, or otherwise job-related, including additional travelling costs and subsistence where the employee is absent from his normal place of work for less than twelve months. (Similarly, by concession A64, where the employee himself bears the cost of an external training course which he attends whilst still being paid his full salary, that cost, including travel and subsistence in some circumstances, is deductible in calculating taxable earnings where the course is of at least four weeks' duration, takes place in the UK, and is job-related.)

Retraining costs (TA 1988, ss 588, 589)

Where a retraining course in the UK for up to one year is made generally available to appropriate employees, the employee is not assessed on the course costs and any incidental travelling expenses paid for by the employer. The employee must have been employed full-time for at least two years, must leave the employment within two years after the end of the course, and must not be re-employed within two years after leaving.

Vocational training (FA 1991, ss 32, 33; FA 1994, s 84; SI 1992/746; FA 1996, s 144)

Tax relief at your top tax rate is available if you pay for your own qualifying vocational training, unless you are under 19 and still in full-time education at school. The training organisation's fees are paid net of basic rate tax, and you are entitled to keep the tax you have deducted whether you are a taxpayer or not. If you pay tax at the higher rate, the extra tax relief due must be claimed and will be given by coding adjustment or in an assessment. The training organisations are able to reclaim the basic rate tax from the Revenue.

The relief applies to study and examination fees paid by UK resident trainees for training leading to National Vocational Qualifications or Scottish Vocational Qualifications. Training for recreational purposes or as a leisure activity does not qualify. For fees paid after 5 May 1996, the relief also applies to any full-time vocational training course for those aged 30 and over, providing the course lasts at least four weeks and not more than a year.

The relief is available even if the course is unrelated to your present work or you have no current job. It is not, however, available if you receive any other public financial assistance for the course, or if any other tax relief or deduction is available for the expenditure, for example where the training is paid for by an employer.

Summary of main benefits provisions

BENEFIT	AMOUNT CHARGEABLE TO TAX FOR P11D EMPLOYEES*
Use of car	Charge based on list price, reduced by ⅓ if business miles 2,500 or more and by ⅔ if business miles 18,000 or more. No reduction for second and subsequent cars, unless business miles in additional car are 18,000 or more, in which case charge reduced by ⅓
Car fuel for private motoring	Scale charge
Car-parking facilities	Not assessable
Use of van	Fixed charge of £500 (£350 if 4 years old or more), or proportionate charge for shared vans
Mobile telephone	Fixed charge of £200
Living accommodation	Letting value (unless job-related)

BENEFIT	AMOUNT CHARGEABLE TO TAX FOR P11D EMPLOYEES*
Provision of services and use of furniture in living accommodation	Cost of services plus 20% p.a. of cost of furniture (but charge cannot exceed 10% of other reckonable earnings from the employment if exempt from living accommodation charge)
Use of other assets (excluding heavy commercial vehicles)	20% of cost
Vouchers other than luncheon vouchers	Full value
Use of employers' credit cards	Cost of goods and services obtained
Medical insurance	Cost to employer
Beneficial loans	Interest at official rate (see page 160) less any interest paid, but no charge if loans total £5,000 or less. See also page 160 re mortgage interest
Loans written off	Amount written off
Creche facilities	Not assessable
Free or subsidised canteen meals	Not assessable if available to all employees
Pension provision under approved schemes	Not assessable

* Non-P11D employees escape tax on benefits except for the following, which are taxed on the same basis as for P11D employees:

Living accommodation
Vouchers other than luncheon vouchers
Use of employers' credit cards
Loans written off

Example 3

An employee is paid a salary of £20,000 in 1996/97.

He is provided with a 2-year old 1500 cc company car with a list price of £12,000, which is completely run by the employer, including the provision of private petrol and a mobile phone for business and private use. He did 10,000 business miles and 5,000 private miles.

He received an overnight allowance which amounted to £649 and in respect of which a dispensation had been granted to his employer by the Revenue.

He paid hotel and meal bills on business trips amounting to £1,539 and spent £250 on entertaining customers. These expenses were reimbursed by his employer. Telephone bills amounting to £250 were paid by his employer, of which £150 was agreed by the Revenue to be for business use.

He received a round sum expenses allowance of £1,200 out of which allowable expenses of £200 are agreed.

Following Revenue agreement of an expenses claim by the employee the assessable earnings are:

	£	£
Salary		20,000
Charge for use of car (£12,000 × 35% = £4,200, less ⅓)		2,800
Scale car fuel charge		890
Mobile phone charge		200
Overnight allowance (covered by dispensation)		—
Hotel and meal bills reimbursed		1,539
Entertaining expenses reimbursed		250
Telephone account paid by employer		250
Round sum expenses allowance		1,200
		27,129
Less: Hotel and meal bills reimbursed	1,539	
Entertaining expenses reimbursed (disallowed to employer)	250	
Proportion of telephone account agreed as relating to employment	150	
Other allowable expenses	200	2,139
Assessable emoluments		£24,990

National insurance

As well as the salary, pay for national insurance will include the round sum expenses allowance (except to the extent of any identified business expenses).

Revenue dispensations are also effective for NI contributions, so there will be no NI on the overnight allowance.

The DSS will accept a private telephone use figure that has been agreed with the Revenue, so that contributions in this example will be due only on £100. If there is no such agreement, pay for national insurance includes payment of telephone bills, except for identified and logged business calls (unless the telephone contract is in the employer's name).

In addition to paying Class 1 national insurance contributions on the salary, the employer will pay Class 1A contributions on the car and fuel scale charges at 10.2% of (2,800 + 890 =) £3,690, i.e. £376, due for payment in June 1997.

Value added tax

The employer will pay output VAT on the car fuel of £33.06 per VAT quarter, unless no VAT input tax is being claimed on fuel for *any* motor vehicle.

PAYE

Tax under Schedule E is normally collected through the PAYE scheme, and employees have not received a tax bill from the Revenue unless there is a significant underpayment. Under self-assessment, employees will be able to have underpayments of up to £1,000 dealt with by coding adjustment if their returns are sent in by 30 September (see page 118). Employers deduct tax (usually on a cumulative basis) and national insurance contributions (on a non-cumulative basis except for company directors) from the weekly or monthly pay (including statutory sick pay and statutory maternity pay), using tables supplied by the Revenue. The total amount deducted in each tax month (ending on the 5th), together with the employer's national insurance contributions, less the amount recoverable for statutory sick pay (if any — see page 217) and statutory maternity pay, is due for payment within 14 days, i.e. by the 19th. Interest is charged on unpaid PAYE and national insurance contributions for any tax year which remain outstanding after the following 19 April. If during the tax year the cumulative tax paid by an employee exceeds the cumulative amount due, the excess is refunded to him by the employer, who then deducts it from the amount due to the Revenue.

Employers who expect their average total monthly payment for PAYE and national insurance contributions (and subcontractors' deductions where applicable) to be less than £600 may pay quarterly instead of monthly. New employers must notify the Revenue accordingly but existing employers need not do so unless they receive a demand from the Collector.

For details on national insurance contributions, including those relating to directors, see chapter 13. For details of statutory sick pay and statutory maternity pay, see chapter 14.

All the necessary documentation is supplied by the Revenue. Basic guidance is provided on the P8 cards. National insurance information is provided by the DSS.

Code numbers

The tax calculation is made using code numbers notified by the Revenue on form P9 or using the specified emergency procedure where no code number

165

is received. Once a code number is issued it remains in force from year to year until the Revenue notify a change.

Your code represents the tax allowances you are entitled to, such as personal allowances and allowable expenses in employment, less a deduction to cover small items of other income like national savings bank interest, or to adjust underpayments in earlier years. Some taxpayers liable only at the lower rate of 20% used to get an extra allowance called 'Taxed Income Relief' to compensate them for having had basic rate tax deducted from their bank and building society interest. This saved them making a repayment claim. Now that savings income is taxed at only 20% this will no longer apply. There is a coding adjustment described as the Allowance Restriction, which adjusts the tax relief on married couple's allowance (and allowances linked to it, such as additional personal allowance) to the appropriate rate, currently 15%. The amount of the restriction varies according to whether the employee is expected to be paying tax at the lower, basic or higher rate of tax.

Your code number is the amount of your allowances less the last digit. For example if your allowances total £3,765 your code number is 376. The code effectively spreads your tax allowances evenly over the tax year. This means that if in any pay period you earn some extra pay, there is no extra tax-free allowance to set against it, so that the whole of the extra suffers tax.

Most codes are three numbers followed by a suffix L, H, P, or V. L denotes personal allowance and H personal allowance plus married couple's allowance or additional personal allowance. P denotes age allowance 65–74 and V age allowance 65–74 plus married couple's age allowance 65–74. The suffixes enable the Revenue to implement changes in these allowances by telling employers to increase the codes by a specified amount. Some codes have suffix T, which means that the code is only to be changed if a specific notification is received from the tax office. A code T may be requested by a taxpayer who wishes his status to remain private.

Some codes have a prefix D or K instead of a suffix. The number following the D or K prefix relates to the tax rate to be used. Prefix D is used if you have more than one employment and your total income will attract higher rate tax. Your allowances are given against the earnings from your main employment and tax is deducted in other employments according to the D code in use. The D code procedure represents an estimate of higher rate tax liability and an adjustment is necessary at the year end when the precise income is known. Prefix K enables tax to be collected during the year where the amount of an employee's taxable benefits or an employed pensioner's state pension exceeds available allowances. The tax deducted under a K code cannot exceed 50% of cash pay (but see below re notional pay). Other codes are BR, which means basic rate tax applies, OT, which means no allowances are available, and NT, which means no tax is to be deducted.

Payments in non-cash form (notional payments) (TA 1988, ss 203F–203K; FA 1994, ss 127–131; SI 1994/1212)

Where employers provide employees with certain marketable assets, or assets which they have arranged for the employee to exchange for cash (see page 154), PAYE and national insurance contributions must be recorded and accounted for at the time the asset is provided, whether or not the employee has sufficient pay to enable the tax and employee's national insurance to be deducted. If the tax and NI are not made good within 30 days from the time the asset is provided, they must be shown as further pay on year-end forms P9D or P11D. The 50% overriding limit on deduction of tax under K codes (see above) is ignored when dealing with the deductions for notional payments.

Tax tables

Tables A, LR, B and C work on a cumulative basis. Table A shows the cumulative free pay each tax week or month for the various code numbers, and it includes the adjustments needed to increase the tax collected from employees with K codes by increasing taxable pay. Tables LR and B show the tax due on taxable pay to date at the lower rate of 20% and the basic rate of 24% up to the basic rate limit and Table C the tax due at the higher rate. Table D is non-cumulative, and is a higher rate tax ready reckoner for use with Table C and for D codes.

Changing jobs or retiring

When you leave your job, then unless the employer will be paying you a pension, he should complete form P45, which is in four parts. He sends the first part to the Revenue and gives you the other three parts, part 1A being for you to retain (you will need it if you have to fill in a tax return) and parts 2 and 3 for your new employer. The P45 shows the total pay and tax to date in the tax year and the code number in use. Passing the form to your new employer when you start another job enables him to continue to deduct tax on the correct basis. Wages in lieu of notice and statutory redundancy pay are not normally treated as pay, but they may be subject to tax under special rules (see chapter 15).

If you cannot produce form P45 to your new employer he will ask you to complete form P46, stating either that this is your first job since leaving school and you have not claimed unemployment benefit, or that this is your only or main job. The P46 procedure enables employers to deduct tax on a cumulative basis straight away for school leavers, so that they get the benefit of the single personal allowance from the beginning of the tax year. Other new employees will usually be allocated a single person's allowance, code 376L, on a non-cumulative basis (called week 1 or month 1 basis), which means they get only one week's (or month's) proportion of the allowance against each week's (month's) pay. If you do not complete either statement on form P46, the employer will deduct tax at the basic rate from the whole of your pay.

Forms P46 are sent to the Revenue unless the employee completes one of the two statements and earns less than £72.50 a week. Forms P46 for such employees must be retained by the employer, together with details of the employee's name, address and amount of pay. If the employee earns more than the national insurance threshold of £61 a week, a deductions working sheet must be prepared.

If you are retiring on pension, your employer will send form P160 to the Revenue (containing similar details to form P45) and give you a copy, which you will need if you fill in a tax return. The employer will deduct tax from your pension on a week 1 or month 1 basis (see above) until the Revenue tell him what code number to use.

Forms P11D

These forms are prepared by employers at the year end and sent in to the Revenue (see below). They summarise the benefits and expenses payments for directors and employees earning £8,500 per annum or more (except those covered by a dispensation — see page 153). They are increasingly subject to close scrutiny and testing by the Revenue as to their accuracy, for example through visits to business premises, knowledge of directors' personal circumstances and a close inspection of the position as regards loans to directors. Care should therefore be taken to ensure that all sections of the form are correctly completed, and in particular that all expenses of the employee met by the employer are declared, a claim being made by the employee in his annual tax return for a corresponding deduction if the expenses are allowable for tax.

The law is to be changed to give statutory effect to the existing practice of annual voluntary settlements, under which employers may make a lump sum payment to the Revenue to cover the tax liability of employees on minor incidental expenses and benefits. Items covered by the settlements do not have to be shown on P11Ds and employees are not taxed on them. Similar arrangements will apply in respect of national insurance contributions.

Substantial penalties may be imposed for failure to submit a form P11D, or for submitting an incorrectly completed form (see page 170).

Forms P11D for 1996/97 onwards will include calculations of the cash equivalents for benefits, and a copy of the form must be provided to the employee by 6 July (see page 169). A copy does not have to be provided to an employee who left during the year unless the employee makes a written request. As far as car benefits are concerned, the employee will need to report the business mileage to the employer, otherwise the employer will have to show the cash equivalent at the maximum level appropriate to the information he holds. The employer will have to show on form P11D benefits that he has arranged for a third party to provide (e.g. where another group company provides cars or medical insurance).

If a third party has provided benefits other than by arrangement with the employer (apart from the exceptions stated on page 156), the third party must give details of the cash equivalent to the employee by 6 July following the relevant tax year. Third parties do not need to send details of the taxable benefits to the Revenue unless they receive a return requiring them to do so.

Employers' records and year end returns

Employers must keep records of pay, tax, employees' and employer's national insurance contributions and the amount of any statutory sick pay and statutory maternity pay (see chapter 14). The totals should be recorded monthly or quarterly either on form P32 or in the payslip booklet.

Details must be provided to the Revenue at the year end for all those who are or have been employed in that year. Employers may either use deductions working sheets P11 supplied by the Revenue and official end of year return forms P14, or use their own pay records and notify the totals on forms P14, or use their own pay records with substitute end of year returns, or keep computerised records and make end of year returns on magnetic tape.

Form P14 is in three parts. Two parts are sent to the Revenue (one of which is for the Department of Social Security) and the third is the form P60 for the employee showing the total pay and tax deducted in the year, and the amounts of statutory sick pay and statutory maternity pay. From 1996/97, forms P14 only need to show statutory sick pay paid in months for which the employer recovered part of it (see page 217): (All sick pay will still be included in the total pay figure.) The forms to be sent to the Revenue at the year end are —

Two copies of form P14 (or substitutes)

Form P35 showing for all employees and former employees the total tax and national insurance contributions, and the amounts recovered in respect of statutory sick pay and statutory maternity pay (see pages 217 and 219). From 1996/97 the amounts *paid* in respect of statutory sick pay and statutory maternity pay do not need to be shown.

Forms P11D showing details of expenses payments and benefits provided to current and former employees earning £8,500 per annum or more and directors

Forms P9D showing expenses payments in excess of £25 to non-P11D employees that have not been treated as pay (other than reimbursed business expenses and expenses paid in accordance with a scale agreed with the Tax Office) and certain other benefits such as the excess of luncheon vouchers over 15p per day.

The time limit for sending in forms P14 and P35 is 19 May, and for sending in forms P11D and P9D, 6 June for years before 1996/97. From 1996/97 onwards, the time limit for sending in forms P11D and P9D is extended to 6 July (e.g. by 6 July 1997 for 1996/97), and a requirement is introduced for copies to be provided to employees by that date. A time limit of 31 May has been introduced from 1996/97 for providing employees with year-end forms

P60. These changes are to give employees information in good time to complete their self-assessment tax returns.

Employers have to give the Revenue details of new and changed arrangements for the provision of cars and car fuel to employees on form P46 (Car). The form must be submitted within 28 days after each quarter to 5 July, 5 October, 5 January and 5 April. Employers' Class 1A national insurance contributions on the car and fuel provision (see page 203) are calculated annually from the P11D entries. For 1996/97, payment has to be made to the Collector of Taxes with the PAYE remittance due on 19 June 1997 (19 July 1997 if you are a small employer making quarterly returns — see page 165) and the payment will be recorded on year end form P35 after 5 April 1998, so that where an employee leaves, records will still need to be maintained for the appropriate period. Employers may apply (on form CA 34 included in their Employer's Pack) to pay Class 1A contributions direct to the DSS rather than paying through the PAYE system. When a business ceases, Class 1A contributions are due within 14 days after the end of the income tax month in which the last payment of earnings is made. If a business changes hands, the employer before the change must similarly pay over Class 1A contributions for any employee not continuing with the new owner within 14 days after the end of the final month. The liability for payment of the Class 1A contributions for continuing employees falls on the successor.

As stated on page 165, interest is charged if PAYE and national insurance contributions for any year to 5 April are paid later than 19 April (which is a month earlier than the due date for submitting the year end forms P14 and P35). For recent rates of interest, see page xxiii.

Automatic penalties are payable by employers who do not send in end of year forms P14 and P35 by 19 May, or who send in incorrect returns (although by concession a penalty will not be charged if the forms are received on or before the last business day within the following seven days). The penalty payable is £100 for every 50 employees (or part of 50) for each month or part month the return is late. For example, someone with 110 employees who does not send in his 1995/96 return until 10 September 1996 (between 3 and 4 months late) would pay a penalty of £300 × 4 = £1,200. Penalties are also charged for late filing of forms P11D and P9D. For each form, there is an initial penalty of up to £300 plus up to £60 a day if the failure continues. If an employer fraudulently or negligently provides incorrect information in a P11D or P9D he is liable to a penalty of up to £3,000 for each form.

Employees' records and self-assessment

With the introduction of self-assessment from 1996/97, all taxpayers are required to keep records relating to their tax liabilities (see page 119). Most employees will not need to fill in tax returns, because their tax will usually be dealt with through the PAYE system (see page 117), but they should still keep records for the statutory period in case there is any query. Employees need to keep records for 22 months from the end of the tax year, unless they are also self-employed, in which case the period is 5 years 10 months. In both cases, the records must be retained until the Revenue complete any enquiry into the taxpayer's affairs.

The main records employees need to keep are year-end certificates P60 and forms P11D (or P9D), forms P45 when they change jobs or P160 if they retire on pension, and records, receipts and vouchers to support expenses claims. They should also keep any other records that relate to their employment income, such as coding notices, information relating to employee share schemes, information re earnings abroad (and proof of any foreign tax deducted), etc.

Tax points

● One of the main reasons for providing benefits rather than cash pay is to enable the employer to save national insurance at 10.2% (and the employee 10% if he earns less than £23,660). It may also be possible to provide the benefits for less than the employee would have paid himself, by use of in-house services, staff discounts, etc. Benefits in the form of gold bullion or commodities, or vouchers to obtain them, are now specifically taxed under PAYE and are chargeable to national insurance (see pages 154 and 167).

● Even if benefits are not caught for national insurance contributions, they limit your free choice of what to spend your money on, so you may still prefer the cash.

● Check whether it is still tax-efficient to pay for an employee's private car fuel. Look at the VAT charge and the national insurance contributions as well as the income tax effect. It may be cheaper to pay the employee extra wages to compensate him for buying his own private fuel.

● Home to work travelling expenses are not allowable but the home and the workbase may be the same place. Area representatives and those holding part-time employments, such as consultants and tribunal members, should seek to establish when they accept their employments that their place of employment is at their home or other workbase, making their travelling expenses from that base allowable.

● There is no tax on an interest-free loan to a P11D employee to buy a season ticket unless the total loans at a nil or beneficial interest rate that are outstanding in the tax year exceed £5,000.

● Employers must be very careful to comply with the requirements of the PAYE scheme. For example, failing to apply the P46 procedure properly for new employees who do not produce form P45 could render the employer liable to account for tax which was not deducted from the amount paid.

Forms P11D must be properly completed and sent in promptly for each employee earning £8,500 per annum or more and each director; severe penalties apply if they are not.

● The Revenue have a programme of visits to employers for the purpose of inspecting records to ensure compliance with PAYE regulations, including reporting requirements. They have issued a leaflet IR71 and a Code of Practice (3) explaining their procedure, which are available from tax offices.

● The definition of 'earnings at the rate of £8,500 per annum' includes certain car expenses met by the employer as well as the car and car fuel scale charges. This brings some employees whose salary is less than £8,500 into the P11D reporting net.

● Remember that an employee's contribution towards the cost of a car (maximum £5,000) and for the private use of a car reduces the car benefit charge, but a contribution towards car fuel is not taken into account unless it covers the whole cost of private fuel.

● If an employer arranges for his employees earning less than £8,500 per annum to eat at a local café which sends the bill to the employer, the employee avoids tax on the provision of the meals. This will not work for P11D employees unless the café can provide a private room, which then effectively becomes the works canteen.

● An arrangement under which your employer is wholly or partly responsible for the finance and management of a childcare scheme is necessary to exempt those benefits from tax. If he simply pays or reimburses your childcare bills, you will pay tax on the benefit.

● If a car is provided for a relative of a P11D employee, the benefit could be charged at 35% of the list price on the P11D employee, but will be charged on the car user according to the user's business mileage if he is also an employee and the duties of the employment are such that the car is required in the performance of those duties (e.g. where the employee is a commercial traveller) and would be provided to any employee in equivalent circumstances.

● You are charged to tax on benefits arising from your employment even though your employer is not the payer. The most common example is tips. Another example is where one of your employer's suppliers pays for you to have a foreign holiday as a sales achievement reward. Details of all such benefits should be shown on your tax return, although you may find that the person making an award has an agreement with the Revenue under which the tax liability falls on him rather than on you.

● Many businesses promote goodwill by providing their customers' employees with entrance to sporting and cultural events, and with entertainment at those events. Such benefits are exempt providing they are not procured by the employer and are not related to services performed or to be performed in the employment.

- Gifts (other than cash gifts) of up to £150 in a tax year to an employee from a third party are exempt by concession, unless they are procured by the employer or relate to services that are part of the employee's normal duties.

- The Revenue frequently reviews the list of professional subscriptions which are allowable in computing the taxable pay of an employee. You should therefore keep a watchful eye on this if your own subscription has not so far been allowed.

- If you *occasionally* work very late, you are not charged to tax if your employer pays for your transport home. Those who regularly work late get no such exemption.

- 'Payment' for PAYE purposes can be triggered much earlier than when money changes hands, especially as regards directors.

- It is important for employees to keep detailed records of business mileage and for employers to have an adequate monitoring system if it would otherwise be difficult to establish that business mileage exceeds 2,500 miles or 18,000 miles per annum as the case may be. Not to do so may prove expensive, particularly now that employers' national insurance contributions are payable on the income tax benefit figures.

- Even if your annual mileage reaches the 18,000 or 2,500 level, changing your car during the year may cause you to lose the scale charge reduction for part of the year. Say you did 1,250 miles in the first nine months, then a further 1,250 in the last three months in a different car, you would only get a reduction in the scale charge for the second car (see page 158).

- If you use your own car for business, mileage allowances based on the Fixed Profit Car Scheme (FPCS) rates (see page xxii) may be received from your employer free of both tax and national insurance. If you pay your own running expenses, you can claim the FPCS rates for the business miles, and if your employer pays you a mileage allowance below the FPCS rates you can claim an allowance for the shortfall.

- Under self-assessment, you need to keep records relating to your tax affairs — see page 170. The Revenue give useful advice in their booklet SA/BK4 Self Assessment — A general guide to keeping records.

11
Share options, share incentives, and profit-related pay

Background

There is a minefield of legislation in this area, some intended to encourage genuine incentives through worker participation but much of it aimed at preventing the avoidance of income tax by directors or employees through the acquisition of shares in the company or group by which they are employed.

There are three sets of provisions designed to give favourable tax treatment to schemes to acquire shares if the necessary conditions are satisfied:

SAYE linked share option schemes (see page 176)
Company share option plans (previously known as executive share
    option schemes) (see page 177)
Approved profit sharing schemes (see page 180)

The profit-related pay provisions enable employees to receive a limited amount of tax-free pay related to profit performance (see page 183).

Under all the approved schemes, employers are required to provide annual returns to the Revenue. Detailed information must also be provided where chargeable events occur in relation to shares (see below). Penalties apply if the company fails to comply. Employees must similarly ensure that appropriate details are included in their tax returns.

There are provisions relating to Employee Share Ownership Plan trusts (see page 181) which enable companies to set up trusts that have more flexibility than approved schemes, although without their tax benefits.

Subject to certain restrictions, employers can get tax relief for the costs of setting up approved share option schemes, profit sharing schemes and employee share ownership plans. For capital gains purposes, on the grant of an option under an approved or unapproved scheme, the employer is treated as receiving the amount, if any, paid by the employee for the option (rather than market value, which usually applies to non-arm's length transactions — see page 60), so no capital gains charge will arise.

Shares valued at up to £3,000 acquired under approved profit sharing and SAYE linked share option schemes may be transferred free of capital gains

174

tax to a single company personal equity plan (PEP) even if they are unquoted — see page 536.

Limits on participation by close company members

A director or employee of a close company (see page 39) cannot participate in profit sharing or SAYE linked option schemes or a profit-related pay scheme if he and his associates own more than 25% of the ordinary share capital. The shareholding limit for non-SAYE linked share option schemes is a holding, with associates, of no more than 10% of the ordinary share capital. For employee share ownership plans there is a 5% limit (which applies to all companies, not just close companies). Apart from these limits, close companies may introduce appropriate schemes so long as the other conditions are satisfied.

Share options

Directors and employees granted rights to acquire shares (TA 1988, ss 135–137, 185, 187 and Sch 9)

Where a director or employee acquires shares in the employing company, or an associated company, by reason of a right to acquire them (an option), favourable tax treatment is given for approved SAYE linked share option schemes and for approved company share option plans (see below). Where the option does not arise under an approved scheme, an income tax charge arises on the difference between the open market value at the time of exercising the right and the cost of the shares, including any amount paid for the option. Similarly, where a right to acquire shares is assigned or released, an income tax charge arises on the consideration received less the cost of acquisition of the rights. An income tax charge also arises where an option holder realises a gain or benefit by allowing the option to lapse, or granting someone else an option over the shares.

Employees and directors are thus prevented from being indirectly remunerated without an appropriate tax charge by the allotment of shares for less than they are worth. The tax charge cannot be avoided by the right being granted or the shares allotted to another person.

The capital gains tax base cost of the shares is the open market value at the time of exercising the option.

Charge on granting a right to acquire shares (TA 1988, s 135(5))

If an option under an unapproved scheme is capable of being exercised more than seven years after it is granted, a charge arises at the time the right is granted on the excess of the then market value of the option shares over the price which, under the option, has to be paid for the shares. The tax paid may, however, be deducted from any tax arising when the option is exercised.

SAYE linked share option schemes (TA 1988, ss 185, 187, Sch 9; FA 1996, s 113)

An exemption from the option charging provisions is given for approved savings-related share option schemes. No charge will arise on the difference between cost and market value when a share option is exercised, nor at the time it is granted, where the cost of the shares is paid out of the proceeds of a linked SAYE scheme. Contributions of between £5 and £250 per month are paid under a SAYE contract with a building society, bank, or the Department of National Savings. The savings are usually deducted from pay. The option will normally be able to be exercised after three years, five years or seven years, when the SAYE contract ends, but may be exercised earlier if the employing company or the part of its business in which the employee works is sold or otherwise leaves the group operating the scheme. If in these circumstances an employee exercises his option within three years of joining the scheme, however, any gain arising will be charged to tax. For options granted on or after the date of Royal Assent to the Finance Act 1996 (and for options granted earlier if the scheme rules are altered accordingly before 5 May 1998), an employee who has been transferred to an associated company which is not participating in the scheme may nonetheless be permitted by the scheme rules to exercise his option within six months after the date his savings contract matures. If an employee dies before completing the contract, the option may be exercised within twelve months after the date of death. If an employee leaves through injury, disability, redundancy or retirement, the option may be exercised within the following six months. An option held by an employee leaving for any other reason must lapse, unless he had held it for at least three years, in which case he may be permitted to exercise it within six months after leaving.

Regardless of the treatment of the option, the SAYE contract itself may be continued by an employee after he leaves, by arrangement with the savings body, so that the tax-free benefits are retained. Payments will then be made direct to the savings body.

The scheme enables an option to be granted now to acquire shares at today's price, the shares eventually being paid for by the proceeds of a linked SAYE scheme. The price at which the option may be exercised must not normally be less than 80% of the market value of the shares at the time the option is granted. The employee does not get tax relief for the SAYE contributions but he gets the benefit of tax-free interest and bonuses, and when the shares are taken up there is no income tax charge on the excess of the market value over the price paid. If the shares are not taken up, the employee retains the proceeds of the SAYE contract together with the tax-free interest and bonuses.

Various conditions must be complied with and in particular the scheme must be available to all directors and employees with five years' service, it must not stipulate a minimum monthly contribution higher than £5 (previously £10) and it must not have features that discourage eligible employees from participating. Companies did not have to include part-time employees for schemes approved before 1 May 1995, but they must do so for schemes approved on or after that date. Part-time directors may still be excluded.

Companies may require scheme shares to be sold if an employee or director leaves the company, thus helping family companies who wish to ensure that their control is not diluted, and scheme rights can be exchanged for equivalent rights in a company taking over the employer company.

The capital gains tax base cost of the shares is the price paid by the employee so that when they are disposed of, the benefit of acquiring them at less than their market value is then partly lost, because the gain is charged to tax (except for the benefit of CGT indexation and any unused annual exemption, which would not have been available if the gain had been charged to income tax). The employee has, however, had the benefit of the SAYE tax-free interest and bonuses. If the opportunity is taken to transfer the shares up to the available £3,000 limit into a single company PEP (see page 536), the capital gain on disposal is tax-free.

Company share option plans (previously known as executive share option schemes) (TA 1988, ss 185, 187 and Sch 9; FA 1996, ss 114, 115 and Sch 16)

Tax advantages have been available for some time under approved non-savings-related share option schemes. It was announced on 17 July 1995 that the tax benefits were to be withdrawn, but the Government has decided instead to limit their scope. Although the changes apply to options granted on or after the date of Royal Assent to the Finance Act 1996, special provisions apply to options granted on or after 17 July 1995 (other than those for which an invitation to apply was made before that date and which were issued within 30 days of the invitation), which effectively make them subject to the new rules. The Revenue are calling schemes under the new rules 'company share option plans' rather than executive share option schemes, reflecting the fact that tax advantages are far more limited under the new schemes.

The new restrictions are that the option must not be granted at a discount (i.e. at an option price below the current market value of the shares) and the total market value of shares that may be acquired under the option and any other approved options held by the employee other than under savings-related schemes must not exceed £30,000. Providing the scheme complies with these and other conditions, there is no tax charge when options are granted. The new restrictions are regarded as included in all schemes from the date of Royal Assent, thus affecting options granted from that time under old or new schemes.

Options granted under the previous rules could be issued at a discount, but tax was charged under Schedule E at the time the option was granted on the excess of the then market value of the shares over the price at which the shares could be acquired under the option plus the amount, if any, paid for the option. If, however, the employer also had an approved SAYE linked share option scheme (see page 176) or an approved profit sharing scheme (see page 180), the price of the shares under the option could be set at a discount of up to 15% without triggering a tax charge at the time the option was granted. The ceiling for the value of options held at the time of the grant was the greater of £100,000 and four times the employee's Schedule E earnings of the current or previous year (excluding benefits and after deducting superannuation contributions).

Under both the old and new rules, there is no tax charge when the option is exercised, providing options under the scheme are exercised between three and ten years after they are granted, and not more frequently than once in three years. Tax will arise only at the time of disposal of the shares, when the total amount paid for the shares, including any discount charged to income tax when the option was granted, will be brought into a capital gains tax computation. If options are exercised in breach of the stipulated time limits, they will be treated in the same way as unapproved options (see page 175).

If the disposal takes place at a time when the scheme is not an approved scheme, the income tax charges under TA 1988, ss 135, 136 (see page 175) or TA 1988, s 162 (where shares are issued partly paid — see page 179) may arise, but the amount charged to tax will exclude any discount that has already been charged to tax when the option was granted.

Before 1 May 1995, schemes had to be restricted to full-time directors and employees, the definition of full-time being 25 hours a week for directors and 20 hours a week for employees. Part-time directors must still be excluded, but part-time employees are no longer excluded where the scheme is registered or amended on or after 1 May 1995.

Schemes may provide that participants must sell their scheme shares when their employment ends but the scheme rights can be exchanged for equivalent rights in a company taking over the employer company.

Share incentives

Issue of shares at an undervalue (TA 1988, s 19)

Unless covered by an approved option scheme, any shortfall between the price at which shares are issued to directors and employees and their market value is taxed as pay under Schedule E.

Issue of shares partly paid up (TA 1988, s 162)

If shares are issued at a price equal to the current market value, with the price being paid by agreed instalments, no charge will arise under the general charging provisions since full market value is being paid, and this will apply even though the market value has increased by the time the shares are paid for. Any growth in value of the shares is liable only to capital gains tax.

Directors and employees earning £8,500 per annum or more who acquire shares other than under the approved schemes and do not pay the full price for shares immediately are, however, regarded as having received an interest-free loan equal to the deferred instalments, on which tax will be charged at the beneficial loans interest rate (see page xxiii) unless the total of all beneficial loans outstanding in the tax year does not exceed £5,000 (see page 160). The loan will be regarded as being repaid as and when the instalments are paid.

Share incentive schemes (FA 1988, ss 77–89)

One way of avoiding the tax charge on shares issued to directors and employees at an undervalue (see above) would be to place restrictions on them in the first place that depressed their market value, and then remove the restrictions at a later date. To stop directors and employees obtaining a tax benefit in this way, tax is charged where the value of shares held by a director or employee increases because of the creation or removal of restrictions or variation of rights relating to the shares or to other shares in the company.

For the charge to apply, the person concerned must have been a director or employee of the company or of an associated company within the seven years before the event causing the increase.

The charge does not apply where the shares were acquired as a result of an offer to the public. Nor does it apply if, at the time of the event causing the increase, the majority of the shares of the class concerned do not belong to directors or employees of the company or to an associated company or its directors or employees; or if the company is 'employee controlled' by reason of holdings of shares of that class.

There are also provisions for charging an increase in value of the shares of a company, called a dependent subsidiary, whose trade is with, and whose performance depends on, other companies in the group.

With certain exceptions, the employee is also charged to tax on the value of any benefit received (a 'special benefit') that is not available to at least 90% of shareholders of the same class.

The charge to income tax arises in the tax year in which the event or special benefit occurs.

Any amount charged to income tax under these provisions is part of the base cost of the shares for capital gains tax.

Approved profit sharing schemes (TA 1988, s 186 and Schs 9 and 10; FA 1996, ss 116–118)

Favourable tax treatment is given to an approved profit sharing scheme under which a company appoints trustees and provides money for them to use to acquire shares in the company. The amount provided by the company is a tax deductible expense.

A director or employee is not charged to tax on shares allocated to him by the trustees under the scheme. He is regarded for capital gains tax purposes as being absolutely entitled to the shares even though they are still held by the trustees, and any dividends arising are regarded as his for income tax purposes.

There is a limit on the value of shares that can be allocated to any one employee in any tax year. For 1996/97 the limit is 10% of the employee's salary (excluding benefits and after deducting superannuation contributions) for 1996/97 or 1995/96, but subject to a minimum limit of £3,000 and a maximum of £8,000.

A scheme will not receive Revenue approval unless it is available on similar terms to all qualifying employees — broadly those with five years' service — but it is recognised that different levels of share allocation may apply to individuals on different salary levels. It must be demonstrated that the scheme does not have characteristics which discourage some of those eligible from participating. Before 1 May 1995, the inclusion of part-time employees was at the employer's discretion. This no longer applies for schemes registered on or after 1 May 1995. Employers still have discretion as to whether to include those with less than five years' service and part-time directors.

No income tax charge arises if the shares are transferred to the employee after three years (five years before Finance Act 1996). The shares must remain in the hands of the trustees for a minimum period which is generally two years, and an income tax charge arises if the shares are disposed of within three years (previously five), equal to their market value when allocated to the employee or the sale proceeds if less. The charge is reduced to 50% if the disposal occurs within the three years because the employee leaves as a result of injury, disability, redundancy, or reaching an age between 60 and 75 as specified by the scheme.

A similar tax charge will also arise if there is a capital receipt, as for example on a rights issue, within three years, but only if it exceeds a stipulated amount (broadly £20 per annum cumulatively up to a maximum £60).

Any amounts charged to income tax are not liable to national insurance.

The income tax charge has no effect on the capital gains tax base cost. Whether shares are disposed of within or after the three-year period the capital gains tax base cost is the market value at the time the shares were appropriated to the employee.

While such schemes appear attractive, there are drawbacks for unquoted companies in that the company cannot choose which employees may participate; there may not be a ready market for the shares if the employee wants to sell them; an immediate market valuation is not available; and the effect on established shareholders has to be considered.

A condition can, however, be imposed that employees must sell their shares when the employment ends.

Capital gains tax share pools

Unless they are subject to any special restrictions, shares acquired under SAYE and other share option schemes (whether approved or not) are pooled with any other shares of the same class in the same company (acquisitions before and after 31 March 1982 being in separate pools — see page 514). Their cost is the price paid for them, plus the amount, if any, paid for the option, plus any amount that has been charged to income tax. The amounts paid attract indexation allowance from the date of payment. Such shares would not, however, go into the CGT pool if you bought and sold them on the same day or within ten days. The sale would be matched with the purchase and no indexation allowance would be available.

Shares acquired under an approved profit sharing scheme are regarded as a separate pool while they are retained by the trustees, with the shares treated as acquired by the employee at market value at the date they are appropriated to him and indexed from that date. After the three-year period of retention, the shares are transferred to the employee's normal pool of shares of that class in that company. A sale at the end of the period of retention is not affected by the same day/ten-day rule referred to above because the shares were treated as owned from the date they were allocated to the employee.

Employee share ownership plans (FA 1989, ss 67–74 and Sch 5; TCGA 1992, ss 227–236; FA 1996, ss 119, 120)

There are provisions to encourage companies to set up trusts that will acquire shares in the company and distribute them to the employees. Revenue approval is not required. The company's payments to the trust are tax deductible. Anyone who owns 5% or more of the company's ordinary share capital is not eligible. All other employees and full-time directors who have been employed throughout a period specified in the trust deed must be included as beneficiaries. The specified period cannot exceed five years, and had to be at least one year for trusts established before the date of Royal Assent to the Finance Act 1996. For trusts established before 1 May 1995, employees working less than 20 hours a week cannot be included, and this continues to be the case for part-time directors. Distributions out of the trust must be on similar terms to all beneficiaries, but allowing for different distributions according to length of service and level of remuneration.

The trustees must use sums received for a qualifying purpose, principally to acquire the company's shares, within nine months of receipt, and must distribute the shares to employees within twenty years of acquisition (seven years for trusts established before 4 May 1994). If any of the conditions are breached, the trust will be charged to tax at 34% on the sums received by it on which tax relief has been given.

There are no special tax reliefs either for the trust or for the employees receiving shares out of it, but it may operate in conjunction with an approved profit sharing scheme trust (see page 180), in which case shares allocated within the approved profit sharing scheme conditions will not be charged to tax. Trusts established on or after the date of Royal Assent to the Finance Act 1996 may also operate in conjunction with an approved savings-related share option scheme.

These provisions may be seen as an extension to the approved profit sharing scheme trusts and savings-related share option schemes, in order to give the trustees more flexibility than is permitted under the approved schemes.

Subject to detailed and complex conditions (in particular the condition that the trust must have a 10% stake in the company either immediately or within 12 months of the sale), a shareholder who sells his shares to the trust may treat the gain as reducing the capital gains tax cost of replacement taxable assets acquired within six months after the sale or of the 10% condition being satisfied, if later. (Alternatively he could claim reinvestment relief if he acquires shares in a qualifying unquoted trading company — see page 62.)

Employers interested in establishing employee share ownership plans may submit draft deeds to the Revenue to see if the proposed trust will qualify.

Priority share allocations for employees (FA 1988, s 68)

When shares are offered to the public, a priority allocation is often made to employees and directors. Where there is no price advantage, a taxable benefit will not arise because of the right to shares in priority to other persons, so long as the shares that may be allocated do not exceed 10% of those being offered, all directors and employees entitled to an allocation are entitled on similar terms (albeit at different levels), and those entitled are not restricted wholly or mainly to persons who are directors or whose remuneration exceeds a particular level. This treatment still applies where the offer to employees is strictly not part of the public offer, as a result of the employees' offer being restricted to shares in one or more companies and the public offer being a package of shares in a wider range of companies.

Where employees get shares at a discount compared with the price paid by the public, the discount is chargeable. The employee's base cost for capital gains tax is the amount paid plus the amount of the discount that was charged to income tax.

Profit-related pay (TA 1988, ss 169–184 and Sch 8)

Part of an employee's pay is permitted to be tax-free where it is related to profits of the employer, and is paid under a scheme which has been registered with the Revenue. Those employed by the Crown or by local authorities are excluded.

The tax-free profit-related pay cannot exceed one-fifth of the employee's total pay of the accounting period (pay for this purpose being exclusive of benefits in kind), with an overriding maximum of £4,000 per annum. Even though this amount is exempt from income tax it is chargeable to national insurance contributions. The maximum tax saving to a 40% taxpayer is £1,600.

The scheme must be registered with the Revenue by the employer or by the parent company in the case of a group scheme. The application must include a certificate from an independent accountant that the scheme complies with the conditions laid down by the legislation. Payments under the scheme cannot be made to an employee who with his associates owns more than 25% of the ordinary share capital of the company. For schemes registered before 1 May 1995, but not for later schemes, employees may be excluded if they work for less than 20 hours a week. Employees may also be excluded if they have not worked for the employer for a minimum period (which cannot exceed three years). The scheme must include at least 80% of employees in a particular employment unit (not counting those who are disqualified as indicated above). There are two methods for calculating the amount which is to be distributed to employees (the 'distributable pool') and the scheme must specify the method to be used. The scheme must provide similar terms for all participating employees, although payments may vary according to remuneration, length of service or similar factors. An independent accountant must submit a report to the Revenue after each profit period. The rules were amended for schemes registered on or after 1 December 1993 to ensure that profit-related pay reflects genuine movements in profits and to ensure that schemes covering particular employment units within a business do not benefit the employees in the unit to a disproportionate extent compared with other employees.

An employee cannot get tax relief on profit-related pay from more than one employment. The Revenue have power to cancel the registration of a scheme in the case of abuse and to recover income tax from the employer where relief has been given since the date of cancellation.

Tax points

- There is no clearance procedure under FA 1988, ss 77–89 (share incentive schemes) and since these provisions tax increases in the value of shares, as distinct from an advantage when they are purchased, it makes the schemes particularly vulnerable to uncertainty.

- In the case of unquoted companies, the value of shares has, when appropriate, to be agreed with the Revenue Shares Valuation Division.

- Group employees may participate in schemes through their parent company.

- For newly-established schemes, part-time employees can no longer be excluded. Part-time directors are still excluded from non-savings-related share option schemes and employee share ownership trusts, and need not be included in savings-related share option schemes and profit sharing schemes.

- Where falls in share values have made approved options unattractive, it is possible for employees to give them up and replace them with more attractively priced options. To avoid possible capital gains problems it is best for there to be a clear break between giving up the old and acquiring the new.

- If you acquire shares under an approved share option scheme and immediately dispose of them, the gain will be subject to capital gains tax (unless covered by reliefs or exemptions). Gains can only be sheltered if the shares are transferred into a single company PEP (see page 536).

- Any income tax charged on an employee under an approved profit sharing scheme (see page 180) is deducted under the PAYE scheme. Where income tax is payable on an event under a share option or incentive scheme, the due date for years before 1996/97 is 30 days after the date of the issue of the assessment.

- Under self-assessment from 1996/97, there are supplementary pages to be completed and sent in with your tax return giving details relating to share schemes and share-related benefits. Any tax due must then be included in your self-assessment. A charge under approved profit sharing schemes is not shown, since tax on such charges is collected through PAYE.

- Employers face penalties if they fail to provide to the Revenue the returns and information required under the provisions outlined in this chapter.

- A profit-related pay scheme can apply to a business as a whole or to any identifiable part for which a separate account can be prepared and certified by an independent accountant but there are rules for schemes registered on or after 1 December 1993 to ensure that employees of a separate PRP unit within a business do not get a disproportionate benefit.

- There are provisions to prevent employers manipulating the rules so that employees are virtually guaranteed profit-related pay whether profits increase or not.

- If your employer wishes you to accept a scheme that replaces part of your existing pay with profit-related pay, you should realise that you are taking the risk that the profit-related pay will not materialise because profits do not increase.

- An approved SAYE share option scheme, company share option plan or profit sharing scheme cannot apply to a subsidiary company unless the parent is a non-close company listed on the Stock Exchange.

12
Directors of small and family companies

Directors and shareholders

In family companies, directors and shareholders are usually the same people, and they can benefit from the company in various ways, e.g.:

Payment of remuneration.
Provision of benefits.
Distribution of income through dividends.

When considering to what extent, and in what form, to withdraw profits, the tax treatment is an important factor. There are other considerations, in particular the effect on pensions. Remuneration and benefits are earned income in the hands of the shareholder, whereas dividends are unearned income. Only earned income is taken into account for pension purposes. Therefore, if you do not have a company pension scheme, taking a low salary means that you can only pay very low personal pension contributions, and if you are in a company pension scheme, you need to watch the definition of final remuneration on which your pension will be based (see page 230).

Profit taken as pay costs the company 10.2% national insurance contributions, but the contributions are deducted in arriving at taxable profits. National insurance contributions are also payable on some but not all benefits in kind. The additional net of tax cost of the national insurance contributions is as follows.

Company's tax rate	*Net cost of NI*
24% (on profits up to £300,000)	7.75%
33% (on profits over £1,500,000)	6.83%
35.25% (marginal small companies rate on profits between £300,000 and £1,500,000)	6.60%

When profits are taken as dividends, they are not deducted in calculating taxable profits, but the company's tax is effectively eliminated to the extent of the tax credits passed on to the shareholders, the net cost being as follows (see example 1).

186

Company's tax rate	*Net cost of dividend*
24%	5%
33%	16.25%
35.25% (marginal small companies rate)	19.06%

Example 1

Company uses 100.00 profits to pay dividend as follows:

Company's tax rate	*24%*	*33%*	*35.25%*
Company profits	100.00	100.00	100.00
Corporation tax:			
ACT (¼ of cash dividend)	19.00	16.75	16.19
Mainstream tax	5.00	16.25	19.06
Cash dividend	76.00	67.00	64.75

As far as the shareholders are concerned, although the tax credit on the dividend is at an effective rate of only 20%, those liable at the basic rate of 24% have no further tax to pay. Higher rate taxpayers, however, have a further 20% to pay, and non-taxpayers and those taxable only at the lower rate can only recover credits at 20% instead of 24%.

For 1996/97, the effective tax rate on a given amount of profits paid as salary or dividend to a director/shareholder liable to tax at 40% and already paying maximum NI contributions is as follows.

Salary payment (not affected by company's tax rate, since taxable profits are reduced by the payment)

Available profit	100.00
Employer's NI on salary (10.2% of 90.74)	9.26
Gross salary	90.74
Tax @ 40%	36.30
Net income	54.44
Effective tax rate	45.56%

Dividend payment

Company's tax rate	*24%*	*33%*	*35.25% (marginal small companies rate)*
Available profit	100.00	100.00	100.00
Corporation tax	24.00	33.00	35.25
Cash dividend	76.00	67.00	64.75
Tax credit 1/4	19.00	16.75	16.19
Shareholder's income	95.00	83.75	80.94

Shareholder's income as above	95.00	83.75	80.94
Tax @ 40%	38.00	33.50	32.38
Net income	57.00	50.25	48.56
Effective tax rate	43%	49.75%	51.44%

Dividends for such director/shareholders are therefore only marginally more tax-effective than salary for companies paying at small companies rate, and are less tax-effective for companies paying at the full or small companies marginal rate.

The position is different for those taxable at less than 40%. Employees' national insurance contributions are payable on earnings up to the upper earnings level (£23,660 for 1996/97 and £22,880 for 1995/96). For those whose income does not exceed those amounts, taking dividends instead of pay will give a substantial extra saving (maximum employees' national insurance contributions for 1996/97 being £2,112 and for 1995/96 £2,047), and also an extra 4% tax saving to the extent that salary is charged at 24% (5% when the basic rate was 25%) and dividends at only 20%. See example 2.

Example 2

Company paying tax at the small companies rate uses profits of £20,000 in the year to 31 March 1997 to make a payment to a director/shareholder who has no other income. Director has available personal allowances of £3,765.

If profit is taken as	salary only £	salary and dividend £
Company's tax position on the payment is:		
Profits	20,000	20,000
Salary	(18,149)	(3,172)
Employer's national insurance	(1,851)	(95)
Taxable profits	—	16,733
Corporation tax at 24%		4,016
Cash dividend		12,717
Tax credit ¼		3,179
Director's income		15,896
Director's tax position		
Salary	18,149	3,172
Dividend	—	15,896
Carried forward	18,149	19,068

Brought forward	18,149	19,068
Personal allowances	(3,765)	(3,765)
Taxable income	14,384	15,303
Tax thereon (£3,900 @ 20%, £10,484 @ 24%)	3,296	
(dividends, therefore all at 20%)		3,061
Tax credit on dividend		(3,179)
Tax refund		(118)
Disposable income:		
Salary	18,149	3,172
Employee's national insurance	(1,561)	(63)
Dividend	—	12,717
Tax/tax refund	(3,296)	118
	13,292	15,944
Saving through paying dividend		£2,652

The saving through paying the dividend is made up as follows:

Increase in income through saving in employer's NI (1,851 – 95)	1,756	
Less part of corporation tax not included in tax credit (4,016 – 3,179)	837	
Extra income available as dividend	919	
Less 20% personal tax	184	735
Reduction in tax rate on dividends compared with salary (10,484 @ 4%)		419
Reduction in employee's NI (1,561 – 63)		1,498
		£2,652

An extra saving of about £129 could be made by fixing the salary at £3,000, thus avoiding employer's and employee's national insurance. The right to short-term and possibly long-term national insurance benefits would, however, be affected (see page 200).

Paying dividends out of earlier profits

Companies paying tax at the small companies rate of 24% cannot pass the whole of the corporation tax on to the shareholders as a tax credit on dividends, because the tax credit is only 20%. The tax credit still, however, represents the major part of the corporation tax.

Companies that have not paid dividends for various reasons in earlier years will even so have paid corporation tax on their profits. Providing cash is available to make the payments, it is possible to pay dividends over and above the profits of the current year and recoup the cost of the ACT by setting it off against earlier tax liabilities and thus obtaining repayment of part of the corporation tax of the previous six years (the ACT set-off being limited to 25% of the profits for the years up to the year ended 31 March 1993, 22½% for the year to 31 March 1994 and 20% thereafter). See example 3.

Example 3

In 1996/97, husband and wife directors have available personal allowances of £3,765 each, and the husband is also entitled to the married couple's allowance of £1,790. They have no sources of income apart from the company.

In the year ended 31 March 1997 the company pays them remuneration of £3,200 each and a dividend of £18,000 each (paying total advance corporation tax of £9,000 to the Revenue and passing on tax credits of £4,500 each). Company's recent results after directors' remuneration are:

Year to 31 March 1991–1996	Profit in each year (no dividends paid)	£20,000

Corporation tax payable @ 25% in each of those years is £5,000 (available in full to set off any carried back ACT for years up to 1993, the set-off being limited to £4,500 for the year to 31 March 1994 and £4,000 for the years to 31 March 1995 and 31 March 1996)

Year to 31 March 1997	Profit	£10,000

Company's tax position for year to 31 March 1997:

	£	£
Profit chargeable to corporation tax		10,000
Corporation tax @ 24%		2,400
ACT paid on dividends of £36,000	9,000	
Maximum set-off for year	(2,000)	(2,000)
Surplus ACT carried back (and repaid) being £4,000 for year to 31 March 1996 and £3,000 for year to 31 March 1995. ACT of year to 31 March 1991 will no longer be available for set-off in years after 31 March 1997 because of the six-year rule.	7,000	
Final corporation tax payable		£400

Directors' tax position in 1996/97:

	Husband £	Wife £
Remuneration	3,200	3,200
Dividend (£18,000 + £4,500)	22,500	22,500
	25,700	25,700
Less: Personal allowances	(3,765)	(3,765)
Taxable income	£21,935	£21,935
Tax thereon @ 20% (because dividends of £22,500 exceed taxable income)	4,387	4,387
Less: Married couple's allowance £1,790 @ 15%	(268)	
	4,119	
Tax credit on dividend	(4,500)	(4,500)
Tax credit repayable	£381	£113

The overall result is that the company has paid a net amount of tax of £2,400 (ACT of £9,000, less £7,000 repaid = £2,000, plus £400 mainstream tax). The directors have recovered £494, further reducing the current tax outlay to below £2,000 on total income of £51,400. There will in addition be an insignificant amount of national insurance on the salaries.

Retention of profits within the company or payment as remuneration or dividends

Retaining profits within the company will increase the net assets and hence the value of the shares if they are subsequently sold on the basis of underlying assets. Having already suffered corporation tax, the retained profits will thus swell the value of the shares for capital gains tax purposes. Reducing retentions through paying remuneration or dividends may therefore ultimately reduce the shareholders' chargeable gains, but this must be weighed against the immediate tax cost. Reducing taxable profit by a permissible contribution to a pension fund from which the director will benefit will often be a better alternative (see below).

Effect on earlier years (TA 1988, s 393A)

A decision on whether to pay remuneration or leave profits to be charged to corporation tax should not be taken by reference to the current year in isolation. The payment of remuneration may convert a trading profit into a trading loss, which, after being set against any non-trading profits of the current year, may be carried back against the total profits of the previous three years, latest first, so long as the trade was carried on in those years (see chapter 26).

Looking into the future

If all current-year profits are used to pay remuneration, there will be nothing against which to carry back any later trading losses. The expected future performance (including any imminent expenditure on equipment and commercial buildings in an enterprise zone) should therefore be taken into account in considering whether to reduce or eliminate profits for the current year.

Pensions (TA 1988, Part XIV, Chapters I–IV)

The company may have its own pension scheme, either through an insurance company or self-administered. Provided that the benefits under the scheme are within the limits laid down by the Revenue, the company's contributions are allowable in calculating its taxable profit, and are not taxable on the director.

If there is no such scheme, a director may pay premiums himself under a personal pension plan. Although the allowable premium is limited annually to a percentage of earnings depending upon age (see chapter 17), you can include the earnings of the previous six years in the maximum premium calculation to the extent that they have not already been used to cover a pension contribution. This may enable you to make a large payment in a single year and take equivalent pay from the company without paying tax, although you would still have to pay national insurance contributions if you were not already paying the maximum and the company would have to pay employer's national insurance contributions in any event. The premium payment might be funded by a loan-back facility arranged by or in conjunction with the insurance company. The company could itself contribute to your pension plan within the available limits, and neither tax nor national insurance would be payable on the amount contributed by the company. Since the income and gains of both company and personal pension funds are usually exempt from tax, paying pension contributions rather than taking salary and investing it privately will be a more tax-efficient method of saving for the future. With company schemes, the permissible benefits may depend upon remuneration, so that restricting salary unduly may affect the available benefits. With personal pension schemes, the benefits depend only upon contributions (which will themselves have been limited by relevant earnings). For further details on pensions, see chapters 16 and 17.

Limits on allowable remuneration

Remuneration, like any other trading expense, must be incurred wholly and exclusively for the purposes of the trade (see chapter 20). If it is regarded as excessive in relation to the duties, part may not be allowed as a deduction in calculating company profits. This should be borne in mind when considering payments of remuneration, either by way of cash or as benefits in kind, to members of a director's or shareholder's family.

Employing a spouse and children in the family company may be useful, particularly if they are not otherwise using their personal allowance, but the amount may be questioned by the Revenue, who will want to be sure that the work done is of sufficient quantity and quality to justify the amount paid. If children are under 16 you must also comply with the regulations as to permitted hours of work, which vary according to local bye-laws. Payments by a farmer to his very young children have been held to be 'pocket money' and disallowed in calculating the taxable profits of the farm.

Waiving an entitlement to remuneration (IHTA 1984, s 14; TA 1988, s 231(3A)–(3D))

There is no income tax on remuneration which is not received, so that an entitlement to remuneration can be waived to assist in a difficult period of trading, or because of a high personal tax rate. It is also specifically provided that no inheritance tax liability arises from such a waiver. The waiver might enable the company to pay higher remuneration to other directors or family members (provided always that it is justifiable under the 'wholly and exclusively' rule) or to increase its profits available for dividends. But if the company is within the definition of a close investment-holding company (see page 39), the Revenue may block the repayment of the tax credit on a dividend if they believe there were deliberate arrangements aimed at generating the tax refund, such as the waiver of dividends by those liable at the higher rate of tax in favour of young family members with unused personal allowances.

Benefits in kind provided by the company

Directors and employees with earnings of £8,500 or more per annum are charged to tax on the cash equivalent of benefits in kind. Directors are caught by these provisions even if they earn less than £8,500 unless they do not own more than 5% of the ordinary share capital (including shares owned by close family and certain other people) and either work full-time or work for a charitable or non-profit-making body.

Benefits may take the form of the outright gift of an asset or of allowing the director/employee to use a company asset. The company is allowed to deduct the cost of providing benefits in calculating its taxable profit, subject to what is said above. The charge on the director/employee is broadly the cost to the company, including VAT where appropriate (whether recovered or not, in the view of the Revenue), or, if the asset remains the company's property, the 'annual value' of its use. The detailed provisions for calculating the charge are in chapter 10.

Using company funds to buy assets that the directors are able to use may be better than providing the directors with funds to enable them to buy the assets themselves, because national insurance contributions would not normally be payable on the benefit of using the assets (see chapter 13 for exceptions). If, however, the expenditure has no relevance to the management or trade of the company, the Revenue would be justified in arguing that it relates to the directors personally, and would look to them to pay in an equivalent amount to the company.

Gifts of company assets (IHTA 1984, s 94; TA 1988, s 418)

Gifts of company assets to directors and employees are covered by the benefits rules mentioned above and explained in detail in chapter 10. If an asset is given to a shareholder who is not a director or employee, the company has to pay ACT on its cost as if it were a dividend, and the total of the cost and the related tax credit is included in the shareholder's taxable income.

If a gift is made to someone who is neither a director/employee nor a shareholder nor connected with them, an apportionment of its value is made among the shareholders for inheritance tax purposes, the shareholders then being treated as having made personal transfers of the amount apportioned to them.

Loans from the company (TA 1988, ss 160, 161, 419–421, 826(4); FA 1996, s 173; Revenue Statement of Practice SP 7/79)

Directors and employees earning £8,500 or more per annum who overdraw their current accounts with the company or who receive specific loans from the company, either interest-free or at a beneficial rate, are treated as having received remuneration equivalent to interest at the 'official rate' (see page 160) on the amount overdrawn or lent, less any amount paid to the company towards the benefit they have received. This does not apply if the total beneficial loans outstanding in a tax year do not exceed £5,000. If the loan is to buy the family home, the tax charge is reduced by the appropriate tax relief on the interest on the first £30,000 of the loan (see page 160). Where a director or employee receives an advance for expenses necessarily incurred in performing his duties, the Revenue do not treat the advance as a loan, provided that

(a) the maximum amount advanced at any one time does not exceed £1,000,
(b) the advances are spent within six months, and
(c) the director or employee accounts to the company at regular intervals for the expenditure.

As well as the tax charge on the director or employee on interest-free or cheap loans, there are tax implications for the company if it is a close company in which the director or employee is a shareholder, and these provisions do not depend on whether any interest is charged. A close company is broadly one controlled by its directors or by five or fewer people. Loans and advances to shareholders (including shareholders who are directors or employees) give rise to a tax liability on the company, except for loans not exceeding £15,000 made to a full-time working director or employee who does not own more than 5% of the ordinary share capital. The company has to notify the Revenue not later than 12 months after the end of the accounting period in which the loan is made, and must pay tax at the ACT rate (currently 1/4) on the amount of the loan or overdrawn account balance.

The tax has previously been payable 14 days after the end of the accounting period in which the loan was made (even though the company did not have to notify the Revenue until much later) and interest on unpaid tax has been charged accordingly. The company has been able to claim repayment of the tax from the Revenue as and when the loan was repaid, and interest on the repayment has run from the date the loan was repaid, or if later, the date the tax was paid.

For accounting periods ending on or after 31 March 1996, the due date for payment of the tax will be 9 months after the end of the accounting period in which the loan is made (i.e. the same as the due date for the corporation tax of that period), and the tax need not be paid at all if the loan has been repaid before the due date. Where the loan is repaid after the tax falls due and has been paid by the company, the tax paid may be reclaimed. The tax repayment will be due 9 months after the end of the accounting period in which the loan is repaid, and will be increased by interest from that 9 months date if relevant.

If a loan or overdrawing is written off by the company, the tax treatment is different for loans made to shareholders by close companies and for other loans.

If a loan by a close company to a shareholder is written off, the shareholder will not be affected unless he is a higher rate taxpayer. Higher rate taxpayers are taxed as if the amount written off was income net of 20% tax, and have to pay the difference between the 20% tax treated as paid and the higher rate of 40%. A loan of £10,000 written off would be regarded as income of £12,500, on which an extra 20% was payable, amounting to £2,500.

If the write-off of a loan is not caught by the close company rules, and it has been obtained by reason of the borrower's employment, whether or not it is at a rate of interest below the 'official rate', the director or employee is treated as having received an equivalent amount of remuneration at that time. (This does not apply to loans written off on death.)

If a non-close company wrote off a loan made to someone who was not a director or employee, there would not usually be any tax consequences for the borrower whether he was a shareholder or not, but the company would not be able to claim a deduction for the write-off unless its business included lending money.

195

As well as the tax aspects, the company law restrictions on directors' loans must also be observed.

Liabilities in connection with directors' remuneration

Remuneration is regarded as paid not only when it forms part of the payroll but also when it is credited to the director's current account with the company and the liability of the company to account for PAYE and national insurance arises at that time. The credit to the current account should therefore be made net of employee's tax and national insurance contributions. Drawings from the account can be made without any further liability once the PAYE and national insurance have been accounted for to the Revenue. If a company pays remuneration to a director and bears the PAYE itself, the amount that should have been borne by the director is treated as extra remuneration and taxable accordingly (TA 1988, s 164).

Where a director receives payments in advance or on account of future remuneration this has to be treated as pay for tax and national insurance purposes at the time of the advance, unless the advances are covered by a credit balance on the director's loan account or are on account of expenses as indicated on page 194.

An advance payment of remuneration is not the same as a loan. The income tax treatment of loans is stated on pages 194, 195. The DSS have revised their earlier view that where a director's private bills are paid by the company and charged to the director's loan account, national insurance contributions are payable. They now state the contributions are only due if a director's account becomes overdrawn *and* the director's earnings are normally paid into that account (see page 202).

It used to be possible to reduce national insurance contributions by paying remuneration at uneven rates and irregular intervals, but this is now prevented by the method of calculating earnings limits. The detailed provisions are in chapter 13.

If employers fail to deduct and account for PAYE and national insurance contributions when due, they may incur interest and/or penalties. Directors may also be personally liable to pay the tax on their remuneration if they knew of the failure to deduct tax.

Tax points

● Always look at the combined company/director/shareholder position in considering the most appropriate way of dealing with available profits, and consider past and future years as well as the current year.

● Make effective use of company or personal pension funds, which should grow faster than individual investments because of their tax exemption. Remember in the case of company pension funds that in calculating corporation tax, relief is only given in the accounting period when the pension premium is paid, so that it is not possible to reduce taxable profits of one year by making a payment in the next year and relating it back. It is therefore essential to anticipate the profit level if a pension contribution is to be used as a way of reducing corporation tax for a particular accounting period.

- A similar timing point applies to dividends, in that ACT on a dividend paid say in August 1996, following a 30 June year end, will be due to be paid to the Revenue under the quarterly system by 14 October 1996, but it will be set against the corporation tax due on 1 April 1998 (for year to 30 June 1997) (see page 33). If the dividend had been paid two months earlier, in June 1996, the ACT would have been payable on 14 July 1996, but would reduce the tax due on 1 April 1997.

- When considering dividend payments, remember that dividends to minority shareholders may affect the valuation of their holdings.

- In considering the payment of a dividend instead of remuneration, remember that future entitlement under a pension scheme may be adversely affected by limiting the amount of remuneration.

- You are not charged either to tax or national insurance contributions on pension contributions by your employer to an approved company scheme or to your own approved personal pension scheme. Your own contributions either to a company or private scheme reduce your income for tax, but not for employees' national insurance contributions.

- Director/shareholders taking a sizeable dividend from a company could avoid higher rate tax, and possibly recover the dividend tax credit, by investing in a commercial building in an enterprise zone (see chapter 32). To retain the tax allowance, however, they would have to leave the money invested for at least seven years, and the commercial viability of the purchase must not be ignored.

- See at the end of chapter 10 the tax point dealing with the provision of a company car to an employee who is a member of a director's family or household.

- Remuneration is regarded as paid when it is credited to an account with the company in the name of a director. The fact that it is not drawn by him but left to his credit in the company (in other words, available for drawing) does not prevent the appropriate tax and national insurance being payable at the time the remuneration is credited. The director's account should be credited only with the net amount after tax and national insurance. If the gross amount is credited, whether or not it is drawn out, and the company fails to account to the Revenue for the tax and national insurance, the director may be personally liable for the failure under the PAYE regulations.

- If your company has failed to pay over the PAYE tax and national insurance on your pay within 14 days of the year end, the Revenue may look to you for payment plus interest, providing you were aware of the company's failure to comply with the PAYE regulations.

● Interest is charged on tax and national insurance contributions that remain unpaid 14 days after the end of the tax year, e.g. from 19 April 1996 for 1995/96.

● If, before a director is credited with additional remuneration, his current account with the company is overdrawn, the Revenue will usually contend that the date on which the additional remuneration can be regarded as credited is that on which the accounts are signed (or the date when a clear entitlement to the remuneration was established — for example a properly evidenced directors'/share-holders' meeting) rather than the end of the accounting year for which the additional remuneration was paid. This can significantly affect the tax charge on the director in respect of beneficial interest (see page 160).

● Benefits in kind assessed to income tax on directors must be distin-guished from personal commitments of a director which are paid for by his family company. The latter, including any VAT, must be reim-bursed to the company by the director or charged against money owed by the company to the director. They are neither allowable in calculat-ing the company taxable profit nor assessable as income on the director.

● For accounting periods ending on or after 31 March 1996, companies are no longer expected to pay the tax due on loans to directors within 14 days of the end of the accounting period. The due date is now the same as that for mainstream corporation tax, i.e. 9 months after the end of the accounting period (see page 195).

● The DSS take the view that if payment of a director's personal bills by his company is not covered by a credit balance on the director's account, and his earnings are normally paid into that account, national insurance contributions are due on the amount paid — see page 196.

13
National insurance contributions — employees and employers

Background

The growing cost of the State pension scheme is causing concern, and it has been suggested that at some future time pensions will not be received as of right but will be subject to means testing. In order to equalise pension ages for men and women without considerably increasing the cost of providing pensions, the State pension age is to become 65 for both men and women from 2020. The change is to be phased in from 2010 to 2020. Women born after 5 April 1955 will be subject to the new retirement age of 65, but women born before 6 April 1950 will still qualify at 60.

A large part of the cost of the social security system is funded from contributions made by people currently earning money either as employees or as self-employed persons. The legislation is in the Social Security Contributions and Benefits Act 1992 (SSCBA 1992). How much you have to contribute and the rules for collecting it depend upon which 'class' of contribution is to be paid. The contribution rates are shown on page xxvii. The functions of the Department of Social Security (DSS) are split between the Contributions Agency and the Benefits Agency. For both Agencies the term DSS has been used in this Guide.

Unless they are 'contracted out' (see page 226), employees and their employers pay Class 1 contributions under the State Earnings Related Pension Scheme (SERPS), the contributions being based on a percentage of earnings. Payments made by employees are known as 'primary' contributions, those by employers as 'secondary' contributions. A separate category of contributions, Class 1A, is payable annually by employers (not employees) on the provision of cars and private fuel to P11D employees — see page 203. Class 1 and 1A national insurance contributions are collected through the PAYE system — for details, see chapter 10. The self-employed pay Class 2 and Class 4 contributions (see chapter 24). Voluntary Class 3 contributions may be paid by those who would otherwise not pay enough contributions to earn a full pension (see below). Details of the various contribution rates are shown on page xxvii.

From 6 April 1996, employers who take on someone who has been out of work for two years or more will get a full rebate of national insurance contributions for that person for up to a year (see page 208).

Pensions

In general, in order to get a full basic pension, Class 1 contributions must be paid or credited equal to 52 times the lower earnings limit (see page 204) in at least nine in every ten years of your working life from 16 to 65 for a man or 60 for a woman, or you must have paid 52 Class 2 or Class 3 (voluntary) contributions for those years. Employees receive a higher pension than the basic amount depending on their earnings. (For this purpose, family credit and disability working allowance paid from 6 April 1995 count as earnings.) For the purpose of the basic pension, you are credited with contributions when you are registered as unemployed or receiving jobseeker's allowance, or unable to work through incapacity or disability, or because you receive invalid care allowance for looking after someone who is disabled, or if you receive maternity allowance or (from 6 April 1995) family credit. If you are an unemployed man aged 60 to 64 you automatically get credits whether or not you are ill or on the unemployment register. Credits will usually be given to those aged 16 to 18 who would otherwise not have paid enough contributions, and also for certain periods of full-time training lasting up to twelve months, but not for longer courses such as university degree courses. Those who stay at home to look after children or sick or elderly people usually get Home Responsibilities Protection, which reduces the number of years needed to qualify for full pension. If you do not earn enough, either as an employee or in your self-employment, to pay the required level of Class 1 or 2 contributions, you may pay voluntary Class 3 contributions to help you to qualify for the retirement and widow's pension. You can check with your local DSS office to see whether your contribution record is not good enough to earn you a full pension. Late contributions can be paid for the previous six years (but sometimes at a higher rate). Married women paying reduced contributions (see page 205) are not entitled to contribution credits and cannot pay Class 3 contributions. They get a pension equal to 60% of the husband's basic pension when the husband is over 65 and the wife is over 60. The same applies to other married women who have not paid enough full rate contributions to earn a higher pension in their own right. A husband with a non-working wife under 60 gets an addition to his pension for her, unless she earns more than £48.25 a week. (This addition counts as his income, not hers.)

Widows usually get a full basic pension at 60 (subject to the contribution requirements), whether it is based on their own or their husband's contributions, unless in the latter case they were too young when their husband died or when their children grew up. But if they remarry before age 60, then unless they are claiming on their own contributions the pension will only be at 60% of the full amount and they will not get a pension until they are 60 and their new husband is 65. Remarriage after age 60 would not affect their entitlement to the full pension.

It has been beneficial for those of pension age who were entitled to invalidity benefit to defer claiming retirement pension, because retirement pension is taxable, whereas invalidity benefit was not. Invalidity benefit (and sickness benefit) were replaced from 13 April 1995 by incapacity benefit, which is taxable after the first 28 weeks, and is not payable after pension age unless the claimant was below pension age when the incapacity began. Anyone receiving the tax-free invalidity benefit on 12 April 1995 will not pay tax on the incapacity benefit while that incapacity lasts. For someone on invalidity benefit and over pension age on 12 April 1995, the benefit of receiving a tax-free amount in the deferral period instead of the taxable retirement pension will still be available while the incapacity lasts.

Persons liable to pay Class 1 contributions (SSCBA 1992, ss 2, 6(1))

Unless specifically exempted (see below), all 'employed earners' and their employers must pay Class 1 contributions. An 'employed earner' is a person who is paid either as an employee under a contract of service or as the holder of an office with earnings chargeable to income tax under Schedule E (see chapter 10).

DSS leaflet NI 39 outlines various criteria which are taken into account in deciding whether a person is employed. For details, see page 260.

Certain people are specifically brought within the liability to Class 1 contributions, including office and similar cleaners, most agency workers (including 'temps' but excluding outworkers), wives employed in their husbands' businesses and vice versa, ministers of religion paid chiefly by way of stipend or salary, and certain part-time lecturers and teachers.

Certain employees and their employers are exempted from payment of Class 1 contributions. These are

(a)   people aged under 16,
(b)   people whose earnings are below the weekly lower earnings limit (£61.00 for 1996/97),
(c)   a wife employed by her husband for a non-business purpose and vice versa,
(d)   people employed for a non-business purpose by a close relative in the home where they both live,
(e)   returning and counting officers and people employed by them in connection with an election or referendum, and
(f)   certain employees of international organisations and visiting armed forces.

Special rules apply to those who go to work abroad — see page 567.

Earnings (SSCBA 1992, ss 3, 4)

Class 1 contributions are calculated on gross pay, which is broadly the same as pay for income tax, but before deducting:

Employees' pension contributions to occupational or private schemes;

Charitable gifts under payroll giving scheme;

and including:

Profit-related pay (even if exempt from income tax) (see chapter 11);

Expenses payments to employees count as pay except to the extent that they are for proper business expenses, for which receipts or records must be available. Reimbursement of an employee's car parking expenses, for example, must be for recorded business-related journeys. From 6 April 1995, where the Revenue have granted a dispensation allowing expenses payments to be ignored for tax purposes, the same treatment will apply for national insurance, and the exemption for personal expenses of £5 a night (£10 if outside the UK) also applies (see page 153). From the same date, contributions are not due on payments for directors' liability insurance, etc. (see page 153).

Contributions are not normally payable on benefits in kind or on tips unless the employer decides how they are to be shared out and the money passes through the employer. Many benefits have, however, been made specifically chargeable (see below). There are also various traps that may cause benefits to be chargeable depending on the way they are provided, and the information in the Employers' Manual on National Insurance Contributions (CA 28) needs to be studied carefully.

One item that needs particular care is the payment by the employer of a debt contracted by the employee, which counts as pay both for national insurance and for income tax. The DSS have, however, now accepted that payment of a director's bills where the payment is charged to the director's account with the company does not count as pay unless the account becomes overdrawn, and even then, only if the director's earnings are normally paid into the account. Those who have been wrongly charged national insurance contributions in these circumstances should apply to the DSS for a refund. If a payment is made under a contract made by the employer, then unless the contract relates to a specifically chargeable item, the payment does not count as pay for national insurance (for example paying the bills for a telephone at an employee's home where the employer has made the contract with the telephone company, or buying a season ticket for an employee).

Pay specifically includes benefits in the form of gilt-edged securities, shares, debentures, units in unit trusts, futures, options, premium bonds, national savings certificates, gold bullion, assets capable of being traded on a recognised investment exchange and (from 6 April 1995) assets (including vouchers) which the employer has arranged for the employees to exchange for cash. The same applies to vouchers to obtain any such assets. Vouchers for private car fuel in a car belonging to the employer are subject to employers' Class 1A contributions — see below. Other vouchers do not count as pay unless they can be exchanged for cash, or a mixture of goods and cash.

Cars and car fuel — Class 1A contributions (SSCBA 1992, s 10)

Class 1A contributions are payable by employers on the provision of cars and private fuel to employees (see page xxviii). Employees' contributions are not, however, payable. The calculated income tax car and fuel benefits are used to determine the chargeable amount and the amount due is payable annually in arrear (see page 170), the 1996/97 payment being due by 19 June 1997 (or 19 July 1997 if quarterly payments are made). Records must be kept in order to substantiate business mileage above the 2,500 threshold, otherwise the full rate will apply, and, similarly, a claim that business mileage is 18,000 or more must be supported by documentary evidence.

If private fuel is provided for use in an employee's own car, Class 1A contributions do not apply but there may be liability for both employer's and employee's Class 1 contributions depending on how the fuel is provided. Broadly contributions will not be due if a credit card, petrol agency card, petrol vouchers or employer's garage account is used providing the garage is told that the fuel is being bought on behalf of the employer. Reimbursement of an employee's fuel expenses will count as pay except to the extent that business mileage can be identified. For 1996/97, mileage allowances for business fuel at the Fixed Profit Car Scheme higher rates (i.e. those up to 4,000 miles — see page xxii) will not count as pay. The AA rates for 10,000 miles of travel were used for 1995/96.

Contracted-out employees

Retirement and widows' pensions consist of two parts, a basic flat-rate pension, and an additional pension related to the level of the employee's earnings. The additional pension is paid under the State Earnings Related Pension Scheme (SERPS).

Employees who are members of occupational pension schemes which meet the requirements of the Occupational Pensions Regulatory Authority can be 'contracted-out' of the additional pension for retirement and part of the additional pension for widowhood by their employers. Contracted-out employees are still eligible for the basic pension from the state but obtain their additional pension from their employer's occupational pension scheme. To help meet the cost of setting up and running a separate pension scheme, contracted-out employees and their employers pay reduced rates of Class 1 contributions. The combined employer/employee contracting-out rebate is 4.8%.

Employees may also contract out of SERPS by entering into personal pension arrangements, to which their employers may or may not contribute (see chapter 17). Both employer and employee continue to pay full national insurance contributions, and the contracting-out rebate is paid by the DSS into the personal pension scheme. At present, the rebate for those with personal pension plans is topped up by a 1% bonus if they are aged 30 or over at the beginning of the relevant year. From April 1997, all contracting-out rebates of Class 1 contributions for both personal pension plans and contracted-out money purchase schemes will be age-related, ranging from 3.4% to 9% for personal pension plans and 3.1% to 9% for money purchase schemes. The rebate for contracted-out salary related schemes will be 4.6%. Employers with a contracted-out money purchase scheme will apply a rebated national insurance contribution for scheme members based on the lowest age-related rebates level. The relevant information will be recorded on year-end forms P14 and the DSS will pay the age-related rebate top-up when they receive the forms P14.

Contribution rates (SSCBA 1992, ss 1, 5, 8, 9)

National insurance rates for 1995/96 and 1996/97 are shown in the tables on page xxvii.

Employers' national insurance contributions are deductible in arriving at their taxable profits, so that the burden of employers' national insurance contributions is reduced by the tax saved on them. Tax on employees' earnings, on the other hand, is calculated on the gross pay before deducting national insurance contributions.

No national insurance contributions are payable by either employee or employer if weekly earnings are below the lower earnings limit (£61 for 1996/97). If weekly earnings exceed that amount, then for 1996/97, employees who are not contracted out pay 2% on the first £61 and 10% on the balance up to the upper earnings limit of £455 per week; their employers pay 3% if weekly earnings are less than £110, 5% if they are less than £155, 7% if they are less than £210 and 10.2% on all earnings of £210 per week and over, with no upper limit. (The 10.2% rate is to be reduced to 10% from April 1997.)

As far as employers' contributions are concerned, there is a disproportionate extra cost when an employee's earnings move from one rate band to another. For example, on earnings of £209 an employer's contributions are 7%, amounting to £14.63. On earnings of £210 the rate is 10.2%, giving contributions of £21.42, so that the extra £1 pay has cost an extra £6.79 contributions. (The employer's contributions are, however, tax deductible, so that the net of tax extra cost will be less.) There is a similar, though less significant, anomaly for an employee in that if wages rise from £60 to £61 per week, the additional £1 will cost national insurance contributions of £1.22.

Contributions for contracted-out employees are payable at the above rates, less a reduction on weekly earnings, for 1996/97, between £61 and £455 of 1.8% for the employee and 3% for the employer.

The reduced rate of employees' contributions for certain married women and widows is shown on page 205.

Employee contributions

Reduced rate for certain married women and widows

Women who were married or widowed as at 6 April 1977 may have chosen on or before 11 May 1977 to pay Class 1 contributions at a reduced rate. If they are still entitled to pay the reduced contributions, they hold a certificate (form CF 383) which must be handed over to the employer to enable him to deduct contributions at the correct rate.

If a married woman is self-employed, the election makes her exempt from paying Class 2 contributions, but not Class 4 contributions (see chapter 24).

The reduced rate for 1996/97, which applies once earnings reach £61 a week and is the same for both contracted-out and non-contracted-out employees, is 3.85% on earnings up to £455 per week.

A wife who pays reduced rate contributions is not eligible to receive contributory benefits, but she can claim retirement and widow's pension on the contribution record of her husband. She is also entitled to receive statutory sick pay and statutory maternity pay. The retirement pension a wife will get is 60% of the husband's basic pension if the husband is over 65 and the wife is over 60 (see page 200). She will not get any earnings-related pension.

The election to pay reduced rate contributions is effective until it is cancelled or revoked. A woman loses the right to pay reduced rate contributions

(a) if she is divorced, in which case the right is lost immediately after the decree absolute, or

(b) if she becomes widowed and is not entitled to widow's benefit, in which case the right is not lost until the end of the tax year in which the husband dies, or the end of the following tax year if he dies between 1 October and 5 April, or

(c) if she pays no reduced rate Class 1 contributions and has no earnings from self-employment for two consecutive tax years.

An election can be revoked in writing at any time and the revocation will, in most instances, take effect from the beginning of the following tax year. If the election is revoked, the wife will start earning a pension, including earnings-related pension, in her own right, and she will also be entitled to claim maternity allowance, unemployment benefit (or, from October 1996, job-seeker's allowance) and incapacity benefit.

Some women on low pay could pay lower contributions if they revoke their reduced rate election, as shown in example 1. But once the election is revoked, it cannot be revived, so if the earnings rise, the contributions will increase. Older women will often be no better off by revoking the election. Those who are considering revoking may get a pensions forecast from the DSS. They should get form BR 19 from their local social security office.

Example 1

A married woman who has made a reduced rate election earns £63 a week.

Her weekly reduced rate contribution is £2.42. If she revoked the election, she would pay full rate contributions of £1.42 a week.

People over pensionable age

No contributions are payable by an employee who is over pension age (65 for a man, 60 for a woman), although the employer is still liable for secondary contributions where earnings reach the lower earnings limit, such contributions always being at non-contracted-out rates.

Employees who are not liable to pay contributions should apply for a certificate of age exception (form CF 384). This should be given to the employer as authority for Class 1 contributions not to be deducted from earnings.

More than one employment

Where a person has more than one employment, he is liable to pay primary Class 1 contributions in respect of each job. There is however a prescribed annual maximum contribution.

The maximum is based on 53 weeks' contributions. The amounts for 1995/96 are:

All employments non-contracted-out	All employments contracted-out	Reduced rate
£2,152.86	£1,777.09	£928.03

Where an employee has both contracted-out and non-contracted-out employments, the contracted-out contributions are converted to the non-contracted-out level to see whether the annual maximum has been exceeded.

If at the end of a tax year an employee's contributions have exceeded the prescribed maximum by a stipulated amount (£2.70 for 1996/97), a refund is available. An employee may obtain a refund by submitting form CF 28F together with evidence of excess payments, e.g. certificates of pay, tax and NIC (forms P60). Refunds of over £30.50 are made automatically, without the need for a claim.

To avoid having to pay contributions in all employments throughout the year and being refunded any excess after the end of the year, an employee may apply to defer some of his contributions. An application form for deferment of contributions can be found in DSS booklet CA 01, and if deferment is granted, a certificate (form RD 950) will be sent to the employers concerned (except those paying the earnings upon which the maximum contributions are calculated) authorising them not to deduct the employee's contributions. All employers must, however, continue to pay employers' contributions.

As an alternative to applying for deferment of contributions, an employee may pay the maximum contributions in advance. Where this is done, all employers will be instructed not to deduct primary contributions.

To prevent abuse of the system, there are 'anti-avoidance' provisions as follows:

(a) Where a person has more than one job with the same employer, earnings from those employments must be added together and contributions calculated on the total;

(b) Where a person has jobs with different employers who 'carry on business in association with each other', all earnings from 'associated' employers must be added together for the purpose of calculating contributions.

These rules will not be enforced if it can be shown that to do so would be impracticable.

Income from self-employment

The position of the employee who also has income from self-employment is dealt with in chapter 24.

Company directors

Directors sometimes receive a salary under a service contract and also fees for holding the office of director. They are often paid in irregular amounts at irregular time intervals, for example a fixed monthly salary together with a bonus after the year end, once the results of the company are known. To ensure that this does not lead to manipulation of liability to pay national insurance contributions, directors in employment at the beginning of a tax year presently have an annual earnings period coinciding with the tax year. Those appointed during a tax year have an earnings period equal to the number of weeks from the date of appointment to the end of the tax year. No Class 1 contributions are due if the director's earnings are less than the annual lower earnings limit (1996/97 £3,172) or a pro-rata limit for directors appointed during a tax year (using the appropriate multiple of the weekly limit).

All earnings paid to a director during an earnings period must be included in that earnings period (irrespective of the period to which they relate). Earnings include fees, bonuses, salary, payments made in anticipation of future earnings, and payments made to a director which were earned while he was still an employee.

If a director resigns, all payments made to him between the date of resignation and the end of the tax year that relate to his period of directorship must be linked to his other 'directorship earnings' of that tax year. If any such earnings are paid in a later tax year, they are not added to any other earnings of the year in which payment is made. Instead, they are considered independently on an annual earnings basis, and Class 1 contributions accounted for accordingly.

Many directors have payments in anticipation of future earnings, e.g. a payment on account of a bonus to be declared when the company's results are known. Liability for Class 1 contributions arises when the payments are made (subject, of course, to the lower earnings limit). The advance bonus payments are added to all other earnings of the annual earnings period. When the bonus is voted (probably at the annual general meeting) the balance, if any, will become liable to Class 1 contributions in the tax year in which the annual general meeting is held. Once a bonus is voted for a past period, it is deemed to be paid whether it is placed in an account on which the director can draw or left in the company, unless exceptionally it is not placed at the director's disposal.

To the extent that a director makes drawings against a credit balance on his director's loan account, no Class 1 liability will arise as these drawings simply reduce the balance of the loan account. If the loan account has been built up from undrawn remuneration, the Class 1 liability will have arisen at the time the remuneration was credited to it.

Proposals are currently under consideration for allowing directors' contributions to be calculated in the same way as for other employees, subject to certain safeguards, rather than by using the 'annual earnings period' rules outlined above. If adopted, it is expected that they will come into force from 6 April 1997.

NIC holiday

The April 1996 supplement to CA 28 contains the detailed provisions of the NIC holiday scheme. Employers may claim back their secondary national insurance contributions in respect of an employee starting work with them on or after 6 April 1996 who has been out of work for two years, providing the employment lasts for at least 13 weeks, the person is under State pension age on the day he/she starts work and he/she agrees to participate. Women paying reduced rate contributions may be included in the scheme. The NIC holiday period lasts for a year from the start of employment, or until State pension age or the end of the employment if sooner.

Employers must apply to join the scheme on form A503 (which the employee should provide), and will receive a deduction certificate entitling them to make the deductions. Contributions are calculated and paid for relevant employees in the normal way. Where contracted-out contributions are paid, the employer can nonetheless recover contributions at the full rate. The amount recoverable is deducted from the monthly PAYE payment. Details of the deductions are shown on tax deduction cards and year-end forms.

Tax points

- If an employee has several employments, he can get back national insurance contributions in excess of the annual maximum. Refunds are not, however, available in respect of employers' contributions.

- If your wife or husband pays maximum contributions in a separate job and also does some work in the family business run by you, you cannot get back employers' national insurance on the earnings from the family business, so it may be more sensible to pay your spouse less than the weekly limit. Remember, however, that earnings of either of you as an *employee* of the family business must be justified if relief for tax is to be given in calculating the business profits.

- Except for company directors, who have an annual earnings period coinciding with the tax year, or for the remainder of the tax year in which they are appointed, national insurance does not work on a cumulative basis. If average earnings will not exceed the national insurance threshold, try to ensure that the actual earnings in any week do not do so, otherwise both employer and employee will be liable to pay contributions for that particular week even though on a cumulative basis the earnings threshold may not have been reached.

- The annual maximum contribution liability is based on 53 weeks' contributions, although there are rarely 53 pay days in a year. If you have more than one job and earn more than £455 a week from one of them, make sure you apply for deferment. You will then not have any more to pay at the year end, whereas if you wait for a refund, you will only get back any excess over *53 weeks'* contributions. Even if you do not earn more than £455 a week from one job, applying for deferment where your *total* earnings exceed that amount is better than waiting for a refund after the year end.

- Since there is no upper limit to the earnings on which employers' contributions are payable, it may be cheaper for the remuneration package to include those benefits in kind which, whilst taxable, do not presently attract a national insurance liability.

- Similarly, dividends paid to shareholders do not attract national insurance contributions. It may be appropriate for shareholders/directors to receive dividends rather than additional remuneration. It is important to ensure that dividends are properly documented so that they cannot be challenged as pay.

This aspect must not, however, be looked at in isolation. Many others are important, e.g. the level of remuneration for company or personal pension purposes, and the effect of a dividend policy on other share-holders. See chapter 12 for illustrations.

● If you can justifiably pay remuneration to your wife or husband up to the limit of the available personal allowance for income tax, consider paying just below the national insurance threshold each week and a bonus to make the wages up to the required amount at the end of March. Employer's and employee's contributions will then only be payable for the week in which the bonus is paid, giving a significant national insurance saving. This will not apply if the wife/husband is a director with an annual earnings period. The effect on benefit entitle-ment should also be considered. The DSS might take action to block the saving, but not retrospectively.

● If you have been paying the reduced married woman's rate of contri-bution, watch the circumstances in which you have to revert to the full rate, for example when you get divorced (see page 205). If you underpay, even by mistake, you will probably have to make up the difference. But you do not have to pay contributions at all from age 60.

● Remember that if you have not paid enough contributions for a year to be classed as a qualifying year, your State pension may be affected (see page 200). Class 3 voluntary contributions can be paid to maintain your contribution record.

● If an employer pays an employee's debt, it counts as pay for national insurance and for income tax. Where possible, make sure the contract is made by the employer.

● For Class 1A contributions on cars and fuel, you need records to show that business miles exceed 2,500 or 18,000 as the case may be. This does not mean *all* business miles must be logged, only enough to show that the appropriate threshold has been reached.

● Records are needed to prove business use in other areas, such as for mileage allowances to those who use their own cars (see page 152 re business mileage rates), and for contributions towards an employee's telephone bill, unless, in the case of telephones, there is a Revenue agreed business proportion, which will now also be accepted by the DSS.

14
Statutory sick pay and statutory maternity pay

Background

The provisions on statutory sick pay (SSP) and statutory maternity pay (SMP) are in the Social Security Contributions and Benefits Act 1992. Most employees are entitled to receive SSP from their employers for up to 28 weeks of sickness absence. From 6 April 1995 SSP is paid at a single flat rate. SMP is paid at two rates, the higher rate being dependent on the employee's earnings and the lower rate being a fixed amount. Both SSP and SMP count as pay for income tax and national insurance contributions. From 6 April 1995, all employers are entitled to recover SSP to the extent that it exceeds a stipulated monthly threshold — see page 217. For weeks beginning on or after 2 April 1995, employers are able to recover 92% of SMP, unless they qualify for Small Employers' Relief, in which case they can recover 100% of the SMP plus a further 5.5% (5% before 5 April 1996) to compensate for the national insurance contributions on the SMP (see page 219). A checklist and worksheet (SP 33) is available to help small employers operate the SSP scheme.

Certain of the rules for SSP and SMP have been relaxed from 6 April 1996. There is also a proposal to allow employers to opt out of the SSP scheme if they pay wages or sick pay at or above the SSP rates. If introduced, it is intended that this will apply from April 1997.

Employees entitled to receive SSP

The definition of an employee is the same as that of an 'employed earner' for Class 1 national insurance contributions (see chapter 13). Married women and widows paying reduced rate Class 1 contributions are therefore entitled to SSP.

An employee is entitled to SSP for each job he has, so that if an individual is employed by two different employers he will be paid SSP by each employer when off work through illness.

An employee is entitled to SSP unless he/she falls into one of the excluded groups (see page 212).

When an employee is being paid SSP he is not entitled to State incapacity benefit. Employees who are not entitled to SSP and employees who have exhausted their SSP entitlement may claim incapacity benefit (see page 201).

Employees excluded from SSP

Employees who, at the beginning of a 'period of incapacity for work' (see below), fall into one of the following categories cannot claim SSP.

(a) People over 65.

(b) Those who have claimed incapacity benefit, severe disablement allowance or maternity allowance within the 57 days before falling ill. An employee who has received one of these benefits will receive a letter from the DSS (known as a 'linking letter') notifying the employer of the period of exclusion.

(c) Those whose average weekly earnings (usually calculated over the previous 8 weeks) are below the lower earnings limit for national insurance contributions (£61 for 1996/97 — see chapter 13).

(d) A person who has not begun work under his contract.

(e) Those who become ill while they are away from work because of a trade dispute, unless the employee can prove that he is not participating in, or directly interested in, the dispute.

(f) A pregnant woman during her disqualifying period of eighteen weeks (see page 213).

(g) Those who have received twenty-eight weeks' SSP from their previous employer(s). This further exclusion does not prevent an employee receiving SSP if he should fall ill more than eight weeks after the end of the previous period of incapacity.

(h) Those who fall ill while in prison or in legal custody.

(j) Those contracted to work for a period not exceeding three months (e.g. seasonal workers). If, however, an employee works on beyond the three months (even though the contract is not formally extended) he will be entitled to SSP thereafter. Moreover, if an employee starts work under a new contract within eight weeks of an earlier contract with the same employer, and the contracts together produce a contract of thirteen or more weeks, the employee will be entitled to SSP.

Those who fall ill while working outside the European Economic Area (i.e. the EU plus Iceland, Liechtenstein and Norway) have previously been excluded from SSP, but for a period of incapacity starting on or after 6 April 1996 this does not apply so long as the employer is liable to pay Class 1 national insurance contributions (see page 567). If the employer's Class 1 liability ends during the incapacity, SSP will continue until stopped for another reason (e.g. reaching maximum entitlement).

Where an employer receives notification of illness from an employee who falls into an 'excluded' category, he must issue the employee with a change-over form SSP 1 (using either the official form or the employer's own version). The form must be issued within seven days of the notification of the illness or, if that is impracticable, on the first pay day in the following tax month. Employers are liable to a fine on conviction if they fail to issue the form within the required period. Form SSP 1 may also need to be issued when entitlement to SSP ends (see page 216).

Pregnancy — disqualifying period

Statutory sick pay cannot be paid during an 18-week disqualifying period. For those entitled to Statutory Maternity Pay or Maternity Allowance, the disqualifying period starts with the beginning of the week in which the employee is first entitled to that payment.

For those not entitled to either of those payments and not already getting SSP, the disqualifying period starts at the earlier of the Sunday of the week in which the baby is born and the Sunday of the week the employee is first off sick with a pregnancy-related illness if after the start of the sixth week before the baby is due.

If SSP is already being paid to a pregnant woman not entitled to SMP or Maternity Allowance, the disqualifying period starts with the earlier of the day after the birth and the day after the first day she becomes sick with a pregnancy-related illness on or after the start of the sixth week before the baby is due.

Qualifying conditions for SSP

For SSP to be payable two qualifying conditions must be met:

(i) there must be a 'period of incapacity for work' ('PIW'); and
(ii) there must be one or more 'qualifying days'.

Incapacity for work

A PIW is a period of four or more consecutive days of incapacity for work, counting rest days and holidays as well as normal working days. A person may be deemed incapable of work on the advice of a doctor or medical officer of health (e.g. where a pregnant woman is advised to stay at home during an outbreak of German measles at her place of work), but a day counts towards a PIW only if the employee is, or is deemed to be, 'incapable by reason of specific disease or bodily or mental disablement of doing work which he/she can reasonably be expected to do under the contract of employment'. The incapacity must exist throughout the day, nightshift workers falling ill during a shift being treated as working only on the day on which the shift began.

If two PIWs are separated by 56 days or less, they are treated as one single PIW (called a linked PIW). See example 1.

Example 1

An employee is incapable of work through illness from Friday 17 May 1996 to Tuesday 21 May 1996 inclusive and from Sunday 7 July 1996 to Thursday 29 August 1996 inclusive.

The two PIWs are separated by 46 days and are therefore treated as a linked PIW.

Tables to help employers work out whether PIWs link are included in the SSP Tables issued by the DSS.

Qualifying days

SSP is payable only in respect of 'qualifying days'. These are days of the week agreed between the employer and employee and will normally be those days on which the employee is required to work. Employer and employee may, however, come to other arrangements if they wish but qualifying days cannot be defined by reference to the days when the employee is sick. There is an overriding rule that there must be at least one qualifying day each week even if the employee is not required to work during that week.

SSP is not payable for the first three qualifying days in any PIW not linked to an earlier PIW. These are 'waiting days'. See example 2.

Example 2

An employee with qualifying days Monday to Friday each week, who had not been ill during September 1996, was ill on the days ringed in October.

M	T	W	Th	F	Sa	Su
	1	2	(3)	(4)	(5)	(6)
7	8	9	10	11	12	13
14	15	16	17	18	19	20
(21)	(22)	(23)	(24)	(25)	26	(27)
(28)	(29)	30	31			

There are three PIWs, from the 3rd to the 6th, from the 21st to the 25th, and from the 27th to the 29th.

In the first, there are two qualifying days which count as waiting days, and no SSP is payable.

In the second, which begins not more than 56 days after the end of the first and is therefore linked with it, the 21st is the third waiting day and SSP is payable for the other four qualifying days.

> The third begins not more than 56 days after the end of the second and is therefore linked with it. As there are three waiting days in the linked PIWs, SSP is payable for each of the two qualifying days in the third PIW.

Amount of SSP

Providing the employee's average weekly earnings are at or above the national insurance lower earnings limit (£61 for 1996/97), SSP is payable on a daily basis at a flat weekly rate of £54.55.

The daily rate of SSP is the weekly rate divided by the number of qualifying days in the week (e.g. an employee who has five qualifying days in a week will receive SSP at a daily rate of £10.91 (£54.55 ÷ 5)).

SSP will usually be paid on the employee's normal pay day.

Wages paid to an employee can be offset against any SSP due for the same day. If the wages are less than the SSP due, the employer must make up the payment to the appropriate rate of SSP.

When SSP ends

SSP ends with whichever of the following first occurs:

(a) the period of incapacity ends and the employee returns to work;

(b) the employee reaches his maximum entitlement to SSP;

(c) the employee's linked PIW has run for three years (which could only happen in exceptional circumstances where there were a large number of very short, four-day illnesses);

(d) the employee's contract of employment ends;

(e) the employee goes abroad outside the European Economic Area, but only if the PIW started before 6 April 1996 (see page 212);

(f) the employee is detained in legal custody;

(g) a pregnant woman employee starts her 18-week disqualifying period (see page 213).

The maximum period for which the employer is liable to pay SSP is normally 28 weeks. Where, however, a new employee commences a PIW within eight weeks of the day when a PIW with a previous employer ended, the weeks of SSP shown on the leaver's statement provided by the previous employer (see below) are taken into account to determine the new employer's maximum SSP liability. The previous period of sickness does not, however, affect the new employer's calculations in any other way and is not treated as a linked PIW.

Where entitlement to SSP ends while the employee is still sick, the employee will be able to claim incapacity benefit. To facilitate the change-over, the employer must issue change-over form SSP 1 to the employee at the beginning of the 23rd week of SSP (or, if sooner, two weeks before the employee's entitlement to SSP is due to end). If the employee's entitlement ends unexpectedly (e.g. through being taken into legal custody), the change-over form must be issued immediately. Form SSP 1 must also be issued at the start of the 18-week pregnancy disqualification period. A fine is payable on conviction for not issuing the form by the required date.

Leaver's statements

If an employee has a PIW which ends not more than 56 days before his employment ceases, and SSP was payable for one week or more, a leaver's statement SSP 1(L) (or the employer's own version of the form) must be issued if requested by the employee, showing the number of weeks' SSP payable (rounded to whole weeks, counting more than three odd days of payment as a week, and ignoring three odd days or less). The statement must be issued not later than the seventh day after the day the employee asks for it or, if that is impracticable, on the first pay day in the following tax month. Employers are liable to a fine on conviction if they fail to issue the form within the required period.

Notification and evidence for SSP

The payment of SSP is triggered by the employee notifying his employer that he is unfit for work. Form SC 2, available from social security offices, may be used for this purpose if employers wish. An employer can draw up his own procedure for notification subject to the following limitations:

(a) reasonable steps must be taken to notify employees of the procedures;
(b) it is not legal to insist that notification
   (i) is made by the employee in person, or
   (ii) is made by a particular time of day, or
   (iii) is made more than once weekly for the same illness, or
   (iv) is made on a form provided by the employer or on a medical certificate, or
   (v) is given earlier than the first qualifying day; and
(c) where the employee is a new employee with a leaving statement from his former employer, the statement must be accepted if it is produced not later than the seventh day after his first qualifying day of sickness.

If no notification procedures have been drawn up, the employee should inform his employer in writing by the seventh day after his first qualifying day of absence. If an employee fails to notify within the laid-down time limits an employer may withhold SSP, but late notification may be accepted if there was good cause for delay.

Having been notified by an employee of his illness, the employer must satisfy himself that the illness is genuine before paying SSP. The DSS expects that employers will obtain 'self-certificates' for the first week of illness and medical notes for longer absences.

An employer may withhold SSP when notification is late, and he may refuse to pay SSP if he feels that the employee is not in fact sick. In both these instances the employer, if required by the employee, must provide written reasons for withholding or refusing to pay SSP. An employee who disagrees with his employer's actions has the right to appeal for an official decision.

Recovery of SSP by employer

From 6 April 1995, employers may recover that part of the SSP paid in a tax month that exceeds 13% of their combined employer/employee national insurance contributions in that tax month (not including any Class 1A contributions). There is no separate relief for small employers.

Example 3

Total employer/employee national insurance contributions for August 1996 are £4,000. 13% thereof is £520. SSP would be recovered as follows:

SSP paid in month	£520 or less	£600	£1,000
SSP recovered	Nil	£80	£480

SSP is recovered from amounts due to be paid over to the Collector of Taxes in respect of Class 1 national insurance contributions. If the total paid exceeds contributions due, the excess can be deducted from PAYE payable to the Collector, and if it exceeds both national insurance and PAYE payable, the employer can either carry the excess forward or apply to the Collector for a refund.

Employees entitled to SMP

To be entitled to statutory maternity pay (SMP), an employee must satisfy the qualifying conditions (see below). Self-employed and unemployed women, and employed women who cannot get SMP, may be able to claim maternity allowance from the DSS. SMP is usually paid for 18 weeks, even if the employee is not returning after the baby has been born. Married women paying reduced national insurance contributions, and widows getting a State widow's benefit, are entitled to SMP if they satisfy the qualifying conditions. SSP and SMP cannot be paid at the same time, and SSP must cease on the last day before the maternity pay period (see page 219) starts, even if for some reason the employee is not entitled to SMP.

Qualifying conditions for SMP

To qualify for SMP an employee must have been employed for at least 26 weeks, including the 15th week before the baby is due. The 15th week is called the qualifying week. The employee's average weekly earnings in the eight weeks ending with the qualifying week must be not less than the lower earnings limit for national insurance contributions (currently £61) and the employer must be liable to pay Class 1 national insurance contributions for her in the qualifying week. The employee must still be pregnant at the 11th week before the expected date of birth. There are special rules for premature births. If an employee satisfies the qualifying rules with more than one employer she can receive SMP from each employer.

Notification and evidence for SMP

To get SMP an employee must give 21 days' notice of maternity absence in a manner prescribed by the employer, and must produce evidence of her expected week of confinement, normally on a maternity certificate form Mat B1 issued by a doctor or midwife, within 3 weeks of the start of the maternity pay period (this 3-week period can exceptionally be extended to 13 weeks).

Employees excluded from SMP

An employee is not entitled to SMP if:

(a)   she is not employed during the qualifying week (see above);
(b)   she has not been continuously employed for 26 weeks;
(c)   the earnings rule (see above) is not satisfied;
(d)   she has not given notice at an acceptable time of the date she is stopping work;
(e)   medical evidence of her expected confinement date is not provided;
(f)   she is in legal custody at any time in the first week of her maternity pay period.

An employee who was abroad outside the European Economic Area (see page 212) at any time in the first week of her maternity pay period (see page 219) was previously excluded from SMP, but where the expected week of confinement is on or after 18 August 1996 this no longer applies if the employer is liable to pay Class 1 national insurance contributions (see page 567).

If an employee is not entitled to SMP at the start of the maternity pay period, she will not be entitled to it at all.

An employee who is not entitled to SMP must be given form SMP 1 within seven days of the decision not to pay it, together with any maternity certificate she has provided. These forms will need to be produced to her social security office if she claims maternity allowance.

Payment of SMP

SMP is payable for a maximum of 18 weeks, called the maternity pay period. The maternity pay period may start at any time from the 11th week before the baby is due to the Sunday after the birth, but if a woman is on sick leave because of pregnancy she will be treated as on maternity leave if there are fewer than six weeks before the baby is due. For a non-pregnancy related sickness, the maternity pay period could be deferred and SSP could still be claimed instead in that last six weeks. The employee cannot do any work for the employer paying her SMP, but may continue to work or start work for another employer before the baby is born without affecting her entitlement. The employer will no longer be liable to pay SMP if, after the baby is born, the employee starts work for a new employer or returns to work for another employer who did not employ her in the qualifying week. SMP will cease also if the employee is taken into legal custody. SMP used to cease if the employee went abroad outside the European Economic Area, but this no longer applies if the expected week of confinement is on or after 18 August 1996.

Amount of SMP

SMP is paid at the rate of 9/10ths of the employee's average weekly earnings for the first six weeks and at the lower rate of £54.55 for the remaining weeks.

Recovery of SMP by employer

Employers other than 'small employers' are able to recover 92% of the gross amount of SMP paid in any month, by deducting it from their payment of Class 1 national insurance contributions (see chapter 13). 'Small employers' are those whose total employer/employee national insurance contributions for the tax year before that in which the SMP 'qualifying week' starts (see page 218) do not exceed £20,000. Such employers can recover all the SMP paid, plus an extra 5.5% (from 6 April 1996 — previously 5%) of the SMP to compensate for the employer's Class 1 contributions on the SMP. If the amount recoverable exceeds the contributions due, the excess can be deducted from PAYE payable to the Collector of Taxes; and if it exceeds both national insurance and PAYE payable, the employer can either carry the excess forward or apply to the Collector for a refund.

Employer's records

Employer's records are particularly important, as the information required to be kept may have to be made available to DSS inspectors. Employers may use record sheets SSP 2 and SMP 2, available from social security offices, if they wish. The form the records take is up to the employer, but the following must be kept:

For SSP

(a) records of dates of employees' PIWs;
(b) all payments of SSP made during a PIW.

For SMP

(a) records of dates of maternity absence;
(b) records of weeks for which SMP not paid, with details;
(c) maternity certificates (forms Mat B1) or other medical evidence, and copies of certificates returned to employees, for example when liability has ended.

For both SSP and SMP

Records must also be kept of the monthly SSP and SMP paid, and certain details need to be included on the end of year returns of pay, tax and national insurance (see page 169).

Records must be kept for a minimum of three years after the end of the tax year to which they relate.

In addition to the records outlined above, the DSS recommends that the following are also retained for further reference:

  (i) records of qualifying days in each PIW for SSP;
 (ii) records of days within each PIW for which SSP was not paid, with reasons (including 'excluded categories', see page 212);
(iii) any leaver's statements from new employees whom the employer did not exclude from SSP;
(iv) copies of SSP leaver's statements issued;
 (v) medical notes and 'self-certificates' relating to PIWs;
(vi) an outline of the employer's SSP and SMP rules;
(vii) a record of when employees report absence through sickness or notify maternity absences;
(viii) a record of all correspondence concerning appeals, etc., with copies of all decisions by Social Security.

15
Golden handcuffs and golden handshakes

A 'golden handcuff' or 'golden hello' is the popular term for a lump sum payment received on taking up an employment, and a 'golden handshake' or 'golden goodbye' the term for a lump sum payment received when you leave an employment.

Lump sum payments on taking up employment (TA 1988, s 313)

Where a lump sum payment is made to a prospective employee, it will be taxed as advance pay for future services unless it represents compensation for some right or asset given up on taking up the employment. It is difficult to show that a payment does represent compensation, and professional advice should be sought if you think a payment you are about to receive is in this category.

Sometimes a lump sum is paid in return for your agreeing to restrict your conduct or activities in some way, for example agreeing not to leave to join a competitor within a certain period of time. Any such special payments are treated as pay in the normal way, both for tax and for national insurance.

Lump sum termination payments (TA 1988, ss 90, 148, 188, 579, 580, 596A, 612 and Sch 11)

Lump sum termination payments are taxable under special rules (see page 222), unless they are already taxable under the normal rules of Schedule E.

A payment will be taxable as earnings under Schedule E if it is a payment for services rendered, i.e. it is really deferred pay. Wages in lieu of notice or compensation for loss of office are taxable as earnings in the normal way if they are specifically provided for in the employment contract (e.g. the contract provides for four weeks' notice to be given, and for wages to be paid for that period if the notice is not given). To be within the special rules, such payments must be by way of compensation because the employer has *broken* the employment contract, or be purely ex gratia payments that are not part of the employer's established practice. Even then, the Revenue may seek to tax them under another heading, if they are paid in return for an agreement by the employee not to pursue any further claims against the employer.

If the payment is made because the job no longer exists, for example redundancy pay over and above the statutory amount, it is not taxable as pay under the normal rules, even where it is covered by contractual arrangements. The important factor is whether the payment is for services rendered by the employee or because his job has ceased to exist.

In the case of an ex gratia payment, it will be more difficult to demonstrate to the Revenue that it was made because of the termination of employment rather than for services rendered. When employment is terminated by the employee's retirement (other than premature retirement through redundancy or disability) or death (other than as the result of an accident), the Revenue consider that ex gratia payments are fully taxable under Schedule E as benefits under an unapproved 'retirement benefits scheme'. This will not apply if the employer gets tax approval for the payments, which will then become 'relevant benefits from an approved scheme', but approval will be subject to the normal rules limiting the maximum lump sum payable, and will not be given if the ex gratia sum is in addition to other lump sum entitlements, except any payable only on death in service. Alternatively, approval need not be sought if the lump sum is the only potential lump sum payable and does not exceed one-twelfth of the pensions earnings cap figure for the year of payment (£82,200 for 1996/97, giving a limit for that year of £6,850). (Revenue Statement of Practice SP 13/91).

For either compensation or ex gratia payments, the following circumstances may give rise to further complication:

  (i) Where the employee is also a shareholder, it may be difficult to show that the payment is not a distribution on which the company would have to pay advance corporation tax, with no deduction being given for the payment in calculating the employer's trading profit (see chapter 3).
 (ii) Where the payment is made at the same time as a change in voting control, a clear distinction must be demonstrated between the payment and the share transactions if the payment is not to be regarded as part of the capital transaction.
(iii) If the employee continues with the employer in a new capacity, either as an employee or perhaps under a consultancy agreement, it becomes that much harder to show that the payment was not for services rendered or to be rendered in the future.

Taxation of the lump sum termination payment

Provided that the payment is not caught either as taxable earnings, or as a distribution, or as part of a capital transaction, it will be taxed according to the special rules for termination payments. Under these, the first £30,000 is exempt and only the balance is taxable as earnings.

Statutory redundancy payments, whilst not themselves taxable, are included within the first £30,000. Most payments in lieu of notice will be covered by the first £30,000 and thus not charged to tax (subject to what is said on page 221).

Exemptions

Some payments are completely exempt from tax, for example those on death in service (subject to what is said above) or in respect of disability, or where the service has been predominantly abroad. There is partial exemption for shorter periods of work abroad.

Lump sums received under approved pension schemes are exempt. They may be boosted by agreed special contributions from the employer to the fund prior to the termination of employment so long as the permitted maximum lump sum is not exceeded (see chapter 16). In view of the Revenue's view on ex gratia payments (see page 222), this route provides an alternative where there is an approved pension scheme.

The £30,000 applies after all other available exemptions.

Application of PAYE

If the termination payment is made before the employee leaves, the employer must deduct and account for PAYE on the excess of chargeable termination payments over £30,000 and also on ex gratia sums on retirement or death for which approval has not yet been granted (tax being refunded as and when approval is received). Details of the termination payment should be provided when sending form P45 to the Revenue. If the payment is made after the employee has left and been issued with form P45, the normal PAYE treatment does not apply. Tax is deducted at the basic rate and details of the payment must be notified to the tax office. Any higher rate tax due will then be collected directly from the employee.

Tax position of the employer (TA 1988, s 90)

To be deducted in arriving at taxable profits, expenses must be wholly and exclusively for the purposes of the trade. Apart from statutory redundancy payments, which are specifically allowable, there is no special rule for termination payments, but it will usually be easier to show that they meet the 'wholly and exclusively' requirement when they are compensation rather than ex gratia payments, and when the trade is continuing rather than when it is not.

Where a trade is permanently discontinued, it is specifically provided that an additional payment up to three times any amount paid under the statutory redundancy pay provisions is allowable as a deduction in computing the employer's profits, any payments in excess of this amount being disallowed.

It may be particularly difficult for the employer to obtain a deduction where the payment is ex gratia and is associated with a sale of the shares or a change in voting control, or where it is an abnormally high payment to a director with a material interest in the company.

National insurance position

Payments that are caught as earnings under the normal Schedule E rules are also liable to national insurance contributions. Otherwise, contributions are not payable.

Counselling services for redundant employees (TA 1988, ss 589A, 589B; FA 1993, s 108)

The provision of counselling services by employers for redundant employees, or payment of an employee's costs for such counselling is specifically exempt from tax for employees, and the cost is fully allowed to employers.

Expenses incurred in obtaining a lump sum payment

Some employees may incur expenses, for example fees to advisers, in obtaining a lump sum payment. These will not reduce the taxable part of the lump sum as they will not have been wholly, exclusively and necessarily incurred in the performance of the duties of the employment. Where an employer pays an employee's legal costs in obtaining a compensation payment, the Revenue will not treat the payment as a taxable benefit if it is made direct to the employee's solicitor following an out of court settlement, or if it is made to the employee under a Court Order.

Tax points

- An ex gratia payment to a director or shareholder of a close company is especially vulnerable to Revenue attack, on either or both of the following grounds:

    (a) it is not a deductible trading expense,
    (b) it is a distribution of profits.

- If an ex gratia payment by a close company is not allowed in calculating profits, the Revenue may contend that each shareholder has made a proportionate transfer of value for inheritance tax. There is a specific exclusion where the payment is allowed in computing profits.

- Ex gratia payments may be taxed as non-exempt 'retirement benefits' — see page 222.

- If an employee who receives a severance payment is allowed to keep a company car as part of the package, the market value of the car will be treated as part of the exempt £30,000 unless it is regarded as a reward for past services, in which case the full market value would be chargeable. To avoid any possible problems, it is better to increase the lump sum and give the employee the opportunity to buy the car at market value. If the lump sum was taxable as an unapproved retirement benefit (see page 222), the value of the car would similarly be taxable.

- If you pay a termination lump sum after an employee has left and been given his P45, tax only has to be deducted at the basic rate. The employee will then pay any higher rate tax due after the year end, when he receives an assessment (or when he sends in his self-assessment from 1996/97).

- Unless you obtain new sources of income to replace your salary, the tax cost of a termination payment in excess of £30,000 may be lower if the termination occurs shortly after 6 April rather than before, because all or part of the payment may fall within the lower or basic rate bands, whereas it might have attracted 40% tax if it was received in addition to a full year's salary.

- It is essential that proper documentation and board minutes are available so that the nature of payments can be demonstrated to the Revenue.

- The tax reliefs for lump sum payments are only available to *employees* taxed under Schedule E and not to those employed under a *contract for services*, whose earnings are charged under Schedule D, Case I or II (see page 260). If, exceptionally, Schedule E earnings are included by agreement with the Revenue in the calculation of self-employed profits, e.g. directors' fees where the directorship is held in a professional capacity and the fees are included as income of the professional practice, this in itself will not prevent a lump sum qualifying for the reliefs outlined in this chapter.

- The chargeable part of a termination payment does not count as relevant earnings for the purpose of calculating maximum contributions to a personal pension plan taken out on or after 1 July 1988. (See chapter 17.) It is included for retirement annuity contracts made before that date.

- A termination payment may affect the former employee's entitlement to social security benefits if he is then unemployed, but the employee will be entitled to unemployment credits for the period covered by the compensation payment so that his national insurance contribution record is not affected.

16
Occupational pension schemes

Background

State pensions are recognised as providing an inadequate income in old age, even though employees' pensions are boosted by an earnings-related addition (SERPS). The Government therefore gives generous tax treatment to occupational pension schemes. The risk for an employee of his contributions being misused will be significantly reduced by a new compensation scheme. From April 1997, where an occupational pension scheme's funds have been misappropriated and the employer is insolvent, compensation may be payable by the Pensions Compensation Board to cover 90% of the loss or to bring the fund up to 90% funding. The compensation scheme will be paid for by a levy on occupational schemes.

Where an employer's scheme provides at least equivalent benefits to the earnings-related State scheme, employees may be contracted out of the earnings-related element of the State scheme, thus paying lower contributions to it. This can be done by guaranteeing minimum contributions to employees' pensions (contracted-out money purchase schemes — COMPS) rather than having to guarantee the benefits on retirement. Contracted-out employees receive their basic pension from the State and the additional benefits from their employer's scheme. The combined employer/employee reduction in contributions for contracted-out employees is 4.8% of earnings between the lower and upper earnings levels (see page xxvii).

Many employers, particularly family companies, remain contracted in to the state scheme and provide their own pension scheme in addition. The employee then gets full benefits under the State scheme (and pays full contributions) plus the additional benefits provided by his employer's scheme. Family companies have the same facility as others for establishing schemes, but there are tighter rules on the calculation of maximum possible benefits where the employee is a shareholder holding 20% or more of the share capital. If a company is an investment company, the scheme must comply with the rules for *automatic* approval (see below) if it is to include 20% directors or directors who are members of a family who control more than 50% of the company's shares.

Employees in a contracted-in scheme are able to contract out of SERPS independently while remaining in their employer's scheme, either by making a free-standing additional voluntary contribution (see page 229) or through a separate personal pension plan (see page 244).

From April 1997 changes are to be made in the way contracted-out schemes interrelate with SERPs, and age-related rebates of Class 1 contributions are to be introduced for contracted-out money purchase pension schemes and personal pensions (see page 204). (At present there is an extra 1% rebate for employees over 30 — see pages 243 and 244.)

Those in personal pension schemes are able on retirement to defer using their pension fund to buy an annuity and have some flexibility as to how much income they draw in the meantime (see page 239). Consideration is being given to the introduction of some flexibility for occupational pensions, which would enable retiring employees to take a reduced pension in earlier years so that they could draw higher pensions later.

Membership of employers' schemes

Employees cannot be compelled to be members of their employers' schemes, unless the schemes are non-contributory and provide only death benefits. Employees are able to take out personal pension plans instead (see chapter 17) or rely on the State pension scheme. Pension rights from an existing occupational scheme may be transferred to a personal pension plan, but if an employee remains in the employment, benefits accrued before 6 April 1988 cannot be transferred unless the scheme permits. It is normally possible to transfer back from a personal pension plan to an employer's scheme if the scheme agrees.

Revenue approval for employers' schemes (TA 1988, ss 590–612)

In order to obtain Revenue approval, the employer must contribute to the scheme but the employee need not.

A pension scheme gains automatic Revenue approval if it conforms precisely to the statutory conditions. The Revenue may, however, approve a scheme which does not precisely conform and nearly all schemes receive this discretionary approval under which greater benefits can be paid (but of course at a higher cost in contributions). The Revenue issue Practice Notes on the manner in which they exercise their discretion, and specialist pensions advisers are able to structure schemes so that they will receive the approval of the Pension Schemes Office (PSO). Schemes may be either 'defined benefit' schemes, under which the benefits depend on final salary, or 'defined contribution' (money purchase) schemes, under which the contributions are fixed and the benefits depend on those contributions and on the investment performance of the scheme. Simplified 'off-the-peg' money purchase schemes that qualify for immediate approval are available to help employers who would not normally provide employees with pension arrangements. These schemes may not include directors of family companies who control 20% or more of the voting rights. The Revenue has issued standard documentation for such schemes.

A pension fund's investment in employer-related investments is limited to 5% of the current market value of the fund (except for small self-administered schemes — see page 234). Self-investments already held at 9 March 1992 can be retained indefinitely, except loans and securities, which could not be retained beyond 8 March 1994 (8 March 1997 for second-tier market investments).

Taxation advantages of Revenue approval

(a) The employer's contributions reduce taxable business profits.
(b) The employer's contributions are not treated as a benefit in kind to the employee, nor do they count as the employee's earnings for national insurance contributions.
(c) An employee's own contributions reduce his earnings for tax purposes (but not for national insurance contributions).
(d) A tax-free lump sum can be paid to the employee on retirement.
(e) Provision can be made for a lump sum to be paid on an employee's death in service, which is usually free of taxation (see page 232).
(f) The income and capital gains of the fund are not taxed.

Retirement age

Normal retirement age may be any age between 60 and 75. (For schemes approved before 25 July 1991, the normal retirement age is 55 for women and 60 for men, with an upper limit for both of 70.) Early retirement may be allowed from age 50 and is also permitted for incapacity.

Maximum contributions

Maximum contributions depend on an employee's earnings, which means the amount on which he is chargeable to tax under Schedule E, including benefits in kind but excluding taxable amounts under share option or incentive schemes or lump sum termination payments.

The maximum combined contributions of employer and employee to an off-the-peg money purchase scheme are 17½% of the employee's earnings, of which the employer must contribute some and the employee cannot contribute more than 15%. For other money purchase schemes, contributions to produce the maximum permitted benefits on retirement may currently be calculated on a level premium basis, thus enabling a substantial fund to be built up at an early stage. The Revenue is, however, considering moving to a percentage of salary basis.

For final salary schemes, there is no specific upper limit on the amount that an employer may contribute, subject only to the requirement that the benefits provided as a result are within the permitted levels and the contributions are not excessive in relation to those benefits. There are, however, regulations to prevent schemes being overfunded (see page 234).

Employers' contributions are deductible only in the accounting period in which they are paid, and not when provision is made in the accounts.

If an employee joins a scheme late, it is possible to make contributions of several times the employee's current earnings in order to fund the maximum benefits. Inflation-proofing may be provided for. Special irregular contributions may be made by the employer in addition to the normal annual contributions. Such irregular contributions may, if they are very large, have to be spread forward over a maximum of four years in calculating the employer's taxable profits, rather than all the relief being given in the year of payment.

An employee need not be required to contribute to a scheme, but if he does the contributions (including any additional or special contributions to obtain additional benefits) must not exceed 15% of his earnings (as defined above). For schemes set up on or after 14 March 1989 and for those joining existing schemes on or after 1 June 1989, there is a limit (referred to as the earnings cap) on the earnings on which contributions may be paid. This limit is usually increased annually in line with increases in the retail prices index (note — not in line with increases in average earnings), and has increased from £78,600 to £82,200 for 1996/97.

Additional voluntary contributions (AVCs)

The benefits available to an employee depend on the funds available in the employer's scheme. An employee wishing to increase his potential pension may pay additional voluntary contributions (AVCs) to the employer's scheme, or to a scheme of his choice (free-standing AVCs). Free-standing AVCs are paid net of basic rate tax and the Revenue pays the tax to the pension scheme. Any AVCs paid must not take the employee's total contributions to more than 15% of his earnings (the earnings being subject to the £82,200 limit where relevant). No part of the additional benefits earned may be taken as a tax-free lump sum, except for AVCs to an employer's scheme under a contract to purchase added years which will produce a precise level of pension and lump sum benefit and AVCs that are paid under arrangements made before 8 April 1987. Some AVCs may have to be refunded on retirement or earlier death if the combined benefits from occupational and free-standing schemes are excessive. Tax is deducted from such refunds at 34% (35% before 6 April 1996). Someone liable at the basic or lower rate is not, however, entitled to a refund. A higher rate taxpayer is treated as having received a sum net of basic rate tax and will be liable to higher rate tax on the gross equivalent. See example 1.

A free-standing AVC may be used to enable an employee to contract out of SERPS individually, even though his employer's scheme is contracted in. The AVC will be boosted by the DSS contracting-out rebate, currently amounting

---

Example 1

Surplus AVCs of £1,000 gross paid to higher rate taxpayer. He receives £660 cash, which is treated as gross income of (660 × 100/76) = £868. Tax at 40% is £347, less £208 treated as paid, so that a further £139 is payable, leaving only £521 in the hands of the taxpayer.

---

to 4.8% (1.8% employee's contribution, 3% employer's contribution) of earnings between the national insurance lower and upper earnings levels. The employee does not, however, get the benefit of an addition for tax relief on the payment by the DSS in respect of his 1.8% share of the contracting-out rebate. If an employee wishes to contract out of SERPS while remaining in his employer's scheme, it is therefore more sensible to do so by means of a personal pension plan, where the DSS payment for the employee's rebate is grossed up for tax relief (see page 244).

Maximum benefits for employees

Basis for calculating maximum benefits

For off-the-peg money purchase schemes, there is no restriction on the benefits, since the restriction is made in the amount contributed. For other schemes, maximum benefits are measured in terms of 'final pensionable remuneration'. Final pensionable remuneration is the greater of the remuneration (as defined on page 228) in any one of the five years before retirement (with averaging for fluctuating payments) or the average of total remuneration for any period of three or more consecutive years ended in the last ten years before normal retirement date.

Unless the 'final remuneration' is that of the twelve months ending with normal retirement date, each year's remuneration included in the calculation may be 'dynamised', i.e. increased in proportion to the increase in the Retail Prices Index for the period from the end of the year up to normal retirement date.

A director who, together with his defined family and trustees, has controlled 20% or more of the employing company's voting rights at any time in the last ten years cannot use a 'best of the last five years' final remuneration calculation and must instead use the three consecutive year averaging of earnings, but the increases from indexing may be taken into account. This averaging provision also applies to employees whose 'final pensionable remuneration' would otherwise exceed £100,000.

For schemes set up on or after 14 March 1989, and those joining existing schemes on or after 1 June 1989, there is an index-linked ceiling, £82,200 from 6 April 1996, on final remuneration taken into account for calculating benefits.

Maximum pension

The maximum pension payable under final salary schemes is 2/3rds final remuneration, at the rate of 1/30th for each year's service up to 20 years. For members of an existing scheme at 16 March 1987, the maximum can apply after 10 years' service. Inflation-proofing may be provided for within the funding of the scheme. Under provisions in the Pensions Act 1995, pension rights built up under final salary schemes from a date to be fixed (probably April 1997) must be inflation-proofed in line with the retail prices index, up to a specified limit, expected to be 5% per annum. Part of the pension may be commuted for a lump sum (see below).

Pensions from other schemes

Benefits at the 1/30th per year rate (or accelerated rate for members of pre-16 March 1987 schemes) may usually be provided in addition to any pension benefits from previous occupations or self-employed pension plans, providing the combined benefits do not exceed 2/3rds of final remuneration.

Lump sums

Part of the maximum available benefits may be commuted to a lump sum. The maximum lump sum is normally 3/80ths final remuneration for each year of service up to 40, giving a maximum of 1½ times final remuneration, but this may be varied or restricted depending on when the employee joined the scheme.

For those joining schemes after 16 March 1987 but before 14 March 1989 (1 June 1989 for schemes in existence at 14 March 1989), there is an overall limit of £150,000.

For schemes set up on or after 14 March 1989 and those who join existing schemes on or after 1 June 1989, the lump sum cannot exceed 1½ times the 'earnings cap' figure of £82,200 (index-linked), giving a maximum lump sum

---

Example 2

An employee retires after 30 years service, his final remuneration being £80,000.

If his pension entitlement is based on the rules applicable from 14 March 1989, the maximum pension is 2/3rds × £82,200 (since he has completed 20 years' service) = £54,800.

The maximum lump sum is the greater of:

3/80 × £82,200 × 30	£92,475
2¼ × £54,800	£123,300

The maximum lump sum is therefore £123,300.

---

of £123,300 using current figures. There is also an alternative to the 3/80ths calculation. If it gives a higher figure, the lump sum is calculated as two and a quarter times the amount of the pension before commutation. This enables late entrants to get the maximum lump sum in appropriate circumstances — see example 2.

In calculating the maximum lump sum payment, lump sums from earlier employments must be taken into account. If dynamised final remuneration is used to calculate the pension, it may also be used to calculate the lump sum. If a lump sum is to be taken, the maximum pension of 2/3rds final remuneration must be reduced.

Provision for dependants

Provision for dependants may be made both for death in service and for death after retirement. Inflation increases may be provided for in both cases. A pension to a surviving spouse may continue for the spouse's lifetime, but children's pensions must cease when they reach age 18 or cease full-time education.

Death in service

When an employee dies in service, a lump sum not exceeding four times final remuneration (which is defined in a more generous way than for other benefits) may normally be paid without attracting inheritance tax. In addition, the employee's own contributions to the pension scheme may be repaid with interest. The pension scheme trustees usually have discretion as to who receives the death in service lump sum, but they generally act in accordance with the employee's known wishes. There may be an inheritance tax problem where the death benefit is to be held in trust for the employee's dependants, because if the employee dies in service after the earliest age at which he could have retired, the capital value of the pension he could have taken immediately before death may be taken into account for inheritance tax. The Revenue have, however, stated that this will not apply in genuine cases of deferred retirement, and will only apply where there is evidence that the intention of deferring benefits was to increase the estate of someone else.

Pensions may also be paid to the surviving spouse and/or dependants. The pension paid to any one person cannot exceed 2/3rds of the maximum pension the employee could have received if he had retired on incapacity grounds at the date of death (with potential service up to normal retirement age being taken into account). The total pensions to spouse and dependants cannot exceed the total incapacity pension the employee could have received.

Death after retirement

Provision may be made for an employee's pension to continue for a set period after retirement despite his earlier death. Separate pensions for spouse and dependants can also be provided, subject to the individual pensions not exceeding 2/3rds of the maximum pension that could have been approved for the employee and the total pensions not exceeding the whole of that maximum. Lump sum benefits will not normally be permitted.

Unapproved pension schemes (TA 1988, ss 595–596B, 605, 606, 611; FA 1989, s 76)

It is possible to set up 'top-up' unapproved pension schemes alongside approved schemes, or to have just an unapproved scheme. Unapproved schemes have both advantages and disadvantages. The employer's contributions are usually deductible in arriving at taxable profits. They are taxed as a benefit on the individual employees (apart from the amount needed to establish and administer the scheme), but national insurance contributions are not payable. If the employer agrees to pay the employee's tax, however, DSS consider that national insurance contributions are due on the amount paid in respect of tax.

Most unapproved schemes are funded schemes. Savings income (including dividend income) within the fund is usually charged at 20% and other income and gains at 24%. Death in service payments are usually free of inheritance tax, providing they are not paid to the employee's estate. The employee can take the benefits on retirement wholly as a tax-free lump sum. He could take a pension instead, but the pension would be taxable, so it would be better to take the cash and buy a life annuity, part of which would then be free of tax (see page 477). Providing the employer's contributions are wholly and exclusively for the trade, there is no limit on the amount that can be contributed, and no limit on the tax-free lump sums that can be paid out.

Measures have been introduced to block the use of offshore funded schemes that pay little or no tax to provide increased tax-free lump sums to employees. For offshore schemes established or varied on or after 1 December 1993, tax will be charged at the employee's marginal rate on any difference between the lump sum received and the employer's and employee's contributions to the fund. See also page 235 re the anti-avoidance provisions that apply if a small self-administered approved scheme becomes unapproved.

Changing employment

When you change employment, then providing you have been in the pension scheme for at least two years, you may either have a preserved pension which will become payable on retirement, or a transfer payment to a new scheme (if the scheme will accept it) or to an insurance company or to a personal pension plan. Where there is a preserved pension under a final salary scheme, it must be increased each year in line with the increase in retail prices (or by 5% if less). For contracted-out schemes, the employer must ensure that the pension must at least equal the guaranteed minimum pension under the State scheme.

Refunds of contributions are not usually available except for periods of employment of less than two years, but where they are made tax is deducted at the rate of 20%.

Pension scheme surpluses (TA 1988, ss 601–603 and Sch 22)

There are special rules for pension scheme surpluses. A fund is in surplus where an objective actuarial valuation, in accordance with guidelines specified by the Government Actuary, shows that the projected value of the scheme's assets is more than 5% higher than the projected cost of paying pension benefits to members. The trustees are required to reduce the surplus at least to the 5% level by a combination of:

(i) increases in pension benefits (within the permissible limits),
(ii) a reduction or suspension of contributions by the employer and/or employees for up to five years, and
(iii) a refund to the employer (subject to stringent conditions, including, for final salary schemes, the need to first provide for inflation-proofing of pensions).

For final salary schemes, trustees also have the option of paying tax on the surplus.

If a refund is made, it cannot reduce the surplus to *below* 5%. The trustees are required to deduct 40% tax at source from any refund they make to the employer and pay it over to the Revenue within 14 days. Interest is charged for late payment. In no circumstances can a company obtain a repayment of the 40% tax because of trading losses or other available reliefs.

Small self-administered pension schemes (SI 1991/1614; TA 1988, ss 591C, 591D)

A self-administered pension scheme is one where the contributions remain under the control of trustees appointed by the company, as distinct from being paid to a pensions provider such as a life assurance company. While it gives maximum flexibility in managing a fund, the pension scheme trustees must invest in the best interests of the members in order to provide their pension benefits. It is possible to have what are often called hybrid schemes where the funds are partly managed by a pensions provider. The fund will also usually hold life assurance cover on the scheme members so that its funds are not unacceptably diminished by the premature death of a member.

A small self-administered scheme (i.e. one with less than twelve members) is subject to specific regulations that control its format, funding and investment powers. It may borrow up to an amount equal to three times the normal annual contribution which it receives from the company plus 45% of the scheme assets. This could be helpful in boosting its funds for, say, the purchase of premises for use by the company. The borrowing is paid off by future annual contributions from the company, and in the meantime the interest cost is covered by the rent charged by the pension fund to the company.

Loans to pension scheme members or their families are forbidden, but loans to the company itself, or to buy shares in it, or the purchase by the trustees and leaseback of the company's premises, may be permitted (subject to certain restrictions), providing each member of the scheme is a trustee, and has given written agreement in advance to the proposed investment.

Specialist advice is essential for such schemes.

Anti-avoidance provisions have been introduced to charge tax at 40% on the market value of the scheme's assets if an approved scheme becomes unapproved (for example, by transferring offshore). The charge also applies to schemes with 12 or more members if a controlling director is a member. The Pensions Scheme Office has taken action to block schemes that purport to avoid the 40% charge.

Payment of pensions

Tax on pensions under occupational schemes is dealt with under the PAYE scheme, with coding adjustments being made where some or all of the available allowances have been used against other income, such as State pensions.

Tax points

- Contributions by employers to approved pension schemes are one of the few benefits for employees earning £8,500 per annum or more and directors that are free of both tax and national insurance, so generous funding of a scheme within the permitted limits is particularly beneficial to them.

- A family company can have an approved pension scheme for its controlling directors. The contribution limits are less restrictive than those for personal pension plans.

- A family company may be able to eliminate taxable trading profits by contributions to a pension scheme, and if the contributions exceed those profits, to carry the resulting loss back against the profits of earlier years. But watch the provisions mentioned on page 229 for the spreading forward of contributions for relief purposes.

- An unapproved scheme is worth looking at, particularly in view of the flexibility it gives on retirement. The whole benefit can be taken as tax-free cash, which can then be divided between husband and wife so as to make the best future use of available allowances and lower tax rates.

- You should remember that once AVCs have been paid into a scheme, you will not benefit from them until you retire. You will then either get an increase in your pension or a return of contributions where your pension has been overfunded. Tax is suffered on any returned contributions at the rate of 34% for a basic rate taxpayer and at almost 48%

for a higher rate taxpayer (see example 1 on page 230), so overfunding should be avoided.

- If you are young and highly mobile, a personal pension plan may be preferable to an employer's scheme because you will be able to take it with you from job to job, whereas there may be problems transferring a fund from one occupational scheme to another. But there is the disadvantage that when negotiating your employment contract you will have to agree with your employer how much the employer will contribute to your personal plan. The higher administration charges also have to be considered.

- If someone deliberately fails to exercise a right in order for someone else or a discretionary trust to benefit, this counts as a transfer for inheritance tax at the latest time the right could be exercised. The value of the transfer is the value of the rights not taken up. This rule may catch some death in service lump sums under pension schemes if the death benefit was held in trust for the family and the employee had deliberately deferred retirement so that the family could benefit. See page 232.

- Where a pension is paid direct to a child, the child's personal allowance will be available to reduce the tax payable, making this more tax-efficient than if the whole pension were paid to the surviving parent who then maintained the child, but the possible effect on other benefits available to the child, e.g. grant aid, must not be forgotten.

- Although benefits in kind may be treated as earnings for calculating maximum pension benefits, dividends received from family companies by working directors may not. This needs to be taken into account in considering whether remuneration or dividends should be paid.

- In the case of a small self-administered scheme, the Revenue will not approve the use of fund monies to acquire premises with private living accommodation or to buy assets from scheme members, nor may the trustees sell assets to scheme members.

- Those who retire before State pension age (65 for a man and 60 for a woman) may need to pay voluntary national insurance contributions to ensure that they get a full basic pension under the State scheme (see page 200). But providing they are registered as unemployed and available for work, contributions will be credited, and unemployed men over 60 are automatically credited with contributions without the need to be registered.

- From 1 April 1996, unemployment benefit (or jobseeker's allowance from October 1996) is reduced to the extent that your occupational pension (or personal pension) exceeds £50 a week. The pension income limit was previously £35 and the restriction applied only to those aged over 55. Anyone under 55 already receiving unemployment benefit before 1 April 1996 will not suffer the restriction until they reach age 55.

17
Providing your own pension

Background (TA 1988, ss 618–626 (retirement annuities), 630–655 (personal pensions))

The self-employed and those not in an employer's pension scheme are entitled to tax relief on premiums they pay to provide their own pension (in addition to earning the State pension by paying national insurance contributions).

The pension scheme rules were changed from 1 July 1988. Pre-1 July 1988 contracts are called retirement annuity contracts and the old rules still apply to those contracts. Contracts starting on or after 1 July 1988 are called personal pension plans and they are subject to the new rules. Most of the rules for old and new schemes are the same, but new schemes must make provision for transfers on change of employment/self-employment. Other differences are indicated later in the chapter.

Personal pension schemes may allow members to direct where their funds are to be invested, subject to various restrictions to ensure that the scheme still meets the conditions necessary for tax approval.

Qualifying individuals

Those who are self-employed, or who are not members of an employer's pension scheme, may contribute to a pension fund for themselves by paying premiums within stipulated limits to one or more pension providers, the premiums being accumulated in a fund free of income tax and capital gains tax. A person who has earnings from both a pensionable employment and one that does not carry any pension rights may pay premiums in respect of the non-pensionable earnings, and husband and wife who each have non-pensionable earnings may each make separate pension provision.

Retirement annuity premiums have to be paid to an insurance company, but personal pension contributions can be paid to a life assurance company, friendly society, bank, building society or unit trust. Under old and new schemes, the retirement benefits themselves are purchased from an authorised insurance company with the fund monies at retirement, and the 'best buy' available at that time can be selected.

It was not possible under the old rules for someone to be in both an occupational scheme and a personal scheme in respect of the same earnings. This also applies to the new pension plans, except where an employee uses a personal pension plan to contract out of the State Earnings Related Pension Scheme (SERPS) (see page 244).

Mis-sold personal pensions (FA 1996, s 148)

It will not normally be beneficial for someone eligible to be in an occupational scheme to which both they and their employer contribute to opt out of the employer's scheme and take out a personal pension plan funded by their own contributions. A review by the Securities and Investments Board found, however, that many people were wrongly advised to do so. Where as a result of the review someone receives compensation for that wrong advice, the compensation is exempt from tax.

Permissible benefits

The retirement benefits must commence not later than age 75 nor earlier than age 50 (60 for old schemes), except in cases of ill health or where the occupation is one in which earlier retirement is customary, for example entertainers and athletes, for whom the Revenue may approve a scheme with an earlier retirement date.

At retirement the whole fund may be used to buy an annuity, which will be taxed as income, or a tax-free lump sum may be taken, with the balance used to buy an annuity. For personal pension plans, the lump sum may not exceed one quarter of the fund. There is no overall maximum, but the index-linked limit for net relevant earnings (currently £82,200 — see below) on which premiums can be based will itself limit the size of the pension fund. For retirement annuity contracts, the maximum lump sum is three times the remaining annual pension, subject to an upper limit of £150,000 for contracts made between 17 March 1987 and 30 June 1988 inclusive.

It is possible for payment of the pension to be guaranteed for up to ten years even if the taxpayer dies within that time. Should death occur before retirement, the contributions are refunded, with or without interest and bonuses. The refund may be to the personal representatives or to any other person. Alternatively, the contract may provide for the death benefits to be held in trust, with the monies payable at the trustees' discretion. If paid to the personal representatives, the sum refunded will form part of the estate for inheritance tax purposes, but tax will not be payable to the extent that the estate is left to the surviving spouse. Inheritance tax will also usually be avoided where the proceeds are held in trust, but where someone works on past the earliest pension age under the policy with the deliberate intention of benefiting someone else, a charge to inheritance tax may arise as with an occupational scheme (see page 232).

Deferring personal pension annuity purchase (TA 1988, s 634A; FA 1995, Sch 11)

Many people have suffered when they retired through having to use their pension fund to buy an annuity at a time when annuity rates were low. For schemes approved or amended after 1 May 1995, those with personal pension contracts may defer buying an annuity until, at latest, age 75. They can still take a tax-free lump sum at retirement date, and they may make taxable income withdrawals from the fund during the deferral period up to a maximum that is broadly equivalent to the annuity they could have taken (with a minimum income withdrawal of 35% of the maximum). The fund will continue to build up tax-free, but further contributions may not be made once any benefits (including income withdrawals) have been taken.

If the pension scheme member dies during the deferral period, a surviving spouse or dependant will be able to take the fund in cash (subject to a tax charge of 35%), or buy an annuity immediately, or continue making income withdrawals and buy the annuity at latest when that person reaches age 75 (or when the pension scheme member would have reached age 75 if earlier). If the survivor dies before buying the annuity, the fund may be paid in cash to his or her heirs (net of tax at 35%). To the extent that a lump sum from the fund forms part of the estate of the deceased, inheritance tax may be payable unless the estate is below the nil threshold or is exempt because of being left to the surviving spouse.

These provisions only apply to those with personal pension contracts. Those with retirement annuity contracts are not able to defer taking the annuity unless they switch into a personal pension contract. A switch might result in a restriction on the lump sum taken at retirement (see page 238) and might involve administration charges.

Allowable contributions

Contribution limits are fixed by reference to 'net relevant earnings'. For a self-employed person, this means his taxable profits, after deducting capital allowances, losses and any excess of business charges (such as patent royalties paid) over general investment income. For an employee, net relevant earnings are those from an employment not carrying any pension rights. The earnings figure includes the cash equivalent of benefits, but is after deducting expenses allowable against those earnings. In line with occupational schemes, an employee's relevant earnings under personal pension plans exclude earnings under share option and incentive schemes and lump sum termination payments. An overall limit applies to net relevant earnings under personal pension plans (but not retirement annuity contracts), the limit being £82,200 for 1996/97 and £78,600 for 1995/96, in line with the limit for occupational pensions. This figure is usually increased annually in line with inflation.

The maximum contributions which may be allowed as a deduction from relevant earnings in any one tax year for someone aged 35 or under (personal pension plans), or 50 or under (retirement annuity contracts) are 17½% of the net relevant earnings, plus any unused relief for the previous six years. Unused relief is the amount that could have been paid in an earlier year by reference to the net relevant earnings of that year, less what was actually paid in respect of that year's earnings. Where there was unused relief at 1 July 1988, when the new scheme started, it counts as unused relief for both personal pension contributions (PPCs) and retirement annuity premiums (RAPs). The percentage limit is increased for taxpayers over 36 (PPCs), 51 (RAPs) at the beginning of the tax year, as follows:

Personal pension plans

	%
age 36 to 45	20
46 to 50	25
51 to 55	30
56 to 60	35
61 and over	40

Retirement annuity contracts

	%
age 51 to 55	20
56 to 60	22½
61 and over	27½

Where someone has pension contracts both under the old and new schemes, the PPC limits are reduced by any RAPs paid. For someone aged 53, for example, with net relevant earnings of £20,000, the maximum RAPs would be 20%, i.e. £4,000, and if premiums of that amount were paid, the amount available for PPCs would be reduced from £6,000 (i.e. 30% of £20,000) to £2,000.

The different age limits for PPCs and RAPs and the fact that PPCs are subject to the earnings cap whereas RAPs are not, makes the calculation of maximum available premiums tricky in some cases. To work out the maximum PPCs payable, add unused PPC relief brought forward to the PPC limit for the year and deduct any RAPs paid in the year. The unused PPC relief carried forward is then the balance remaining after deducting the PPCs paid. To work out the unused relief carried forward for RAPS, any PPCs paid in the year are deducted. This can have the effect of 'capping' the RAPs payable, even though the £82,200 earnings limit only applies to PPCs. The capping can, however, be overcome by paying PPCs (and RAPs if required) in one year and only RAPs in the next year. See examples 1 and 2.

The opportunity of using unused past relief can substantially reduce or even eliminate the net relevant earnings for the tax year, but, as indicated in example 3, it is not necessary to utilise all the unused past relief in one year. Any contribution made uses up first the available relief for the current year, then any unused relief for the previous six years, earliest first.

Example 1

Man aged 30 with relevant earnings of £100,000 in 1996/97 and no unused relief brought forward can pay retirement annuity premiums (RAPs) up to 17½% of that amount, i.e. £17,500, but his limit for personal pension premiums (PPCs) is 17½% of £82,200, i.e. £14,385.

If he wants to pay any PPCs, the maximum amount of his combined RAPs and PPCs is restricted to £14,385, because any RAPs have to be deducted to arrive at the amount available for PPCs. Say he paid £10,000 PPCs and £4,385 RAPs. He would then have no unused PPC relief to carry forward, but would have unused RAP relief carried forward of (17,500 − 4,385 − 10,000) = £3,115. If the limits remained unchanged in 1997/98, and he paid no PPCs in that year, he could pay RAPs of (17,500 + 3,115) = £20,615, so that over the two years he would have paid (14,385 + 20,615) = £35,000.

Example 2

Man aged 53, with earnings of £120,000, has a personal pension contribution limit for 1996/97 of 30% of £82,200 and a retirement annuity premium limit of 20% of £120,000. He is in the following position if he makes the payments shown:

Max PPC	Less RAP paid	Available	PPC paid	Unused relief c/fwd
£	£	£	£	£
24,660	10,000	14,660	8,660	6,000

Max RAP	Paid	PPC paid	Unused relief c/fwd
£	£	£	£
24,000	10,000	8,660	5,340

If the limits and earnings remained unchanged for 1997/98, the maximum PPC for that year would be £24,660 + £6,000 b/fwd = £30,660, reduced by any RAP paid, and the maximum RAP would be £24,000 + £5,340 = £29,340.

Employees making personal pension plan arrangements may elect to contract out of the State Earnings Related Pension Scheme (SERPS), still, however, contributing for a basic retirement pension. It is also possible for an employee in a contracted-in pension scheme to remain in the scheme but contract out of SERPS independently through a personal pension plan. See page 244.

An employer can contribute to the personal pension scheme of an employee, but the maximum contribution levels (17½% or higher) cover the combined contributions (but not those by the DSS — see below). Employers' contributions cannot be backdated to earlier years (see below), nor can unused relief brought forward be used to cover an employer's contribution (see page 240).

Example 3		£	£
Net relevant earnings in 1996/97			15,000
17½% thereof		2,625	

Unused relief for earlier years:

	Appropriate percentage of net relevant earnings, say	*Less* contributions already relieved for that year, say	
1995/96	3,500	2,000	1,500
1994/95	2,500	2,200	300
1993/94	2,900	1,700	1,200
1992/93	3,000	1,000	2,000
1991/92	2,000	500	1,500
1990/91	2,200	1,400	800

Maximum relief available for year 1996/97	9,925

The minimum contribution required for 1996/97 in order to avoid wasting any unused relief would have to be:

17½% of £15,000 (relevant earnings for 1996/97)	2,625
Unused relief for 1990/91	800
	£3,425

The unused relief for 1991/92 to 1995/96 inclusive would then be available to increase the funding limit for 1997/98.

Backdating of contributions to earlier years (TA 1988, ss 619(4), 641; FA 1996, Sch 17 para 2 and Sch 21 paras 17, 18)

A claim may be made for a contribution paid in one tax year to be treated for all purposes as a payment in the previous tax year (or, if there were no net relevant earnings in the previous year, as a payment made two years earlier). Thus in example 3, the contribution of £3,425 could have been paid wholly or partly in 1997/98 and by election treated as relating to 1996/97. This gives a breathing space to establish what the maximum allowable contribution is for a particular year, and also to provide the cash resources to make the payment. It is a useful provision since it is not possible to carry forward an excess of contributions, over the allowable limit, for relief in a later year. Indeed, any excess personal pension contributions (but not excess retirement annuity contributions) have to be refunded. If contributions have been paid by both employee and employer, the employee's contributions are refunded first.

For years before 1996/97, backdating claims had to be made before 6 July following the end of the tax year in which the premium was paid, and were given effect by adjusting the tax liability of the earlier year. Under self-assessment, claims must be made by the 31 January following the tax year in which the premium is paid. The tax saving resulting from backdating is worked out by reference to the tax position of the earlier year, but the legislation provides that the claim is treated as relating to the later year, and affects the tax liability of that later year. This treatment strictly applies to a payment carried back from 1996/97 to 1995/96. The Revenue have, however, announced that the previous treatment will apply for one more year and such payments will be taken into account in calculating the provisional half-yearly payments on account to be made for 1996/97 (as to which see page 120).

Example 4

Pension premium of £6,000 is paid in December 1996, which will save tax at the basic rate. It would be beneficial to treat the premium as paid in 1995/96 (providing there were sufficient relevant earnings), so that tax would be saved at 25%, rather than in 1996/97 when the saving would be 24%. The reduction of tax of £1,500 will be reflected in the 1995/96 assessment and in the half-yearly provisional payments to be made on account for 1996/97 on 31 January 1997 and 31 July 1997, each of which would accordingly be reduced by (£6,000 @ 25% = £1,500 ÷ 2 =) £750.

If the payment and backdating claim were not notified to the Revenue until after 31 January 1997, and had not been taken into account in the provisional payment due on that day, the taxpayer would be able to claim back the overpayment and would receive interest on it from the payment date until repayment.

Contracting out of the State Earnings Related Pension Scheme (SERPS) by employees not in an employer's scheme

Since 1 July 1988, employees not in an occupational scheme have been able to contract out of SERPS by taking out an appropriate personal pension plan (i.e. one that satisfies conditions laid down in the legislation). The premium under the plan is paid net of basic rate tax and the Inland Revenue pay the tax into the plan. The employee and his employer continue to pay full national insurance contributions, but the DSS pay into the plan the contracting-out rebate (currently 4.8% of earnings between lower and upper levels). Up to 5 April 1993 they also paid an incentive payment of a further 2% of those earnings. From 6 April 1993 the DSS will pay in an additional rebate of 1% for those who are 30 or over at the beginning of the relevant tax year. (See page 204 for changes being introduced from April 1997.) Since personal pension plans qualify for tax relief whereas national insurance contributions do not, the DSS will also pay in tax relief on the gross equivalent of the employee's 1.8% share of the 4.8% rebate. See example 5.

Example 5

Employee aged 33 in non-pensionable employment who earns £250 a week contracts out of SERPS by contributing £12 a week to an appropriate personal pension plan.

Earnings on which contracting-out rebate is paid are £250 less £61 lower earnings level, i.e. £189.

Weekly investment in plan in 1996/97 is as follows:

	£
Employee pays £12 less 24% tax (£2.88)	9.12
Inland Revenue pays in the tax relief of	2.88
DSS pays:	
Contracting-out rebate	
Employer's contribution 3% × £189	5.67
Employee's contribution 1.8% × £189	3.40
Tax relief on gross equivalent of employee's	
contribution (£3.40 × 100/76 @ 24%)	1.07
Over 30s rebate 1% × £189	1.89
	£24.03

The part of the pension funded by the DSS payment can only be paid from age 65 (60 for women), it cannot be commuted for a lump sum and it must include provision for index-linking and for widows'/widowers' pensions.

Contracting out of SERPS and remaining in an employer's scheme

An employee who is in an occupational scheme that is contracted in to SERPS may remain in the employer's scheme but opt out of SERPS by means of an individual personal pension plan. The way that this is done is that the employee and employer continue to pay full national insurance contributions, and the payment into the personal pension plan is made solely by the DSS, who contribute the same amount as indicated in example 5 for employees not in a pension scheme, i.e. currently 4.8% of the employee's earnings between the lower and upper earnings levels (5.8% for employees over 30) plus tax relief on the employee's share of the contracting-out rebate.

Funding the contributions

Two often expressed objections to personal pension provision are, first, the cost and, second, the fact that you cannot use the fund until retirement.

Although it is not possible for a lender to take a charge on a personal pension fund, several pension providers have arrangements under which a lender will make an appropriate advance to a taxpayer with a sufficiently large accumulated fund, or who is paying regular contributions to a fund, usually in the latter case based on a multiple of recurrent contributions and the age of the taxpayer. The terms of the advance are usually that interest is payable year by year but capital repayments are taken from the eventual tax-free lump sum on retirement. Whether security for the borrowing is required often depends upon the trade or profession carried on by the taxpayer.

The loan could itself be used to fund contributions to the scheme, so that in example 3 (on page 242) a substantial part of the £9,925 maximum contribution might be funded from a loan made at the same time through the pension provider.

Tax relief on the interest paid will not be available unless the borrowing is for a qualifying purpose, such as the limited relief available on the acquisition of a main residence and the relief for the acquisition of a business property or a partnership share (see chapter 2). There will thus not be any relief in the case of a loan used to pay pension scheme contributions.

Term assurance and pensions for dependants (TA 1988, ss 621, 636, 637)

The return of contributions on death prior to retirement is in itself a form of lump sum provision. The amount refunded is the gross contributions, usually with reasonable interest, whereas the cost to the payer was net of tax relief, so that a cash profit automatically arises. Clearly, the longer the contributions have been paid the greater the capital sum on death before retirement or lump sum following retirement.

To cover the possibility that death might occur before a reasonable sum has been built up, the taxpayer may also pay a premium to provide a lump sum on death before age 75. Such a policy may be written in trust, which has the advantage of making the sum quickly available instead of waiting for probate, and also avoids the sum assured swelling the estate for inheritance tax. Relief for premiums paid is given at the payer's top tax rate, thus giving opportunity for life cover with tax relief, even though tax relief is not now available on ordinary life assurance policies taken out after 13 March 1984.

Alternatively or additionally, a premium may be paid to provide a pension for dependants.

The allowable premiums for the term assurance (and/or dependants' pensions for old schemes) are subject to a limit of 5% of net relevant earnings, the 5% being part of, and not additional to, the 17½% (or higher because of age) limit (see above).

Way in which relief is given

Retirement annuity relief is given to the self-employed by deduction in the tax assessment (including a self-assessment) and to employees by coding adjustment.

The way in which personal pension plan relief is given depends on whether the pension plan is taken out by a self-employed person or by an employee. Premiums paid by the self-employed are paid in full and tax relief is given in the assessment on the self-employed earnings. Premiums paid by employees are paid net of basic rate tax, and relief at the higher rate, where relevant, is given by coding adjustment. Where an employee contracts out of SERPS, however, there is no higher rate relief on the part of the DSS contribution that relates to the employee's contracting-out rebate.

Where basic rate tax is deducted at source by an employee, the relief is retained whether the employee is a taxpayer or not. This could give the opportunity for an employee with relatively low non-pensionable earnings to get tax relief on a substantial premium in one year, even though earnings were largely covered by the personal allowance. See example 6.

Example 6

A married woman aged 40 has unused relief brought forward of £3,000. Her only income was a salary of £5,000 in 1996/97, giving an allowable premium for that year of £1,000. If she paid the maximum allowable premium of £4,000 gross, £3,000 net, the position would be:

	£
Salary	5,000
Personal pension premium paid	(4,000)
Personal allowance	(3,765)
Taxable income	Nil

Amount invested in pension fund is £4,000 at a net cost of £3,000.

Had she been self-employed, the maximum tax-efficient premium would have been £1,235 (i.e. £5,000 – £3,765).

If someone is both employed and self-employed, he can pay a single personal pension contribution relating to both sources of earnings, with the basic rate tax deducted from the employed earnings element, but separate contribution certificates will have to be provided showing that the contribution re the employment earnings was paid net of basic rate tax and the contribution re the self-employment was paid in full.

Payment of pensions (TA 1988, s 648A)

Up to 5 April 1995, retirement annuities and personal pension plan annuities were paid net of basic rate tax. Those on low incomes who had not used their allowances and/or lower rate tax band therefore had to claim repayments, and higher rate taxpayers had extra tax to pay. From 6 April 1995 the annuities are taxed through the PAYE scheme in the same way as occupational pensions, with tax being charged at the appropriate rate and coding adjustments being made where some or all of the available allowances have been used against other income, such as State pensions.

Late assessments and investigation settlements (TA 1988, ss 625, 642; Revenue Statement of Practice SP 9/91)

Assessments are sometimes made more than six years after the tax year to which they relate, usually owing to the fraudulent or negligent conduct of the taxpayer (see chapter 9). Where an assessment becomes final and conclusive more than six years after the tax year to which it relates, a taxpayer may utilise any unused relief created by the assessment to cover a contribution in excess of the 17½% (or higher because of age) limit (see above) for the year of payment, provided that he both makes the additional contribution and makes an election within six months after the assessment becomes final and conclusive. Relief is then given against the earnings of the year of payment. (Only the contribution related to the unused relief need be made within the six-month period. The contribution under the normal rules could be made in the following year and carried back.)

Strictly, this relief is only available where assessments are formally determined, but the Revenue will allow it where an investigation settlement is concluded in the more usual way by their acceptance of an offer in respect of tax, interest and penalties rather than by the formal determination of assessments.

Tax points

- Contributions to personal pension plans attract tax relief at your top rate making them a highly efficient means of providing for the future.

- The person through whom you arrange your pension contract may rebate part of his commission to you, or net it off against the premium, or invest it on your behalf. The Revenue had announced that they would regard such sums as your taxable income, but they no longer intend to do so.

- Consider tax-efficient term assurance under the personal pension scheme rules as an alternative to life assurance. But remember that a term assurance can only provide a lump sum on death before age 75, not on surviving to a certain age as with an endowment policy.

- Also bear in mind that life assurance contracts taken out before 14 March 1984 will probably still entitle you to 12½% income tax relief on the premium payments, so if you are considering replacing existing life cover, it may be more appropriate to surrender later policies.

- An inheritance or unexpected windfall may be used to fund an exceptional personal pension contribution supported by current earnings and unused past relief.

- Even though non-pensionable earnings have been eliminated by personal allowances, they still qualify as relevant earnings for the calculation of relief. Thus a working wife may have paid very little tax on modest earnings because of her tax allowances, but those earnings can nonetheless create unused relief to support a pension contribution in a later year when her earnings have increased enough for the set-off to be beneficial. Also, if she is an employee, she can get tax relief on a premium even though all or part of her salary is covered by her personal allowances.

- Where someone who is UK resident has non-pensionable earnings abroad that escape tax because of the 100% deduction for long absences (see page 558), those earnings even so create unused relief that can be used to cover a pension premium in the following six years.

- There are special rules for doctors and dentists, who, despite having to pay pension contributions under the National Health Service Acts, can also make personal pension contributions along the lines of this chapter, subject to certain modifications because of the NHS pension contributions. The calculation rules are complicated and should be considered very carefully in deciding to what extent relief is available.

- Some building societies and other lenders will permit the borrower to pay only interest during the period of a loan, with an undertaking that the loan itself will be repaid from the tax-free lump sum on retirement.

- You can delay buying an annuity with your personal pension fund when you retire, which is useful if annuity rates are low. You are, of course, taking the risk that the annuity rates may have fallen even further at the time when you want to buy the annuity.

- If, after retiring from a pensionable employment, you then have earnings from a non-pensionable employment, you may make further pension provision by paying contributions under a personal pension plan.

- If a person works on after the earliest permitted retirement age under a pension contract and dies before drawing the pension, the value of the pension rights immediately before his death may be taken into account for inheritance tax — on the same grounds as those indicated on page 236 for employees in occupational schemes.

- Trading losses set off against other income (see chapter 25) must even so be taken into account in calculating unused relief by reducing the next available profits from the trade.

- If you retire early and register as unemployed, unemployment benefit (or jobseeker's allowance from October 1996) is reduced to the extent that a personal pension or occupational pension exceeds £50 a week. The pension income limit was previously £35 and the restriction applied only to those aged over 55. If you are under 55 and were already receiving unemployment benefit before 1 April 1996, you will not suffer the restriction until you reach age 55.

- New pension contracts have to be under the personal pension contract rules, so that it is only possible to vary the mix of retirement annuity and personal pension contributions where there is an existing variable retirement annuity contract.

18
Sole trader, partnership or company?

Non-tax considerations

The alternatives when you start in business or need to consider a change in how you operate are to become a sole trader, to form a partnership with others or to form a limited liability company. A sole trader or partner is liable for the debts of the business to the full extent of his personal assets, and can in the extreme be made bankrupt. A company shareholder's liability is normally limited to the amount, if any, unpaid on his shares. Protection of private assets is usually one of the main reasons for trading through a company. However, lenders, landlords and sometimes suppliers often require directors to give a personal guarantee in respect of the company's obligation, which reduces significantly the benefit of limited liability. There are also major compliance requirements for a company under the Companies Acts, including the possible need to prepare and publish audited accounts, which must be sent promptly to the Companies Registry (see page 137). Companies whose turnover is £90,000 or less need not, however, produce audited accounts, and companies with turnover between £90,000 and £350,000 may submit unaudited accounts accompanied by an accountant's report (called a compilation report).

The general commercial and family considerations must be weighed alongside the comparative tax positions when choosing what form the business is to take.

Comparative income tax and national insurance position for the unincorporated trader and the company director

As a sole trader or partner, you will pay income tax at 40% on all your income (after personal allowances) in excess of £25,500, whether you leave the profits in the business or withdraw them. This threshold is available to each of a husband and wife partnership. If you are a controlling director/ shareholder you can decide how much profit to take in the form of remuneration or dividends (on which you will pay income tax) and how much to leave to be taxed at corporation tax rates. (Your remuneration or dividend need not be withdrawn from the company, it can be left to your credit on loan account. The important point is whether more tax will be paid overall if it is treated as your personal income rather than as company profit.) The corporation tax rate on profits up to £300,000 is 24% (see page 30 for further details). Once profits reach a certain level, therefore, it is better from the immediate tax point of view to operate as a company in order to take advantage of the lower company tax rates.

But you also need to look at the national insurance position. A sole trader or partner pays class 2 national insurance contributions of £6.05 a week, amounting to £315 in 1996/97, and class 4 contributions of 6% on profits between £6,860 and £23,660, giving a maximum class 4 liability for 1996/97 of £1,008. The maximum total class 2 and class 4 contributions for 1996/97 are therefore £1,323. In a husband and wife partnership both have to pay class 4 national insurance contributions. They also both have to pay class 2 contributions unless the wife elected not to do so on or before 11 May 1977 and holds a certificate of exemption. The national insurance contributions on remuneration drawn from a company depend on the earnings (see page 204). The employee's contribution is 2% on the first £61 of weekly earnings and 10% on the next £394 up to the upper earnings limit of £455 per week. The employer's contribution is 10.2% on all earnings if they are £210 per week or more. (The 10.2% rate is to be reduced to 10% from April 1997.) If remuneration of £23,660 is taken (i.e. the upper limit for employee's contributions, £455 × 52), the combined employer's and employee's contributions in 1996/97 would be £4,525. The employer's share (£2,413) is, however, allowable as a deduction in calculating the profits of the company which are liable to corporation tax (reducing the figure to £3,946 with corporation tax at 24%). In broad terms, the extra national insurance cost of operating through a company at that profit level is therefore around £2,600.

The overall tax position is also affected by whether profits are withdrawn as salary or dividends, 20% of the tax paid by the company on dividends being able to be passed on to the shareholder as a tax credit. That tax credit covers the shareholder's tax liability on the dividend unless his income exceeds the basic rate threshold, because the charging rate on dividends (and other savings income) up to the basic rate threshold is only 20%. This gives the possibility of an extra 4% tax saving for basic rate taxpayers on paying dividends instead of salary. For an illustration, see page 188.

Four other points should be borne in mind. First, some benefits, in particular unemployment benefit (or jobseeker's allowance from October 1996) and earnings-related retirement pension, are not available to the self-employed. Second, to obtain a deduction in calculating taxable profits, earnings as a director or employee are required to be 'wholly and exclusively for the purposes of the trade', so particularly where a wife or husband does not work full-time in a business, the earnings may be challenged by the Revenue as excessive in calculating the taxable profit of the company. There is no such requirement for a wife or husband who is an active partner, albeit working less than full-time, although artificial arrangements will not work (see page 340). Third, capital gains tax retirement relief on a company shareholding is only available to full-time working directors and employees. Part-time directors do not qualify (see page 58). Again, there are no such restrictions where a partner working less than full-time disposes of all or part of his partnership interest. Fourth, the rate of inheritance tax business property relief may be lower when operating through a company (see page 79).

The profit level at which the retentions after tax and national insurance will be less operating through a company than as a sole trader or partner is not a static figure but one which will vary according to whether there are other sources of income, how much remuneration is drawn from the company, and whether any dividends are paid. Example 1 shows that in 1996/97 if an individual with no other income draws a salary of £29,265 from a company to leave him with taxable income equal to the basic rate band of £25,500, the profit level at which the tax burden using the company format equates with that of an individual trader is £48,374. The turning point would be at a lower profit level on a salary of less than £29,265 and a higher level on a salary above £29,265 (and would in any event be nearly double for a husband/wife partnership). There could, however, be further tax liabilities on the company retentions at a later date, but these may never materialise, through changes in tax rates, exemptions, etc., and in the meantime cash will have been conserved in the company.

Paying tax on the profits (TMA 1970, ss 59A, 59B; TA 1988, ss 5, 10; FA 1994, ss 192, 193)

Directors' remuneration is subject to tax and national insurance under the PAYE scheme immediately it is paid or credited to the director's account, with corporation tax on any profits left in the company being payable 9 months after the year end. Before the introduction of self-assessment in 1996/97, income tax on self-employed business profits was paid in two equal instalments on 1 January and 1 July, the interval between earning the profits and paying the first instalment being anything from 9 to nearly 21 months depending on the choice of accounting date. This gave the self-employed a significant cash flow advantage.

Following the introduction of self-assessment for individuals from 1996/97, coupled with the change to a current year basis of assessment, the advantage of the unincorporated business over the company in terms of the payment dates is not so clear-cut. The unincorporated business makes provisional payments of tax half-yearly on 31 January in the tax year and 31 July following. The provisional payments are based on the total income (not just the business profits) of the previous tax year, with an adjustment to the correct figure, including any tax due on capital gains, on the following 31 January. The extent to which the unincorporated business will be better off than the company from a cash flow point of view will depend on whether directors' remuneration has been taken (and if so, how much and when), and whether the provisional income tax payments are significantly less than the full amount due. See example 2.

Example 1

Business profits before tax and national insurance are £48,374 and there are no other sources of income. A sole trader is liable to income tax on the full amount. If a company director drew a salary of £29,265 in equal monthly amounts during 1996/97 (which after the personal allowance of £3,765 leaves income of £25,500 to use the lower and basic rate tax bands), the comparative position is:

	Trader		Company director
Profits/remuneration	48,374		29,265
Personal allowance	3,765		3,765
Taxable income	44,609		25,500
Tax thereon: On 3,900 @ 20%	780		780
21,600 @ 24%	5,184		5,184
19,109 @ 40%	7,644		
44,609			
	13,608		5,964
Class 2 NI (flat rate)	315	Employee's NI	
Class 4 NI (maximum)	1,008	(maximum)	2,112
Total personal tax and NI	14,931		8,076
Company's tax and NI:			
Profits		48,374	
Less: Director's remuneration		(29,265)	
Company's NI thereon		(2,985)	2,985
Taxable profits		16,124	
Tax thereon @ 24%		(3,870)	3,870
		12,254	
Total tax and NI liabilities	14,931		14,931
Drawn or undrawn profits	33,443		33,443
	£48,374		£48,374

Each extra £1 of profit would cost the sole trader 40p in tax and the company 24p.

Possible further tax liabilities if company retentions of £12,254 are paid out:
   If distributed as dividends, maximum of
      (40–20)% on £15,318 (i.e. £12,254 plus tax credit £3,064,
      the 20% tax credit being passed on to the shareholder
      from company's corporation tax) £3,064
   If taxed as capital gains, 40% on £12,254 .... £4,902

Example 2

Say accounts of a business that started in 1995 were made up for the year to 31 December 2000. The profits of that year would be part of the total income of 2000/2001 and tax on that total income would be payable provisionally in two equal instalments on 31 January 2001 and 31 July 2001, based on the previous year's income. The correct figure of tax on the income plus capital gains of 2000/2001 would be notified by 31 January 2002, and a balancing payment or repayment would be made accordingly. The first provisional payment for 2001/2002 would also be due on 31 January 2002.

If the business had been a company, tax on the undrawn profits of the year to 31 December 2000 would have been due on 1 October 2001, with PAYE tax and national insurance being payable at the time when any remuneration was drawn and corporation tax having been paid in advance if dividends were paid.

There is an additional flexibility open to unincorporated businesses. By choosing an accounting date early in the tax year, say 30 April, they may benefit from lower tax rates and thresholds in the year of assessment compared with those in force when most of the profits were earned (although the rates can of course go up as well as down). This was particularly beneficial under the 'previous year basis' rules, but still applies under self-assessment. The possible advantage may, however, be counterbalanced by the current year basis rules for taxing profits when the business ceases. For the detailed rules on how profits are charged to tax, see chapter 21.

Losses (TA 1988, ss 380–385, 393, 574–576; FA 1991, s 72; TCGA 1992, s 253; FA 1994, ss 209, 210)

If a new business is expected to make losses in its early years, it is essential to bear in mind the different loss reliefs available to individuals and to companies. (These are dealt with more fully in chapters 25 and 26.) The income tax loss rules are changing as a result of the changes in the way self-employed profits are taxed (see page 350). The following provisions relate to new businesses starting on or after 6 April 1994.

Individuals can claim generous reliefs for trading losses in a new business. Losses in any of the first four tax years of a new business may be carried back to set against *any* income of the previous three tax years, earliest first. The tax liability of the earlier years is recalculated accordingly to establish the tax saving. For loss claims relating to 1996/97 and later years, however, effect is given to the saving by reducing the tax liability of the tax year of loss rather than that of the tax year in which the loss has been set off, so the tax saving is not boosted as it used to be by interest on overpaid tax (repayment supplement). For losses in later years (or instead of a carry-back claim for opening year losses) a claim may be made to set them against the total income of the tax year in which the loss is sustained or the previous tax year, and tax will be discharged or repaid. The losses may be boosted, or indeed created, by capital allowances. In some circumstances, trading losses may be set against capital gains. Unrelieved trading losses may always be carried forward to set against future trading profits of the same trade.

If a new company makes trading losses, they may only be set against any current profits of the company, such as bank interest or chargeable gains, or carried forward against the company's later *trading* profits. Trading losses of an established company may be set against the profits from other sources, if any, in the same accounting year, then against the total profits of the previous three years, latest first, with any balance being carried forward against trading profits. Established companies can thus claim more generous loss reliefs than established unincorporated businesses.

Funds introduced to a limited company to support losses, either as share capital or on loan, do not qualify for any immediate relief (but see page 12 as regards relief for interest payable on any borrowing to enable the funds to be introduced). There are two relieving measures for shares and loans, but they are only available when shares are disposed of or when money lent becomes irrecoverable. The provisions are as follows:

(a) An individual can set a capital loss on the disposal of shares that he had *subscribed for* in an unquoted trading company against any of his income in the same way as a trading loss, as an alternative to setting the capital loss against capital gains.

(b) The loss of money loaned to the company (or paid to cover a bank guarantee) may be deducted against the lender's capital gains.

To get the first relief, you need to dispose of the shares, or they need to have become virtually worthless, probably because the business has failed. The second relief is also only likely to be available because the company is in financial difficulties. The distinction between the shares relief being given against income and the loan relief only against capital gains is important, because relief against income gives more flexibility and the opportunity for early relief. With income and capital gains tax rates now being the same, consideration of the tax rate at which the loss is relieved is of less significance.

These two relieving measures are available both to working directors and to others providing funds to a company.

Pensions

If you are self-employed, you are entitled to relief at your top rate of tax on premiums paid to provide a pension when you retire. The maximum allowable premium is presently between 17½% and 40% of your profits (subject to a £82,200 ceiling for 1996/97 — see page 239), depending on your age. If the maximum premium is not paid in any year, the unused relief may be carried forward to enable larger premiums to be paid in the next six years. Company directors/employees in non-pensionable employment can also take advantage of these provisions, but it is often preferable for a family company to operate its own pension scheme.

Company pension schemes are less restrictive in that the only limit on the company's contributions to an approved scheme is that the retirement benefits provided must not exceed certain limits and the scheme must not be overfunded, although the same £82,200 ceiling applies in calculating maximum benefits. The company scheme can be contributory or non-contributory, the company's contributions reducing the company's taxable profits and not being charged either to tax or national insurance on the employee, and the individual's contributions, if any, being allowed against his earnings from the company (although not deducted from pay in calculating employers' and employees' national insurance contributions).

For details on company and personal pension schemes, see chapters 16 and 17.

Capital gains

Where realised chargeable gains are not covered by available reliefs, the first £6,300 of the total gains in 1996/97 is exempt from tax for individuals (£6,300 each for husband and wife), tax being charged at the appropriate income tax rate of 20%/24%/40% on the remainder. Companies are not entitled to any exemption and pay corporation tax on the full amount. The rate of tax on the company's gains for the year to 31 March 1997 is therefore either the small companies rate of 24%, the full rate of 33% or the marginal rate of 35.25% if profits lie between £300,000 and £1,500,000. ACT on dividends may, however, be set against the corporation tax on capital gains. This means that the effect of gains being realised within a company depends on the company's tax rate and the way in which the gains are passed to the shareholder. The possible effect if the gains are passed on as a dividend is shown in example 3. If the gains are retained within the company until the shareholder disposes of his shares or the company goes into liquidation, the shareholder will be liable to capital gains tax on the increase in value of his shareholding, and since the gain will have borne corporation tax when it was made this would effectively give a double tax charge. Reliefs may, however, be available at the time the shares are disposed of (see below).

Whether or not a business is incorporated, the increase in the value of its chargeable assets may lead to chargeable gains in the future, and in the case of a company there is the possibility of further personal chargeable gains where the share value is increased by profit retentions. Death is an effective, albeit unwelcome, way of escaping capital gains tax liabilities. Legatees effectively take over the assets at their market value at the date of death and thus get a tax-free uplift in base cost where values have risen.

Less drastically, two important reliefs lessen the capital gains tax impact, and both reliefs are available to sole traders, partners and company shareholders who are full-time working directors or employees.

Example 3

Company makes a gain of £10,000 in year to 31 March 1997, which is passed on to shareholders as a dividend.

| | Rate of tax on profits | | |
	24%	33%	Marginal rate of 35.25%
	£	£	£
Company gain	10,000	10,000	10,000
Corporation tax	(2,400)	(3,300)	(3,525)
Leaving for cash dividend	7,600	6,700	6,475
Tax credit on dividend at 20/80ths	1,900	1,675	1,619
Shareholder's income	9,500	8,375	8,094
Maximum income tax @ 40%	3,800	3,350	3,238
Leaving shareholder with net cash of	£5,700	£5,025	£4,856
Combined company and personal tax	£4,300	£4,975	£5,144
i.e.	43%	49.75%	51.44%

If in the first instance (i.e. company's tax rate 24%), the shareholder had not been liable to tax because of available reliefs, and had been able to recover the tax credit of £1,900, the net tax suffered would be (2,400 – 1,900) = £500, representing a tax rate of 5% on the gain. The total tax on the gain could therefore be anything from 5% to 51.44%.

Subject to certain restrictions, gains on the disposal of a business, or of an interest in a business, or of shares in your personal trading company in which you work full-time are exempt up to a maximum of £250,000, with 50% exemption on gains between £250,000 and £1,000,000, if you are over 50 (or if you are forced to retire before age 50 through ill health). A personal company is one in which you hold 5% or more of the voting rights.

If you make gifts of chargeable business assets, the gifts are treated as disposals at open market value, which may give rise to chargeable gains. You and the donee may, however, jointly claim to treat the gain as reducing the donee's capital gains tax cost, and thus avoid an immediate tax charge. For those entitled to retirement relief, the gifts relief may be used to cover gains in excess of that relief.

A further relief is available where gains (whether arising through the business or otherwise) are wholly or partly reinvested in ordinary shares in a qualifying unquoted trading company. The reinvested gains are treated as reducing the acquisition value of the shares.

See chapter 4 for a fuller treatment of these provisions.

Inheritance tax (IHTA 1984, ss 103–114)

There is usually no inheritance tax to pay on gifts in lifetime or on death of all or part of your business, whether you operate as an individual or through a company. Business property relief is available at the rate of 100% on transfers of all or part of an individual's business and on transfers out of unquoted shareholdings (providing the company carries on a qualifying business — see page 80 — and providing any lifetime gifts of such property, or qualifying replacement property, are still retained by the donee when the donor dies). Shares on the Unlisted Securities Market or Alternative Investment Market count as unquoted shares. For details, see chapter 5.

If you want to pass on your business gradually to other members of the family, the company format has the edge in terms of flexibility, since it is easier to transfer shares 'than to transfer a part of an unincorporated business.

Raising finance

The enterprise investment scheme gives a qualifying company an advantage over an unincorporated business in attracting funds from outside investors. Tax relief at 20% is given on up to £100,000 invested for at least five years in shares of qualifying unquoted trading companies, and gains on disposal of the shares are exempt from tax. Similar provisions apply to investments in venture capital trusts, which are quoted companies that invest in unquoted companies. The detailed rules are in chapter 29.

Changing from one format to another

It is a simple matter for an unincorporated business to change from a sole trader to a partnership or vice versa (see page 325). Where an unincorporated business is to be incorporated, careful planning is necessary to ensure the best tax position and to minimise the disadvantages — see chapter 27. Unfortunately there are no special tax provisions to help companies who wish to disincorporate. If the company has accumulated trading losses, these cannot be transferred to the shareholders. If the shareholders take the company's assets into personal ownership in order to use them in a new unincorporated business, the disposal by the company will be an open market value disposal for the purpose of calculating a taxable gain, and where there are trading losses, any capital gains can only be reduced by current and not by brought forward losses. Corporation tax will then be payable on any remaining gains. The consequences of either paying out gains as dividends or as capital distributions in a liquidation are illustrated in chapter 28. If the company's disposal of any of the assets should yield a capital loss, no relief would be available unless the company had gains against which to set it, and the shareholders would be acquiring the assets at a lower capital gains tax base cost than was paid by the company.

Tax points

● Don't let the tax tail wag the commercial dog. Consider *all* aspects of alternative business forms.

● If profits are at or above the £48,000 level, operating through a company will reduce the tax rate on retained profits up to £300,000 from the top income tax rate of 40% to the corporation tax rate of 24%. There are long-term factors to consider, but these will probably be outweighed by the short-term advantage.

● The loss rules for individuals, particularly the three year carry-back of new business losses, make an unincorporated start an attractive proposition where there is heavy initial expenditure, particularly on revenue items but also on capital items which attract tax allowances. The business can later be converted to a company if appropriate.

● To get income tax relief on a capital loss where shares are disposed of in an unquoted trading company, the shares must have been issued *to you* by the company. Shares acquired by transfer from a previous shareholder do not qualify.

● The possible double tax charge where a company first sells chargeable assets at a profit, thus paying corporation tax on the profit and also increasing the value of its shares, can be avoided by shareholder/ directors retaining personal ownership of assets such as freeholds or leaseholds and allowing the company to use them. But inheritance tax business property relief at 50% is only available on those assets where a shareholder *controls* the company, whereas the 50% reduction is available to any partner who personally owns assets which are used by the partnership. See chapter 27 for the effect of charging rent.

● Although chargeable gains are now taxed at income tax rates, they are none the less still chargeable gains. Thus, any available income tax deductions, such as allowances for buildings in enterprise zones, cannot be set off against them. But a dividend from a company, even if payable out of a capital profit, counts as income in the hands of the shareholder, and deductions could then be set off , with an appropriate repayment of the tax credit attaching to the dividend.

19
Starting up a new small or part-time business

Is it a self-employment?

It is important to establish at the outset whether your activities amount to self-employment or whether you are an employee. You may be neither employed nor self-employed but receiving casual sums taxable under the 'any other income' provisions (for example receiving payments for writing the occasional article, but not often enough to be regarded as an author). Exceptionally, the activity may not be taxable at all.

The distinction between employment and self-employment is important in deciding whether tax and employees' national insurance should be deducted from payments (and employers' national insurance paid), what expenses may be deducted from the income in calculating the tax liability, and whether the recipient should register for VAT.

The main distinction between employment and self-employment used to be whether payment was under a contract of service chargeable under the PAYE rules or a contract for services entitling you to payment against your invoice or fee note, to be included in your self-employed accounts. But the decision is now not so clear-cut, and depends on the overall circumstances rather than just the form of the contract. The Revenue and DSS have published a joint booklet IR 56/NI 39 outlining the main points they look at. (A separate version of the booklet — IR 148/CA 69 — is published for contractors in the construction industry — see chapter 44.) Factors pointing to employment are that you work wholly or mainly for one business, you need to carry out the work in person, you have to take orders as to how and when to do it, to work where those providing the work tell you to, and to work set hours at an hourly, weekly or monthly rate, and you get paid for overtime, sickness and holidays. Factors pointing to self-employment are that you risk your own capital and bear any losses, you control whether, how, when and where you do the work, provide your own equipment, are free to employ others to do the work and are required to bear the cost of correcting anything that goes wrong. None of these factors is conclusive — indeed many of them will be irrelevant in particular cases — and all the circumstances have to be taken into account. The decision affects your status both for income tax and national insurance, and a decision taken by one department will be accepted by the other. The tax/national insurance treatment is not, however, conclusive for VAT.

You can challenge a ruling by the Revenue, the DSS or Customs that you are an employee, and some taxpayers have recently had some success, but it could be costly and time consuming. A few years ago, the Revenue targeted the entertainment profession for particular scrutiny. From 6 April 1990, they treated as employees all entertainers on standard Equity contracts who joined the profession after 5 April 1987. As a result of recent court decisions in the taxpayers' favour, the Revenue have now revised their view and will normally treat entertainers as self-employed except where they are permanent members of an orchestra, opera, ballet, theatre company or similar body. (Such people may nonetheless have other earnings that are treated as being from self-employment.) Affected taxpayers have been invited to have their tax liabilities recomputed back to 6 April 1990, but this will inevitably cause considerable difficulty and inconvenience. Those who have been reclassified as self-employed should also be treated as such for national insurance, although the profession are asking the DSS to treat them as a special case and to continue to allow them to pay contributions as employees, so that they may claim benefits accordingly. Where entertainers remain taxable as employees under the Revenue's revised view, the fees they pay to their agents (including VAT) are specifically allowed as a deduction from their earnings (subject to an overall maximum deduction in any tax year of 17½% of the employment earnings) (TA 1988, s 201A).

For VAT, particular care is needed with licensing and franchise arrangements, and even if someone is regarded as self-employed, they may be treated as the agent of the licensor/franchisor, so that the VAT liability depends on the licensor's/franchisor's VAT status. In two cases involving driving instructors, the instructors in one were held to be agents (even though accepted as self-employed by the Revenue and DSS), while the others were held to be self-employed principals. And in two hairdressing cases, one group of stylists working under a franchise arrangement were treated as self-employed principals, whereas the others were held to be agents of the salon owner.

Many businesses which use part-time assistance are justifiably wary of paying fees in full, since they could be held liable for the PAYE and national insurance they should have deducted if someone is later held to be an employee, and possibly interest and penalties as well. Some businesses will, however, accept an assurance from a tax office or accountant that the income is included in self-employed accounts of the recipient and that the payment should not be taxed under PAYE.

Someone who occasionally buys and sells may contend that his activities are not a trade but remain a hobby, a collector's activity or an investment, such as collecting and restoring antique furniture, sometimes selling the occasional piece at a profit. It is important to establish that the Revenue agree with this contention and not to leave it until they make a challenge, otherwise you could be faced with interest and penalties for non-disclosure. It may be the Revenue rather than the taxpayer who take the view that an activity is a hobby, particularly where there are losses, because to accept that it is a commercial activity would open the way for loss reliefs against other income. Each case depends on the facts, with appropriate rights of appeal if the Revenue do not see it in the same way as the taxpayer.

Where a self-employment has been established, you will have responsibilities in relation to tax, national insurance and VAT. The three Government departments dealing with these matters have combined to produce a booklet CWL1 setting out the basic requirements for those starting in business and dealing with record-keeping, employing staff and other points. The leaflet incorporates a form CWF1 to be sent to the DSS covering all the information you need to provide for all three departments. The following points should be borne in mind.

Computation of taxable profits

The detailed rules for calculating profits are in chapter 20. Chapter 22 deals with capital allowances for the purchase of buildings, equipment, etc. A newly-established business is often run from your home, perhaps using your existing car for any business travelling that is required. You can claim for the business proportion of car expenses, and also the business proportion of capital allowances on the value of the car when you started using it for business. You can also claim a deduction for business calls made from your home telephone. Where you run the business from your home, expenses of part of the home can be allowed against taxable profits if they are wholly and exclusively for the business, so that a fixed proportion of, for example, the light and heat can be charged for the part of the residence which is used for the business, such as a study/office, surgery, workshop, etc. You will be liable to pay business rates on that part of the property, as well as paying the council tax on the rest of the property, unless you can show that the business use does not stop you continuing to use that part of the property for domestic purposes. If paid, business rates will be allowable against your profits. Where business rates are not paid, you will be able to treat as a business expense an appropriate proportion of the council tax according to the business use of the home.

If no part of your home is used wholly and exclusively for the business, your capital gains tax owner-occupier exemption will not be affected. If part of your property is so used, that part will be outside the capital gains tax owner-occupier exemption. Any gain need not be charged to tax immediately if you sell the property and continue the business from a new residence, because a claim may be made for the gain to be regarded as reducing the cost for capital gains tax of the business part of the new residence (see page 55), although it would not be necessary to make that claim if the chargeable gain was covered by the annual capital gains tax exemption (see example 1).

Example 1

House bought January 1986 for £60,000, sold January 1996 for £140,000, indexation allowance £33,660.

Used to January 1991 wholly as residence
    then 1/6th for self-employment
    for remainder of period

Total gain (140,000 − (60,000 + 33,660))   £46,340

Chargeable gain:
    Business use 1/6th for 5 years out
    of 10, 1/6 × 5/10 × £46,340   £3,862

Covered by 1995/96 annual exemption of £6,000 unless already used.

Yet another possibility is retirement relief if you cease to trade after you are 50 years of age or earlier because of ill health (see page 57).

Employing staff (FA 1989, s 43)

If you employ staff in the business, you will need to operate the PAYE scheme (see chapter 10). The Revenue will supply you with all the necessary documentation. It is important to make sure that PAYE is operated properly, particularly where you take on casual or part-time employees. Even if you pay someone less than the tax and national insurance threshold, you must still deduct tax if they have significant other earnings. Form P46 must be completed for any employee who does not produce form P45 (employee's leaving certificate). In a new small business, the first employees are very often members of the family and the PAYE rules apply equally to them. In addition, the salary payments must be both justified and paid. The Revenue will, for example, be unwilling to accept that an amount drawn for house-keeping or personal use includes family wages, and will also be better able to challenge the validity of the expense if it is left as an amount owing rather than having actually been paid. Payments of wages must in any case be made within nine months after the end of the accounting period if they are to be allowed for tax against the profits of that period rather than a later period.

If family wages can be justified for the work done, they enable personal allowances to be used if not already covered by other income. Although the single person's allowance is £3,765, there will still be a cost unless the wages are kept below the national insurance level of £3,172 (see example 2).

Paying a wife below the national insurance threshold does mean that she is not building up any state pension entitlement in her own right, nor can she claim contributory benefits, but she will get a pension based on her husband's contributions when he is 65 and she is 60 (see page 200).

Example 2

If a husband pays his wife a wage of £3,150 in 1996/97, it will reduce his profit for tax, his wife will pay no tax providing she has no other income, and neither he nor she will pay any national insurance contributions thereon. If he pays her an extra £615, making a wage of £3,765, he will save tax on the £615 against his profit and the wife will still pay no tax on it, but there will be a cost of paying it, as follows:

Employee's contributions:		
2% of £3,172	63	
10% of £593	59	122
Employer's contributions 3%	113	
Less tax relief for expense against		
husband's profit, say 24%	27	86
Total national insurance cost		208
Offset by tax relief on extra wage of £615		
against his profit, at say 24%		
(ignoring any possible saving in		
class 4 national insurance)		(148)
Net cost of paying extra £615		£60

How are profits charged to tax?

For businesses starting after 5 April 1994, the first profits usually form the basis of the first two years' assessments (see page 287). A part-time start may therefore help to reduce the tax burden for those years so long as the transition from the part-time activity to full-time self-employment cannot be argued by the Revenue as the start of an entirely new trade. Linking a slow start with a 30 April year end may be particularly helpful (see example 3), although the initial and ongoing advantage where profits are rising needs to be set against the possible disadvantage of a higher taxable profit when the business ceases (see page 288).

Loss relief

If losses are incurred in the first four tax years of a new business, they may be treated as reducing any income of the previous three tax years, earliest first, or set off against any other income and chargeable gains of the tax year of the loss. Tax will then be discharged or repaid accordingly, although from 1996/97 where a loss is carried back to an earlier year, the claim is treated as relating to the loss year and affects the tax liability of that year even though the tax saving from the claim is calculated by reference to the tax position of the earlier year. Capital allowances may be taken into account in the loss claims. See chapter 25 for details of the claims.

Example 3

Trader starts business on a part-time basis on 1 May 1995 and makes up accounts to 30 April 1996, showing a profit for the first year of £12,000. He then devotes all his time to the business and makes a profit of £24,000 in the year to 30 April 1997. The tax position on those profits is as follows:

1995/96	1.5.95–5.4.96	11/12 × £12,000	£11,000
1996/97	1.5.95–30.4.96		£12,000
1997/98	1.5.96–30.4.97		£24,000

Although £11,000 of the £12,000 profit is taxed twice, a deduction of £11,000 will be given against profits when the business ceases (or sometimes earlier).

The effect of choosing a 30 April year end is that the taxable profits of the current year were largely earned in the previous year. The actual profit in 1996/97 was 1/12 of £12,000 and 11/12 of £24,000 = £23,000, whereas the taxable profit is £12,000.

Pension provision

Earnings from a small business can support a personal pension premium, both in respect of the self-employed earnings and for the family employees. It does not matter that the self-employed taxpayer or family employee is also in separate pensionable employment. If you do not pay premiums out of early profits because you want to use the profits to build up the business, or for any other reason, the earnings will enable you to make a larger premium payment within the next six years, even if you paid no tax on the earnings when they were earned, because they were covered by allowances. See chapter 17 for details.

VAT registration

You need to register for VAT at the end of any month if your turnover in the previous twelve months exceeded £47,000. You are required to notify Customs and Excise and you will then be registered unless you can show that your turnover will not exceed £45,000 in the coming twelve months. If you expect your turnover in the next *30 days* to exceed £47,000, you must register immediately. You need to watch these limits carefully because there are severe penalties for not complying with the rules. Even if your turnover is below the limit you may wish to register voluntarily in order to recover VAT input tax on your purchases. But this will not be to your advantage unless most of your customers are VAT registered (see chapter 7).

National insurance

A self-employed person pays class 2 contributions, of £6.05 a week, and also class 4 contributions, at 6% on profits between £6,860 and £23,660 in the tax year 1996/97. The detailed provisions are in chapter 24. Note particularly the provisions for deferring contributions if you are both employed and self-employed. Neither deferment nor a refund affect the liability of the employer to pay employers' contributions.

If your self-employed earnings were below £3,260 in 1995/96 and your circumstances have not materially changed, or are expected to be below £3,430 in 1996/97, you can apply for a certificate of exception from Class 2 contributions (see chapter 24). But you need to consider the effect of not paying on your benefit entitlement, particularly retirement pension, and you may think it best to pay Class 2 contributions even though your earnings are small. Class 2 contributions may be refunded in some circumstances where the small earnings exception would have applied if claimed — see chapter 24.

Occasional earnings not treated as from self-employment

If you are not treated as self-employed, occasional earnings are taxed under Schedule D, Case VI according to the amount earned in the tax year, with a deduction for justifiable expenses. From 1996/97, all income tax that is to be paid directly to the Revenue will be accounted for by making two provisional payments on 31 January in the tax year and 31 July following, with a balancing payment if necessary on the next following 31 January. If you are also an employee, the Revenue will sometimes, for convenience, offset small amounts of occasional earnings against your tax allowances when arriving at your PAYE code number.

Any losses can be set off against any income from other sources charged under Case VI, but it is unlikely that there will be any, in which case the losses are carried forward to reduce any future Case VI profits.

Tax points

- Do not forget to show the self-employment on your tax return or delay in advising the Revenue and submitting accounts, otherwise interest for late payment of tax, and sometimes penalties for negligence, may arise. If your turnover is below £15,000 you can send in a simple three-line account — see page 124.

- Similarly, wages paid to your wife from your self-employment should be shown on her tax return.

- If early earnings are small and covered by allowances, they can still create unused relief for personal pension premium purposes, enabling you to pay a larger premium later on when you can afford to do so (see chapter 17). The same applies to small earnings of a spouse.

- Disabled people and people who have been unemployed for six weeks or more, or on certain Government training schemes, may be entitled to a cash business start-up allowance if they become self-employed, subject to criteria established by Training and Enterprise Councils. To prevent the allowance being taxed more than once because of the opening year rules, it is taxed separately from the profit. It still counts as trading income for Class 4 national insurance contributions and for personal pension premiums.

- You need to notify the DSS when you become self-employed, either to make arrangements to pay Class 2 contributions (quarterly or by direct debit — see page 343), or to apply for a certificate of exception on the grounds of small earnings (see page 266).

- The time limits for lodging DSS applications for deferral and exception from national insurance contributions are important, and applications have to be renewed each year. There could also be a cost of making late payments, either in lost or delayed benefits, or increased contributions. Class 2 repayments are available to some people with small earnings, but again only if claimed within the time limit.

- Do not take people on without making sure of their employment status. If you make a mistake you have only limited rights to recover underpaid tax and national insurance from the worker, and you may have to pay interest and penalties as well.

- A useful test on the self-employed status is whether there is a risk of loss as well as gain, normally implying self-employment; and whether you have to carry out corrective work without payment.

- The Inland Revenue and DSS each have one nominated officer at each office who is responsible for queries and decisions about employment status. A written decision made after investigation by one department will be accepted by the other so long as all the facts have been accurately and fully given and the circumstances remain the same.

- Do not forget to register for VAT if appropriate. You need to check at the end of every *month* to make sure that the annual turnover limit has not been exceeded. See chapter 7.

20
How are business profits calculated?

Background (TA 1988, ss 18, 832)

Trading profits are charged to tax under Schedule D, Case I. Profits from carrying on a profession or vocation are charged under Schedule D, Case II. The same rules are, however, used to calculate profits under both headings. It is usually obvious that a trade is being carried on, but the charge under Case I is extended beyond what would normally be regarded as trading and can cover occasional transactions and those to which an investment motive cannot be attributed, where the circumstances point to a trading intention.

Important indicators of possible trading, when there is any doubt, are the nature of the asset itself (whether it is income producing, or something you get enjoyment from owning, which will indicate investment rather than trading), your reason for acquiring it, how long you owned it, whether you worked on it to make it more saleable, your reason for selling and how often such transactions were undertaken.

General rules for computing profits (TA 1988, s 74)

Whether the business is that of an individual trader, a partnership or a company, profits are calculated according to normal commercial accounting rules unless those rules conflict with the Taxes Acts as interpreted by the courts. The two most important rules for expenses are first that they must be wholly and exclusively for the purposes of the trade, and second, that they must be of a revenue, and not capital, nature.

'Wholly and exclusively'

You cannot claim a deduction for an expense that is for both business and private purposes, such as the rental paid by sole traders or partners for a telephone they use both for business and private calls, but part of a mixed expense may be wholly and exclusively for the purposes of the trade and thus be a valid deduction in calculating profits, such as the charges for the business telephone calls.

If you are a sole trader or partner, some of your car mileage is wholly and exclusively for business, some is purely for private purposes, and some may be partly both. No part of a business trip combined with a holiday satisfies the rule, even though the business derives benefit from the trip, but a conference fee within that trip might qualify. See example 1. The same applies to mixed business and living accommodation, where again it may be possible accurately to separate the business and private areas (see page 262). Where expenditure is for the sole purpose of the business, any incidental private benefit would be ignored. So that if, for example, a trader went away to a two-day business conference, and went to the theatre in the evening, this would not invalidate the business purpose of the conference trip, unless the whole trip had been planned for mixed business/private purposes.

The Revenue might sometimes allow relief for a part of mixed expenses by concession.

Example 1

A trader's recorded mileage in a twelve-month period of account was as follows:

Purely business journeys		5,000
Purely private journeys	4,000	
Home to business	2,000	
Journeys for combined business/private purposes	1,000	
		7,000
		12,000

Allowable business proportion is 5/12ths.

In the case of a company, there can be no private use by the company itself. Where a company or unincorporated employer incurs expenses that benefit employees or directors, the usual treatment is that the expenses are allowed in calculating the taxable profits of the employer, but are treated as taxable earnings of the employee or director (see chapter 10). Sometimes, directors' fees, wages paid or the cost of benefits provided to members of the family who do not work full-time may not be allowed in full if the payment is considered excessive in relation to the work done, because it would then not be regarded as wholly and exclusively for the business. It is also particularly important where a business employs family members that the wages payment is properly made (see page 263).

In the case of family and similar companies, a distinction must be drawn between company expenditure which benefits a shareholder who is a director and the payment by the company of the personal debts of the shareholder/director, for example school fees, private entertaining, or expenses of a private residence. Unless the amount has been treated as a payment of salary, it is regarded as a loan which the shareholder/director must repay to the company and it is neither an allowable business expense nor taxed as a benefit on the shareholder/director. The loan has tax consequences both for the company and the director — see pages 194, 195, and possible national insurance consequences — see page 196.

If a loan to a director or employee is written off, the amount written off would be allowed as a deduction against the profit providing it could be shown that the loss of the money lent was connected with the trade. It would usually be treated as taxable pay of the director or employee (but not for an employee who had left, unless he was a P11D employee — see pages 150, 195).

Where an employer takes out insurance against loss of profits as a result of the death, accident or illness of a key employee, the premiums would usually be allowable to the employer and any policy proceeds treated as a trading receipt. If in the event of accident or illness the benefits of the policy were passed on to the employee, they would be taxed either as normal pay if the employee had a contractual right to them or as sick pay.

Capital or revenue

Revenue expenditure is an allowable expense against your profit (unless specifically prohibited, such as business entertaining expenses).

A capital expense cannot be deducted in calculating profits, although many items of capital expenditure may attract capital allowances (see chapter 22). The usual definition of a capital expense is one made 'not only once and for all, but with a view to bringing into existence an asset or an advantage for the enduring benefit of the trade'. One person's stock in trade will be another person's fixed assets. Your business premises are clearly a capital item, but if you build and sell factories, they will be trading stock and the cost will be taken into account in calculating your profit. Cars used by you and your employees are capital items, but cars held for sale by a motor dealer are trading stock. Normally, repair expenditure is revenue expenditure and is allowable, but if you buy a capital asset that cannot be used in your business until it is renovated, the cost of renovating it is part of the capital cost. The distinction is often hard to draw, and has led to many disputes between the taxpayer and the Revenue which have had to be settled by the courts.

Similar considerations apply in deciding whether a particular item is income chargeable under Schedule D, Case I or II or a capital profit.

Allowable and non-allowable expenses

The principles outlined above provide a broad guide to what expenses are allowed. Some specific examples are given in the table on page 276, including items specifically allowed or disallowed by the Taxes Acts.

Payment of remuneration (FA 1989, s 43)

Directors' and employees' pay may only be taken into account as an expense of the accounting period to which it relates if it is paid within nine months after the end of the period. Otherwise it may only be deducted in the accounting period in which it is paid.

Business entertaining (TA 1988, s 577)

The cost of business entertaining and business gifts (apart from the exception noted on page 276) is not allowable. Expenditure on entertaining staff (and their guests) will normally be allowable, unless it is incidental to entertaining those with whom the employer does business, but there will be a benefits charge on P11D employees (subject to the exception noted on page 156).

The VAT position is slightly different. Input VAT on business entertaining is disallowed, but where proprietors or employees act as hosts at meals with clients, etc. while away from work on business, a deduction may be claimed for the VAT other than that relating to the clients (unless business entertainment was the main purpose of the trip). As far as staff entertainment is concerned, Customs consider that the proportion of input VAT relating to *guests* at a staff function should be disallowed, and they usually allow only 50% of the remaining input VAT to be recovered.

Any disallowed VAT is not allowable when calculating taxable profit, except for the disallowed amounts relating to staff entertaining.

Bad and doubtful debts (TA 1988, s 74(1)(j)(2); FA 1994, s 144)

Bad debts and specific provisions for bad debts may be deducted from profits for tax purposes. A *general* provision for bad debts cannot, however, be allowed against taxable profits.

A creditor may treat a debt as bad if he has released the debt in a voluntary arrangement under the 1986 Insolvency Act. The debtor in a voluntary arrangement will not have to bring into his trading profit debts that have been released in this way.

Interest paid (TA 1988, ss 74(1)(a), 349, 360, 362, 363, 787; FA 1996, ss 80, 82)

Interest paid on business borrowings must be wholly and exclusively for the purposes of the business. Companies pay bank interest in full. Most other interest paid by companies is paid net of income tax (at the then basic rate of 25% before 6 April 1996 and at the lower rate of 20% thereafter), and the company pays over to the Revenue the income tax it has deducted. Interest relating to the trade is deducted from the company's trading profits. See page 27 for details and for the treatment of other interest. Individuals normally pay interest in full and deduct interest relating to the trade as a trading expense. Partners may obtain tax relief for interest on a loan used for lending money or introducing capital to a partnership by deducting the interest from their total income (see pages 11 and 333). So may those who introduce funds into their family company (see page 12).

Where interest is paid on borrowing to acquire a property that is partly private and partly business, the interest has to be split to arrive at the part that is allowable as a business expense and the part that is for the living accommodation. This will depend on the respective values of the parts of the property.

Now that MIRAS interest saves only 15% tax, and is in any event not available on a loan above £30,000, individuals should consider business borrowings instead, or if they are partners, borrowing money individually to lend to the firm (see page 11), so that profits can be fully withdrawn from a business. Capital can also be withdrawn (except to the extent that it represents asset revaluations), leaving the business to obtain funding from partners' loans or from other sources. If, however, withdrawing funds leads to a proprietor's capital/current account with the business becoming overdrawn, interest on business borrowings that had enabled the drawings to be made would not be wholly and exclusively for the trade. And partners must not withdraw their capital *after* making loans to the business, because they would be regarded as merely withdrawing what was introduced, and they would not get relief for interest on the loans.

There are some anti-avoidance provisions affecting both individuals and companies, and professional advice is essential. There are specific anti-avoidance provisions to prevent partners substituting personal loans for business borrowings to gain an advantage at the time of the changeover to the current year basis — see page 294.

Lease of cars (CAA 1990, s 35(2)–(4); FA 1996, Sch 39 para 1(3)(4))

If you buy a car costing more than £12,000 (£8,000 for expenditure under a contract entered into before 11 March 1992), capital allowances are restricted (see page 308), but the full cost will be allowed to you eventually, except to the extent that the car is used privately by a sole trader or partner. There is no private use restriction for a company, but the car user will be taxed on the benefit. As far as expenditure on repair and maintenance is concerned, the cost of the car does not affect the allowability of that expenditure, so that sole traders and partners get relief for the business proportion and companies get relief in full.

If instead you lease a car with a retail price when new of more than £12,000, part of the leasing cost is disallowed, so that you do not get tax relief at all for that part. You can only deduct from profit the proportion of the total hire charge that £12,000 plus one half of the excess of the retail price over £12,000 bears to the retail price, and for cars used by sole traders and partners, the allowable amount must be further restricted by the private proportion. (If there is a subsequent rebate of rentals, the amount brought in as a taxable receipt is reduced in the same proportion.) See example 2. Lease contracts may either be operating leases (contract hire), under which the lease rental covers repair and maintenance as well as the provision of the car, or finance leases, under which only the car is provided and repair and maintenance costs are borne by the lessee (see below). Where you acquire a car on contract hire, you should try to get the contract hire company to split the lease rental between the amount paid for the car and the repair and maintenance charge. The £12,000 restriction will then only apply to the car hire payment.

Example 2

Car with retail value of £30,000 leased on 1 May 1996 for £9,000 a year.

Allowable hire charge:

$$9,000 \times \frac{12,000 + (\frac{1}{2} \text{ of } 18,000)}{30,000} = £6,300.$$

The £6,300 will be further restricted if the car is used privately by a sole trader or partner.

No tax relief is available for the remaining £2,700.

See page 274 for the VAT position on leased cars.

Finance leases

Although for accounting purposes an asset you acquire under a finance lease is treated as owned by you, it is in law owned by the lessor so the lease rental payments are a revenue expense allowable against your profit, restricted as indicated above if the leased asset is a car costing more than £12,000. The Revenue have issued a Statement of Practice (SP 3/91) giving their view as to how lease rentals are to be spread over the term of the lease for tax purposes. The date of payment is not the decisive factor and all relevant circumstances must be taken into account.

Goods for own use

If you are a retailer, you must include in sales the retail value of goods taken from stock for your own use (the wholesale price being used for a wholesaler). Services are valued at cost, so no notional profit has to be included for services provided free of charge to, say, a relative. Where business is carried on through a limited company, the directors are charged on goods and services taken for their own use under the benefits rules (see chapter 10) and the cost will be allowed in calculating the company profits, unless some of the directors' total remuneration including benefits is considered not to be wholly and exclusively for the trade (see page 192).

Stock and work in progress — valuation (TA 1988, ss 100–102; FA 1995, s 140)

Stock is valued at the lower of cost or realisable value, opening and closing stock being brought into the accounts in determining profit. Work in progress is similarly brought into account, and may be valued on any one of three bases, provided that the chosen base is used consistently.

(a)   Cost including production overheads.
(b)   Cost plus all overheads.
(c)   Cost plus overheads plus profit contribution.

The value of a proprietor's or working partner's own time is not a contributory part of cost, so this element need not be included in a work in progress valuation, only being reflected in profit when it is billed out.

When a trade ceases, stock is valued at the price received, if sold to an unconnected UK trader. If the UK trader is connected with the vendor (e.g. through a family link, or as companies in the same group), then the stock is valued at an arm's length price. If, however, that value is greater than both the actual sale price and the cost of the stock, the two parties may make a claim to use the higher of cost and sale price instead of arm's length value. Stock that is disposed of other than by being sold to a UK trader, for example taken by a trader for his personal use, is valued at open market value.

Value added tax

If you are VAT registered, VAT will not normally be taken into account either as part of your turnover or part of your expenses. You will collect VAT for Customs and Excise on your supplies of goods and services and recoup any VAT that anyone has charged you. VAT on business entertaining expenditure (subject to what is said on page 271) and cars cannot, however, be recovered from Customs unless, in the case of cars, they are used *wholly* for business purposes, e.g. by private taxi firms, self-drive hire firms, driving schools and, from 1 August 1995, leasing companies — see page 97. The unrecovered VAT on entertaining cannot be recovered against your profit either, because business entertaining is not allowed in calculating taxable profits (subject to what is said on page 271). But disallowed VAT on cars forms part of the cost for capital allowances (see chapter 22). Where assets are leased, the VAT included in the leasing charges is normally recoverable, but if there is any private use of a leased car on which the lessor recovered the input VAT, the lessee may only recover 50% of the input VAT on the leasing charges. The balance would then form part of the lease charges deducted from profits. (There would be no 50% restriction on any input tax relating to a charge for repairs and maintenance if the charge was made in a separate contract as mentioned on page 273.) Private car fuel is subject to a VAT scale charge (see page 98). Unlike the provisions for income tax and national insurance, the VAT scale charge applies to private fuel provided for any employees, no matter what they earn, and no matter whether the car is provided by the employer or belongs to the employee. The VAT accounted for to Customs on the fuel may be included as part of the travelling expenses allowed against your profit, except any relating to private use by a sole trader or partner, which will be disallowed along with the private expenditure itself (see page 269).

If you are not registered for VAT, any VAT you have suffered (other than on business entertaining expenses, which are wholly disallowed) will form part of your expenditure. It will either be part of the cost of a capital item and may qualify for capital allowances or it will be an expense in arriving at your profit. The same applies where although you are registered for VAT, some of the supplies you make are exempt from VAT. You may then not be able to recover all your input VAT from Customs, and the non-deductible amount will be taken into account as part of your expenditure for income tax or corporation tax.

National insurance

The national insurance contributions you pay on your employees' wages, and on the provision of cars and private fuel to staff, are allowable against your profit. No part of a sole trader's or partner's own Class 2 and Class 4 contributions is allowed against profit, and from 6 April 1996, the deduction that was previously allowed against *total* income for half of the Class 4 contributions is no longer available (but the rate of Class 4 contributions has been reduced from 7.3% to 6% to compensate).

Change to current year basis

There are anti-avoidance provisions to prevent businesses seeking to benefit disproportionately from the averaging of two years' profits for 1996/97, or from the overlap relief provisions for a period before 6 April 1997. These will in some circumstances affect the calculation of profits for the relevant years — see page 293.

Non-trading income and capital profits

Any non-trading income of sole traders and partners included in the business accounts is not charged to tax as part of the business profits. The precise nature of the income will determine under what head it is taxed, for example interest under Schedule D, Case III (unless tax has been deducted at source) and rent under Schedule A. By concession, the Revenue will allow small amounts of rental income to be included in the trading income if they are

EXAMPLES OF ALLOWABLE AND NON-ALLOWABLE EXPENDITURE

Allowable	*Not allowable*
Staff wages and benefits in kind	Drawings on account of profits by a sole proprietor or partners
Employer's national insurance contributions on employees' wages and on the provision of cars and fuel	Profit shares in the form of interest on partners' capital
Counselling services for redundant employees	Self-employed national insurance contributions
Rent of business premises	Cost of improvements, extensions, additions to premises and equipment
Business rates	
Repairs	Depreciation (capital allowances are available on certain assets — see chapter 22)
Premium for grant of lease for 50 years or less, but limited to the amount taxed on the landlord as extra rent (see chapter 32), spread over the term of the lease	Expenses of private living accommodation (unless assessable on directors or employees as a benefit in kind)
Interest on business borrowings	
Cost of raising loan finance (excluding stamp duty), for example debentures (not share capital)	Legal expenses on forming a company, drawing up partnership agreement, acquiring assets such as leases
Advertising	Illegal payments such as bribes
Business travel	Payments made in response to threats, menaces, blackmail and other forms of extortion
Bad debts written off and provision for specific bad debts	
Legal expenses on debt recovery, trade disputes, defending trade rights, employees' service agreements and, by concession, renewing a short lease (i.e. 50 years or less)	Fines, and normally any legal expenses connected therewith
	Business entertaining expenses including the VAT thereon (except on a reasonable scale when entertaining staff)
Contributions to local enterprise agencies and training and enterprise councils	Gifts to customers, except gifts with a conspicuous advertisement that cost not more than £10 per person per year and are not food, drink, tobacco or gift vouchers
Gifts to educational establishments of equipment manufactured, sold or used in the donor's trade	Charitable subscriptions and donations, unless exceptionally the donation satisfies the wholly and exclusively rule (but see chapter 43 re allowance of company donations as charges on income)
Non-recoverable VAT relating to allowable expenses, for example where turnover is below VAT threshold, or relating to private petrol for employees	
	Donations to political parties
	Taxation (but see opposite column as regards VAT)

from subletting a part of business premises that is temporarily surplus to requirements. Under self-assessment from 1996/97, tax on all sources of income (and capital gains) will be calculated as a single figure. It will still be necessary to keep different sources of income separate, however, particularly because of the treatment of losses. In the case of a partnership, non-trading income will usually be included in the accounts for the purposes of division between the partners, but it will have to be separated from the trading profit, and up to and including 1995/96 appropriate assessments will be made on each partner under other Schedules or Cases. Partners are currently charged jointly on their trading profits and separately on other income and capital gains, but from 1994/95 for new businesses and from 1997/98 for existing businesses, partners will be taxed separately on all their partnership income and gains (see chapter 23).

A company's non-trading income is also excluded from the trading profit, but the company is charged to tax in a single assessment on all its sources of income plus its chargeable gains, as indicated in chapter 21.

Capital profits of sole traders and partners are liable to capital gains tax, subject to any available reliefs and to the annual exemption. See chapter 4.

Tax points

● Try to avoid mixing business and private expenditure. Make sure you do not cloud a genuine business expense with a private element.

● If you are a retailer, use your business connections to make private purchases at lower cost, rather than taking goods out of your own stock and suffering tax on a figure equivalent to the profit you would have made if you had sold them to a customer.

● Since any expense for the benefit of staff is normally allowable in computing profits, it will sometimes be cheaper because of the saving in national insurance contributions to provide acceptable benefits than to pay higher salaries. The employee may be taxable on the benefits but not always at the full value, and sometimes not at all (see chapter 10).

● If you claim a deduction that is not commercially justifiable, you may have to pay interest on tax underpaid as a result, and possibly a penalty as well. This is very important when considering the 'wholly and exclusively' business element of a mixed expense, such as accommodation and motor expenses. An inaccurate claim and/or providing insufficient information to the Revenue can be costly in the long run.

● Wages payments to a wife must not only be commercially justifiable for her participation in the business but must be properly made and recorded in the business books. The Revenue will usually challenge the charge if it has not been separately paid, but has instead been regarded as included in the amount drawn by the husband or for housekeeping, with an accounting entry being made to create the wages charge.

- Similar considerations apply where mature children are able genuinely to participate in the business, for example in farming, retail and wholesale trades.

- Remember that wages paid after the end of an accounting period must be paid within nine months if they are to be deducted from the profits of that period, otherwise they will be deducted from profits in the period of payment.

- Although expenses, incurred by a company, from which a director or employee derives a personal benefit are allowable in computing trading profit and taxed as earnings of the director or employee, this must be distinguished from using company funds to meet the private expenditure of a director/employee who is a shareholder. This will be treated as a loan from the company, which will have tax and possibly national insurance consequences both for the director and the company — see page 198.

- Where you use part of your home for business, you will usually pay business rates. If you do not, you can claim the appropriate part of your council tax as a business expense — see page 262.

- When considering whether a partnership should be financed by partnership borrowing or by the personal borrowing of the partners, remember that the anti-avoidance legislation on the transition from the previous year to the current year basis of assessment may deny some of the relief for interest paid personally (see page 294).

- The anti-avoidance rules will also cancel any advantage obtained by artificially increasing some years' profits and reducing others, and also possibly charge a penalty on top (see page 293).

- With the introduction of self-assessment from 1996/97, you must make sure you keep all business records relating to your tax affairs for at least 5 years 10 months after the end of the tax year, and sometimes longer. Penalties of up to £3,000 per tax year apply if you do not. See page 119. The Revenue have issued a useful booklet SA/BK3 on record-keeping for the self-employed.

21
How are business profits charged to tax?

Companies (TA 1988, ss 8–12)

Although taxable business profits for individuals and companies are calculated on similar lines, the way company profits are taxed is much more straightforward. A company's trading profits are taxed with its other profits, such as interest, rents and chargeable gains, by reference to chargeable accounting periods (see page 28). A chargeable accounting period can be as short as the company wishes but cannot exceed twelve months. If a company makes up an account for say fifteen months it is split into two chargeable accounting periods for tax purposes, the first of twelve months and the second of three months. Capital allowances (see chapter 22) are then deducted in arriving at the trading profits. The capital allowances are not calculated for the fifteen-month period and divided pro rata. They are calculated for the separate periods of twelve and three months according to the events of those periods.

Example 1

A company makes trading profits of £150,000 in the 15 months to 31 March 1997. The profits will be charged to tax as follows:

	12 months to 31.12.96 £	3 months to 31.3.97 £
12/15, 3/15	120,000	30,000
Less capital allowances (say)	10,000	8,000
	£110,000	£22,000

The due date for payment of corporation tax is nine months and one day after the end of the chargeable accounting period, i.e. 1 October 1997 for the twelve-month account and 1 January 1998 for the three-month account in example 1.

If companies delay payment it will cost them interest, because when the tax for the period is finally determined, any shortfall between that amount and the amount paid suffers interest from the original due date (see page 38).

279

Individuals — position for years before 1996/97

For the self-employed person and those in partnership, tax on business profits and some other sources of income has for many years been charged on the 'previous year basis', which means that the liability for one tax year is normally worked out by taking into account the income of the previous tax year (or for business profits, the income of the accounting year ending in the previous tax year). The rules have been radically changed from 1996/97, with the introduction of the current year basis for measuring all income and self-assessment for calculating and paying tax. For new sources on which income first arises after 5 April 1994 the taxable income is worked out according to the current year basis rules from the start (see page 287), although such income will not be 'self-assessed' until 1996/97.

Normal basis of assessment (TA 1988, s 60)

Income tax on trading profits for years before 1996/97 is payable in equal instalments on 1 January within the tax year and 1 July following it, or 30 days after the assessment is issued if later. Thus the tax for 1995/96 is payable in equal instalments on 1 January and 1 July 1996. Class 4 national insurance contributions are included in the amount payable.

An individual (or partnership) is free to choose the annual date to which accounts are made up and it is usual, but not compulsory, for accounts to be made up to a calendar month end. The 1995/96 assessment for an established trader would be based on the result of his accounting period of twelve months ended in the previous tax year 1994/95, i.e. between 6 April 1994 and 5 April 1995, for example:

> Year ended 30 April 1994
> Year ended 31 May 1994
> Year ended 30 November 1994
> Year ended 31 March 1995

The earlier the accounting date in the tax year the greater the time interval between earning the profits and paying the tax on them (see example 2).

Example 2	Due date of payment of tax for 1995/96	Interval between end of accounting year and payment date
Year ended 30.4.94	1.1.96	20 months
	1.7.96	26 months
Year ended 31.10.94	1.1.96	14 months
	1.7.96	20 months
Year ended 31.3.95	1.1.96	9 months
	1.7.96	15 months

An established trader or partnership was able to alter the interval by changing the previously adopted accounting date (see page 286).

Assessment in early years (TA 1988, ss 61 and 62)

Under the previous year basis, special rules applied in the early years. These rules do not apply to businesses starting on or after 6 April 1994 (see page 287), and there are also some special transitional rules for businesses starting shortly before 6 April 1994 (see page 292). Significant tax advantages could be obtained under these rules (and to a lesser extent under the current year basis rules and the transitional provisions) by careful choice of the date to which accounts are to be made up and the length of the account. Professional advice is essential.

For the tax year in which a pre-6 April 1994 business started, the tax charge was based on the profit from the date of commencement to the following 5 April. If necessary, profits are apportioned on a time basis. The second tax year's tax charge was based on the profits of the first 12 months' trading and the charges for later years would under the old rules normally have been based on the profits of the accounting year ended in the previous tax year. Any available capital allowances (see chapter 22) were deducted once the taxable profit was worked out (see page 283). See example 3.

Example 3

Trade commenced on 1 January 1993. Profits before capital allowances were £3,650 for the year ended 31 December 1993 and £12,000 for the year ended 31 December 1994.

Year of Assessment	Basis period		Assessment* £
1992/93	1.1.93–5.4.93	95/365ths × £3,650	950
1993/94	1.1.93–31.12.93		3,650
1994/95	1.1.93–31.12.93		3,650
1995/96	1.1.94–31.12.94		12,000

* Any capital allowances will be deducted from this figure.

When the first accounts were prepared for a period other than 12 months, it might not have been possible to base the charge for the third tax year on the profits of 12 months ended on the chosen accounting date in the previous tax year. In these circumstances, the charge for the third tax year was again based on the profit of the first 12 months' trading.

Regardless of the dates to which accounts are made up, some profits were used more than once in establishing the taxable profits for the early years. In example 3 the first year's profits were used to work out taxable profits for 27 tax months (3 months in 1992/93 and the whole of 1993/94 and 1994/95). This overlap was, under the old rules, balanced by profits for an equivalent time not being charged to tax when an established trade ceased (see page 284). If profits increased year by year, the opening year rules and subsequent previous year basis of assessment worked in the taxpayer's favour, because the taxable profits were less than the profits currently being earned. The

---

Example 4

(all calculations taken to the nearest month for simplicity — any available capital allowances would be deducted from the assessable amounts)

Trade commenced on 1 January 1993. Profits of the 4 months to 30 April 1993 are £1,000, those of the year to 30 April 1994 are £15,000 and those for the year to 30 April 1995 are £2,400.

The tax charge for the first year, 1992/93, is based on the profit from 1.1.93 to 5.4.93, i.e. three-quarters of £1,000 = £750.

The profits charged to tax for the **second** and **third** tax years are as follows:

Year of assessment	Basis period			Assessments
Normal basis				
			£	£
1993/94	1.1.93–30.4.93	£1,000	1,000	
	1.5.93–31.12.93	8/12 × £15,000	10,000	
				11,000
1994/95	1.1.93–31.12.93			
	(As for 1993/94)			11,000
				£22,000

With taxpayer's claim to be taxed on actual profits				
			£	£
1993/94	6.4.93–30.4.93	1/4 × £1,000	250	
	1.5.93–5.4.94	11/12 × £15,000	13,750	
				14,000
1994/95	6.4.94–30.4.94	1/12 × £15,000	1,250	
	1.5.94–5.4.95	11/12 × £2,400	2,200	
				3,450
				£17,450

Clearly it is in the taxpayer's interest to be taxed in 1993/94 and 1994/95 on the profits actually earned in those tax years.

The normal rules will apply to 1995/96, which will be based on the profit of £15,000 for the year to 30 April 1994, and the transitional provisions will apply to 1996/97 (see page 291).

---

trader in example 3 was taxed on £3,650 in 1994/95, although his profits for the year to 31 December 1994 were £12,000. But if profits fell, the multiple assessment of the initial higher profits could cause hardship. The taxpayer was therefore able to claim within six years after the end of the third tax year to have the tax charges for both the second and third tax years (not just one of them) based on the actual profits made in those tax years rather than on the profits of the earlier period. This meant that later, lower profits were multiple-assessed instead of the earlier, high ones. See example 4 above.

Different rules apply if the business was new because of a change of partners. These are dealt with in chapter 23.

Capital allowances in early years (CAA 1990, s 160)

Where expenditure qualified for capital allowances, the first allowance normally reduced the profit of the accounting year in which the expenditure was incurred (see chapter 22).

Where an early accounting period of a new trade that started before 6 April 1994 was used to work out taxable profits for more than one tax year, the first allowance for capital expenditure in that accounting period was given in the earliest relevant tax year (see example 5). These rules do not apply when profits are charged on the current year basis, because capital allowances are treated differently (see page 287).

Example 5

In examples 3 and 4, capital allowances would be given as follows:

Expenditure incurred	Allowances start in tax year
Example 3	
1.1.93–5.4.93	1992/93
6.4.93–31.12.93	1993/94
1.1.94–31.12.94	1995/96
Example 4 (after taxpayer's claim to be taxed on actual profits)	
1.1.93–5.4.93	1992/93
6.4.93–5.4.94	1993/94
6.4.94–5.4.95	1994/95
6.4.95–30.4.95*	1996/97

* This will be part of the transitional basis period for 1996/97, which will run to 30 April 1996 — see page 301.

Assessment on cessation of trade (TA 1988, s 63)

Under the previous year basis rules, the taxing of profits more than once in the opening years is compensated by the rules for taxing profits when a business ceases. The final assessment for the tax year in which the business ceases is based on the profit from the beginning of that tax year (i.e. 6 April) to the date of cessation, and replaces the assessment based on the profits of the 12 months account ended in the previous tax year. This means that some profits are never assessed at all. However, just as the taxpayer could choose which profits are taxed more than once at the start of the business, so the Revenue has the right to decide which profits are not charged when the business ceases. The profits charged to tax for the two tax years before the final tax year may, at the option of the Revenue, be revised to the profits actually made in those tax years instead of the profits of the accounts ended in the previous tax years. As with the taxpayer's claim in the opening years, this revision must be made for both tax years or for neither. See example 6.

Choice of cessation date

A significant tax advantage can sometimes be obtained under the 'previous year basis' rules where a choice of cessation date is possible. There is a cessation for tax purposes:

> When trading comes to an end.
> When a trader dies (although, by concession, profits can at present continue to be taxed on the previous year basis if the trade is continued by the spouse — see page 464).
> When partners change in a partnership before 6 April 1997 (although the partners may choose to continue to be taxed on a previous year basis, see chapter 23).
> When a trader or partnership transfers its trade to a company (see chapter 27).

If your profits are rising, you will normally be better off delaying the cessation until just after the next 5 April, so that the profits that escape tax are later, higher profits. If your profits are falling you should cease earlier rather than later, because the later the cessation the smaller the escaping profits.

Capital allowances in closing years (CAA 1990, s 160)

For capital allowances purposes, expenditure in the period for which profits escape tax on cessation is regarded as incurred in the next period unless that is the last tax year, in which case it is regarded as incurred in the previous period. This ensures that no qualifying capital expenditure or sales are omitted. See example 7.

Example 6

A trader who has prepared accounts to 30 April for many years ceases to trade on 31 August 1996, the recent and final profits (before capital allowances) having been:

		£
Year ended	30.4.93	24,000
	30.4.94	30,000
	30.4.95	36,000
	30.4.96	48,000
Four months to	31.8.96	15,000

The taxable profits (before capital allowances) for the last three tax years are worked out as follows:

Year of assessment	Basis period		Assessments
		£	£
1996/97	6.4.96–30.4.96	1/12 × £48,000	4,000
	1.5.96–31.8.96		15,000
			£19,000

and either
Normal preceding year basis

1995/96	1.5.93–30.4.94	30,000
1994/95	1.5.92–30.4.93	24,000
		£54,000

or
Revenue's revised actual basis

1995/96	6.4.95–30.4.95	1/12 × £36,000	3,000
	1.5.95–5.4.96	11/12 × £48,000	44,000
			47,000
1994/95	6.4.94–30.4.94	1/12 × £30,000	2,500
	1.5.94–5.4.95	11/12 × £36,000	33,000
			35,500
			£82,500

Although following revision by the Revenue the total profits charged to tax for 1994/95 and 1995/96 will be increased by £28,500 (from £54,000 to £82,500), the profits of the 23 months from 1 May 1992 to 5 April 1994, amounting to £51,500, will not be taxed at all.

Example 7	Normal basis	Revenue's revised basis
In example 6 the 'profits gap' was	1.5.94–5.4.96	1.5.92–5.4.94
It is added to the basis period for	1995/96	1994/95
Which then covers capital		
expenditure and sales from	1.5.93–5.4.96	1.5.92–5.4.95

These rules do not apply when profits are charged on the current year basis, because capital allowances are treated differently (see page 287).

When a business ceases, the assets on which allowances have been claimed are normally treated as sold for either the actual sale proceeds or the open market value if not sold (but see page 303 re connected persons).

Change of accounting date (TA 1988, s 60)

A change of accounting date by a trader or a partnership that affects the basis period for 1995/96 or an earlier year is dealt with under the previous year basis rules and profits either escape being taxed or get taxed more than once at that time, with a corresponding adjustment to the length of the period for which profits escape tax when the trade ceases. This has provided an opportunity to reduce assessments overall as long as the change was commercially justifiable. The detailed provisions are beyond the scope of this book, but broadly the Revenue practice is to charge tax for the tax year(s) directly affected by the change on the profits of 12 months to the new accounting date in the previous tax year, and to adjust the previous year's assessment according to recent average profits, unless the adjustment would be insignificant.

Such changes of accounting date create overlaps or gaps in basis periods for capital allowances. Any overlapping period is treated as being in an earlier rather than a later basis period. A gap between basis periods is treated as part of the later period, unless that is the final tax year of trading, in which case it is treated as part of the earlier period.

Partnership

There are some special points to be considered about the way assessments are divided between partners, what happens on a change of partners and the treatment of losses and capital gains. Different rules apply to partnership changes after 5 April 1997 (or after 5 April 1994 if the partners do not choose to continue to be taxed on the previous year basis). The provisions are dealt with in chapter 23.

Individuals — new current year basis rules and transitional provisions (FA 1994, ss 200–205 and Sch 20; FA 1995, ss 122, 123 and Sch 22)

Introduction of current year basis

Business profits and other sources of income that have been taxed on the 'previous year basis' will be charged on a current year basis from 1997/98, 1996/97 being a transitional year. For sources of income acquired on or after 6 April 1994, the current year basis applies straight away.

Treatment of businesses ceasing before 6 April 1999 (FA 1994, Sch 20 para 3)

The rules outlined earlier in this chapter apply to businesses in existence at 5 April 1994 that cease before 6 April 1997. They also apply to existing businesses ceasing in 1997/98 if the Revenue so direct (which they will if the aggregate profits of 1995/96 and 1996/97 on a strict tax year basis are more than the taxable profits using the normal rules). For existing businesses ceasing in 1998/99 the Revenue will have the right to adjust the 1996/97 assessment to the actual profit of that tax year rather than the averaging provisions that apply under the current year basis (see page 291).

Capital allowances under the current year basis (FA 1994, ss 211–214)

Under the current year basis, capital allowances are treated as a trading expense and balancing charges as a trading receipt of the accounting period. If the accounting period is shorter or longer than 12 months, the annual writing-down allowances will be reduced or increased proportionately. To prevent businesses in existence at 5 April 1994 suffering any loss of allowances for 1996/97, for which profits are averaged (usually over two years) to arrive at the taxable amount, the capital allowances changes will apply to those businesses from 1997/98. See page 300.

New businesses starting on or after 6 April 1994

In the first tax year, new businesses are taxed on their profit from the start date to the end of the tax year. The second year's charge is normally based on the profits of the accounting year ended in the second tax year. Part of that profit has usually already been taxed in the first year, and this is called the 'overlap profit' (see example 8). Overlap profits can also occur on a change of accounting date, and as a result of the transitional rules when existing businesses change over to the current year basis.

Where profits need to be apportioned, the apportionment may be made in days, months, or months and fractions of months providing the chosen method is used consistently. If a business makes up accounts to 31 March, the Revenue are prepared to treat the year to 31 March as being equivalent to the tax year itself, so that for such a business starting on say 1 April 1995 the result of the first five days would be treated as nil, giving a nil profit for 1994/95. The profit of the first 12 months to 31 March 1996 would be taxed in 1995/96 and there would be no overlap profits and no overlap relief. The effect of the rules for overlaps is that the business is taxed over its life on the profits made. There is, however, no provision for any inflation-proofing of overlap profits.

Example 8

Business starts 1 January 1995 and makes up accounts annually to 31 December. It ceases on 30 June 1999. Profits after capital allowances were as follows:

		£
Year to 31.12.1995		12,000
1996		15,000
1997		14,000
1998		17,000
6 months to 30.6.1999		10,000
		68,000

The profits are charged to tax as follows:

			£
1994/95	1.1.95 – 5.4.95 3/12 × £12,000		3,000
1995/96	1.1.95 – 31.12.95		12,000
	(Overlap profit £3,000)		
1996/97	1.1.96 – 31.12.96		15,000
1997/98	1.1.97 – 31.12.97		14,000
1998/99	1.1.98 – 31.12.98		17,000
1999/2000	1.1.99 – 30.6.99	10,000	
	Less overlap profit	3,000	7,000
			68,000

Thus the business is taxed over its life on the profits earned.

A record needs to be kept not only of the amount of overlap profits but also the length of the overlapping period. If an overlapping period shows a loss, it must be recorded as an overlap of nil for the appropriate period. This is important because overlap relief is given either when the business ceases or partly or wholly at the time of an earlier change of accounting date to the extent that more than 12 months' profit would otherwise be chargeable in one year (see example 12 on page 290).

If the first accounts are made up to a date in the second tax year, but for a period of less than 12 months, the charge for the second tax year is based on the profits of the first 12 months.

Example 9

Business starts 1 January 1995 and makes up first accounts for 9 months to 30 September 1995, then annually to 30 September.

The taxable profits are arrived at as follows:

1994/95	1.1.95 – 5.4.95	$3/9 \times$ 1st profits
1995/96	1.1.95 – 31.12.95	Profits of 1st 9 months plus $3/12 \times$ profits of yr to 30.9.96
1996/97	1.10.95 – 30.9.96	
Overlap profits are:		$3/9 \times$ 1st profits plus $3/12 \times$ profits of yr to 30.9.96

If accounts are made up to a date in the second tax year, and are for 12 months or more, the charge for the second tax year is based on the profits of 12 months to the accounting date (see example 10 and also example 5 on page 329 re the admission of a new partner).

Example 10

Business starts 1 October 1994 and makes up first accounts for 15 months to 31 December 1995, then annually to 31 December.

The taxable profits are arrived at as follows:

1994/95	1.10.94 – 5.4.95	$6/15 \times$ 1st profits
1995/96	1.1.95 – 31.12.95	$12/15 \times$ 1st profits
1996/97	1.1.96 – 31.12.96	

Profits of 1st 15 months have therefore been used to charge tax for 18 months, so overlap profits are:

$$3/15 \times \text{1st profits}$$

If the first account is made up for more than 12 months and no account ends in the second tax year, the charge for the second tax year is based on the profits of the tax year itself, and the charge for the third tax year is based on 12 months to the accounting date.

Example 11

Business starts 1 January 1995 and makes up first accounts for 16 months to 30 April 1996, then annually to 30 April.

The taxable profits are arrived at as follows:

1994/95	1.1.95 – 5.4.95	$3/16 \times$ 1st profits
1995/96	6.4.95 – 5.4.96	$12/16 \times$ 1st profits
1996/97	1.5.95 – 30.4.96	$12/16 \times$ 1st profits

Profits of first 16 months have therefore been used to charge tax for 27 months, so overlap profits are:

$$11/16 \times \text{1st profits}$$

Change of accounting date

Under the current year basis, changes of accounting date are not permitted more than once in every five years unless the Revenue is satisfied that the change is for commercial reasons, and notice of the change has to be given to the Revenue by 31 January following the tax year of change.

The rules for dealing with the change broadly ensure than 12 months' profit is charged in each tax year, except the first year and the last year. If accounts are made up to a date earlier in the tax year than the previous date, profits of 12 months to the new date will be charged, but this will result in overlap profits for which relief will be due later. The overlap profits and period to which they relate will be combined with any earlier overlap profits (including transitional overlap profits) and overlap period to give a single figure for a single period. If accounts are made up to a date *later* in the tax year, more than 12 months' profits will be charged in the year of change, but a proportion of the available overlap relief will be deducted, according to how many more than 12 months' profits are being taxed. If the earlier overlap period(s) showed a loss rather than a profit, however, there would be no overlap relief due, so that the charge on more than 12 months' profit would stand. The *length* of the total overlap period is not affected by the fact that one or more earlier overlap periods showed a loss (see page 288). This is particularly important when calculating how much relief may be given when more than 12 months' profit would otherwise be charged in one year.

Example 12

Business starts on 1 January 1995 and makes a loss in the year to 31 December 1995, profits arising thereafter. There is no taxable profit in 1994/95 or 1995/96, but the overlap period is from 1 January 1995 to 5 April 1995, i.e. (to the nearest month) 3 months, the overlap profit being nil. If the accounting date was later changed to 30 June, this would give a further overlap of 6 months. The combined overlap period would be *9 months*, with an overlap profit of nil plus a 6 months' proportion of the profit at the time of the later overlap.

If the accounting date was subsequently changed again to, say, 30 September, 15 months' profit would be charged at that time, less a deduction for a 3 months' proportion of the overlap profit, but this would amount to *3/9ths* not 3/6ths.

Even where losses are not involved, the overlap profit may have been seriously eroded by inflation, so that the amount deductible when more than 12 months' profits would otherwise be charged, or on cessation, may be at a very much lower level than the profits currently being charged.

Example 13

Say a business started on 1 January 1995, making up accounts to December, and the overlap profit for the 3 months to 5 April 1995 amounted to £6,000. If the business had continued with a 31 December year end until 31 December 2005, making profits in that year of £96,000, and had then made up a 9-month account to 30 September 2006, the assessment for 2006/07 would be based on the profits of 12 months to 30 September 2006, so that 3/12 of the profits of the year to 31 December 2005, i.e. £24,000, would be taxed twice. That amount would be an additional overlap profit, which would be combined with the earlier overlap profit of £6,000, giving total overlap profits of £30,000 for 6 months. Overlap relief for that amount would be given either on cessation or in an earlier year to the extent that more than 12 months' profit would otherwise be taxed.

Alternatively, say that instead of making up accounts to 30 September 2006, the business had made up a 14-month account to 28 February 2007, showing a profit of £112,000. The profits of the year to 31 December 2005 would be taxed in 2005/06. The profits of the 14 months to 28 February 2007 would be taxed in 2006/07, reduced by 2 months' overlap relief, i.e. 2/3 of £6,000 = £4,000 (although 2 months at the then profit rate represents profits of £16,000). The balance of the overlap relief of £2,000 would be given on cessation or when tax was again being charged for a period exceeding 12 months.

Transitional provisions for businesses in existence at 5 April 1994

So that the previous year basis can be replaced by the current year basis rules, the tax charge for 1996/97 will normally be based on the average of the profits of the two years' accounts ended with the annual accounting date in 1996/97. This means that one year's profit will escape tax at that time. (On the other hand only half the expenditure in that two-year period will be tax-relieved.) Taxpayers may if they wish make up a single account for the whole of the transitional period, but this might not be appropriate for various reasons, for example if there would otherwise be a loss in one of the periods (see page 292), and annual accounts may be required for purposes other than tax.

The profit for the period from the end of the basis period for 1996/97 to 5 April 1997, which is included in the taxable profits for 1997/98, represents a transitional overlap profit, relief for which will be given when the business ceases (or possibly earlier if the accounting date is changed — see page 290). In working out the transitional overlap profit, the profits of the relevant accounting period are taken into account *before* deducting capital allowances.

This only applies to overlap relief under the transitional provisions on the change to the current year basis and not to normal overlap relief arising in businesses that start on or after 6 April 1994, or arising as a result of a change of accounting date from 1997/98 onwards.

Example 14

In example 3 on page 281, the first year's profit to 31 December 1993 (before capital allowances) was used to work out taxable profits before capital allowances for 27 months, representing an overlap of 15 months. Say subsequent profits before capital allowances were then as follows:

		£
Year to	31.12.95	15,000
	31.12.96	18,000
	31.12.97	16,000

Taxable profits before capital allowances would be:

1996/97	Average of 2 yrs to 31.12.96,	
	i.e. half of (15,000 + 18,000)	16,500
1997/98	Year to 31.12.97	16,000

Transitional overlap profit 1.1.97 – 5.4.97   3/12 × 16,000   4,000

The transitional overlap profit of £4,000 would reduce the taxable profit of the year in which the business ceased, or of an earlier tax year if an account was made up for longer than 12 months.

Thus 12 months' profit escapes tax in 1996/97 and a further 3 months on or before cessation, compensating for the 15 months' overlap in taxable profits when the business started.

If a loss occurs in one of the two years to which averaging applies, it is treated as nil to arrive at the aggregate profits (so that there will effectively be only one year's profit to be averaged, which will be halved to arrive at the 1996/97 taxable amount). Loss relief claims may then be made in the normal way for the loss (see chapter 25).

Where a business started shortly before 6 April 1994 and the profits of the tax year itself are taxed in 1995/96 (usually where a taxpayer has exercised his option for actual basis for the second and third tax years, but also applying to certain partnership changes), averaging does not apply for 1996/97 and the profits of the tax year itself are taken instead.

Change of accounting date during transitional period

If the 1996/97 assessment for a business in existence at 5 April 1994 is affected by a change of accounting date, the averaging rules for the transitional basis period still apply so that a 12 months' proportion is taken of the total profits from the end of the 1995/96 basis period to the accounting date in 1996/97. This may enable more than 12 months' profit to escape tax at the time of the change to the current year basis.

Example 15

In example 3 on page 281, the first 12 months' profits were used to work out 27 months' taxable profits, giving an overlap of 15 months. The basis period for 1995/96 was the year to 31.12.94. Say the business had then made up accounts for 15 months to 31 March 1996, then for 12 months to 31 March 1997. The 1996/97 assessment would be a 12 months' average of the profits for the 27 months from 1.1.95 to 31.3.97. Profits for 15 months would therefore drop out of assessment, compensating for the 15 months' overlap on commencement, and there would be no overlap relief on cessation.

Businesses can therefore avoid the adverse effects of inflation on the overlap relief arising at the time of the change to the current year basis by switching to a 31 March year end before 1 April 1997, but they will then be taxed each year on the profits earned in the year, rather than profits some of which were earned earlier. A change of accounting date that brings the end of the 1996/97 basis period closer to 5 April 1997 is specifically excluded from the anti-avoidance rules that have been introduced to stop people manipulating their results to benefit from the change to the new system (see below).

Anti-avoidance provisions

There are anti-avoidance provisions to prevent people obtaining an undue advantage from the rules for changing to the current year basis. The provisions apply to all accounting periods that affect the income taxed in 1996/97 and the overlap period to 5 April 1997. The actions that may trigger the anti-avoidance provisions are a change or modification of accounting policy (including a change of accounting date, subject to the exception noted above), transactions with close family, partners or other connected persons, reciprocal or self-cancelling arrangements and changes in business behaviour (such as invoicing patterns, debt collection, payments on account). The provisions do not apply to bona fide commercial transactions or changes or to transactions or changes for which a tax advantage was not the main anticipated benefit. There will also be de minimis thresholds to exclude small amounts and to exclude businesses with a low turnover, but these limits have not yet been announced.

Where profits are shifted into the 1996/97 basis period, so that without the special rules only half of the profits would be taxed, the other half is also included, uplifted by one-quarter. (The provisions are adapted appropriately if the basis period for 1996/97 is not 24 months, as in example 15.)

> **Example 16**
>
> £5,000 profits artificially shifted from year to 31.12.94 (the profits of which are assessable in 1995/96) into year to 31.12.95. Only half thereof would therefore be included in averaging calculation for 1996/97 assessment under the normal rules.
>
> Other half, i.e. £2,500, multiplied by 1¼, i.e. £3,125, is added to 1996/97 assessment.

If profits are artificially moved into the transitional overlap period to 5 April 1997 (see page 291), the avoidance is countered by excluding from overlap relief 1¼ times the relevant amount.

> **Example 17**
>
> Profit of year to 30.6.97 increased by £10,000 to £30,000 by shifting expenditure from that year into year to 30.6.98.
>
> Transitional overlap relief on profit from 1.7.96 to 5.4.97 would normally be 9/12 of £30,000, i.e. £22,500. This is reduced by [(9/12 × £10,000) × 1¼ =] £9,375, giving overlap relief of £13,125.

If a partnership is caught by the anti-avoidance provisions relating to the transitional overlap period that runs from the accounting date in 1996/97 to 5 April 1997, and a partner retires during that overlap period, he will be charged tax personally for *1996/97* on the amount of the transitional relief restriction he would otherwise have suffered.

The uplift of one-quarter in taxable profits illustrated in examples 16 and 17 will not apply if the taxpayer states in his tax return the extent to which amounts in the return are affected by the anti-avoidance provisions. The effect of the transactions will then merely be nullified by including the appropriate amounts in 1996/97 profits, or excluding them from overlap relief, as the case may be.

The anti-avoidance rules also apply to non-trading income under Schedule D, Cases III, IV and V that is presently charged on the previous year basis. Any deliberately diverted income that would otherwise be excluded from the 1996/97 assessment under the averaging provisions will be included, plus an uplift of one-quarter. The transitional overlap relief of a partner will be reduced by 1¼ times the attempted avoidance where overlap relief applies to a partner's share of non-trading income (see page 331). In both cases the one-quarter uplift will not apply if the fact that a specified amount has been diverted is disclosed in the tax return.

There are also anti-avoidance provisions to prevent partners obtaining an advantage by replacing business borrowings (for which no tax relief would be obtained on part of the interest because of the averaging provisions for 1996/97) with personal loans which they introduce into the business (the whole of the interest on which would normally qualify for relief). Unless the new borrowing was taken out before 1 April 1994, the interest allowed as a deduction in arriving at the total income of the individual partner will be restricted to what would have been allowed under the averaging provisions. This will not apply to bona fide commercial transactions, transactions not aimed at tax avoidance and situations where the aggregate interest on the new borrowing is below a stipulated threshold (not yet fixed).

Pre-trading expenditure (TA 1988, s 401; FA 1993, s 109; FA 1995, s 120; FA 1996, Sch 14 para 20)

Some expenditure, for example rent and rates, may be incurred before trading actually starts. So long as it is a normal trading expense and is incurred not more than seven years before the trade starts (five years for trades started before 1 April 1993), then for businesses commenced before 6 April 1995 it may be treated by individual traders and partnerships as a separate loss of the first tax year of trading and loss relief may be claimed for it. The types of loss relief available are dealt with in chapter 25. Where the expenditure is incurred by a company, or in a new sole trade or partnership that commenced on or after 6 April 1995, it may be treated as an expense of the first trading period. The different treatment for individuals for pre-6 April 1995 businesses ensures that they do not get the benefit of deducting the expense more than once because of the rules for taxing profits in the opening years (see page 281). This restriction is not necessary under the current year basis of assessment, although it will in fact apply to businesses starting between 6 April 1994 and 5 April 1995, even though they are taxed under the current year basis.

Post-cessation receipts (TA 1988, ss 103–110; FA 1996, s 128(4), Sch 17 para 5)

Income may arise after a business has ceased which has not been included in the final accounts. This may be because of the nature of the business and is particularly relevant for barristers because their accounts are traditionally based on cash received rather than on earnings. Whatever the reason, the income is charged to tax under Schedule D, Case VI. The chargeable amount may be reduced by any expenses, capital allowances or losses that could have been set against the income if it had been received before the business ceased. The taxable amount is treated as income of the tax year in which it is received, unless it is received within six years after cessation, when the taxpayer can elect to have it treated as arising in the tax year when trading ceased. The carry-back election must be made within one year after the 31 January following the tax year in which the income was received (two years after the end of the tax year of receipt for claims for 1995/96 and earlier years). The amount of tax payable on the additional income will be calculated by reference to the tax position of the earlier year, but it will be treated as additional tax payable for the tax year in which the amounts were received.

Post-cessation expenses (TA 1988, s 109A; FA 1995, s 90)

From 29 November 1994, certain expenditure incurred by sole traders or partners in the seven years after a trade or profession has ceased that has not been provided for in the final accounts and cannot be set against any post-cessation receipts may be set against the total income and capital gains of the tax year in which it is incurred. This applies to professional indemnity premiums, cost of remedying defective work plus any related damages and legal expenses, bad debts and debt recovery costs. For the relief to apply, a claim must be made within one year after the 31 January following the tax year in which the expenditure was incurred (two years after the end of the tax year for expenditure in 1994/95 or 1995/96).

Tax points

● The way the self-employed are taxed has been changed from 6 April 1996, and the 'previous year basis of assessment' no longer applies. Although the aim is stated to be simplification, an inevitable result is the loss of the tax planning opportunities previously available. Significant savings can still be made in the short term.

● Choosing an accounting date early in the tax year gives more time for planning the funding of tax payments. It also means that you are paying tax each year on profits that were largely earned in the previous year, giving an obvious advantage if profits are rising. When the business ceases, however, the final tax bill may be particularly high, because the profits then being earned may be very much higher than the early overlap profits for which relief is given on cessation.

● If you are intending to cease an unincorporated business, you should, if possible, postpone cessation to a date after the next 5 April if profits are rising, but cease before that date if profits are falling. The maximum possible profits will then escape assessment.

● This chapter contains examples of claims which are available to taxpayers. There is always a time limit involved, which depends on the type of claim being made. The legislation should be checked for the time limit whenever a claim is available. There is a general time limit under self-assessment of approximately five years ten months where no other time limit is specified (the previous general limit was six years).

● In example 3 on page 281, the tax and Class 4 national insurance for 1992/93 (due 1.1.93 and 1.7.93) and the first instalment for 1993/94 (due 1.1.94) were due before the first accounts to 31.12.93, on which the tax is based, were available. The same might have applied to the second instalment of tax for 1993/94 (due 1.7.94) and so on. In such cases, you should not delay informing the Revenue that you have started to trade. For years before 1996/97, they will issue estimated assessments (see chapter 9) and amend them later when the accounts are available. If the Revenue are not told until you send in the first accounts, they may seek to charge interest on overdue tax and national insurance, and penalties because of your earlier failure to notify them. From 1995/96, the time limit for notifying liability to income tax or capital gains tax if a return is not received is six months from the end of the tax year, e.g. by 5 October 1997 for someone who starts a new business between 6 April 1996 and 5 April 1997. The Revenue will not issue estimated assessments under the self-assessment system, but the taxpayer himself may have to make an estimated assessment and amend it later, because the information may not be available in time. Penalties for late notification of liability still apply, and also penalties for late returns, together with interest and surcharges on late payments (see page 122).

- New businesses may often incur interest charges on underpaid tax under self-assessment, because interest will run from the 31 January filing date for the return (or three months after the return is issued, if later) on what the tax finally turns out to be. If you start business say on 1 January 1997 and make up accounts to 31 December 1997, tax is due on 31 January 1998 on the profit from 1 January to 5 April 1997. You are unlikely to have completed the December 1997 accounts by that date. If you underestimate the tax due, interest will run on the underpayment from 31 January 1998 (although the tax itself will not be due until 30 days after you file an amendment to your return).

22
Capital allowances

Background

Capital expenditure cannot be deducted in calculating income profits, but taxable profits may be reduced by allowances that are available on certain capital expenditure when the expenditure is incurred and/or by 'writing-down allowances' over the later years of the ownership of the assets.

The law on capital allowances is in the Capital Allowances Act 1990 as amended by later Finance Acts. References in this chapter are to the 1990 Act unless otherwise stated.

The most important allowances available to companies, sole traders and partnerships are those in respect of expenditure on:

Plant and machinery
Industrial buildings
Agricultural buildings
Hotels
Buildings in enterprise zones, other than dwelling houses
Patents
Know-how
Scientific research
Mineral extraction

Agricultural buildings allowances are dealt with in more detail in chapter 31.

Dwellings let under the assured tenancy scheme qualify for relief, broadly on expenditure incurred before 15 March 1988 or under a contract entered into before that date. Later expenditure does not qualify for allowances. The allowances are similar to industrial buildings allowances, being given at 4% of the building cost per annum, with initial allowances having been given for expenditure between 10 March 1982 and 31 March 1986. The detailed provisions are in earlier editions of this book.

Plant and machinery allowances are available not only to businesses but also to employees who have to provide plant and machinery for use in their employment, and to those who let property, in respect of landlord's fixtures, fittings, etc., but not on furniture, etc. let in a dwelling house (for which a wear and tear allowance is usually given instead — see pages 445 and 449). The most common example of qualifying expenditure on plant and machinery by an employee is the provision of a car, but another might be a musical instrument purchased by an employee of an orchestra. A landlord of let property may obtain relief on such items as lifts. Industrial and agricultural buildings allowances are also available to landlords when qualifying buildings are let.

If an asset is used partly for private purposes by sole traders or partners, or by employees claiming allowances for their own plant and machinery, allowances are given only on the appropriate business fraction.

Expenditure qualifying for relief (ss 11, 60, 153, 154)

Capital allowances are available when expenditure is incurred on a qualifying asset, even if the expenditure is funded by means of a loan or bank overdraft. Interest on such funding is, however, allowed as a business expense and not as part of the cost of the asset. Where an industrial building is let at a premium on a long lease (more than 50 years), the landlord and tenant may elect for the premium to be treated as the purchase price for the building, so that industrial buildings allowances may be claimed by the tenant. If the tenant himself incurs capital expenditure on a qualifying building, he is entitled to allowances on that expenditure.

When an asset is purchased under a hire-purchase agreement, the expenditure is regarded as incurred as soon as the asset comes into use, even though the asset is not strictly owned until the option-to-purchase payment is made. The hire-purchase charges are not part of the cost but are allowed as a business expense, spread appropriately over the term of the agreement.

Where assets are acquired on a finance lease, then although for accounting purposes they are treated as owned by the lessee, they belong in law to the lessor and it is the lessor who gets the capital allowances. See page 273 for the treatment of the lease payments.

Subsidies or contributions from third parties must in general be deducted from the allowable cost. Regional development grants, however, are specifically excluded from this requirement and do not have to be deducted.

If the qualifying expenditure on an asset is restricted because the owner has received a contribution or subsidy from someone else, the third party may claim allowances on the contribution, even though strictly he does not have an interest in the asset.

Where value added tax has been paid and cannot be recovered, for example on motor cars or, in the case of other asset purchases, because of the partial exemption rules or because the trader is not VAT registered, it forms part of the allowable expenditure for capital allowances. Capital allowances computations have to be adjusted where input VAT on land and computers is later adjusted under the capital goods scheme (see page 313).

Basis periods (ss 140, 141, 144, 145, 160; FA 1994, ss 211–214 and Sch 20 para 9)

Corporation tax

For a company, allowances are first given by reference to the expenditure incurred in the company's chargeable accounting period, so that where a period of account exceeds 12 months, it is split into a 12-month period or periods and the remainder, and relief for capital expenditure is first given according to the chargeable period in which the expenditure is incurred.

Income tax — current year basis rules

The treatment of capital allowances for individuals is different under the 'previous year basis' rules and the 'current year basis' rules. Under the current year basis, capital allowances are treated as trading expenses, and balancing charges as trading receipts, of the accounting period. If the accounting period is longer or shorter than 12 months, writing-down allowances are increased or reduced accordingly (the £3,000 maximum allowance for cars costing more than £12,000 — see page 308 — being similarly increased or reduced). If an account exceeds 18 months, however, capital allowances are calculated as if it was one or more periods of account of 12 months plus a period of account covering the remainder of the period. The aggregate allowances for the separate periods are then treated as a trading expense of the whole period. This prevents undue advantage being gained as a result of the long account. See example 3 on page 308.

The current year basis rules apply from the outset for businesses starting on or after 6 April 1994 and from 1997/98 for businesses in existence before that date (so that allowances are not lost as a result of the averaging rules for 1996/97). Transitional provisions apply for 1996/97 (see below). For businesses in existence at 5 April 1994, any unused allowances brought forward to the first account ended after 5 April 1997 will be treated as trading expenses of that account.

Income tax — previous year basis rules

Under the previous year basis rules, allowances are given for tax years, according to the expenditure incurred in the relevant basis period. For traders and partnerships the basis period is the accounting period on which the assessment for the relevant tax year is based. Thus expenditure incurred by an established business in the year ended 31 December 1994 would first qualify for allowances in 1995/96, when the profits of the year to 31 December 1994 are charged to tax.

Because of the previous year basis rules for taxing profits in the opening and closing years and on changes of accounting date, there may be overlaps and gaps in basis periods (see chapter 21). Where expenditure is incurred in the basis period for more than one assessment, it is regarded as being incurred in the first period (see example 5 on page 283). Where it is incurred in a period whose profits escape tax, it is regarded as incurred in the next period, unless the next period is the last tax year of the business, in which case it is regarded as being incurred in the previous period (see example 7 on page 286).

Transitional provisions for 1996/97

The basis period for 1996/97 for businesses in existence at 5 April 1994 runs from the end of the basis period for 1995/96 to the 1996/97 accounting date, which will normally be a two-year period (subject to the rules for overlaps and gaps in basis periods — see pages 283 and 284). There is, however, only one year's writing-down allowance for 1996/97.

Example 1

In an old-established business, accounts are made up annually to 30 June. The basis period for 1995/96 is the year to 30 June 1994. The basis period for 1996/97 runs from 1 July 1994 to 30 June 1996, all additions and disposals in that two-year period being brought into the computation.

If the business decided to change its accounting date and made up a 21-month account to 31 March 1997, the basis period for 1996/97 would cover all additions and disposals from 1 July 1994 to 31 March 1997 (2 years 9 months).

In either case, only one year's writing-down allowance would be available.

Basis periods for non-trading individuals

For employees and landlords who are individuals, the basis period is the income tax year itself.

Date expenditure is incurred (s 159)

This is generally the date on which the obligation to pay becomes unconditional (i.e. normally the invoice date), but if any part of the payment is not due until more than four months after that date, that part of the expenditure is regarded as incurred on the due date of payment. The due date of payment is also substituted where the unconditional obligation to pay has been brought forward to obtain allowances earlier. It sometimes happens that, under large construction contracts, the purchaser becomes the owner at an earlier date than the time when the obligation to pay becomes unconditional, e.g. on presentation of an architect's certificate. Where, in those circumstances, ownership passes in one basis period, but the obligation becomes unconditional in the first month of the next, the expenditure is regarded as incurred in the earlier period.

Way in which capital allowances are given (ss 9, 24, 140, 141, 144, 145, 145A and Sch A1; TA 1988, s 379A; FA 1995, Sch 6 para 19)

Allowances for sole traders and partners under the previous year basis rules are available against the trading profits for the relevant tax years. A claim may be made to use the allowances to increase a loss, or turn what would otherwise be a profit into a loss (see chapter 25). Any unrelieved allowances are carried forward to set against later trading profits. Under the current year basis rules, allowances are treated as trading expenses of the accounting period and if a loss arises the allowances will therefore already be included in it. On the transition to the current year basis for businesses that were in existence at 5 April 1994, any unrelieved allowances carried forward to the first account ended after 5 April 1997 will be treated as trading expenses of that account.

Allowances for a trading company are deducted in computing trading profit, and as with the unincorporated trader, might turn a profit into a loss, for which the usual relief for company trading losses could be claimed (see chapter 26).

Allowances claimed by individual or corporate investors are given first against rent income (and for individuals they will be deducted as an expense in arriving at the profit of the 'Schedule A business' — see page 444). A claim may be made to set any excess allowances against other income in the case of the individual, or against other profits in the case of a company. The time limit for such a claim for companies is two years after the end of the accounting period. For individuals the time limit from 1996/97 onwards is one year from 31 January following the tax year in which the accounting period ends (two years after the end of the relevant tax year for years up to 1995/96). For the individual investor, the excess allowances will be set against any other income of the same tax year or of the following tax year. See example 7 on page 316. A corporate investor may deduct the excess allowances from the total profits (including capital gains) first of the same accounting period and then of the previous accounting period. For both individuals and companies, allowances that have not been set against other income or profits will be carried forward against future rent income.

Both individuals and companies must make a specific claim for capital allowances (and in the case of plant and machinery, there is a separate requirement to give written notification — see page 305).

A company's claims must be made in its corporation tax return (CT 200) or in an amended return. The time limit for making or amending claims is two years from the end of the accounting period or, if later, the time when the profits or losses of the period are finally settled (but not later than six years after the end of the accounting period).

For years before 1996/97, an individual's claims are made in his tax return, and cannot strictly be revised once the assessment on the profits has become final, but the Revenue may allow claims to be revised where a claim was made early in the tax year and circumstances changed before the end of that year (Statement of Practice A26). Under self-assessment from 1996/97, capital allowances will be claimed in tax returns or amended returns, so they will be subject to the same time limits as for other entries in returns, i.e. any amendment must normally be made within 12 months after the 31 January filing date for the return (see page 118).

Some allowances need not be taken in full, e.g. first-year and writing-down allowances on plant and machinery and initial allowances on industrial buildings. This may enable you to make better use of other available reliefs and allowances (see Tax points at the end of this chapter).

Balancing allowances and charges (ss 4, 5, 24)

When an asset is sold, a 'balancing allowance' is given for any amount by which the sale proceeds fall short of the unrelieved expenditure on the asset. If the proceeds exceed the unrelieved expenditure, the excess is included in taxable income by means of a 'balancing charge'. If the proceeds exceed the original cost, however, the excess over cost is dealt with under the capital gains tax rules (see page 309), except for sales of know-how (see page 318).

For plant and machinery, balancing allowances and charges are normally dealt with on a 'pool' basis for most assets (see page 306).

Connected persons, etc. (ss 26, 77, 78, 152, 157, 158)

If an asset is withdrawn from a business for personal use or sold to a connected person for use other than in a business, the amount to be included as sales proceeds is usually the open market value. (The definition of 'connected person' is broadly the same as that for capital gains tax — see page 60 — although it is slightly wider.)

On a sale of plant and machinery between connected persons, open market value is not used for the seller if the buyer's expenditure is taken into account for capital allowances (so that, for example, inter-group transfers are taken into account at the price paid). On a sale of assets other than plant and machinery, open market value will apply unless a joint claim is made by seller and buyer, within two years after the transfer, for the transfer to be treated as made at written-down value.

Where the sale of an asset to a connected person takes place at the time when the business itself is sold, the assets are treated as being sold at open market value. But the seller and buyer may make a joint election, within two years from the date of the sale, for the transfer to be treated as made at the tax written-down value, so there will be no balancing adjustment on the seller and the buyer will take over the allowances from that point. The most common example of the application of these rules is when a business is transferred to a company (see page 380).

Plant and machinery

What is plant and machinery?

Plant and machinery is not defined in the tax legislation, although it is clear as far as machinery is concerned that as well as items that would generally be regarded as such, the term includes motor vehicles and ships. As to what is and is not plant, the question has come before the courts many times. The main problem lies in distinguishing the 'apparatus' *with* which a business is carried on from the 'setting' *in* which it is carried on. Items forming part of the setting do not qualify for allowances unless they do so as part of the building itself and not as plant, for example where it is an industrial building, or unless the business is one in which atmosphere, or ambience, is important, but, even so, allowances for plant will not be available on expenditure on an asset which becomes part of the premises, such as shop fronts, flooring and suspended ceilings. (Although initial expenditure on a shopfront is disallowed, the cost of a subsequent replacement will be allowed as a revenue expense against the profit, but excluding any improvement element.) Lifts and central heating systems are treated as plant, while basic electricity and plumbing systems are not. Specific lighting to create atmosphere in a hotel and special lighting in fast food restaurants have been held to be plant. A tenant who incurs expenditure on items that become landlord's fixtures can nonetheless claim allowances — see page 448.

An attempt was made in the Finance Act 1994 to clarify the boundaries between buildings and plant, and to limit the extent to which expenditure can be regarded as being on plant rather than on the building. The new provisions do not affect items that the courts have already held to be plant. (Sch AA1; FA 1994, s 117).

Expenditure on computer hardware is capital expenditure on plant and machinery. Allowances will usually be claimed under the 'short-life assets' rules (see page 306). Unless it is developed 'in house', computer software is usually licensed for lifetime to a particular user or users rather than being purchased outright. Despite the fact that a license to use software is an intangible asset, it is specifically provided that capital expenditure on licensed software and electronically transmitted software qualifies for plant and machinery allowances.

If licensed software is acquired on rental, the rentals will be charged against profit over the life of the software. Where a lump sum is paid, the Revenue normally take the view that the cost of software with an expected life of less than two years may be treated as a revenue expense and deducted from profit. Otherwise it will usually be treated as capital expenditure for which plant and machinery allowances may be claimed (under the short-life asset rules if appropriate — see page 306). The treatment of in-house software is broadly similar, being either treated as capital or revenue depending on the expected period of use.

Certain items that are not plant are specifically allowable as such, for example certain expenditure by traders on fire safety, heat insulation in industrial buildings, and expenditure on safety at sports grounds.

Notification of expenditure (FA 1994, s 118; FA 1996, s 135(5) and Sch 21 para 48)

Expenditure on plant and machinery must be notified to the Revenue, the notification being a separate matter from the requirement for a claim to be made, although it will usually be combined with a claim. The notice will usually be given in the tax computations accompanying returns. It will not be enough merely to give a global figure of expenditure, but a breakdown into broad categories should be sufficient. If the allowances are to commence in the first available period, then the notice must be given to the Revenue within two years after the end of the chargeable period for companies and within one year after 31 January following the tax year in which the accounting period ends for individuals (this time limit replacing the previous two-year time limit for 1996/97 onwards). Expenditure incurred by a company in the year to 31 December 1995 would therefore have to be notified by 31 December 1997. If the expenditure had been incurred by an individual, it would have been during the transitional basis period for 1996/97 (i.e. the two years to 31 December 1996), and the time limit for notification would have been 31 January 1999.

If expenditure is notified late, writing-down allowances will commence in the first later accounting period for which the notice is in time, providing the plant and machinery is still owned at some time in that period. If, for example, a company's expenditure for the year to 31 December 1995 was not notified until March 1998, writing-down allowances would commence in the year to 31 December 1996, providing the plant and machinery was owned at some time in that year.

Allowances available (s 24)

The allowances available are writing-down allowances of 25% per annum on the reducing balance method. In the first year of business for individuals and partnerships under the previous year basis rules, the writing-down allowance is reduced according to the length of the basis period, and it is also reduced proportionately for companies in respect of accounting periods of less than 12 months. Under the income tax current year basis rules, the writing-down allowance is proportionately reduced or increased if the accounting period is less than or more than 12 months, but with special rules if it exceeds 18 months (see page 300 and example 3 on page 308).

Pooling expenditure (s 25)

All qualifying expenditure on plant and machinery is included in a single 'pool' except for the following:

At the taxpayer's option, assets that are expected to be disposed of within five years ('short-life assets').

Any asset with part private use by a sole trader or partner.

Assets for foreign leasing.

Any 'car' costing over £12,000 (£8,000 for cars bought before 11 March 1992).

Any other 'cars' — defined as all other motor vehicles except those primarily suited for carrying goods, those not commonly used as private vehicles and unsuitable to be so used, those let on a short lease (i.e. where the car is normally hired to the same person for less than 30 consecutive days and for less than 90 days in any twelve months), and those let to someone receiving mobility allowance or disability living allowance.

Cars under the last heading are kept in a separate 'pool' — see page 309.

The writing-down allowance at the rate of 25% per annum (reducing balance method) is calculated on the unrelieved expenditure brought forward from the previous period, plus expenditure in the period, less any sales proceeds (up to, but not exceeding, the original cost — see page 309). If the proceeds exceed the pool balance, a balancing charge is made.

A balancing allowance will not arise on the main pool, except on a cessation of trade where the total sales proceeds are less than the pool balance. See example 2. See also example 3, which illustrates the special rules mentioned on page 300 for income tax accounting periods that exceed 18 months.

De-pooling of short-life assets (ss 37, 38; FA 1996, s 135(4) and Sch 21 para 30)

Some assets have a very short life and depreciate very quickly. The normal pooling system does not give relief for such assets over their life span because even though they have been disposed of, any unrelieved expenditure remains in the pool to be written off over future years (unless the business has ceased, when a pool balancing adjustment will be made — see above). An election may be made to have the capital allowances on specified items of plant and machinery calculated separately under the 'short-life assets' provisions. A balancing allowance or charge will then arise if the asset is disposed of within four years from the end of the accounting period in which it is acquired. If the asset is still held at the end of that period, the tax written-down value is transferred into the main pool. Cars and any other assets which would not in any event have been included in the main pool of expenditure cannot be dealt with under the short-life assets rules. The election for this treatment is irrevocable, and must be made within the specified time limit. The time limit for companies is two years after the end of the accounting period in which the expenditure is incurred. The same time limit used to apply to individuals, but from 1996/97 it is changed to one year after the 31 January following the tax year in which the accounting period in which the expenditure was incurred ends. The Inland Revenue have issued guidelines (Statement of Practice SP 1/86) on practical aspects of these rules, including provisions for grouping classes of assets where individual treatment is impossible or impracticable.

Example 2

A trader has the following transactions in plant in the years ended 31 December 1994, 1995 and 1996:

		£
June 1994	Proceeds of sales	3,000
December 1994	Purchase from associated business	1,000
January 1995	Proceeds of sales	8,500
June 1995	Arm's length purchase	15,000
December 1996	Arm's length purchase	10,000

The pool balance brought forward at 1 January 1994 is £8,000.

The allowances are calculated as follows:

1995/96 (based on year to 31 December 1994)	
Pool value brought forward	8,000
Additions December 1994 (dealt with as a sale in the computations of the associated business)	1,000
	9,000
Less sales proceeds June 1994	(3,000)
	6,000
Writing-down allowance 25% (reduces taxable profit)	(1,500)
	4,500
1996/97 (based on two years to 31 December 1996)	
Additions June 1995 and December 1996	25,000
	29,500
Sales proceeds January 1995	(8,500)
	21,000
Writing-down allowance 25% (reduces taxable profit)	5,250
Balance carried forward	£15,750

The balance carried forward attracts a 25% per annum writing-down allowance in accounting period commencing 1 January 1997 and later periods, on the reducing balance method.

Example 3

22-month account is made up from 1 January 2000 to 31 October 2001. Pool balance brought forward is £100,000. The only additions were new plant costing £20,000 in March 2001. The allowances will be calculated as follows:

	£
Year to 31.12.2000	
Pool balance brought forward	100,000
WDA 25%	25,000
	75,000
10 mths to 31.10.2001	
Additions	20,000
	95,000
WDA 25% × 10/12	19,792
Written-down value carried forward	75,208
Total allowances for period treated as trading expense	£44,792

Without the rule for accounts longer than 18 months, allowances would have been:

£120,000 @ 25% × 22/12 =	£55,000

Assets with part private use (s 79)

Any asset that is privately used by a sole proprietor or by a partner in a business is dealt with separately. This does not apply to assets used by directors of family companies. The use of company assets for private purposes by directors or employees does not affect the company's capital allowances position, but results in a benefits charge on the director/employee (see chapter 10).

Allowances and charges on privately-used assets are calculated in the normal way, but the available allowance or charge is restricted to the business proportion.

There is no 'pooling' of privately used assets. A separate calculation is made for each asset which is so used, and an individual balancing adjustment is made when it is disposed of.

Cars costing more than £12,000 (ss 34–36)

Each car that costs more than £12,000 (£8,000 for cars bought before 11 March 1992) is dealt with separately, and the available writing-down allowance is £3,000 (£2,000 for pre-11 March 1992 purchases) per annum or 25% of the unrelieved balance, whichever is less. If such a car is used privately by a sole trader or partner the available amount is further restricted by the private proportion. When the car is sold a balancing allowance or charge arises. See page 272 for the treatment of a car with a value of more than £12,000 that you lease instead of buy.

Car pools (s 41)

Any car costing over £12,000 and/or with part private use by a sole trader or partner is dealt with in a separate individual pool. All other cars are dealt with in the car pool (see page 306 for the definition of 'car').

The expenditure on the car pool qualifies for writing-down allowances of 25%. Sales proceeds are deducted before the writing-down allowance is calculated, and a balancing charge is made if the sales proceeds exceed the pool balance. If all the items in the car pool are disposed of, a balancing allowance or charge arises. The car pool will then be reopened as and when a further car is acquired.

Films (s 68; F(No 2)A 1992, ss 41–43)

Expenditure on the production and acquisition of films is treated as revenue expenditure and not capital expenditure, with the cost being written off over the income-producing life of the film. This does not apply to qualifying European Union (EU) films. For such qualifying films, pre-production expenditure up to 20% of the total budgeted expenditure, and abortive expenditure, may be written off as it is incurred, and production expenditure may be written off at a flat rate of $33\frac{1}{3}\%$ a year from completion of the film. The $33\frac{1}{3}\%$ relief also applies to expenditure on acquiring qualifying EU films. An alternative treatment may be claimed for qualifying EU films, under which allowances may be claimed under the normal plant and machinery rules instead, but this would give lower allowances.

Assets for foreign leasing (s 42)

Assets leased to non-UK residents who do not use them for a UK trade are kept in a separate pool, normally attracting writing-down allowances at 10%, balancing charges where the sales proceeds exceed the tax written-down value, and a balancing allowance where the tax written-down value exceeds the proceeds on a cessation of trade. In some circumstances, no allowances at all are available.

Effect of capital allowances on capital gains computation (TCGA 1992, ss 41, 55(3))

Capital allowances are not deducted from the cost of an asset in computing a capital gain, but are taken into account in computing a capital loss. There will only be a gain if an asset is sold for more than cost, and in that event any capital allowances given will be withdrawn by the cost being taken out of the capital allowances computation (except for certain industrial buildings allowances — see page 313 — and agricultural buildings allowances — see chapter 31) and will not therefore affect the computation of the gain. Now that indexation allowance cannot create or increase a loss for capital gains purposes, capital losses will not normally arise.

For plant and machinery that is moveable rather than fixed, there is no chargeable gain if it is sold for £6,000 or less. Where the proceeds exceed £6,000, the chargeable gain cannot exceed 5/3rds of the excess of the proceeds over £6,000 (see page 541).

If plant and machinery is fixed rather than moveable, gains are not exempt but they may be deferred if the item is replaced (see page 55).

Where the asset was acquired before 31 March 1982, plant and machinery is not covered by a general 31 March 1982 rebasing election (see page 49) so computations have to be made both under the old rules and the new. See example 4.

Example 4

Plant cost £50,000 in September 1981 and is sold in July 1996 for £110,000. The value of the plant at 31 March 1982 was £55,000. Indexation allowance from March 1982 is, say, 90%.

Since the plant is sold for more than cost, the capital allowances will be fully withdrawn by deducting £50,000 from the pool balance. The capital gains computation is as follows:

	Old scheme £	New scheme £
Proceeds	110,000	110,000
Cost/31 March 1982 value	(50,000)	(55,000)
	60,000	55,000
Indexation allowance at 90% on 31 March 1982 value	(49,500)	(49,500)
	10,500	5,500

Chargeable gain is the lower of the two, i.e. £5,500. If the plant is fixed plant, the gain will be eligible for rollover relief. If it is moveable plant, the gain will be fully chargeable.

Industrial buildings

Definition (s 18)

Industrial buildings are broadly those in use for the purpose of qualifying trades, the most common of which are manufacturing or processing goods or materials. Buildings used to store goods and materials before and after manufacture or processing are included. Offices, shops, hotels, wholesale warehouses and buildings used as retail shops (including repair shops) are excluded from the definition, but hotels qualify for allowances under a separate heading (see page 315). The Revenue treat a vehicle repair work-shop as an industrial building if it is completely separate from the vehicle sales area, does not have a reception, and public access is discouraged. Allowances would be restricted to the extent that vehicles for resale were repaired in the workshop. Where part of a building is outside the definition (for example offices in a factory), the whole building qualifies for allowances providing the expenditure on the non-industrial part does not exceed 25% of the total cost. This applies only where the non-industrial part is housed within the same building, not where it is a separate building. Where a building is in an enterprise zone, there is no restriction on the use to which it may be put, except that a private dwelling does not qualify, and much more generous allowances are available (see page 315).

Allowances for new buildings and additional capital expenditure on existing buildings (ss 3–5, 8, 10, 12, 13, 15, 21; FA 1993, s 113)

Allowances are given on the cost of construction and no allowances are available for the cost of the land, although site preparation works qualify. Where a building is bought from the builder, allowances are available on the amount paid. Where additional capital expenditure is incurred on an existing qualifying building, the additional expenditure qualifies for allowances as if it were a separate building. This enables a tenant to get allowances on any capital expenditure he incurs on a qualifying building, and it is specifically provided that if any repair expenditure on a qualifying building is disal-lowed as a business expense, it is treated as qualifying capital expenditure. Furthermore, expenditure on items that become part of the building does not qualify for plant and machinery allowances and counts instead as part of the building expenditure — see page 304.

The allowances available used to be an initial allowance on construction expenditure incurred in the basis period, and annual writing-down allowances for any basis period at the end of which the building was in qualifying use, until the expenditure was fully relieved. Initial allowances were generally withdrawn for expenditure incurred after 31 March 1986, except for buildings in enterprise zones (see page 315). A 20% initial allowance was, however, reintroduced for new industrial buildings that were contracted for between 1 November 1992 and 31 October 1993 inclusive and brought into use by the end of 1994. The 20% initial allowance is also available on buildings bought unused where the seller incurred the expenditure on the building in the year to 31 October 1993, and on buildings bought unused from the builder in the year to 31 October 1993, even if wholly or partly built earlier. The initial allowance is given according to the basis period in which the qualifying expenditure is incurred.

The remainder of the expenditure, or the whole of the expenditure where the 20% initial allowance is not available, is written off by writing-down allowances at the rate of 4% of the construction cost per annum starting when the building is brought into use, until the cost has been fully written off. (Writing-down allowances are at the rate of 2% per annum on capital expenditure incurred before 6 November 1962, such buildings having a tax life of 50 years. The allowances were introduced in 1946/47 for existing as well as new buildings, available for the remainder of an existing building's 50-year life.) The rates of initial allowance from 11 March 1981 until 31 March 1986 were as follows:

Date expenditure incurred	Rate
11 March 1981 to 13 March 1984	75%
14 March 1984 to 31 March 1985	50%
1 April 1985 to 31 March 1986	25%

The allowances were at various rates for earlier years, having commenced on 6 April 1944.

Example 5

A factory built in Spring 1996 is bought from the builder for £500,000 in October 1996 by a trader making up accounts to 31 December. The building is brought into use immediately. Allowances will be given as follows:

1996/97	
Cost	500,000
Writing-down allowance 4%	(20,000)
Balance of expenditure	£480,000

Relieved by writing-down allowances of £20,000 per annum for 24 years from 1997/98 to 2020/2021 (unless the building is sold within that time).

Had the building not been brought into use until say February 1997, the first writing-down allowance would have been given in 1997/98.

If a building is sold before the expenditure has been fully relieved, there is a balancing adjustment between the seller and the buyer, and the buyer is entitled to writing-down allowances over the remainder of the building's tax life (see below). Second-hand purchasers are not entitled to initial allowances.

Sale of the building (ss 4, 5, 15)

This will involve a balancing adjustment on the seller (unless the building is sold after the end of its tax life — see below) and a possible claim for relief by the purchaser.

Whilst there are rules to deal with periods of non-industrial use, the basic adjustment is to give the seller a balancing allowance to make up any shortfall between the unrelieved expenditure and the sale proceeds, or to make a balancing charge to withdraw excess allowances if the sale proceeds exceed the unrelieved expenditure. (See page 357 for the treatment of a balancing charge arising when a building is disposed of after the trade has ceased.)

Providing he uses the building for a qualifying trade, the purchaser gets allowances on the part of the original building cost remaining unrelieved after the balancing adjustment on the seller. This amount is relieved by way of equal annual allowances over the remainder of the 'tax life' of the building. No matter how much the purchaser pays for the building, the maximum amount on which he can claim relief is the original building cost, which may have been incurred many years earlier and bear little relation to current prices. No relief is available for the cost of the land whether relating to new or used buildings. The tax life of industrial buildings is 25 years from the date the building is first used for expenditure on or after 6 November 1962 and 50 years for expenditure before that date. See example 6. If a building's tax life has already expired, there is no balancing adjustment for the seller and the purchaser cannot claim any allowances at all, unless additional capital expenditure on the building had been incurred at a later date, in which case that expenditure would be treated as if it related to a separate building with its own tax life (see page 311).

Where plant and machinery is purchased with a building, the purchase price needs to be apportioned and plant and machinery allowances can then be claimed on the appropriate part of the purchase price. There is no restriction of plant and machinery allowances to the original cost of the items.

Interaction with VAT capital goods scheme (s 159A; FA 1991, Sch 14)

Input tax adjustments under the VAT capital goods scheme (see page 101) are reflected in capital allowances computations. Changes to VAT paid in respect of an industrial building will be added to or deducted from the unrelieved expenditure on the building and writing-down allowances recalculated over the remainder of the building's tax life. Similarly, adjustments for VAT on computers will be made in the plant and machinery pool or short-life asset computation in the period in which the VAT adjustment is made. Where the original expenditure qualified for the special 20% initial allowance on industrial buildings, any additional VAT liability will be treated as additional expenditure qualifying for extra initial or first-year allowance, the extra allowance being given in the adjustment period.

Example 6

The construction costs of an industrial building in December 1985 were £100,000, the land cost being £25,000. Initial allowance of £25,000 and annual allowances of £4,000 for 11 years, totalling £69,000, have been claimed.

The building (including £40,000 for the land) is sold in November 1996 for

(a) £68,000   (b) £112,800   (c) £200,000

The vendor's position is

	(a)	(b)	(c)
	£	£	£
Sale proceeds	68,000	112,800	200,000
Land included	40,000	40,000	40,000
Building proceeds	28,000	72,800	160,000
Building cost	100,000	100,000	100,000
Cost of owning building	72,000	27,200	Nil
Allowances already given	69,000	69,000	69,000
Balancing allowance/(charge)	£3,000	£(41,800)	£(69,000)

In the case of (c) there would also be a capital gain:

Proceeds (land and buildings)	200,000
Cost (land and buildings)	125,000
Chargeable gain (before indexation allowance)	£75,000

The purchaser would get reliefs as follows.

	(a)	(b)	(c)
Cost to him (building only)	£28,000	£72,800	£160,000
Restrict to original cost if less than purchase price			£100,000
Annual allowance 1/14th*	£2,000	£5,200	£7,143

(*14 years of 25-year life remaining, ignoring fractions of year for illustration.)

If the building had been built in June 1970, there would have been no balancing adjustment for the seller and no allowances to the buyer, because it would be over 25 years old. The capital allowances given would not be deducted from the cost to calculate the capital gain.

If the building had been built in 1960, there would still be 14 years remaining out of the writing-down life of 50 years (for expenditure incurred before 6 November 1962), but the allowances would relate to any unallowed balance of the 1960 building cost.

Hotels (ss 7, 19)

Relief is available for construction costs in respect of a qualifying hotel or hotel extension. The hotel or extension must be of a permanent nature, be open for at least four months between April and October, and when open must have at least ten letting bedrooms offering sleeping accommodation. It must provide services of breakfast, evening meal, making beds and cleaning rooms. The relief works in the same way as that for industrial buildings (see above). The annual writing-down allowance is 4% of cost, and the 20% initial allowance was available for qualifying expenditure in the year to 31 October 1993. If the hotel is in an enterprise zone, it qualifies for the allowances described below, with no restriction on months of opening or number of bedrooms, etc.

Buildings in enterprise zones (ss 1, 4A, 6, 10A, 10B, 17A; FA 1994, ss 120, 121)

When an area has been designated as an Enterprise Zone by the Secretary of State, expenditure incurred or contracted for within ten years after the creation of the zone on any buildings other than dwelling houses qualifies for an initial allowance of 100%, or whatever lower amount is claimed. (If part of a building was used as a dwelling, the whole expenditure would still qualify, providing the expenditure on that part did not exceed 25% of the total building cost.) Any expenditure on which initial allowance is not claimed qualifies for writing-down allowances of 25% of cost (straight line method) until it is written off in full. See page 302 for the way in which an investor may get relief for the allowances he claims, which is illustrated in example 7 on page 316. Where fixed plant or machinery is an integral part of the building, it can be treated as part of the building for the purposes of claiming enterprise zone allowances. Balancing allowances or charges apply on the disposal of buildings in enterprise zones using the same rules as for industrial buildings (see page 312), and treating the life of the building as being 25 years. This means that if the building is sold in the early years, the seller will usually lose all or a large part of the benefit of the 100% allowances. It used to be possible to avoid a balancing charge by granting a long lease on a building rather than selling it. For interests in enterprise zone buildings acquired on or after 13 January 1994 (except those under a contract entered into before 13 January 1994 that became unconditional before 25 February 1994), the granting of a lease will be treated as a sale, triggering a balancing charge, if it takes place within seven years after the date of the contract to acquire the interest in the building. This treatment will not apply to leases granted after more than seven years. If, however, there is a guaranteed exit arrangement, the seven-year period will not apply and a balancing charge will be made on the granting of a lease at any time within the building's 25-year life.

Example 7

In September 1995, i.e. in the tax year 1995/96, a single man purchased a workshop in an enterprise zone from a developer for £72,000 (including land £6,000), the first letting taking place in the following tax year, i.e. 1996/97. He had rent income from another property of £8,000 in 1995/96 and he had other income of £40,000. His total income in 1996/97 was £60,000 and is expected to continue at that level. The allowance he can claim in 1995/96 is any amount up to a maximum of 100% of £66,000. The amount claimed can be set against just his rent income of that year and later years, or alternatively against his total income of either 1995/96 or 1996/97 or both years, any unrelieved balance then being set only against rental income in later years. If he claimed the maximum, however, and extended the claim in 1995/96 to his other income, he would lose all personal allowances in that year. He could instead claim allowances as follows.

Initial allowance	20,500
which can be utilised as follows:	
Against rent income of 1995/96	8,000
	12,500
Then against other income of 1995/96	40,000
Leaving taxable income (just below basic rate threshold after personal allowance) of	£27,500

The unrelieved expenditure is £45,500 (£66,000–£20,500) and this is relieved as follows:

1996/97 (25% × £66,000)	16,500
1997/98 (25% × £66,000)	16,500
1998/99 (the remainder)	12,500
	£45,500

If he wanted to eliminate his taxable income in 1995/96 he could instead claim initial allowance of £44,475 for that year and then claim relief as follows.

	1995/96	1996/97	1997/98
Total income	48,000	60,000	60,000
Initial allowance	44,475		
Writing-down allowance		16,500	5,025
Leaving taxable income (before personal allowance) of	£3,525	£43,500	£54,975

This would save lower and basic rate tax in 1995/96 at the expense of additional higher rate tax in 1997/98 and 1998/99.

Purchase within two years after first use

Someone who acquires an enterprise zone building within two years after it is first used is treated as if he had acquired an unused building, so that he can claim the 100% initial allowance or 25% writing-down allowance as indicated above. As far as any subsequent second-hand purchaser is concerned, the position is the same as for purchasers outside the first two years (see below), but the 25-year life of the building dates from the date of first use by the person who acquired it within the first two years of use.

Purchase more than two years after first use

Where the first disposal of an enterprise zone building occurs more than two years after it is first used, the purchaser cannot claim the 100% or 25% enterprise zone allowances. He gets writing-down allowances only, normally on the lower of the price paid by him and the original construction cost. The writing-down allowance is calculated by spreading the unrelieved expenditure over the balance of the building's 25-year life which is unexpired at the date of purchase. Where, however, a building is transferred between connected persons (say husband and wife), they may make a claim to treat the transfer as being at written-down value (see page 303), so that the benefit to the vendor of the higher enterprise zone building allowances is not lost as a result of the transfer.

Limits on enterprise zone allowances

Where part of the expenditure on a building was incurred neither within the ten-year life of the enterprise zone, nor under a contract entered into within the ten-year period, that part of the expenditure qualifies only for the normal level of buildings allowances (i.e. for industrial buildings or hotels), or not at all if it is a non-qualifying building.

Enterprise zone allowances cannot be claimed on expenditure incurred more than 20 years after the site was included in the enterprise zone, no matter when the contract was entered into.

Way in which allowances are given

Enterprise zone allowances may be claimed both by traders and investors. The treatment is dealt with on page 302.

Patents (TA 1988, ss 520–522, 524, 528)

Expenditure incurred in devising and patenting an invention (or an abortive attempt to do so) is allowable as a business expense. Where, however, patent rights are purchased, writing-down allowances at 25% on the reducing balance method are available, with all expenditure on patent rights after 31 March 1986 being pooled.

Balancing charges arise in the usual way, and a balancing allowance will be given on any unallowed expenditure, if the last of the rights come to an end without subsequently being revived or on the permanent discontinuance of the trade.

Expenditure before 1 April 1986 is relieved by way of capital allowances in equal annual instalments over seventeen years, or over the period for which the rights were acquired, whichever is less. So if accounts were made up to 31 March and patent rights with twelve years to run were purchased for £1,800 in January 1986, allowances of £150 p.a. are given for twelve years, commencing in 1986/87 in the case of an individual or in the accounting period ended 31 March 1986 for a company.

Although a balancing charge can never exceed the allowances given, there are specific provisions to charge a capital profit on patent rights as income rather than as a capital gain. The profit is not dealt with as part of the business profits but is charged to income tax under Schedule D, Case VI over six years in equal instalments, commencing with the tax year in which it is received, unless the taxpayer elects to have the whole sum charged in the year of receipt.

Patents allowances granted to non-traders can only be set against income from the patent rights and not against any other income.

Know-how (TA 1988, ss 530–533)

'Know-how' is defined as any industrial information or techniques which are likely to assist in a manufacturing process, or the working of a mine, or the carrying out of agricultural, forestry or fishing operations.

Capital expenditure on the acquisition of know-how for use in a trade qualifies for an annual writing-down allowance of 25% on the reducing balance method. Any additional expenditure is added to the unrelieved balance and any sale proceeds are deducted from it before calculating the writing-down allowance. If the sale proceeds exceed the tax written-down value, a balancing charge is made and this is not restricted to the allowances given, so that the balancing charge will include any excess of the proceeds over the original cost.

If know-how is sold as part of a business, the payment is regarded as being for goodwill and thus dealt with under the capital gains rules, unless both seller and buyer elect within two years of the disposal for it to be treated as a sale of know-how.

If the trade ceases during the writing-down period but the know-how is not sold, relief for the unallowed expenditure is given by way of a balancing allowance.

Scientific research (ss 136–139)

Capital expenditure for the purposes of scientific research is allowed in full, when incurred, in taxing trading income. Expenditure on land and dwelling houses does not generally qualify for relief.

Proceeds of sale or compensation payments on destruction (not exceeding the allowance given) are treated as a trading receipt, with open market value sometimes being substituted for those proceeds.

If the sale takes place in the same basis period as the expenditure is incurred, any deficiency between the cost of expenditure and the proceeds is allowed as a deduction in calculating trading profits.

Mineral extraction (ss 98–121)

Expenditure on mineral extraction qualifies for writing-down allowances on a reducing balance basis at the following rates:

	Rate
Pre-trading expenditure	10%
Acquisition of a mineral asset (mineral deposits, land comprising mineral deposits, etc.)	10%
Other qualifying expenditure	25%

A balancing charge will be made if sales proceeds exceed tax written-down value. A balancing allowance will be given in the chargeable period when the mineral extraction trade ceases, or when particular mineral deposits cease to be worked, and in the case of pre-trading expenditure, when trading commences or exploration is abandoned before then.

Tax points

● A specific claim for capital allowances must be made by individuals, partnerships and companies, so it is important to ensure that the appropriate entry is made on the tax return and supported by computations.

● For plant and machinery allowances there is now the additional requirement for the expenditure to be notified within two years from the end of the period, or within one year from the return due date under self-assessment — see page 305. To avoid any possible loss of relief, you should ensure that all plant and machinery expenditure is automatically notified within the time limit (by letter if, exceptionally, the final tax computation is not ready), whether or not a claim is to be made. The notification should show a breakdown of the amounts expended into the various categories of expenditure, e.g. office furniture, computers, lorries.

- If claiming the maximum allowances means wasting personal allowances, you can reduce your claim for certain allowances — see page 303. You will then get writing-down allowances on an increased amount in future years.

- Alternatively, for any year when you are charged under the previous year basis rules, you can use capital allowances to turn a trading profit into a loss which you can relieve against other income (see chapter 25). This flexibility is not available under the current year basis, because the capital allowances claimed are automatically included in the loss.

- Companies can revise capital allowances claims within two years (and sometimes within up to six years). Individuals are able to revise claims for years before 1996/97 if the circumstances fall within a Revenue Statement of Practice (see page 303). Following the introduction of self-assessment in 1996/97, the capital allowances will form part of an individual's self-assessment and the claim may be amended within one year from the 31 January filing date for the return, i.e. within one year ten months from the end of the tax year in which the account ends.

- Companies will benefit by not taking allowances, where they want to leave profits high enough to take advantage of reliefs which are only available in the current period, such as group relief for losses or double tax relief. The amount on which writing-down allowances can be claimed in later years is increased accordingly.

- Allowances available on capital expenditure incurred on commencing trading on your own or in partnership may contribute to a trading loss, which may be carried back against the income of earlier years (see chapter 25).

- Whereas you get only 25% writing-down allowance when you buy cars, if you lease a car instead, you can set the whole of the leasing charge against your profit, subject to disallowance of any private element and the restriction on the allowable hire charge where the car cost the leasing company more than £12,000 — see page 272.

- When you buy or sell a group of assets, such as goodwill, plant and machinery and trade premises, some will be subject to capital allowances at different rates and some will not qualify for allowances at all. It is essential that the price apportionment is realistic and is agreed with the other party at the time of purchase or sale in order to avoid complications when you submit the tax computations.

- If there is doubt as to whether a contract for the purchase of plant or machinery is a hire-purchase contract or a leasing contract, it is advisable to check with the finance company as to the nature of the payments to them to ensure the correct treatment in tax computations.

- Writing-down allowances at 25% on the reducing balance method will write off about 90% of the expenditure in eight years. The option to keep short-life assets out of the plant and machinery pool enables you to shorten this time to five years or less if the assets are sold or scrapped within that period.

- If you take over a business from someone with whom you are connected, the election to continue the predecessor's capital allowances computation has to be made within two years after the change (see page 303). Do not forget the time limit.

- Plan the expenditure on any non-qualifying parts of a new industrial building (for example, offices) to ensure, if possible, that it does not exceed the allowable 25% for non-qualifying expenditure.

- Since the purchase of land does not qualify for industrial buildings allowances, more tax-efficient use of capital expenditure can be achieved by constructing on leasehold land.

- If you want to invest in an enterprise zone building but the cost is too high, you can participate on a co-ownership basis or through an enterprise zone property trust.

- The allowances for buildings in enterprise zones are available for any commercial buildings and not just industrial buildings — see page 315.

23
Partnerships

Assessment (TA 1988, ss 60–63, 111; TCGA 1992, s 59)

The rules for taxing partners are changed with the introduction of the current year basis of assessment. The new rules apply straight away to new partnerships commencing on or after 6 April 1994 (including those treated as new businesses because no election for continuity of assessments has been made (see page 325)), and from 6 April 1997 to partnerships in existence at 5 April 1994. New rules also apply from 1996/97 (when self-assessment starts) in relation to partnership tax returns. The new provisions are dealt with on page 328.

Unless and until the current year basis provisions apply, the trading profits of a partnership are charged to tax by a joint assessment covering all the partners. The assessment is normally calculated in the same way as an assessment on any self-employed person (see chapter 21). Thus the profits of an established partnership for the year ended 31 August 1994 will be assessed in 1995/96. The 1996/97 assessment for such a partnership would be based on the average of the profits for the two years to 31 August 1996 (see page 291).

One assessment on the trading profits is made in the partnership name, any partner being liable for the whole of the tax if it is not paid. The liability of one of the partners, or of any group of partners, can never be separated from that of the other partners.

There is no joint assessment on non-trading income or on capital gains of the partnership. Here, each partner is charged on his share, and there can be no claim against the others if he does not pay. Thus each partner will receive an assessment in respect of his share of interest received, or of rent where there is co-ownership of land (see page 324).

Under the current year basis, partners will be separately liable for their own tax on all sources of income. For partnerships in existence at 5 April 1994, the new rules apply from 1997/98, and they will receive a partnership assessment on the trading profits for 1996/97 (see page 332).

Division of assessments on business profits (TA 1988, s 277)

To arrive at each partner's income for tax purposes under the previous
year basis rules (and the transitional rules for 1996/97), the taxable profits
of each tax year are divided amongst the partners in the way they share
profits for that tax year. This division may not be in the same proportions
as those used to divide the profits on which the tax charge is based. See
example 1.

Example 1

A, B and C, who have been in business for many years, share
profits equally in the year ended 30 November 1994. The profit is
£60,000, each taking a £20,000 share. From 1 December 1994 they
have amended the profit-sharing ratio to 2:1:1.

The profit of £60,000 is charged to tax in 1995/96 and the
assessment is divided as follows:

A   £30,000   B   £15,000   C   £15,000

Furthermore, the 1994/95 assessment, based on the profits of the
year to 30 November 1993, will be apportioned, and the proportion from 6 April 1994 to 30 November 1994 will be shared
equally and that from 1 December 1994 to 5 April 1995 shared
2:1:1.

B and C therefore benefit by having their taxable profits reduced
compared with their actual profits, at the expense of A, who is
taxed on more profits than he has had.

Had the change in profit-sharing taken place a year later on
30 November 1995, the difference between taxable and actual
profit shares would not have been so marked, because the
assessments affected would be 1995/96 and 1996/97, and the
transitional averaging rules for 1996/97 would mean that half of
the 1996/97 assessable profits (i.e. relating to the year to 30
November 1996) would have been shared in the same ratio as
that in which they were taxed.

Sometimes, the profit-sharing arrangement may not be a straight split but
may provide for interest on partners' capital, partnership salaries or perhaps
a system of slices by which profits are disproportionately divided. The
division for tax purposes takes into account any variation of profit-sharing
arrangements during a tax year. See example 2.

Example 2

The profit of X, Y and Z for the year ended 30 June 1994 is £40,000, shared in the ratio 3:1:1, so that X has £24,000, and Y and Z £8,000 each.

They continue sharing in this way until 5 October 1995, when the arrangements are changed to give interest on partnership capital amounting to £4,000, £1,000 and £700 per annum respectively, annual partnership salaries of £7,500, £12,000 and £10,000 respectively, with the balance being shared equally.

The taxable profit for 1995/96 of £40,000 is divided for tax purposes as follows:

	Total	X	Y	Z
Profit from 6.4.95 to 5.10.95				
(½ of that of year to 30.6.94)	20,000			
Split 3:1:1		12,000	4,000	4,000
Profit from 6.10.95 to 5.4.96				
(½ of that of year to 30.6.94)	20,000			
Interest on capital (6 months)	(2,850)	2,000	500	350
Partnership salaries (6 months)	(14,750)	3,750	6,000	5,000
Balance remaining (split equally)	2,400	800	800	800
Division for tax purposes	40,000	18,550	11,300	10,150
Whereas accounts profit was divided	40,000	24,000	8,000	8,000

The June 1995 profit, which was shared according to the old arrangements, will be averaged with the June 1996 profit, a quarter of which was also shared on the old arrangements (up to 5 October 1995), to arrive at the 1996/97 assessment. The whole of that assessment will be split between the partners under the new sharing arrangements.

Non-trading income

As stated on page 322, each partner is taxed separately on his share of non-trading income, such as interest and rents.

Untaxed interest will have been taxed according to the income arising in the previous tax year for years up to 1995/96, and is taxed on the average of the two years to 5 April 1997 for 1996/97 (see chapter 37). Taxed income is charged according to the amount received in the tax year.

Rental income should strictly be calculated over the tax year from 6 April to 5 April, but many non-statutory arrangements were made before 1995/96 (see page 446). From 1995/96 the legislation provides that all rents are to be calculated on a strict tax year basis. But from 1997/98 this will not apply to partnerships, and any untaxed non-trading income will be calculated for the same periods as the trading profits (see page 331). Where partners have used a current year accounts basis for rents before 1995/96, they may continue to do so for 1995/96 and 1996/97, to avoid having to change the treatment twice in quick succession. (Further information is given in the Revenue's Tax Bulletin of February 1996.)

If new sources of non-trading income arise (or an incoming partner first takes a share of such income) on or after 6 April 1994, the current year basis rules apply to that income or that partner's share of it straight away, even though the current year basis will not apply to the trading income until 1997/98 if a continuation election (see below) is made.

Change of partners (TA 1988, ss 61, 62, 113)

If all the old partners sell out to new partners, then clearly the old trade has ceased for tax purposes. But for changes occurring before 6 April 1997, there is a cessation of trade for tax purposes whenever a new partner is introduced or an existing partner leaves the partnership, or when a sole trader takes in a partner. If, however, there is at least one individual who continues, and all those who were proprietors or partners before and after the change elect in writing to the Revenue within two years after the date of the change, assessments on the trading profits will continue on the normal previous year basis. (But see above for the position on non-trading income.) If the election is not made in relation to a change occurring after 5 April 1994, the partnership is treated as a new business from the date of the change, and the new current year basis rules apply (see page 287).

The Revenue apply the two-year time limit very strictly. They have, however, issued a statement (SP 9/92, 23 November 1992) indicating the very limited circumstances in which a late election may be accepted. On the same day they also issued an extra-statutory concession (A80) under which a firm of 50 or more partners (or with at least 20 non-resident partners) may make an election covering all future changes until one or more partners notifies the Revenue that they wish to withdraw from the arrangement, providing any new partners also make an election and the Revenue are indemnified against any claims by current or former partners that the elections have not been properly made.

Since, in calculating the tax payable by a partnership under the previous year basis rules and for the transitional year 1996/97, the taxable profit is divided between the partners in the way in which they share profits in the year of assessment, it follows that where a continuation election is made on a change of partners, the tax assessment will be divided between different persons from those who actually shared the profits. See example 3.

The partners cannot alter the statutory rules for dividing the taxable profit, and the *total* tax payable as a result of the statutory division will depend on each partner's personal circumstances. They could, however, agree to bear the calculated tax charge in a different way, so that, for example, C in example 3 did not bear any of the tax on profits which he did not share. This will not normally be done in an established partnership, since C will after all have received partnership income from 1 July 1995 onwards, and it is from this date that he is being included in the division of the assessment and paying tax on his share (and on the facts given in the example, he is better off than he would have been without a continuation election).

Example 3

Profits in the year ended 30 June 1994 £30,000, and in the year ended 30 June 1995 £33,000, were divided equally between the then partners A and B.

C is admitted as a partner on 1 July 1995. A, B and C share profits equally thereafter. Profits for the year to 30 June 1996 were £57,000, and for the year to 30 June 1997 £66,000.

All three partners sign and submit to the Revenue an election for continuity within two years after 1 July 1995.

Profits for tax purposes will be charged under partnership assessments up to 1996/97 and individually on each partner from 1997/98. They are divided as follows:

	Total	A	B	C
1995/96 £30,000 (profits of year to 30.6.94)				
To 30 June 1995, say 3 months	7,500	3,750	3,750	—
1 July 1995 to 5 April 1996, say 9 months	22,500	7,500	7,500	7,500
	30,000	11,250	11,250	7,500
1996/97 £45,000 (half of profits of 2 years to 30.6.96)	45,000	15,000	15,000	15,000
1997/98 (profits of year to 30.6.97)	66,000	22,000	22,000	22,000
Total for 3 years	141,000	48,250	48,250	44,500
Transitional overlap profits* 1.7.96–5.4.97	49,500	16,500	16,500	16,500

C is charged to tax on a share of the profits of £30,000 to 30 June 1994 and £33,000 to 30 June 1995 even though he did not actually share in those profits. But the periods for which he is taxed are those during which he has been a partner, and the amounts on which he is taxed are in fact less than his actual profit shares. If the continuation election had not been made, the position would have been as follows:

	Total	A	B	C
1995/96 (old firm**)				
(profits to 30.6.95)	8,250	4,125	4,125	—
1995/96 (new firm)				
(profits 1.7.95–5.4.96)	42,750	14,250	14,250	14,250
1996/97				
(profits of year to 30.6.96)	57,000	19,000	19,000	19,000
1997/98				
(profits of year to 30.6.97)	66,000	22,000	22,000	22,000
Total for 3 years	174,000	59,375	59,375	55,250
Overlap profits*				
1.7.95–5.4.96	42,750	14,250	14,250	14,250

All partners are therefore better off through the election for continuity, because they are each able to benefit from tax being charged on earlier, lower profits.

* Capital allowances have been ignored for simplicity, but in fact transitional overlap relief is calculated on profits before capital allowances and normal overlap relief on profits after capital allowances (see page 291).

** A and B might also suffer an increase in the taxable profits for 1993/94 and 1994/95, because the Revenue would be able to base the tax charge on actual profits for those tax years if higher than the normal previous year basis assessments (see page 284).

The tax position for the new firm where a change occurred before 6 April 1994 and a continuation election was not but could have been made depends on the circumstances. If the change was from sole trader to partnership or vice versa, the normal opening year rules apply (see page 281). If there were two or more partners in both the old and new firms, then, subject to the transitional provisions set out later in this paragraph, the assessments are arrived at as follows. The taxable profits for the first four tax years in the new partnership are based on the actual profits made. The partnership can elect for the assessments of the fifth and sixth tax years to be based on the actual profits made in those years (instead of the election applying in the second and third tax years as is the case when the normal new business rules apply). This election must be made within six years after the end of the sixth year of assessment in the new partnership. These provisions will be superseded by the current year basis rules from 1997/98 (see page 328). If the 1995/96 assessment is based on the actual profits under these special rules, averaging will not apply to 1996/97 and the assessment for that year will also be based on actual profits of the tax year.

Capital allowances (CAA 1990, ss 77, 152)

Where a continuation election is made on a change of partners before 6 April 1997, capital allowances are computed as if no change had taken place. If the continuation election is not made, allowances are computed as if the assets had been disposed of and reacquired at market value, except that for plant and machinery, the partners may elect within two years after the change for a deemed disposal value equal to the written-down value brought forward by the old firm, so that there will be no balancing adjustment, but the old firm will get no allowance in the tax year of transfer.

Current year basis and self-assessment (TMA 1970, ss 12AA–12AC; FA 1994, ss 184–186, 215, 216; FA 1995, s 117; FA 1996, s 123)

Partnerships commencing on or after 6 April 1994 and existing partnerships for which an election for continuity is not made on a change of partners before 6 April 1997 are taxed on the new current year basis rules (see page 287).

Partnerships in existence at 5 April 1994 who continue after 5 April 1997 will be charged on the current year basis from 1997/98. Their trading profits will be taxed on the averaging basis for 1996/97 (see page 291), so that one year's profit will escape assessment at that time. The 1996/97 assessment will be divided according to the existing rules, i.e. in the way the partners share profits in the tax year. See page 331 for the treatment of non-trading income.

Under the current year basis, partners no longer have joint liability for tax on the partnership trading profits. Partnership profits will, however, still have to be agreed globally, no partner being able to agree his share of profits independently of the others. It is only the liability for the tax that is separated under the new rules.

Sharing profits and losses

The anomalies under the previous year basis where there are changes in profit shares and/or partners, and where partners make different loss claims, do not arise under the current year basis. The profits of the accounting period are divided between the partners according to the sharing arrangements in the period. Each partner's share of the profit is then treated as arising to him individually, and the rules for opening and closing years and for overlap relief depend on when he joins and leaves the firm (see examples 4 and 5). Losses are similarly shared on an accounting period basis and treated as arising to the partners individually, loss claims being made accordingly.

Example 4

Facts as in example 1 on page 323, but change in profit sharing was made from 1 December 1999. The profits for tax purposes will be shared in the same way as the accounts profits, the profit of the year to 30 November 1999 (taxable in 1999/2000) being shared equally and that of the year to 30 November 2000 (taxable in 2000/2001) being shared 2:1:1.

Example 5

D and E commenced in partnership on 1 January 1995, making up accounts annually to 31 December and sharing profits equally. F joined them as an equal partner on 1 July 1996 and E left the partnership on 28 February 1997. Profits and their division between the partners for the first three years are as follows:

Yr ended	Profits	D	E	F
	£	£	£	£
31.12.95	40,000	20,000	20,000	
31.12.96	60,000	25,000	25,000	10,000
31.12.97	90,000	42,500	5,000	42,500
Total profits for period		87,500	50,000	52,500

Assessments and overlap profits available for relief will be:

	D	E	F
	£	£	£
1994/95			
1.1.95–5.4.95	5,000	5,000	
1995/96			
1.1.95–31.12.95	20,000	20,000	
Overlap profits	(5,000)	(5,000)	
1996/97			
1.1.96–31.12.96	25,000		
1.1.96–28.2.97 (25,000 + 5,000)		30,000	
Less overlap relief		(5,000)	
		25,000	
1.7.96–5.4.97:			
To 31.12.96 10,000			
To 5.4.97 3/12 × £42,500 10,625	10,625		20,625
1997/98			
1.1.97–31.12.97	42,500		42,500
Overlap profits			(10,625)

> *Profits assessed over 3 years and overlap profits available for relief*
>
> | | | | |
> |---|---|---|---|
> | Total assessable profits | 92,500 | 50,000 | 63,125 |
> | Overlap profits | (5,000) | — | (10,625) |

Any non-trading partnership income is divided according to the sharing arrangements in the accounting period in the same way as the trading profits (see page 331).

A change in partners is not regarded as a cessation of the partnership unless none of the old partners continues after the change, so partnership continuation elections will no longer be relevant.

Effect of continuation election for partners joining a partnership, which existed at 5 April 1994, between 6 April 1996 and 5 April 1997

If a partner joins between 6 April 1996 and 5 April 1997 and a continuation election is made, the current year basis rules are used to arrive at a notional basis period for that partner for 1996/97, in order to establish the basis period for 1997/98 and to decide how much normal overlap relief and/or transitional overlap relief the partner is entitled to.

Example 6

Old-established partnership of A and B makes up accounts to 31 May annually. C joins as a partner on 1 December 1996 and a continuation election is made.

The 1996/97 assessment (based on the average of the profits of the two years to 31 May 1996) will be divided as follows:

6.4.96 to 30.11.96 (8/12ths) Between A and B
1.12.96 to 5.4.97 (4/12ths) Between A, B and C

To establish basis periods for C from 1997/98 onwards, a notional current year basis period is arrived at for 1996/97 as if the new rules had applied when he joined. His basis periods will therefore be:

1996/97 1.12.96–5.4.97 (notional basis period)
1997/98 1.12.96–30.11.97 (actual basis period)
1998/99 1.6.97–31.5.98 (actual basis period)

C will be entitled to transitional overlap relief on his share of the profits from 1 December 1996 to 5 April 1997 and to normal overlap relief on his profits share from 1 June 1997 to 30 November 1997.

Non-trading income

Under the current year basis, partnership non-trading income is shared for tax purposes according to the sharing arrangements in the accounting period, as it was under the previous year basis. Unless tax has been deducted at source, however, such income is treated as if it arose from a separate trade that commenced when the partner joined the firm. It is therefore taxed according to the same periods as the trading income. This means that there may be overlap relief on commencement and possibly on a change of accounting date. The overlap relief for non-trading income will be allowed to the extent that more than 12 months' income would otherwise be charged in one year as a result of a change of accounting date, and otherwise in the tax year in which a partner ceases to be a partner (even if the source of income ceased earlier). The deduction will be given against the untaxed non-trading income of the relevant tax year. If it exceeds that untaxed income it will be relieved against other income of that tax year.

Example 7

Interest received in full for many years by an established partnership making up accounts annually to 30 April is payable in June and December. In 1996/97 the interest received in June and December 1995 and June and December 1996 will be averaged and the partners will each be taxed on their shares of the averaged amount. In 1997/98 they will each be taxed on their shares of the interest received in the accounting year to 30 April 1997, i.e. the June and December 1996 interest, which has already been taken into account in 1996/97. Overlap relief will therefore apply to each partner's share, and will be given not when the source of interest is disposed of but when the partner leaves the firm (unless more than 12 months' income would otherwise be chargeable in an earlier year as a result of a change of accounting date).

Where partnership non-trading income is received net of tax (or, in the case of dividends, accompanied by a tax credit), then although it is divided according to the sharing arrangements of the accounting period, each partner will, in his self-assessment, apportion his shares to the relevant tax years. Each partner will therefore have to be provided with details not only of the amounts of income but also of the tax deducted. Apportioning the income on a time basis may clearly lead to anomalies where tax rates change.

For partnerships in existence at 5 April 1994, there may be overlaps in respect of the non-trading income on the transition to the current year basis. Where the 1996/97 basis period for the non-trading income ended on 5 April 1997, which would normally be the case (see page 324), any overlap with 1997/98 will give rise to normal overlap relief rather than transitional overlap relief, as illustrated in example 7 (and will not therefore be subject to the anti-avoidance provisions on page 294). Where rents are charged on an accounts basis for 1996/97 (see page 325), the profits for the period from the accounting year-end in 1996/97 to 5 April 1997 will be transitional overlap profits qualifying for transitional overlap relief (and will be subject to the anti-avoidance provisions if appropriate). Relief for transitional overlap profits will be given in the same way as for normal overlap profits (see above).

Even though continuity elections may be made in respect of the trade for partnership changes up to 5 April 1997, so that the current year basis does not then apply until 1997/98, any new partner joining on or after 6 April 1994 would be taxed on the current year basis straight away in respect of his shares of non-trading income.

Partnership tax return and assessments on partners

It has been common practice for partnership tax returns not to be completed, and for the tax position to be dealt with by the submission of the relevant accounts and tax computations even though the law requires a return to be made. Commencing with the year 1996/97, a partnership tax return *must* be sent to the Revenue, showing the names, tax districts and references of each partner, together with a statement showing each partner's share of profits, losses and charges on income. Relevant accounts, computations and information, including capital gains details, will be included with the return. The return will normally relate to the accounting year ended in the tax year, except for 1996/97, which will usually cover two years' accounts. The return will not include calculations of tax payable, because these will be in each partner's separate return. The partnership return must be submitted by the 31 January following the tax year, e.g. by 31 January 1998 for 1996/97. (Different dates apply to partnerships with corporate partners.) The provisions for amending returns and for Revenue enquiries into them are the same as for individual returns (see pages 118, 123).

Each partner will include his share of the partnership income and gains in his self-assessment return for the tax year to which the income or gain relates, which may not be the same tax year as that in which it was reported by the partnership. For example a disposal of a chargeable asset in January 1998 in the accounting year to 30 June 1998 would be reported in the partnership return for 1998/1999, but the gain would be dealt with in each partner's personal return for 1997/98. And three-quarters of a partner's share of any non-trading income taxed at source in that accounting year would be apportioned to 1997/98, along with a quarter of any such income in the year to 30 June 1997.

For 1996/97 *only*, for partnerships in existence at 5 April 1994, there will still be a partnership assessment on the trading or professional profits. Tax on that assessment will be paid by the partnership, with the usual rights of appeal (the instalments being due on 1 January 1997 and 1 July 1997), and each partner will get a credit for his share of the tax in his self-assessment.

Partnerships taxed on the *current year basis* for 1994/95 or 1995/96 are not strictly required to make a return for either of those years, but the Revenue are asking them to do so, and will use their general powers to obtain information if they do not. The current year basis assessments will be individual assessments, with each partner having an individual right of appeal, but the Revenue will seek to have appeals for all partners heard together, late appeals being accepted in these circumstances.

Anti-avoidance provisions

The anti-avoidance provisions to prevent a tax advantage being obtained by manipulating the rules for the change to the current year basis are dealt with on page 293. If a partner retires in the transitional overlap period, he is charged in *1996/97* on the transitional relief restriction he would otherwise have suffered.

Work in progress (TA 1988, s 104(4); Revenue Statement of Practice SP 3/90)

Profit is affected by the amount of work in progress at the start and end of an accounting period. The Revenue will accept that the accounts of established professional practices can be prepared without including work in progress, so that an increase or decrease in work in progress over the accounting period does not affect the profit. If it is then decided that work in progress should in future be included, tax is payable on the amount that is introduced into the accounts. If, on the other hand, work in progress is currently taken into account and you wish to exclude it, tax will have been paid on its value up till then and tax will again be paid when the work is invoiced. There is no relief for the double charge.

Where work in progress is included, there is a choice as to whether it is valued at cost including production overhead, cost plus all overhead, or cost plus overhead plus profit. A change in the way in which work in progress is valued will affect the profit figure, and while the tax arising will usually be dealt with in one year only, the Revenue may seek to spread the effect over a number of past years, particularly if they consider that earlier valuations were not properly made.

Changes both in the way work in progress is valued and in the way it is accounted for are often made in the interests of consistency when two firms merge. This is a complex area, on which professional advice is essential.

Introducing funds to a partnership (TA 1988, ss 362, 363)

If a partner who is not a limited partner (see page 339) borrows to introduce funds to a partnership, either as capital or on loan, interest on the borrowing is allowable at his top tax rate. If, however, a partner then withdraws all or part of his capital, the introduced funds will be treated as repaid up to the amount of the withdrawal, restricting or eliminating the amount on which interest relief is available. This provision does not apply if the partner withdraws his capital *before* introducing new funds. The partnership would, however, need to be able to bridge the gap between the withdrawal of the existing funds and the introduction of the new. See page 272.

If borrowings are made by the partnership itself, the interest is allowed as a business expense, and when profits are averaged to arrive at the 1996/97 assessment the effect will be that relief will be given for only part of the interest paid. See page 294 for the anti-avoidance provisions preventing partners obtaining a tax advantage by replacing business borrowings with personal loans.

Consultancy

An outgoing partner may perform consultancy services for the partnership. He will be taxed on the income either under Schedule E, if the services are provided under a contract of service, or under Schedule D, Case I or II, if performed under a contract for services (see page 260). The payments will be an allowable deduction in calculating the taxable profits of the partnership so long as they satisfy the 'wholly and exclusively' rule (see chapter 20).

Trading losses (TA 1988, ss 380–390)

Chapter 25 deals with the calculation of the available loss reliefs and ways in which relief may be given. Relief for partnership trading losses may be claimed by each partner quite independently of the others. Thus one partner may decide to carry forward his share of the loss, another to set his against other income of the same tax year, another to set it against any income of the next tax year, another to carry back against the income of previous years in the early years of his being a partner, and so on.

Where there have been changes in profit-sharing arrangements, the ability of partners to make different loss claims can result under the 'previous year basis' rules in the total relief available being greater than the actual loss, because a claim under TA 1988, s 380, against other income of the tax year of loss and the following year, requires losses to be split according to the sharing arrangements of the tax year itself, while carrying forward a loss under TA 1988, s 385 requires a split on the accounts year basis. This anomaly does not apply under the current year basis rules (see page 328).

The carry-back loss rules for the first four years of a new trade only apply to a new partner, not to the continuing partners, whether or not the change of partnership has been treated as a cessation and restart. There is an anti-avoidance provision blocking carry-back claims by a new partner if he is joining his spouse in a continuing business.

Partnership assets (TCGA 1992, ss 59, 286; Revenue Statements of Practice D12 (17/1/75), SP 1/79 and SP 1/89)

When partners join or leave a partnership, this will usually involve a change in the persons who are entitled to share in the partnership assets. There is no capital gains tax consequence if an incoming partner introduces cash which is credited to his capital account. Nor is there normally any capital gains tax consequence when an outgoing partner withdraws his capital account. In the first instance, an incoming partner is paying in a sum which remains to his credit in his capital account, whilst in the second instance, an outgoing partner is only withdrawing what belongs to him.

If, however, before an outgoing partner withdraws his capital account, that capital account has been credited with a surplus on revaluation of partnership assets (e.g. premises or goodwill), his leaving the partnership will give rise to a realised capital gain in respect of the excess on revaluation, and to that extent his withdrawal of capital is chargeable to capital gains tax. The chargeable gain cannot be avoided by his leaving his capital on loan to the partnership, but it might be covered by retirement relief.

This charge will arise not only when a person ceases to be a partner, but whenever a partner's capital account includes a revaluation of chargeable assets and his entitlement to share in the assets is reduced. He is treated as having disposed of a proportion of the chargeable assets equivalent to the drop in his entitlement. The change will usually correspond with the change in the profit-sharing ratio, except where income and capital profits are shared differently, when the capital ratio will apply.

A payment by an incoming partner to the existing partners for a share in the chargeable assets such as goodwill or premises will constitute a disposal by the existing partners for capital gains tax, and a cost for capital gains tax to the incoming partner. The same applies where cash passes on a variation of profit-sharing arrangements without a change in partners. It makes no difference whether the cash is left in the partnership (by a credit to the capital account of those disposing) or is withdrawn by them, or indeed is dealt with outside the partnership itself. The test is whether a partner receives consideration for reducing his share in the partnership. Conversely, if he does not receive consideration, whilst there is still a disposal in the sense that his partnership share is less than it was, then, unless the partners have a family connection, the market value of the assets is not substituted for the purpose of calculating and charging the gain that could have been made, and thus no chargeable gain arises.

Example 8

X and Y are in partnership. Z is admitted as a partner, sharing equally in both capital and income. He introduces £45,000 as capital which is credited to his capital account. The £45,000 is neither a

---

capital gains tax base cost for Z nor a disposal by X and Y. The partnership assets include premises worth £180,000, which cost £63,000 when acquired in 1983.

Consider the following alternatives:

(1) Before Z's admission, X and Y revalue the premises up to £180,000 by crediting each of their capital accounts with £58,500.

On Z's admission they each make a chargeable gain of:

	£
Value of premises reflected in their capital account (½ each)	90,000
Share of premises retained after Z's admission (⅓ each)	60,000
Disposal proceeds	30,000

Less cost:

Cost was ½ each × £63,000	31,500	
Cost is now ⅓ each × £63,000	21,000	
Cost of part disposed of		10,500
Gain (subject to any available indexation allowance)		£19,500

The cost of Z's share in the premises is £60,000 (⅓ × £180,000), equivalent to the disposal proceeds of X and Y.

(2) The premises are not revalued on the admission of Z.

There is then no deemed gain by X and Y, and the cost for capital gains tax purposes for each of X and Y is ⅓ × £63,000 = £21,000. Z's cost will be £21,000 plus indexation allowance to date. On future disposals, X and Y will each get indexation allowance from 1983 on £21,000 and Z from the date he acquired his share on £21,000 as increased by indexation allowance to that date.

(3) Z privately pays £60,000 (£30,000 each) to X and Y, for a ⅓rd share in the partnership premises.

X and Y are treated as receiving £30,000 each as in (1).

The capital gains cost for future disposals in the case of (1) and (3) is:

	X	Y	Z
Original cost	31,500	31,500	—
On introduction of Z	(10,500)	(10,500)	21,000
Gains on which X and Y are assessable (subject to indexation)			39,000
	21,000	21,000	60,000

On future disposals, X and Y will each get indexation allowance on £21,000 from 1983 and Z on £60,000 from the date he acquired his share.

Annuities to outgoing partners (TA 1988, s 628 and Revenue Statements of Practice D12 (17/1/75) and SP 1/79)

An outgoing partner may be paid an annuity by the continuing partners when he retires. He will not be subject to capital gains tax on the capitalised value of the annuity so long as the annuity is regarded as reasonable recognition for past services to the partnership. For this purpose, the average of the partner's best three years' assessable profit shares out of the last seven is calculated and the annuity is considered reasonable if it does not exceed the fraction of that average amount obtained from the following table:

Years of service	Fraction
1–5	1/60 per year
6	8/60
7	16/60
8	24/60
9	32/60
10	2/3

The annuity is a charge against the income of the paying partners. They will deduct basic rate income tax when making the payment and claim relief at the higher rate where appropriate by an adjustment in the partnership or personal assessments.

Capital gains tax reliefs

Retirement relief (TCGA 1992, s 163, Sch 6; FA 1996, s 176)

The relief on gains up to £250,000 and on one half of the gains between £250,000 and £1,000,000 (see page 57) applies to the disposal of a partnership share or of business assets owned personally by a partner and used in the business of the partnership. He must be 50 years of age or over (55 for disposals before 28 November 1995), or be retiring before age 50 through ill health. Husband and wife partners can each get the relief if the conditions are satisfied. To qualify for the maximum relief there must be ten years' qualifying trading. If there are less than ten qualifying years but at least one, the available relief is reduced according to the number of qualifying years (see example 8 on page 59).

A mere sale of assets by the partnership when a partner is eligible for retirement relief will not entitle that partner to the relief on his share of the gain. There must be a reduction of his interest in the partnership.

Where an asset used by the partnership is owned personally by a partner, retirement relief is restricted when the partner disposes of the asset if the partnership pays rent, and if a full market rent is charged for any part of the ten-year qualifying period relief is lost for that part of the period. The relief is, however, still given on that part of the gain equivalent to the share of income profits to which the retiring partner was entitled, since he is regarded as not having been able to pay rent to himself. The Revenue take the view that if, instead of rent, it had been agreed to pay the partner an appropriate amount by way of a first slice of profits, the retirement relief is still restricted.

Replacement of business assets (TCGA 1992, ss 152–157)

Rollover relief for the replacement of business assets (see page 55) is available where an asset owned personally by a partner and used in the partnership is disposed of and replaced. This is not affected by the payment of rent by the partnership.

Death of a partner

Where a partner dies in service:

(a) if the death occurs before 6 April 1997, any election which is made for continuity of assessments must be signed by his personal representatives, otherwise a cessation of the partnership cannot be avoided;
(b) any gains arising on the disposal of his share in partnership assets by reason of the death are exempt, like gains on any other chargeable asset held at death;
(c) the annuity referred to earlier (on page 337) may be paid to his widow or dependants.

Inheritance tax

The interest of a deceased partner in the partnership (including his capital account) qualifies for the 100% business property relief unless the surviving partners are obliged to acquire his share, in which case it is regarded as an entitlement under a contract for sale and not therefore eligible for relief. Relief is not lost where there is an option, as opposed to an obligation, for the share to be acquired by the surviving partners.

Although the option to pay tax by ten annual instalments applies to the transfer of a partnership share, the introduction of the 100% relief has made the instalment option irrelevant for such transfers. The instalment option is still relevant for transfers of land owned by an individual partner and used in the business, the rate of business property relief for such land being 50% (see chapter 5). Interest is, however, charged on the full amount of tax outstanding rather than just on overdue instalments.

Value added tax

Customs and Excise need to be notified of a change of partner within 30 days, but not of a change in profit-sharing arrangements. The registration number will normally continue. A retiring partner remains liable for VAT due from the partnership until the date on which Customs are notified of his retirement.

National insurance

For the national insurance position of partnerships, see page 347.

Stamp duty

There is no stamp duty on a partnership agreement. When a partnership is dissolved, the division of assets on the dissolution attracts only a 50p stamp as a conveyance or transfer other than on sale.

Stamp duty arises on a document evidencing a payment by one person to another for a share in the partnership (but not where an incoming partner merely introduces capital to his own capital or current account), and also when the partnership transactions involve documents requiring to be stamped, for example in respect of land transactions. Stamp duty on all transactions other than those relating to land and buildings is to be abolished from some as yet unspecified date (see chapter 6).

Miscellaneous

A *salaried partner* is not the same as a partner who is allocated a salary as part of the profit-sharing arrangement. Senior employees are often described as partners in professional firms. They remain liable to income tax under Schedule E as employees, receiving a salary for the duties of their employment.

The share of a *sleeping partner* ranks as unearned income and cannot therefore support a pension premium.

A *company* may be a partner with individuals. In this case the profit share of the company for the relevant accounting period is liable to corporation tax, whilst the share applicable to the partners who are individuals is charged to income tax. Under the previous year basis rules, capital allowances are computed for the accounting period and the shares of the individuals are apportioned to the tax years comprised in that period. Under the current year basis, capital allowances are deducted as a trading expense in arriving at the profit for both company and individual partners.

A partnership may include a *limited partner* under the Limited Partnership Act 1907, whose liability is limited to the amount of the partner's agreed capital contribution. The limited partner, who may be either an individual or a company, cannot take part in the management of the partnership, although he is not barred from taking part in a non-managerial capacity. If the profit share of a limited partner ranks as unearned income, it cannot be used to support a pension premium. Certain reliefs available to a limited partner cannot exceed the amount of the partner's agreed capital contribution plus undrawn profits. The reliefs concerned are reliefs for trading losses (including capital allowances) against income other than trading income (see pages 352 and 366), interest paid in connection with the trade by an individual, trade charges on income paid by a company, and certain capital allowances in connection with the trade for which relief is given by discharge or repayment of tax (such as some buildings allowances).

Husband and wife partnerships. The national insurance cost of employing a wife is usually greater than if she were a partner with the husband. Moreover, if she is a partner, capital gains tax retirement relief will apply to the disposal of her share as well as his, whereas as an employee of a sole trader she is not entitled to retirement relief. The tax advantages of a wife being a partner must be weighed against her legal liability as a partner. Taking a wife into partnership may be regarded as an appropriate way of getting the best out of independent taxation, but it must be genuine, with the wife's share being appropriate to her contribution to the business, otherwise there is the risk of the partnership arrangement being treated as a settlement by the husband, in which case the income would remain his.

Partnership itself, and matters arising, need not be governed by *formal written agreement*. In the absence of such agreement, sometimes indeed despite it, the Revenue will require other evidence of partnership, for example the name of, and operating arrangements for, bank accounts, VAT registration, names on stationery, contracts, licences, etc.

The overseas aspect of partnerships is dealt with in chapter 41.

Tax points

- For partnership changes before 6 April 1997, an election for assessments on the business profits to continue on a preceding year basis can be made so long as there is one individual engaged in carrying on the business both before and after the change. For changes on or after 6 April 1997, partnerships will automatically be regarded as continuing if there is at least one existing partner who continues.

- To avoid the risk of a partner not being prepared to sign a continuation election on a change before 6 April 1997, include a provision in the partnership agreement or dissolution arrangements requiring an incoming or outgoing partner to sign one if asked to do so by the other partners.

- An election for continuity is not always advantageous, and a comparison of the alternatives should be made in respect of the old and new partnerships taken together.

  An agreement between the partners that a disadvantaged partner is compensated for any extra tax suffered is always possible and may persuade an otherwise dissenting partner to join in the election.

- Calculate annuities to retiring partners within the allowable capital gains tax limits, leaving them taxable only as income in the hands of the recipient and allowable for income tax to the payers. An inflation-linked increase to an annuity which is initially within the allowable limits will not affect the capital gains exemption.

- A pension payment by continuing partners to a retired partner, whilst assessable as income on the recipient, is not regarded by the Revenue as deductible in calculating the partnership taxable profits. The annuity arrangements in the previous tax point are a more tax-efficient way of providing income to a retired partner.

- Because of the previous year basis that has applied to existing partnerships for years before 1996/97, tax has usually been payable some time after the profits are earned and this is still relevant for 1996/97. It is sensible to set aside sufficient funds to pay the liability on trading profits on the half-yearly due dates of 1 January and 1 July, retaining an appropriate part from each partner's profit share for this purpose. When self-assessment applies, partners will be responsible for paying their own tax, and the half-yearly instalments (which will be due on 31 January and 31 July) will be on account of a partner's total income tax liability, not just his partnership share — see page 120. Although self-assessment generally applies from 1996/97, it applies from 1997/98 as regards payment of tax on partnership profits. In some circumstances it may still be prudent for partnerships to retain part of a partner's profit to meet the tax liability on partnership income, releasing it to the Revenue as part of each partner's personal liability on the due dates.

- To get maximum retirement relief, you do not need to have owned the business assets for ten years, only your interest in the business. If husband and wife intend to retire at the same time but one will be too young to claim any retirement relief, and the other has owned his/her interest in the business for ten years but will not use the maximum relief available, an interest in partnership assets may be transferred by the younger to the elder before they put the business up for sale. There should preferably be a significant time interval between the transfer and the disposal, otherwise the Revenue may seek to deny the relief by treating the disposals as a series of transactions with a tax-avoidance motive.

- If you have the choice of borrowing to buy your home and borrowing to introduce funds to a partnership (other than as a limited partner), the partnership borrowing will save you tax at your highest rate, whereas the home loan will only save you 15% tax.

- If one spouse takes the other into partnership, it should not be forgotten that the new partner has to pay Class 2 national insurance contributions. It can be costly to remember this only after the partnership has traded for some time.

- A capital gain may arise where partners sell partnership assets (e.g. land) to raise funds to pay out a retiring partner. The partners will, however, be able to deduct the gain from the cost of acquisition of the outgoing partner's share of any of the remaining business assets of the partnership that qualify for rollover relief rather than pay tax on it.

- A merger of two or more firms is strictly a cessation of each firm and the commencement of one new firm. The converse applies where one firm splits into two or more new firms. In both cases it may not be clear whether the rules for partnership changes apply. The Revenue issued a Statement of Practice (SP 9/86) explaining their view and have now issued further guidance covering the change to the current year basis in their SAT 1 (1995) guide. This area is one where professional advice and consultation with the Revenue is essential.

- Income and capital profit-sharing ratios need not always be the same. Established partners can retain the right to the whole of the future increase in value of partnership premises, to the exclusion of incoming partners, by excluding the incoming partners from the capital profit-sharing ratio.

  Any running expenses of those premises, including interest on borrowing, remain allowable in calculating trading profit, which is divided in the income-sharing ratio.

- Under the previous year basis rules, when a partner's loss claim includes his share of capital allowances, the other partners must countersign the claim because of the resultant effect on all partners of a reduction in the total capital allowances available to be carried forward.

- Under the current year basis, your share for any accounting period of partnership non-trading income taxed at source must be apportioned over the tax years to which it relates. Except for a 31 March year-end, this means that part of the income must be included in your return for the tax year before that in which it is shown in the partnership return. And a capital gain must similarly be dealt with by you in the tax year of disposal, although the disposal will be reported by the partnership according to the accounting year in which it occurs. (See page 332.)

24
National insurance contributions for the self-employed

Background

A self-employed person over the age of 16 must, unless specifically exempted, pay both Class 2 and Class 4 contributions. Class 2 contributions are payable at a flat weekly rate and entitle the contributor to incapacity benefit, basic retirement pension, widow's benefit and maternity allowance. They do not count for unemployment benefit or the earnings-related supplement to retirement pension. Class 4 contributions are payable at a fixed percentage on profits chargeable to income tax under Schedule D, Case I or II (see chapter 21). They carry no entitlement to benefits of any kind. The legislation is in the Social Security Contributions and Benefits Act 1992 (SSCBA 1992). See page 200 for the position on receiving contribution credits in order to satisfy the contribution requirements for State pensions.

Class 2 contributions

Payment (SSCBA 1992, s 11; SI 1993/260)

Those who become self-employed must notify the DSS and make arrangements to pay their Class 2 contributions, unless they are not liable to pay (see page 344). Payment is made either by monthly direct debit or quarterly in arrear. Those who pay quarterly get a bill from the DSS showing the amount payable.

The weekly rates for 1995/96 and 1996/97 are:

1995/96	£5.75
1996/97	£6.05

If Class 2 contributions are paid late, they may affect your entitlement to benefits. If they are paid after the end of the tax year following the one in which they were due, they normally have to be paid at the highest rate applicable between the due date and the payment date.

Exempt persons

Class 2 contributions are payable by 'self-employed earners', which means those who are 'gainfully employed' other than as employees. The Class 2 net is wider than Class 4, because it includes a 'business', whereas Class 4 only covers a trade, profession or vocation.

The following people are, however, not liable to pay Class 2 contributions:

(a) men and women over state pension age (men 65, women 60);

(b) married women who chose on or before 11 May 1977 to pay reduced rate Class 1 contributions or to pay no Class 2 contributions (provided that this election has not been automatically revoked by divorce or possibly revoked by widowhood — see page 347);

(c) someone with small earnings who obtains a certificate of exception (see below);

(d) someone who is not 'ordinarily' self-employed (see page 345);

(e) someone who, for a full week, is
  (i) incapable of work, or
  (ii) in legal custody or prison, or
  (iii) receiving incapacity benefit or maternity allowance;

(f) someone who, for any day in a particular week, receives invalid care allowance.

In the case of (e) and (f), the exemption is applicable only to the particular week concerned.

Special rules apply to those who go to work abroad — see page 567.

Small earnings

You may apply for a certificate of exception for a tax year if you can show that:

(i) your net earnings for that tax year are expected to be less than a specified limit; or

(ii) your net earnings for the previous tax year were less than the limit specified for that year and that circumstances have not materially altered.

In this context 'net earnings' are earnings shown in the profit and loss account as opposed to taxable earnings. Business start-up allowance (see page 267) is not included. If employed earnings on which Class 1 contributions have been paid are included in the accounts, these are not counted in net earnings. Where an accounting period overlaps 5 April, earnings are strictly apportioned on a time basis between tax years but in considering (ii) above, the DSS will normally take the accounts year ended in the previous tax year.

The small earnings exception limits are:

1994/95	£3,200
1995/96	£3,260
1996/97	£3,430

Certificates of exception must be renewed each tax year and can be applied for on form CF 10 in DSS leaflet CA 02. Exception from payment cannot apply from a date earlier than 13 weeks before the date of the application.

Not paying contributions will affect your retirement pension (see page 200) and other contributory benefits. You need not apply for a certificate of exception if you don't want to, in which event self-employed contributions will be payable unless you are not 'ordinarily' self-employed — see below.

If you paid contributions but could have claimed exception, you may apply for a refund. Refund claims must be made by 31 December after the end of the relevant tax year. Where repayments are concerned, the earnings will be calculated strictly over the tax year, which means claims may have to be made before the exact earnings are known.

Persons not 'ordinarily' self-employed

When someone applies to pay Class 2 contributions he may be informed by the DSS that they consider that he is not ordinarily self-employed and that there is therefore no liability to pay contributions. There is no statutory definition of 'not ordinarily self-employed' but the example quoted by the DSS in leaflet CA 02 is of a person employed in a regular job whose earnings from spare-time self-employment are not expected to exceed £800 in a tax year.

If you are in this category, you do not have to apply for a certificate of exception. You would be eligible for relief under the small earnings rule anyway, but this lower limit avoids the need to apply for a certificate. If you are not paying contributions as an employee you may wish to pay voluntary Class 3 contributions to maintain your contribution record for retirement/widow's pension (see page 200).

More than one self-employment

People who are self-employed have to pay only one weekly Class 2 contribution no matter how many self-employed jobs they may have. In deciding whether you are entitled to a certificate of exception on the grounds of small earnings, self-employed earnings from all sources are added together.

Class 4 contributions

Payment (SSCBA 1992, ss 15–17 and Sch 2 paras 2, 3; FA 1994, Sch 19 para 45)

Class 4 contributions are payable at a percentage rate on profits chargeable to income tax under Schedule D, Case I or II which fall between specified upper and lower limits.

Contribution rates and limits for 1995/96 and 1996/97 are:

Year	Rate	On profits	Maximum
1995/96	7.3%	Between £6,640 and £22,880	£1,185
1996/97	6%	Between £6,860 and £23,660	£1,008

One half of the Class 4 contributions used to be deductible from total income in calculating your income tax liability, the deduction being made in the self-employed assessment. The deduction is no longer given from 1996/97, but this has been compensated for by the reduction in the rate of contributions from 7.3% to 6%.

If you have more than one self-employment, all the profits are added together when calculating your Class 4 liability.

In general, 'profits' are computed in the same way for Class 4 contributions as for income tax but certain special rules apply, for example losses allowed under TA 1988, ss 380, 381 (see chapter 25) against non-trading income and capital gains for tax purposes are set only against trading income for national insurance, and may thus be carried forward against future profits for calculating Class 4 contributions. Retirement annuity and personal pension premiums cannot be deducted in calculating Class 4 contributions.

For years before 1996/97, Class 4 contributions are calculated and collected by the Inland Revenue together with income tax payable under Schedule D, Case I or II; the contributions are therefore payable at the same time as the income tax liability on the relevant profits. From 1996/97, the provisional half-yearly payments made on 31 January and 31 July under self-assessment will include Class 4 national insurance contributions based on the previous year's figures, with any balancing adjustment made in the return on the following 31 January.

Exempt persons

The following people are not liable to pay Class 4 contributions:

(a)   men and women over state pension age (men 65, women 60) at the beginning of the tax year;

(b)   individuals who are not resident in the UK for income tax purposes;

(c) trustees and executors who are chargeable to income tax on income which they receive on behalf of other people (e.g. incapacitated persons);

(d) 'sleeping partners' who supply capital and take a share of the profits but take no active part in running the business;

(e) divers and diving supervisors working in connection with exploration and exploitation activities on the Continental shelf or in UK territorial waters;

(f) someone who is under 16 on 6 April in a particular tax year and holds a certificate of exception for that year. Application for an exception certificate should be made on form RD 901; application need only be made once as any certificate granted will cover all the relevant tax years;

(g) someone who is not 'ordinarily' self-employed (see under Class 2 above).

Late payment of contributions

Class 4 contributions are collected along with Schedule D, Case I or II income tax for years before 1996/97, and under the self-assessment provisions from 1996/97. The income tax rules for charging interest (see pages 19 and 20) apply if they are paid late and also the penalties in cases of fraudulent or negligent conduct (see page 143).

Partnerships (including husband and wife partners)

Each partner is liable to both Class 2 and Class 4 contributions (unless a wife is exempt from Class 2 contributions — see below), the Class 4 profit limits applying to each partner's profit share.

When computing the Class 4 liability of partnerships, including husband/wife partnerships, the Revenue add the separate liabilities together and collect the total liability from the partnership, together with the income tax payable on the business profits. For partnerships starting after 5 April 1994, each partner will pay his own tax and Class 4 contributions. This will apply to existing partnerships as well from 1997/98. Where a partner carries on a further trade or trades, the profits of all such businesses are considered together when calculating his overall Class 4 liability. Class 4 contributions are payable only up to a single upper earnings limit regardless of how many businesses are involved.

Married women

If you were married or widowed before 6 April 1977, you could elect on or before 11 May 1977 not to pay full national insurance contributions. If you have made the election, you pay Class 1 contributions as an employee at a reduced rate, and you do not have to pay Class 2 self-employed contributions. You do, however, have to pay Class 4 contributions.

You lose the right to pay no Class 2 and reduced rate Class 1 contributions in some circumstances. For details, and further points on the reduced rate election, see page 205.

Self-employed and employed in the same tax year

If you are both self-employed and an employee, you are liable to pay Class 1, 2 and 4 contributions, and if you have more than one employment you will be liable to Class 1 contributions in each employment. There are, however, two separate maximum figures above which contributions will be refunded.

The Class 4 maximum is worked out by taking 53 Class 2 contributions plus the maximum Class 4 contributions, and is £1,328.65 for 1996/97. If your total contributions under Classes 1, 2 and 4 exceed this amount, you may claim a refund of the excess up to the amount of Class 4 contributions paid.

The overall maximum for all contributions is based on 53 times the maximum weekly Class 1 contribution, and is £2,152.86 for 1996/97. If your total contributions exceed this amount by £2.70 or more, the excess will be refunded.

Where you expect your contributions to exceed the maximum, you should apply to defer payment of Class 4, 2 or 1 contributions as appropriate (in that order).

Application for deferment of Class 4 and 2 contributions must be made on form CF 359, which is part of leaflet CA 03 — 'NI contributions for self-employed people, Class 2 and Class 4'. Where deferment is granted, responsibility for the computation and collection of Class 4 contributions is transferred from the Inland Revenue to the DSS. Application for deferment of Class 1 contributions should be made on form CF 379, which is part of leaflet CA 01 — 'National Insurance contributions for employees'.

If you feel you have overpaid contributions you may apply to the DSS for a refund. This could happen, for example, if you have several businesses and the profits of those businesses have been totalled incorrectly in arriving at your overall Class 4 liability, or if you have paid Class 1 contributions that have not been taken into account in calculating your Class 4 liability.

Tax points

● Make sure you notify the DSS of any weeks for which a Class 2 contribution is not due, for example when you are receiving incapacity benefit, so that an adjustment can be made.

● If you are both employed and self-employed, make sure you claim deferment if you are eligible. This is better than waiting till after the year end for a refund. As well as the cash flow benefit, there is another advantage if your employed earnings exceed £455 per week. If you apply for deferment on the self-employed earnings, you will have no liability at the year end because you are already paying maximum contributions. If instead you pay employed and self-employed contributions, the amount refunded is any excess over the stipulated maximum, which is based on 53 weeks' contributions. Weekly paid employees rarely have 53 pay days in a tax year, and monthly paid employees always have the equivalent of 52 weeks' contributions, so that any refund is reduced by the extra week's contribution.

- If you have applied for deferment of Class 4 contributions, make sure that tax relief is given against your income for half of any Class 4 contributions that you do eventually pay for years before 1996/97.

- If you are a married couple who both work in the business, consider whether it is better for the wife to be a partner or employee. Whilst the national insurance aspect cannot be considered in isolation, it would usually be better for her to be an employee if she earns less than £61.00 a week and to be a partner if she earns more.

- Remember that trading losses set off against non-trading income for income tax purposes are carried forward against trading profits for Class 4 contributions purposes. You will need to claim this relief from the DSS. It will not usually be given by the inspector of taxes.

- Make sure you notify the DSS as soon as your self-employment commences. A small earnings exception may be asked for at the same time if the early profits are anticipated to be minimal.

- Where Class 2 contributions are payable, the DSS preferred method is by monthly direct debit, but you will get a cash flow advantage by opting to pay quarterly in arrear.

- Do not delay making payment of contributions. Class 2 contributions paid more than one year after the end of the contribution year in which they were due are payable at a higher rate.

- If you take your wife or husband into partnership do not forget that a liability to Class 2 contributions will almost certainly arise. The arrears will have to be paid later if this is overlooked.

- If you are a married woman who has elected not to pay Class 2 contributions, watch the circumstances in which contributions become payable, for example following widowhood or divorce.

25
Losses of sole traders and partners

Introduction

Not all sources of income may give rise to losses. For example, where a source provides income in the form of interest on investments, losses will not arise. Losses may arise in a trade, profession or vocation carried on in the UK or abroad, or in a business of property letting. Capital losses may arise on the disposal of chargeable assets. Losses relating to rented property may normally be relieved only against rental income, and are dealt with in chapter 32. Relief for losses relating to businesses controlled abroad is restricted to profits from the same source (see chapter 41). Capital losses are normally set against capital gains of the same tax year, with any balance carried forward against later gains (see chapter 4), although capital losses on certain unquoted shares may be set against income (see page 531). Other aspects relating to capital losses are dealt with in context in other chapters. The remainder of this chapter deals with losses of UK trades. The rules for trading losses apply equally to losses in relation to professions or vocations.

The rules for calculating trading losses before the change to the current year basis of assessment broadly provide for them to be computed on a strict tax year basis. This leads to complications and anomalies, particularly in the opening years of a business. The rules are very much simpler under the current year basis. The current year basis applies to new businesses commencing on or after 6 April 1994, and to existing businesses from 1997/98, 1996/97 being a transitional year. Although trades ceasing before 6 April 1998 may not come within the current year basis provisions for calculating profits (see page 287), the current year basis rules apply as appropriate to loss claims for 1996/97 and 1997/98. The loss rules under the current year basis are dealt with on page 358.

Loss relief under the 'previous year basis' rules

Calculation of loss

The rules for calculating the trading loss of an accounting period are the same as those for calculating profits (see chapter 20). There are, however, special rules as to the way in which relief is given for the loss, and, in particular, in calculating what part of the loss of an accounting period is available for relief in the opening years of a new business. Where a loss occurs in a partnership, each partner may choose what loss claim(s) to make for his share of the loss quite independently from how the other partners relieve their loss shares (see page 334).

Loss reliefs available

There are various ways in which relief for trading losses may be claimed:

Carry forward against later profits of same trade (TA 1988, s 385).

Set against general income of current tax year then, if the taxpayer wishes, against capital gains of that year. If the same trade is still carried on by the taxpayer in the *following* tax year, similar claims may be made in that tax year (TA 1988, s 380 and FA 1991, s 72). (For losses in 1996/97 and later years, Section 380 losses will be able to be carried one year *back* instead of one year forward — see page 361.)

In a new trade, carry back against general income of previous three tax years, earliest first (TA 1988, s 381).

When a loss occurs on ceasing to trade, carry back against trading income of previous three tax years, latest first (TA 1988, ss 388, 389). (For trades ceasing in 1996/97 and later years, terminal losses will be given against the income of the *final tax year* before being carried back — see page 362.)

Assessments (TA 1988, s 60)

The first thing a trading loss does is to fix the assessment based on the accounting period at Nil. See example 1. However, this does not give relief for the loss.

Example 1

The results of a sole trader or the shares of a partner are as follows:

Year ended 31 December 1992	Profit	£8,000
1993	Loss	(£7,000)
1994	Profit	£10,000

Assessments based thereon:

1993/94	£8,000
1994/95	Nil
1995/96	£10,000

Loss carried forward (TA 1988, s 385)

The most straightforward way of obtaining relief for a loss is by carrying it forward to reduce later income of the same trade, so that in example 1 the loss of £7,000 would reduce the 1995/96 assessment to £3,000. The set-off can only be made against profits of the *same* trade, so that a change in activity will cause relief to be denied.

There are obvious disadvantages in carrying forward a loss. The trade may cease, or its nature change, before the loss is fully relieved. The relief is against the first available profits and the size of those profits may leave insufficient income to utilise the taxpayer's personal allowances, so that if the taxpayer in example 1 had personal allowances in 1995/96 of £3,525 and no other income, tax relief on allowances of £525 would be wasted.

It is not possible to set off only £6,475 of the losses brought forward and leave £3,525 taxable profit in order to use personal allowances. There is also a considerable delay before the loss results in a cash saving by reducing or eliminating a tax bill. If the loss in example 1 of the year to 31 December 1993 was carried forward, it would reduce the 1995/96 tax bill, which is payable in equal instalments on 1 January 1996 and 1 July 1996, so that relief in cash terms is delayed for at least two years.

Loss set against other income (TA 1988, s 380)

Relief may be obtained more quickly by setting off the loss against any other income of the tax year in which the loss is incurred or of the next tax year (providing the trade is still carried on in that year), or, if the loss is large enough, of both tax years. This claim, however, cannot be made for losses incurred in 'hobby' trades as distinct from commercial activities. The set-off is also specifically prohibited for the sixth year of a consecutive run of farming and market gardening losses (reckoned before capital allowances) (TA 1988, s 397).

Strictly, a loss for set-off against other income should be calculated by reference to an income tax year, arrived at by splitting accounts, so that in example 1 the position for the income tax year 1992/93 would be:

¾ × £8,000	6,000	
¼ × (£7,000)	(1,750)	
Surplus	£4,250	(so no loss claim)

and for the income tax year 1993/94:

¾ × (£7,000)	(5,250)	
¼ × £10,000	2,500	
Loss	£(2,750)	

The loss of £2,750 represents the loss of 1993/94, for which relief may be claimed against the income of 1993/94 or of 1994/95 (or, if the loss had been large enough, of both years).

It is important to remember that these calculations do not relate to assessments. Those have been calculated at example 1. These calculations are of the loss for which relief may be claimed.

Since the accounting loss incurred was £7,000 and only £2,750 would be relieved by reference to the loss actually incurred in the income tax year 1993/94, the balance of the loss, i.e. £4,250, would be carried forward. However, the Revenue will in practice usually accept that the loss of an accounting year may be treated as being the loss of the tax year in which the accounting year ends, so that the loss of £7,000 in the accounting year ended 31 December 1993 may be regarded as the loss of the income tax year 1993/94. The Revenue will not follow this practice in the first three years of assessment of a new business, nor in the last year of assessment. In those years, the loss of the income tax year itself must be calculated by splitting the accounts. But otherwise their practice is normally followed. As well as being more straightforward than splitting accounts, the Revenue concession usually operates in the taxpayer's favour, giving an immediate loss claim of £7,000 in example 1 rather than £2,750 now and £4,250 carried forward.

If an accounts basis loss claim is made in the tax year before that in which the trade ceases, and a loss also occurs in the final trading period, the loss of the period from the accounting date to 5 April in the penultimate year will not qualify for relief under Section 380 (although terminal loss relief may be available — see page 357). Some relief for such a loss may be available under the Revenue's extra-statutory concession A88.

Sometimes a strict basis loss claim would benefit the taxpayer. In example 1, the position on the concessionary basis would be:

1993/94 (based on profit of year to 31 December 1992)	8,000	
Less loss claim under Section 380	(7,000)	£1,000
1994/95 (based on result of year to 31 December 1993)		Nil
1995/96 (based on result of year to 31 December 1994)		£10,000

Unless there were other sources of income, the loss claim would result in personal allowances being wasted in 1993/94. If the loss was calculated on the strict basis, giving a loss for 1993/94 of £2,750 as shown above, the position would be:

1993/94 (8,000 – 2,750)	£5,250
1994/95	Nil
1995/96 (10,000 – 4,250)	£5,750

In addition to a strict claim possibly avoiding personal allowances being wasted, it may also enable a claim to be made for an earlier year. If the loss in example 1 had related to accounts to 30 April 1993 instead of 31 December, there would be a loss on the strict basis one year earlier than the concessionary basis, i.e. in the tax year 1992/93 instead of 1993/94, as follows:

1/12 × £8,000	667
11/12 × (£7,000)	(6,417)
Loss available for relief	£(5,750)

The balance of the loss of (7,000 − 5,750 =) £1,250 would be carried forward. The benefit of claiming loss relief against the income of a year earlier would need to be weighed against the smaller loss available to set against current income compared with £7,000 on the concessionary basis.

The assessable income against which relief is given is all income from whatever source and not just the income from the trade. (Indeed, there will usually be no income from the trade itself in the second year of claim because the assessment for that year is based on the result of the previous period, in which the loss was incurred.) The set-off cannot be restricted to part of the income, and as with the carry-forward loss claim, the loss set-off must be made *before* deducting personal allowances, so that in some cases they may be wasted.

Extending Section 380 claim to capital gains (FA 1991, s 72)

A Section 380 claim may be extended to include set-off against capital gains, in either or both of the tax year of loss and the following tax year, providing the trade is still carried on in that tax year. The claim against income of the year must be made first (personal allowances therefore being wasted, except where married couple's allowance is transferred) and the loss available to set against capital gains is also reduced by any other loss relief claimed, for example under Section 380 in the following year or by carry-back under Section 381 in a new business (see page 355). The amount of capital gains available to relieve the trading loss is the amount of the capital gains less any capital losses of the relevant year less unrelieved capital losses brought forward from earlier years. Having identified the amount *available* for relief in this way, that amount is then treated as an allowable loss of the relevant year and is therefore given in *priority* to brought forward capital losses. The claim may mean wasting all or part of the annual exemption. See example 2. Where there are capital losses brought forward that already reduce gains to the exempt level, the trading loss claim would give no immediate tax saving and it would be a question of whether it would be preferable to have unrelieved trading losses carried forward or unrelieved capital losses carried forward. See example 3.

Example 2

Trader makes loss of £15,000 in year to 31 December 1995, and claims Section 380 relief for 1995/96 against his total income for that year of £10,000 (being trading profits for year to 31 December 1994 of £7,000 plus other income £3,000), and against his capital gains. His gains and losses of the year were £12,000 and £2,000 respectively.

The Section 380 claim against income covers £10,000 of the loss, and wastes personal allowances (although if he is married, the married couple's allowance may be transferred to his wife).

The claim against the net capital gains of £10,000 covers the remaining £5,000 loss, with the balance of gains of £5,000 covered by the annual exemption, but with £1,000 of the annual exemption wasted.

Example 3

Facts as in example 2, but there are capital losses brought forward of £5,500.

If relief for the trading loss is claimed against capital gains, the gains available are £10,000 less £5,500 = £4,500, leaving £500 trading loss to be carried forward. The gains of the year of £10,000 are reduced by trading losses of £4,500 to £5,500, which will be covered by the annual exemption, and the brought forward capital losses of £5,500 will still be carried forward.

If the claim against gains had not been made, the gains of £10,000 would be reduced by £4,000 of the capital losses brought forward, leaving gains of £6,000 covered by the annual exemption and unrelieved capital losses carried forward of £1,500, in addition to unrelieved trading losses carried forward of £5,000.

New trades — carry-back of losses (TA 1988, s 381)

Where a loss occurs in any of the first four tax years of a new sole trade, or of a new partner's membership of a partnership, relief may be claimed against that person's general income of the three previous tax years, earliest first. There is no set-off against capital gains. As with Section 380 (see page 352), this carry-back claim cannot be made unless the trade is carried on on a commercial basis. Where a loss is large enough, a claim under Section 380 may be preceded or followed by a Section 381 claim.

Example 4

Trade started 1 August 1993.
Year ended 31 July 1994   Loss   (£10,800)
Year ended 31 July 1995   Profit   £2,400
There will be Nil assessments for 1993/94, 1994/95 and 1995/96 (see chapter 21), so, unless there are other sources of income, there would be no loss claims at all under Section 380, nor under Section 385 until 1996/97.

For the first three years of assessment, the calculation of a loss for claims under Sections 380 and 381 must be made on the basis of the loss in the tax year itself, not in the accounting year ended within it.

The losses on this basis are:

	1993/94	1994/95
8/12 × (£10,800)	(£7,200)	—
4/12 × (£10,800)		(3,600)
8/12 × £2,400		1,600
		(£2,000)

Relief is available by
carry back against general

income of:	First	1990/91	1991/92
	Then	1991/92	1992/93
	Then	1992/93	1993/94

There would be a loss of £1,600 not covered by the carry-back claims and this would be carried forward under Section 385 to set against later trading profits. If the losses of £7,200 and £2,000 were not fully relieved under the carry-back claims, any balance remaining would also be carried forward.

If there were also losses in 1995/96 and 1996/97 (making with 1993/94 and 1994/95 the first four years of assessment) relief for those losses would be available as follows:

For losses incurred in		1995/96	1996/97
Relief would be available by carry back against general			
income of:	First	1992/93	1993/94
	Then	1993/94	1994/95
	Then	1994/95	1995/96

Capital allowances (TA 1988, s 383)

Where there are losses or where capital allowances exceed profits, unused capital allowances relating to the loss period may be carried forward to set against later trading profits or used to increase Section 380 and/or Section 381 loss claims. The choice of including or excluding capital allowances again gives flexibility in arriving at the best loss claim bearing in mind available personal allowances. Even more flexibility is available for allowances on plant and machinery, because the capital allowances claim itself can be reduced to whatever amount is required (see pages 303 and 320).

For the accounting year ended in 1995/96, there are strictly no capital allowances that may be included in a 1995/96 loss claim, because that accounting year is part of the two-year basis period for 1996/97. This has, however, been varied by a Revenue statement in the February 1996 Tax Bulletin (see page 359).

Loss on cessation of trade (terminal loss) (TA 1988, ss 388 and 389)

Losses towards the end of a business clearly cannot be carried forward against future profits. A Section 380 claim may be made to set the loss against other income of the tax year in which the trade ceases, if there is any (see page 352). Alternatively, or if the loss is large enough, additionally, a claim may be made to set the loss of the last twelve months of trading (called a terminal loss), or the balance of such a loss after Section 380 relief, against the *trading* income (after capital allowances) of the three tax years prior to that in which the trade ceases, *latest* first. If there are unrelieved capital allowances for that twelve months, they may be included in the claim. See example 5.

Where an industrial building, qualifying hotel or enterprise building is sold after the cessation of a trade and a balancing charge arises, unrelieved trading losses, expenses and capital allowances may be carried forward to set against the balancing charge. This relief was previously given by concession but has been made statutory by Finance Act 1996 (CAA 1990, s 15A; FA 1996, Sch 39 para 1(2)(4)).

Time limits for claims

TA 1988, s 380	Set-off against income and gains of same tax year or following year	Within two years after the end of the year of assessment to which the claim relates
TA 1988, s 381	Set off new business losses against income for three previous tax years, taking earlier before later years	Within two years after the end of the year of assessment in which the loss occurs
TA 1988, s 385	Carry forward against future profits of same trade	Within six years after the end of the year of assessment to which the claim relates
TA 1988, ss 388, 389	Carry back of terminal losses	Normal six-year time limit since no other time limit specified

Example 5

Trade ceases 30 September 1995.

Previous accounts have been to 31 December, recent results and assessments (see chapter 21) being:

Period to 30 Sept. 1995   Loss (£9,000) 1995/96 assessment Nil

Year to 31 December 1994   Profit £2,400 Escapes assessment

Year to 31 December 1993   Profit £1,000 Assessed in 1994/95

Year to 31 December 1992   Profit £5,000 Assessed in 1993/94

Year to 31 December 1991   Profit £7,000 Assessed in 1992/93

Terminal loss:
1 October 1994 to 5 April 1995

First three months	Profit	600
Next three months	Loss	(3,000)
		(2,400)
6 April 1995 to 30 September 1995		(6,000)
		(£8,400)

This may be carried back against trading assessments for:

1994/95	£1,000
1993/94	£5,000
1992/93	£7,000, reducing it to £4,600

Alternatively a Section 380 claim may be made to set the 1995/96 loss of £6,000 against any income or chargeable gains of that year — which could arise through balancing charges on the disposal of assets on which capital allowances have been claimed and through chargeable gains on the sale of business assets, in addition to any regular sources. If loss relief were obtained in that way, only the balance of the terminal loss of £2,400 would be the subject of a terminal loss claim. It may, however, be preferable to leave other income to cover personal allowances in 1995/96 and claim terminal loss relief on the full amount as illustrated.

Formal claims for relief must be made within these time limits, except for Section 385, where the Revenue will accept a computation indicating that the loss is being carried forward.

Loss relief under the current year basis and transitional provisions (FA 1994, s 209 and Sch 20 para 8; FA 1995, s 118)

The calculation and treatment of losses is changed under the current year basis of assessment. The new rules apply immediately to new businesses commencing on or after 6 April 1994. For existing businesses, some of the changes apply from 1996/97 and some from 1997/98.

Position for 1996/97

1996/97 is a transitional year prior to the start of the current year basis and the assessment for businesses that started before 6 April 1994 is usually arrived at by averaging the previous and current years' profits. If a loss is incurred in one of those years, it is counted as nil in the averaging calculation and the rules described earlier in this chapter will apply to the calculation of the loss.

Having calculated the loss according to the old rules, the treatment will depend on the tax year to which the loss relates. A loss of 1995/96 will be dealt with under the old rules, so that Section 380 relief will be available in 1995/96 and/or 1996/97, and if the trade ceased in 1995/96 terminal loss relief will be given according to the rules on page 357. A loss of 1996/97 will be dealt with under the revised rules applying from that year (see page 361), so that a Section 380 claim for 1996/97 may be made against the income of 1996/97 and/or 1995/96, and if the trade ceases in 1996/97, a terminal loss claim for that tax year will be set against the trading income of that year before being carried back against the trading income of the previous three tax years.

The averaging calculation will be made *before* taking capital allowances into account, and the allowances will then be deducted from the averaged profit. The basis period for the 1996/97 allowances will usually be the two years to the accounting date in 1996/97. If there is a loss in the account ended in 1996/97, the 1996/97 allowances may be added to the loss for the purposes of a Section 380 claim. If there is a loss in the account ended in 1995/96, then strictly there are no capital allowances available to augment a Section 380 claim for that year (see page 356). The Revenue have, however, stated in their February 1996 Tax Bulletin that as an alternative to setting the 1996/97 allowances as computed against the averaged profit, or using them to augment a 1996/97 loss, notional allowances may be calculated for 1996/97 in order to increase the *1995/96* loss claim. The notional allowances will be based on the accounting year ended in 1995/96 rather than on the transitional averaging basis. Any allowances taken into account in this way for a 1995/96 loss claim will reduce the actual capital allowances claimed for 1996/97 (or will possibly eliminate the 1996/97 allowances altogether, or turn them into a balancing charge). If a loss claim is to be made for 1996/97 as well, only the reduced amount will be available to include in that claim.

See example 6.

Calculation of loss

Under the current year basis, losses from 1997/98 onwards (or from the outset for businesses starting on or after 6 April 1994) are calculated using

Example 6

In an old established business, a trader makes a loss of £10,000 in the year to 31 December 1995 and a profit of £15,000 in the year to 31 December 1996. The 1996/97 assessment will be half of £15,000, i.e. £7,500, and the loss of £10,000 may be treated as the loss of 1995/96, for which relief may be claimed in 1995/96 and/or 1996/97.

Say the 1996/97 capital allowances computation, based on the two years to 31 December 1996, was as follows:

		£
Written-down value brought forward		15,000
Year to 31.12.1995	Additions	20,000
	Disposals	(3,000)
Year to 31.12.1996	Additions	—
	Disposals	(14,000)
		18,000
Writing-down allowance		(4,500)
Written-down value carried forward		13,500

The allowances of £4,500 would reduce the 1996/97 assessment to £3,000. Alternatively, notional allowances could be calculated as follows for 1996/97 (based on the year to 31 December 1995, ended in 1995/96):

		£
Written-down value brought forward		15,000
Year to 31.12.1995	Additions	20,000
	Disposals	(3,000)
		32,000
Writing-down allowance		(8,000)

These allowances could be added to the 1995/96 loss of £10,000 for a 1995/96 loss claim. The amount of £8,000 so used would be set against the actual 1996/97 allowances of £4,500, resulting in a balancing charge for that year of £3,500, which would increase the assessable profit of £7,500 to £11,000. The capital allowances written-down value carried forward would remain at £13,500, since net allowances of £4,500 have been given (£8,000 in the 1995/96 loss claim less balancing charge of £3,500 in the 1996/97 assessment).

the same basis periods as those used for calculating profits. So a loss of the year to 31 August 1997 would be regarded as a loss of 1997/98 in the same way as a profit of that year would be taxed in 1997/98. Where a loss would be taken into account in two successive tax years (for example, in the first trading period of a new business or on a change of accounting date), it is only taken into account in the first year.

Example 7

Trader starts in business on 1 June 1995 and makes a loss in the year to 31 May 1996. The assessments for 1995/96 and 1996/97 will therefore be Nil.

10/12ths of the loss will be regarded as the loss of 1995/96 and 2/12ths as the loss of 1996/97.

When claiming to carry back a loss in any of the first four tax years of a new business under Section 381 (see page 355), the effect of the switch to an accounting period basis may be to restrict the claims available if the accounting date is early in the tax year.

Example 8

New business starts 1 May 1995. If accounts are made up annually to 31 March, Section 381 claims will be possible in respect of losses made in the 11 months to 31 March 1996, and the years to 31 March 1997, 1998 and 1999. If accounts are made up annually to 30 April, Section 381 claims will only be possible in respect of the loss of the year to 30 April 1996 (the claim being split as to 11/12ths in 1995/96 and 1/12th in 1996/97), and the years to 30 April 1997 and 1998.

Way in which relief may be claimed

The way in which relief for the loss may be claimed under the current year basis is the same as under the rules applying previously, with the following differences:

(a) From 1996/97 (or from the outset for businesses starting on or after 6 April 1994), relief against other income and gains under Section 380 may be claimed in the year of loss and/or the *previous* year, rather than the *following* year. For example a 1997/98 loss may be set against income of 1997/98 and/or 1996/97. If relief is claimed in a tax year both for a loss of that year and a loss carried back from the following year, the current year's loss is relieved first.

(b) In order for a loss to be carried back under Section 380, the trade does not have to have been carried on in the previous year.

(c) Since capital allowances are treated as trading expenses from 1997/98 (or from the outset for businesses starting on or after 6 April 1994), there will no longer be the flexibility of including or excluding them when making loss claims. Plant and machinery allowances can still be varied by using the disclaimer provisions (see page 303).

(d) From 1996/97 (or from the outset for businesses starting on or after 6 April 1994), terminal loss relief is given against any trading income of the year of cessation, then the previous three years. The requirement to claim the relief against trading income of the final year in addition to that of earlier years removes the flexibility of not claiming relief against a balancing charge in the final year, in order not to waste personal allowances (as illustrated in example 5 on page 358).

(e) From 1996/97 onwards for both new and existing businesses, the time limits for claims (see page 357) are somewhat shortened, in that the two-year period is shortened to a period of one year from 31 January following the tax year of loss (e.g. by 31 January 1999 for claiming relief in 1995/96 and/or 1996/97 for a 1996/97 loss) and the six-year period becomes five years from 31 January following the tax year of loss.

Where new businesses claim loss relief under the current year basis in 1994/95 or 1995/96 the old time limits will apply.

Repayment supplement (TMA 1970, Sch 1B para 2; TA 1988, s 824; FA 1994, Sch 19 para 41; FA 1996, Sch 17 para 2)

A loss claim will either prevent tax being payable or cause tax already paid to be repaid. For years before 1996/97, a tax-free repayment supplement is paid to individuals receiving a repayment more than one year after the end of the tax year to which it relates. The supplement runs from the end of the tax year following that for which the repayment is made (or from the end of the tax year in which the tax was paid, if later) to the end of the tax month in which the repayment is made. The rate of interest changes from time to time (see page xxiii). The supplement applies to all loss claims but is particularly beneficial in relation to carry-back claims on new business losses.

Under the self-assessment rules that apply from 1996/97, repayment supplement runs from the date of an overpayment rather than one year after the end of the relevant tax year, but the rate of interest is lower than that charged on unpaid tax. Furthermore, where a loss is carried back and set against the income of an earlier tax year, then although the tax saving is calculated by reference to the tax position of the earlier year, the adjustment is made by reducing the tax liability of the loss year (see page 119) and supplement will run from the payment dates for that year. This significantly reduces the benefit of carrying back new business losses for up to three years (see page 355).

Pre-trading expenditure (TA 1988, s 401; FA 1995, s 120)

Where expenditure is incurred within seven years before a trade commences and it would have been allowable as a trading expense if incurred afterwards (see chapter 20 for allowable and non-allowable expenses), then for businesses started before 6 April 1995, the expenditure may be treated as a loss of the first tax year and relief claimed under Sections 380, 381 or 385. This would cover, for example, rent paid on business premises before starting to trade. For businesses started on or after 6 April 1995, such expenditure is treated as an expense of the first trading period, and will therefore already be incorporated into a loss (see page 295).

Losses of limited partners (TA 1988, ss 117 and 118)

Some partnerships have 'limited partners', whose liability for partnership debts is limited to a fixed capital contribution. These limited partners may be either individuals or companies. A loss claim by such partners in any year against income other than from the trade cannot exceed the total of the limited partner's fixed capital contribution plus undrawn profits at the end of that year. The loss claims referred to are those under Sections 380 and 381 for individuals, and under TA 1988, s 393A(1) or the group relief provisions for companies (see pages 366 and 375).

There is no restriction on the right of limited partners to carry forward their unused losses against later profits from the same trade.

National insurance

Losses reduce your profit for Class 4 national insurance as well as for income tax. If you claim income tax relief for your loss against non-trading income or against capital gains, you can still set the loss against future trading income for Class 4 national insurance purposes.

Example 9

Using the figures in example 2 on page 355, the trader has set £3,000 of his loss of the year to 31 December 1995 against unearned income and £5,000 against capital gains in 1995/96.

The loss will be treated as nil in arriving at the average profits of the two years to 31 December 1996 for assessment in 1996/97. The assessment will therefore be on half of the profit of the year to 31 December 1996. That assessment will be reduced by £8,000 for Class 4 national insurance purposes. If it is insufficient, the balance of the £8,000 will be carried forward to set against later profits.

Where a loss claim results in Class 4 contributions being refunded, the refund attracts repayment supplement.

Tax points

●   The earliest relief is not always the best. The key questions are how much tax will you save, when will you save it and how much tax-free repayment supplement will be received. Watch the effect of changes in tax rates and allowances in the various years.

● Claiming carry-back relief under Section 381, instead of current year relief under Section 380, for a first year loss leaves other income of the loss year available for a possible carry-back claim under Section 381 for a loss in later years.

● The tax-free repayment supplement on loss claims under Section 381 can substantially boost the repayment for losses in 1995/96 or earlier years. The supplement is likely to be much less on claims under Section 380, and on *all* loss claims from 1996/97 because of the changed rules for giving effect to the claim (see page 362).

● Loss relief against general income is restricted to those losses incurred in a demonstrably commercial trade and this may be difficult to prove. This is particularly so in the case of a new trade, so that a viable business plan is often essential to support a carry-back claim under Section 381.

● A loss in the opening years carried back under Section 381, in preference to a claim under Section 380, must be fully relieved under Section 381 before the balance of available losses can be relieved under Section 380. It is not possible to carry back sufficient of the loss to relieve income of the third year back and then not to proceed against the income of the second year back and then the first. The carry-back facility must be exhausted if claimed at all, before a Section 380 loss claim is made in respect of the balance remaining unrelieved.

If there is a loss in the next year of trading this forms an entirely new claim. Relief for that loss can be claimed under Section 380 in preference to Section 381, but if a Section 381 claim is embarked upon first, the same remarks as above apply, so that the carry-back facility must be exhausted in respect of that particular loss before the balance can be relieved under Section 380.

● If a loss is large enough, claims for relief under Section 380 before the current year basis applies may be made both for the tax year of loss and the following tax year. Normally the loss would be set against the first year's income before the second. The Revenue have stated that a taxpayer may make the second year's claim before the first, or make both claims together and stipulate that the loss is to be relieved against the second year's income before the first. This may or may not be beneficial depending on the total income and available allowances of each year. Under the current year basis rules, Section 380 relief may be claimed for the tax year of loss and/or the *previous* tax year. The taxpayer will still be able to stipulate the priority of the claims in the same way as before.

● If including capital allowances in a loss claim under the 'previous year basis' rules means wasting personal allowances, the capital allowances can be left out altogether, or the claim for allowances on plant and machinery can be reduced to an appropriate level, so that the total allowances added to the loss claim are less. Under the current year basis, capital allowances are treated as trading expenses, and so cannot be left out of a loss claim, so the only way of using allowances to vary the amount of the loss is by disclaiming plant and machinery allowances.

● Before the introduction of self-assessment, it has not always been possible to agree the amount of a loss claim before the time limit for claiming runs out. The Revenue have, however, usually been prepared to accept an unquantified claim made within the time limit, with the figures being agreed later. The claims procedure under self-assessment is far more formalised and there are time limits both for making claims and for amending them (see page 118). Claims will not be subject to Revenue agreement, but the Revenue may challenge their validity if they open an enquiry (see page 123).

26
Company losses

Introduction

Companies may incur losses in their trades, in the course of letting property, in relation to investment income if expenses exceed the income, and in their capital transactions. In some cases the losses will relate to activities outside the UK. The overseas aspect is dealt with in chapter 41. The treatment of losses on rented property is dealt with in chapter 32. The treatment of capital losses is dealt with in chapter 4 and in context in various other chapters. From 1 April 1996, the loss of money lent is regarded as an income loss rather than a capital loss. Such losses are dealt with in this chapter at page 368.

Reliefs available for trading losses

As for individuals and partnerships (see chapter 25), trading losses of companies are calculated in the same way as trading profits, but the company's losses already include any capital allowances which have been claimed, whereas for individuals and partnerships, capital allowances may (until the current year basis applies) be included in or excluded from a loss claim. The following alternatives are available for obtaining relief for a company's trading loss:

> Set-off against current profits from other sources (TA 1988, s 393A(1)).
> Carry-back against earlier profits from all sources (TA 1988, s 393A(1)(2)).
> Carry-forward against future trading profits (TA 1988, s 393(1)).
> Set-off against franked investment income (TA 1988, s 242).
> Group relief (TA 1988, s 402).

Set-off against current profits (TA 1988, s 393A(1))

A trading loss of a company, which includes its capital allowances, can be set against any profits of the same chargeable accounting period, thus reducing or eliminating the corporation tax bill. Profits for this purpose include not only all sources of income (other than UK dividends, which are not liable to corporation tax) but also capital gains (see page 25). (See page 369 for the treatment of charges on income.) A claim against current profits in respect of a non-trading deficit takes priority over this claim (see page 368).

Carry-back against previous profits and carry-forward (TA 1988, ss 393(1), 393A(1)(2))

After a trading loss has been set against all profits of the current period, any balance may be carried back and set against the profits of the previous three years, latest first, so long as the trade was carried on in the earlier period.

As with the claim against current profits, the set-off in the carry-back period is not limited to trading profits and is made against profits of any description. See example 1. (See page 369 for the treatment of charges on income.) If in the period of set-off there is a non-trading deficit for which relief is claimed against the profits of that period, that claim takes priority over the claim to set off carried back trading losses (see page 368).

Any loss not relieved against current or previous profits may be carried forward for set-off against future trading profits of the same trade, without time limit on its use unless there is a change of ownership to which the anti-avoidance provisions outlined on page 377 apply. Although any carried-forward losses cannot normally be relieved after a trade ceases, the provisions outlined on page 357 apply equally to a company, so that where a

---

Example 1

In its year to 31 March 1996 a company made a trading loss of £70,000. It has no franked investment income and no associated companies. Its other results and loss claims arising are:

	Year ended 30.9.93 £	Year ended 30.9.94 £	6 mths to 31.3.95 £	Year ended 31.3.96 £	Loss and Loss claims £
Trading profits	20,000	16,000	12,000	—	(70,000)
Investment income	4,000	7,000	8,000	6,000	
Capital gains	—	5,000	3,000	1,500	
Total profits	24,000	28,000	23,000	7,500	
Loss set-off:					
Against profits of same period				(7,500)	7,500
Against previous profits for up to 36 months:					
6 mths to 31.3.95			(23,000)		23,000
yr to 30.9.94		(28,000)			28,000
yr to 30.9.93	(11,500)				11,500
Profits remaining in charge	£12,500	—	—	—	

If the loss had not been fully relieved, it could have been set against 6/12 of the profits of the year to 30 September 1992.

building is sold after the cessation and a balancing charge is made to withdraw excess capital allowances, unrelieved trading losses may be set against that balancing charge.

Claims to set off losses against current and previous profits of any description are only permitted if the company carries on business on a commercial basis with a view to the realisation of profit. There is no commercial basis restriction for carrying losses forward, since the permitted set-off is only against trading profits of that same trade.

Non-trading losses relating to loans (FA 1993, s 130; FA 1994, s 160; FA 1996, s 83, Sch 8 and Sch 14 paras 69, 75)

For accounting periods ending after 31 March 1996 (subject to transitional provisions for accounting periods straddling that date), new rules apply for the treatment of interest paid and received by companies, and to profits and losses on loans (see page 27). Where a loan is for the purposes of the trade, the income and expenses and profits or losses on disposal are brought into the calculation of the trading profit or loss. For loans that do not relate to the trade, the various amounts are aggregated and if there is a surplus it is merged with any foreign exchange or financial instruments profit (see page 575) and taxed under Schedule D, Case III. If there is a loss, i.e. a 'non-trading deficit', it is merged with any foreign exchange or financial instruments loss (see page 575), and relief for *all or part of the loss* may be claimed as follows:

(a) Against any other profits (including capital gains) of the deficit period.

(b) By way of group relief (see page 377).

(c) Against Schedule D, Case III profits of the previous three years, latest first (so far as that period falls after 31 March 1996). (If this relief is claimed, the claim must relate to the *whole* of any deficit not relieved under (a) or (b), so far as the earlier profits permit.)

(d) Against *total* non-trading profits (including capital gains) of the next following accounting period.

Treatment of any remaining deficit

Any part of the deficit for which relief is not claimed under (a) to (d) above is carried forward to set against Schedule D, Case III profits in the following year. If it forms part of a Schedule D, Case III deficit for that following year, it may not form part of a claim for that year under (a) to (c) but it may form part of a claim under (d) to be set against *total* non-trading profits of the next following year.

Priority of reliefs

Relief against the other profits of the same accounting period under (a) above is given *after* relief for brought forward trading losses but *before* relief for current or carried back trading losses (see pages 366, 367) or for carried back non-trading deficits under (c).

Carry-back relief for any accounting period under (c) above is given against the profits of the period of set-off *after*:

> relief for a deficit incurred in an earlier period, relief for trade charges, relief claimed against the profits of the set-off period under (a), group relief under (b), and current or carry-back relief for trading losses (see pages 366, 367).

Charges on income (TA 1988, ss 338, 393(9), 393A(7)(8); FA 1996, Sch 8 para 3 and Sch 14 para 16)

Charges on income comprise payments such as patent royalties and charity covenants, which are paid net of basic rate income tax, and the company accounts to the Revenue for the income tax deducted. The main category of charges on income used to be loan interest paid, but from 1 April 1996 all interest paid and received is now brought together under Schedule D, Case III, along with profits and losses on loans, and separate rules apply if there is a deficit (see above).

Charges may be deducted not just from trading profits but from total profits, including capital gains. The treatment of charges and the way they interact with loss claims is different according to whether or not they are paid wholly and exclusively for the purposes of the trade. If there are trading losses and/or non-trading deficits (see above), the losses and/or deficits are set off in priority to both trade and non-trade charges of the same period. Where losses and/or non-trading deficits are carried back, they are set off *after* trade charges, such as patent royalties, but *before* non-trade charges, such as charity covenants. Where *trade* charges exceed the available profits, the excess may be *carried forward* as a trading loss. In a continuing business, excess charges, whether trade charges or non-trade charges, may never be carried back against previous profits. When a business ceases, however, unrelieved *trade* charges (but not non-trade charges) of the final accounting period may be treated as part of the trading loss that may be carried back under the provisions on page 367.

If the charges are not paid wholly and exclusively for the purposes of the trade (for example, charity covenants), and the company has insufficient profits against which to set them in the accounting period in which they are paid, they may not be carried forward for relief against later profits. They may, however, be the subject of a group relief claim (see page 377), or relief may be claimed against surplus franked investment income (see page 373).

Effect of carry-back of losses on tax paid and ACT set-off

Loss relief may be obtained at one of three possible corporation tax rates: at the small companies rate if the loss set-off is against profits charged at that rate; at the full corporation tax rate if the set-off is against profits in excess of the upper limit for marginal small companies relief; and at a higher marginal rate on profits between the small companies rate marginal relief upper and lower limits. For the year to 31 March 1997, the rates are 24%, 33% and 35.25% respectively. For the five years to 31 March 1996, the rates were 25%, 33% and 35% respectively. Higher rates applied for earlier years. See page xxiv for further details.

Carry-back loss claims will result in corporation tax already paid being repaid, or in tax otherwise due not having to be paid. The carry-back will also affect the calculation of the maximum advance corporation tax set-off which may be made, so that if ACT has either been paid in that period or carried back or forward to it, the loss claim may require the ACT set-off to be adjusted, and surplus ACT may arise as a result. See example 2.

For the treatment of surplus ACT, see page 34. Where surplus ACT arises as a result of a loss claim, the time limit for a claim to carry back the surplus ACT is still two years from the end of the accounting period in which the surplus arose, so it will often not be possible to make the claim in time and the surplus ACT may have to be carried forward. But a provisional claim to carry back surplus ACT may be made after the end of the accounting period of loss, but within the time limit, even if the amount of the loss and surplus ACT have not been quantified at that time. Such a provisional claim could not, however, cover surplus ACT that arose as a result of events outside the time limit. If in example 1, the result of carrying back the loss of the year to 31 March 1996 was that surplus ACT then arose in the year to 30 September 1993, the surplus ACT could not have been carried back from that year, because the time limit for the ACT carry-back claim would be 30 September 1995, at which time the loss available for carry-back had not occurred. The Revenue have stated, however, that where surplus ACT arising from a loss claim is carried forward, it is treated as part of the ACT of the year to which it has been carried, so that in the example, surplus ACT of the year to 30 September 1993 could be carried forward to 30 September 1994 and treated as paid in that year. A claim to carry back surplus ACT for up to six earlier years would then be in time if made by 30 September 1996.

Interest calculations (TA 1988, ss 825, 826)

Where the accounting period for which a repayment is made ends on or before 30 September 1993 (i.e. before the introduction of Pay and File — see page 25), the interest added to the repayment will be calculated under the repayment supplement provisions (see page 38), so that supplement will be paid at the same interest rate as that charged on overdue tax, but will normally be paid only from twelve months after the due date of payment of corporation tax for the relevant period. Where the repayment relates to an accounting period ended after 30 September 1993, it will attract interest from nine months after the end of the relevant period or, if later, from the actual date of payment of tax for that period (see page 38), although the rate at which interest will be payable is lower than the rate charged on overdue tax. This is illustrated in example 2. The latest available interest rates are set out at page xxiii.

For calculating interest on repayments resulting from current and carried back losses, a repayment is normally treated as relating to the *loss* period, but a repayment relating to an accounting period falling *wholly* in the twelve months before the loss period is treated as relating to that accounting period.

Carried back ACT is normally treated for the purposes of calculating interest on a repayment as ACT for the year in which the related dividend was actually paid rather than for the year to which the ACT has been carried back, so that the interest calculation will depend on the due date of payment of corporation tax for that later period. Interest will run from an even later date where surplus ACT arises (or is carried forward and deemed to arise) in an accounting period ended after 30 September 1993 *and* as a result of carrying back a loss further than twelve months. Interest on any repayment resulting from carrying back such ACT will be related to the normal due date of payment for the *loss* period and will be paid from that date if the ACT has been carried back to an accounting period ending after 30 September 1993 and from one year after the corporation tax payment date for the loss period if the ACT has been carried back to an accounting period ending on or before 30 September 1993.

See examples 2 and 3.

Example 2

A company has the following results.

Year ended 31 March	1994 £	1995 £	1996 £
Trading profit (loss)	50,000	20,000	(40,500)
Investment income	3,000	3,000	3,000
Chargeable gains	4,000	2,500	2,000
Total profits	57,000	25,500	5,000

ACT maximum set-off before loss relief:			
22½% × profits of £57,000	12,825		
20% × profits of £25,500		5,100	
20% × profits of £5,000			1,000
If loss relief under TA 1988, s 393A(1) is claimed:			
Profits	57,000	25,500	5,000
Less loss	(10,000)	(25,500)	(5,000)
Total profits	47,000	—	—
ACT maximum set-off following loss relief:			
22½%× £47,000/Nil/Nil	10,575	—	—

Any tax repayment for the year to 31 March 1995 resulting from carrying the loss back 12 months will attract interest from the corporation tax payment date for that year, i.e. from 1 January 1996. The repayment for the year to 31 March 1994 will attract interest from 1 January 1997 (the payment date for corporation tax for the *loss* year to 31 March 1996).

Assuming a dividend was paid in the year to 31 March 1995, surplus ACT would arise as a result of carrying the loss back 12 months. Any repayment relating to the carry-back of the ACT on that dividend to the year to 31 March 1994 would attract interest from 1 January 1996 (the corporation tax payment date for the year in which the dividend was paid). If the surplus ACT was carried back to the year to 31 March 1993 or earlier, repayment supplement would be payable from 6 January 1997 (one year after the corporation tax payment date for the year in which the surplus arose).

If on the other hand surplus ACT arose in the year to 31 March 1994, it would be as a result of carrying the loss back more than 12 months. Any repayment relating to the carry-back of that surplus ACT would relate to the year to 31 March 1993 or earlier and would attract repayment supplement from 6 January 1998, one year after the corporation tax payment date for the *loss* period. Note that the carry-back claim would have to be made by 31 March 1996, and it would have to be a provisional claim, since the loss, although incurred by that date, would not have been quantified, so that the precise amount of surplus ACT could not be ascertained.

Example 3

Loss in year to 31 December 1996, after relief in that year, is carried back to years ended 31 December 1995 and 31 December 1994.

Repayments relating to loss claim will carry interest as follows:

Year ended	Interest from
31.12.96	1.10.97
31.12.95	1.10.96
31.12.94	1.10.97

Repayments resulting from carrying back surplus ACT will carry interest as follows:

Surplus ACT arising in year ended	Interest from
31.12.95	1.10.96
31.12.94	1.10.97

Surplus ACT of years before the year to 31.12.94 would have to be carried forward and treated as arising in the first later period for which a carry-back claim could be made within the two-year time limit, say year to 31.12.94, for which a provisional claim could have been made by 31.12.96. Since the year to 31.12.94 is a Pay and File year, repayment supplement on any corporation tax repaid for periods before 1.1.93 (as a result of the ACT carry-back) would run from 6.10.98, one year after the payment date for the loss year.

Relief for losses, etc. against dividends from other UK companies (franked investment income) (TA 1988, s 242; FA 1996, Sch 14 para 12)

Although franked investment income (i.e. dividends from United Kingdom companies, including the attached tax credits) is not chargeable to corporation tax, it nonetheless forms part of the fund of corporate profit. When all other loss reliefs are exhausted, it is possible to set any remaining trading losses against such dividend income (unless it has itself been used to make a dividend payment), thus obtaining a refund of the dividend tax credits, rather than carry forward the loss to set against future trading profits. The accounting periods in respect of which such a claim may be made are the same as for normal current and carry-back loss claims, i.e. the current period and the previous three years. The relief obtained is, however, only at the lower rate of income tax, i.e. 20%, rather than the corporation tax rate. (For losses set against dividend income received before 6 April 1993, the relief is obtained at 25%.)

The claim is subject to adjustment in a later year if the company pays dividends in excess of dividends which it receives. The adjustment is rather complex, but it effectively means that the company gives back to the Revenue the tax credit originally refunded and obtains relief for the trading loss at the corporation tax rate then applicable to its trading profits.

Claims to set unrelieved amounts against surplus franked investment income may also be made in respect of Schedule D, Case III non-trading deficits (see page 368), excess charges on income and excess management expenses of investment companies. These claims follow similar rules for those for trading losses, although there are some differences.

Time limits for claims

TA 1988, s 393A; FA 1996, s 83(2)(a)(c)	Set off trading losses or non-trading deficits against profits of same accounting period and previous accounting periods	Within two years after the end of the accounting period of loss or deficit, or such further period as the Board allow
FA 1996, s 83(2)(d)	Set off non-trading deficit against total non-trading profits of next accounting period	Within two years after the end of that next accounting period, or such further period as the Board allow
TA 1988, s 393(1)	Carry forward trading losses against later trading profits from same trade	No claim is required. Losses are entered on the corporation tax return and any unrelieved amounts are carried forward automatically*
FA 1996, s 83(3)	Carry forward non-trading deficit against later Schedule D, Case III profits	No claim is required
TA 1988, s 242	Set trading loss or non-trading deficit against an excess of dividends received over those paid (surplus franked investment income)	Within two years after the end of the accounting period of loss or deficit, or such further period as the Board allow
TA 1988, s 239(3)	Carry back surplus ACT to set off in previous six years	Within two years after the end of the accounting period in which the surplus arises (see page 370)

* For accounting periods ending on or before 30 September 1993, the time limit was within six years after the end of the accounting period of loss.

Group relief for losses (TA 1988, ss 402–413; FA 1996, s 83, Sch 8 para 2 and Sch 14 para 22)

Trading losses

In a group consisting of a holding company and its 75% subsidiaries, trading losses may be surrendered from one company to one or more other companies within the group, provided that all the companies are resident in the UK. This enables the company to which the loss has been surrendered to reduce its taxable profits by the surrendered amount. The loss available to be surrendered must relate to an accounting period of the loss-making company that corresponds with that of the claimant company. This will not pose any difficulty when accounts within the group are prepared to the same date, but where accounts are prepared to different dates, part of the loss period will correspond with part of one accounting period of the claimant company and the remainder with part of the next accounting period. The loss available for relief and the profits against which it may be set must be apportioned accordingly. Relief is also proportionately restricted if the parent/subsidiary relationship does not exist throughout the accounting period, usually on a time basis, but by reference to what is just and reasonable where a time basis would give an unreasonable result.

The set-off rules are quite flexible, and broadly the loss-making company may surrender any part of its trading loss (without first claiming other reliefs available), up to a maximum of the available total profits of the claimant company or companies for the corresponding period. The profits of the claimant company available for relief are profits from all sources, including capital gains, but after deducting charges on income.

Relief for surrendered losses is not, however, available against the dividend income of a claimant company.

A significant factor in deciding the optimum loss claim is the rate of tax saving. Other things being equal, it will be best to surrender the loss against profits being charged at the small companies marginal rate (or indeed not to surrender it at all if the company's own profits are charged at that rate). The rules enable the loss to be divided among several group companies in order to obtain the maximum loss relief. See example 4.

Where a loss would otherwise be unrelieved, it might be appropriate for a profit company in a group to disclaim some of the allowances on its plant and machinery, to give it a higher profit against which to make a group relief claim (see pages 303 and 320). The profit company would then have a higher pool balance carried forward on which to claim capital allowances in the future, whereas if it has insufficient current profit to cover the loss available for surrender, the surrendered loss has to be restricted.

The group relief provisions are also available in certain circumstances to a consortium of companies that owns at least 75% of the ordinary share capital

Example 4

Company A has been the wholly owned subsidiary of Company B for many years. (Small companies rate marginal relief limits are therefore reduced for each company to £125,000 and £625,000 for the year to 31 March 1994 and £150,000 and £750,000 for the years to 31 March 1995, 1996 and 1997.) Both companies prepare accounts to 31 March, and for the year to 31 March 1996, results are as follows:

Company A has a trading loss of	£80,000
and other profits of	£10,000
Company B has total profits of	£205,000

In the year to 31 March 1995, Company A had total profits of £170,000. Company A's profits for the year to 31 March 1997 will be below £150,000.

Company A may claim its own available loss reliefs and not surrender any part of the loss to Company B; or it may surrender the full £80,000 and pay tax on its own profits of £170,000 in 1995 and £10,000 in 1996; or it may surrender any other amount up to £80,000, as the companies wish, and claim its own loss reliefs on the balance.

Rates of tax at which relief is available:	On Company A's profits	On Company B's profits
Year to 31 March 1996	25% on £10,000	35% on £55,000
		25% on £150,000
Year to 31 March 1995	35% on £20,000	No relief available
	25% on £150,000	
Year to 31 March 1997	24%	

By a combination of claims against Company A's own profits and group relief, tax can be saved on £70,000 of the loss at 35%.

One alternative is to surrender £50,000 of the loss to Company B, achieving a 35% tax saving thereon against Company B's profits, and to claim relief for £30,000 against Company A's own profits, giving relief on £10,000 at 25% in the year to 31 March 1996 and £20,000 at 35% in the year to 31 March 1995.

A second alternative is to surrender £55,000 to Company B and claim relief for £25,000 against Company A's profits (£10,000 in the year to 31 March 1996 and £15,000 in the year to 31 March 1995). The rate of tax saved is the same for both alternatives, so the choice would depend on to what extent the tax repaid under the carry-back claim attracted interest, and the effect of the loss set-off on ACT.

of a trading company or of a holding company with 90% trading subsidiaries, with the consortium members each owning at least 5% of that ordinary share capital. Losses in proportion to the consortium member's shareholding in the consortium-owned company can be surrendered both from the trading companies to the consortium companies and from the consortium companies to the trading companies.

Group relief for other unrelieved amounts

In addition to trading losses, group relief may also be claimed in respect of excess charges on income and excess management expenses of investment companies.

A further category has been introduced from 1 April 1996, enabling a group relief claim to be made for all or part of a non-trading deficit relating to loans (see page 368). Reflief is given as if the deficit has been a trading loss, so that the same rules apply.

Procedure for group relief claims (TA 1988, Sch 17A)

Companies may make, vary and withdraw group relief claims up to the later of two years after the end of the claimant company's accounting period and the date that the profits and losses for the period are determined, but not normally beyond six years after the end of the period. Each group company makes initial claims for specified amounts of group relief and shows amounts available for group relief surrenders on its own individual corporation tax return (CT 200) or amended return. Claims must show the name and tax district reference number of the surrendering company and be accompanied by a copy of the surrendering company's consent. The surrendering company will send the notice of consent to its own tax district. Where original claims are to be varied, groups may make a single amending return.

Anti-avoidance provisions

There are provisions to prevent a purchased company being used to obtain relief that would not otherwise be available for trading losses and surplus ACT. The provisions apply if either:

(a) within a period of three years there is both a major change in the nature or conduct of a trade carried on by a company and a change in its ownership; or

(b) after the scale of activities in a trade carried on by a company has become negligible and before any considerable revival, there is a change in ownership. (TA 1988, ss 245, 768, 768A).

The provisions prevent losses (and surplus ACT) incurred before the change of ownership being carried forward, and prevent losses (and surplus ACT) in an accounting period *after* the change of ownership from being carried back to an accounting period *before* the change. The Revenue have issued Statement of Practice SP 10/91 giving their views on the meaning of a 'major change in the nature or conduct of a trade'.

Where there is a change in ownership of an investment company, there are provisions to prevent the company carrying forward unrelieved management expenses, charges on income and non-trading deficits on loans (TA 1988, ss 768B, 768C and Sch 28A; FA 1996, Sch 14 paras 39, 40, 54).

Where one company transfers a trade to another and a 75% interest in the first and second companies is owned by the same persons, the trade is treated for certain purposes as continuing. Thus the accumulated trading losses incurred by the first company are available for relief against future profits of the trade in the hands of the successor company. The loss relief available for carry-forward into the successor company is restricted if it does not take over the predecessor company's unpaid liabilities (TA 1988, ss 343, 344).

The 75% link for group relief purposes (see page 375) is defined very much more restrictively than simply 75% of ordinary share capital, to prevent companies taking advantage of the provisions by means of an artificial group relationship (TA 1988, s 413 and Sch 18).

Group relief is not available for a part of an accounting period in which arrangements exist whereby the loss-making company could cease to be a member of the group (TA 1988, s 410).

Tax points

● When considering loss claims, always look at the amount of tax saved. For the five years to 31 March 1996, set-off of losses may save tax at 33% if profits are charged at the full rate, 35% where the set-off is within the marginal small companies tranche of profits, or only 25% if profits are charged at the small companies rate. For the year to 31 March 1997, the respective rates are 33%, 35.25% and 24%.

● Until Finance Act 1996, unrelieved interest could not be carried back against earlier profits, except for bank interest relating to trade borrowing, which was included within a trading loss. The new rules for the treatment of loans enable *all* unrelieved interest to be carried back, but the carry-back for interest that does not relate to the trade will be only against non-trading profits relating to loans (see page 368).

● Remember that group relief for losses is not available if there is less than a 75% link between holding and subsidiary companies.

● If two or more companies are controlled by the same individual(s), group relief is not available. But unused losses are still available against the profits of the trade if that trade is transferred from one company to another under the same control (see above).

- Watch the anti-avoidance provisions on group relief. An arrangement made part-way through an accounting period to sell a loss-making subsidiary will prevent group relief being claimed for the remainder of the accounting period even though the parent/subsidiary relationship exists throughout.

- Exceptional revenue expenditure, such as extraordinary repairs, or establishing or boosting a company pension scheme within permissible limits, may result in a normally profitable trade incurring a loss. When a company is planning such expenditure or considering when, or indeed whether, it should be incurred, the carry-back of losses against profits of the previous three years, resulting in tax not having to be paid, or being repaid, is an important consideration.

- Although losses may be carried back three years and surplus ACT six years, the resulting repayments do not attract interest for that length of time — see page 371.

27
Transfer of business to limited company

Choice of date

When the trade of an individual or partnership is transferred to a company the trade has ceased for income tax purposes, so that the closing year rules dealt with in chapter 21 apply. The new current year basis rules will broadly apply to cessations after 5 April 1997, but there are some transitional provisions affecting cessations occurring up to 5 April 1999 (see page 287).

For trades ceasing before 6 April 1997 (or 6 April 1998 if the Revenue so direct), the Revenue will have the option of charging tax for the two tax years before the last according to the profits actually made in those years rather than on the normal basis (and see page 287 re the possibility of the 1996/97 assessment being adjusted to actual profits where there is a cessation in 1998/99). Some profits will, however, still escape tax, provided that the trade has been carried on long enough for the early profits to have been taxed more than once. The transfer date will determine what profits escape assessment, so it is important to make an appropriate choice. If profits are rising it will generally be better to delay the transfer until after the end of a tax year (see page 284).

Once profits are taxed on the current year basis (see page 287), there will no longer be any opportunity to vary the profits that escape assessment on cessation. The amount of any overlap profit will be calculated at the time of the overlap, and that is the amount that will be deducted from the final year's profits. The timing of the cessation will still need to be considered in the light of expected income in the years affected, for example the deduction of the overlap profit may reduce higher rate tax, or possibly create a loss to be carried back against the previous year's income.

Capital allowances (CAA 1990, ss 77, 78, 152, 157, 158)

Normally the cessation of trade would involve a balancing allowance or charge on the disposal to the company of plant and equipment and, where relevant, industrial buildings.

The sole trader or partners and the company may usually, however, jointly elect within two years after the transfer date for the assets to be treated as transferred at the tax written-down value. If the election is not made, the transfer is deemed to be at market value, with a resulting balancing allowance or charge on the sole or partnership trade, and the company getting writing-down allowances on that market value.

Unused trading losses (TA 1988, s 386)

If there are unused trading losses, these cannot be carried forward to a company as such, but they may be relieved against income received by the trader or partners from the company, either in the form of directors' fees or dividends, so long as the business is exchanged for shares and the shares are still retained at the time the loss is set off. Other available loss claims may be made first, e.g. under TA 1988, s 380 against income of the year of loss (or the previous year under the current year basis rules), or terminal loss relief for a loss of the last twelve months against the trading income of the previous three years (see chapter 25), and the relief against income from the company would then be available on the balance of unrelieved losses.

Capital gains tax (TCGA 1992, ss 17, 18, 286)

When the transfer takes place, the general rule is that those assets chargeable to capital gains tax which have been transferred will be treated as being disposed of to the company at their open market value. Current assets (stock, debtors, etc.) are not chargeable assets, and moveable plant and machinery, although chargeable unless valued at £6,000 or less for each item (see chapter 39), will not normally be valued at more than cost, so the most likely assets on which a liability may arise are freehold or leasehold premises, fixed plant and machinery and goodwill.

An obvious way of avoiding the charge on premises is for the proprietor or partners to retain ownership and to allow the company to use the property either at a rent or free of charge. This will also save the stamp duty that would have been incurred on the transfer. Further stamp duty can be saved if the business debts are collected by the proprietor/partners instead of being transferred to the company.

The only way of not transferring the goodwill is if the sole trader/partners continue to own it whilst licensing the company to carry on the trade, but unless this is commercially practicable, sensible and properly done, the goodwill will automatically be transferred with the trade. The valuation of goodwill depends not only on the size of the profits but also on the extent to which the profits depend on the skills of the proprietor or partners, the nature of the trade and many other factors.

Any gain arising may be covered by the annual exemption or possibly retirement relief if the sole trader or partners are over 50 (55 for transfers before 28 November 1995) or retire through ill-health. Otherwise the capital gains tax effect must be considered. See example 1.

Example 1

The net assets of a trader at the time of incorporation of his business were:

		£
Freehold premises } at current market value		204,000
Goodwill		120,000
Plant and equipment (cost £320,000)		140,000
Net current assets other than cash		256,000
Cash and bank balances		80,000
		£800,000

The premises had been acquired for £120,000 and the trade newly commenced after 31 March 1982. Assume indexation allowance to date of transfer to be £32,000 on the premises.

The potential chargeable gains on incorporation are:

			£
Freehold premises—market value		204,000	
Less: Cost	120,000		
Indexation allowance	32,000	152,000	52,000
Goodwill — market value		120,000	
Less: Cost	Nil		
Indexation allowance	Nil	—	120,000
			£172,000

The gain on the premises can be avoided by the trader retaining ownership, but the goodwill will be treated as transferred, unless it is possible to retain it while licensing the company to use it and that arrangement is properly made.

There are three alternatives for reducing or eliminating an immediate capital gains tax charge. One is the rollover relief of TCGA 1992, s 162, which requires *all* the assets (except cash) to be transferred to the company, and defers gains only to the extent that the consideration is received in the form of shares in the company. The second is a combination of retaining some assets in personal ownership and using the business gifts relief of TCGA 1992, s 165 (outlined on page 60) to defer the gains on other chargeable assets (notably goodwill), the company then being treated as acquiring those assets at market value less the gains. Under this alternative, any consideration received from the company for the assets that are transferred need not be shares and a credit may be made to a director's loan account or cash taken instead. The third is the reinvestment relief outlined on page 62. This is only available if the company is a qualifying unquoted trading company.

Capital gains rollover relief on transfer (TCGA 1992, s 162)

If relief under section 162 were claimed in example 1, all assets other than the £80,000 cash would have to be transferred.

The chargeable gains on the disposal of the business are calculated, and they are treated as reducing the tax cost of the shares received in exchange for the business. The lower base cost for the shares will of course increase the potential capital gains tax liability in the future, but further reliefs may be available at the time the shares are disposed of, for example retirement, reinvestment or gifts relief, or total exemption if the shares are still held at death. See example 2.

The difference between the £700,000 par value of the shares and the £720,000 assets value in example 2 represents a share premium. It is almost inevitable that the par value will not correspond with the asset values since those values cannot be precisely determined before the transfer date.

Example 2

In consideration of the transfer of the trade in example 1, the trader receives 700,000 shares of £1 each, fully paid, in the new company, transferring all assets except the cash of £80,000.

The base cost of the shares will be:

700,000 shares	(£800,000 assets – £80,000 cash)	720,000
Less gains otherwise arising on premises and goodwill		172,000
Cost of 700,000 shares for capital gains tax purposes		£548,000

If the transfer is made only partly for shares, and partly for cash or credit to a director's loan account, then only proportionate relief is given. See example 3.

Example 3

Suppose the consideration of £720,000 in example 2 was satisfied as to £480,000 shares and £240,000 cash. Only two-thirds of the chargeable gains can be deducted from the base cost of the shares.

		Shares	Cash
Consideration		480,000	240,000
Gains	£172,000	114,667	£57,333
Cost of shares for capital gains tax purposes	£365,333		

The £57,333 is charged to capital gains tax (subject to any available exemptions and reliefs).

Obtaining the maximum deferral of gains under section 162 therefore requires the consideration for the shares to be locked in as share capital. If the consideration is provided through leaving money on director's loan account, tax will not be deferred, but the money can later be withdrawn at no personal tax cost.

The section 162 relief is given automatically without the need for a claim, although the Revenue will not object if the transferor has acquired business assets and wants to claim the business assets rollover relief instead (see page 55). It appears, however, that the Revenue would require section 162 to be applied even if gains were covered by, say, the annual exemption. To avoid the problem, the appropriate part of the consideration resulting in chargeable gains equal to available exemptions could be left on director's loan account, so that a gain would be immediately realised, as shown in example 3.

See page 51 for the treatment of disposals after 5 April 1988 that are affected by deferred gains on assets acquired before 31 March 1982.

Gifts of business assets (TCGA 1992, s 165)

If the premises were retained in personal ownership, saving capital gains tax and stamp duty, and further stamp duty was saved by not transferring debtors, this would leave the gain on the goodwill to be considered. The business gifts relief enables the whole of the gain on goodwill to be deferred providing any consideration received does not exceed the capital gains tax base cost of the goodwill. In example 1, that cost was nil, so that the full gain on the goodwill could be deferred only if nothing was charged for it. Goodwill will have a capital gains tax cost either if it was purchased or if it had a value at 31 March 1982.

The disadvantage of charging consideration equal to the capital gains tax base cost is that the transferor is only credited in the accounts of the company with that amount (before reckoning indexation allowance), not with the market value at the time of transfer, and that lower value (plus any available indexation allowance up to that time) will be the company's acquisition cost on which future indexation allowance will be calculated.

The chargeable asset could be transferred at a figure in excess of capital gains tax base cost, but less than market value, available exemptions being set off against the gains arising. This has the advantage of more cash being received on the transfer or a higher credit to the director's account, and in either case a higher base value for the asset in company ownership. The business assets gifts relief eliminates the chargeable gain on the difference between market value and the value used for the transfer.

Reinvestment relief (TCGA 1992, ss 164A–164N)

The disadvantage of the section 162 rollover relief is that all assets must be transferred to the company, whereas it may be preferred to retain premises in personal ownership. The disadvantage of the business gifts relief is the reduced value at which the company is regarded as acquiring the gifted assets. Both disadvantages can be eliminated if the company is a qualifying unquoted trading company by claiming reinvestment relief instead (see page 62). You need only transfer such assets as you wish, and they will be transferred at full market value. Money need only be locked into share capital to the extent necessary to cover the gains.

Example 4

In example 1, providing the company is a qualifying unquoted trading company, the premises could be retained personally and the goodwill and other assets except cash transferred to the company for £516,000. The consideration for the transfer could be shares worth £120,000 and £396,000 on director's loan account.

The gain of £120,000 on the goodwill could be offset by a claim for reinvestment relief of the same amount, or a smaller amount if other reliefs and exemptions were available.

There is no difference in the transferor's position at example 4 whether he simply lets the goodwill accrue to the company on the transfer of the trade, covering the otherwise chargeable gain by the gifts relief of section 165, or whether he takes shares in the company equivalent to its value. In the first instance his shareholding will have a true value £120,000 greater than he has paid for it because the value of the company will reflect the goodwill for which it has not paid. In the second instance the cost of the shareholding will reflect the market value of the goodwill upon its sale, but an otherwise chargeable gain of £120,000 will be deducted from its cost because of reinvestment relief.

But in so far as the company is concerned, its cost upon a future sale of the goodwill is £120,000 when acquired with the other assets for part cash/part shares consideration, compared with nil cost if acquired by the business gifts route. The reinvestment route will therefore be preferable to the business gifts route where the company is a qualifying company.

Retirement relief (TCGA 1992, ss 163, 164 and Sch 6)

Retirement relief is available both to sole traders and partners and to full-time working directors and employees who own 5% or more of the voting rights in a trading company (see page 57). For the purpose of the ten-year qualifying period, the periods of operating the unincorporated and incorporated businesses are taken together.

If husband and wife partners incorporate their business, however, and one of them then works only part-time in the company, he/she will lose the entitlement to retirement relief.

Stamp duty

Stamp duty is a fixed or ad valorem charge on certain documents, and if there is no document no duty is normally payable.

Stock and plant can be transferred to the company by delivery, so no stamp duty will be payable, and the company can either pay cash or credit the director's loan account.

Stamp duty will arise on the agreement for the transfer of the trade to the company according to the value of the assets transferred. As already indicated, the stamp duty can be reduced by not transferring premises to the company and by the sole trader or partners collecting the debts instead of assigning them.

Value added tax (VATA 1994, s 49; SI 1992/3129, para 5; SI 1995/2518, paras 5, 6)

On the transfer of a business to a company, VAT will not normally arise on the assets transferred and the company will take over the VAT position of the transferor as regards deductible input tax and liability to account for output tax (see page 101). This VAT-free treatment does not apply to transfers of land and buildings in respect of which the transferor has opted to charge VAT (see page 454), or of commercial buildings that are either unfinished or less than three years old, unless the transferee company gives written notification before the transfer that it has opted to charge VAT. Otherwise, VAT must be charged. A claim may be made by the trader or partners and the company for the existing VAT registration number to be transferred to the company. It is advisable to contact the appropriate VAT office in good time to obtain the necessary forms and ensure that the various requirements are complied with.

Inheritance tax

There will not usually be any direct inheritance tax implications on the incorporation of a business, but two situations need watching.

The first is the effect on the availability of business property relief where partners form a company. A partner who personally owns assets such as premises used in the business is entitled to business property relief at the rate of 50%. Relief at the 50% rate is available to a shareholder only if he is a controlling shareholder, and no relief is available at all for such assets owned by minority shareholders. Shares of husband and wife are related property and the available rate of relief is determined by their joint holdings.

The second situation arises where assets have been transferred using the capital gains provisions for gifts to the company of business assets (TCGA 1992, s 165). Such gifts will not be potentially exempt for inheritance tax since they are not to an individual or qualifying trust fund. They may be covered by the 100% business property relief, but if not, the amount of the transfer of value is the amount by which the sole trader's or partner's estate has fallen in value. In measuring that fall in value, the value of the shares acquired in the company (enhanced by the gifted assets) will be taken into account. The result may be that there is no transfer of value. If there is a transfer of value, no tax may be payable, because of annual exemptions and the nil rate threshold. If tax is payable, the tax may be paid by instalments if the company as donee pays the tax.

See chapter 5 for further information on inheritance tax.

National insurance

If a sole trader or partner becomes a director and/or employee in the company, national insurance contributions are payable by both the employer and the employee, and the burden is significantly higher than the maximum self-employed contributions under Classes 2 and 4. See chapter 18 for further details.

Business rates

Although the incorporation of a business means a change of occupier for rating purposes, any transitional relief to which the unincorporated business was entitled is available to the company (see page 116).

Tax points

- Choose the transfer date with care to maximise the profits that escape income tax. With steadily rising profits this means after 5 April rather than before.

- Where you want to claim relief under TCGA 1992, s 162 on the transfer of a business, minimise the amount locked up in share capital by not transferring cash. If the cash is needed to assist the liquidity of the company, it can always be introduced on director's loan account.

- Rollover relief on the replacement of business assets (see page 55) can still be claimed on premises owned personally and used in the owner's personal trading company — see page 57. A personal company is one in which the individual owns at least 5% of the voting rights.

- The payment of rent by the company for property owned personally by the former sole trader or partners will affect their entitlement to retirement relief for capital gains tax — see page 59. It will not, however, affect business property relief for inheritance tax.

- You cannot get the best of all worlds on incorporation of a business. Maximising the capital gains deferral can only be done at extra cost in terms of stamp duty and with the disadvantage of locking funds into share capital. Retaining some assets and using gifts relief on those that are transferred saves stamp duty and enables you to fund the company by making loans to it, but your director's account is credited with a lower figure in respect of the gifted assets and that value becomes the company's base value for capital gains. This could also significantly reduce the indexation allowance when the company disposes of the assets. Using reinvestment relief to eliminate the chargeable gain on the transfer of assets will ensure that the company's base value is increased, but the agreement for the transfer of the assets will attract stamp duty.

- When considering how much of the proceeds for the transfer of the business should be locked in as share capital, do not forget that funds may need to be drawn for the payment of taxation relating to the former sole trade or partnership. Unless the potential tax has been included in the last sole trade or partnership accounts as a liability, or there are sufficient funds on directors' loan account, it will not be possible to withdraw the required funds from the company without incurring a further tax liability on remuneration or dividends.

- It may be possible to reduce the problems of locking in share capital by using redeemable shares, which can be redeemed gradually as and when the company has funds and possibly using the annual capital gains exemption to avoid a tax charge on the shareholder. There are, however, anti-avoidance provisions, and also a clearance procedure, and professional advice is essential.

- It is sometimes worth considering transferring chargeable assets, such as goodwill, at their full value, with a corresponding credit to your director's account. This will increase the capital gains tax payable at the time, but will provide a higher facility to draw off the director's loan account at no future personal tax cost. This is particularly relevant where the chargeable gains would in any event be covered by retirement relief, which may otherwise be lost because of your later reduced participation.

28
Selling the family company

Background

There are two ways in which the family company may be sold — selling the shares or selling the assets and liquidating the company, and the most difficult aspect of the sale negotiations is usually reconciling the interests of the vendors and the purchasers.

The vendors will often prefer to sell the shares rather than the assets to avoid the double capital gains tax charge which will arise on the assets sale and on the distribution to the shareholders if the company is wound up. The purchaser may prefer to buy assets in order to be able to claim capital allowances on purchases of equipment, plant and qualifying buildings, and because buying assets is frequently more straightforward, involving fewer legal formalities than a share purchase, with consequently lower costs. Stamp duty is currently charged both on share transactions and on the acquisition of property. Yet again, the vendors may intend staying in business, so that a sale of assets by a trading company, with the company then acquiring replacement assets, may give an opportunity for rollover relief. If the vendors plan to invest in another company, then providing that company is a qualifying unquoted trading company for reinvestment relief (see page 62), all or any part of the gains on the disposal of the shares in the existing company (and any other gains they may have) may be treated as reducing the capital gains cost of shares acquired in the new company.

A share purchaser will take over any latent liabilities and obligations of the company. The purchaser will clearly require indemnities and warranties from the vendors, but the vendors will want to limit these as much as possible, and in any event the purchaser would have the inconvenience of enforcing them or perhaps be unable to do so if the vendor had insufficient funds or was not able to be contacted.

The outcome will depend on the future intentions of the vendor, the relative bargaining strength of each party and the adjustments each agrees to in order to resolve points of difference.

Selling shares or assets

Part of the sale consideration may relate not to tangible assets but to the growth prospects or the entrepreneurial flair of those involved with the company, and where goodwill is a substantial factor, the valuation placed on it will be an important part of the negotiations, providing flexibility in agreeing a price.

The tax cost of selling the shares can be significantly less than that of selling the assets followed by a liquidation. See example 1 for a straight comparison of a share sale and an assets sale based on the same values. So long as the ACT can be set off, the disadvantage could be mitigated, but not eliminated, by the company paying a dividend equivalent to the profit less tax on the sale of its assets, and then distributing the remainder of its funds upon liquidation. See example 2. Knowing the tax advantage of the share sale to the vendor, coupled with the potential tax liability if the company in its new ownership sells its premises and goodwill, the purchaser may well seek a reduction in price if this route is to be followed.

Example 1

Company was formed in 1986 and 1,000 £1 shares were issued at par. Balance sheet of company immediately prior to intended sale in September 1996 was:

	£		£
Share capital	1,000	Net current assets	50,000
Accumulated profits	99,000	Premises at cost	50,000
	£100,000		£100,000

A sale is now proposed on the basis of the goodwill and premises being worth £350,000.

If the shares are sold:

Assets per balance sheet		100,000
Increase in value of premises and goodwill (350,000–50,000)		300,000
Sale proceeds for shares		400,000
Cost	1,000	
Indexation allowance, say	600	1,600
Chargeable gain		£398,400
Capital gains tax @ 40% (ignoring any set-offs and exemptions and assuming that the shareholders' lower rate bands have been fully utilised)		£159,360

If assets are sold and company is liquidated:

Assets per balance sheet		100,000
Increase in value of premises and goodwill	300,000	
Less provision for corporation tax on sale		
(£300,000 less, say, £30,000 for		
indexation on cost of premises)		
Gain £270,000 @ say 33%	89,100	210,900

Amount distributed to shareholders on liquidation		
(ignoring liquidation costs)		310,900
Cost of shares	1,000	
Indexation allowance, say	600	1,600
Chargeable gain		£309,300

Capital gains tax @ 40% (ignoring any set-offs and exemptions and assuming that the lower rate bands have been fully utilised)	£123,720

Amounts received by shareholders:

	Proceeds	Capital gains tax	Net
On sale of shares	400,000	159,360	240,640
On liquidation	310,900	123,720	187,180
Extra cost of liquidation route			£53,460

Example 2   £

Assets on balance sheet per example 1 are £100,000.

Profit after tax on sale of assets	210,900
Dividend September 1996	(210,900)

ACT of £52,725 on dividend is set off against the liability of £89,100 on sale of the assets.

Distribution on liquidation	100,000
Indexed cost of shares	1,600
Chargeable gain	£98,400
Capital gains tax @ 40%	£39,360

Received by shareholders:

Dividend	210,900	
Less higher rate tax on		
(210,900 + tax credit (¼) 52,725 =)		
£263,625 @ (40% − 20%)	52,725	158,175
On liquidation	100,000	
Less capital gains tax	39,360	60,640
		£218,815

Comparison of amounts received by shareholders in example 1 and in this example:

	Share sale	Asset sale/ liquidation	Asset sale/ dividend/ liquidation
	£	£	£
Value of assets	400,000	400,000	400,000
Corporation tax		(89,100)	(89,100)*
Shareholders' higher rate tax			(52,725)
Shareholders' capital gains tax	(159,360)	(123,720)	(39,360)
	£240,640	£187,180	£218,815

* Comprising ACT £52,725 and mainstream tax £36,375.

Where the company was established before 31 March 1982, the value of its chargeable assets and of the shares at that date may be substituted for cost, and indexation also calculated on that value, if it reduces the gains or if an election has been made to use 31 March 1982 value for all assets. Whilst the chargeable gains may be correspondingly less, the same principles apply.

Other factors

The disadvantages of selling assets may be mitigated if the company has current (as distinct from brought-forward) trading losses which may be set off against the gains on the assets.

If it is intended that the company shall continue trading in some new venture rather than be wound up, it may be possible to roll over or hold over the gains by the purchase of new assets. Alternatively, if the new trade commences before the old trade ceases, trading losses may arise in that new trade against which the gains may be set under the normal rules for set-off of trading losses.

Paying a dividend out of accumulated profits

Advance corporation tax on dividends can be set off against corporation tax on any profits, including capital gains, and if the maximum ACT set-off has not been made by the company in the previous six years, then to the extent that a dividend could be paid without creating unrelieved ACT, the net amount received by the vendor could be increased. See example 3. The overall effect of paying dividends would, however, need to be considered very carefully.

Example 3

If in examples 1 and 2 the accumulated profits of £99,000 were distributed as a dividend in September 1996, and the ACT of £24,750 was fully recoverable against corporation tax liabilities of earlier years, the after-tax benefit to the shareholders would in either case be:

	£
Higher rate tax on (99,000 + tax credit (¼) 24,750 =)	
£123,750 @ (40% – 20%)	24,750
Compared with capital gains tax @ 40%	
if £99,000 included in a distribution on liquidation	39,360
	£14,610

Capital gains tax retirement relief

Shareholders over age 50 (55 for disposals before 28 November 1995) who are directors or employees working full-time in a managerial or technical capacity and owning 5% or more of the voting rights are entitled to complete exemption on chargeable gains up to a maximum £250,000 and on a maximum of one-half of the gains between £250,000 and £1,000,000. The gain on which relief is given is restricted to the business assets proportion of the gain on the shares if the company's assets include shares in other companies or other investments, but on a disposal of shares in the holding company of a family trading group, it is the group's assets that are taken into account and holdings of shares in other group companies are ignored. If there are no chargeable assets at all there is no restriction on the relief. In some circumstances a small amount of investment assets could eliminate the relief altogether (see example 4). This problem could be overcome by disposing of the investment assets before the sale of the company.

Example 4

Company's assets before sale are:

	£
Quoted shares	500
Net current assets	249,500
	250,000

Since there are chargeable assets but no chargeable business assets, the business assets proportion of any gain on disposal of the company is nil, so retirement relief is not available. If, however, the shares were sold prior to the sale, there would be no restriction on the available retirement relief.

There is no difference in the retirement relief available to a shareholder on a sale of shares and a return of monies through a liquidation. Retirement relief is available in both cases on the business assets proportion of the shareholder's gain. The return of funds to the shareholder on a liquidation will still be less because of the corporation tax paid by the company on the sale of assets. A shareholder whose retirement relief would eliminate his gains would, however, prefer to receive funds on a liquidation rather than an income dividend. There may be a problem in reconciling the best interests of different shareholders where not all of them are entitled to retirement relief. Retirement relief is not available to the company itself, irrespective of the age of the shareholders, as distinct from its being available to each shareholder depending upon age, participation in the company and the length of time for which the shares have been held.

If the controlling shareholders personally own the premises from which the company's business is carried on, retirement relief is given on any gain on the disposal of the premises at the time of a share disposal or a return of monies to the shareholders on a liquidation. The relief is, however, restricted if the company pays rent, and if the rent is the full market rent, no relief is available.

In some husband/wife companies, retirement relief may be increased by appropriate transfers of shares between them. This should be done well in advance of the disposal of the company, otherwise it may be vulnerable to attack on anti-avoidance grounds. See examples 5 and 6.

Payments in compensation for loss of office

Compensation and ex gratia payments are dealt with in detail in chapter 15. There are two aspects, first whether the director/shareholder will be exempt from tax on the first £30,000 of the payment, and second whether the payment will be deductible as an expense against the company profits.

As far as the individual is concerned, in order for the £30,000 exemption to apply, the company must be able to demonstrate that any payments are wholly unassociated with a sale of the individual's shares in the company and moreover do not represent an income dividend. Ex gratia payments may also be challenged as being benefits under an unapproved retirement benefits scheme (see page 222).

As far as the company is concerned, the company must show that the payments are wholly and exclusively for the purposes of the trade, which is more difficult if the payment is ex gratia rather than compensation for loss of office. Where the company's trade ceases following a sale of the assets, an ex gratia or compensation payment cannot satisfy the 'wholly and exclusively' rule because there is no longer any trade. The part of the company's payment that can be set against the company's trading profits in those circumstances

Example 5

Husband and wife are both over 50 and both have owned 50% of the shares in their family trading company for 20 years, but wife has only worked part-time. Total gains on the shares are expected to be £250,000.

If no action is taken, husband's gains of £125,000 would be exempt. Wife's gains of £125,000 would be fully chargeable.

If wife transferred her shares to husband, the full gains of £250,000 would be exempt.

The same would apply if both had worked full-time but only one was over 50.

Example 6

Husband and wife have run their family trading company for 20 years and are both over 50 and both work full-time, but husband owns 90% of the shares and wife 10%. Total gains on the shares are expected to be £1,000,000.

If no action is taken, husband will be exempt on gains of £250,000 and will get 50% relief on the remaining £650,000, and wife will be exempt on gains of £100,000. If shareholdings are equalised, each will be exempt on £250,000 and get 50% relief on the remaining £250,000.

This would not have been possible if the wife had owned less than 5% of the shares, since she needs to have held at least 5% for 10 years to get the full relief.

is limited to the amount of statutory redundancy pay to which the director is entitled plus a sum equal to three times that amount (see page 223). Where a compensation or ex gratia payment is made prior to a sale of the shares, the company's trade continuing, this restriction will not apply.

Whether there is a sale of the shares or an assets sale followed by a liquidation, the compensation payment will reduce the value of the company's assets, and thus the amount of disposal proceeds on which the shareholder's capital gains tax liability will be calculated.

Payments into a pension scheme

Prior to selling the shares, the cash resources of the company, and thus, effectively, the eventual sale proceeds, may also be reduced by an appropriate pension scheme contribution, the benefits of which may be taken partly as a tax-free lump sum and partly as a pension. Again, the trading profits prior to the sale are reduced, with a corresponding saving in corporation tax. This is of course only acceptable if the levels of contributions and benefits payable are within the stipulated limits. Company pension schemes are dealt with in chapter 16.

Selling on the basis of receiving shares in the purchasing company (TCGA 1992, ss 126–140 and Sch 6 para 2)

Where, as consideration for the sale of their shares, the vending shareholders receive shares in the company making the acquisition, then each vending shareholder is normally treated as not having made a disposal of the 'old shares', but as having acquired the 'new shares' for the same amount and on the same date as the 'old shares'.

Where the consideration is part shares/part cash, that part received in cash is liable to capital gains tax, whilst the 'new shares' again stand in the shoes of the old. See example 7.

Example 7

Shares cost £1,000. As a result of an acquisition of the entire share capital by another company, the shareholder receives cash of £4,000 and shares in the acquiring company valued at £6,000. The capital gains position is:

	Cash £	Shares £
Cost of £1,000, divided in proportion to the proceeds	400	600
Proceeds:		
Cash	4,000	4,000
New shares	6,000	
Total consideration	10,000	
Chargeable gain (subject to indexation allowance and available exemptions)	£3,600	
Cost of 'new shares'		£600

Where part of the consideration depends upon future performance, say the issue of further shares or securities if a profit target is met, the value of the right to receive further shares is itself part of the disposal proceeds at the time the original shares are sold, and it is not strictly covered by the rules allowing the new shares to stand in the shoes of the old. By concession D27, the Revenue will allow the taxpayer to claim that the later shares or securities are part of the original transaction so that any capital gains are rolled over until the shares or securities are sold. The concession does not apply if the future consideration is cash. In that event, the whole of the right to future consideration is liable to capital gains tax at the time of the sale, with a further liability on the difference between that value and the consideration itself when it is received.

Where the vendor is entitled to retirement relief, he can claim that the provisions treating the new shares as standing in the shoes of the old do not apply, so that he can realise gains to use the retirement relief. He cannot, however, do this for only some of the shares which he has received in exchange. He may therefore be left with an immediate capital gains tax bill on any balance of gains over the retirement relief available, even though he has not received any cash.

Stamp duty

Stamp duty will normally be payable on the consideration whether the sale is of assets or shares. The rate of duty payable on the sale of shares by the shareholder is ½%. The duty on assets sold by the company would normally be at 1%.

Stamp duty on the sale of assets can only be reduced to the extent that assets may be transferred by delivery, such as plant and machinery, or where the vendor company does not assign its debtors but appoints the purchaser as its agent to collect the debts.

Value added tax (VATA 1994, ss 49, 94, Sch 9 Group 5; SI 1992/3129, para 5; SI 1995/2518, paras 5, 6)

Where the family company is sold by means of a share sale, the sale does not attract value added tax because the shares are not sold in the course of business but by an individual as an investment.

Where all or part of the business is sold as a going concern by one taxable person to another, no value added tax is charged by the vendor and the purchaser has no input tax to reclaim on the amount paid (subject to the exception stated on page 386 for land and buildings). The going concern treatment only applies, however, where the assets acquired are such that they represent a business which is capable of independent operation.

Where the 'going concern' concept does not apply, value added tax must be charged on all taxable supplies, and any related input tax suffered by the seller will be recoverable. Taxable supplies will include goodwill, stock, plant and machinery, and motor vehicles (except that cars on which input tax was not recovered when they were acquired will only be chargeable to the extent, if any, that the disposal proceeds exceed original cost). Business premises on which the seller has exercised his option to tax will also be included, and the seller can therefore recover any VAT relating to the costs of sale, for example on legal and professional fees. The disposal of book debts, and of business premises over three years old on which the option to tax has not been taken, is an exempt supply and does not attract VAT. For partially exempt businesses there are some complex rules as to how the sale of the business is treated.

It is important to ensure that the purchase agreement provides for the addition of value added tax and that the purchase consideration is allocated over the various assets acquired. If value added tax is not mentioned in the purchase agreement, the price is deemed to be VAT-inclusive.

Tax points

- When a company ceases to trade, this denotes the end of a chargeable accounting period, and if there are current trading losses these cannot be relieved against chargeable gains arising after the cessation. But gains are deemed to be made on the contract date, not on completion, so if the company enters into the contract for sale of the chargeable assets while it is still trading, the right to set off current trading losses against chargeable gains in that trading period will be preserved.

- ACT must relate to a dividend paid in a 'chargeable accounting period' in order for a company to be able to set it off against earlier corporation tax liabilities. If a dividend is paid after a trade has ceased, make sure that the company still has some chargeable income, such as interest on bank deposits.

- Compensation for loss of office and ex gratia payments upon cessation of employment can only be expected to escape Revenue challenge if they are genuine payments for breach of contract or reasonable ex gratia amounts bearing in mind years of service, etc. and even so, ex gratia payments may not qualify for the £30,000 exemption (see page 394 and chapter 15).

- When selling shares in a family company with significant retained profits, the Revenue may argue that the increased share value as a result of the retained profits represents not a capital gain but sums that should have been paid out as income, and that they are chargeable as such. Whilst the rate of capital gains tax is now the same as that for income tax, retirement relief and reinvestment relief will only be available against a capital gain. You should therefore ensure that Revenue clearance is obtained for the proposed sale. On the other hand, income can be sheltered by investment in an enterprise zone building, whereas a chargeable gain cannot.

- When buying the shares in a company, you should look particularly for any potential capital gains liabilities which will be inherited, such as the crystallisation after ten years of gains on depreciating business assets which have been held over because the company acquired new qualifying assets, or, if the company you are purchasing is leaving a group, the crystallisation of gains on assets acquired by it from another group company within the previous six years. Moreover, the accounts value of the company assets may be greater than the tax value because earlier gains have been deducted under the rollover relief provisions from the tax cost of the assets now held or the assets have been revalued for accounts purposes. Thus a chargeable gain may arise on the company even though the item is sold for no more than its value in the accounts.

- If you buy a company with unused trading losses or surplus advance corporation tax, you will not be able to use them when you restore the company to profitability if the change of ownership takes place within a period of three years during which there is also a major change in the nature or conduct of the business. There is also a restriction on availability of trading losses where the company being acquired has succeeded to the trade of another company without taking over that other company's liabilities (see page 378).

- The capital gains retirement relief is available to sole traders, partners and qualifying shareholders. It is not available to reduce gains that a company makes on a sale of chargeable assets prior to liquidation of the company.

- If a company has investment assets, retirement relief is restricted, or possibly not available at all — see page 393.

- The share capital in a family company is sometimes sold on the basis that the family shareholders receive shares in the purchaser company in exchange. In these circumstances, the new shares take the place of the old shares in the personal capital gains tax position of the vendor shareholders, and no capital gains tax is payable at that time. A proportionate part of the gain is chargeable where the purchase consideration is part cash/part new shares. If you are eligible for retirement relief, try to ensure that sufficient cash is received to use the retirement relief available. Alternatively, you can claim for the gain on the shares not to be rolled over by reference to the shares received in exchange, but this may leave you with an immediately chargeable gain if the retirement relief does not fully cover it.

- The purchase consideration may partly depend on the company's future profit performance, sometimes referred to as an 'earn out', and when it is received it may be partly in cash and partly in the form of shares in the purchasing company. The capital gains tax position is complicated and professional advisers have to look very carefully at this aspect, if possible obtaining the views of the Revenue when they apply for clearance on the share sale.

- To get the maximum retirement relief, you need to have been in business for a total of ten years either as a sole trader, partner or full-time director or employee of a trading company in which you own 5% or more of the voting power. Although the disposal date for capital gains tax is the date of the contract, you are allowed to count the period up to completion as part of the ten-year period if the business activities continue up to the completion date.

● A private company may avoid the costs of putting a company into formal liquidation by distributing the assets and then having the company struck off the companies register as a defunct company. (The procedure for doing this has been formalised and simplified from 1 July 1995.) Although strictly the distribution of assets in these circumstances is an income distribution on which the shareholders would be liable for income tax, the Revenue will usually agree to treat it as if it were a capital distribution in a formal liquidation (concession C16). It is essential to get the formal approval of the company's tax district, which will require certain undertakings.

● Because there are so many pitfalls and problems when selling or buying a family company, it is essential to get expert professional advice.

● Retirement relief is still available where your family business is run through a number of companies which have been associated with each other, even though you cannot be said to have worked full-time for any of them because of your involvement with them all.

29
Encouraging business efficiency

Background

There are specific tax provisions to encourage investment in new and expanding companies and to enable companies that have become unwieldy to split into smaller units without adverse tax consequences. There are also specific provisions covering the purchase by a company of its own shares, enabling a company to resolve conflicts with disaffected shareholders by buying them out, and also making investment under the Government schemes more attractive through enabling the investor to withdraw his funds after the appropriate period.

Although the aims are reasonable, the provisions are for the most part extremely complex and regarded by some as unnecessarily restrictive. This chapter gives only an outline of the provisions, professional advice being essential.

Enterprise investment scheme (TA 1988, ss 289–312; FA 1994, s 137 and Sch 15; FA 1995, ss 66, 67 and Sch 13; FA 1996, s 134(3), Sch 20 paras 22, 23 and Sch 21 para 7)

The enterprise investment scheme ('EIS') was introduced from 1 January 1994 to replace the business expansion scheme ('BES'). The chief drawback to the EIS is that income tax relief is given only at 20%, rather than at the investor's marginal rate as with the BES. Unlike the BES, the EIS does not cover investment in private rented housing. In some respects, however, the EIS provisions are less restrictive.

Relief is given where a 'qualifying individual' subscribes for 'eligible shares' in a 'qualifying company' carrying on, or intending to carry on, a 'qualifying business activity'. The definition of these terms is complex, but is broadly as follows. A 'qualifying individual' is one who is not 'connected' with the company, which mainly excludes someone who is an employee or director, or who controls more than 30% of its capital. (Someone who was not connected with the company before the shares were issued may, however, become a paid director without affecting his entitlement to relief.) Non-residents are eligible, but the reliefs can only be given against UK tax liabilities. Eligible shares are new ordinary shares that are not redeemable for at least five years. A 'qualifying company' carrying on a qualifying business activity is an unquoted trading company carrying on business wholly or mainly in the UK whose trading activities are not specifically excluded. Shares on the Unlisted Securities Market (USM) do not count as unquoted shares, but shares on the Alternative Investment Market (AIM) are treated as unquoted. Companies that do not qualify include those providing finance, legal and accountancy services and leasing. The relief is subject to detailed anti-avoidance provisions.

Claims for relief cannot be made until a certificate has been received from the company, issued on the authority of an inspector of taxes, stating that the relevant conditions have been satisfied. The time limit for claiming the relief is five years from the 31 January following the tax year in which the shares are issued. If any of the requirements for a 'qualifying individual' or 'qualifying company' are breached during a 'relevant period' (broadly, in the five or three years respectively after the issue of the shares), the relief will be withdrawn.

Limitation on the raising of funds

There is a limit of £1 million on the amount any company can raise in one tax year or within six months of an earlier issue in a previous tax year (increased to £5 million for ship operating or chartering companies).

Amount of relief

The maximum amount on which an individual can claim relief in any tax year is £100,000, this limit being available to each of husband and wife. Relief is given in the tax year when the shares are purchased, but one-half of the amount subscribed before 6 October in any tax year can be carried back for relief in the previous tax year, up to a maximum carry-back of £15,000. (From 1996/97, although the tax saving from the carry-back claim will be calculated by reference to the tax position of the earlier year, it will reduce the tax liability of the tax year in which the shares are subscribed for, so that any interest on overpaid tax will run only from the payment date for that year — see page 119.) The claim for carry-back must be made at the same time as the claim for relief, and the carry-back cannot increase the relief for a tax year to more than £100,000. The minimum subscription by an individual to one company is £500 except where the investment is made through an investment fund approved by the Revenue. Income tax relief is given at 20% in calculating the individual's income tax liability for the year.

Withdrawal of relief

The shares must be held for a minimum of five years, otherwise the relief is withdrawn completely if the disposal is not at arm's length and the tax saving is lost on the amount received for an arm's length bargain. Relief is also withdrawn if the individual receives value from the company within that time. 'Value' is exhaustively defined and includes the repayment of loans that had been made to the company before the shares were subscribed for, provision of benefits, and purchase of assets for less than market value.

An amount received in respect of an option to sell EIS shares will cause the loss of an appropriate amount of relief, but an arrangement to sell them (say to the controlling shareholders) after the qualifying five-year period will not.

Capital gains exemption for EIS shares (TCGA 1992, s 150A; FA 1994, Sch 15 para 30; FA 1995, Sch 13 para 2)

There is no charge to capital gains tax if shares for which EIS relief has been given are disposed of at a profit after the five year retention period (except to the extent that gains become chargeable under the reinvestment relief provisions outlined below). Where shares are disposed of at a loss, any EIS relief that has not been withdrawn is deducted from the allowable cost. A loss can be relieved either against chargeable gains, or against income (under the provisions outlined on page 531).

Example 1	
	£
Cost of shares acquired under EIS	10,000
Income tax relief at 20%	2,000
Net cost of investment	8,000
Disposed of six years later for	6,500
Cost net of EIS relief	8,000
Loss available for relief	£1,500

Where shares have been acquired at different times, disposals are identified with shares acquired earlier rather than later. If any of the earlier disposals qualified for BES relief, or the earlier business start-up relief, those disposals are identified first with business start-up shares, and then with BES shares, before any other shares.

Capital gains EIS reinvestment relief (TCGA 1992, s 150C and Sch 5B; FA 1995, 13 Sch para 4)

A claim may be made for all or any part of a chargeable gain on the disposal of *any* asset (or a chargeable gain arising under the venture capital trust provisions — see page 528) to be deferred to the extent that it is matched by a subscription for EIS shares within one year before and three years after the disposal. The relief is only available if the investor is resident and ordinarily resident in the UK. The deferred gain (as distinct from the gain on the EIS shares, which is considered separately) becomes chargeable on the disposal of the shares, other than to a spouse, or if the investor becomes non-resident within 5 years of acquiring the shares, or ceases to qualify for the EIS relief, or the company ceases to qualify within 3 years. The deferred gain is not triggered if the investor (or spouse to whom the shares have been transferred) dies.

Where the gain is triggered, it may be further deferred by another EIS investment (or investment in a venture capital trust — see page 528, or under the general reinvestment relief provisions — see page 62) if the conditions are satisfied.

Withdrawal of investment after relevant period

Potential investors may see a disadvantage in their being locked in as minority shareholders. The company may, however, build up reserves by retaining profits, and use the reserves to purchase its own shares after the five-year period, using the rules described below.

Venture capital trusts

Those who wish to support new and expanding companies but are unwilling to invest directly in unquoted shares may obtain similar relief to that available under the EIS through venture capital trusts. These trusts invest in unquoted companies but are themselves quoted (see page 528).

Purchase by company of its own shares (TA 1988, ss 219–229)

Where an unquoted trading company or the unquoted holding company of a trading group buys back its own shares (or redeems them or makes a payment for them in a reduction of capital) in order to benefit a trade, the transaction is not treated as a distribution, and thus liable to income tax in the hands of the vending shareholder, with the company being liable for advance corporation tax, but as a disposal on which the vending shareholder is liable to capital gains tax. This does not apply if there is an arrangement the main purpose of which is to get undistributed profits into the hands of the shareholders without incurring the tax liabilities on a distribution.

The main requirements are that the shareholder must be UK-resident, he must normally have owned the shares for at least five years, and he must either dispose of his entire holding or the holding must be 'substantially reduced'.

A company may apply to the Revenue for a clearance that the proposed purchase will not be treated as a distribution.

Any legal costs and other expenditure incurred by a company in purchasing its own shares will not be allowable against the company's profits.

Management buyouts

The provisions enabling a company to purchase its own shares could assist a management buyout team to acquire the company for which they work, in that only shares remaining after those bought in by the company need then be acquired by them.

If only part of a trade is to be acquired, the existing company could transfer the requisite assets into a subsidiary company using the reconstruction provisions of TA 1988, s 343, the buyout team then buying the shares in the subsidiary.

Alternatively, if the buyout team form an entirely new company and purchase assets from their employing company, capital allowances will be available where appropriate and the new company may be able to raise some of the funds it needs through the enterprise investment scheme, or by attracting investments from venture capital trusts (see page 528) or from individuals who wish to shelter capital gains by reinvesting them in a qualifying trading company (see page 62).

Demergers (TA 1988, ss 213–218)

The aim of the demerger legislation is to remove various tax obstacles to demergers, so that businesses grouped inefficiently under a single company umbrella may be run more dynamically and effectively by being allowed to pursue their separate ways under independent management. The detailed provisions are very complex, the following being an outline.

A company is not treated as having made a distribution for corporation tax purposes (and the members are not treated as having received income) where the company transfers to its members the shares of a 75% subsidiary, or transfers a trade to a new company in exchange for that new company issuing shares to some or all of the transferor company's shareholders.

In order for these provisions to apply, all the companies must be UK-resident trading companies, the transfer must be made to benefit some or all of the trading activities, and the transfer must not be made for tax avoidance reasons.

The distribution by the holding company of shares in subsidiaries to its members is also not treated as a capital distribution for capital gains tax purposes, and the capital gains charge when a company leaves a group on assets acquired within the previous six years from other group companies (see page 610) does not apply.

There are detailed anti-avoidance provisions, and there is also provision to apply for Revenue clearance of proposed transactions.

Enterprise zones

Certain areas in which the Government particularly wants to encourage investment have been designated as enterprise zones. Those who set up business within an enterprise zone get certain advantages for a limited number of years, such as not paying business rates and entitlement to 100% relief for expenditure on buildings for use in the trade. The relief for expenditure on buildings is also available to landlords and is dealt with in chapter 22. If you are considering buying a building in an enterprise zone, make appropriate comparisons to ensure that the cost is not higher because of tax relief on construction expenditure and the other known advantages of operating from a designated area.

It used to be possible to dispose of your investment in an enterprise zone building without losing the benefit of the 100% allowances by granting a lesser interest, such as a long lease, rather than selling. This is no longer possible, because such a disposal now triggers the withdrawal of the allowance (see page 315).

Other measures to stimulate business enterprise (TA 1988, ss 79, 79A)

Businesses may claim a deduction from their profits for contributions they make up to 31 March 2000 to local enterprise agencies, training and enterprise councils (TECs), Scottish local enterprise companies and business link organisations.

Local enterprise agencies are bodies approved by the Secretary of State that promote local industrial and commercial activity and enterprise, particularly in forming and developing small businesses. TECs are private companies whose directors are mainly local businessmen. They work under contract to the Department of Employment's Training Agency and are mainly concerned with Government training programmes. Scottish local enterprise companies are similar to TECs but cover economic development and environmental functions as well as training. Business link organisations are authorised by the Department of Trade and Industry to use the 'Business Links' service mark and provide a single point of access for TECs, local enterprise agencies, chambers of commerce and local authorities.

Tax points

- The detailed conditions and anti-avoidance rules in relation to most of the provisions dealt with in this chapter are too extensive to deal with in detail, but should be looked at carefully by interested companies and investors.

● Although qualifying companies or fund managers will issue certificates to individuals investing under the enterprise investment scheme, each individual must make a specific claim for income tax relief to his own tax district within the time limit indicated on page 402. Capital gains relief for reinvestment in EIS shares must also be claimed, but no time limit is specified, so the general time limit of 6 years (5 years 10 months under self-assessment from 1996/97) will apply.

● When you reinvest gains into EIS shares, you can effectively get up to 60% tax relief at that time (20% income tax relief on the shares and 40% capital gains relief on the deferred gains for a higher rate taxpayer). Although the capital gains relief is only a deferral, further deferral may be possible when the deferred gains are triggered. The gains may eventually become chargeable unless they have not been triggered before your death.

● You cannot get EIS reliefs if you are connected with the company. Relief from capital gains tax on reinvested gains may be available instead under the general reinvestment relief outlined on page 62, but no income tax relief is available.

● Shares in USM companies do not qualify for EIS relief, but shares in companies on the Alternative Investment Market (AIM) are treated as unquoted, so EIS relief is available providing the company is a qualifying company.

● The Revenue will not usually give a clearance under the demerger provisions where companies in the same ownership are first merged and then demerged so that each company ends up in the ownership of independent people.

30
Your family home

General

The tax system encourages you to own your own home by usually exempting any capital gain when you sell it and by giving relief for interest paid on loans up to a maximum of £30,000 to buy it, although the rate of tax relief on the interest is now only 15%. The £30,000 is a joint limit for husband and wife. For loans after 31 July 1988 to unmarried home sharers, it applies to the property and not each individual borrower. An unmarried couple will retain relief on up to £60,000 borrowed on or before 31 July 1988, but will be restricted to the joint £30,000 limit if they move house, or remortgage the property. Where there is more than one loan, relief is given on the earliest loans first, and when the total qualifying loans exceed £30,000 no relief is given on the excess. Relief is not available on home improvement loans. If, however, you obtained such a loan before 6 April 1988, you continue to get relief so long as the borrowing falls within the £30,000 overall limit. You will lose this relief if you remortgage the property. The disallowance of home improvement loans stops you getting interest relief if you borrow to undertake a 'do-it-yourself' conversion of non-residential or derelict property, such as a barn. You can, however, reclaim the VAT on the building materials.

If the loan is not used for a qualifying purpose, then even if it is from a building society and secured on the house, it will not qualify for relief.

You can sometimes get relief from capital gains tax and for income tax on interest payments for a property you intend to occupy in the future, and for those already occupied by a dependent relative at 5 April 1988 (see page 409). Interest and capital gains relief is also sometimes available on existing loans in respect of a property occupied at 5 April 1988 by a former or separated spouse — see chapter 33. The £30,000 interest relief limit is an umbrella figure, however, that must cover all such qualifying loans to one borrower, and in all cases relief is now restricted to the 15% rate of tax.

If you are 65 or over, you can get relief for interest on up to £30,000 of a loan secured on your home that you use to buy a life annuity (see page 478). The rate of tax relief on such interest is 24%.

Leasehold reform

Where flat tenants buy their freeholds under the new leasehold reform provisions, various tax points need to be borne in mind, particularly where some tenants buy and some do not. Someone has to be responsible for dealing with the tax on any income, such as ground rents and interest on the maintenance fund, and there are also capital gains tax considerations. Professional advice is essential.

Buying and not moving in immediately (TA 1988, s 355)

If you do not move into your house immediately, you still get tax relief on interest on a loan to buy it providing you move in within twelve months after the making of the loan. (See also page 418 re job-related accommodation and page 420 re bridging loans.)

For capital gains purposes, the Revenue will, by concession, allow you to treat any non-occupation in the first twelve months as covered by your owner occupier exemption if you do not move in because you are having the property built, or you are altering or redecorating the property, or because you remain in your old home while you are selling it.

Empty property may be liable to council tax, but newly built or structurally altered property is not subject to the tax for up to six months after the work is substantially completed, and there is no charge on any unfurnished property for up to six months.

Dwelling occupied by a dependent relative (TA 1988, s 355(1)(a); FA 1988, s 44; TCGA 1992, s 226)

If on 5 April 1988 you owned a property that has been continuously occupied rent-free by a dependent relative since that date, the property is exempt from capital gains tax when you dispose of it. Payment of council tax by the relative does not affect the exemption. Relief is also available for interest on borrowing to buy the property (and on borrowing for any other property similarly occupied) so long as your total qualifying loans are within the £30,000 borrowing ceiling.

Relief for interest will not continue if there is a change of occupant after 5 April 1988 even if the new occupant is also a dependent relative. The same applies to the capital gains tax exemption, but the period from 31 March 1982 which did qualify for the exemption is taken into account in calculating any chargeable gain.

'Dependent relative' is defined as your own or your spouse's widowed mother, or any other relative unable to look after themselves because of old age or infirmity. There is no income restriction.

See page 476 for a tax-effective way of providing a home for a dependent relative now.

If your home is let (TCGA 1992, s 223(4); F(No 2)A 1992, s 59 and Sch 10)

Income tax

A 'rent a room' relief is available for owner-occupiers and tenants who let furnished rooms in their only or main residence. You must occupy the property as your main home at the same time as the tenant for at least part of the letting period in each tax year. The relief is available both where the rent comes under the 'Schedule A business' rules (see page 444) and where substantial services are also provided so that the rent is charged as trading income (see chapter 21). (If you let part of your property unfurnished in the same year, however, the relief cannot be claimed.) No tax will be payable if the gross rents for the tax year, before deducting expenses, do not exceed £3,250. If the letting is by a couple, the relief is £1,625 each. The rent taken into account for the relief is the payment for the accommodation plus payments for meals, cleaning, laundry, etc. It is not clear whether a separate contribution from the tenant towards council tax, light and heat and telephone counts as rent, but it is arguable that such contributions need not be taken into account. You can claim for the relief not to apply for a particular year, for example if your expenses exceed your rent and you want to claim relief for a loss. The time limit for the claim for years before 1996/97 is one year after the end of the relevant tax year, extended from 1996/97 to one year from 31 January following the end of the relevant tax year (or longer at the Revenue's discretion). If your rent exceeds £3,250, you can choose to pay tax either on the excess over £3,250 or on the rent less expenses under the normal rules described below. If you want to pay on the excess over £3,250 you must make a claim to do so, and that basis will then apply until you withdraw your claim. The time limit for such a claim is the same as that for electing for the relief not to apply at all.

If the 'rent a room' relief does not apply, then unless the letting amounts to a trade (see above), the letting income is chargeable to income tax along with other letting income, if any, after setting off appropriate expenses (see page 444). It is normally treated as unearned income, but if the letting qualifies as furnished holiday accommodation (see page 451), the income is treated as trading income, and can therefore support a self-employed pension premium (see chapter 17). For the treatment of mortgage interest when you let part of your home, see page 413.

Capital gains tax

As far as the capital gains exemption is concerned, the last three years of ownership always count as a period of residence (see page 419), so if you move out and let the property during that time it will not affect your exemption. You would also get relief for interest paid on the whole of your borrowing during that time against your rents (not under the MIRAS scheme), at your top tax rate and with no £30,000 restriction (see page 444).

If you live in the property while letting part of it, your capital gains exemption is not affected if the letting takes the form of boarders who effectively live as part of the family. Where, however, the letting extends beyond this, or you let the whole property, other than during the last three years of ownership or during another allowable absence period (see page 419), the appropriate fraction of the gain on disposal is chargeable but there is an exemption of the smaller of £40,000 and an amount equal to the exempt gain on the owner-occupied part.

Example 1

The gain on the sale of a dwelling in 1996/97 is £80,000. The agreed proportion applicable to the let part is £48,000, the exempt gain being £32,000.

The £48,000 gain on the let part is reduced by the lower of

(a) £40,000 and
(b) an amount equal to the exempt gain, i.e. £32,000.

Therefore a further £32,000 is exempt and £16,000 is chargeable (but the £6,300 annual exemption will reduce the gain still further if not already used).

Where a married couple jointly let part of the home, each is entitled to the residential lettings exemption of up to £40,000.

The exemption is not available if the let part of the property is effectively a separate dwelling, such as a self-contained flat with its own access. But where part of the home is let, without substantial structural alterations, it will qualify, even if it has separate facilities.

The Revenue have taken the view that the residential lettings exemption is only available where the letting has some degree of permanence, but they have lost a case on the point in the Court of Appeal, where it was decided that the exemption was available to the owners of a small private hotel who occupied the whole of the property during the winter months, with one or two guests, but moved to an annexe during the summer. The exemption can be claimed only if the property qualifies as your capital gains tax exempt residence for at least part of your period of ownership, so it cannot be claimed on a property which, although you live in it sometimes, has never been your only or main residence for capital gains tax purposes. Subject to that, it can be claimed where all of the property has been let for part of your period of ownership, or part of the property has been let for all or part of your period of ownership.

The position of furnished holiday lettings (see page 451) is not clear. Gains on such property are specifically eligible for rollover relief when the property is sold and replaced, but providing you comply with the rules outlined above, it would seem that the residential lettings exemption could apply instead. To continue to get the other benefits of the furnished holiday lettings provisions, you would have to make sure that you complied with the rules for such lettings (in particular ensuring that neither you nor anyone else normally occupied the accommodation for a continuous period of more than 31 days for at least seven months of the year).

Council tax and business rates

If the let part of your property is self-contained living accommodation that counts as a separate dwelling, the tenants will be liable to pay the council tax. But for any period when it is not anyone's only or main home, for example when it is untenanted, you will be liable to pay 50% of the council tax (subject to certain exemptions, for example unfurnished property for up to six months — see page 111). If the let part of your home is not self-contained, you will be liable to pay the council tax, but you will usually include an appropriate amount in the rent to cover the proportion applicable to the tenants. If you do not live in the property while it is let, the council tax will be paid by tenants who occupy it as their main home, except for multi-occupied property such as bed-sits, where you will remain liable. If the let part is let as short-term living accommodation, and is therefore no-one's only or main home, you will pay 50% of the council tax unless the property is available for short-term letting for 140 days or more in a year (for example self-catering holiday accommodation), in which case you will pay business rates instead. If you offer bed and breakfast facilities in your own home, you will not be liable to business rates providing you do not offer accommodation for more than six people, you live in the house at the same time and the house is still mainly used as your home. If part of your home is let for business purposes rather than as living accommodation, business rates will be payable on that part.

Any council tax or business rates paid on let property will be deducted from the rent in arriving at your taxable letting income.

How relief is given for allowable interest (TA 1988, ss 353–358, 366–379; FA 1994, s 81 and Sch 9; FA 1996, s 76)

Most loans for home buying are now covered by the Mortgage Interest Relief At Source (MIRAS) scheme, which applies to the first £30,000 of qualifying loans, but some lenders are not authorised to operate the scheme.

If the loan falls within the MIRAS scheme, you deduct income tax at 15% when paying the interest, so that for gross interest of £1,000 you pay a net amount of £850. If you are over 65 and the loan is to buy a life annuity (see page 478) the tax relief is at 24%, so that for gross interest of £1,000 you would pay £760 net.

For loans above £30,000 made after 5 April 1987, MIRAS applies to the first £30,000 and the interest on the balance above £30,000 is paid in full. Lenders do not have to include loans above £30,000 made on or before 5 April 1987 in the MIRAS scheme, although they may do so if they wish. In any event, an increase above the £30,000 limit of up to £1,000 due solely to the addition of unpaid interest is ignored and the loan remains within the MIRAS scheme. When the balance on a loan falls below the £30,000 limit, the interest is brought within the MIRAS scheme from the beginning of the following tax year if MIRAS is not already in operation on the allowable part of the loan.

For loans outside MIRAS, interest has to be paid in full and the tax relief has to be claimed. This will normally be done in your tax return and the relief will be given by coding adjustment or by reducing the amount of tax payable on your income. A certificate of interest paid, supplied by the lender, is essential in these cases.

Non-taxpayers benefit from the MIRAS scheme because they are allowed to retain the tax deducted. Non-taxpayers whose home loans are not within MIRAS cannot get any tax relief for the interest.

Where part of your property is let or used for business, strictly the interest on the loan cannot be split. By concession A89, the Revenue allow such a loan to be treated as two separate loans. Relief for the private proportion is given at 15% as a reduction of your tax bill (restricted to relief on £30,000 if the private proportion of the loan is higher than £30,000). Relief for the balance is given by setting it against the business profit or letting income as the case may be, thus saving tax at your top tax rate with no restriction on the amount of the loan. Where you have a MIRAS loan, the loan cannot remain in MIRAS if more than one-third of the home is used for business or letting. You would have to notify the lender if that applied, the loan would then be taken out of MIRAS and you would claim relief for both parts of the loan as indicated above.

A loan may remain in MIRAS if the one-third limit is not exceeded. You then need to make a claim to get the extra relief for the non-residential proportion over and above any relief at 15% retained under MIRAS. If the proportion of the loan relating to the residence is £30,000 or more, the whole of the MIRAS relief will relate to the residential use, and relief will be available in full for the business or let proportion of the interest. If, however, the proportion of the loan relating to the residence is less than £30,000, some of the MIRAS relief will relate to the business or let proportion, and this will have to be taken into account in calculating the relief due at your top tax rate for the interest deduction against the business or letting income (see examples 2 and 3). The adjustment is rather complicated, as the examples show. It is not clear how this will be done under self-assessment, but the simplest way would be to deduct the relevant amount of interest in full from the business or letting income, and then increase the final amount of tax payable by the tax saving already obtained through the MIRAS scheme. If this were done for the MIRAS loan in the first part of example 3, £1,000 would be deducted from rent, saving tax of £240. The final figure of tax payable would then be increased by £21.

Example 2

MIRAS loan at or below £30,000

15% relief will be given on *all* the interest. If, say, 1/4 of the property was used for business, extra relief would be due on 1/4 of the interest at (20% – 15% =) 5% for a lower rate taxpayer, (24% – 15% =) 9% for a basic rate taxpayer and (40% – 15% =) 25% for a higher rate taxpayer, and at an intermediate rate for someone whose income straddled two different rate bands.

MIRAS loan above £30,000 but residential proportion below £30,000

Say loan was £36,000, with 1/4 of the property let, so the loan relating to the residential use would be £27,000 and that relating to the letting £9,000. MIRAS relief would be given on 30/36ths of the interest. 27/30ths of the MIRAS relief would relate to the residential use and 3/30ths to the letting. Relief at the taxpayers's marginal rate on £9,000 would be reduced by 3/30ths of the tax saved through MIRAS.

Residential proportion of MIRAS loan above £30,000

The relief through MIRAS would relate solely to the residence, and full relief would be available on the business/let proportion.

Example 3

One-third of home is let, so home loan to a basic rate taxpayer of £42,000 is split as to £28,000 residential (below the £30,000 limit, therefore relief available on full amount) and £14,000 let proportion. Gross interest in 1996/97 is £3,000.

If loan not in MIRAS

Relief totalling £540 will be claimed in the tax return as follows:

1/3 × £3,000 = £1,000 interest deduction against rental income, saving tax at 24% = £240.
2/3 × £3,000 = £2,000 @ 15% = £300 relating to home loan, deducted from tax payable.

If loan in MIRAS

MIRAS relief will be $\dfrac{30,000}{42,000}$ × £3,000 @ 15% = £321

of which 28/30, i.e. £300, relates to the residential use and 2/30, i.e. £21, to the letting. The balance of relief relating to the letting of (240 – 21) = £219 will be claimed in the tax return.

If one-quarter of the home had been let, the loan would be split as to £31,500 relating to the residence (above the £30,000 limit, therefore relief restricted) and £10,500 relating to the letting. The position would then have been:

If loan not in MIRAS

Relief totalling £501 would be claimed in the tax return as follows:

1/4 × £3,000 = £750 interest deduction against rental income, saving tax at 24% = £180.

$$3/4 \times £3,000 = £2,250 \times \frac{30,000}{31,500} @ 15\% = £321$$

relating to home loan, deducted from tax payable.

If loan in MIRAS

MIRAS relief would be $\dfrac{30,000}{42,000} \times £3,000 @ 15\% = £321$

all of which would relate to the residential use. The relief relating to the letting of £180 would be claimed in the tax return.

Special rules apply if your home is let while you live in job-related accommodation (see page 418) or while you are working away (see page 420).

If you are married and buying your home in joint names, interest is regarded as being paid equally. Now that home loan interest only saves 15% tax, it will not usually make any difference to the joint tax bill who gets the tax relief, but if the loan is outside MIRAS and one of you is a taxpayer and the other is not, you can elect (on form 15(1990) available from the tax office) to have all the interest treated as paid by the taxpaying spouse, no matter how much interest each of you actually pays. For years before 1996/97, the election must be made within twelve months after the end of the tax year to which it first applies, extended from 1996/97 to one year from 31 January following the end of the relevant tax year (or longer at the Revenue's discretion). You can vary your election or withdraw it (on form 15–1(1990)), if you wish, within the same time limit.

See page 468 for the position on separation and divorce.

Interest relief — unmarried home sharers (TA 1988, ss 356A–356D)

For loans made before 1 August 1988, unmarried home sharers could each claim interest relief on a loan of up to £30,000, and can continue to do so providing the loan is still outstanding.

For later loans, the £30,000 limit applies to the property and not to each borrower. The £30,000 limit also applies to loans that replace pre-1 August 1988 loans, and pre-1 August 1988 loans that are re-secured on another property (see page 420). The £30,000 limit is divided between the borrowers in equal shares. Relief cannot be given to one borrower for interest paid by another. It is, however, possible for a borrower who does not fully use his or her share of the limit to transfer it to another sharer. See example 4.

Example 4

Three unmarried sharers borrow the following sums for an equal share in a residence:

A	£25,000
B	£9,000
C	£4,000

The balance of the £10,000 qualifying loan limit to which each of B and C is entitled, but which they have not fully used, can be transferred to A, giving relief for the borrowing as follows:

A (£10,000 + £1,000 + £6,000)	17,000
B (£10,000 − £1,000 to A)	9,000
C (£10,000 − £6,000 to A)	4,000
Interest relief given for borrowing of	£30,000

Ways of funding a mortgage

There are many ways of arranging the borrowing to buy your house. You can have a conventional repayment mortgage, where you repay both capital and interest over the period of the mortgage. You can have an endowment mortgage, under which you pay only interest on the borrowing, and pay endowment insurance premiums to produce a lump sum to repay the capital. Any profit element in the lump sum is tax-free (see page 549). Another option is a mortgage linked to a Personal Equity Plan (PEP) (personal equity plans are explained on page 536). This is similar to an endowment mortgage, but it has extra tax advantages, although on the other hand it carries more risk. Interest is paid on the loan, and a further monthly payment is made, but it is invested in equities and/or unit trusts through the PEP. Dividends and capital gains on the investments are free of tax. To cover the early years when the fund is small, you have to take out temporary life assurance for the amount borrowed, but this is relatively cheap. PEP mortgages are more flexible than endowment mortgages.

The most tax effective choice of all for those who are able to contribute to personal pension plans (see chapter 17) is a pension mortgage. Some lenders will also lend on the basis of a company pension scheme. Again, interest is paid on the amount borrowed, and temporary life assurance is taken out to cover the borrowing, but the capital is repaid out of the lump sum entitlement from the pension fund. Tax relief on the contributions to the pension fund is obtained at the payer's highest tax rate, as well as the fund itself being free of tax. You should remember, however, that you are using part or all of the lump sum that was really intended to support you in retirement.

To help those who have difficulty meeting early high repayments, there are various deferred interest or 'low start' mortgages on offer, and they are usually structured in such a way that MIRAS relief is still effectively obtained on the deferred interest, either by using two separate accounts or two separate loans. The schemes must ensure that the interest for which relief is given is actually paid, even though it is paid out of a separate unqualifying loan. Less interest at the beginning does of course mean more interest later on, but you may then be in a better financial position.

You need to think carefully about the different choices available, and consider the advantages and disadvantages of each.

More than one home (TA 1988, s 355(1)(a); TCGA 1992, s 222(5)(6))

Capital gains tax

You may notify the Revenue within two years after acquiring a second home which of the two is to be the exempt home for capital gains tax. After doing so, you may later notify a change of choice from a specified date, which cannot be earlier than two years before the date of the later notification. If you do not make a notification, and a dispute between you and the Revenue is taken to appeal, the main residence will be decided by the Appeal Commissioners as a question of fact. Provided that both houses have been your main residence for capital gains tax at some time, the last three years of ownership of both will in any event be counted as owner-occupied in calculating the exempt gain. The Revenue no longer consider that an election is required where you have a residence that you own and a second residence that you neither own nor lease (e.g. accommodation with relatives, or a hotel room). A property that you rent would, however, need to be taken into account even if it had no capital value (see Revenue's Tax Bulletin October 1994).

A married couple living together can only have one qualifying residence and where there are two or more residences owned jointly, or each owns one or more residences, the notice as to which is the main residence needs to be given by both. Where both spouses own a residence when they marry, a new two-year period starts for notifying which is the main residence. A new two-year period does not start if on marriage one spouse already owns more than one residence and the other owns no property. If a couple jointly own more than one property before and after marriage, a new two-year period still begins, because the election after marriage must be a joint election.

Mortgage interest relief

For mortgage interest relief, it is a question of fact which is your main residence. In the event of a dispute between you and the Revenue, it would be decided on appeal by the Appeal Commissioners.

The qualifying residence for interest relief need not be the one to which the capital gains exemption applies. In both cases, however, it is necessary for the house to be or have been your residence, and a pure investment property could not qualify.

Council tax

For council tax, you pay 50% of the tax on a property which is no-one's only or main home (except in Wales where you may pay more — see page 115). The question of which of two or more homes is your only or main home for the council tax is a question of fact, decided in the first place by the local authority, but you may appeal against their decision. In some circumstances, one of the properties might be the main home of one spouse and the other property the main home of the other, in which case the resident partner would be liable to pay the council tax at each property, with a 25% single resident reduction if the property was not also the main residence of anyone else over 18. This could apply, for example, if a wife lived at a house in the country and her husband at a house in town, going to the other house at weekends, etc. But the length of time spent at the property would not necessarily be the deciding factor and all relevant circumstances would be taken into account. If the second home was a holiday property available for short-term letting for 140 days or more in a year, it would be liable to business rates rather than the council tax.

If your second home is a caravan, it will not usually be liable to council tax. The site owner where the caravan is kept will pay business rates, which will be included in his charge to you. Touring caravans kept at your home when you are not touring will not be subject to council tax.

Job-related accommodation (TA 1988, ss 356, 375A; TCGA 1992, s 222(8); FA 1995, Sch 6 para 18)

If you live in accommodation related to your employment, for example as a hotel manager or minister of religion, or to your self-employment, for example as the tenant of licensed premises, you may wish to acquire a residence for your future occupation. Tax relief is allowable at 15% on interest paid on borrowing of up to £30,000 for its acquisition, and the house qualifies for capital gains tax exemption, even though you do not live there.

If you let the property, then unless the rent is insufficient to cover the interest paid, it would be better to claim relief for the interest against the letting income, because the £30,000 limit would not apply and relief would be given on the full amount of the loan at your top tax rate providing the interest is wholly and exclusively for the purposes of the letting. You would also be entitled to relief for home improvement loans. On the other hand, if you are a non-taxpayer, you are better off with MIRAS relief, because the 15% tax relief may be retained. If you have a MIRAS loan and you want to claim the interest relief against letting income instead, you can notify the Revenue that you want the loan taken out of MIRAS. The notification must be made within 22 months after the end of the tax year. Strictly the loan cannot then go back into MIRAS so long as you receive letting income from any property, but the Revenue have stated that the loan may be put back into MIRAS when the home is no longer let. If the home loan is not in MIRAS, you have a free choice as to whether to claim the relief as a home loan at the restricted rate of 15% or against letting income.

Unless the house is someone's only or main home (for example if you let it long-term), you will pay 50% of the council tax on it.

Periods of absence (TCGA 1992, s 223)

Provided that a house has at some time been your only or main residence, the last three years of ownership are always exempt from capital gains tax, whether you are living there or not. Other periods of absence also qualify for exemption provided that the house was your only or main residence at some time both before and after the period of absence, and that no other residence qualifies for relief during the absence (see page 417). If you are going to occupy rented property while you are away, then even though your tenancy has no capital value, the property you are occupying would strictly 'qualify for relief'. In those circumstances the Revenue will probably accept a main residence election for your own property, so that the rules for qualifying periods of absence can apply.

If you acquire an interest in a property from your spouse (including an acquisition as legatee when your spouse dies), your period of ownership is treated as starting when your spouse acquired the property, and your tax position would take into account any part of that period when your spouse was not resident in the property.

The qualifying periods of absence are any or all of the following:

(a) three years for any reason whatsoever (not necessarily a consecutive period of three years);
(b) up to four years where the duties of a United Kingdom employment require you to live elsewhere; and
(c) any period of absence abroad where the duties of employment require you to live abroad.

If those periods are exceeded, only the excess is counted as a period of non-residence. If you have to move to another place of employment, so that it is not possible to have a period of residence immediately after an employment-related absence, that condition is waived.

You can thus have long periods of absence without losing any part of the capital gains tax exemption.

Periods of absence before 31 March 1982 are ignored in calculating the chargeable gain, which depends on the proportion of residence/deemed residence to the total period of ownership after 30 March 1982.

For interest relief purposes, the Revenue, by concession A27, similarly disregard temporary absences of up to one year, or up to four years where required by your employment (or any longer period in the case of certain civil servants posted overseas). If the property is let during the absence, the same treatment applies as that stated for job-related accommodation on page 418. You may choose how to claim relief for non-MIRAS loans, and for MIRAS loans you may make an irrevocable election to take the loan out of MIRAS and claim relief against rents instead. Unless you are a non-taxpayer and would benefit from being able to retain the 15% relief on a MIRAS loan, it will usually be preferable for the interest to be allowed against the rent, saving tax at your highest tax rate and with no restriction on the amount of the qualifying loan. Where relief is claimed against rents, interest on loans for home improvement will also qualify.

There are no special council tax provisions about permitted absences, other than the exemptions listed on page 111 and the 50% discount for a property that is no-one's only or main home.

Moving home (TA 1988, ss 191A, 191B, 355(1A)(1B), 357A–357C, Sch 11A; TCGA 1992, s 223; FA 1993, ss 56, 57)

Owning two houses at the same time is usually covered for capital gains tax purposes by the exemption of the last three years of ownership. For interest relief purposes, a separate £30,000 limit applies to a bridging loan for a statutory period of one year, generally extended to two years by Revenue concession. Bridging loan interest is normally paid gross and tax relief is obtained through a coding adjustment or in an assessment, the claim being supported by a certificate of interest paid. Where someone moves out and puts their home up for sale without buying another home, relief will continue to be given (through the MIRAS scheme where relevant) for one year, or more at the Revenue's discretion. This will apply, for example, where two people who are buying houses on mortgage get married and either sell both houses and buy a third, or go to live in one of the houses and sell the other. If the couple continue to use both houses as residences, they will need to elect which of them is to be their qualifying main residence (see page 417). Relief will also continue to be available where someone transfers an existing qualifying loan to a new property, the loan that then qualifies being restricted to the lower of the amount of the existing loan and the cost of the new home (and the £30,000 restriction is applied to that qualifying loan). This will be of some help to those whose homes are worth less than the amount of their mortgage (see example 5). You will not, however, get relief on any part of the earlier loan that was for home improvement (see page 408).

Example 5

Existing loan £80,000. House sold for £60,000 and new home bought for £50,000, the borrower paying £10,000 off the loan. The lender transfers the balance of £70,000 to the new property. The qualifying loan will then be £50,000 (being the lower of £80,000 and £50,000), on which three-fifths of the interest qualifies for MIRAS relief (i.e. the interest on a loan of £30,000).

Employees earning £8,500 per annum or more and company directors are charged to tax on the benefit of certain low rate or interest-free loans from their employers (see page 160). This includes bridging loans, but there are specific statutory provisions covering removal and relocation expenses, under which employees are not taxed on qualifying expenses paid by their employers up to a limit of £8,000 (see page 153). If the £8,000 limit has not been fully used, any balance is available to cover an equivalent amount of the notional interest chargeable to tax on a low rate or interest-free bridging loan from the employer. This is done by working out a number of days for which the bridging loan is not charged to tax, rounding up if not an exact number of days.

The taxable interest, and any interest actually paid, on £30,000 of the bridging loan will qualify for a tax reduction at 15% under the normal bridging loan rules.

See page 154 for the tax treatment if you sell your home to your employer or to a relocation company.

As far as council tax is concerned, the same points apply as stated on page 420 for 'Periods of absence'.

Part use for business purposes (TCGA 1992, s 224)

Interest on that part of any borrowing attributable to the use of part of your home exclusively for business is allowed as a business expense, and the £30,000 limit then applies to the remainder of the loan (see page 413).

You will pay business rates on the business part of the property (allowable against your profits for tax). Where part of the property is used for both business and domestic purposes, and the business use does not prevent the continued domestic use, such as a study where you do some work and your children do their homework, business rates will not be payable, and you will be able to claim a deduction against your profit for the appropriate propor-tion of your council tax.

As far as capital gains tax is concerned, the private residence exemption is not available on any part of your property that is used *exclusively* for business purposes. Where a replacement property is acquired that is similarly used partly for business, rollover relief may be available to defer the gain (see page 55) and if you eventually dispose of the property when you retire, the gain may be covered by retirement relief (see page 57). Your capital gains exemption is not affected if none of your home is *exclusively* used for business purposes.

When a claim for Schedule E expenses has included part of the home expenses (TCGA 1992, s 158(1)(c); SP 5/86)

If you use your home in connection with your employment, part of your home expenses, such as rent, insurance, heat and light, may be allowed as an expense against your earnings (see page 152). When an expenses deduction is not based on any specific proportion of the house being so used, the Revenue may well not seek to tax any part of a capital gain when you sell the house. The position is not, however, free from doubt, and where expenses are deducted under Schedule E, the possible effect on the capital gains exemption when you dispose of the property should be carefully considered. A claim for rollover relief (see page 55) is possible where the employer does not make any payment or give other consideration for his use of the property nor otherwise occupy it under a lease or tenancy. Alternatively, any gain might be wholly or partly covered by your annual capital gains tax exemption.

Selling to make a profit, including selling off part of the garden

The capital gains tax exemption for your main residence does not apply if you acquired the property with the intention of reselling at a profit, and if after acquiring a property you incur expenditure wholly or partly to make a gain on sale, an appropriate part of the gain will not be exempt (TCGA 1992, s 224). The Revenue have stated, however, that expenditure to get planning permission does not affect the exemption.

The capital gains exemption covers grounds not exceeding half a hectare (approximately 1¼ acres), or such larger area as is appropriate to the size and character of the house. If you sell some of the land, perhaps for building plots, the sale is covered by the exemption so long as the land is sold before the house and immediately surrounding grounds.

In exceptional circumstances, the Revenue may assert that selling part of the garden, or frequent buying and selling of properties (particularly when accompanied by substantial work on them while owned), amounts to a trade, resulting not only in the loss of the capital gains tax exemption but also in the taxation of the profits as income.

Tax points

● Now that tax relief on home loans is restricted to 15%, consider whether you could pay for the home in full and borrow for other tax allowable purposes on which relief at your top tax rate is still available. For other allowable interest, see pages 11, 12. See also pages 271, 272.

● If you acquire a second home, consider carefully which is your main residence for mortgage interest and council tax purposes and which you wish to treat as your capital gains tax exempt residence, remembering that the last three years of ownership of a house which at some time has been your main residence for capital gains tax can in any event be counted as years of owner-occupation in the capital gains tax calculation.

● If you are living in job-related accommodation, be certain to tell the Revenue about the acquisition of a dwelling for your own occupation, thus avoiding any doubt that you regard it as your main residence for capital gains tax, and for claiming relief for interest paid on borrowing for its purchase.

● When considering the business proportion of mixed premises for the purpose of claiming relief for expenses, bear in mind the possibility of capital gains tax when the premises are sold.

● To qualify for 'rent a room' relief (see page 410), you need to live in the property at the same time as the tenant for at least part of the relevant period. You can then still claim the relief for that tax year even if you have left the property. But if you do not live in the property at all while it is tenanted, rent a room relief is not available.

● If you take in a lodger under the 'rent a room' provisions, make sure you tell your contents insurer. Even so, you will probably be covered for theft only if it is by breaking and entering. You should also check with your mortgage lender.

● The maximum £40,000 capital gains tax exemption where the family home has been let (£40,000 each if jointly let by husband and wife) applies where it is wholly let for residential occupation for part of the period of ownership, or partly let for residential occupation at some time during the period of ownership. Because of the residential requirement, it could not exempt that part of a gain which was chargeable because part of the accommodation was used by the family company for trading purposes.

● Where a house has separate buildings to accommodate staff, they may count for the capital gains exemption if they are 'closely adjacent' to the main property, but not if they are so far away that the house and buildings cannot really be regarded as a single dwelling.

- Since you cannot get tax relief on a loan to buy a home for a former/separated spouse or a dependent relative, consider jointly owning the property with the occupant, with the occupant paying the interest and claiming the tax relief.

- Interest on home improvement loans taken out on or after 6 April 1988 does not qualify for relief. When moving house, it will therefore pay to maximise the borrowing for the purchase, within the £30,000 limit, rather than borrow less at the outset and then have to top it up with non-qualifying home improvement loans.

- If you undertake a barn conversion yourself, you cannot get relief for interest on borrowing to cover the expenditure, because it counts as home improvement. You can, however, reclaim the VAT on the building materials.

- If you remortgage your home, you will get tax relief only on an amount equal to your previous qualifying loan, even if it was below £30,000. Any additional borrowing will not qualify for tax relief unless it is for a qualifying purpose — see pages 11, 12; and if any part of the earlier qualifying loan covered home improvements, you will lose your tax relief on that part of the replacement loan.

- Each of husband and wife has a separate annual capital gains tax exemption and each can use the 20% and 24% rate bands, so far as not used against income, to restrict the tax charge on gains. Joint ownership of a second home might therefore reduce the capital gains tax on an eventual sale.

- If you are selling off part of your garden, make sure it is sold before the house and immediately adjoining land.

- If you have converted part of your home into a self-contained flat for letting, you will be liable to pay 50% of the council tax on it if it is untenanted, except for the first six months if it is unfurnished.

- As a bed and breakfast provider you will not pay business rates providing you do not offer accommodation for more than six people, you still live there as well and the property's main use is still as your home, and because of the 'rent a room' relief there will be no income tax to pay if the gross income does not exceed £3,250 in a tax year.

31
A country life: farms and woodlands

Farming and market gardening profits

The profits of farmers and market gardeners are calculated in the same way as those of other businesses, but because of the particular characteristics of farming, various special rules apply, some of which are mentioned below.

The Revenue published Business Economic Note 19 on farming stock valuations in 1993, and in their May 1993 Tax Bulletin they gave their view of the treatment to be followed if a change in the basis of valuation was to be made. The valuation of cattle bred on the farm can be included at 60% of market value, and likewise that of home-reared sheep and pigs at 75% of market value, but no reduction is permissible for mature bought-in animals.

There are many different grants and subsidies available to farmers. The general tax treatment is that where the amounts are to meet particular costs, they should be set against those costs (and the costs net of such amounts would then be included, where appropriate, in stock valuations). Where they are to subsidise the sale proceeds of a particular crop they should be recognised as income when the crop is sold. This applies, for example, to Arable Area Payments, including set-aside. Animal grants and subsidies will normally be taken into account either at the end of the retention period or when they are received. (See Revenue's Tax Bulletins of February and December 1994.) Superlevy payments for exceeding milk quota are an allowable expense, but purchases of extra quota to avoid superlevy are capital expenditure. Amounts received for loss of milk, beet or potato quota will be treated as income or capital depending on whether they are compensation for loss of profit or of the quota itself. In the event of receipts for loss of milk and potato quotas being treated as capital, rollover relief (see page 55) is available.

It is common in farming for members of the family to be employed on the farm. As with all businesses, expenses must be 'wholly and exclusively for the purposes of the trade', and there has been a court decision that a farmer's wages to his young children were pocket money and were therefore neither allowable as an expense in calculating farm trading profits nor to be treated as the children's income to enable their personal allowances to be used. The fact that the children were below legal employment age was taken into account, although it was not conclusive.

It is essential that proper professional advice is sought on the agreement of taxation liabilities.

Farming as a single trade (TA 1988, s 53)

All farming carried on by one farmer is treated as a single trade, so that several holdings are treated as a single business and a move from one farm to another will not be treated as the cessation of one business and the commencement of another. The single trade treatment applies whether the farmer is a sole trader, a partnership or a company.

Loss relief (TA 1988, ss 380–383, 385, 388, 389, 397)

The usual reliefs for losses in early and later years and on cessation of trading are available to farming businesses and the usual restriction applies to prevent losses being set against other income if the business is not operated on a commercial basis (see chapter 25). In addition, a loss in the sixth tax year of a consecutive run of farming and market gardening losses (calculated before capital allowances) can only be relieved against later profits of the same trade. The same applies to a loss in a company accounting period following a similar five-year run of losses (before capital allowances). The restriction does not apply if a competent farmer or market gardener could not have expected a profit until after the six-year loss period. By extra-statutory concession B5, an owner-occupier who would otherwise be caught by the 'commercial basis' or six-year run of losses rules may claim to set a loss off against his total income of the same tax year and/or the following tax year, to the extent that it consists of maintenance, repairs, insurance or management expenses (not loan interest). If losses are required to be carried forward, any related capital allowances are similarly treated. Once one year shows a profit, another six-year period then applies to later losses.

Averaging (TA 1988, s 96; FA 1994, ss 214(1)(a), 216(3)(a); FA 1996, s 128(3) and Sch 17 paras 3, 4)

The results of an individual farmer or market gardener or of a farming or market gardening partnership may be averaged over two tax years if the profit of one year is less than 7/10ths of the profit of the other year, with marginal relief if it is more than 7/10ths but less than 3/4.

If profits are averaged, the average figure is then used as the result of the second year and it may again be averaged with the result of the third year and so on. Losses are counted as nil profits in the averaging calculation, with relief for the loss being available separately. On the transition to the current year basis for businesses in existence at 5 April 1994, the taxable profit of 1996/97 will be calculated as a 12 months' average of the profits from the end of the basis period for 1995/96 to the accounting date in 1996/97 (which will be a two-year period unless the accounting date is changed). This average figure is the taxable profit of 1996/97 to compare with the previous or following year for a farmer's averaging claim.

Under the 'previous year basis' rules, profits before capital allowances are taken into account for averaging, but when the current year basis applies the profits will be after deducting capital allowances. For businesses in existence at 5 Apri 1994, if a claim is made to average 1995/96 and 1996/97 the profits will be taken into account *before* capital allowances, and if a claim is made to average 1996/97 and 1997/98, averaging will apply to the profits *after* capital allowances. If both claims are made, therefore, the revised profit for 1996/97 after the first claim (to average 1995/96 and 1996/97) will be reduced by capital allowances to decide whether averaging applies to the second claim (to average 1996/97 and 1997/98).

Under the current year basis, averaging claims will not be made by partnerships. The individual partners will be able to make separate claims on their profit shares if they wish.

Where the first of the two tax years to be averaged is 1995/96 or an earlier year, the time limit for the averaging claim is two years after the end of the second tax year. Where the first of the two years to be averaged is 1996/97 or a later year, the time limit is one year from 31 January following the end of the second tax year. Averaging may not be claimed by farming companies nor in relation to any profits charged to tax under Schedule A (see chapter 32).

An averaging claim cannot be made in the first or last tax year of trading.

Averaging enables farmers to lessen the effect of high tax rates on a successful year when preceded or followed by a bad year. The tax payable under the various alternatives needs to be calculated, taking into account, if appropriate, the possibility of not claiming plant and machinery capital allowances or claiming a reduced amount (in which case the written-down value carried forward to attract writing-down allowances in later years would be increased).

For claims relating to 1996/97 and later years (and therefore presumably applicable to a claim to average 1995/96 and 1996/97), the adjustment to the tax of an earlier year resulting from a farmer's averaging claim is *calculated* by reference to the tax position of the earlier year, but the adjustment is made to the tax payable for the *later* year. Interest on overpaid or underpaid tax, where relevant, would therefore run from the payment date for the later year (see page 119). This means that increasing the tax for an earlier year at the expense of a later year will not in itself be disadvantageous and only the overall effect needs to be considered. See examples 1 and 2.

Example 1

Farmer's profits before capital allowances are as follows:

Year ended 31 December		£
1994	Profit	40,000
1995	Loss	(7,000)
1996	Profit	34,000
1997	Profit	38,000

The capital allowances are £4,000 for 1995/96, £4,500 for 1996/97 and £3,000 for 1997/98.

Assessable profits may variously be as follows:

	No averaging £	Averaging 1995/96 and 1996/97 only £	All three years averaged £
1995/96	40,000*	28,500*	28,500*
1996/97	17,000#	28,500*	29,500##
1997/98	35,000**	35,000**	29,500##

*	Before capital allowances
**	After capital allowances
#	Transitional averaging calculation of half of profits before capital allowances, i.e. half of (34,000 + nil), loss of £7,000 being available for relief separately
##	£28,500 less CAs £4,500 = £24,000 + £35,000 = £59,000 × half = £29,500

Example 2

Assume the farmer in example 1 is a single man with no other sources of income, and that allowances and tax rates remain unchanged for 1997/98. The position would therefore be:

	Basic rate threshold £	Personal allowance £	Income limit for higher rate tax £
1995/96	24,300	3,525	27,825
1996/97	25,500	3,765	29,265
1997/98*	25,500	3,765	29,265

* assumed

After capital allowances but before loss relief the assessable profits are:

	No averaging £	1995/96 and 1996/97 averaged £	All three years averaged £
1995/96	36,000	24,500	24,500
1996/97	12,500	24,000	29,500
1997/98	35,000	35,000	29,500

The loss of the year to 31 December 1995 may be treated as a loss of 1995/96, for which relief may be claimed under TA 1988, s 380 in 1995/96 or 1996/97. If it is carried forward under TA 1988, s 385, then it will in any event be relieved in 1996/97 because of the change to the current year basis. It cannot be used to reduce the higher rate tax of 1997/98. (Losses are dealt with in chapter 25.)

With no averaging, but claiming relief for the loss of £7,000 in 1995/96 to save higher rate tax in that year, higher rate tax would be payable on £1,175 in 1995/96 and on £5,735 in 1997/98.

If 1995/96 and 1996/97 are averaged (and the loss relief claimed for either year), there is no higher rate tax in 1995/96, but higher rate tax is still payable on £5,735 in 1997/98.

If all three years are averaged, and loss relief is claimed in 1996/97 to save higher rate tax in that year, higher rate tax is payable only in 1997/98, and only on £235.

Although the 1997/98 capital allowances could be increased by disclaiming allowances in 1996/97, this would make the overall position worse, because the 1997/98 allowances would be increased by only 25% of the disclaimed amount, whereas the 1997/98 profit would, through averaging, be increased by *one half* of the disclaimed amount, thus increasing the higher rate tax.

Herd basis (TA 1988, s 97 and Sch 5; FA 1994, Sch 19 para 43)

Farm animals and other livestock are normally treated as trading stock. A production herd may, however, effectively be treated as a capital asset if an election is made for the herd basis. The election is irrevocable.

The time limit for making the election (applicable as far as individuals are concerned to years before 1996/97) is two years from the end of the first tax year or company accounting period for which the tax liability will be affected by the purchase of the herd, or if later, two years after the end of the business's first period of account (see example 3).

From 1996/97 for individuals and partnerships, and for accounts ended on or after a date to be fixed for companies (not later than 31 March 1998), the time limit for the election will depend on the accounting period in which the herd is first kept. The time limit for companies will be two years from the end of that account, and for individuals and partnerships one year from the 31 January following the tax year in which that account ends (unless it ends in the first tax year of trading, in which case the time limit for individuals but not partnerships is extended by one year). The limits will no longer be affected by loss claims. See example 4.

Example 3

A production herd is acquired in May 1994 by an established business that makes up its accounts to 31 December.

If the result of the year to 31 December 1994 is a profit, the time limit for making the election is 5 April 1998 for a sole trader or partnership and 31 December 1996 for a company.

If the result of that year is a loss, the time limit is two years from the end of the tax year or company accounting period in which relief for the loss is first given, so that if a sole trader claimed relief for the loss in 1994/95 the time limit for the election would be 5 April 1997, and if a company had no other profit in the year to 31 December 1994 and claimed relief against the profits of the year to 31 December 1993, the time limit would be 31 December 1995.

If the year to 31 December 1994 was the first account of a new sole trade or partnership business, then although the first tax year of charge would be 1993/94, the time limit for the claim would be 31 December 1996 and not 5 April 1996.

Example 4

Facts as in example 3, but the herd is acquired in May 1998, in the accounting period to 31 December 1998. The time limit for the claim is 31 December 2000 for a company and 31 January 2001 for individuals and partners, whether the business makes a profit or a loss.

The limit would remain the same if the year to 31 December 1998 was the first year of business for a sole trader, because the account ends in the second tax year. If accounts had been made up to 5 April and the year to 5 April 1999 had been the first accounting year of a sole trader, then the relevant account would end in the first tax year, i.e. 1998/99, and the time limit would relate to the following year, i.e. 1999/2000, so that it would be 31 January 2002.

A change in the partners in a farming partnership (whether or not there is an election for the continuation of assessments) requires a new herd basis election to be made even where the farming business has owned the herd for several years. There are, however, anti-avoidance provisions to prevent the change being used solely or mainly for the purposes of obtaining a benefit resulting from the right to make a herd basis election or flowing from the election.

Under self-assessment, partnerships will still make a single election for the herd basis, even though partners are assessed separately.

A production herd is a group of living animals or other livestock kept for obtaining products such as milk, wool, etc. or their young.

The effect of the election is that the initial purchase of the herd and any subsequent purchases that increase the herd attract no tax relief, but a renewals basis applies where animals are replaced, so that the cost of the replacement is charged as an expense and the sale proceeds are brought in as a trading receipt. If the whole or a substantial part of the herd is sold and not replaced, no part of the proceeds is charged as income, because it represents the sale of a capital asset, and capital gains tax does not arise since the animals are wasting assets on which capital allowances are not available and are therefore exempt (see chapter 4).

Compensation for compulsory slaughter

By concession, where compensation is paid for compulsorily slaughtered stock to which the herd basis does not apply, the compensation may be left out of account in the year of receipt and brought in over the next three years in equal instalments.

Farm plant and machinery

Capital allowances on farm plant and machinery are available in the usual way (see chapter 22).

Agricultural buildings allowances (TA 1988, s 379A; CAA 1990, ss 123–133, 145; FA 1993, s 114 and Sch 12)

The owners or tenants of agricultural land may claim agricultural buildings allowances in respect of expenditure incurred by them on the construction of buildings, fences, roads and on the installation of services, including up to one-third of the cost of a farmhouse (see page 435). Any grants received are deducted from the allowable cost. Farm shops count as agricultural buildings, but the allowable expenditure is restricted if the shops also sell bought-in items.

Expenditure incurred before 1 April 1986

The provisions for agricultural buildings allowances were different for expenditure incurred before 1 April 1986. In most cases such expenditure will have been fully written off by 1993/94, or at latest by 1995/96 (or in the case of a company, usually by 31 March 1994, or at latest by 31 March 1996). For details, see earlier editions of this book.

Expenditure incurred on or after 1 April 1986

Expenditure incurred on or after 1 April 1986 is relieved by writing-down allowances at 4% per annum over 25 years. Until the introduction of the current year basis (which as far as capital allowances are concerned will apply from 1997/98, or from the outset for businesses starting on or after 6 April 1994 — see page 287), the allowances for sole traders and farming partnerships normally commence in the tax year following the accounts year in which the expenditure is incurred. For non-trading agricultural landlords they commence in the tax year in which the expenditure is incurred. For both trading and non-trading companies the allowances commence in the accounting period in which the expenditure is incurred.

A special 20% initial allowance was available for expenditure under a contract entered into between 1 November 1992 and 31 October 1993, providing the buildings or works were brought into use before 1 January 1995. The taxpayer could claim less than the full initial allowance if he wished. The first writing-down allowance was not given in the same period as the initial allowance unless the buildings or works were brought into use by the end of that period. Unless there is a sale on which a balancing adjustment is made (see below), the 25-year writing-down period will be shortened according to how much of the initial allowance was claimed.

A balancing allowance or charge may be made when agricultural buildings or works are disposed of or scrapped, but only if the former and new owners, if there is a disposal, or the owner, if there is no disposal, makes an election to that effect. The purchaser then gets allowances for the remainder of the 25-year period, normally on what he pays or on what the first user paid, whichever is lower. The time limit for making the election, applicable as far as individuals are concerned to years before 1996/97, is two years after the end of the relevant tax year or company accounting period, as the case may be. From 1996/97, the time limit for individuals is one year from the 31 January following the end of the tax year.

The joint election for the balancing adjustment will not usually be made, because it will be to the advantage of one of the parties at the expense of the other.

If the election is not made, the seller gets a final writing-down allowance which is proportionate to the length of the part of his basis period up to the date of sale, and the buyer gets the remaining allowances, with his first writing-down allowance depending on the part of his basis period that occurs after the date of sale. Where the basis periods of individual traders differ there has sometimes been an unallowed balance at the end of the 25-year period, which is added to the allowance of the final tax year. A shortfall will not occur under the current year basis rules, because allowances are given by reference to accounting periods rather than tax years.

If a farming tenant vacates his holding and does not receive any consideration for his unrelieved agricultural buildings expenditure from the incoming tenant, the landlord is entitled to relief for the balance over the remaining writing-down period.

In the case of a farming trade, the allowances are given against the trading profits and may therefore turn a profit into a loss, or increase a loss, for which the usual loss reliefs are available (see chapters 25 and 26).

For agricultural landlords, either individuals or companies, the allowances are set against rental income under Schedule A (and are treated as expenses of an individual's 'Schedule A business' from 1995/96 — see page 444). For individuals, a claim may be made for any excess allowances to be set against other income of the same tax year and/or the next tax year. For companies, excess allowances may be set against other profits of any description (including capital gains) of the same accounting period, then against the profits of the previous accounting period. (See page 302.) For both individuals and companies, if any balance still remains it will be carried forward against rental income.

Where a building is sold for more than cost, the full cost will be taken into account in the capital gains computation, despite any allowances that have been given against income.

VAT

For VAT purposes, most of a farm's outputs will be zero-rated, but there may also be standard-rated outputs, such as sales of equipment, shooting rights, holiday accommodation, and exempt outputs such as rents for residential caravan sites, possibly leading to partial exemption restrictions. Some farming subsidies and grants, such as set aside, are outside the scope of VAT. The usual input tax restrictions for entertaining, private use, etc. apply (see chapter 7). For the treatment of land and buildings, see below.

If milk quota is sold separately from land, it is standard-rated. If the sale is linked to a supply of land the VAT liability is the same as the liability for the land.

Flat rate farmers (VATA 1994, s 54; SI 1992/3221; SI 1995/2518, Regs 202–211)

Farmers may opt to become 'flat rate farmers' for VAT purposes, regardless of their turnover, providing they satisfy the Commissioners that the total flat rate compensation they will be entitled to in the year after they join the scheme will not exceed the input tax they could have claimed by £3,000 or more. They will not need to register for VAT and will therefore make no VAT returns, but will be able to add a fixed flat rate compensation percentage of 4% to their sale prices when they sell to VAT registered businesses, which they will keep to offset the input tax they have suffered. The registered businesses will be able to reclaim the compensation amount charged to them on their VAT returns. Farmers below the registration threshold need not become flat rate farmers unless they wish to.

Agricultural landlords (TA 1988, ss 53, 379A; CAA 1990, ss 123–133; FA 1995, Sch 6 para 19)

Income from letting agricultural land is taxed in the same way as for any investment property (see chapter 32). New rules apply for individuals (not companies) from 1995/96 under which all rental income is charged as the profits of a 'Schedule A business'. If expenses exceed income, an agricultural landlord who is an individual may claim to set the loss off against his total income of the same tax year and/or the following tax year, to the extent that the loss consists of agricultural buildings allowances (see page 433) and/or maintenance, repairs, insurance or management expenses (not loan interest). Company agricultural landlords can claim relief for excess agricultural buildings allowances as indicated on page 433. The treatment of other deductions is the same as for non-agricultural landlords (see page 447).

The occupation of land managed on a commercial basis is treated as a trade, thus applying where an agricultural landlord receives income from grazing. It follows that the land arguably qualifies as a business asset on which rollover relief for capital gains tax is available if it is sold and the proceeds reinvested in a qualifying replacement asset within one year before and three years after the sale (see chapter 4).

Although gifts relief for capital gains tax normally applies only to business assets or to gifts that are immediately chargeable to inheritance tax, it applies to agricultural property held as an investment providing the conditions for inheritance tax agricultural property relief are satisfied (see page 80).

Value added tax (VATA 1994, Sch 8 Group 5, Sch 9 Group 1, Sch 10)

Grants of long or short leases of agricultural land and buildings, and rents received therefrom, are exempt from VAT, but the landlord has the option to charge VAT. Written notice must be given to Customs within 30 days. VAT is then charged from the day the landlord exercises his option, or any later date he specifies. (If the landlord is not already VAT registered, he will have to become registered to take this option.) If the option is taken, then from 1 March 1995 it can be changed within three months from the time it takes effect, or otherwise not until twenty years after it takes effect. Where a landlord has interests in several different estates, an election can be made for specific discrete areas (such as one farm). This applies from 1 March 1995. Previously one election covered all the land and buildings owned, leased or licensed by the landlord that formed a single estate. The landlord will be able to increase existing rents by the VAT charged if the lease allows VAT to be added or is silent as to VAT. If not, the rent will have to be treated as VAT-inclusive.

Following the exercise of the option, VAT will have to be charged not only on rents and lease premiums, but also on any sale proceeds as and when any of the land and buildings are sold (subject to what is said on page 454). An apportionment will be made in each case, however, to exclude any private dwelling/charitable element. Making the election will enable the landlord to recover any VAT he suffers, for example on the acquisition of the property, or on repairs, and the farmer tenants will usually be VAT registered and will therefore be able to recover the VAT charged.

Small agricultural holdings

The profits of a commercial smallholding are taxed as trading profits, but, if losses arise, the Revenue may contend that the trade is not conducted on a commercial basis with a view to profit, so that the losses may only be carried forward against future income from the smallholding and not set against any other income. This is quite separate from their right to disallow farming losses from the sixth year onwards (see page 426).

The smallholder may seek voluntary VAT registration even though his taxable supplies are less than £47,000 p.a., because he will then be able to reclaim input tax on his expenditure and he will have no liability on his supplies, which are zero-rated. Customs and Excise are required to register anyone making taxable supplies who seeks voluntary registration. The smallholder may alternatively join the flat rate scheme (see page 433).

The farmhouse (TCGA 1992, ss 222–224; IHTA 1984, s 115(2))

The restriction for agricultural buildings allowances of the qualifying capital expenditure on a farmhouse to a maximum of one-third recognises that the domestic and business activities overlap. In arriving at the farm profits, an appropriate part of the establishment charges of the farmhouse is allowed. The Revenue used to allow one-third of the expenses to be claimed in most cases, but will now require the claim to be based on the extent to which the particular farmhouse is used for business.

Customs will adopt a similar approach in relation to the recovery of input VAT on farmhouse expenses such as light and heat. They will, however, normally allow a sole proprietor or partner working full-time to recover 70% of the input VAT on repair and maintenance costs (but not more than 30% on alterations and extensions that are predominantly of a private nature).

The business expenses deduction will not jeopardise the capital gains tax private residence exemption (see chapter 30) provided that no part of the farmhouse has been used exclusively for business purposes. Where part is so used and a chargeable gain arises, rollover relief may be claimed if the farmhouse is replaced (see page 55). If the farmhouse is disposed of on retirement over age 50 or as a result of ill-health, the gain may be reduced by retirement relief (see page 57). The capital gains tax exemption usually extends to grounds up to half a hectare, but for a farmhouse a larger area may be allowed because of the situation and character of the farmhouse and immediately surrounding grounds. The capital gains tax exemptions and reliefs are dealt with in chapter 4.

Agricultural property relief for inheritance tax is available on the farmhouse providing the owner also owns the agricultural land, the farmhouse is 'of a character appropriate to the property', and occupation of the farmhouse is ancillary to that of the agricultural land.

Land let by partners to farming partnership, or by directors to farming company (TCGA 1992, ss 152–158, 164 and Sch 6)

Where land is owned personally by a partner or director, and let to the farming business, any rent paid is allowed as an expense of the business and treated as unearned income in the partner's or director's hands. If interest is paid on a loan to buy the land, it may be deducted from the rent (or any other rent) so long as the letting is on a commercial basis (see chapter 32 for the detailed treatment of let property).

The charging of a commercial rent will, however, affect retirement relief when the land is disposed of by an individual aged over 50 or retiring earlier through ill-health. If no rent is charged, then retirement relief is available provided that the land is disposed of in conjunction with the disposal of an interest in the partnership or shares in the company. Proportionate relief will be given where a rent below the market rent is charged.

Capital gains tax rollover relief may sometimes be claimed if the land is disposed of and the proceeds used to acquire a qualifying asset within one year before and three years after the sale. Charging rent as indicated above does not affect this relief. See page 57.

Capital gains tax (TCGA 1992, ss 52(4), 155, 164I; FA 1995, s 46)

Various capital gains tax aspects are dealt with elsewhere in this chapter. As far as rollover relief for replacement of business assets is concerned, some categories of qualifying asset specifically relate to farming, namely milk and potato quotas and ewe and suckler cow premium quotas (see page 55). It is the view of the Revenue that quota is a separate asset from land, and where nothing was paid for the quota there will be no allowable cost to set against the gain. This view has been upheld in a recent decision of the Special Commissioners. It is understood that quotas are regarded as having an indefinite life, and therefore as being non-depreciating assets for rollover relief. Where quota and land is transferred in a single transaction, values have to be apportioned on a just and reasonable basis. See also page 425.

Farmers need to be particularly careful in relation to retirement relief. Although the relief gives exemption from tax on gains on business assets, it is available only where there is a disposal of all or part of a business, as distinct from a mere sale of a qualifying business asset. Sales of part of the farm land do not therefore qualify, and in a recent case it was held that where milk quota was sold a year after dairy farming ceased, the quota having been leased in the meantime, the gain on the sale of the quota did not qualify because it did not take place as part of the cessation of dairy farming.

Where a tenant receives statutory compensation for improvements at the end of the tenancy, the compensation is not liable to capital gains tax.

Farming companies are qualifying companies for reinvestment relief, so gains on the disposal of any assets may be deferred when shares are acquired in a qualifying unquoted farming company (see page 62).

Inheritance tax (IHTA 1984, ss 115–124; FA 1995, s 155; FA 1996, s 185)

When agricultural property is transferred, agricultural property relief is given on the agricultural value, and where the property is also business property, business property relief is given on the non-agricultural value. The detailed rules for each relief are in chapter 5.

The rate of relief for some tenanted agricultural property was 50%, as against 100% for owner-occupied land, but relief at the 100% rate is now available for all qualifying tenanted property where the letting commences on or after 1 September 1995, including successions to tenancies following the death of the previous tenant on or after that date (see page 81). The grant of the tenancy itself is specifically exempt from inheritance tax so long as it is made for full consideration. Although tenanted property normally has to be owned for seven years to qualify for agricultural property relief (see page 80), the period is only two years where the tenant is a partnership in which the donor is a partner or a company controlled by the donor.

The relief applies to lifetime transfers which are not potentially exempt, or which, having been so, become chargeable because the donor dies within seven years, and to transfers on death. The relief is only available in calculating the tax or additional tax payable as a result of the donor's death within seven years if the donee still owns the property (or qualifying replacement property) when the donor dies, or if earlier, when the donee dies.

Where relief at the time of the transfer is at 100%, there will be neither a chargeable transfer nor a potentially exempt transfer at that time, but the transfer will be counted at death if the donor does not survive the seven-year period. Where relief is at the 50% rate, and two years' annual exemptions are available (see page 70), a combination of the 50% relief and the annual exemptions totalling £6,000 will eliminate a transfer of £12,000.

The introduction of the 100% rate of agricultural property relief has changed the effect of making lifetime gifts, because a lifetime gift will attract capital gains tax (although payment can be deferred by claiming gifts relief), whereas on death there is a capital gains tax-free uplift in asset values. The previous compensating benefit of the lifetime gift in terms of the gifted assets not forming part of the death estate if the donor survived for seven years no longer applies, since the 100% relief has reduced the taxable amount to nil. There is, of course, no certainty that the present generous regime will continue.

Stamp duty

Stamp duty is payable on the sale of farm land and buildings. It is not usually payable on a gift, but if say mortgaged farmland was transferred from a farmer to a family farming partnership, or from one family partnership to another, and the transferee took over liability for the mortgage, the amount of the mortgage would be subject to stamp duty (unless it was £60,000 or less and the transaction was certified not liable to duty).

Woodlands and short rotation coppice

The tax treatment of woodlands is dealt with below. Short rotation coppice is treated as farming, rather than under the woodlands provisions (see page 440).

Income tax

There used to be an income tax charge on woodlands, but this was abolished from 6 April 1988. This means that for newly acquired land, relief for losses incurred and interest paid in the initial planting period cannot be claimed. There is, however, no income tax charge on profits and there has been an increase in the Government grants given for investment in woodlands.

Capital gains tax (TCGA 1992, ss 158, 250)

There is no charge to capital gains tax on trees that are standing or felled. Proceeds of sale of timber are therefore not charged to tax at all. The land is, however, a chargeable asset for capital gains purposes. It is therefore important on acquisition and disposal to establish the different values applicable to the timber and the land.

For commercially run woodlands, gains on sale of the land may be deferred by rolling them over against the cost of replacement assets where the land sale proceeds are reinvested in qualifying business assets within one year before and three years after the sale. If a gain is made on a disposal by way of gift, it will not qualify for gifts relief (see page 60) unless the woodlands operation is a trade. For a disposal by someone over 50, or retiring earlier through ill health, retirement relief (see page 57) is also only available if the business is run as a trade (as distinct from having been taxed as such).

Where woodlands are owned by a company, the land is a qualifying asset for rollover relief as far as the company is concerned, but an individual will not get rollover relief when he sells his shares and reinvests the proceeds (unless he qualifies for reinvestment relief — see page 62, enterprise investment scheme relief — see page 403, or relief for investment in a venture capital trust — see page 529). He will not be entitled to gifts relief or retirement relief in respect of the shares unless the company is a trading company and the other conditions for relief are satisfied (see pages 57–61).

Value added tax (VATA 1994, Sch 1 para 9)

A commercially run woodland is within the scope of VAT, the supply or granting of any right to fell and remove standing timber being standard-rated. It is possible to register for VAT before making taxable supplies, the intention to make taxable supplies being sufficient for registration purposes even though they will not be made for some years. Having registered, you can recover input tax on goods and services in connection with the woodlands operation.

Inheritance tax (IHTA 1984, ss 125–130)

Where an estate on death includes growing timber, an election may be made to leave the timber (but not the land on which it stands) out of account in valuing the estate at death. The election must be made within two years after the date of death and is only available if the deceased either had been beneficially entitled to the land throughout the previous five years or had become entitled to it without consideration (for example by gift or inheritance). (Commercially managed woodlands will usually qualify for 100% business property relief, in which case the election would not be made — see below.)

The election may not be made if the occupation of the woodlands is subsidiary to the occupation of agricultural land, but agricultural relief would be given if the necessary conditions were fulfilled.

Following the election, when the timber is later disposed of by sale or gift, there will be a charge to inheritance tax on the sale price or, if the disposal is for less than full consideration, the market value, less allowable expenses in both cases. Allowable expenses are the costs of sale and expenses of replanting within three years after disposal, or such longer time as the Revenue allow.

The net disposal proceeds or market value are treated as value transferred at the date of death, forming the top slice of the property passing on death, but using the scale and rates current at the time of disposal to find a notional liability on the estate first excluding and then including the timber proceeds, the tax on the timber proceeds being the difference between the two. The tax is due six months after the end of the month in which the disposal takes place, with interest on overdue tax at the death rate. The person entitled to the sale proceeds is liable for the tax. Where there are no proceeds because the disposal is by way of gift, the tax arising out of this disposal may be paid by instalments over ten years.

A lifetime gift of woodlands either attracts inheritance tax or is a potentially exempt transfer (see chapter 5). Where the disposal is one on which tax is payable following its being left out of account on an earlier death, the value transferred by the lifetime transfer is reduced by the tax charge arising out of the previous death.

If the person who inherits woodlands on which an election has been made dies before the timber is disposed of, no inheritance tax charge can arise in respect of the first death. Furthermore, a new election may then be made on the second death.

Where woodlands are managed on a commercial basis, despite there being no income tax charge, they qualify for 100% business property relief so long as they have been owned for two years (see chapter 5). Where tax is payable, it may be paid by instalments in the case of a death transfer where the value has not been left out of account and where, exceptionally, a lifetime transfer is not potentially exempt. If an election is made to leave the timber out of account on a death, business property relief is given on the net sale proceeds when it is disposed of, but only at 50% rather than 100%. This will be relevant where the election has already been made, but clearly no new elections will be made where the 100% business property relief is available.

Short rotation coppice (FA 1995, s 154)

Short rotation coppice, which is a way of producing a renewable fuel for 'green' biomass-fed power stations from willow or poplar cuttings, is regarded as farming for income tax, corporation tax and capital gains tax, and as agricultural land for inheritance tax.

The Revenue consider that the initial cultivation costs of the short rotation coppice are capital expenditure, the net amount of which (after deducting any Woodland Grants offset against the expenditure) may be used to roll over gains on disposals of other business assets. The expenditure (net of both Woodland Grants and any rolled over gains) will be allowable in calculating gains when the land is disposed of, providing the coppice stools are still on the land at that time.

Subsequent expenditure after the initial cultivation will be revenue expenditure. Set-aside receipts are to be treated as normal farming income (see page 425), rather than being regarded as income from the coppice.

See Revenue's Tax Bulletin October 1995.

Council tax and business rates

Agricultural land and buildings are exempt from business rates. Any buildings or parts of buildings that are for domestic rather than agricultural use will attract 50% of the council tax if the building or part is no-one's only or main home. If it is someone's only or main home, the residents will be liable to pay the council tax. The valuation will take into account the restricted market for the property because of the agricultural use. In Scotland only, unoccupied, unfurnished property previously used in connection with agricultural land or woodlands, etc. is exempt from council tax.

Tax points

- If you have a smallholding which is likely to show consistent losses, you are unlikely to be able to relieve them against other income, and treating the smallholding as a trade may prejudice your capital gains tax private residence exemption. It may be preferable to make a yearly note in your tax return that the working of the holding is not by way of trade but only for the maintenance of the holding and that no profits arise.

- If you are making losses and are in danger of falling foul of the six-year rule (see page 426), see if you can show a small profit in one year, perhaps by delaying repairs or other expenses. The six-year cycle will then start again. If you are caught by the six-year rule, there is a useful concession (extra-statutory concession B5) enabling you to set some of your unrelieved farm expenses against other income.

- Where a smallholding or market garden is clearly a trade, make sure if possible that no part of the dwelling house is used exclusively for business, to avoid any possible loss of the private residence capital gains exemption.

- When buying a holding with agricultural buildings, remember that what you pay for them does not necessarily entitle you to any capital allowances. You cannot get allowances on any more than that part of the seller's expenditure for which relief has not yet been given.

- If you are an individual agricultural landlord and have incurred expenditure on agricultural buildings, you may make a claim to set the available allowances against any income to the extent that your total rental income is insufficient. Relief can be given in the tax year itself or the following year. Company landlords may claim to set excess allowances against their total profits (including capital gains) of the same accounting period and then the previous accounting period.

- Owning agricultural land personally and renting it to your partnership or company will not stop you getting capital gains tax rollover relief if the land is sold and replaced, but the payment of rent does restrict your entitlement to retirement relief (see page 436).

- Rollover relief (page 55) is not available to agricultural landlords except in the circumstances indicated in the previous tax point.

- Gifts relief *is* available to agricultural landlords if the conditions are satisfied (see page 60).

- Farming is no longer an excluded trade for reinvestment relief — see page 62.

- A farmer's averaging claim will affect income for two or more years. From 1996/97, however, the averaging claim has no effect on the dates on which tax is due for payment (see page 427). Note that the claim will affect the permissible levels of personal pension contributions for the years concerned.

- There are a number of specialist organisations ready to advise on an investment in woodlands, not only from the taxation point of view but also on the question of cash grants through the Forestry Commission, and on estate management.

32
Investing in land and buildings

Introduction

The provisions in this chapter apply to both commercial and private investment properties in the UK. The detailed treatment of let agricultural buildings is covered in chapter 31. The tax advantages of investing in enterprise
zone buildings and the special provisions relating to the grant of a lease on
an enterprise zone building are dealt with in chapter 22. The treatment of
non-residents who let UK property and UK residents who let property
overseas is dealt with in chapter 41.

Income from land and buildings

Income from UK land and buildings is usually charged to income tax as
investment income, except for furnished holiday lettings, which are treated
as trading income (see page 451). The distinction between trading income
and investment income is important in relation to relief for contributions to
provide your own pension. It is also important for capital gains purposes
because a property that provides you with investment income will not
qualify for rollover relief (see page 55) when it is replaced (unless it is
compulsorily purchased — see page 452) nor retirement relief if the property
is sold after you reach age 50 (see page 57), and gifts relief (see page 60) will
not usually be available either. As far as inheritance tax is concerned,
business property relief is not available where the business consists of
making or holding investments. This is taken to include land which is let (see
page 80), and the relief has recently been denied in a case before the Special
Commissioners where the owners played a very active role in the letting,
management and maintenance of their properties. Relief is, however, available to landlords of let agricultural property (see page 437).

For years up to 1995/96, income tax on rental income was payable on a
provisional basis on 1 January in the tax year, with an adjustment to the
correct figures once the result for the year was known. From 1996/97, the
self-assessment rules apply (see page 20). Companies pay corporation tax on
all their profits under the Pay and File system, the due date normally being
nine months after the end of the accounting period (see page 36).

In order to make it easier for individuals to self-assess their liability to income tax, the rules for taxing rents were simplified from 6 April 1995. The new rules apply only to individuals. Companies are still taxed on the same basis as previously. The tax treatment of individuals is dealt with on pages 444 to 446 and that of companies on pages 446 to 449. The treatment of furnished holiday lettings, which applies both to individuals and companies, is dealt with on page 451. The treatment of lease premiums, where the treatment is again broadly the same for individuals and companies, is dealt with on page 450.

Tax treatment of individuals (TA 1988, ss 15, 21; FA 1995, s 39 and Sch 6)

Special rules apply where you let furnished rooms in your own home, and in some circumstances the letting may amount to a trade. This is dealt with in chapter 30, from page 410. Unless these special rules apply, then from 6 April 1995, all income from UK property (including the right to use a fixed caravan or permanently moored houseboat) will be treated as the profits of a 'Schedule A business', whether there is just one letting or a number of lettings, whether the property is let furnished or unfurnished, and no matter whether repairs are the responsibility of the landlord or the tenant (although income from furnished holiday lettings will effectively be kept separate and the provisions outlined on page 451 will apply).

Where rental income was first received in 1994/95, taxpayers were invited to calculate income under the new rules from the outset, to avoid the need for the transitional adjustments outlined on page 446.

Calculation of Schedule A profits

The income charged to tax is that of the tax year from 6 April to 5 April. (Different rules apply to partnerships — see page 331.) Although the income is investment income, the general accounting rules for working out trading profits apply, so that allowable expenses are broadly those that are wholly and exclusively for the purpose of the lettings, and adjustments are made for rent and expenses in arrear or in advance. (In small, simple cases, the Revenue will accept computations on the basis of amounts received and paid, with no adjustments for amounts in arrear or in advance.) Interest payable, including interest payable to a non-resident lender, is allowed as a trading expense, subject to the 'wholly and exclusively' rule.

Where capital allowances are available (for example on agricultural or industrial buildings, or on plant and machinery provided in commercial or industrial buildings or used in estate management), they are deducted as an expense. Capital allowances are not available on furniture, etc. in a dwelling house, but relief for wear and tear of furniture may be claimed either on the renewals basis or by way of a wear and tear allowance of 10% of rents (as outlined on page 449).

In some circumstances, where your letting income is small, you need only include total figures of rent, expenses and net income on your tax return — see page 126.

Treatment of losses (TA 1988, s 379A; FA 1995, Sch 6 para 19)

If losses arise, they will normally be carried forward to set against later Schedule A income. Relief is, however, available against other income of the same and/or the following tax year in respect of excess capital allowances (see page 302) and certain agricultural expenses (see page 434). If there are unrelieved losses under the old rules at 5 April 1995 they will be treated as Schedule A losses brought forward to 1995/96.

Interest paid by those in job-related accommodation or working away from home

Special rules apply to interest paid by someone who lets their home while they live in job-related accommodation (see page 418) or while they are working away (see page 420).

National insurance contributions

Property letting will rarely be regarded as self-employment for national insurance purposes, although if the extent of the landlord's involvement in managing the lettings and looking after the properties is substantial (which might be particularly relevant for furnished holiday lettings — see page 451), it is possible that the activities will constitute a business, in which case Class 2 national insurance contributions (but not Class 4 contributions) will be payable (see page 344). Even though rents are now *treated* as being from a business for Schedule A income tax, this is not the same as saying that a business actually exists, and it does not alter the national insurance position.

Rental income ceasing in 1995/96

If someone ceased to let property at some time in 1995/96, and no new source of property income was acquired in that year, the new treatment does not apply and the 1995/96 income is calculated under the previous rules, which are broadly the same as those for companies, as outlined on pages 446 to 449. Relief for interest relating to unfurnished property is only allowable under the old rules if the property has been let at a commercial rent for at least 26 weeks out of 52 and, when not so let, was available for letting or was being repaired or improved or was used as the only or main residence of the borrower. Relief is not available if the borrowing is by way of overdraft rather than a specific loan. For furnished lettings, relief is available under the old rules if the interest is wholly and exclusively for the purposes of the letting, with no restriction on the number of weeks for which the property has been let.

Transitional provisions

Before 1995/96, income from furnished lettings under Schedule D, Case VI was often calculated on the basis of the results for a current or previous accounting period rather than for the current tax year. Although Schedule A income from unfurnished lettings should strictly have been based on the result of the tax year, in practice it has sometimes been calculated in the same way as for Schedule D, Case VI. Because of the variety of practices that were in use, no transitional rules were enacted, and the Revenue have dealt with the transition from the old rules to the new on a just and reasonable basis. Details are contained in their Press Release of 10 February 1995. Any necessary adjustments will usually have been made in the 1994/95 assessment, unless this had already been finalised, in which case they will be made for 1995/96. Any adjustments relating to interest paid will be made in the 1995/96 assessment.

Tax treatment of companies

Income from unfurnished lettings

The following provisions apply to income from unfurnished lettings. The rules for furnished lettings (other than furnished holiday lettings) are dealt with on page 449. As indicated on page 449, however, a company landlord may choose to have the part of the furnished lettings rent that relates to the property rather than the furniture charged under the following rules instead of the furnished lettings rules.

Calculation of rent (TA 1988, ss 15, 33A, 41)

Rent is taken into account for tax purposes when it is due and payable, the date when it is actually received not being relevant and no apportionment being made over the period which it covers. See example 1. Anti-avoidance provisions have been introduced to prevent connected persons, such as companies in the same group, exploiting these provisions by getting a deduction for the payment in an earlier period than that in which the rent is charged to tax. If rent due from a connected person is allowed as a deduction to that person in an earlier period than that in which it is payable, it is treated as income of that earlier period.

You can deduct rent not received from the amount chargeable if you have tried but failed to collect the rent, or if you have not enforced your right to the rent in order to avoid hardship to the tenant.

Example 1

Rent of £2,000 per quarter is due in advance on the usual quarter days under a seven-year lease commencing on 29 September 1996.

If the company makes up accounts to 31 March, the rental income included in the profits of the year to 31 March 1997 is:

	£
29 September 1996	2,000
25 December 1996	2,000
25 March 1997	2,000
	£6,000

even though on a day to day basis only a little over £4,000 relates to that year, and whether or not rent is in fact received on those dates.

Allowable expenses (TA 1988, s 25)

Allowable expenses include business rates or council tax if appropriate (see page 456), rent payable to a superior landlord, maintenance, repairs and redecorations, insurance and management expenses, including advertising for tenants, and any other expenses which under the terms of the lease are to be met out of the rent. Improvement expenditure, on for example building extensions or installing central heating or double glazing, is not allowable in calculating income, although it will be counted as part of the cost for capital gains purposes. Where repair and maintenance expenditure is made unnecessary because of improvements, additions and alterations, a deduction from rent is allowed by Revenue concession B4 for the estimated amount that would have been spent on the repairs. No similar concession applies to deductions for repairs against trading profits. See page 449 for the treatment of interest on borrowings.

Where the rent is sufficient, taking one year with another, to meet the landlord's outgoings, the lease is called a 'full rent lease'.

Normally, expenses incurred when a property is not let would not be allowed, but, for leases at a full rent, periods when a property is empty between the time of acquisition and being let at a full rent, and between full-rent leases, are regarded as part of a continuing lease, enabling expenses during the void periods to be deducted against rents as if the property had been let continuously. This does not apply, however, to expenditure on newly acquired property to rectify dilapidations arising before the company bought it. Such expenditure will form part of the cost for capital gains purposes and is not allowable in calculating taxable income.

Several properties (TA 1988, s 25)

Where the company has several let properties, whether the expenses of each have to be isolated against the rent of each depends on the type of lease.

For full-rent leases under which the company is responsible for the repairs (known as landlord's repairing leases), total expenses may be set against total rents to arrive at the net income from the properties. If expenses exceed rents, the excess is carried forward to set against later rents on such properties. Expenses of any property let at a full rent under a tenant's repairing lease are first set against the rent of that property, and then against the surplus on landlord's repairing lease properties (if any), any balance being carried forward to set against a future profit on the same tenant's repairing lease property, and indeed this may be the only way of getting relief if it is the only property involved.

Where properties are let below a full rent, losses may only be set against any future profit on that particular property and only while it is let to the same tenant under the same lease. If the rent is increased to a full rent, brought forward losses cannot be set off.

The total of the income less expenses from all properties can conveniently be called the 'net rents'.

Capital allowances (TA 1988, s 32; CAA 1990, ss 51–59)

The capital allowances available on let agricultural buildings are dealt with in chapter 31, and chapter 22 deals with allowances on industrial buildings, hotels and buildings in enterprise zones.

As far as plant and machinery is concerned, allowances are available where expenditure is incurred on machinery or plant for the maintenance, repair or management of premises where the rents are charged under Schedule A — see chapter 22. Except for furnished holiday lettings (see page 451), allowances are not available on furniture let in a dwelling house, but a wear and tear allowance is usually given instead (see page 449).

A business tenant may claim allowances on expenditure he incurs on such items as lifts, heating and ventilating equipment, etc. even though in law they become landlord's fixtures. Where such fixtures are not bought outright but are acquired on lease, either by a landlord or a tenant, an election may be made for allowances to be given to the equipment lessor, instead of to the landlord or the tenant as the case may be. Appropriate adjustments are made when rights under the equipment lease are transferred. The lessor will be taxed on the payments he receives under the lease, with those payments being allowed in calculating the rent income of the lessee.

Furnished lettings (TA 1988, s 15)

Furnished lettings of UK property are taxed under Schedule D, Case VI, but the company may choose to have the property proportion of the rent included with unfurnished lettings under Schedule A, leaving only the payment for the furnishings and/or services to be charged under Schedule D, Case VI. The advantage of separating the furnishings rent and the property rent is that the property rent may enable a set-off to be made for losses on unfurnished properties that would otherwise have to be carried forward.

The expenses of furnished lettings are, as with Schedule A, allowed broadly on a common-sense basis. See below for relief for interest. Additionally, relief is given for wear and tear on furnishings in residential property. Relief may be claimed either on a renewals basis (so that nothing is allowed when furniture, etc. is first bought, but as and when any item is replaced the full cost of the replacement is allowed), or more usually, by a wear and tear allowance. By concession B47, the Revenue accept a figure of 10% of the rent for this purpose, but any additions to rent for council tax, water rates and other sums for services which would normally be borne by a tenant are deducted, if material, before calculating the 10% relief. Where the 10% allowance is claimed, no further deduction is allowed for renewing furniture and furnishings, such as suites, beds, carpets, curtains, linen, crockery or cutlery, nor for items such as cookers, washing machines or dishwashers. But an additional deduction may be claimed for renewing fixtures such as baths, washbasins and toilets.

The Revenue will rarely accept that a furnished letting amounts to a trade, and their attitude has been supported by the courts. Income from furnished holiday lettings is, however, generally treated as trading income (see page 451).

Relief for interest

Interest on borrowing by property letting companies to buy or improve the let property used to be a 'charge on income' and as such, was deducted from the company's total profits from all sources. If it exceeded the profits, the unrelieved amount could be carried forward to set against later profits from all sources.

From 1 April 1996 all interest on company borrowings is dealt with under the rules outlined on page 27. Interest relating to furnished holiday lettings (see page 451) will thus be deducted from the income from those lettings, since expenses may be deducted as if such lettings were a trade. All other interest relating to let property will be taken into account in arriving at the overall non-trading surplus or deficit on loans. If there is a deficit, relief will be available as indicated on page 368. Where deficits are carried forward, the new provisions are less generous than the old, because such deficits may be set only against non-trading profits rather than total profits.

Where a premium is charged (TA 1988, ss 34, 37, 87; TCGA 1992, Sch 8 para 5; FA 1995, Sch 6 paras 9, 12, 14, 37)

There are two sorts of premium, one where an existing leasehold interest is assigned, the other where a lease or sublease is granted. The first is a disposal for capital gains purposes.

The treatment of the second depends on the length of the lease. If a lease is granted for more than 50 years, it is treated as a disposal for capital gains purposes. There are both capital and income aspects if the lease is of 50 years duration or less (known as a short lease), in that the premium is partly treated as income and partly as a disposal for capital gains. The income portion is treated as additional rent and is the amount of the premium less 2% for each complete year of the lease except the first. The amount by which the premium is reduced is treated as the proceeds of a part disposal for capital gains, the cost of the part disposed of being the proportion of the total cost that the capital portion of the premium bears to the full premium plus the value of the freehold reversion. See example 2.

The income portion of a premium on a short lease is wholly charged in the year the lease is granted, although the lease may run for anything up to 50 years.

Since the income part of the premium is treated as additional rent, any expenses of the letting can be relieved against it. The premium might in fact have been charged to recover some extraordinary expenses, perhaps necessitated by a previous defaulting tenant. For individuals, the income portion of a premium is brought in as part of the overall income of the Schedule A business (see page 444).

Where a premium on a short lease is paid by a business tenant, he may deduct the income portion (i.e. after the 2% deduction) as a business expense, but spread over the term of the lease rather than in a single sum (see example 2). A similar deduction could be claimed by a tenant who sublets, his deduction depending on the length of the sublease. Any deductions allowed in calculating income are not allowed in calculating the capital gain if the lease is disposed of.

Any expenditure on the acquisition of a lease is treated for capital gains purposes as wasting away during the last 50 years (or shorter period for which the lease was granted) and only the depreciated cost (using a special table in TCGA 1992, Sch 8) may be used. If a lease is held for its full term, no allowable loss may be claimed for the unrelieved expenditure on acquisition, so that any expenditure for which relief has not been given in calculating income will not have been allowed for tax at all.

Example 2

Individual charges a premium of £8,000 on granting a lease for 21 years commencing 20 June 1996. The cost of the freehold was £15,000 in 1985. The value of the freehold reversion after the grant of the lease was £24,000.

The amount included in assessable rent for 1996/97 is:

	£
Premium	8,000
Less Treated as part disposal for capital gains (21–1) = 20 years at 2%=40%	3,200
Amount treated as additional rent	£4,800

The chargeable gain (before indexation allowance) is:

Capital proportion of premium	3,200
Less Allowable proportion of cost	
$15,000 \times \dfrac{3,200}{8,000 + 24,000}$	1,500
	£1,700

If the tenant was a business tenant, he could claim a deduction for £4,800 spread over 21 years, i.e. £229 per annum, in addition to the deduction for the rent paid. If he assigned the lease within the 21 years, the allowable cost for capital gains would be the premium paid of £8,000 less depreciation under TCGA 1992, Sch 8, less the total annual deductions allowed.

Furnished holiday lettings (TA 1988, ss 503, 504; CAA 1990, s 29; TCGA 1992, s 241)

As with other furnished lettings, the 'rent a room' relief exempting gross rent of up to £3,250 a year is available to those who let rooms in their homes and this may be more beneficial than the furnished holiday lettings treatment described below (see page 410).

Income from furnished holiday lettings of UK property is broadly treated as trading income (although it remains chargeable under Schedule A for individuals and Schedule D, Case VI for companies, rather than Case I). If interest is paid on a loan to purchase or improve the property, it will be allowed as a trading expense (restricted if necessary by any private use proportion). Capital allowances (see chapter 22) on plant and machinery, such as furniture and kitchen equipment, and loss relief (see chapters 25 and 26) may be claimed, and the income qualifies as relevant earnings for personal pension purposes (see chapter 17). For years up to 1995/96 income tax was payable by equal instalments on 1 January in the tax year and 1 July following. The self-assessment provisions apply thereafter (see page 20).

Corporation tax is payable on the normal due dates. The property is eligible for capital gains rollover relief either when it is itself replaced, or as a qualifying purchase against which gains on other assets may be set, and for retirement and business gifts reliefs (see pages 55–61). If the property has been the main residence for capital gains tax, it may also be possible to claim the residential lettings exemption (see page 411). Despite the trading treatment, individuals do not have to pay Class 4 national insurance contributions, because Class 4 contributions only apply where profits are charged under Schedule D, Case I or II. Class 2 contributions would, however, usually be payable unless the landlord's activities in managing the properties were insufficient to be regarded as carrying on a business (see page 344).

To qualify, the accommodation must be let on a commercial basis; it must be available as holiday accommodation for at least 140 days in the tax year, and actually let as such for at least 70 of those days. The 70 days test may be satisfied by averaging periods of occupation of any or all of the holiday accommodation let furnished by the same person. The accommodation must not normally be in the same occupation for a continuous period of more than 31 days during at least seven months of the year, which need not be continuous but includes any months containing any of the 70 let days. Where only part of the let accommodation is holiday accommodation, apportionments are made on a just and reasonable basis.

The letting of holiday caravans is, depending on the scale, either treated as a trade or as a furnished letting. In the latter case, the income may be treated as trading income from furnished holiday accommodation if the conditions are satisfied. Long-term lets would accordingly not qualify. Caravans occupying holiday sites are treated as plant and machinery qualifying for capital allowances, even if they are on hard standings and not required to be moved.

Income from letting caravan sites is charged as unearned income under Schedule A, unless the activity really amounts to a trade, embracing services, shops, restaurants, etc. in which case the whole income will be treated as earned income from a trade.

For the treatment of furnished property, including holiday property and caravans, in relation to council tax and business rates, see page 456.

Capital gains on sale of investment properties (TCGA 1992, ss 243–248, Revenue Statement of Practice SP 13/93)

The usual capital gains tax principles apply (see chapter 4), including the relief dealt with in chapter 30 (page 411) where part of the property is owner-occupied, and that dealt with above where the property is let as furnished holiday accommodation. Apart from those instances, there is no rollover relief on disposal and replacement of investment properties except where the disposal is occasioned by compulsory purchase. In this case, there is no tax charge if the proceeds are reinvested in another property, provided that the reinvestment is made within the period beginning one year before and ending three years after the disposal. The replacement property cannot, however, be the investor's capital gains tax exempt dwelling house at any time within six years after its acquisition. As an alternative to rollover relief where part of a holding of land is compulsorily purchased, small proceeds (not defined but probably not exceeding 5% of the value of the holding) may be treated as reducing the capital gains cost of the holding rather than being charged as a part disposal.

Compulsory purchase includes not only purchase by an authority but also purchase of the freehold by a tenant exercising his right to buy.

If a lease is surrendered and replaced by a new lease on similar terms except as to duration and rent payable, the surrender is, by concession (D39), not treated as a disposal for capital gains tax.

See page 434 for the availability of capital gains gifts relief for agricultural landlords.

Property dealing, etc.

Although the income from letting is assessed under Schedule A or Schedule D, Case VI as the case may be, any surplus on disposal of a property may even so be liable to income tax or corporation tax, either specifically under TA 1988, s 776 (see page 609), or as a trading transaction, instead of as a chargeable gain. Whether or not a trade may be inferred is dealt with in chapter 20, but the letting, whilst not conclusive, will at least indicate an investment motive and be influential in the surplus being treated as a capital gain.

Housing investment trusts (TA 1988, ss 508A, 508B, 842; FA 1996, s 160 and Sch 30)

From the date of Royal Assent to the Finance Act 1996, the rules for approved investment trusts (see page 527) will be amended to allow such trusts to invest in residential property. The property must be acquired on or after 1 April 1996 and must be either unlet or let on assured shorthold tenancies when acquired, and must subsequently be let on assured tenancies. The property must be either freehold or long lease property at a low rent, costing not more than £125,000 in Greater London and £85,000 elsewhere. Housing investment trusts will pay corporation tax at the small companies rate (currently 24%) on net rental income, and any capital gains on the properties will be exempt.

VAT (VATA 1994, Sch 8 Group 5, Sch 9 Group 1, Sch 10)

The VAT position on land and buildings had to be changed as a result of EU regulations and is now very complex. Sales of new commercial buildings and commercial buildings that are less than three years old are standard-rated.

Sales or leases for more than 21 years of new residential properties (including dwellings created by the conversion of non-residential property) and new buildings occupied by charities for charitable purposes are zero-rated. (Shorter leases are exempt and cannot be subject to the option to charge VAT — see below.)

Unless the vendor has exercised his option to charge VAT (see below), all sales of buildings that are more than three years old are exempt, and grants of long or short leases (other than those mentioned above) are also exempt, except for holiday accommodation (see page 455). Rents received are exempt unless the landlord has opted to charge VAT.

Most landlords letting domestic property will be exempt from VAT. Any VAT they are charged will therefore form part of their costs, and must be taken into account in fixing their rents. Landlords letting commercial property will be in the same position, unless they opt to charge VAT (see below). If the expenditure is revenue expenditure, such as repairs, the unrecovered VAT may be claimed as part of the expense against the rent. If it is capital expenditure, such as on property conversion, reconstruction, extension, improvement, etc., no deduction can be claimed against the rent, but the unrecovered VAT will form part of the capital cost in a capital gains computation when the property is disposed of.

Option to charge VAT

In all situations where exemption applies (other than leases of residential/ charitable property for less than 21 years, pitches for residential caravans and mooring facilities for houseboats), the owner/landlord has an option to charge VAT (but if he is not already VAT registered he has to become registered in order to take this option). Customs must be notified in writing within 30 days. The effect of taking the option is that VAT is then charged not only on rents and lease premiums but also on any sale proceeds when buildings are sold. Although the sale of tenanted property may represent the disposal of part of a business, the provisions relating to the sale of a going concern (see page 101) do not apply to land on which the seller has exercised the option to tax unless the buyer notifies Customs before the sale that he has also exercised the option. In the absence of such an election, the going concern treatment is not available and VAT must be charged on the sale.

Making the election enables the landlord to recover any VAT he suffers, and could be particularly beneficial where he has to incur substantial repair expenditure. But if most of his tenants are partially exempt, part of the VAT will be an extra cost to them, so the overall effect needs to be considered carefully. Following the election, the landlord will be able to add VAT to the rent unless the lease specifically prevents him from doing so. In that event, the rent he receives will have to be treated as VAT inclusive until such time as it may be increased on a rent review.

The option may be exercised separately in relation to each building (but not separate parts of a building) and in relation to discrete areas of agricultural land, such as one farm (see page 434). Once taken, the option can only be revoked by that owner within three months from the date it has effect and before it has had any tax consequences, or twenty years after it has effect. A new owner may or may not exercise the option as he wishes.

Anti-avoidance provisions apply to lease and lease-back schemes, under which the option to tax cannot be taken on a lease between connected persons where either party is exempt or partially exempt, although Customs may allow it by concession in some circumstances.

Holiday accommodation, etc.

The provision of short-term holiday accommodation in hotels, boarding houses, caravans, etc. is charged to VAT at the standard rate but reduced charges apply if a tenant stays for more than four weeks. If you sell or lease holiday accommodation, including time share accommodation, that is less than three years old, then both the initial charges and any periodic charges, such as ground rent and service charges, are also standard-rated. If the property is over three years old, the initial charges are exempt from VAT but periodic charges are still standard-rated. The standard rate applies to charges for pitching tents and to seasonal pitch charges for caravans (charges for non-seasonal pitches being exempt). If the pitch charges to the caravan owners include water, gas and electricity and the landlord can ascertain how much is provided to the caravans as distinct from the rest of the site (shops, swimming pools, etc.), this can be divided by the number of caravans and shown separately on the bills, and VAT need not then be charged on those services. VAT is also not charged on any part of the pitch charge that represents business rates on the individual caravans (but it is charged on any business rates element that relates to the rest of the site).

The sale of building plots for holiday accommodation is standard-rated.

'Self-supply' provisions

For commercial buildings, there have been special provisions to charge VAT if, within the period from the time the building was first planned to ten years after its completion, it was either occupied by the person who had it built or was leased rather than sold. The provisions broadly ensured that those who are partly exempt from VAT could not avoid a VAT cost by having a building built on their own land (unless the original cost of the land plus the construction expenditure was less than £100,000). The provisions also covered certain reconstructions, extensions and enlargements of existing buildings.

The charge has been abolished for all developments commencing on or after 1 March 1995. Developments started before and in progress at that date will suffer the self-supply charge not later than 1 March 1997, unless the developer repays to Customs any input tax recovered to date, in which case the self-supply charge will not be made.

Stamp duty on buying

When property is purchased for £60,000 or less, no stamp duty arises. If the purchase price exceeds that amount, duty is payable on the whole of the purchase price at 1%. Any stamp duty paid forms part of the cost for capital gains tax purposes on a subsequent disposal.

Where VAT is included in the cost of property, stamp duty is charged on the VAT-inclusive amount.

Council tax and business rates

The detailed council tax and business rates provisions are in chapter 8, which outlines the exemptions and discounts available.

When considering liability to council tax and/or business rates, each self-contained unit is looked at separately. Where there is mixed business and domestic use, business rates are payable as well as the council tax, even if there is no separate business part of the property, unless the business use does not materially detract from the domestic use. Any charges that fall on a landlord are allowable according to the normal expenses rules.

Let property that is domestic property and is not someone's only or main home is liable to a 50% council tax charge, unless any other discount or exemption applies (see chapter 8). Where let property is someone's only or main home, that person is liable to pay the council tax and there are no council tax or rates implications for the landlord, unless the property is multi-occupied property, such as bedsits, with rent paid separately for different parts of the property, in which case the council tax is payable by the landlord.

Non-domestic property, such as commercial property, boarding houses, etc., is liable to business rates. Staff accommodation, however, is domestic property. If the owner lives there as well, he is liable to pay the council tax. If he does not live there, the staff are liable to council tax if it is their only or main home. If the domestic accommodation was no-one's only or main home, the owner would be liable to pay 50% of the council tax. In the case of self-catering holiday accommodation, business rates are payable if it is available for short-term letting for 140 days or more in a year. This is independent of the number of days for which the property is actually let. Bed and breakfast accommodation is not subject to business rating providing it is not offered for more than six people, the provider lives there at the same time and the bed and breakfast activity is only a subsidiary use of the home. Where holiday property is not business rated, the 50% council tax charge is payable on any self-contained accommodation that is not someone's only or main home (see page 115 for special provisions for Wales).

If someone lives in a caravan as his or her only or main home, he or she will pay the council tax. For other caravans, the site owner will pay business rates on the caravans and pitches, passing on the charge to the caravan owner in the site rents. (Note that this part of the site rent is not liable to VAT — see page 455).

Time shares

If you buy a time share, you may be concerned with taxation in respect of income from it, or on a capital gain when you sell it.

The nature of the rights acquired depends on the particular agreement, but most time share agreements do not give you any rights of ownership over the property itself, but merely a right to occupy it at a certain time.

If you let your time share, you will be liable to tax on the income less expenses under Schedule A. Where time share property is abroad, income is from a foreign possession charged under Schedule D, Case V (see pages 556 and 561). Many people will not have any time share income, but will sometimes exchange time shares. If this is done on a temporary basis, there are no tax implications, but a long-term arrangement could be treated as a part disposal for capital gains tax.

When you sell a time share, you will be liable to capital gains tax on the profit, after taking into account the cost and indexation allowance in the usual way. If the time share has less than 50 years to run, a depreciated cost must be used (on a straight line basis).

Time share property in the UK is usually subject to business rates. The owner of time share property charges value added tax on the selling price for the time share if it is less than three years old and on any service charges made, including business rates. If the property is over three years old, the sale proceeds, but not the service charges, are exempt from VAT.

Tax points

- If interest paid cannot be relieved against rents, individuals cannot set it against a capital gain on disposal of the property but investment companies can — see pages 368 and 449.

- Management expenses are allowed as a lettings expense. This should cover a landlord's expenses of travelling to his properties wholly for the purposes of property management. The Revenue have been reluctant to allow a deduction, particularly if the landlord lives some distance away. They may not be justified in refusing, since they lost a case on the point before the General Commissioners and did not take the case any further, and the new rules from 1995/96 for calculating rent using commercial accounting principles should strengthen the taxpayer's right to the deduction.

- In the current economic climate you may be incurring losses on furnished holiday accommodation that you want to set against other income. Make sure that you can demonstrate to the Revenue that the letting is in fact commercial and that all the various conditions are satisfied.

- The fact that property is being let does not of itself prevent an income tax charge instead of a chargeable gain on a disposal if a trading motive can be proved. Facilities for sheltering income and chargeable gains are available, but it is important to establish which tax a disposal is subject to so that the proceeds can be invested in an appropriate purchase (see page 62 and chapter 29).

- The value added tax provisions relating to property letting, including holiday letting, are extremely complex. Make sure you look carefully at the appropriate Customs and Excise booklets relating to your circumstances.

- If you normally let your property for long-term residential use but it is empty for a period of time, you will be liable to pay council tax on it, subject to any available discounts and exemptions (see page 456).

- Bed and breakfast providers can escape business rates if they offer the facility as a subsidiary use of their own homes for not more than six people. Otherwise, business rates are payable.

- If you borrow to buy property abroad, income tax relief is available on the interest from 6 April 1995.

- An investment in a property in an enterprise zone can be particularly tax-efficient so long as the price is right. See pages 315 and 406.

- Under self-assessment, you must keep the records relating to your property income for at least 5 years 10 months after the end of the tax year — see page 119. Penalties of up to £3,000 per tax year apply if you do not. The Revenue have issued a useful booklet SA/BK3 on the record-keeping requirements.

33
Husband, wife and children

General

The incomes of husband and wife are taxed independently. Each is entitled to a personal allowance and the husband gets a married couple's allowance (see below). A wife may, however, claim half the married couple's allowance as of right, and all of it if both agree.

A married couple's gains are also taxed independently, each being entitled to the annual exemption, currently £6,300. Losses of one spouse may not be set against gains of the other, but transfers of assets between husband and wife who are living together are not chargeable to capital gains tax. Any indexation allowance arising to the date of transfer increases the original cost for the purpose of calculating the gain on an eventual disposal (subject to rules to ensure that the indexation allowance does not create or increase a loss when the other spouse disposes of the asset — see page 65). This provision enables couples to plan in advance and make appropriate transfers one to the other before negotiating disposals to third parties, so that, for example, one spouse does not have gains in excess of the exempt threshold while the other has unrelieved losses, or so that tax is charged at a lower rate where one spouse's tax rate is higher than the other's. Where capital losses are brought forward from before the introduction of independent taxation on 6 April 1990, each spouse's losses must be separately identified so that they are set only against that person's gains.

Husband and wife are each responsible for completion of tax returns and for payment of the tax.

For inheritance tax purposes, husband and wife have always been treated as separate taxable persons, each having separate exemptions and a separate nil rate threshold. Transfers between the two are exempt unless one of them is not domiciled in the United Kingdom, in which case the transfers to the non-domiciled spouse are exempt up to £55,000, and potentially chargeable on the excess over that amount should the donor not survive for seven years. For the meaning of domicile, see page 554.

Stamp duty is not normally charged on the value of assets transferred between husband and wife, but see page 462 re mortgaged property.

Married couple's allowance (TA 1988, ss 256, 257A, 257BA, 257BB; FA 1994, s 77 and Sch 8)

The married couple's allowance is given as a reduction of your tax liability and saves tax only at 15%. The tax saving in 1995/96 was £258, and it has increased to £268.50 for 1996/97 following the increase in the allowance from £1,720 to £1,790.

The allowance is given in full in the year of separation or death of either spouse, but it is reduced in the year of marriage (see page 463).

The married couple's allowance is normally given to the husband. A married woman may, however, claim half the basic married couple's allowance (not any age addition for the over 65s) as of right, and the couple may jointly claim for the wife to get the whole of the basic allowance, providing in each case the claim is made *before* the tax year in which it is first to apply, except in the year of marriage when the claim may be made within that year (see page 13 for the detailed provisions). If you tick the appropriate box on your 1996 tax return, the Revenue will send you a claim form enabling the 1997/98 allowance to be transferred. The latest draft of the self-assessment return does not provide a box to be ticked, and states instead that you should write to the Revenue if you want to make a change.

A wife can use the transferred allowance to reduce any of her tax for the year, even if the tax relates to income arising before marriage or after the date of separation or of her husband's death.

Whichever of you gets the allowance, if your tax bill is too low to use the tax reduction, you may notify the Revenue that you want to transfer the surplus allowance to your spouse. There is a box to tick on tax returns if you want to apply for a transfer notice form (form 575). For years before 1996/97, the claim to transfer the surplus may be made at any time in the six years *after* the tax year, reduced from 1996/97 onwards to five years from the 31 January following the tax year.

Since the allowance is given as a fixed amount of tax saving, transferring all or half of it to the wife will not save tax unless the husband has insufficient income to pay tax. A transfer to the wife may, however, improve cash flow if, say, the husband would get the reduction in the tax on self-employed profits that he pays half-yearly as part of his provisional and balancing payments under self-assessment whereas the wife is an employee who would reduce her PAYE tax from the beginning of the tax year.

Using available allowances and the lower rate band

Some people on low incomes, particularly married women with very little earned income, will need to make sure that they make the best use of their allowances and the 20% tax rate band.

You will get a cash flow advantage if you receive income equal to your available personal allowance in full, without tax being deducted by the payer. Investments that always pay interest gross are national savings bank accounts and offshore accounts with banks and building societies. If you will not be liable to tax at all, you can claim to receive interest from other banks and from building societies without tax being deducted rather than having to reclaim the tax later (see chapter 37). The claim to receive it in full cannot be made if you expect some of your income to be liable to tax, even if you will be entitled to reclaim all or most of the tax deducted by the bank or building society.

Transferring property from one spouse to another (TA 1988, ss 282A, 282B, 660A; FA 1995, Sch 17)

In order to take best advantage of being taxed separately, it may be sensible for property to be transferred from husband to wife or vice versa. Any such transfers are fully effective for tax purposes providing the transfer is an outright gift of the property with no question of the transferring spouse controlling it or deriving a benefit from it. It is not possible to transfer a right to income while retaining a right to the capital (but see below re jointly owned property). The rules do not prevent the spouse who gave the property getting it back later as a gift, or after the other spouse's death, providing there were no 'strings' on the transfer in the first place. And where property is transferred into the joint names of husband and wife and they own it under the normal 'joint tenants' provisions, the Revenue do not regard this as breaching the 'outright gift' rules, even though the property goes automatically to the survivor when one dies (see below).

Such transfers will be beneficial where a wife or husband would otherwise waste their personal allowance or 20% rate band, or where one spouse would be paying higher rate tax while the other did not fully use the basic rate band. You must make sure you have evidence of transfers in the proper legal form.

Stamp duty is not charged on gifts (except possibly in relation to mortgaged property — see page 462).

Where husband and wife are living together and one spouse acquires the other's interest in the family home in lifetime or on death, the joint period of ownership after 31 March 1982 is taken into account for the purpose of the capital gains private residence exemption (see page 419).

Jointly owned property

Husband and wife are normally treated as owning joint property as 'joint tenants', which means that each has equal rights over the property and when one dies, it goes automatically to the other. The joint tenancy can, however, be severed, and replaced by a 'tenancy in common', in which the share of each is separate, and may be unequal, and may be disposed of in lifetime or on death as the spouse wishes. If you do this, make sure you have proper documentary evidence of what you have done.

Where property is in joint names, it is treated as being owned equally for income tax purposes unless it is actually owned in some different proportions *and* you make a declaration to that effect. Such a declaration takes effect from the date it is made, providing notice of the declaration is given to the Revenue (on form 17) within 60 days. The form only covers the assets listed on it. Any new assets must be covered by a separate form. Special provisions apply to joint mortgage interest on your home (see page 415).

The tax treatment of joint ownership may be useful to overcome one practical difficulty of maximising the benefits of independent taxation — that the richer spouse may be unwilling to transfer property to the other. The reluctant spouse could transfer an asset into joint ownership as tenants in common, retaining 95% ownership and giving the spouse a 5% share; if no declaration of the actual shares is notified to the Revenue, the tax law treats the income as being shared equally.

Any sort of property may be transferred — land and buildings, shares, bank accounts, etc. When you open joint bank and building society accounts, you normally declare that they are in your joint beneficial ownership. You can still later change your ownership to tenants in common, although the bank or building society are likely to act on the basis of your original declaration, so that they would treat the account as belonging to the survivor when one dies. In that case your personal representatives need to be left clear instructions so that they can deal properly with your estate. Another point that needs to be watched is in relation to mortgaged property. If the spouse to whom the property is transferred takes over responsibility for the mortgage, the mortgage debt is treated as consideration for the transfer and is liable to stamp duty (unless covered by the £60,000 limit for certified transactions — see page 89). This will not apply if the spouse who is transferring the property undertakes to pay the mortgage. (See also page 469 re separation and divorce.)

Regardless of the way income is treated for income tax purposes, it is the underlying beneficial ownership of assets that determines the capital gains tax treatment. Again, it is essential to have evidence of the shares in which property is held.

Children (TA 1988, s 660B; FA 1995, Sch 17)

The income of your children is theirs in their own right, no matter how young they are, and they are entitled to the full personal allowance and lower rate tax bands. For a child under 18 and unmarried, this does not apply to income that comes directly or indirectly from you, which is still treated as your own income with the following exceptions.

Each parent can give each child a capital sum (say a bank or building society deposit) from which the child receives no more than £100 gross income per annum. (But if the income exceeded the limit, the whole amount and not just the excess over £100 would be taxed on the parent.)

The national savings 'children's bonus bonds' for under 16-year olds (see page 495) can be given in addition.

A parent may pay premiums (maximum £270 per annum) on a qualifying friendly society policy for a child under 18 (see page 549).

A parent may establish an 'accumulation and maintenance' settlement for his children, the income from which is not treated as his in certain circumstances (see chapter 42).

A parent may establish a 'bare trust' for a child, under which the income counts as the child's income rather than the parent's so long as it is not actually paid to or for the benefit of the child (see chapter 42).

Parent/child covenants used to save tax, but this only applied up to 5 April 1995 to covenants made before 15 March 1988 that were still in force and does not apply in any event after that date.

Student grants

The parental contribution to student grants depends on the parents' income and although broadly the same rules apply as for income tax, it is worth finding out the detailed provisions and taking steps where appropriate to reduce the income of years that count for grant purposes, e.g. by making maximum payments into a personal pension plan.

Year of marriage (TA 1988, s 257A)

If a couple marry in 1996/97, the husband is entitled to the married couple's allowance of £1,790, reduced by £149.17 for each complete tax month prior to the date of marriage. Thus if you marry on 25 January 1997, the allowance is reduced by 9 × £149.17, i.e. by £1,342, giving a married couple's allowance of £448 on which the tax saving at 15% is £67.20. The provisions enabling all or half of the married couple's allowance to be transferred to the wife apply to the reduced amount.

The additional personal allowance (see page 15) is not available in the year of marriage in respect of a child born after the marriage, although this allowance can continue in the year of marriage for a child of either husband or wife before marriage. In the case of a child of the husband, the proportion of the married couple's allowance could not be claimed as well (see page 13).

Death of the husband

In the year of her husband's death, a widow may reduce her tax bill by 15% of £1,790 (for 1996/97) in respect of the widow's bereavement allowance, which is also given in the next tax year provided that she has not remarried before the start of it. If the widow has a qualifying child living with her (see page 15), she may also claim a deduction of the same amount in respect of the additional personal allowance in the year of her husband's death, and that allowance continues for so long as there is a qualifying child or children living with her and she remains unmarried at the beginning of the tax year.

In the year of her husband's death, the widow can also receive the benefit of any of the married couple's allowance which cannot be used against the husband's tax bill up to the date of death. This might be particularly relevant where the husband died early in the tax year. The husband's executors must notify the Revenue that the surplus married couple's allowance is being tranferred to the widow.

A woman who has claimed all or half of the basic married couple's allowance will get the widow's bereavement allowance tax deduction instead in the year of her husband's death, the married couple's allowance being automatically transferred back to reduce the tax on the husband's income. If his income is insufficient to use his allowances, the widow will be entitled to the benefit of any surplus married couple's allowance, without the need for a claim.

All the allowances available to a widow in the year of her husband's death may be given against the tax on income arising both before and after the date of death.

Her income will include any she is entitled to from the assets in her husband's estate. By Revenue concession A7, a widow who acquires from her husband's estate a business or other source of income (such as a national savings bank account) which has been charged to tax on a previous year basis has been able to avoid the business or source of income being treated as ceasing and a new business/source starting. Because of the change to the current year basis, the concession has been withdrawn from 6 April 1995 for businesses/sources that started on or after 6 April 1994. For businesses/sources established before 6 April 1994 it is to be withdrawn from a date to be fixed (not before 6 April 1997).

Some of the State benefits a widow gets are taxable and some are not (see table on page 149). If a widow qualifies for any of the non-taxable benefits, she may be better having her widow's pension reduced and drawing the non-taxable benefits in full instead. A widow who remarries before age 60 may also be worse off in terms of her State retirement pension — see page 200.

See page 419 for the capital gains position when a widow aquires her late husband's interest in the family home.

Death of the wife

The husband is entitled to the full married couple's allowance for the tax year in which his wife dies. For later years until remarriage, he loses his entitlement, but he may claim the additional personal allowance if he has a qualifying child living with him (see page 15). Investment income arising on the wife's assets following death will be assessed through her estate and will form part of the husband's income to the extent that he is the ultimate beneficiary. Revenue concession A7 outlined above also applies (until its withdrawal) to a husband taking over sources of income from his deceased wife.

If all or half of the husband's basic married couple's allowance has been claimed by the wife, and her income in the year of her death is insufficient to cover her allowances, any surplus married couple's allowance can be transferred back to the husband, providing the wife's personal representatives notify the Revenue accordingly.

See page 419 for the capital gains position when a widower acquires his late wife's interest in the family home.

Separation (TA 1988, ss 257F, 259, 260, 261A)

If husband and wife separate and the separation is likely to be permanent, the married couple's allowance is available (in full) for the year of separation but not in later years. The allowance will go to the husband, unless a claim has been made to transfer half or all of it to the wife. The date of separation is a question of fact.

Before 6 April 1990, when husband and wife were taxed jointly, a husband could continue to get married man's allowance up to the year of divorce if he wholly maintained his separated wife by unenforceable payments. This does not apply to the married couple's allowance. Where, however, a couple separated before 6 April 1990 and the husband was entitled to the married man's allowance under the old provisions, he will continue to get married couple's allowance so long as the conditions are satisfied.

Additional personal allowance may be claimed by both husband and wife in the year of separation if each has a qualifying child resident with him or her for all or part of the remainder of the year (see page 15). If husband and wife both claim in respect of the same child the allowance is apportioned between them, but two allowances are available if each has a different qualifying child resident with him or her for at least part of the year (subject to what is said below about cohabiting couples). The available allowance is, however, reduced by any married couple's allowance to which husband or wife is entitled. If half of the basic married couple's allowance has been claimed by each, each can only claim half of the additional personal allowance. If the couple have claimed that the wife should get all of the married couple's allowance she cannot claim the additional allowance at all in that year. In that case, if the husband has a qualifying child resident with him for all or part of the remainder of the year, he will be entitled to a full additional personal allowance, unless he is over 65, in which case the age addition to the married couple's allowance will reduce his additional personal allowance.

The additional personal allowance will continue in later years so long as the conditions are satisfied. If, however, husband and wife remain apart but either or both of them live with someone else as man and wife, only one additional personal allowance is available per household. So if, say, two unmarried people live with each other and each has a qualifying child from a former marriage, only one additional personal allowance will be available and it will be given in respect of the youngest qualifying child.

To get the additional personal allowance for a qualifying child, you have to show that the child is resident with you for all or part of the year. The Revenue view is that 'resident for part of the year' means more than just the occasional short visit. Although this view is not necessarily correct, if the child does not live with you permanently it is better to avoid a challenge by making sure that the child does have his/her own room and belongings at your home and spends some significant time there.

Reconciliation

If a couple become reconciled in a later tax year, the full married couple's allowance is available in the year of reconciliation (unless they had divorced). If the reconciliation takes place in the same tax year as the separation, they will usually be taxed as if they had not been separated.

Maintenance payments

The tax treatment of maintenance payments depends on whether the payments are to the spouse or to the children, and when the maintenance first became payable. The extent to which the payer gets relief and the recipient is taxed on the maintenance is outlined below. All maintenance that qualifies for relief is paid in full, without any deduction of tax. The tax relief due is given to the payer and any tax due is collected from the recipient by means of an adjustment to the PAYE coding for employees, and otherwise in an assessment or, from 1996/97, self-assessment.

Maintenance payments to spouse (TA 1988, ss 347A, 347B; FA 1988, s 38; FA 1994, s 79)

Payments made after 14 March 1988, except those under obligations which then existed (see below) (TA 1988, s 347B)

Where you pay maintenance to your separated or divorced spouse by court order, Child Support Agency assessment or written agreement, you can claim a maintenance relief deduction from your tax bill for 1996/97 of 15% of £1,790 (£1,720 for 1995/96), or 15% of the amount paid if less. You cannot save tax on more than £1,790 even if you pay maintenance to more than one person. Your spouse is not taxed on the amount received. The full allowance is available in the year of separation, as well as the married couple's allowance. Payments due after your spouse remarries do not qualify for relief. Maintenance relief is available to European Economic Area (EEA — see page 132) nationals resident in the UK and to UK nationals paying maintenance by order or written agreement of an EEA country.

Payments under obligations existing at 15 March 1988 (FA 1988, ss 38–40)

Special provisions apply to payments you make under pre-15 March 1988 obligations. For 1996/97, the first £1,790 (£1,720 for 1995/96) of qualifying maintenance to your spouse (and children where relevant — see below) saves you tax at 15%. The balance qualifies for relief at your top tax rate. The spouse is liable to tax on the maintenance, except for the first £1,790.

Where maintenance has been increased since 1988/89 , the amount on which you qualify for relief is limited to the maintenance paid in that year, and your spouse pays tax only on that amount, less £1,790.

If the 1988/89 maintenance figure has been increased to more than the current maintenance relief limit, you may be better off claiming under the new rules, and for years before 1996/97 you can make a claim to do this within twelve months after the end of the tax year to which you want the new rules first to apply, increased from 1996/97 onwards to one year from the 31 January following the tax year. If, for example, the maintenance paid in 1988/89 was £1,500 and it is later increased to £2,000, switching to the new rules from 1995/96 would allow you relief on £1,720 instead of £1,500 for that year, and on £1,790 in 1996/97.

Maintenance payments to children (TA 1988, ss 347A, 347B, 348, 683; FA 1988, s 38; FA 1994, s 79; FA 1996, s 149)

From 6 April 1995, the only circumstances in which maintenance payments made direct to your children continue to qualify for tax relief are where they are made under a pre-15 March 1988 court order. Even then, relief ceases once they become 21. Before 1996/97, relief remained available if the child was already over 21 on 6 April 1994, but this no longer applies from 6 April 1996. The first £1,790 of the total qualifying maintenance payments to your spouse and children under 21 saves tax at 15%. The balance saves you tax at your top tax rate. The amount qualifying for relief is, however, restricted to the level of maintenance payable in 1988/89.

467

Maintenance that qualifies for relief under these provisions is treated as your child's income, against which the child's personal allowance may be used if not already used against other income.

Where you pay maintenance under a pre-15 March 1988 agreement, rather than a court order, it no longer qualifies for tax relief from 6 April 1995.

Divorce

The tax position of divorced couples is broadly the same as that of separated couples, except that the married couple's allowance given to some married men who were separated before 6 April 1990 (see page 465) is not available in any circumstances in tax years after that in which the divorce occurs. There are some provisions, for example the rules for employee benefits and close company associates, that continue to apply up to divorce even though the couple are not living together.

For policies entered into before 14 March 1984, a divorced wife continues to be entitled to life assurance relief on a policy on her husband's life taken out before the divorce. If she wishes to protect herself against the loss of maintenance on her husband's death, this can be done with her husband's co-operation if he takes out a policy on his own life in trust for her, or she herself takes out a policy on his life. There will be no tax relief on the premium unless the policy was taken out before 14 March 1984.

Separation and divorce — the family home (TCGA 1992, ss 222, 223; FA 1985, s 83; TA 1988, ss 354, 355; FA 1988, s 44; Stamp Duty (Exempt Instruments) Regulations 1987 (SI 1987/516))

Two aspects are important — relief for mortgage interest paid and the capital gains tax position.

Where your former or separated spouse occupies the family home, relief for mortgage interest paid by you is not available unless you have put the property up for sale, in which case relief on a loan up to the £30,000 limit (see chapter 2) may continue for 12 months or possibly longer, even if you are claiming relief for a loan to buy another home. If the mortgage interest is paid by the spouse who remains in the home (possibly using money provided by you), the spouse can claim relief on the interest on up to £30,000 of borrowing, even if you remain the legal owner. You will have your own limit of £30,000 for borrowing to buy another home.

There are transitional provisions to enable interest relief to be claimed where the loan existed (or was under written offer), and the former or separated spouse was resident in the property, at 5 April 1988. (Replacement loans do not qualify for relief.) In these circumstances, however, the £30,000 mortgage interest relief limit has to cover the borrowing on your own home, on a home occupied rent-free by a dependent relative at 5 April 1988 and on a home provided for a divorced or separated spouse.

For capital gains tax, the family home will cease to be the main residence of the spouse who leaves it. His or her share of any calculated gain on a subsequent sale will therefore be chargeable to the extent that it relates to the period of non-residence, subject to any available exemptions or reliefs. The last three years of ownership always count as a period of residence, even if a new qualifying residence has been acquired. If the property is disposed of more than three years after a spouse leaves it, part of the calculated gain will be assessable, but only in the proportion that the excess period over three years bears to the total period of ownership since 31 March 1982. Even then the chargeable gain may be covered by the annual exemption of £6,300. There is a Revenue concession (concession D6) covering absences of more than three years following separation or divorce, but only where the property is eventually transferred to the spouse remaining in it as part of the financial settlement, and an election for a new qualifying residence has not been made by the spouse moving out in the meantime.

If property is transferred from one spouse to another on break-up of a marriage, stamp duty is not payable, even if the acquiring spouse takes over a mortgage. This exemption applies to all property, not just the family home.

Capital gains tax — other chargeable assets (TCGA 1992, ss 58, 165)

The inter-spouse exemption only applies to assets transferred in a tax year when you are living together. In later tax years, capital gains tax is chargeable in the normal way, and this must be remembered when considering a matrimonial settlement following separation. In the case of certain assets transferred from one to the other before the divorce, it may be possible to avoid gains being charged to tax at that time if husband and wife elect, under the 'business gifts relief', for the recipient to adopt the original cost plus indexation allowance to date in calculating the tax payable on an eventual disposal (see chapter 4). The business gifts relief will not usually be available after divorce since the transfer of assets will then be regarded as being for consideration and therefore not eligible for gifts relief.

Inheritance tax (IHTA 1984, s 18(1))

The spouse exemption for inheritance tax is not lost on separation but continues until the time of divorce. Even then there is an exemption for transfers to former spouses for the maintenance of themselves and the children. See chapter 5.

Living together without being married

An unmarried couple can get the equivalent of the married couple's allowance in the form of the additional personal allowance if they have a qualifying child (see page 15). But only one claim may be made per household, even if each has a qualifying child. The allowance is given in respect of the youngest qualifying child. When two people claim the relief for the same child, the relief is apportioned, the split being made according to how long the child resides with each claimant in the tax year, unless they have agreed some other split. Claimants other than the child's own parent are not entitled to the relief unless they maintain the child.

An unmarried person is not entitled to tax relief on payments under a maintenance order awarded to a cohabitee in respect of their children.

See page 415 for mortgage interest relief for unmarried home sharers.

Council tax

Couples who are living together as husband and wife, whether married or not, are jointly liable for payment of council tax. This only applies for any part of the year when they are living together, and would not apply after separation or divorce. A partner is not liable unless the authority has issued a bill to him or her (see page 112).

Tax points

- If all or half of the 1997/98 married couple's allowance is to be transferred to the wife, you must claim *before* 6 April 1997. The claim form is available from your tax office and you can get it by ticking a box on your 1996 tax return. Wives can claim half the allowance as of right, and all of it with the husband's agreement. This may give you a timing benefit when paying tax (see page 460).

- The Revenue require a separate form 17 (notification of unequal shares) for any new jointly owned assets. This needs to be borne in mind if you have a joint share portfolio, where there may be frequent changes.

- If you change your ownership of bank and building society accounts so that you hold them as tenants in common rather than joint tenants, make sure you have proper evidence that you have done so.

- Although the capital gains tax private residence exemption does not apply to a second home, if you own the second home jointly you will be entitled to two annual exemptions when you sell it (unless used against other gains).

- In a bona fide husband and wife partnership where both play a significant role in the business, profits can be shared so as to maximise the benefit of independent taxation and of capital gains retirement relief when you retire.

- If your joint wealth is substantial, you may be able to save inheritance tax by rearranging the ownership of assets between you. See chapter 35 for details.

- In appropriate circumstances, separated parents with two qualifying children can each claim additional personal allowance. But make sure you satisfy the rules — see page 465.

- If you are cohabiting, remember that the social security regulations are different from those relating to tax. They should be researched before making financial arrangements between you and for children.

34
Especially for the senior citizen

General (TA 1988, ss 256, 257, 257A, 257BA, 257BB; FA 1994, s 77)

Married couples

The incomes of husband and wife are taxed independently. Each is entitled to a personal allowance based on their age, available against any income, earned or unearned, and saving tax at their highest tax rate. The allowances for 1996/97 are as follows:

Under 65	£3,765
65 to 74	£4,910
75 and over	£5,090

Note that even if a wife gets State pension at 60, she does not get the higher tax allowance until she is 65.

In addition, there is a married couple's allowance, based on the age of the older spouse, as follows:

Both under 65	£1,790
Elder 65 to 74	£3,115
Elder 75 or over	£3,155

The married couple's allowance saves you tax at only 15%. The allowance normally goes to the husband, but a wife may claim half of the basic married couple's allowance (not any addition for those over 65) as of right, and all of it if both agree. The husband always gets any extra allowance for the over 65s. For the detailed provisions, see chapter 33. Note particularly pages 465, 466 on the possible adverse effect of transferring the allowance if a couple entitled to the increased allowances for those over 65 become separated or divorced.

There were transitional provisions for certain husbands with older wives to prevent their allowances being lower when independent taxation was introduced from 6 April 1990, but these are no longer relevant.

The entitlement to age allowances is subject to an income restriction — see page 473.

If your tax bill is lower than the tax saving on your married couple's allowance, any excess may be transferred to your spouse. You have to make a specific claim to do this — it is not automatic. There is a box to fill in on your tax return if you want the Revenue to send you the necessary form.

Single people

Single people are entitled to a personal allowance at the same levels as those stated above for married people, and are subject to the same income limit (see below). A single woman gets state pension at age 60, but is not entitled to a higher tax allowance until she is 65.

Income limit for age allowances

The benefit of higher personal allowances is withdrawn to the extent that income exceeds a specified limit, £15,200 for 1996/97. Each of a married couple has his or her own limit. The personal allowance is reduced by half the excess of income over that limit until it reaches the normal personal allowance level, currently £3,765.

The married couple's age allowance is similarly subject to the income limit, but the amount available depends on the husband's income only, even if the extra allowance is being given because of his wife's age rather than his. After the personal allowance has been reduced to £3,765, the married couple's allowance is similarly reduced by half of the excess of his total income over £15,200 which has not already been taken into account to reduce his personal allowance, until it reaches the normal married couple's allowance, currently £1,790 (which may have been transferred to the wife).

Once income reaches a certain level, all the benefit of the increased personal allowances, and increased married couple's allowances where relevant, is lost and only normal allowances are given. The maximum income levels at which age allowance and married couple's allowance are available are shown on page 14.

Example 1	(a) £	(b) £
Single person, aged 67, has income in 1996/97 of:		
Pension	10,000	10,200
Savings income	5,200	5,200
	15,200	15,400
Personal allowance (over 65)		
Unrestricted	4,910	
Restricted by ½ of £200		4,810
Taxable income	10,290	10,590

Tax thereon:

Non-savings income	3,900/ 3,900 @ 20%	780	780
	1,190/ 1,490 @ 24%	285	357
Savings income	5,200/ 5,200 @ 20%	1,040	1,040
	10,290 10,590	£2,105	£2,177

Additional tax payable on extra £200 income is £72, i.e. 36%.

Example 2

Facts as in example 1 but extra income is savings income.

	(a)	(b)
	£	£
Pension	10,000	10,000
Savings income	5,200	5,400
	15,200	15,400
Personal allowance as before	(4,910)	(4,810)
Taxable income	10,290	10,590

Tax thereon:

Non-savings income	3,900/ 3,900 @ 20%	780	780
	1,190/ 1,290 @ 24%	285	309
Savings income	5,200/ 5,400 @ 20%	1,040	1,080
	10,290 10,590	£2,105	£2,169

Additional tax payable on extra £200 income is £64, i.e. 32%.

If the pension had been only £8,700 and the remaining income was savings income, the position would be:

	(a)	(b)
Pension	8,700	8,700
Savings income	6,500	6,700
	15,200	15,400
Personal allowance as before	(4,910)	(4,810)
Taxable income	10,290	10,590

Tax thereon:

Non-savings income	3,790/ 3,890 @ 20%	758	778
Savings income	6,500/ 6,700 @ 20%	1,300	1,340
	10,290 10,590	£2,058	£2,118

Additional tax payable on extra £200 income is £60, i.e. 30%.

As a further variation, if the savings income had been £6,500 and the remaining income was pension, the position would be:

	(a)	(b)
Pension	8,700	8,900
Savings income	6,500	6,500
	15,200	15,400
Personal allowance as before	(4,910)	(4,810)
Taxable income	10,290	10,590

Tax thereon:

			(a)	(b)
Non-savings income	3,790/	3,900 @ 20%	758	780
	—/	190 @ 24%	—	45
Savings income	6,500/	6,500 @ 20%	1,300	1,300
	10,290	10,590	£2,058	£2,125

Additional tax payable on extra £200 income is £67, i.e. 33½%.

The reduction of the age allowance by £1 for every £2 of income over £15,200 is sometimes called the age allowance trap, because it may have the effect of costing you tax at 36% on the excess over £15,200. Where there is savings income taxed at 20%, the tax on the excess will be somewhere between 30% and 36%, depending on the level of non-savings income. See examples 1 and 2 above.

If you are in this position, you should consider reducing your taxable income by switching to tax-exempt investments such as Tax Exempt Special Savings Accounts and national savings certificates. In both cases, maximum returns are obtained by leaving the money invested for the prescribed period, but some withdrawal of funds is possible, particularly with savings certificates. For details, see chapters 36 and 37.

Where you pay charges on income, such as convenanted payments to charity (see page 9), the payments reduce your income for age allowance purposes.

Pensions and State benefits

There are various points you need to know about pensions, both from employers and from the State. An increase in State pension will result in a larger deduction of tax from an occupational pension. This is because the State pension increase takes up another slice of your tax allowances, reducing the amount available to set against your occupational pension. You are still better off overall. Some people with small occupational pensions may not get the full benefit of their allowances through their tax deductions and will need to claim a refund — see below. Some State benefits are taxable and others, including some widows' benefits, are not (see Table on page 149), so you need to take care where you have a choice. For general points on State benefits, see chapter 13.

475

Tax refunds

If you pay too much tax, you will be entitled to a refund. State pensions are received in full, and take up the first slice of your allowances, and occupational and personal pensions are taxed through the PAYE scheme, so in many cases the allowances and lower rate band of tax have already been taken into account and the correct amount of tax has been paid. Before 1996/97, tax was deducted at 25% from savings income, so that refund claims were necessary to the extent that tax had been paid at 25% rather than the lower rate of 20%. From 1996/97 all savings income (including dividends) is charged at the lower rate of 20% unless total income exceeds the basic rate threshold of £25,500, so that far fewer refund claims will be necessary. They will still be relevant in some circumstances, such as where pension income is insufficient to use available allowances (see example 5 on page 22). You may be able to avoid overpaying tax by registering to receive bank and building society interest in full, but only if you will not be liable to pay tax at all — see page 503. You can, however, claim a refund of tax deducted from bank and building society interest without waiting till the end of the tax year if the refund is £50 or more.

Providing a home for a dependent relative (IHTA 1984, s 53; TCGA 1992, ss 73, 225)

A gain on the disposal of a property provided rent-free for a dependent relative, such as a parent over 65, used to be exempt from capital gains tax but this no longer applies unless the relative was in the property on 5 April 1988 and still lives there. It is, however, possible for you to acquire a property, put it into trust and allow an elderly relative to live in it rent-free for life, the property then reverting to you when the relative dies. There would be no income from the property, therefore no income tax to pay, capital gains tax would not be payable when you reacquired the property, and providing the relative does not outlive you, inheritance tax would not be chargeable on the value of the property in the trust, since the property will have reverted to you in your lifetime. If the property was already owned for a time before it was put in trust and was not exempt as your private residence, there would be a chargeable gain at that time equal to the difference between its value when transferred to the trust and the indexed cost. Professional advice is essential.

Maximising investment income

Now that those with income below the basic rate threshold of £25,500 pay tax on their savings income plus a further £3,900 at 20%, and at 24% on the remainder, and with capital gains now being taxed at income tax rates, it may be sensible for you to reappraise your investments following retirement with a view to maximising income instead of concentrating on capital growth. You should, however, remember that each of husband and wife is exempt from capital gains tax on the first £6,300 of chargeable gains, so that investments with the potential of realising such gains should not be ignored.

Purchased life annuities

A purchased life annuity is where you receive an annual sum for your lifetime in exchange for a capital payment. The characteristic of a purchased life annuity is that part of it is regarded as a return of capital and thus escapes tax; from April 1996 the income element is regarded as savings income and tax is deductible at only 20% (see page 16). The older you are the greater the tax-free capital element of the annuity. You do, of course, sacrifice the capital required to buy the annuity, and this loss of capital must be weighed against the greater income arising. You may think the loss of capital is worthwhile to enable you to improve your standard of living, particularly if you have no dependants or others you want to leave your capital to. See example 3. The annuity rates vary from time to time and it is essential to get proper professional advice before making this sort of arrangement.

Example 3

	Tax calculation	Cash available
Income of a single taxpayer aged over 75 is	5,240	5,240
Personal allowance (75 and over)	5,090	
Tax at 20% on	150	30
Net spendable income		£5,210

A life annuity is purchased for £16,000. Suppose it produces £2,800 for the taxpayer's lifetime, of which £1,750 is regarded by the Revenue as a return of capital.

The effect on the net spendable income is:

Net spendable income as before		5,210
Capital element of annuity received in full		1,750
Income element of annuity	1,050	
Less tax at 20%	210	840
Net spendable income increases to		£7,800

The net spendable income has been increased by £2,590 but £16,000 capital has been lost forever to achieve that increase.

Making the most of the dwelling house

Your home is often your most significant asset, yet it can be your biggest liability in the sense that you have to maintain it, and in most cases it does not produce income.

Sometimes the money to purchase a life annuity (see page 477) is raised by a loan secured on your home (a home income plan). Interest on the first £30,000 of the loan is allowed for tax and relief may be given under the MIRAS scheme. This interest qualifies for tax relief at the basic rate, currently 24%, even though relief on other home loans is restricted to 15%. If you leave the property and put it up for sale, you will still be entitled to relief on interest for a further 12 months, or longer at the Revenue's discretion. The interest paid clearly reduces the extra income from the annuity and careful calculations are necessary to see if the result is a meaningful increase in your spending money.

If you decide to let part of your home, you will not have to pay income tax on the rent unless it exceeds £62.50 a week — see page 410. The letting will not cause you to lose your capital gains tax private residence exemption (see chapter 30) when you sell the property provided that the gain on the let part does not exceed that on the exempt part, subject to a maximum exempt gain on the let part of £40,000. Taking in boarders who live as part of the family does not affect your capital gains tax exemption at all.

Another possibility is a home reversion scheme, under which you sell all or part of your house to the reversion company for much less than its value (the discount usually being at least 50%) in return for the right to live in it until you die. Some schemes give you a lower initial sum but give you a share in future increases in value of the property. The initial cash sum does not attract capital gains tax but shares of future increases in value may be liable. The investment of the initial capital sum gives you extra spendable income.

There are numerous life assurance/annuity schemes, some of them involving the value of your home. Proper financial advice is essential and you must also be sure that the scheme gives you security of income and does not put your home at risk.

Helping the family

You may be in a position to give financial help to your family rather than requiring help from them. Income tax and possibly capital gains tax advantages may be obtained by placing funds in a 'bare trust' — see page 582. As far as inheritance tax is concerned, the following gifts may be made without inheritance tax consequences:

(a) habitual gifts out of income that leave you with enough income to maintain your usual standard of living;

(b) gifts of not more than £250 per donee in each tax year;

(c) the first £3,000 of total gifts in each tax year, plus any unused part of the £3,000 exemption for the previous tax year. This exemption applies to gifts on an 'earliest first' basis, so if you gave away nothing last year and give £5,000 in May and £5,000 in June, the May gift is exempt and £1,000 of the June gift is exempt.

Even if the gift is not exempt, there is still no immediate inheritance tax to pay since lifetime gifts (other than to discretionary trusts) are only brought into account for inheritance tax if you do not survive the gift by seven years. In the meantime they are called 'potentially exempt transfers' (see page 72). If you do not survive the seven-year period, there is still no question of inheritance tax being payable if the gift is within the nil rate band for inheritance tax, currently £200,000. This nil band is used against the earliest gifts in the seven years before death. Any gifts over and above the nil band are chargeable, but the tax is reduced on a sliding scale if you have survived the gift by more than three years. All non-exempt gifts within the seven years before death do, however, affect how much of the nil rate band is available against the death estate.

Husband and wife have always been treated separately for inheritance tax, each being entitled to the available exemptions.

Tax position on death

When you die, your wealth at death and the chargeable transfers you have made in the previous seven years will determine whether any, and if so how much, inheritance tax is payable (see chapter 5). There is no inheritance tax on assets passing to your husband or wife. There is no liability to capital gains tax on any increase in the value of your assets up to the date of your death, and those who acquire the assets are treated as having bought them at their market value at the date of your death. Further details on the position at death are in chapters 33 and 35.

If capital gains have been made in that part of the tax year before your death, they will be chargeable if they exceed the annual exemption of £6,300. Any capital losses in the tax year of death may be carried back to set against gains on which tax has been paid in the three previous tax years, latest first, and, in that event, tax will be repayable to the estate. From 1996/97, interest on the repayment will run from the payment date for the tax year of death (see page 119).

As far as income tax is concerned, the income to the date of death is charged to tax in the usual way, and a full personal allowance is available. In the case of a married couple, the married couple's allowance is available in full in the year of the wife's death but not in later years. If the husband dies first, any part of the tax saving on the married couple's allowance that is not used against his tax bill may be transferred to the widow, and she can use it against any of her tax for the year, on income arising both before and after her husband's death. A widow is also entitled to a tax deduction in respect of the widow's bereavement allowance in the year of her husband's death and in the following year unless she has remarried before the beginning of it. In 1996/97 the allowance reduces her tax bill by 15% of £1,790, i.e. £268.50. On remarriage she cannot transfer any unused tax saving to her new husband. If all or half of the married couple's allowance had been transferred from the husband (see page 460), the widow will get the widow's bereavement allowance deduction instead in the year of her husband's death and the married couple's allowance will automatically be transferred back to be used against the husband's tax bill to the date of death, but with any tax reduction not used against his tax still being available to the widow.

A widow with a qualifying child may claim a tax deduction in respect of the additional personal allowance (see page 15), commencing in the year of her husband's death. A widower can only claim for years after that in which his wife died.

Private medical insurance (FA 1989, ss 54–57; FA 1994, s 83 and Sch 10)

Tax relief is available for premiums paid for private medical insurance where the insured person is over 60, or, if the insurance relates to a married couple, where one of them is over 60, at the time of payment. Relief is also available to someone else, such as your son or daughter, if they pay premiums on your behalf, but no further relief is available if the payer is already entitled to tax relief on the payment. So you cannot claim relief if the premium is paid by your employer (who gets tax relief for the payment in calculating his profits), even though you will be taxed on the benefit if you are a P11D employee (see page 157) . The person who is to pay the premium must complete a declaration of eligibility for tax relief on a form supplied by the insurer.

The relief is at the basic rate of tax, and it is deducted when you pay the premium, so that you pay a net sum. You may retain the tax deducted even if your income is too low to attract tax.

Council tax

Your property is exempt from council tax if it is left unoccupied while you are a long-term hospital patient, or are being looked after in a residential care home, or are living elsewhere to receive care (see page 111). You may qualify for a one-band reduction for council tax if your home has special features because you or another resident is disabled (see page 113). Other discounts may be available (see page 112).

People on low incomes are entitled to council tax benefit of up to 100% (see page 114).

Tax points

- The marginal tax rate for those over 65 with income over £15,200 ranges from 30% to 36%, so that investments that produce tax-free income or capital gains should be considered in those circumstances.

- In reckoning the income for age allowances, any investment bond withdrawals over the 5% limit have to be taken into account even though there is no tax to pay on that excess at the higher rate (see chapter 40). Conversely, an amount paid under a deed of covenant to a charity will reduce the income when calculating whether age allowances are to be restricted.

- There is no point in increasing available income now if this jeopardises your capital and causes worry and uncertainty for the future.

- If you have a life annuity 'home income plan' and you have to leave your home, you can still get relief for loan interest for a limited time providing the property is put up for sale. You will not get the relief if you are not trying to sell it.

- Now that lifetime transfers are potentially exempt from inheritance tax and no longer have to be reported, it is more important than ever to keep accurate records of gifts out of income and capital so that there can be no doubt about dates and amounts of gifts. Personal representatives are responsible for enquiries about transfers in the seven years before death and carefully kept records will be essential for the avoidance of doubt.

- If, because of disability, you have to provide, adapt or extend a bathroom, washroom or lavatory in your private residence, the cost is not liable to VAT. There is, however, no income tax relief on the cost, nor any income tax relief on interest you pay on money borrowed to pay for the work, where the loan was made after 5 April 1988. Relief for income tax on interest paid after 5 April 1988 on loans made before then continues to be available (but not on replacement loans).

- If your wife is over 65 and does not have enough income of her own to cover her personal allowance, you should consider transferring some of your assets to her if this is practicable, so that the income from them will then be hers and not yours (see page 461). Interest on national savings bank accounts is paid gross, and the wife's allowance can be used to cover interest she has from such accounts. Interest on other bank and building society accounts can only be paid gross if you are able to register because you will not be liable to tax at all (see chapter 37). If you cannot do this, there will be a cash flow advantage with national savings bank interest, but you need to compare the rates of interest on offer as well.

- If it is not appropriate to transfer assets from one spouse to the other, placing them in joint ownership but in unequal shares will still have the effect of the income being split equally even if the ownership share of the one spouse far exceeds that of the other (see page 462).

- The income limit for age-related married couple's allowance depends on the husband's income, even if the allowance is given because of the wife's age. It does not matter how high the wife's income is.

- If a husband's income is too low to use the age-related married couple's allowance, the unused amount can be transferred to his wife and the full amount transferred is available to her, with no income restriction.

35
Making a will and post-death planning

If you die without making a will

If you die without making a will, the rules of intestacy require your estate to be divided in a particular way. If you are married, your spouse automatically acquires the matrimonial home if you own it as joint tenants (see page 484, and the intestacy rules apply only to the remainder of your estate. If, on the other hand, the house was owned either by you alone or jointly with your spouse as tenants in common (see page 484), your share would form part of your estate and would be subject to the intestacy rules. As far as the spouse is concerned, from 1 January 1996 the spouse will not inherit under the intestacy rules unless he/she survives the deceased spouse by at least 28 days. The intestacy rules applicable in England and Wales are set out in the following table.

Where there is a surviving spouse Are there any:			Spouse takes:	Remainder
Children and their issue*	Parents	Brothers and sisters and their issue*		
No	No	No	Whole estate	
Yes			Personal chattels + £125,000 + life interest in half of residue	Children (or their issue*) share half residue and take spouse's share on his or her death
No	Yes		Personal chattels + £200,000 + half of residue absolutely	Parents share half of residue absolutely
No	No	Yes	"	Brothers and sisters (or their issue*) share half of residue absolutely

Where there is no surviving spouse

If there are children, or their issue*, they take the whole estate absolutely.

If there are no children or their issue*, the whole estate goes to surviving relatives in the following order of precedence, each category taking the whole estate to the exclusion of any later category:

Parents
Brothers and sisters (or their issue*)
Half brothers and sisters (or their issue*)
Grandparents
Uncles and aunts (or their issue*)
Parents' half brothers and sisters (or their issue*)

If there are none of these relatives, the estate goes to the Crown.

* 'Issue' means children and their children, grandchildren, great grandchildren, etc., each such person being entitled to an appropriate proportion of the deceased parent's share.

The share of anyone under 18 is held on trust to age 18.

It is possible for those entitled under an intestacy to vary their entitlement (see page 487), but if there are beneficiaries under 18, this cannot be done without court consent.

General considerations

In making the best arrangements from a taxation point of view, you should not forget that the prime objective is to ensure that those left behind are properly provided for in a sensible, practical and acceptable way. There are important tax implications, which it can be expensive to ignore, but they should not be allowed to override the main aim.

Where the court considers that the terms of a will or the intestacy rules do not make reasonable financial provision for certain people, such as a spouse, former spouse who has not remarried, child, or cohabitee, they may make an appropriate order, for example for the payment of a lump sum or maintenance. Such orders take effect as if they had applied at the date of death and override the provisions of the will or intestacy rules.

Inheritance tax: spouse exemption (IHTA 1984, s 18; TCGA 1992, s 58)

Gifts between husband and wife are exempt from inheritance tax for both lifetime and death transfers (unless the donee is not domiciled in the UK, in which case gifts are exempt up to a limit of £55,000 — see chapter 5). Transfers between husband and wife in a tax year when they are living together are also exempt from capital gains tax, and there is no stamp duty on gifts.

Since husband and wife are each entitled to the inheritance tax nil rate threshold (currently £200,000) before transfers become chargeable, it is clearly sensible for the joint wealth to be arranged in such a way that each takes advantage of it. The tax advantage may, however, be lost on death if the estate is then left to the surviving spouse. If, say, each had £200,000 wealth and made no transfers in the seven years before death, no tax would arise if each left the wealth to the next generation, because it would be covered by the nil rate threshold. But if the wealth were left to the surviving spouse, that spouse would then have £400,000 (ignoring any capital variation in the meantime) which would attract a tax liability of £80,000 (at current rates) on the second death.

Bypassing your spouse will not be practicable if he/she is left with inadequate assets to maintain his/her standard of living. The surviving spouse can still have the benefit of the joint capital during his/her lifetime whilst preserving the family wealth for the next generation through the use of life assurance to cover the tax liability on the second death. This is dealt with later in the chapter.

Providing the nil rate threshold is used, there is no inheritance tax incentive to equalise estates in lifetime, and indeed it may be better to leave the excess over the nil rate threshold to the surviving spouse so that tax would be paid later rather than earlier, and the surviving spouse would be able to make further tax-exempt gifts and gifts within the nil rate threshold as it increased year by year. But for income tax, it will be tax-efficient for each spouse to have sufficient income to use the lower and basic rate bands, capital gains also being charged at marginal income tax rates, so the overall position needs to be looked at.

Jointly owned assets

There are two ways in which assets may be held jointly — as joint tenants or as tenants in common. If you hold an asset with someone else as a joint tenant, it automatically passes to the other joint tenant(s) when you die. With a tenancy in common, each has a separate share which can be disposed of in lifetime or on death as the person wishes. Husband and wife are presumed to own assets as joint tenants, and other people are presumed to own them as tenants in common, but if they want to vary the normal presumption this can be done. It must, however, be done in the proper legal manner appropriate to the asset.

The appropriate share in a jointly held asset still forms part of a person's estate for inheritance tax whether the asset is held on a joint tenancy or as tenants in common, but where assets are held jointly by husband and wife, any assets passing to the spouse are covered in any event by the spouse exemption. Holding as joint tenants has the advantage in the case of a joint bank or building society account that when your spouse dies, all that is needed to enable you to take over sole ownership of the account is production of the death certificate. You do not have to wait for grant of probate or administration. But a joint account has other tax implications, particularly in relation to independent taxation of husband and wife since in many cases the share of income accruing to the wife will not give the best income tax position.

The joint ownership principles must be borne in mind when planning the use of the nil rate threshold for inheritance tax, and action taken to vary the normal presumptions where necessary (see page 461).

Legacies and their effect on the spouse exemption

Unless a will states otherwise, legacies are payable out of the residue of an estate, after inheritance tax has been paid, reducing the amount available to the person entitled to the balance of the estate — called the residuary legatee. The legacies are not themselves reduced by inheritance tax unless the will specifically says so. It follows that the amount available to a residuary legatee is often less than is apparent at first sight.

If the residuary legatee is the surviving spouse, this has an effect on the tax payable because the exempt part of the estate (which goes to the spouse) is first reduced by the tax. In example 1, out of a gross estate of £400,000, A's children receive legacies totalling £260,000, leaving an apparent residue of £140,000 for the widow. She does not, however, get £140,000, but only that amount less the tax on the rest of the estate. This is calculated by working out the tax on a figure sufficient to leave the legacies intact, called grossing-up. The tax amounts to £40,000 as shown in the example. If the will had provided that the children should pay the tax on their legacies, the widow would have received £140,000 and the total tax payable by the legatees on £260,000 would have been £24,000 (40% of the £60,000 excess over £200,000). The children could have provided for this liability by insuring their father's life, using the proceeds of the policy to pay the tax on the legacy.

Where there are deaths in quick succession (IHTA 1984, s 141)

Where at the time of someone's death, his estate has been increased by a lifetime or death gift made to him within the previous five years, the tax charge on the second transfer is reduced by quick succession relief. Although the relief is deducted from the tax payable on the second transfer, it is calculated as a percentage of the tax paid on the earlier transfer (see chapter 5).

Quick succession relief is therefore not relevant in the case of assets acquired from a spouse, in lifetime or on death, or where they have been acquired in lifetime but no tax has been paid by reference to that transfer. While not

Example 1

A has made no transfers in the seven years before his death in 1996/97. He leaves an estate of £400,000 as follows:

£65,000 to each of his four children = £260,000
Residue to his wife

The inheritance tax position on A's death is as follows:

	Gross £	Tax £	Net £
Net legacies			260,000
Gross equivalent and tax thereon	300,000	40,000	

The estate will accordingly be divided as follows:

Gross estate	400,000
Legacies to children	(260,000)
Inheritance tax payable out of residue	(40,000)
Remainder to widow, covered by spouse exemption	£100,000

losing sight of the overriding principle of family provision, there are cases where it is clearly not sensible to increase a person's estate by incoming transfers, if they have adequate resources already. Thus it will often be more tax-efficient to leave to grandchildren instead of to children. This gives the added advantage that the income arising is then that of the grandchildren in their own right, on which they will not have to pay tax if it is covered by their available income tax allowances.

Simultaneous deaths and survivorship clauses (IHTA 1984, s 92)

Where two closely related people die at the same time, or in circumstances in which it is impossible to decide who died first, neither estate has to be increased by any entitlement from the other in calculating the inheritance tax payable. This is not so if it is clear who died first. It is therefore often advisable to include a survivorship clause in a will making a bequest conditional on the beneficiary outliving the deceased by a given period, and this is effective for inheritance tax providing the period does not exceed six months. This is particularly useful to a husband and wife who wish to leave their estates to each other to make sure that there is adequate provision for the survivor's lifetime. If the wills include an appropriate survivorship clause, then if they both die within six months, the estate of the first will not pass to the second, inheritance tax being payable at each death on the value of the separate estates. This will often attract less tax than if no tax was paid on the first death, but tax was calculated on the combined estates for the second, with the second spouse to die having had little or no benefit from the assets in the meantime. The assets in each estate and the extent to which the inheritance tax nil rate band is available need to be taken into account.

A 28-day spouse survivorship period is now also prescribed under the intestacy rules (see page 482).

Variations and disclaimers (IHTA 1984, ss 17, 142, 143; TCGA 1992, s 62)

It is possible for those entitled to a deceased's estate (either under a will, on an intestacy or otherwise) to vary the way in which it is distributed, or to disclaim their entitlement, provided that they do so within two years after the death and notify the Revenue within six months after the date of the variation or disclaimer. (Court consent is needed if there are beneficiaries under 18.) If an original beneficiary has died, his personal representatives can act in his place. Inheritance tax is then charged as if the revised distribution had operated at death. Such a variation or disclaimer can also be effective for capital gains tax purposes if an appropriate claim is made (subject to what is said below about trusts), and the ultimate beneficiary takes the asset at the market value at the date of death, so that any increase in value since death is not charged until the beneficiary disposes of the asset. As far as income derived from the assets is concerned, the personal representatives will have paid basic rate tax on it (or lower rate tax if it is savings income), but the income is regarded as having been received not by the person who actually receives it following the variation but by the original beneficiary, and any tax due in excess of the basic (or lower) rate on the income up to the date of variation or disclaimer will be calculated by reference to the original beneficiary's tax rates. It may be appropriate for the person actually receiving the income to agree to pay any income tax at the higher rate. Where a variation includes the setting up of a trust, those whose entitlement goes into the trust will be regarded as settlors of the trust fund for income tax and capital gains tax, so that for example parents whose share is given up in favour of infant children will still be taxed on the income so long as the children are under 18 and unmarried, and trustees' capital gains may be treated as the original beneficiary's gains if that person is a beneficiary under the trust.

A deed of variation or disclaimer could be used to advantage where, for example, an estate has been left to the surviving spouse without the deceased's nil rate threshold having been used. If the surviving spouse is already adequately provided for, part of the estate could be diverted to, say, the children. It could also be useful where, for example, children have sufficient assets of their own and would prefer legacies to go to their own children, subject to what is said above about trusts.

Where quoted shares fall in value within the twelve months after death and are sold, cancelled, or dealings are suspended within that period, the lower value may be substituted in calculating tax on the death estate (see page 78). The reference to cancellation is apparently intended mainly to apply to liquidations, but it may be that the liquidation is not completed within the twelve-month period, so that the relief cannot be claimed. One way of avoiding the tax liability on the higher death value of the shares would be to use a deed of variation to re-direct the shares to an exempt beneficiary, such as a spouse, so that there would be no tax payable on that higher value.

Deeds of variation and disclaimer can be used to lessen the overall tax burden on death, but it is necessary for all concerned to consent to the arrangement, and they should usually be regarded as something in reserve rather than a substitute for appropriate planning.

Two other ways of building flexibility into a will are worth consideration. It is possible for someone making a will to leave a 'letter of wishes' asking the personal representatives to give effect to the requests in the letter. This is particularly useful for dealing with chattels and personal effects, and is treated for inheritance tax purposes as if it had been part of the will. The other useful provision is the ability to create a discretionary trust by will, out of which the trustees can make distributions within two years of the death, which are again treated as having been made by the will.

Insurance

Life assurance may often be useful in planning for inheritance tax. It is not always possible to reconcile making adequate provision for the family with reducing the tax liability, and insurance may then be used to cover the anticipated liability.

There is no point in insuring your own life for the benefit of your estate, because the proceeds would then form part of the estate and attract inheritance tax. Furthermore, they would not be available until the grant of probate or administration is obtained. If, however, a policy on your life is arranged by someone with an insurable interest, say your children, or you take out a policy yourself and pay the premiums, with the proceeds in trust for someone else, again say your children, the funds will not be taxable in your estate. If you pay the premiums on a trust policy, each payment is a separate gift, but you will usually be able to show that it is normal expenditure out of income, and thus exempt from inheritance tax, or, if not, covered by the annual exemption of £3,000 for transfers out of capital.

Tax points

- Equalising estates of husband and wife was previously sound practice in most cases to make use of lower inheritance tax rates, making sure that the benefit was not then lost on the first death by bringing the estates together again. Now that there is only a single 40% rate above the exempt threshold of £200,000, no extra savings will be made once each has used that nil threshold. It may be better to leave most of the excess over the nil threshold to the surviving spouse, to avoid tax on the first death and give maximum flexibility for the future. The income tax and capital gains tax position needs to be looked at as well.

- Whilst it is beyond the scope of this book to deal in detail with discretionary trusts, it is possible, in order to use up the £200,000 nil threshold, to leave £200,000 or other appropriate amount to a trust where the trustees have a discretion as to what they do with the income. You could include your wife/husband as one of the beneficiaries. The supporting capital is thus not transferred to your spouse directly to swell his/her estate for tax purposes on eventual death, but any shortage of income may be made good by the trustees exercising their discretion to pay income to him/her. Professional advice is essential since this is a very complicated area.

- A discretionary trust is also useful where there is some uncertainty at the time of making the will as to who should benefit. A transfer of the capital to one or more individuals by the trustees within two years after your death will be treated for tax purposes as having been made by your will, and will have the same effect.

- Where tax at death cannot be avoided, consider covering the liability through life assurance, the policy being written so that the proceeds belong to those who will have to bear the tax.

- If you leave your entire estate to your spouse, he/she can make lifetime transfers out of your combined wealth to an extent which he/she sees as sensible depending on the family circumstances from time to time. Those transfers may be completely exempt if they are covered by annual or marriage exemptions, or potentially exempt, becoming completely exempt if your spouse survives for seven years after making them (and where they exceed the nil rate threshold they would be subject to tapering relief on survival for three years). Unless you use appropriate trust provisions, you cannot ensure that your spouse will carry out your wishes, since if it is left to him/her unconditionally, it is up to the spouse what he/she does with it.

- Although those entitled to your estate have the right to vary the way it is to be distributed, it is useful for your will to contain authority for a deed of variation, since this makes it clear to the beneficiaries that they would not be acting against your wishes.

- If you are apprehensive about leaving outright bequests to certain people, but still want them to benefit, you could leave an amount in trust for them to receive the income it produces, and in certain circumstances, the capital. There are only minimal, if any, taxation disadvantages and it may give you the comfort of knowing that, for example, an adult child, whilst able to benefit immediately from the income, does not have an outright capital sum until a later stage when he/she is better able to manage it.

- Since all gifts to your spouse are exempt from inheritance tax, it will often be more tax effective to leave agricultural and/or business property to someone else, otherwise agricultural and business property relief will be wasted. The tax position should not, however, override family and commercial considerations.

- Where business property and agricultural property reliefs are at the rate of 100%, deferring gifts of such property until your death avoids any charge to capital gains tax and also any problems of the relief being withdrawn at death because the donee has disposed of the property. But today's reliefs may not be available tomorrow, and you may still prefer to make lifetime gifts now, deferring any capital gains tax under the gifts relief provisions (see page 60).

- Although wealth left to the next generation will be liable to inheritance tax on your death, whereas it will not be liable if left to your spouse, tax is avoided on any increase in value between your death and that of your spouse, if the next generation inherits at the death of the first rather than the second parent.

- Changing legislation, as well as family circumstances, make it important to review wills regularly.

36
Tax on your investments

Introduction

This chapter outlines the tax position on the main forms of investment available to the majority of taxpayers. More detailed information is given in chapter 37 on investing in banks and building societies and in chapter 38 on stocks and shares. The following investments are not dealt with in this chapter but are covered in the chapters indicated:

(a) Industrial buildings (chapter 22).
(b) Unquoted trading companies through the enterprise investment scheme (chapter 29).
(c) Single premium life assurance policies — investment bonds (chapter 40).
(d) Chattels and valuables (chapter 39).

The information given on each type of investment is so that you can see the effect of taxation on the income and capital growth. It is not intended to replace advice on the investments themselves, which you should seek from appropriate sources.

Tax on investment income

On many investments, tax is deducted at source, and from 6 April 1996 the rate of tax deducted is the lower rate of 20% rather than the basic rate. This is the same as the effective tax rate on dividends (a tax credit of £20 being received with a cash dividend of £80, which represents 20% of the tax credit-inclusive amount). On other investments, interest is received in full. In either case, an individual is liable to tax at the rate appropriate to his income, so he may have to pay some more tax or get some back. From 1996/97, tax on interest received gross, and higher rate tax on taxed income, is included in the provisional half-yearly payments on 31 January in the tax year and 31 July following for continuing sources, with any balance being part of the overall balancing payment due on 31 January following the tax year. For employees or pensioners with small amounts of untaxed interest, the tax may be collected by adjusting their PAYE codings.

Where income tax is deducted from a company's income, the company still has to pay corporation tax on the income, but gets a credit against its tax payable for the income tax deducted (see page 36 and also page 496 re interest on government stocks).

Investing in building societies and banks (other than the National Savings Bank)

Most people who invest in building societies and banks invest in normal interest-bearing accounts. The interest on such accounts is received after deduction of tax (at the lower rate of 20% from 6 April 1996), unless you are able to register to receive interest in full because your total income is expected to be covered by your personal allowances (see page 503). If after the end of the tax year the tax deducted is more than your liability, you may claim a repayment of tax from the Revenue. You can claim a repayment before the end of the year if it amounts to £50 or more. If you have received interest in full and it is found at the end of the tax year that some tax is due, the tax will have to be paid. There are other types of investment on offer — for example, the Tax Exempt Special Savings Account (TESSA). For details on the tax treatment of the various accounts, see chapter 37.

National Savings Bank accounts

The National Savings Bank operates both ordinary and investment accounts. Interest on both types of account is credited annually on 31 December without deduction of income tax (see page 491 for the way in which tax is collected).

The first £70 of interest on ordinary accounts is exempt from tax (for husband and wife, £70 each). The rate of interest is, however, not very attractive, being 2.75% on balances of £500 or more and 1.75% on lower balances, although interest rates on many other accounts where the interest is fully taxable are currently not very high. Ordinary accounts do have the convenience of allowing regular customers to withdraw up to £250 cash straight away.

The investment account usually pays interest at a competitive rate and will give you a cash flow advantage compared with investing in other banks or building societies if, although you are not exempt from tax, you have spare personal allowances to cover the interest received. Receiving the interest in full to start with saves you having to wait for a tax repayment. One month's notice is required for withdrawals.

Fixed interest national savings certificates

These certificates may be attractive to those paying income tax at the higher rate, since the interest, at rates guaranteed for five years, accumulates over the period of the investment, and when the certificates are cashed the capital appreciation is totally free from income tax and capital gains tax. They may also be attractive to someone whose income would otherwise exceed the age allowance income limit (see page 473). The minimum purchase is £100. New issues are made fairly frequently, so you need to check the details of the issue currently on offer. A maximum holding of certificates is prescribed for each issue, that for the 43rd issue being £10,000, but an additional £20,000 may be held if existing matured certificates (including index-linked and yearly plan certificates) are reinvested. The certificates may be wholly or partly repaid, so that regular withdrawals could be made to provide an effective tax-free income, although at a lower rate of return. The certificates are repaid at their purchase price in the first year (except for reinvested certificates, which carry interest for each complete three months in the first year), but after that, the tax-free yield rises each year. The compound tax-free interest rate for the 43rd issue if held for the full five years is 5.35% per annum. The annual interest earned is 3.75% in the first year, 4.15% in the second year, 5% in the third year, 6.15% in the fourth year and 7.75% in the fifth year. After five years, the certificates only earn interest at the lower general extension rate, so they should be reinvested into other issues.

National savings index-linked certificates

As with the fixed interest certificates, index-linked certificates are subject to a minimum purchase of £100. They provide inflation proofing over five years, plus guaranteed extra interest on an increasing scale each year, but biased to discourage early repayment. The original purchase price is index-linked in line with the increase in the retail prices index, and the index-linking and extra interest are earned monthly from the date of purchase (subject to the rules for early encashment). At the end of each year, the index increases and extra interest are capitalised, and the total amount then qualifies for index-linking and extra interest in the following year. The compound extra interest over the full five years on the current 9th issue is 2.5% in addition to the inflation proofing.

The certificates may be wholly or partly repaid. If they are cashed within the first year, only the amount invested is repaid (except for reinvested certificates, which earn index-linking and interest for each complete month). If they are cashed after the first year, they qualify for the index increases plus extra interest for each complete month they have been held since the date of purchase. Although the extra interest rates are guaranteed for only five years, the certificates may be held for longer, and after the fifth year they attract interest at an indexed extension rate. You need to check whether there is a better rate on offer by reinvesting in a current issue. Any increase in the value when the certificates are cashed is free of income tax and capital gains tax.

There is a limit on the holding of certificates in each issue, a maximum of £10,000 being prescribed for the 9th issue, but an additional £20,000 may be held if existing matured certificates (including fixed interest and yearly plan certificates) are reinvested.

These certificates are suitable for taxpayers who are prepared to forgo immediate income to protect their capital in real terms, and the extra interest improves the return and is itself fully index-linked once earned. Those who want regular income could make partial withdrawals of their investment, but at a lower rate of return on the certificates cashed.

National savings capital bonds

Capital bonds may be purchased by investing £100 upwards, with an upper limit of £250,000 (excluding any holdings in Series A). The bonds are for a five-year period at a guaranteed rate of interest, which works out at 6.65% per annum compound on Series J if you hold the bonds for the full five years. The interest is added to the bond each year. They may be cashed in early on two weeks' notice but there will be no interest if they are repaid in the first year, and you will earn a lower rate unless you hold the bonds for the full five years.

Although the interest is taxable, it is received in full and tax is accounted for later (see page 491). The disadvantage for taxpayers is that tax is payable every year even though no income is received from the bond until the end of the five-year period, unless it is wholly or partly cashed in, in which case lower interest rates apply.

National savings income bonds

National savings income bonds are intended for those who wish to invest lump sums at an attractive rate of interest, and to receive a regular income from their capital. Interest is paid by monthly instalments, either by post or direct to a bank account. Although the interest is taxable, it is received in full and tax is accounted for later (see page 491). The bonds are particularly beneficial for those whose income is not high enough for tax to have to be paid. The minimum holding is £2,000 and the maximum £250,000 (in units of £1,000), for either an individual or joint holding. Three months notice is required to obtain repayment.

National savings pensioners' bonds

National savings pensioners' guaranteed income bonds are similar to the ordinary income bonds, but ordinary income bonds carry a variable interest rate and the minimum and maximum holdings are higher. Pensioners' bonds enable those over 60 to invest between £500 and £50,000 (£100,000 for a joint holding) in bonds carrying interest fixed at 7% gross (on the current Series 3 issue) for the first five years. The interest is paid monthly direct into a building society or bank account. Repayment may be made without notice at any fifth anniversary, or otherwise after 60 days' notice (no interest being paid during the notice period). Although the interest is taxable, it is received in full and tax is accounted for later (see page 491).

National savings first option bonds

'First Option' bonds offer fixed rates of interest guaranteed for a year at a time. Unlike other national savings products, tax is deducted from the interest (at the lower rate of 20% from 6 April 1996), the net interest being added to the bond annually. Those liable to higher rate tax will have further tax to pay, and those not liable to pay tax will be able to claim a refund (see page 491). The minimum holding is £1,000 and the maximum £250,000, and bonds can be held indefinitely or cashed at any anniversary date without penalty. Bonds cashed in the first year do not earn any interest. If cashed between anniversary dates, they attract half the normal interest rate from the previous anniversary date. The rate of interest for the first year on the bonds currently on offer is 5% net after 20% tax (6.25% gross). There is an increased rate of 5.2% net (6.5% gross) for balances of £20,000 or more.

Children's bonus bonds

National Savings children's bonus bonds for children under 16 are in units of £25 and the maximum holding per child is £1,000 in issue H plus any holdings in earlier issues. The current issue H carries a guaranteed return over the first five years of 6.75% per annum compound. The bonds may be cashed in before the end of the five years on one month's notice, but no interest is earned if they are cashed in the first year and only 5% per annum is earned on later early repayments. At the end of five years they may be held for a further five years at revised guaranteed rates of interest, except that they mature at the holder's 21st birthday and no further returns are earned after that time.

All returns are exempt from tax, and parents may provide the funds without affecting their own tax liability.

Premium savings bonds

Any person over 16 can buy these bonds and an adult can buy them for a child under 16. The minimum purchase is £100, and the current maximum holding is £20,000. They do not carry interest, but, once a bond has been held for a clear calendar month, it is included in a regular monthly draw for prizes of various amounts. All prizes are free of income tax and capital gains tax and the bond itself can be encashed at face value at any time. This gives you the chance to win a tax-free prize, but at the cost of not receiving any income or protection of the real value of your capital.

Local authority stock, bonds and loans

Some local authority stocks are listed on the Stock Exchange and interest on the stocks is paid after deduction of income tax. Local authorities also raise money by unlisted temporary loans, mortgages and non-negotiable bonds. Interest on these items will usually be paid after deduction of income tax (at the lower rate of 20% from 6 April 1996 rather than the basic rate), although if your income is not more than your available personal allowance you can register to receive interest gross in the same way as with bank and building society interest (see page 503).

Local authority stocks, bonds and loans that are transferable are subject to the accrued income provisions described below (page 497). They are also within the definition of 'qualifying corporate bonds' and are exempt from capital gains tax. See page 532.

From 1 April 1996, income, gains and losses relating to a company's holdings of local authority stocks, etc. are taken into account in calculating the company's income, and disposals are no longer within the capital gains regime (see pages 27 and 531).

Government stocks

These represent borrowings by the British government, and they vary considerably in terms of interest. Some are issued on an index-linked basis so that the interest paid while the stock is held and the capital payment when it is redeemed are dependent on increases in the retail prices index. With the exception of 3½% War Loan, income tax is usually deducted at source (at the lower rate of 20% from 6 April 1996 rather than the basic rate). It is possible, however, to purchase stocks that are on the National Savings Stock Register through your local post office, and you then receive interest without deduction of tax. See page 491 for the way in which tax is accounted for.

Most of the stocks have a redemption date upon which the par value, or index-linked value as the case may be, is paid to the holder, so if you buy them below par you will have a guaranteed capital gain at a given date, which is exempt from capital gains tax. The gain on non-index-linked stock will be fixed in money terms whereas on index-linked stock it is fixed in real terms. In the meantime, the value of the stock will fluctuate with market conditions, so that there may be opportunities to make tax-free capital gains before the redemption date. If, however, you make losses they are not allowable for set-off against chargeable gains.

Government stocks can be useful as a means of providing for future known commitments, such as school fees, and if you are inclined to overspend, the government stock is not as readily accessible as a building society account.

Looked at on a pure money return basis, however, a purchase for capital growth may sometimes be no better for a higher rate taxpayer than an investment producing a greater income with no growth prospects. It depends upon the rates of interest being paid from time to time, and the price at which government stock can be purchased.

For individuals, interest on government stocks is subject to the accrued income scheme (see below).

As far as companies are concerned, the treatment of all loans, including government stocks, has changed from 1 April 1996 (see page 27). The broad effect is that both income from loans and profits and losses on disposal of them are taken into account in calculating a company's income, and the capital gains exemption for government stocks no longer applies (see page 531). In the case of indexed gilts, the index increase in each year will be excluded from the taxable income (FA 1996, s 94). Other indexed securities will normally be treated in the same way as other loan stock.

Companies will normally receive interest on government stocks net of lower rate income tax. They will recover the tax through the quarterly accounting system on form CT 61 or by deduction against mainstream tax, the gross interest being included in the profits charged to corporation tax (see page 36). From 2 January 1996, companies are able to receive interest gross if they open a special 'STAR' account at the Central Gilts Office of the Bank of England. If they do so, they must account for income tax quarterly on form CT 61 (with an advance payment on a separate return on 14 March for the quarter to 31 March). (TA 1988, ss 51A, 51B; FA 1995, ss 77, 78; SI 1995/2934 and SI 1995/3224).

Company loan stock

Company loan stock is normally within the definition of 'qualifying corporate bonds' and exempt from capital gains tax in the same way as government stocks, although for companies gains and losses are brought into account when calculating the company's income (see page 531). Company loan stock is not likely to be so attractive to the individual taxpayer, however, because it is not so readily marketable, there is a greater degree of risk, brokers' commission charges are higher and it is not possible to acquire it through the post office and thus receive interest without deduction of tax. The 'accrued income' rules for reckoning interest on a day to day basis apply (see below). It is now possible to hold company loan stocks in a Personal Equity Plan (PEP) — see page 536.

Accrued income scheme (TA 1988, ss 710–722; FA 1996, s 158 and Sch 14 para 36)

The accrued income scheme applies to interest-bearing marketable securities such as government stocks and to most local authority and company loan stock. It also applies to building society permanent interest bearing shares (see page 504). It does not apply to ordinary or preference shares in a company, units in unit trusts, bank deposits or securities within the 'discounted securities' provisions on page 533.

From 1 April 1996, the accrued income scheme no longer applies to such securities if they are held by companies, following the changed treatment for loans to and by companies (see page 27). Nor does it apply to an individual if the nominal value of all accrued income scheme securities held does not exceed £5,000 at any time either in the tax year in which the next interest payment on the securities falls due or in the previous tax year. If, for example, you buy or sell securities in February 1996 on which interest is paid in June and December, the two tax years to look at are 1996/97 (in which the June interest date falls) and 1995/96 (the previous year). If the interest had been payable in March and September the two tax years to look at would have been 1995/96 (the interest date year) and 1994/95.

Where the scheme applies, interest received is included in income according to the amount accrued on a day to day basis, so that selling just before an interest date does not enable income tax to be avoided on the interest by effectively receiving it as part of the sales proceeds. If you sell before a security goes 'ex dividend', you will be taxed on the accrued interest to the settlement date and the buyer's taxable income will be correspondingly reduced. If you sell ex dividend (so that you get the full interest at the payment date), your taxable income will be reduced and the buyer's increased by the interest applicable to the period between the settlement date and the interest payment date. The accrued income adjustments are made in the tax year in which the next interest payment date falls. See example 1.

Example 1

An individual investor has owned £10,000 12% stock for some years. Interest is payable half-yearly on 12 June and 12 December. Stock goes ex dividend on 6 May 1996.

If sold for settlement on 28 April 1996 (i.e. sold cum dividend)

Buyer receives the full 6 months' interest on 12 June 1996, but effectively 'bought' part of this within his purchase price. The interest accrued from 13 December 1995 to 28 April 1996 is:

$$£600 \times \frac{138}{183} = £452.46$$

Seller's taxable income is increased (by an accrued income charge) and buyer's taxable income reduced (by accrued income relief) of £452.46.

If sold for settlement on 13 May 1996 (i.e. sold ex dividend)

Seller receives the full 6 months' interest on 12 June 1996, but effectively 'bought' part of this by receiving reduced sale proceeds. The interest from 14 May 1996 to 12 June 1996 when he did not own the stock amounts to:

$$£600 \times \frac{30}{183} = £98.36$$

Seller's taxable income is reduced (by accrued income relief) and buyer's taxable income increased (by an accrued income charge) of £98.36.

The accrued income adjustments are made in the tax year in which the next interest payment date falls, 1996/97 in this example.

Where a sale is through a bank or stockbroker, the accrued interest is shown on the contract note.

The accrued income scheme applies not only to sales but also to any other transfers, except that it no longer applies on death where the death occurs on or after 6 April 1996.

Accrued income charges and reliefs must be shown in the investor's tax return (see chapter 9, page 127). Most securities covered by the accrued income scheme are exempt from capital gains tax (see page 532).

Ordinary shares in listed companies

The tax legislation used to refer to shares listed on the Official List of the Stock Exchange as quoted securities. This has now changed to listed securities (FA 1996, Sch 38).

Ordinary shares are 'risk capital' and investors have to be prepared to accept the risk element in return for seeking rising income and capital appreciation. Although listed shares are readily marketable, the price can fluctuate considerably, so they are not recommended if you may need to make an unplanned sale to meet unexpected commitments.

Dividends attract a tax credit (effectively a proportion of the company's corporation tax, passed on with the dividend) which in 1996/97 amounts to one-quarter of the cash amount, or 20% of the total of the cash dividend and the credit. Even though the tax credit represents only 20% tax on the total amount, you have no further tax to pay if you are a basic rate taxpayer. If you are liable to tax at the higher rate you must pay the extra tax of 20% on the total of the cash received and the tax credit (or 25% of the cash dividend). If you are not liable to tax, the tax credit is repayable. Gains on disposal are chargeable to capital gains tax in the usual way.

Dividends are included in your income as they arise and are not subject to the 'accrued income' provisions that apply to government, local authority and company loan stocks.

Investment in ordinary shares can be free of income tax and capital gains tax if you invest through a Personal Equity Plan — see page 536.

The detailed treatment of shares, and further information on company loan stock and government stocks, is in chapter 38.

Unit and investment trusts and venture capital trusts

The tax treatment of investments in these trusts is dealt with on pages 526–530.

Purchased life annuities

If you pay a lump sum to a life assurance company to get a fixed annual sum in return, the annual sum is partly regarded as a non-taxable return of capital, thus giving a comparatively high after-tax income, and the after-tax income is even higher for basic rate taxpayers now that they only pay tax on savings income at 20%. You have, however, effectively spent your capital to secure the annual income and thus at the end of the annuity term the capital is exhausted.

It is therefore common for purchased life annuities to be acquired in conjunction with life assurance policies, part of the annual income being used to fund the life assurance premium so that at the end of the annuity period the life assurance policy proceeds can replace the purchase price of the annuity. There are numerous variations on this sort of arrangement — see chapter 40.

Tax points

- If you have spare personal allowances, national savings bank accounts still have a cash flow advantage over other bank accounts and building society accounts unless you can register to receive the bank or building society interest in full, without tax being deducted. This needs to be weighed against the interest rates on offer. See chapter 37.

- Index-linked national savings certificates offer inflation proofing plus some guaranteed extra interest, the best return being available if you invest for a full five years.

- Although investing for the full term shows the highest returns with national savings certificates, they can be repaid gradually over the period, giving the opportunity to draw an effective tax-free income.

- Some of the National Savings products are attractive to higher rate taxpayers because of the tax-exempt income. The Department of National Savings issues a booklet describing its products, which is useful to have so that you can keep up to date with what is on offer.

- Once your national savings certificates have matured they attract the general extension rate of interest, which is lower than other rates available. Make sure you reinvest matured certificates into one of the current issues.

- There can appear to be a disproportionate extra charge on dividends, or other savings income from 6 April 1996, if an increase in other income takes the total income over the basic rate threshold. For an illustration, see page 18.

• If you are a small investor, you can benefit from a wide range of investments through a unit or investment trust. The trust is exempt from tax on its gains. You pay tax on income and gains in the normal way. See pages 526–528.

• If you have a reasonable amount of capital, you can use the certain increase in the value of dated government stocks to hedge the maximum loss on the purchase of ordinary shares. Suppose that you had £10,000 to invest and safety of capital was important.

		£
Invest in £10,000 nominal of dated government stock at £90 per £100		9,000
Invest in ordinary shares		1,000
		10,000
Surplus on government stock if held to redemption	1,000	
Less maximum loss on ordinary shares	1,000	—
Original investment intact		£10,000

Income will have been received in the meantime, with the possibility of capital appreciation on the ordinary shares.

• For those who are liable to tax, capital bonds (see page 494) have the disadvantage of tax being payable every year even though no income is received until the end of the investment period.

• If you have children under 16, you can invest the maximum £1,000 in *each issue* of children's bonus bonds. The current issue pays tax-free interest of 6.75% if held for five years (5% if cashed in other than in the first year) — see page 495.

• You are now eligible to acquire pensioners' bonds if you are over 60 (previously 65). The current rate of interest is 7%, and although it is taxable, you will not pay more than 20% tax unless your income exceeds the basic rate threshold of £25,500 (but see page 475 if you are over 65 and have income above the age allowance income limit of £15,200).

37
Investing in banks and building societies

Investing in building societies and banks (other than the National Savings Bank) (TA 1988, ss 477A, 480A, 481, 482)

Investing in building societies and banks is usually regarded as a low risk investment. If the bank or building society should fail, however, the maximum compensation is currently 75% of £20,000 for investment in a bank and 90% of £20,000 for a building society investment.

Building societies and banks, including the National Savings Bank, notify the Revenue how much interest has been paid to customers, no matter how small.

Income tax is not deducted from bank and building society interest paid to companies (see page 28), Personal Equity Plan managers (see page 537) and charities (see page 592).

Apart from tax-exempt accounts such as SAYE accounts (which may no longer be opened by new depositors unless linked to an employee share option — see page 176) and TESSAs (see page 505), interest paid to individuals by building societies and by banks other than the National Savings Bank is paid after deduction of tax (at the lower rate of 20% from 6 April 1996 rather than the basic rate) unless either you can register to receive it in full (see page 503) or the interest is paid in full because it arises under one of the following headings.

(a) Certificates of deposit (including 'paperless' certificates) and sterling or foreign currency time deposits, providing the loan is not less than £50,000 and is repayable within five years.
(b) General client deposit accounts with building societies or banks operated by solicitors and estate agents.
(c) Offshore accounts, i.e. held at overseas branches of UK and foreign banks and building societies.
(d) Bank and building society accounts held by someone who is not ordinarily resident in the UK and has provided a declaration to that effect.

Interest under headings (a) and (b) is taxed in the same way as national savings bank interest (see page 506). Interest on offshore accounts under heading (c) is taxed as income from a foreign possession — see page 556. Interest under heading (d) usually escapes UK tax (see page 566).

Interest counts as income for tax purposes according to the date when it is credited to your account. It is not apportioned over the period when it accrues. Whether tax has been deducted by the payer or not, you may have to pay some more or claim some back, depending on your tax rate. For the way in which this is done, see page 491.

Bank and building society interest paid to trustees is also net of tax, unless it is excluded under heading (a) or (c) above or it is paid to non-resident trustees of discretionary and accumulation trusts of which the beneficiaries are not ordinarily resident in the UK, providing the trustees have provided the bank or building society with a declaration to that effect.

Receiving bank and building society interest in full (TMA 1970, s 99A; TA 1988, ss 477A, 480A, 480B)

Although tax is normally deducted from interest paid by banks and building societies, you can register to receive the interest in full if you expect your total taxable income to be below your available allowances. The relevant forms R85 may be obtained from banks, building societies and local authorities (see page 495) or from your tax office. A separate form is needed for each account. A parent can register the account of a child under 16 if the child's total income will be less than the personal allowance (£3,765 for 1996/97), providing not more than £100 income arises from parental gifts (a separate £100 limit applying to income from gifts from each parent).

Even though the interest is received in full, the special rules for charging National Savings Bank interest outlined on page 507 do not apply and the interest is taxed as income of the tax year in which it is credited to your account.

You must give written notice straight away to banks and building societies who are paying you interest in full if your circumstances change and you are no longer eligible to receive gross interest. You should also let your tax office know about any tax you may have to pay. Where tax has been underpaid, it will be collected either by adjustment to a PAYE coding or by assessment (or self-assessment). A penalty of up to £3,000 may be charged if you fraudulently or negligently certify that you are entitled to register to receive interest in full, or if you fail to notify that you are no longer entitled to receive interest in full.

It is not possible to register some accounts and not others. You must expect to have *no tax liability at all* in order to be eligible. If you cannot register, say because your income is just above your available allowances, you will be entitled to a refund of any tax overpaid, and a refund can be claimed as soon as at least £50 tax is owing to you. You do not have to wait until the end of the tax year.

Building societies: conversion to banks, takeovers, mergers (FA 1988, Sch 12; TCGA 1992, s 217)

Building societies are able to convert to companies under the Building Societies Act 1986. If they do, they are subject to normal company and bank legislation. Possible adverse consequences of conversion for building society members are prevented by specific rules which provide that members are not liable to capital gains tax on rights to acquire shares in the company in priority to other subscribers, or at a discount, or on rights to acquire shares free of charge; these provisions apply whether the rights are obtained directly or through trustees. If any cash payment is made to the members (for example as compensation for not being allowed to vote on conversion), it will be liable to capital gains tax, as will the proceeds subsequently received when free shares are disposed of. Such gains may, however, be covered by the annual capital gains tax exemption if not already used.

The same treatment applies when a building society is taken over by a company, rather than being converted. If building societies merge, however, the Revenue have stated that any cash payments on the merger are chargeable to income tax. Such payments would be treated in the same way as other income from the building society. Tax would be deducted at 20%, higher rate taxpayers would have to pay a further 20% and non-taxpayers would be able to claim a repayment.

Taxpayers with either capital gains or income under the above provisions will need to make appropriate entries on their tax returns.

Building society permanent interest bearing shares (FA 1991, ss 51, 52, Schs 10 & 11)

Building societies may issue a special type of share — permanent interest bearing shares (PIBS). These shares are acquired through and listed on the Stock Exchange and are freely transferable, dealing charges being incurred on buying and selling. You are not entitled to compensation if the building society fails, and the shares are irredeemable, so what you get back on sale will depend on prevailing interest rates and the soundness of the building society. The tax treatment of the shares is different from that of other building society shares. Tax is deducted from interest on the shares by the building society (except for certain interest to non-residents) and you cannot register to receive it in full. The shares are within the definition of qualifying corporate bonds (see page 532) and are exempt from capital gains tax, so that no allowable losses may be created. They are also within the accrued income scheme (see page 497), so that adjustments for accrued interest are made when they are transferred. For companies, neither the capital gains treatment nor the accrued income scheme applies from 1 April 1996 (see page 27).

Where the shares are issued to existing members in priority to other people this will not result in a capital gains tax charge.

Tax Exempt Special Savings Accounts (TESSA) (TA 1988, ss 326A, 326B, 326BB, 326C; FA 1995, s 62; FA 1996, Sch 6 para 7)

Anyone over 18 may open a tax exempt special savings account (TESSA) with a bank or building society (or EU authorised institution), husband and wife being entitled to one each. If the qualifying conditions are satisfied for five years (or until death if earlier), the interest earned during that period is totally tax-free.

Except for follow-up TESSAs (see below), not more than £3,000 may be deposited during the first twelve months from the date the account is opened, nor more than £1,800 in any later year, nor more than £9,000 in total (so that someone investing the maximum in the first four years can only invest £600 in the last year). Depositors may withdraw interest credited, providing an amount out of the interest equivalent to basic rate tax, or lower rate tax for withdrawals of interest credited on or after 6 April 1996, is left in the account. Such withdrawals need not be declared on tax returns.

At the end of the five-year period the full amount in the account may be withdrawn. Alternatively, within six months after the end of the five-year period, all or part of the capital invested in the TESSA, but not the accrued interest, may be reinvested in a follow-up TESSA. If the full £9,000 is reinvested, no further investments may be made in the follow-up account. If less than £9,000 is reinvested, further investments may be made in the next four years until the £9,000 limit is reached, the £1,800 limit applying to investments in the later years. Those opening their first TESSA are still limited to the £3,000 maximum in the first year.

The tax-exempt status is lost if the balance on the account falls below an amount equal to the sums deposited plus tax at the appropriate rate on all interest credited, or if the account is assigned or used as security for a loan. The appropriate rate of tax is the basic rate of 25% for interest credited before 6 April 1996 and the lower rate of 20% thereafter. If the tax-exempt status is lost, all interest credited to that point is treated as taxable income of the tax year in which the rules were breached, even though some of it may relate to earlier years. If the breach of the rules occurs on or after 6 April 1996, tax will be deducted from the interest at only 20%, even though the 25% rate may have applied when the interest was earned. The interest must be shown on your tax return and you may have to pay some more tax or claim some back, depending on your tax rate.

Investing in the National Savings Bank (TA 1988, s 325)

The main investments offered by the National Savings Bank are outlined in chapter 36. National savings certificates, children's bonus bonds and premium savings bonds are exempt from tax. First option bonds (see page 495) are taxable, but unlike other national savings investments, the interest is paid net of tax and is treated in the same way as interest from other banks and building societies, so that you may have to pay more tax or claim some back, depending on your tax rate.

Interest on other accounts with the National Savings Bank and on capital and income bonds, including pensioners' bonds, is received in full and is charged to tax under the provisions of Schedule D, Case III. The first £70 of interest received on *ordinary* accounts is exempt from tax. Husband and wife get an exemption of £70 each. Any unused part of the £70 exemption cannot be transferred to the other spouse, but interest up to £140 is exempt when the account is in joint names. There is no exemption for interest on investment accounts, income bonds or capital bonds.

Changes to tax treatment of National Savings Bank and other interest received without tax being deducted (TA 1988, ss 64, 66, 67; FA 1994, ss 206, 207(4) and Sch 20 paras 4, 5; FA 1995, Sch 22)

Until the introduction of the current year basis of assessment, National Savings Bank interest and interest under headings (a) and (b) on page 502 has been taxed according to the following rules. The same provisions also apply to interest on offshore accounts (heading (c) on page 502), even though such interest is taxed as income from a foreign possession. (These provisions do *not* apply to interest received in full on bank and building society accounts because the holder has certified that he is a non-taxpayer — see page 503).

The tax charge for such sources has normally been on the interest received in the previous tax year, with special rules for the opening and closing years. Technically *each* deposit in a bank account is a separate source of income, and *each* withdrawal the cessation of a source, requiring the opening and closing years' rules to be applied as necessary. The Revenue have tended, however, to ignore the movement on accounts unless a substantial tax advantage was being obtained by the movement of funds into and out of them, in which case the strict rules would be applied.

The rules for taxing interest are being changed so that tax will always be charged on the interest received in the current tax year and no special rules will be needed for the years in which sources of income are acquired or disposed of. Transitional provisions apply for 1996/97 for accounts, deposits and bonds on which interest has been received before 6 April 1994. The new rules will not, however, apply if the final interest from such a source is credited before 6 April 1998, so that the old rules would apply in those circumstances to both 1996/97 and 1997/98. For accounts, deposits and bonds on which interest is first received on or after 6 April 1994, the new rules apply straight away.

The old rules for the opening and closing years are as follows.

For the first two and the last tax years, tax is charged on the interest credited in the tax year itself. In the third tax year, tax *may*, at the option of the taxpayer, be charged on the interest credited in that year rather than on the previous year's interest, and the same applies to the last but one tax year at the option of the Revenue. See example 1.

Example 1

A National Savings Bank investment account was opened in November 1991 and is closed on 5 August 1996. Interest credited and related assessments are as follows:

Interest credited		Assessments	
December 1991	£10	1991/92	£10
December 1992	£80	1992/93	£80
December 1993	£130	1993/94	£80*
December 1994	£150	1994/95	£130
December 1995	£178	1995/96	£178**
August 1996	£65	1996/97	£65

* Taxpayer will not opt to be taxed on actual interest of £130 rather than previous year's interest of £80
** Revenue will opt to tax actual interest of £178 rather than previous year's interest of £150

Those with sources of income from which interest has been received before 6 April 1994 and which continue beyond 5 April 1998 will get the benefit of one year's interest escaping tax in 1996/97. Tax for that year will be charged on half of the total interest received in 1995/96 and 1996/97. Tax for 1997/98 will then be charged on the interest received in that year. See example 2.

Example 2

National savings bank investment account opened February 1992, on which interest is credited as follows:

December 1992	£80	Taxed in 1992/93
December 1993	£110	Taxed in 1993/94 and again in 1994/95 (taxpayer not opting for actual basis of £130)
December 1994	£130	Taxed in 1995/96
December 1995	£120 ⎤	Half of £246, i.e. £123,
December 1996	£126 ⎦	taxed in 1996/97
December 1997	£125	Taxed in 1997/98

Someone who first received interest in 1993/94 will be taxed under the old rules for the first three years, including the right to be taxed on the actual income of the third year, i.e. 1995/96. If that right is exercised, the tax charge for 1996/97 and later years will be based on the actual income of each year and the two-year averaging will not apply.

There are anti-avoidance provisions to prevent people making arrangements to divert income into the two-year period that is to be averaged to arrive at the 1996/97 assessment. The provisions do not apply if obtaining a tax advantage was not the main purpose of the arrangements, or if the amount concerned is below certain thresholds that have not yet been fixed. Where the provisions apply, the taxable interest of 1996/97 will be increased by 1¼ times the amount that would otherwise have escaped tax through averaging. The one-quarter uplift will not apply if the taxpayer states in his tax return the extent to which amounts in the return are affected by the anti-avoidance provisions. The effect of the transactions will then merely be nullified by including the appropriate amount in 1996/97 income. In addition to the anti-avoidance provisions, the Revenue have the power to treat a significant addition to an existing account as a new source, so that the current year basis applies straight away to that addition.

Death of account holder or spouse

When interest is taxed on the new current year basis, there are no special rules at the time of the death of the account holder or his spouse. The following rules apply for any tax years in which interest is being taxed on the previous year basis.

When a single person or a married person with his/her own account dies, any interest credited between 6 April and the date of death is charged to tax in the tax year of death, with the Revenue option applying to the previous tax year. Interest credited after the date of death is charged on the personal representatives. By Revenue concession A7, these rules need not apply to an account if it is left to a surviving spouse, and the previous year basis and transitional provisions for the change to the current year basis will apply unless the Revenue are asked to apply the closing year rules. Under the concession, the interest charged to tax in the tax year of death is therefore that of the previous tax year, split on a time basis between the deceased's estate and the survivor. The concession is not relevant when the current year basis of assessment applies.

In the case of a joint account between husband and wife, Revenue concession A7 (outlined above) applies (unless the Revenue are asked not to apply it), so that the interest charged in the year of death is that of the previous tax year, or the average of the interest received in 1995/96 and 1996/97 if death occurs in 1996/97, an appropriate proportion applying to the estate of the deceased. If the concession does not apply, the surviving spouse will continue to be taxed on the previous year basis on his or her share of the interest until the changeover to the current year basis, but the rules for new accounts will apply to the interest relating to the share acquired from the other spouse.

Partners and other joint owners

The assessment is not joint. Each partner or co-owner is assessed on his share. For further details, see chapter 23.

Tax points

● If you close your National Savings Bank investment account, try to time it so that you maximise the saving from one year's interest not being charged to tax.

● If you do not register to receive bank and building society interest in full, even though you are entitled to do so, you will still get the overpaid tax back. You can claim before the end of the tax year if you are owed £50 or more. If you do not know your tax office, fill in form R95 in leaflet IR 111 (which is obtainable from any tax office or tax enquiry centre).

● Make sure you do not register to receive bank and building society interest in full unless you expect all your income to be covered by your available allowances. Even if some tax will be repayable, you are not eligible to register unless you will have no tax liability at all.

● If you have registered to receive bank and building society interest in full because your income is less than your available tax allowances, there is now no difference between investing in the National Savings Bank and investing in other banks and building societies. You need to compare the rates of interest on offer. If you cannot register but have allowances available to set against interest, you will still get a cash flow benefit from a National Savings Bank account, because for other accounts you will usually have to wait for a tax refund.

● Even if most of your bank and building society interest will be covered by your allowances, you cannot register some accounts and not others. It is all or nothing.

● If you receive a cash windfall on a building society takeover/ conversion, it will be liable to capital gains tax, but tax will not be payable if it is covered by your annual exemption (£6,300 for 1996/97). A cash windfall on a building society *merger* is liable to income tax, and will be received net of 20% tax, but you will not have any more tax to pay unless you are a higher rate taxpayer.

● It is only the general client deposit accounts maintained by solicitors and estate agents on which interest is received without tax being deducted, and not their normal accounts for office monies.

● A joint bank or building society account of husband and wife is normally treated as owned in equal shares, with the survivor automatically entitled to take over the whole account when the other dies, and it is unlikely that banks and building societies would be prepared to vary this treatment. It is, however, possible for the underlying beneficial ownership to be altered, so that specific action could be taken to sever the joint tenancy and the account could be held as tenants in common (see page 461) in whatever proportions you wish, providing the spouse giving up part of his or her share does so as an outright gift. If the account continued to be treated as a common pool from which each could and did draw freely, the Revenue would be unlikely to accept that an outright gift had been made.

- If you do take specific action to hold a bank or building society account as tenants in common, then although the bank may regard the account as going automatically to the survivor when the other died, the survivor would have to account to the personal representatives for the deceased spouse's share.

38
Investing in stocks and shares

Background

The term 'quoted securities' has in general been replaced in the tax legislation by 'listed securities', meaning listed in the Official List of the Stock Exchange. Many of the capital gains provisions, however, deal with stocks and shares acquired many years ago, in respect of which the old terminology may still apply. For simplicity, the terms 'quoted' and 'unquoted' have been retained in this chapter.

When you invest through the Stock Exchange, the principal securities you may acquire are company shares or loan stock, government stocks, local authority loan stock and building society permanent interest bearing shares (see page 504). You may also invest in unquoted company stocks and shares and unquoted local authority loans. From 1 April 1996, gains and losses made by a company in relation to loans (both ordinary debts and loan stock) are taken into account in calculating the company's income, and the capital gains provisions do not apply (see page 513).

Unquoted local authority loans are dealt with on page 495. Unquoted company stocks and shares are dealt with in this chapter. The treatment of foreign stocks and shares is dealt with in chapter 41 at pages 555 (capital gains) and 556, 557 (income), 'foreign' meaning that the issuing company is not resident in the UK.

Tax treatment of dividends and interest

Dividends

Dividends paid by companies on their shares represent a distribution of profits to the members. The company pays part of its corporation tax in advance (ACT) when it pays a dividend, and a tax credit equal to one-quarter of the dividend (representing 20% of the total of the dividend plus the credit — see page 32) is passed on to the shareholder at the same time. Even though the tax credit on the dividend is only at an effective rate of 20%, it is regarded as covering the income tax liability of a basic rate taxpayer. Those entitled to refunds can, however, only recover the actual tax credit, and higher rate taxpayers have a further 20% to pay. Dividends received by companies are not chargeable to corporation tax — see page 32.

Scrip options

If you take scrip shares instead of a dividend from a UK resident company (a scrip option), the cash dividend forgone is treated as your income, unless it is substantially different from the market value of the shares, 'substantially' being interpreted by the Revenue as 15% or more either way. In that event your deemed income is the market value of the shares on the first day of dealing. Lower rate tax on the notional dividend is treated as paid (but you cannot claim a refund if you are a non-taxpayer). Those liable to higher rate tax will pay tax at 20% on the grossed-up amount (TA 1988, ss 249–251). If scrip options are taken up by personal representatives, the gross equivalent is treated as income of the estate. The gross equivalent is treated as income liable to the 35% rate of tax where scrip options are taken up by trustees of discretionary trusts. The capital gains tax effect is dealt with on page 526. Where scrip dividends are issued to a company, they are not treated as income, and have a capital gains base cost of nil. This also applies to scrip dividends issued to a life interest trust unless the scrip dividend is income of the life beneficiary under trust law. If the trustees take the view that the scrip dividend belongs to the life tenant, the shares are effectively treated as acquired directly by the life tenant outside the trust's holding of shares, except in Scotland, where the rules are different (see Revenue Statement of Practice 4/94), and the life tenant would be treated as having notional income in the same way as if he had acquired the shares directly. As far as the company issuing the scrip dividend is concerned, the issue does not count as a distribution and therefore ACT does not have to be paid (TA 1988, s 230).

Foreign income dividends

For the treatment of 'foreign income dividends' (i.e. UK dividends paid out of foreign profits) see page 571.

Interest

From 6 April 1996, interest paid by companies on both quoted and unquoted stocks, and by local authorities and the Government on quoted stocks, is normally paid after deduction of lower rate tax (but see page 497 re the option available to companies). As with dividends, basic rate taxpayers have no further tax to pay, non-taxpayers can recover tax at only the 20% rate and higher rate taxpayers have a further 20% to pay. Tax is not deducted from interest on 3½% War Loan, and on some other government stocks if they are on the National Savings Stock Register and are bought from the post office. Income tax at the appropriate rate on such gross interest is collected through the self-assessment system. (See page 497 for the special accrued income scheme provisions that may apply to individuals in relation to interest-bearing securities.) The treatment of interest received by companies is dealt with on page 27.

There are some special provisions for personal investors covering discounted securities (see page 533).

Capital gains tax treatment of stocks and shares

For capital gains tax, shares and interest-bearing stocks are treated differently. Government stocks, qualifying corporate bonds and local authority stocks are exempt from capital gains tax, so that you will make neither chargeable gains nor allowable losses when you dispose of them (subject to some special rules for losses on qualifying corporate bonds — see page 532). Other interest-bearing stocks are chargeable to capital gains tax, but they are subject to different rules for identifying disposals with acquisitions from those relating to shares. The provisions are outlined below, but this area has become one of the most complicated in the tax legislation and it is not possible to deal with all the complexities.

Even more complexity has been added by the introduction of separate provisions for companies in relation to loans, whether they are in the form of loan stock or simple debts. From 1 April 1996 all interest paid and received by companies, and all gains and losses on the disposal of interest-bearing assets, are broadly taken into account in calculating a company's income, subject to transitional provisions (see page 27). In general, a company's chargeable assets in the form of loans will be treated as disposed of and reacquired on 31 March 1996, but with any chargeable gain or allowable loss not being brought into account until they are actually disposed of. Companies may, however, elect to treat a deemed capital loss as an income loss incurred at 31 March 1996 (FA 1996, Sch 15 paras 8, 9). There are exceptions to the general provisions, some of which are referred to on page 531, which deals with the basic rules for loan stock. Other points relating to capital gains are dealt with elsewhere in this chapter.

Capital gains when shares are disposed of (TCGA 1992, ss 35, 53–55, 104–110 and Sch 2; FA 1994, s 93)

When shares are disposed of, a capital gains computation is made. The general rules for calculating gains and losses outlined in chapter 4 apply, but because of the special problems associated with shares (bonus and rights issues, takeovers, mergers, etc.), the need to deal with shares already on hand on 6 April 1965 when capital gains tax started, and with those on hand when indexation was introduced on 31 March 1982, and the calculation and treatment of the indexation allowance, there are inevitable complications for shareholders with even a modest portfolio.

Shares acquired before the commencement of indexation

If a general rebasing election has been made (see page 49), all shares of the same class in the same company held on 6 April 1982 (1 April 1982 for companies) are treated as acquired at their 31 March 1982 market value and are regarded as a single asset. (No special provision is made for acquisitions by individuals from 1 to 5 April 1982, but logically such acquisitions should be included at cost.) Any such holding is called the '1982 holding' in the legislation, but it is referred to in this chapter as the pre-1982 pool. The legislation does not provide for shares acquired before 6 April 1965 to be merged with those acquired afterwards, but since they are all regarded as costing the same amount it is considered that they need not be kept separate.

If the rebasing election has not been made, then unless some of the shares in the company were acquired before 6 April 1965, the single asset treatment still applies but there will be two values for the pre-1982 pool, namely cost and 31 March 1982 value. If some of the shares were acquired before 6 April 1965, then they must be kept separate from the pre-1982 pool. This does not apply to *quoted* shares if an election had been made (under provisions introduced in 1968) to treat them as acquired at their market value on 6 April 1965, in which case they will be included in the pre-1982 pool at that value. The treatment of unpooled pre-6 April 1965 acquisitions is dealt with on page 521.

Where the rebasing election is not made, the 31 March 1982 value is still used to calculate the gain or loss unless using the cost would show a lower gain or loss. If one calculation shows a loss and the other a gain, the transaction is treated as giving neither gain nor loss. In both calculations, the indexation allowance is based on the *higher* of the cost and 31 March 1982 value.

Where 31 March 1982 valuations of unquoted holdings are needed by several shareholders, the Revenue Shares Valuation Division will open negotiations with the shareholders or their advisers before being asked by a tax office, providing all shareholders with similar holdings will accept the value agreed. Someone with pre- and post-6 April 1965 unquoted holdings may, by concession, have them valued as a single holding, which may give a higher value per share. This does not affect the rules for matching disposals with acquisitions (see page 515).

Shares acquired after indexation was introduced

New rules were introduced from 6 April 1985 (1 April 1985 for companies), under which each holding of quoted or unquoted shares of the same company and class acquired on or after 6 April 1982 (1 April 1982 for companies) is regarded as a single asset, called the 'new holding' in the legislation, but referred to in this chapter as the post-1982 pool. The post-1982 pool grows with acquisitions and is depleted by disposals (see identification rules below).

Identification of disposals

When shares are disposed of, there are rules to relate the disposal to specific shares acquired. These rules do not apply to disposals of scrip and rights shares, because scrip and rights shares are treated as acquired when the original shares were acquired, and thus both the pre- and post-1982 pools will grow by the appropriate number of scrip or rights shares (see page 523). Apart from scrip and rights shares, the following rules apply to match disposals with acquisitions.

There are two identification rules that override the normal rules dealt with below. Shares of the same company and class that are purchased and sold on the same day are matched with each other. If the 'same day' rule does not apply, disposals by a company that owns 2% or more of the issued shares of a particular class are matched with acquisitions in the previous month (latest first) then with acquisitions in the following month (earliest first).

Where neither of these special rules applies, disposals are identified as follows.

(a) First with acquisitions within the previous nine days (and no indexation allowance is available).
(b) Second with those in the post-1982 pool, i.e acquired from April 1982 onwards.
(c) Third with those in the pre-1982 pool, i.e. acquired up to April 1982.
(d) Fourth (where no rebasing election has been made) with those acquired before 6 April 1965 (unless, in the case of quoted shares, they are included in the pre-1982 pool because of an election to include them at 6 April 1965 values). Each acquisition is dealt with separately and later acquisitions are treated as sold before earlier acquisitions, i.e. 'last in, first out'.

Indexation allowance

For pre-1982 pools of shares held at 6 April 1982 (1 April 1982 for companies), the indexation allowance is calculated by taking the increase in the retail prices index between March 1982 and the month of disposal. Where the rebasing election has been made to treat all assets acquired before 31 March 1982 as being acquired at their market value on that date, the indexation allowance is based on that 31 March 1982 value (see

example 6). Where the election has not been made, the indexation calculation is based on the higher of the value of the shares at 31 March 1982 and
their cost or, for shares held at 6 April 1965, their 6 April 1965 market
value when using that value to calculate the gain or loss (see pages 521,
522).

Indexation allowance on post-1982 pools (see page 514) is worked out
from the date expenditure is incurred. The holdings are maintained at
both an unindexed value and an indexed value, and the indexed value is
uplifted by further indexation every time an event occurs that alters the
value of a holding (such as a purchase or a sale). Unlike other indexation
allowance calculations, the indexation adjustment on the post-1982 pool
should strictly not be rounded to three decimal places. If the index has
fallen since the previous event, no adjustment is made to the indexed
value. The post-1982 pool rules were introduced on 6 April 1985 (1 April
1985 for companies) and an opening figure for the indexed value was
required at that date, working out indexation allowance on each acquisition from 6 April 1982 (1 April 1982) onwards. (If the calculation was
delayed until the time of the first event affecting the value of the holding,
it would not significantly affect the figures.) It was common practice from
1985 to keep records only of the indexed value of shareholdings, since up
to 30 November 1993 the gain or loss was the difference between the
disposal proceeds and the indexed cost. Now that indexation allowance
cannot create or increase losses, it will be necessary to re-establish
unindexed values for each holding.

Where the rebasing election has been made, the pre-1982 pool can be
maintained at both unindexed and indexed values in the same way as the
new holding, although this is not provided for in the legislation. This can
still be done even if there is no rebasing election, but figures would be
required both for indexed cost and indexed 31 March 1982 value (basing
indexation allowance in both cases on the higher of those two figures, but
not so as to create or increase a loss. (For an illustration, see example 9.)

Where partly paid shares are acquired, the instalments of the purchase price
qualify for indexation allowance from the date the shares are issued, unless
they are paid more than twelve months later, in which case they qualify from
the date they are paid. This does not apply to the privatisation issues, which
qualify for indexation from the date of issue even if some instalments are
paid more than twelve months later. (Any privatisation issue vouchers that
are used to reduce bills are deducted from the allowable cost. Any free shares
acquired later are added to the holding and treated as acquired at market
value on the first day of dealing in them.)

See examples 1 to 7 and refer to the general computation rules in chapter
4.

The figures used in the examples are not intended to be indicative of probable values and are used merely to illustrate the rules. In many cases, 31 March 1982 values will be higher than earlier costs and the irrevocable rebasing election will have been or will be made. But the election needs to be considered in the light of all the chargeable assets held on 31 March 1982 and not just the particular asset sold.

Example 1

Shareholder acquired 5,000 shares in AB plc in May 1987 for £7,500 and a further 2,000 shares in December 1990 for £4,000. Say he sold all the shares in February 1996 for (a) £17,000 or (b) £13,000 or (c) £10,000. The retail prices index was 101.9 for May 1987, 129.9 for December 1990 and 150.9 for February 1996. The capital gains computation is:

AB plc post-1982 share pool

	Number of shares	Unindexed value £	Indexed value £	Proceeds £	Gain (loss) £
May 87 Bought	5,000	7,500	7,500		
Dec 90 Indexn on £7,500 from May 87 $\dfrac{129.9}{101.9} - 1$			2,061		
Bought	2,000	4,000	4,000		
	7,000	11,500	13,561		
Feb 96 Indexn on £13,561 from Dec 90 $\dfrac{150.9}{129.9} - 1$			2,192		
	7,000	11,500	15,753		
(a) Sold	(7,000)	(11,500)	(15,753)	17,000	1,247
	7,000	11,500	15,753		
(b) Sold	(7,000)	(11,500)	(15,753)	13,000	—
	7,000	11,500	15,753		
(c) Sold	(7,000)	(11,500)	(15,753)	10,000	(1,500)

Note that the *gain* in (a) is the difference between proceeds and indexed value, i.e. £1,247, the *loss* in (c) is the difference between proceeds and unindexed value, i.e. £1,500, and if as in (b) the proceeds lie between unindexed and indexed values, the indexation allowance reduces the gain to nil.

INVESTING IN STOCKS AND SHARES   38

Example 2

Quoted shares in CD plc are acquired by an individual as follows:

	Number	Cost £
1.1.59	2,000	2,000
10.9.64	500	1,000
Between 6.4.65 and 5.4.82 (pre-1982 pool)	5,000	35,000
Post-1982 pool:		
Between 6.4.82 and 5.4.85	4,000 }	42,000 }
31.5.85	2,000 }	24,000 }
Sales	Number	Consideration
28.11.94	2,000	38,000
16.2.96	10,000	160,000

Market value £3 per share at 6 April 1965 and £8 per share at 31 March 1982. No election had been made to include shares acquired before 6 April 1965 in the pre-1982 pool nor a rebasing election to treat all assets acquired before 31 March 1982 as being acquired at 31 March 1982 value.

The relevant increases in the retail price index are .899 between March 1982 and February 1996, .005 between April 1985 and May 1985, .526 between May 1985 and November 1994 and .039 between November 1994 and February 1996.

Sales identified on 'last in, first out' basis (see page 515)

	£	Gain £
Sale of 2,000 on 28.11.94 out of post-1982 pool	38,000	
Indexed cost (see example 3)	(35,826)	2,174
Chargeable gain on CD plc shares in 1994/95		2,174
Sale of 10,000 on 16.2.96:		
Sale out of post-1982 pool 4,000/10,000 × 160,000	64,000	
Indexed cost (see example 3) but cannot create loss	(74,446)	—
Sale of 5,000 shares in pre-1982 pool Gain (see example 4)		4,040
Sale of 500 shares acquired 10.9.64 and of 500 shares out of 2,000 acquired 1.1.59, each show gains of £404 (see example 5)		808
Giving total chargeable gains on CD plc shares in 1995/96 of		£4,848

Example 3

CD plc post-1982 pool	*Number of shares*	*Unindexed value*	*Indexed value*
		£	£
At 6.4.85 per example 2 (acquisitions between 6.4.82 and 5.4.85)	4,000	42,000	42,000
If at 6.4.85 the entire holding had been sold, the indexation allowance would have been, say			4,200
Giving indexed value at 6.4.85 of			46,200
May 85 Indexn on £46,200 from Apr 85 (.005)			231
Bought	2,000	24,000	24,000
	6,000	66,000	70,431
Nov 94 Indexn on £70,431 from May 85 (.526)			37,047
			107,478
Cost of shares sold (one-third of holding)	2,000	22,000	35,826
	4,000	44,000	71,652
Feb 96 Indexn on £71,652 from Nov 94 (.039)			2,794
			74,446
Cost of shares sold	4,000	44,000	74,446

Example 4

CD plc pre-1982 pool

5,000 shares cost £35,000, value at 31.3.82 £8 each = £40,000.

	£		£
Sale proceeds 16.2.96 5,000/10,000 × 160,000	80,000		80,000
Cost	(35,000)		
31.3.82 value			(40,000)
Indexation allowance .899 on 31.3.82 value	(35,960)		(35,960)
	9,040	or	4,040
Lower gain			£4,040

Example 5

CD plc

	Number of shares	Cost (£)
Pre 6.4.65 acquisitions per example 2:		
1.1.59	2,000	2,000
10.9.64	500	1,000

Identified with sales on 'last in, first out' basis.

Sale 16.2.96 of 500 shares acquired 10.9.64:

	£	£
Using old 6.4.65 rules		
Sale proceeds 500/10,000 × 160,000	8,000	8,000
Cost 10.9.64	(1,000)	
6.4.65 value		(1,500)
Indexation allowance .899 on 31.3.82 value (500 @ £8 each = £4,000, which is higher than both cost, £1,000 and 6.4.65 value, £1,500)	(3,596)	(3,596)
	3,404 or	2,904
Lower gain is		£2,904

	£
Using 31.3.82 value	
Sale proceeds	8,000
31.3.82 value	(4,000)
Indexation allowance (as above)	(3,596)
Gain	£404
Gain is lower of £2,904 and £404	£404

Sale 16.2.96 of 500 shares acquired 1.1.59:

	£	£
Using old 6.4.65 rules		
Sale proceeds 500/10,000 × 160,000	8,000	8,000
Cost 1.1.59 500/2,000 × 2,000	(500)	
6.4.65 value		(1,500)
Indexation allowance .899 on 31.3.82 value of £4,000	(3,596)	(3,596)
	£3,904	£2,904
Lower gain is		£2,904

	£
Using 31.3.82 value	
Gain is as above	£404
Gain is lower of £2,904 and £404	£404

Example 6

Facts as in example 2, but rebasing election has been made to use 31.3.82 value for all pre-31.3.82 acquisitions.

Treatment of sale of 2,000 shares on 28.11.94 and of 4,000 out of 10,000 shares sold on 16.2.96 is unchanged, since they comprise the post-1982 pool. The gain in 1994/95 thus remains at £2,174 and there is neither gain nor loss on the disposal of the 4,000 shares in 1995/96.

Since the pre-1982 pool and the shares acquired before 6 April 1965 are all treated as acquired at their 31.3.82 value of £8, the gain or loss on the remaining 6,000 shares sold on 16.2.96 can be worked out in a single calculation. Since 31.3.82 value was used to work out gains in any case, rebasing would show the same result as follows:

	£	£
Sale proceeds 6,000 shares		
6,000/10,000 × 160,000		96,000
31.3.82 value (£8 each)	48,000	
Indexation allowance .899	43,152	91,152
Gain in 1995/96 on CD plc shares		
as in example 2		£4,848

Shares held on 6 April 1965 (TCGA 1992, Sch 2, Parts I and III)

If the rebasing election has been made to treat all assets acquired before 31 March 1982 as acquired at their market value on that day, gains and losses will be computed on that basis for both quoted and unquoted shares (as in example 6).

Where the rebasing election has not been made, the procedure is as follows.

For unquoted securities, the legislation requires two computations to be made, as follows.

(a) (i) Calculate the gain or loss over the whole period of ownership.
   (ii) Adjust for indexation allowance based either on cost or 31 March 1982 value, whichever is higher (but not so as to create or increase a loss), then calculate the proportion of the resulting gain or loss that relates to the period after 5 April 1965 (but ignoring any period of ownership before 6 April 1945).
   (iii) As an alternative to the result in (ii), the taxpayer may make an irrevocable election to have the result computed by reference to the value of the asset on 6 April 1965, with indexation allowance based on the higher of 6 April 1965 value and 31 March 1982 value (but the indexation allowance cannot create or increase a loss). If this calculation would give a loss instead of a gain, the transaction is deemed to

give neither gain nor loss. The election cannot give a greater loss than the amount by which the cost exceeds the sale proceeds.

(Losses will rarely arise under either calculation because the costs of many years ago are being compared with current sale proceeds.)

(b) Calculate the gain or loss as if the shares had been bought on 31 March 1982 at their market value on that date. Indexation allowance is based on the higher of 31 March 1982 value and either cost or 6 April 1965 value according to which was used to give the result in the first computation (but not so as to create or increase a loss).

If both computations show a loss, the lower loss is taken, and if both show a gain, the lower gain is taken. See example 7. If one computation shows a gain and the other a loss, the result is treated as neither gain nor loss. If, however, the first computation has already resulted in no gain, no loss, that result is taken and the 31 March 1982 value calculation is not made. Where a gain arises it will be obvious in many cases that the lower gain will result from using the 31 March 1982 calculation, without making the alternative calculation. As far as losses are concerned, there can only be an allowable loss if the sale proceeds are below both the cost and the 31 March 1982 value.

For quoted securities, unless a rebasing election has been made, or the shares on hand at 6 April 1965 are included at their value at that date in the pre-1982 pool (see page 514), two computations are also made. The procedure is similar to that for unquoted securities, except that time apportionment does not apply. In the first computation, the sale proceeds are compared with both the cost and the 6 April 1965 value and the lower gain or lower loss is taken. If one method shows a gain and the other a loss, the computation is treated as giving rise to neither gain nor loss. Indexation allowance is deducted in each case (based on the higher of the cost/6 April 1965 value and 31 March 1982 value) but not so as to create or increase a loss. The second computation treats the shares as acquired at 31 March 1982 value (but indexation allowance is nonetheless based on cost/6 April 1965 value if it exceeds 31 March 1982 value). The lower gain or lower loss produced by the two computations is then taken. If one computation shows a loss and the other a gain, the result is neither gain nor loss. If the first computation has already given a no gain/no loss result, then the second computation is not made. See example 5 on page 520. As with unquoted securities, it will often be obvious that the lower gain will result from the 31 March 1982 calculation. Losses will not arise except to the extent that the proceeds are less than the lowest of the cost, 6 April 1965 value and 31 March 1982 value.

The above examples show that where a taxpayer has acquired shares at various times before and after 31 March 1982 the rules may require several calculations to be made. If the rebasing election has been made, the position is very much simpler and there are only two share 'pools', one covering all acquisitions up to 5 April 1982 (the pre-1982 pool) and the other all later acquisitions (the post-1982 pool). Even so, complications arise through scrip and rights issues, takeovers, etc. The calculations can be simplified by using publications such as Extel and D & B Securities Taxation (formerly Stubbs) to obtain 31.3.82 values and other relevant information.

Example 7

1,500 unquoted shares acquired 6 January 1958 for £2 per share. Market value considered to be £3 per share at 6 April 1965 and £8 per share at 31 March 1982. No rebasing election had been made to treat all assets acquired before 31 March 1982 as being acquired at 31 March 1982 value.
The shares were sold in January 1996 for £15 per share.
Increase in retail prices index from March 1982 to January 1996 is 89.1%.

First computation

Using time apportionment		Using 6 April 1965 market value	
Sale 1,500 shares @ £15	22,500	Sale	22,500
Cost 6.1.58 @ £2	(3,000)	6.4.65 MV 1,500 @ £3	(4,500)
Indexation allowance*	(10,692)		(10,692)
Overall gain	8,808		

Proportion after 6.4.65

$$\frac{6.4.65 - 6.1.96}{6.1.58 - 6.1.96} = \frac{30.75}{38}$$

| Gain | 7,127 | | 7,308 |

Therefore, election not made to use 6.4.65 value
and gain is   £7,127

Second computation

Sale 1,500 shares @ £15	22,500
31.3.82 value @ £8	(12,000)
Indexation allowance £10,692	
but cannot create loss	(10,500)
Result is	No gain/no loss

The overall result is that there is neither chargeable gain nor allowable loss.

*Indexation allowance is 89.1% on March 1982 value of £8 per share.

Scrip and rights issues (TCGA 1992, ss 57, 122, 123, 126–132)

Scrip and rights issues are identified with the shares out of which they arise, although the amount paid for a rights issue (or treated as paid for a scrip dividend — see page 512) only attracts indexation allowance from the time of payment (or entitlement to the dividend).

If rights are sold nil paid, the proceeds are treated as a part disposal of the holding, unless they do not exceed 5% of the value of the holding, in which case they are deducted from the cost instead. The Revenue will not insist on this if the taxpayer would prefer the part disposal treatment, for example because the gain was covered by the annual exemption. (The value of the holding is arrived at by taking the ex-rights value of the existing shares plus the proceeds for the rights shares sold. If not all the rights shares were sold, those retained would also be valued at nil-paid price in this calculation.) For post-1982 pool calculations (see page 516), the indexed pool is increased by indexation before making the deduction. For pre-1982 pools and other acquisitions (see page 514), the legislation provides that the indexation allowance on a later disposal is first calculated on the full cost then reduced by an indexation amount on the rights sale proceeds from the date of receipt. This ensures that the correct amount of indexation allowance is given. It is,

---

Example 8

A taxpayer acquired 2,000 shares in EF plc on 23 February 1986 for £4,000. On 10 December 1987 there was a scrip issue of 1 for 2. On 19 October 1996 there was a rights issue of 1 for 6 at £3 per share. The ex-rights value of the shares was £3.40, giving a value of £10,200 for 3,000 shares.

EF plc post-1982 pool

Rights taken up:

	Shares	Unindexed value £	Indexed value £
23.2.86	2,000	4,000	4,000
10.12.87 Scrip	1,000		
	3,000		
19.10.96 Rights	500		
Indexn February 1986 to			
October 1996, say .6			2,400
Rights cost		1,500	1,500
	3,500	5,500	£7,900

Rights sold nil paid for 40p per share = £200, which is less than 5% of (£10,200 + £200):

	Shares	Unindexed value £	Indexed value £
As above	3,000	4,000	6,400
Rights proceeds		(200)	(200)
	3,000	3,800	6,200

---

however, more straightforward to operate pre-1982 pools on an indexed basis (see page 516), so that the sale of rights nil-paid can be treated in the same way as for post-1982 pools (see example 9).

Example 9

In addition to the post-1982 pool in example 8, the taxpayer had acquired 3,000 shares for £3,000 on 11 April 1979. These shares comprise the pre-1982 pool. The 31 March 1982 value of the shares was £1.20 per share. Rebasing election not made.

EF plc pre-1982 pool

Rights taken up:

	Shares	Unindexed cost	Indexed cost	Unindexed 31.3.82 value	Indexed 31.3.82 value
		£	£	£	£
At 31.3.82	3,000	3,000	3,000	3,600	3,600
10.12.87 Scrip	1,500				
	4,500				
19.10.96 Rights Indexn March 1982 to October 1996 (say 93% × £3,600)	750		3,348		3,348
Rights cost		2,250	2,250	2,250	2,250
	5,250	5,250	8,598	5,850	9,198

Rights sold nil paid for 40p per share:

	Shares	Unindexed cost	Indexed cost	Unindexed 31.3.82 value	Indexed 31.3.82 value
		£	£	£	£
At 31.3.82, adjusted for scrip and indexn as above	4,500	3,000	6,348	3,600	6,948
19.10.96 rights proceeds		(300)	(300)	(300)	(300)
	4,500	2,700	6,048	3,300	6,648

Although examples 8 and 9 show small proceeds on a sale of rights being deducted from the value of the holding, if treating them as a part disposal would produce a gain covered by the annual exemption, the part disposal treatment would be better. The part of the cost of the holding that is taken into account against the cash proceeds is arrived at in the same way as for cash on a takeover (see page 533).

Scrip dividend options (TCGA 1992, s 141)

If you take scrip shares instead of a dividend, the capital gains tax cost is the amount treated as your net income (see page 512), not the grossed up equivalent. There is neither reckonable income nor any capital gains tax cost where the recipient is a company. The same will apply if the recipient is a life interest trust unless the trustees treat the shares as income of the life tenant (see page 512). Where trustees adopt that treatment, the scrip shares do not go into the trust's holding at all, and are regarded as belonging to the life tenant directly, even if held by the trustees (except in Scotland, where the treatment is different).

Many enhanced scrip offers have been made where the value of the shares is usually 50% more than the cash dividend alternative, and the offers have included an option for the scrip shares to be sold immediately at a set price. Unlike the treatment of nil-paid sales of rights, scrip shares sold in this way are first regarded as purchased for the amount of the shareholder's notional income (see page 512) and added pro rata to pre- and post-1982 holdings after first adjusting for indexation. The shares sold are then treated as sold out of the post-1982 pool in priority to the pre-1982 pool.

Unit and investment trusts and open-ended investment companies

Unit trusts (TA 1988, ss 468–470; FA 1989, s 80; TCGA 1992, s 100; FA 1994, Sch 14; FA 1996, Sch 6 paras 10–12, Sch 10 para 4)

Unit trusts enable an investor to obtain a wide spread of investments, within a professionally managed fund. There are various types of funds to suit particular circumstances, for example some aimed at capital growth and some at maximising income. Most unit trusts are authorised unit trusts (i.e. authorised under the Financial Services Act 1986, which places certain restrictions on the investments the trust is able to make). Authorised unit trusts are exempt from tax on capital gains.

From 1 April 1996, all authorised unit trusts pay corporation tax on their income (net of management expenses and interest) at a rate equal to the lower rate of income tax, currently 20%. Before 1 April 1996, this applied only to those trusts that made a claim showing that the market value of the trust's interest-bearing investments did not exceed 60% of the total market value of its investments at any time in the period. Authorised unit trusts are able to pay 'foreign income dividends' (see page 571).

The position of individual investors is broadly similar to what it would have been if they had invested directly. Individuals investing directly could not, of course, obtain tax relief on the costs of managing their portfolio. Distributions on and after 6 April 1996 will carry a tax credit of 20%, whether they are from equity based funds or from funds that invest wholly or partly in interest-bearing securities. (Foreign investors are able to receive interest free of UK tax in some circumstances, or may be able to claim double tax relief.) An individual investor's gains are similarly taxed as if the funds had been invested directly, except that gains on sales of gilt units are taxable, whereas gains on gilts themselves are not (see page 532).

Companies that invest in authorised unit trusts may receive either interest distributions or dividend distributions. From 6 April 1996, the rate of tax in respect of both types of distribution is 20%. (Unit trusts may only pay interest distributions where their interest-bearing investments comprise more than 60% of the total market value of the trust fund.) Dividend distributions received by companies are franked investment income and are not liable to corporation tax. Interest distributions are brought into account under Schedule D, Case III on a 'mark to market' basis (the income tax suffered at source being deducted from tax payable), as are gains and losses on disposals of unit trust investments (see page 27).

Open-ended investment companies (FA 1995, s 152)

Provision is being made for open-ended investment companies (OEICs) to be permitted under UK law. The shares in OEICs may be continuously created or redeemed, depending on investor demand. They will be treated in essentially the same way as unit trusts, and existing unit trusts will be able to convert into OEICs if they wish.

Investment trusts (TA 1988, s 842; TCGA 1992, s 100)

Investment trusts are actually companies and not trusts, and you buy shares in them in the usual way. Some trusts with a limited life are split level trusts, i.e. they have income shares that receive most of the trust's income and a fixed capital sum on liquidation, and capital shares that receive little or no income but get most of the capital surplus on a liquidation.

Investment trusts are exempt from tax on their capital gains if they are approved investment trusts (approval has to be given every year by the Inland Revenue) but the gains may only be reinvested and cannot be distributed as dividends. They are charged to corporation tax in the normal way (except in relation to certain rental income — see page 453), which puts them at a disadvantage as against unit trusts.

Savings schemes

Both unit trusts and investment trusts operate monthly savings schemes, which give the investor the advantage of 'pound cost averaging', i.e. fluctuations in prices are evened out because overall you get more units/shares when the price is low and less when it is high. Such schemes give calculation problems for capital gains tax, because the indexed pool cost needs to be increased every month (see page 516). Investors may, however, apply to be treated as if they had made a single annual investment in the seventh month of the trusts' accounting year, which cuts the calculations down significantly.

Personal Equity Plans (PEPs)

Investors can invest up to £6,000 in each tax year in unit and investment trusts and open-ended investment companies through PEPs, providing the trust/company holds at least half of its own investments in UK ordinary shares or broadly comparable EU shares.

As an alternative, PEP investments may be made in trusts/companies that have more than half their investments in shares other than UK and EU shares, but subject to a limit of £1,500.

For details of the PEP scheme, see page 536.

Venture capital trusts (TA 1988, ss 332A, 842AA and Schs 15B and 28B; TCGA 1992, ss 151A, 151B and Sch 5C; FA 1995 ss 70–73 and Schs 14–16)

From 6 April 1995, individuals may invest in qualifying unquoted trading companies through a venture capital trust (VCT). VCTs are quoted companies holding at least 70% of their investments in shares or securities they have subscribed for in qualifying unquoted companies trading wholly or mainly in the UK, at least 30% of such holdings being in ordinary shares, and no single holding being more than 15% of total investments. Companies on the Alternative Investment Market (AIM) count as qualifying unquoted companies providing they are carrying on a qualifying trade. The VCT must not retain more than 15% of its income from shares and securities. VCTs are exempt from tax on their capital gains.

The main exclusions from the definition of qualifying trading company are companies dealing in land or providing finance, legal and accountancy services and leasing.

Individual investors aged 18 or over are entitled to two income tax reliefs and two capital gains reliefs as follows.

Income tax reliefs

When new ordinary shares are *subscribed for*, income tax relief at 20% may be claimed on up to £100,000 of the amount subscribed each year. The relief will be withdrawn to the extent that any of the shares are disposed of within five years (other than to the holder's spouse, or after the holder's death). If the disposal is at arm's length and at a loss, relief is withdrawn in the proportion that the consideration received on disposal bears to the amount subscribed. Where shares are acquired from a spouse, the spouse is treated as if he or she had subscribed for the shares. The relief will also be withdrawn if the VCT loses its qualifying status within the five-year period.

Dividends from ordinary shares in VCTs are exempt from tax to the extent that not more than £100,000 in total of shares in VCTs are *acquired* each year (whether acquired by subscription or by purchase from another shareholder). Individuals are also entitled to receive a refund of the tax credits on those dividends via the VCTs.

Capital gains reliefs

Gains arising on the disposal of VCT shares that were acquired by subscription or purchase up to the £100,000 limit in any year are exempt from capital gains tax (and any losses are not allowable). There is no minimum period for which the shares must be held. Where gains are chargeable, they may be deferred if reinvested in new VCT shares, EIS shares (see page 403) or other qualifying unquoted shares under the reinvestment relief provisions (see page 62).

A claim may be made for all or any part of gains on the disposal of *any* assets by someone resident or ordinarily resident in the UK to be deferred to the extent that they are reinvested, within one year before or one year after the disposal, in VCT shares on which income tax relief is given and which (where relevant) are still held at the time of the disposal. The *deferred* gains (not the gains on the VCT shares themselves) will become chargeable if the VCT shares are disposed of (other than to a spouse), or the investor (or spouse who has acquired the shares) becomes non-resident within five years of acquiring the shares, or the VCT loses its approval, or the income tax relief is otherwise withdrawn. The deferred gain is not triggered by the death of the investor (or spouse to whom the shares have been transferred). Where deferred gains are triggered, they may again be deferred if further reinvested in new VCT shares, EIS shares (see page 403) or other qualifying unquoted shares under the reinvestment relief provisions (see page 62), if the conditions are satisfied.

Example 10

In December 1996 an investor buys shares in a qualifying venture capital trust from an existing shareholder for £40,000. On 1 March 1997 he subscribes £90,000 for further shares, so that his total investment in the year is £130,000.

He will get 20% income tax relief on the £90,000 subscribed for new shares. No relief is available for the purchased shares.

Dividends on the shares bought for £40,000 and on £60,000 of the shares subscribed for will be exempt from tax. Capital gains exemption will apply to the same amount.

Gains of up to £90,000 on *any* assets disposed of between 1 March 1996 and 1 March 1998 may be deferred against the shares subscribed for.

Capital gains share pools

Shares in a VCT that are eligible for CGT exemption on disposal are kept separate from any pool of non-eligible shares in the VCT. Any disposals are identified first with shares acquired before the trust became a VCT. To decide whether other disposals relate to shares in excess of the £100,000 limit in any year, disposals are identified with shares acquired earlier rather than those acquired later. Where shares are acquired on the same day, shares in excess of the £100,000 limit are treated as disposed of before qualifying shares.

If a VCT loses its qualifying status, shares eligible for the CGT exemption are treated as disposed of at market value (any gain being covered by the exemption) and immediately reacquired at market value, thus going into the pool of non-eligible shares at that value.

Shares of negligible value (TCGA 1992, s 24; FA 1996, Sch 39 para 4)

Where shares (or any other assets) have become of negligible value, you may establish an allowable loss by claiming to be treated as if you had actually disposed of them either on the date of the claim or at a stipulated time within the two tax years before the tax year in which the claim is made, providing the shares were of negligible value on the chosen date (see page 63). The loss cannot be increased by indexation allowance. Details of quoted shares that are regarded as being of negligible value, and the date from which that applies, are published by the Revenue. In the case of unquoted shares, the fact that the shares are of negligible value has specifically to be agreed with the Revenue. Even though shares are on the Revenue's list, you do not have to make a negligible value claim unless and until you wish to do so. If a claim has not been made before the time when the shares cease to exist, they are treated as disposed of at that time.

Relief against income for losses on shares in unquoted trading companies (TA 1988, ss 574–576; FA 1994, s 210 and Sch 20 para 8)

Where an individual sells shares at a loss, the loss is normally relievable, like any other capital loss, against gains on other assets. Where, however, the shares are in an unquoted UK trading company and were acquired by subscription as distinct from transfer, relief may be claimed instead against any other *income* of the tax year of loss or of the previous tax year. The claim takes priority over any claim for relief for trading losses. For the years 1994/95 and 1995/96, claims must be made within two years after the end of the tax year of loss. From 1996/97, claims must be made within one year from 31 January following the tax year of loss (e.g. by 31 January 1999 for a 1996/97 loss).

Relief is available under these provisions for a loss on shares acquired under the enterprise investment scheme (see page 403).

Capital gains on government, local authority and company loan stocks (TCGA 1992, ss 104–106, 108, 115–117 and Sch 9; FA 1996, ss 92, 96 and Sch 14 para 61)

Companies

Before 1 April 1996, the provisions outlined below for individuals also applied to companies. Loan stock was broadly exempt for capital gains purposes, which denied relief for losses as well as exempting gains. From 1 April 1996, gains and losses on disposal are brought into account in calculating a company's income, as outlined on page 513 (with the exception of holdings of 3½% Funding Stock 1999/2004 and 5½% Treasury Stock 2008/12, which will remain subject to the capital gains exemption).

The disposal of securities which can be converted into or exchanged for shares will be dealt with under the capital gains provisions where there is more than a trivial likelihood at the outset that the conversion etc. rights will be exercised, providing they cannot be redeemed for a 'deep' return over the issue price if they are not converted.

Subject to transitional provisions, neither the accrued income scheme provisions (see page 497) nor the provisions for deep discounted and deep gain securities (see page 533) apply to companies from 1 April 1996. Interest, gains and losses on securities formerly covered by those provisions are dealt with according to the normal rules for loans outlined on page 27.

Individuals

No chargeable gains or allowable losses arise on disposals by individuals of British Government stock and qualifying corporate bonds (with the exception of certain losses as indicated below). Qualifying corporate bonds are quoted or unquoted non-convertible sterling loan stock purchased or issued on commercial terms after 13 March 1984. Building society permanent interest bearing shares (see page 504) are also within the definition of qualifying corporate bonds. Profits and losses on certain securities issued at a discount are dealt with under the income tax rather than the capital gains provisions (see page 533). Index-linked securities that are outside the discounted securities provisions (i.e. those that are linked to the value of chargeable assets) are also outside the definition of qualifying corporate bond and are thus chargeable to capital gains tax.

The capital gains exemption for qualifying corporate bonds cannot be used to avoid income tax by selling just before an interest date, because of the accrued income provisions (see page 497). There are special provisions for company reorganisations to ensure that the appropriate exemption is given on loan stock converted into shares or vice versa.

Disposals of interest-bearing stocks that are not government stocks or qualifying corporate bonds (i.e. non-sterling loan stock, loan stock that may be converted into shares, loans that are not commercial loans and loan stock acquired before 14 March 1984) are subject to capital gains tax (unless they are discounted securities within the income tax charge), but the computation differs from that for shares in the following respects.

The post-1982 pool provisions dealt with on page 514 do not apply to these securities, so that each acquisition of such securities is treated as a separate asset.

Disposals are not identified according to the rules on page 515. They are normally identified with acquisitions in the previous twelve months on a 'first in, first out' basis, then with any other acquisitions on a 'last in, first out' basis. These general rules are subject to certain anti-avoidance provisions.

Losses on qualifying corporate bonds (TCGA 1992, ss 251, 253–255; FA 1996, Sch 14 paras 65, 66 and Sch 39 paras 8, 9)

Since qualifying corporate bonds are exempt from capital gains tax, no allowable loss can arise under the normal rules. For qualifying corporate bonds issued after 14 March 1989 (or held on that date by the person who made the loan), relief for losses may be claimed according to the rules outlined on page 63 if the claimant made the loan to a UK resident trader. Someone to whom the bond has been assigned cannot claim the relief. A claim may be made when the value of the loan has become negligible (see page 63). Where unquoted bonds were issued before 14 March 1989 in exchange for other shares or securities, and they do not strictly qualify for this loss relief because the money has not been used in a trade, the relief is given by Revenue concession (D38). See page 535 for the treatment of losses on qualifying corporate bonds acquired on a takeover.

The provisions in this section do not apply to companies in relation to disposals on or after 1 April 1996, because the new treatment for companies of gains and losses relating to all loans applies from that date (see page 513).

Securities issued at a discount (FA 1996, Sch 13)

The deep discounted securities provisions no longer apply to companies from 1 April 1996 (subject to transitional provisions), so what follows relates only to private investors.

Before Finance Act 1996, there were numerous different rules for dealing with securities that were at a deep discount, or at a deep gain, or were indexed or convertible into shares. These have been replaced from 6 April 1996 by a single set of rules for private investors covering all securities issued at a discount. The accrued income scheme (see page 497) does not apply to securities within these provisions. Securities are discounted securities where their issue price is lower than the redemption price by more than ½% per year between issue and redemption, or, if that period exceeds 30 years, by more than 15%. The provisions do not cover shares, gilt-edged securities (except for gilt strips, for which there are special rules), indexed securities that are linked to the value of chargeable assets, and life assurance policies.

There is no capital gains tax charge on discounted securities, and investors will be charged to income tax under Schedule D, Case III (or Case IV for foreign securities) in the tax year of disposal or redemption on the profit made. If a loss arises, a claim may be made by the first anniversary of 31 January following the relevant tax year to set the loss against the income of that tax year. Trustees may only set losses against income from discounted securities of the tax year of loss or, if that is insufficient, of a later tax year. When someone dies, they are treated as disposing of the securities to the personal representatives at market value at the date of death, and transfers from personal representatives to legatees will be treated as at market value at the date of the transfer.

Takeovers, mergers and reconstructions (TCGA 1992, ss 57, 116, 126–131, 135; FA 1996, s 177)

An exchange of new shares for old does not normally involve a chargeable gain, the new shares standing in the shoes of the old both as regards acquisition date and cost. This often happens when one company (whether or not its shares are quoted on the Stock Exchange) acquires another (either quoted or unquoted) by issuing its own shares to the holders of the shares in the company which is being taken over.

Where both cash and new shares are received, a partial disposal arises, in the proportion that the cash itself bears to the cash and market value of the securities acquired in exchange.

Example 11

X owns 10,000 shares in a company, A, which cost £6,000 in September 1983.
Company A is taken over by company B on 6 May 1996, indexation allowance from September 1983 to May 1996 being, say, 78%.

(a) 12,000 shares in company B, valued at £15,000, are received in exchange for the 10,000 shares in company A.
No chargeable gain arises on the £9,000 excess value of the company B shares over the cost of the company A shares.
Instead the 12,000 shares in company B are regarded as having the same £6,000 base value as the 10,000 company A shares which they replace.

(b) 12,000 shares in company B, valued at £11,250, together with £3,750 in cash are received in exchange for the 10,000 shares in company A, the shares in company A having an indexed cost of £10,680. The cash represents ¼ of the total consideration and the shares ¾.
The 12,000 shares in company B have base values as follows:

Unindexed value ¾ × £6,000	£4,500
Indexed value ¾ × £10,680	£8,010

The indexed cost to set off against the £3,750 cash received for the part disposal is ¼ × £10,680 = £2,670.

When part of a takeover package takes the form of shares to be issued at some future date, the number of such shares depending for example on future profits, the current value of that future right should strictly be calculated and treated as part of the disposal proceeds, with an immediate capital gains tax liability arising. By Revenue concession D27, a taxpayer may elect for the shares to be dealt with under the normal takeover provisions outlined on page 533. The concession does not apply if the future consideration is cash rather than shares. This can present a problem, because if the amount eventually received turns out to be less than the amount taken into account at the time of the takeover, losses will occur against which there may be no matching gains at that time.

As indicated on page 532, qualifying corporate bonds are not chargeable assets for capital gains tax, and can create neither a chargeable gain nor allowable loss (subject to the special rules on page 532). Sometimes on a takeover or reorganisation qualifying corporate bonds may be exchanged for shares or vice versa. When qualifying corporate bonds are exchanged for shares, the normal rules outlined above do not apply and the shares are treated as acquired at their market value at the date of the exchange. If shares are exchanged for qualifying corporate bonds, the gain or loss at the date of the exchange is calculated and 'frozen' until the qualifying corporate bonds are disposed of, when the frozen gain or loss crystallises. From the date of the exchange, no further indexation allowance is available and no gain or loss can be established on the bonds themselves (with the exception stated on page 505). In some cases, this could mean that a gain is chargeable even if the qualifying corporate bonds have become virtually worthless. One solution is to give them to a charity. The frozen gain on the shares would not then be charged, nor would the charity have any tax liability when it disposed of the bonds. A frozen gain escapes charge if the taxpayer dies. If a frozen gain arises on shares held by personal representatives, however, it is charged when the loan stock is disposed of by the personal representatives, or when disposed of by a legatee following the transfer of the stock to him by the personal representatives.

Where a frozen gain would otherwise become chargeable, it may be deferred if an equivalent investment is made in unquoted shares under the reinvestment relief provisions (see page 62). Where shares are exchanged partly for cash and partly for qualifying corporate bonds, reinvestment relief may be claimed on the gain on the cash element.

A company's frozen gains or losses on corporate bonds at 31 March 1996 are taken into account in the transitional provisions for the changed treatment of company loans.

Disposal by gift (TCGA 1992, ss 67, 165)

Where shares or securities are disposed of by gift, the proceeds are regarded as being their open market value. If a gain arises, the donor and donee may make a joint election for the donee to adopt the donor's base cost for capital gains tax purposes, as increased by the indexation allowance to the date of the gift, but this right is only available if the gift is of shares or securities in an unquoted trading company, or in a quoted trading company in which the donor owns 5% of the shares, or if the gift is immediately chargeable to inheritance tax, or would be if it were not covered by the donor's annual inheritance tax exemption (see page 60).

If a loss arises on a transaction with a connected person (which broadly means close family of the donor and of his spouse, trustees of family trusts and companies controlled by the donor) the loss is not allowed against gains generally but only against a gain on a subsequent transaction with the same person.

Stamp duty

Stamp duty is currently payable on most transactions in stocks and shares, usually at ½%, but higher rates apply in some circumstances. The provisions are outlined in chapter 6.

Personal Equity Plans (PEPs) (TA 1988, s 333; TCGA 1992, s 151; SI 1989/469)

The Personal Equity Plan scheme is designed to encourage savings through the purchase of shares. Every individual aged 18 and over who is resident and ordinarily resident in the UK is able to invest up to £6,000 in each tax year in a Personal Equity Plan (£6,000 each for a married couple). A further £3,000 a year may be invested in a single-company PEP. Shares can be transferred free of capital gains tax into a single-company PEP from approved savings-related share option and profit sharing schemes (see chapter 11), and unlike other PEP investments (see below) such shares may be unquoted.

PEPs are managed by unit and investment trusts, banks, building societies, insurance companies, stockbrokers and other financial advisers. Any capital gains and dividends on the plan investments are entirely tax-free, and will remain so for as long as the investment is held within the plan. On the other hand, any losses arising on disposals within a plan are not allowable losses. The plan managers are able to reclaim from the Revenue the tax credits on dividends, thus increasing the value of the plan. Dividends and credits may be retained within the plan or passed on to shareholders. Where gains, dividends and tax credits are reinvested, the total value of the plans held is permitted to go up to that extent each year by more than the annual limit. Investors may pay in cash to take up rights issues on shares they already hold in the plan but this can only be done within the subscription limits and not in addition to them.

Subject to some special rules as to what part of the £6,000 investment may be in unit and investment trusts and open-ended investment companies (see page 528), the plan managers may invest the money in UK ordinary shares that are quoted on the Stock Exchange or on the Unlisted Securities Market, comparable European Union shares, quoted corporate bonds and convertibles of UK non-financial companies, and quoted UK and EU preference shares. In order to qualify, corporate bonds must have a minimum five-year term and carry a fixed rate of interest. Shares on the new Alternative Investment Market (AIM) cannot be held directly in a PEP, although they may be included in the investments of a unit trust or investment trust for PEP purposes. Investors (or plan managers on their behalf) are able to switch from one qualifying investment to another without any capital gains tax effect. It is also possible to arrange with the plan manager to transfer a PEP to a different plan manager, although there will be costs involved. Investors who acquire new issue shares outside the plan, including the privatisation issues and building society shares, are able, with the plan manager's approval, to transfer the shares into the plan, subject to the overall annual subscription limit.

When an investor wishes to withdraw all or part of his investment, the withdrawals may be either cash or the investments themselves. If investments are withdrawn, their base cost for capital gains tax purposes is their market value at the date of withdrawal. There is no loss of the tax advantages already obtained when funds or shares are withdrawn. If an investor dies, the personal representatives are treated as acquiring the plan at its market value at the date of death and the tax exemption ceases to apply.

Plan managers may hold cash on deposit within a plan before it is invested or reinvested in ordinary shares. The investment should take place as soon as possible, and for a single-company PEP the cash must be substantially invested within 42 days. Tax is not deducted from any interest received by the plan managers on the cash deposit, and the interest is not subject to tax at all if it is reinvested in shares or unit trusts. Otherwise, it is taxed in full when withdrawn (at the lower rate of 20%) unless it is not more than £180.

Although a small investor's own capital gains tax exemption would usually cover gains he made if he invested other than through a PEP, the other tax advantages make them an attractive investment. The benefits are, however, reduced by the plan manager's charges.

Tax points

- Selling quoted shares is often a convenient way to realise capital gains and use the annual exemption, currently £6,300. If you wish to continue to hold shares that offer such opportunities, you can arrange to buy them back again the next day (called 'bed and breakfast') but this cannot be done without both the sale and purchase being fully completed, with the consequent costs involved, including the difference between buying and selling prices. Share portfolios should be looked at for suitable opportunities before the end of each tax year. The complicated calculation of the potential gain should be borne in mind when working out what can be sold without attracting tax.

- If you take 'enhanced' scrip shares instead of a cash dividend, you will be treated as having taxable income equal to the value of the shares on the first day of dealing (see page 512). They are still scrip shares, so are pooled with the existing holding(s). Even if all or any of the shares are immediately sold, the ten-day rule does not apply to match the shares sold with the scrip shares acquired, and the cost of sale is arrived at by taking a proportionate part of the indexed pool cost (the shares sold being matched first with the post-1982 pool even though some of the scrip shares acquired went into the pre-1982 pool).

- If you are a small investor, unit and investment trusts can be a useful way of getting the benefit of a wide spread of investments, with the added advantage of expert management. Such trusts are exempt from tax on their capital gains. You pay capital gains tax in the usual way when you dispose of your investment in the trust. The investment is particularly tax efficient when made through a personal equity plan.

- Investing regular amounts on a monthly basis into a unit or investment trust evens out the ups and downs of share prices.

- When you reinvest gains into venture capital trust shares, you can effectively get up to 60% tax relief at that time (20% income tax relief on the shares and 40% capital gains relief on the deferred gains for a higher rate taxpayer). As and when the deferred gains are triggered, further deferral may be possible, and the gains will escape tax altogether if not triggered before your death.

- The new 'corporate bond' PEPs may be of interest to those who are looking for greater certainty of income than is available through PEP investments in ordinary shares. There is, however, more opportunity for capital growth with ordinary shares, and even fixed interest bonds are not risk-free.

- When a PEP investor dies, his personal representatives should notify the PEP plan manager promptly, because the tax exemption ceases at the date of the investor's death.

- If you give away shares, they are regarded as sold for market value, but tax does not have to be paid at that time if they qualify for gifts relief. The relief is available on a holding of quoted shares if you control 5% or more of the voting power (see page 60).

- See page 535 re avoiding a frozen gain crystallising on qualifying corporate bonds that were acquired on a takeover, etc. by giving them to a charity.

- Now that indexation allowance cannot increase a loss, you may wish to make a negligible value claim as soon as shares have been included on the Revenue's list (see page 530). But if, say, making the claim immediately would cause annual exemption to be wasted, you should defer it to a later year.

- If there is some control over the time of payment of a dividend, as with a family or other small company, watch that the date of payment does not aggravate an already high taxable income where the income of the major shareholders varies from year to year.

- When acquiring unquoted trading company shares, they should if possible be subscribed for and not taken up by transfer, so that if a loss arises on disposal it may be relieved against income rather than against capital gains which are perhaps covered by the annual exemption.

- If you buy government stocks on the National Savings Stock Register you will receive the interest in full and pay the income tax later, rather than receiving the interest net if you acquire the stocks on the Stock Exchange. The end result will be the same but your cash flow will be improved.

- If you hold not more than £5,000 nominal value of government stock or other securities to which the accrued income scheme applies, remember that the accrued interest will not be charged to income tax (see page 497). The securities will usually be exempt from capital gains tax (see page 532). If they are not, the accrued interest will be taken into account for capital gains tax in arriving at the cost or proceeds as the case may be.

- If you hold more than £5,000 nominal value of accrued income scheme securities, you will need to consider what adjustment is required when you dispose of any of them. Details must be shown on your tax return. If you deal through a bank or stockbroker, the amount of accrued interest will be shown on your contract note. Accrued income charges or reliefs are taken into account in the tax year in which the next interest payment is made on the stock.

- Since each acquisition of shares before 6 April 1965 is a separate asset for capital gains tax purposes, unless an election has been made to include those holdings in the pre-1982 pool at their market value at 6 April 1965, or a rebasing election has been made to treat all assets owned on 31 March 1982 as acquired at their market value on that day, it follows that a disposal of a holding will sometimes be treated as several disposals for capital gains tax purposes. If the disposal qualifies for the business gifts relief, this may give the opportunity of electing for the gifts rollover relief to apply to only some of the disposals, leaving the gain on others to be covered by the annual exemption if not otherwise used. Where there is only a post-1982 pool and/or a pre-1982 pool, gifts could be made at different times to enable the exemption to be used.

- With the rate at which you pay capital gains tax depending upon your level of income, the timing of disposals can be important where your level of income varies.

- Since husband and wife are both entitled to an annual capital gains tax exemption of £6,300, it may be appropriate to split share portfolios so that each may take advantage of it. Transfers between husband and wife are not chargeable disposals. If shares are held jointly in unequal shares, watch the provisions about notifying the Revenue for income tax purposes (see page 462).

39
Chattels and valuables

What are chattels? (TCGA 1992, ss 21, 263, 269)

Chattels are tangible movable property, for example coins, furniture, jewellery, works of art, motor vehicles. Although currency comes within the definition, sterling currency is specifically exempt from capital gains tax, as is foreign currency for personal use abroad. Motor cars (other than one-seater cars) are also specifically exempt from capital gains tax. One-seater cars and other motor vehicles are exempt as wasting assets unless they have been used in a business (see below).

Income tax

If you invest in valuable objects, the appreciation in value does not generally attract income tax (nor sometimes capital gains tax), but on the other hand there is no tax relief for expenses of ownership such as insurance or charges for safe custody.

A succession of profitable sales may suggest to the Revenue that chattels and valuables are held for trading purposes rather than investment, particularly where the scale and frequency of the sales, or the way in which they are carried out, or the need for supplementary work between purchase and sale, suggest a trading motive. Indeed, even a single purchase and sale has on occasion been held to be a trading transaction. However, an important indicator of trading is the lack of significant investment value or pride of ownership. Where chattels have those qualities, a trading motive is more readily refuted.

Capital gains tax (TCGA 1992, ss 44, 45, 262)

The capital gains tax treatment of a chattel depends on the nature of the chattel, and sometimes on its value.

Motor cars, sterling currency, and foreign currency for own use abroad are completely exempt, as indicated above. If other chattels have a predictable life of 50 years or less (called wasting assets), they are totally exempt from capital gains tax unless they are used in a business and capital allowances have been, or could have been, claimed on them. Plant and machinery is always regarded as having a predictable life of 50 years or less. So privately owned items such as greyhounds and yachts (and even collectors' items if they are 'machinery') are exempt because they are wasting assets. If an asset is exempt, there can be neither a chargeable gain nor an allowable loss. In many cases, therefore, the exemption denies you relief for a loss rather than exempting a gain.

In the case of chattels that are not wasting assets, and business chattels (whether they are wasting assets or not), any gain is exempt if the chattel is bought and sold for £6,000 or less. Where the proceeds exceed £6,000, the chargeable gain cannot exceed 5/3rds of the excess proceeds over £6,000. If the chattel is sold at a loss for less than £6,000, it is treated as sold for £6,000 to calculate the allowable loss. This means that there can only be an allowable loss if the chattel cost more than £6,000, and if it is a business chattel there will not be an allowable loss in any event (see below).

See examples 1 and 2.

Example 1

	£	£
Sale proceeds of antique dresser in June 1996 are		7,200
Cost was	3,550	
Indexation allowance, say	1,020	4,570
Chargeable gain		£2,630
But limited to 5/3 × (7,200–6,000)		£2,000

No allowable loss could arise on the dresser, no matter what the sale proceeds, because proceeds of less than £6,000 are treated as £6,000 to calculate a loss, and indexation allowance is not available.

Example 2

Painting that had cost £10,000 in January 1989 was sold for £8,000 in June 1996. Indexation allowance is not available and the allowable loss is £2,000. If the painting had been sold for £5,000, it would be treated as sold for £6,000, giving an allowable loss of £4,000.

As far as business chattels are concerned, capital allowances are taken into account in computing income liable to income tax or corporation tax. If the chattel is sold for more than cost, the capital allowances will be withdrawn, so that they will not affect the computation of a capital gain. Where a business chattel is sold for less than cost, the capital allowances computation will automatically give relief for the loss on sale in arriving at taxable income, so there will be no allowable loss for capital gains purposes.

Items comprising a set or collection are treated as separate assets unless they are sold to the same or connected persons (as defined in TCGA 1992, s 286 — see page 60), in which case the sales are added together and treated as arising on the occasion of the last sale. Splitting up a set and selling it to different unconnected people would usually not be sensible because it would substantially reduce its value.

Coins (TCGA 1992, ss 21, 262, 269)

Coins may either be currency, i.e. legal tender, or they may be demonetized. Coins are within the definition of a chattel, and if they have a predictable life of more than 50 years, which obviously applies to collectors' items, the exemption for chattels that are wasting assets is not available.

Foreign currency for your own personal use abroad is exempt from capital gains tax under a specific provision. The same applies to sterling currency (which includes post-1838 sovereigns). Demonetized coins (including pre-1838 sovereigns) are subject to the chattels rules and any gain is exempt if the coin is sold for £6,000 or less.

Where a coin is still legal tender, i.e. is currency, the £6,000 exemption is not available and the coin is chargeable to capital gains tax in the normal way. An example is Krugerrands, which are legal tender in South Africa.

Collectors' coins are normally liable to VAT at the standard rate, whether they are legal tender or not, unless they are dealt with under the special scheme for antiques and collectors' pieces or under the global accounting scheme for second-hand goods (see page 98).

Gifts of chattels

A gift of a chargeable asset is treated as a disposal at open market value at the date of the gift. In order to arrive at an estimated valuation, some evidence of the transaction in the form of correspondence, etc. is advisable. If the value is below the £6,000 exempt level, no tax charge will arise, but the valuation at the time of the gift counts as the cost of the asset to the donee when calculating the capital gains position on a subsequent disposal by him.

If the value of the gift exceeds the £6,000 exempt level and there is a chargeable gain, tax may not even so be payable because the gain, together with other gains, may be within the annual exemption of £6,300. For gifts of business assets, certain other gifts for public benefit, etc. and gifts into and out of discretionary trusts, it is possible for donor and donee to claim gifts relief, so that the donor pays no tax on the gift and the donee acquires it at indexed cost for the purposes of a future sale by him (see page 60).

For inheritance tax purposes, a gift of a chattel may be covered by the annual exemption. If not, it will either be a potentially exempt transfer, or a chargeable transfer if it is to a discretionary trust, but if the donor does not survive the gift by seven years, the value at the time of the gift will be taken into account in calculating the inheritance tax payable at death. The person who received the gift will be primarily responsible for the inheritance tax triggered by the death within seven years, although the Revenue have the right to look to the estate of the donor if necessary. There will not be any potential liability if the gift was within the nil rate band, but, if there is, it may be worth insuring against by a term assurance policy on the life of the donor in favour of the donee.

Tax points

- Details of chattel acquisitions are frequently required at a later date, perhaps for capital gains tax purposes or to demonstrate that funds for some other investment or business enterprise were available from their sale. Evidence can be provided by purchase invoices that identify the object, and/or by having substantial items included specifically on a household contents insurance policy when they are acquired.

- A profit on the sale of a vintage or classic car is exempt from capital gains tax (unless it is 'unsuitable to be used as a private vehicle') but if you buy and sell with the aim of making a profit rather than holding the car as an investment you are likely to be held to be trading and thus liable to income tax (or corporation tax).

- 'Machinery' is always exempt from capital gains tax unless it is used in a business. A private individual will therefore not pay tax on a gain on a valuable antique machine, such as a clock. The same would apply to a gain by a private individual on a vintage or classic vehicle not covered by the cars exemption.

- Be aware of the trading trap if you regularly buy and sell chattels and valuables.

40
Sensible use of life assurance

Background

You cannot get tax relief on life assurance premiums (except as indicated below for term assurance within a personal pension plan) unless the policy was taken out before 14 March 1984 and has not subsequently been amended (whether or not by a clause in the policy) to increase the benefits or extend the term. There are, however, still tax advantages for qualifying policies, because of the treatment of the proceeds.

Relief for premium payments (TA 1988, s 274)

Where term assurance is included in a personal pension plan, you get relief at your highest tax rate (see chapter 17). Apart from that, the rate of relief available on a qualifying policy taken out before 14 March 1984, and not subsequently amended, is 12½% of the premiums paid, subject to maximum allowable premiums of either £1,500 or one-sixth of your total income, whichever is higher.

Qualifying policy (TA 1988, ss 266, 267, 272–274 and Sch 15)

The definition of 'qualifying policy' is complex, but broadly the policy must be on your own or your spouse's life, it must secure a capital sum on death, earlier disability or not earlier than ten years after the policy is taken out, the premiums must be reasonably even and paid at yearly or shorter intervals, and there are various requirements as to the amount of the sum assured and sometimes as to the surrender value. Providing these conditions are satisfied, the policy proceeds are tax-free (subject to what is said on page 545 as regards early surrender). The offer of a free gift on taking out a policy could breach the 'qualifying policy' rules, but by concession a gift valued at up to £30 will be ignored.

Purchased life annuities (TA 1988, ss 1A, 656–658; FA 1996, s 73)

A qualifying policy is sometimes useful to higher rate taxpayers in conjunction with a purchased life annuity (see chapter 36).

Only part of the purchased annuity is liable to income tax (tax being deducted at 20% from 6 April 1996 — see page 16), the remainder being regarded as a return of capital.

Instead of making a conventional investment and losing a substantial part of the income in tax, a higher rate taxpayer could purchase a life annuity and use the net income arising to fund a qualifying life policy, the profits on maturity of the policy being tax-free. Whilst the reduction in tax rates has reduced the advantages of this form of investment, it can still be attractive in some circumstances, but specialist advice is essential.

If you are an older taxpayer, a variation is available under which only part of the net annual sum from the annuity is used to pay the premiums on a qualifying policy to replace the initial cost of the annuity, the remainder being retained as spendable income. It is also possible to use your house as security to borrow the money to buy an annuity if you are 65 or over but the annuity rates will often make this impracticable and specialist advice is again essential (see chapter 34).

Early surrender of qualifying policies (TA 1988, ss 540, 541, 547)

Where a qualifying policy is surrendered less than ten years after the policy is taken out (or, for endowment policies, before the expiry of three-quarters of the term if that amounts to less than ten years), any profit arising is charged to tax at the excess of higher rate tax over basic rate to the extent that the profit falls within the taxpayer's higher rate income tax band (but top-slicing relief is available — see page 547), and see below under 'Non-qualifying policies' for the way in which the profit is taken into account where there is savings income.

Details of gains must be shown on your tax return, as for non-qualifying policies (see below).

Non-qualifying policies (TA 1988, ss 540–549)

If a policy is not a qualifying policy, there is no relief for premium payments even for policies taken out before 14 March 1984. Whenever the policy was taken out, the proceeds are not wholly tax-free. They are free of capital gains tax, but if the capital appreciation comes within the higher rate tax band when it is added to your income in the tax year of surrender or assignment, it is chargeable to income tax at the excess of higher rate tax over basic rate, subject to certain special provisions which are outlined below. Although savings income is treated as the top slice of your income for all other purposes (see page 16), life policy gains are added in last of all in order to calculate any tax liability.

Gains must be shown on your tax return. Your insurance company should be able to provide you with the relevant details. If you are calculating your own

545

tax, you should ask the Revenue for a special working sheet to work out the tax on the life insurance gains.

Investment bonds

A non-qualifying policy usually takes the form of a single premium investment bond. When invested by the life office, the single premium should grow more rapidly than an equivalent amount in the hands of a higher rate taxpayer reinvesting net income from a conventional investment. You are able to make withdrawals of not more than 5% of the initial investment in each policy year (ending on the anniversary of the policy) without attracting a tax liability at that time, such withdrawals being treated as partial surrenders which are only taken into account in calculating the final profit on the bond when it is cashed in. The 5% is a cumulative figure and amounts unused in any year swell the tax-free withdrawal available in a later year, which could be useful if you want to save the withdrawal facility for some particularly heavy item of expenditure. If you withdraw more than the permitted 5% figure, you will be charged to tax on the excess, but only if, taking into account the excess, your taxable income exceeds the basic rate limit, so that if the excess occurs in a year when you are a basic rate taxpayer no charge will normally arise. The same applies to the position when you finally cash in the bond, because if this can be arranged in a year when your income, even with the addition of the bond profit, will not attract the higher rate, no tax will normally be payable (and see below as regards top-slicing relief). Thus it may be possible to surrender in a year when your income is low, for example because of business losses or following retirement. If the bond is cashed in on your death, any mortality element of the profit as distinct from the surplus on the underlying investments is not taxable, and since the income of the year of death will usually not cover a full tax year, even on the taxable portion there may be little tax liability at the higher rate. There is no charge to tax if a new policy is issued under the terms of an option contained in the maturing policy and the whole of the proceeds under the maturing policy are retained by the insurance company and applied in paying one or more premiums under the new policy.

There is no relief if there is a loss when the bond is cashed in, but if any deficiency exceeds the cumulative 5% tax-free withdrawals, a higher rate taxpayer may deduct the excess from his income in calculating the amount of extra tax payable on income above the basic rate threshold.

There is one instance where the cashing-in of a bond, or an earlier chargeable event, may result in a tax charge, even when you are not a higher rate taxpayer, and that is where you are entitled to a higher personal allowance because you are aged 65 or over, and/or a higher married couple's allowance because you or your wife is aged 65 or over. Although the bond profit or excess withdrawn is only chargeable to tax if your taxable income exceeds the basic rate limit, it still counts as part of your total income for the purposes of age-related allowances. Any loss of age-related allowances will thus indirectly result in a tax charge.

Top-slicing relief on policy surrenders (TA 1988, s 550)

In the tax year when you cash in the bond (or indeed when a chargeable event arises on a qualifying policy) top-slicing relief is available to lessen the impact of the higher rate charge. The surplus on the bond is divided by the number of complete policy years (ending on the anniversary of the policy) that the bond has been held, and the amount arrived at is treated as the top slice of your income to ascertain the tax rate, which is then applied to the full profit. The longer the bond has been held the smaller the annual equivalent on which the tax charge is based. See example 1.

Example 1

		£
Taxpayer purchases investment bond for		10,000
He takes annual withdrawals of £500 for		
six years(covered by 5% rule)	3,000	
He cashes in bond in 1996/97 for	11,800	14,800
Profit liable to tax in 1996/97		£4,800

His taxable income after all allowances and reliefs is £25,100, leaving £400 available within the basic rate limit.

Annual equivalent of bond profit		
(1/6th × £4,800)	800	
Tax thereon as extra income: 400 @ 24%	96	
400 @ 40%	160	256
Less basic rate tax on £800 @ 24%		192
Tax at excess rates on £800		£64
Tax charge on full profit of £4,800 is £64 × 6, i.e.		£384

Top-slicing relief is only available when you pay tax above the basic rate. It does not enable you to avoid losing age-related allowances if the bond profit or excess withdrawal takes your income above £15,200.

An astute investor will usually want to switch investments from time to time, say from equities to properties, then to gilts and so on. For a small administration charge, a life office will let you switch the investments underlying your bond, and the switch has no adverse tax effect.

To give added flexibility in the timing of bond surrenders, it is possible to take out a number of smaller bonds, so that they need not all be cashed in the same tax year. Not only can the original investment be cashed over a number of years but the amount liable to tax in any year is itself top-sliced in arriving at the tax payable. This type of arrangement may be used as an alternative to a purchased life annuity in order to pay the premiums on a qualifying policy, and also to pay large items of recurrent expenditure such as school fees.

Trust policies

Where someone is entitled as of right to the income from a trust fund (called an interest in possession), the fund itself is regarded as belonging to that person for inheritance tax purposes.

If you take out a policy on your own life in trust for, say, your children, the policy is treated as belonging to them, and, when the proceeds are received, there is no inheritance tax charge because the child has held an interest in the trust fund throughout, which now comprises cash instead of a life policy. Nor is there any inheritance tax when the trustees pay the cash to the child, because the trust fund was always regarded as belonging to him. See example 2.

Example 2

In September 1996, a taxpayer takes out a qualifying policy on his own life assuring £100,000 on his death and pays the first annual premium of £5,000.

The policy is gifted to trustees for the benefit of his son, but he continues to pay the annual premiums of £5,000.

The effect is:

The gift of the annual premiums will be covered by the inheritance tax exemption for gifts out of income.

The son will receive the eventual proceeds without any tax charge whatsoever.

This is a useful way of providing for an anticipated inheritance tax liability by putting funds in the hands of those who will inherit the estate.

It is possible for husband and wife to arrange the policy so that the proceeds do not arise until the second death. The surviving spouse can then take the whole of the deceased's estate at the first death without inheritance tax, because of the surviving spouse exemption, and the liability to inheritance tax on the second death will be covered by the policy proceeds in the hands of the policy beneficiaries.

Endowment mortgages

Endowment mortgages are a combination of a loan on which you pay interest, plus a life assurance policy which is intended to pay off the loan when it matures. No capital repayments are made to the lender, so the interest cost never falls because of capital repaid. The profit element in the policy when it matures is not liable to tax.

Policies which were taken out before 14 March 1984 still attract 12½% life assurance tax relief on the premiums.

If the mortgage is reduced because capital becomes available, or is repaid early, usually on change of residence, it is worth considering whether the existing endowment policy should be retained, if it is a pre-14 March 1984 policy, in order to preserve tax relief on the premiums, so that it will only be any new policy to support an additional amount of borrowing that will not attract the premium relief. If the existing policy were surrendered and a new policy taken out to cover the whole borrowing, no life assurance relief would be available.

Pension mortgages

Some building societies and banks will grant mortgages or loans with no capital repayments, but with an undertaking that the borrowing will eventually be repaid out of the capital sum received from a pension plan (see chapters 16 and 17), the borrowing in the meantime being covered by temporary life assurance. The lender cannot take a charge on the pension contract, but you can give an undertaking to use the lump sum from the plan to discharge the loan.

The effect is that tax relief at your various marginal rates over the period of your pension plan is obtained on the capital repayment since the fund used to make the repayment has been built up from premiums upon which the tax relief has been obtained at the time of payment. Unless these arrangements are part of an overall plan to provide adequately for your retirement, you will, however, have used part of the money that was intended to finance your retirement to pay off your mortgage.

Friendly societies (TA 1988, ss 459–467; FA 1995, Sch 10)

Whereas the profits of other life assurance companies are taxable, the profits of friendly societies arising from life or endowment business are generally exempt from income tax and corporation tax. The exemption applies where the premiums in respect of the policies issued by the friendly society do not exceed £270 a year (or £25 a month), or the annuities which they grant do not exceed £156 a year.

Policies taken out by children under 18 qualify for the exemption and payment of the premiums by a parent will not contravene the income tax rules about parental gifts (see page 463); there will therefore be no tax charge on the parent.

The society's tax exemption gives an added advantage to a qualifying policy with a registered friendly society, although the restrictions on premiums and annuities limit the scope accordingly.

Tax points

- With the abolition of premium relief for life assurance policies taken out after 13 March 1984, those who seek term assurance should consider arranging it under the personal pension provisions if they are self-employed or employees who have chosen to make personal pension provision (see chapter 17).

- A qualifying policy taken out before 14 March 1984 will continue to attract life assurance relief at 12½% on the premiums. Whether or not linked to a mortgage, this should be taken into account in considering early surrender.

- There is no point in taking out a policy on your own life to cover any inheritance tax arising on your death if the policy forms part of your estate. Although it will produce a capital sum, that sum will increase the taxable estate, and moreover will not be available until a grant of probate or administration has been obtained. A policy for the benefit of someone else will escape tax in your estate and the policy monies will be available to that person on production of the death certificate and appropriate claim form.

- A wide range of ways of investing through life assurance and purchased annuities is on offer by the various life offices, and an arrangement can often be tailored to your specific requirements. There are several schemes aimed at reducing inheritance tax. Specialist advice on what is available is essential.

- A single premium bond can be a simple and convenient way of investing without the need for any complex records such as those required when you invest on the Stock Exchange.

- Bonds are also a convenient way to get into and out of the property market by choice of appropriate funds, and you can give away one of a series of property fund supported bonds much more easily than giving land itself, with no inheritance tax charge if the gift is covered by exemptions, or if you survive for seven years after making it.

- There is no magic way of paying school fees. Sensible use of the types of life assurance contracts mentioned in this chapter will help, but early planning is essential, and contracts should be taken out soon after the child is born.

- There is a limit to the amount within a pension fund which can be taken as a lump sum. If you undertake to use your lump sum to repay a loan, the lender needs to be satisfied that the level of regular contributions is sufficient to produce a high enough lump sum to discharge or substantially reduce the debt (leaving you to draw the pension itself). The longer the period before retirement the bigger the fund that will be established.

- Friendly society policies for children are a tax-efficient way of using some of your income for your children's benefit. For other tax-efficient parent/child arrangements, see page 463.

- Your insurance company may rebate commission to you, or net it off against the premium, or invest it on your behalf. The Revenue had announced that they would regard such sums as your taxable income, but they no longer intend to do so.

41
The overseas element

Background

There are two main aspects to the overseas element: the tax treatment of UK citizens and UK resident companies with income or assets abroad; and the tax treatment of foreign nationals or foreign-resident companies with income or assets in the UK. In all cases, the tax liability may be affected by double taxation relief.

An individual's liability to UK tax depends on where he is resident, ordinarily resident and domiciled. For a company, ordinary residence and domicile are not normally significant, and the company's tax liability depends only on its residence. Within the scope of this book it is only possible to give a brief outline of the meaning of residence, ordinary residence and domicile. The Inland Revenue publishes a useful booklet IR 20, 'Residents and Non-residents — Liability to Tax in the United Kingdom', covering the provisions in more detail.

The overseas element also affects the taxation of trusts. This aspect is dealt with briefly on page 576.

Where UK tax is payable, the normal provisions for charging interest and penalties apply. Repayment supplement on overpaid tax is not paid to non-resident individuals (other than EU residents) for years before 1996/97. Thereafter, supplement is payable to both residents and non-residents.

Residence and ordinary residence of individuals (TA 1988, ss 207, 334–336; TCGA 1992, s 9; FA 1993, s 208)

Residence is a question of fact and usually requires physical presence in a country. The residence of husband and wife is determined independently. It is possible for an individual to be resident in more than one country for tax purposes. Ordinary residence is broadly equivalent to habitual residence. You are regarded as remaining resident and ordinarily resident in the UK despite a temporary absence abroad unless the absence spans a complete tax year.

Strictly you are either resident or non-resident for the whole of a tax year, but by Revenue concession A11 a tax year may be split into resident and non-resident periods as indicated below.

If you leave the UK to take up full-time employment abroad for a period which will span a complete tax year, you are regarded as not resident and not ordinarily resident from the day after you leave and as a new resident when you return, providing your UK visits do not overstep the limits for visitors (see below).

If you leave the UK for any other purpose you may be provisionally treated as not resident and not ordinarily resident if you can produce evidence of leaving the UK permanently, e.g. selling your house here and buying one abroad, and the provisional ruling will be confirmed when your absence has spanned a complete tax year. If evidence is not available at the start of the absence, you will provisionally be treated as remaining UK resident for a period of up to three years, and if your UK visits have averaged less than 91 days a tax year, you will be treated as not resident and not ordinarily resident from the time of leaving. If you have property in the UK available for your use, you will need to be able to show that retaining the property is consistent with your stated intention of living permanently abroad.

New permanent residents and those who intend to stay for two years or more are regarded as resident from the date of arrival in the UK, although this treatment might be revised if the circumstances changed and the UK stay was in fact short-term. Those whose intended stay was less than three years would not initially be regarded as *ordinarily* resident. Someone who does not know how long he is going to stay will be regarded as ordinarily resident from the beginning of the tax year after that in which the third anniversary of his arrival falls, or earlier if it becomes clear before then that he intends to stay on a long-term basis, or if he remains in the UK and purchases accommodation in the UK or leases it for a period of three years or more.

Those who visit the UK for a temporary purpose will not be regarded as UK resident, even if they have accommodation available here. Visitors will, however, be regarded as resident in any tax year in which their visits add up to 183 days in total. If UK visits, while not amounting to 183 days a year, average 91 days a year or more for four consecutive tax years (but excluding any days spent in the UK because of exceptional circumstances beyond the individual's control), a visitor is then regarded as becoming both resident and ordinarily resident in the UK. If it was clear at the outset that he was going to make regular, substantial visits, he may be regarded as resident and ordinarily resident from the start.

Residence of companies (FA 1988, s 66 and Sch 7; FA 1994, ss 249–251)

Under UK tax law, any company that is incorporated in the UK is treated as being UK resident no matter where it is managed and controlled. Companies incorporated abroad are regarded as UK resident if they are managed and controlled here. If a non-resident company transfers its central management and control to the UK it is treated as resident from the time of the transfer. Where, however, a company is treated as non-resident under the terms of a double tax treaty, this overrides these rules and the company is regarded as not being UK resident.

A company may have more than one country of residence. Anti-avoidance provisions apply to dual resident companies (see page 607).

Domicile

Domicile is different from nationality and residence and a person can only have one domicile at any one time. An individual's domicile is usually the country in which he has his permanent home. A domicile of origin is acquired at birth and under UK law this is the father's domicile for legitimate children and the mother's domicile for illegitimate children. A wife's domicile is ascertained independently of her husband's.

The domicile of origin may be abandoned and a domicile of choice acquired. This necessitates positive action, e.g. changing residence, making a will under the laws of the new country, obtaining citizenship of the new country. A high standard of proof is required to establish a change of domicile.

Domicile sometimes has an extended meaning for inheritance tax — see chapter 5. It has no relevance for companies.

Registration to vote in the UK as an overseas elector does not affect domicile for UK tax purposes (FA 1996, s 200).

Effect of residence, ordinary residence and domicile on UK tax position for individuals

Income tax is charged broadly on the world income of UK residents, subject to certain deductions for earnings abroad and for individuals who are not ordinarily resident or not domiciled in the UK. Individuals are normally charged on the full amount of foreign income arising abroad, whether it is brought into the UK or not. Someone resident in the UK who is not UK domiciled, or not ordinarily resident in the UK, is, however, charged only as and when income is brought into the UK (see page 557). Where tax is charged on the amount that arises abroad, the income to be brought into account is the sterling equivalent of the overseas amount at the date it arises. An average exchange rate for the year may be used, using rates published by the Revenue. Non-residents are liable to income tax only on income that arises in the UK and even then special rules apply (see later in this chapter, in particular pages 563 and 566). Where the UK chargeable income is high enough they pay higher rate tax. Non-residents are not entitled to personal allowances except as indicated on page 563.

Capital gains tax is charged on individuals who are resident *or* ordinarily resident in the UK — on world gains if domiciled in the UK, and on gains arising in or remitted to the UK if domiciled elsewhere. The gain or loss on the disposal of property abroad is arrived at by comparing the sterling equivalent of the cost at the date of purchase with the sterling equivalent of the proceeds at the date of sale (subject to indexation allowance). Foreign stocks and shares are subject to the same provisions as UK stocks and shares (see chapter 38), so that the capital gains tax pooling rules apply to shares, and the special matching rules apply for identifying disposals of loan stock (see page 532). Non-residents carrying on business in the UK through a UK branch or agency are charged to tax on gains on assets used in the branch or agency — see page 567. Other non-residents who are not ordinarily resident in the UK are not charged to capital gains tax on the disposal of UK assets.

For the mortgage interest and capital gains position on your private residence when you are absent abroad, see pages 419, 420.

If you are emigrating and you sell qualifying business assets (see page 55) in a tax year when you are UK resident, investing the proceeds in qualifying replacement assets abroad within three years, the gains on the UK assets may be rolled over against the cost of the replacement foreign assets (whether or not you are resident in the UK at the time of acquisition of the replacement assets). If the replacement assets are then sold in a tax year when you are not resident and not ordinarily resident in the UK (and are not carrying on a business in the UK through a branch or agency), you will escape UK tax on the rolled over gains. (You may, however, have a liability in your new country of residence.)

If you become not resident and not ordinarily resident within six years after receiving a gift on which capital gains tax was deferred under the gifts relief provisions, the gain is chargeable to tax (see page 61). Becoming non-resident within a specified period also triggers gains deferred under the reinvestment relief provisions (the relevant period being three years — see page 62), and under the enterprise investment scheme or venture capital trust provisions (the relevant period being five years in each case — see pages 403 (EIS) and 529 (VCTs)).

There are provisions to prevent a UK resident individual avoiding tax by transferring assets abroad while retaining a right to benefit from them (see page 608).

Residence has no bearing on inheritance tax, which applies to an individual's world-wide property if he is domiciled in the UK and to his UK property if he is domiciled elsewhere.

Basis of charge for foreign income of individuals (TA 1988, ss 18, 19, 65, 65A, 118A–118K, 192, 391; FA 1994, s 207 and Sch 20 paras 6, 7; FA 1996, Schs 7 and 29)

Foreign income is taxed as part of an individual's total income at the lower, basic and higher rates as the case may be. Foreign investment income is treated in the same way as UK investment income, and thus taxed at only 20% except for higher rate taxpayers. This does not apply where the recipient is charged to tax only on the amounts remitted to the UK (see page 557), such remittances being taxed at the same rates as non-savings income. Note that 'foreign income dividends' are not foreign income. They are dividends paid by UK companies out of foreign profits. For the tax treatment, see page 571.

The basis of charge under Schedule E for income from employment is the earnings received in the tax year and the rules are outlined on page 8. Deductions are available as indicated on pages 558, 559.

Other income from abroad may be charged under Schedule D, Case IV (covering foreign securities such as foreign government stocks and foreign debentures) or Schedule D, Case V (covering foreign 'possessions', which includes all other non-employment income, such as from shares in foreign companies, bank accounts abroad, foreign businesses and foreign property). Property income from abroad is dealt with on page 561 (but see page 457 for foreign time shares). A self-employed UK resident will usually be charged on his profits under Schedule D, Case I, whether they are earned in the UK or abroad, subject to some special provisions for partners in firms controlled abroad (see pages 560, 561).

Interest on foreign government stocks, and also some other interest under Schedule D, Case IV and some dividends under Schedule D, Case V, are received from a UK paying or collecting agent, such as a bank, and tax is usually deducted at source. The rate of deduction was reduced to the lower rate of 20% from 6 April 1996. Tax will not be deducted where the recipient is exempt from tax, such as a charity or pension fund, and may be deducted at a reduced rate where relief is given for foreign tax (see page 569). A bank that merely clears a cheque for a foreign dividend or interest is not required to deduct tax.

Foreign fixed interest stocks are subject to the accrued income scheme (see page 497), unless you are only liable to tax on income remitted to the UK (see page 557). The special rules for scrip dividends (see page 512) do not apply to scrip dividends from non-UK resident companies. There are anti-avoidance provisions to counter the rolling-up of income in an offshore fund with the intention of realising it in a capital form. The provisions are dealt with briefly on page 608.

Except where tax is deducted at source as explained above, and subject to the special rules outlined below for those who are taxed only on what is received in the UK, tax under Schedule D, Cases IV and V other than on the profits of a foreign business is charged in the same way as for Schedule D, Case III (see page 506). For years up to 1995/96, tax has been charged on the income arising in the previous tax year with special rules for the first three and the last two tax years. For sources of income in existence at 5 April 1994, tax for 1996/97 will be charged on the average of the income of 1995/96 and 1996/97 (see page 569 for the effect of the averaging on claims for relief for overseas tax) and from 1997/98 the charge will be based on the income of the tax year itself, i.e. on a current year basis. The current year basis applies from the outset to foreign sources from which income first arises on or after 6 April 1994. The same provisions apply as on page 507 where 1995/96 is the third year in which income arises and a taxpayer has chosen to be taxed on the actual income of that year, and where a pre-6 April 1994 source of income ceases before 6 April 1998. There are anti-avoidance provisions to prevent the deliberate diversion of income into the two-year period that is to be averaged (see page 293).

Where a business is carried on abroad, tax under Schedule D, Case V is charged under the current year basis according to the same rules as for Schedule D, Case I, i.e. on the profits of the accounting year ending in the tax year rather than on the profits of the tax year itself. For businesses in existence at 5 April 1994, the 1996/97 assessment will be arrived at by averaging the profits of the tax years 1995/96 and 1996/97, but the 1997/98 profits will be those of the accounting year ending in that tax year, so transitional overlap relief will apply. Some Case V businesses have already been taxed on an accounts basis in earlier years, and the transitional provisions for those businesses will mirror those for Schedule D, Case I (see chapter 21).

For individuals who are resident, ordinarily resident and domiciled in the UK, tax is charged on only 90% of foreign pensions (except where the pension is paid as a result of Nazi persecution, in which case it is not chargeable at all).

If you are resident but not ordinarily resident or not domiciled in the UK, you are not charged to tax on income from abroad unless you remit it to the UK. If you do remit it, you are charged on the full amount remitted, with no percentage deduction, and basic rate taxpayers have to pay the basic rate rather than the lower rate on remittances of foreign investment income (see page 556). There are rules to decide whether you are remitting income or other sums.

Where you are charged on the amount remitted, the rules outlined above for Schedule D, Cases IV and V apply to the amount remitted rather than to the income arising. The first year of charge is the year in which income is first remitted to the UK. If your first remittance from a foreign source is received in the UK on or after 6 April 1994, the current year basis rules apply from the outset. Where you have earned income chargeable on the amount remitted under Schedule E, you are charged to tax in the year in which the earnings are remitted to the UK.

Deductions available for UK citizens with earnings from employment abroad (TA 1988, ss 19, 192 and Sch 12)

If your employment abroad spans a complete tax year and all your duties are performed abroad, you will normally be treated by concession as non-resident from the date of leaving and as a new resident when you return. Otherwise you will remain UK resident.

Notice that it is not the length of the absence but whether it spans a tax year that is important, so that if you were working away from 1 April 1995 to 30 April 1996, a period of thirteen months spanning a tax year, you would be non-resident for that period, but if you were working away from July 1995 to December 1996, a period of eighteen months that does not span a complete tax year, you would remain resident throughout.

If you are non-resident, you escape UK tax on all foreign income, but income arising in the UK is still taxable.

If you are resident, you are technically liable to tax on your earnings both in the UK and abroad, but a deduction of 100% is allowed for earnings during a 'long absence' working abroad, which makes the earnings exempt from UK tax. No deduction is available for short absences. A period of non-residence does not count towards the qualifying period for the 100% deduction. You may therefore be better off using the strict rules to decide whether you are resident or non-resident for the whole of a tax year, rather than the concessionary treatment of regarding the year as split into resident and non-resident parts (see page 553).

The 100% deduction is given in respect of earnings abroad during a qualifying period of at least 365 days. The 365 days do not have to coincide with a tax year. Thus in the above illustration the absence from July 1995 to December 1996 which *did not* establish non-residence for a tax year, *does* give an entitlement to the 100% deduction from the earnings abroad, but the non-resident period from 1 April 1995 to 30 April 1996 could not count as part of a qualifying absence for the 100% deduction if after again becoming resident you once more go to work abroad. A qualifying period is one consisting either wholly of days of absence or of days of absence linked by UK visits that do not overstep certain limits. A day does not count as a day of absence unless you are absent at the end of it, i.e. midnight. The limits are that UK visits must not exceed 62 consecutive days and that the days spent in the UK must not exceed one-sixth of the total days in the period. (More generous limits, of 183 consecutive days and one-half of the total days in the period, apply to seafarers.) This one-sixth rule cannot be calculated as a proportion of the total spell of employment abroad but must be considered at the end of each absence. See example 1.

If, although he satisfies the 365-day qualifying period rules, an employee has both overseas earnings and UK earnings, i.e. for work during his UK visits, the 100% deduction applies only to the overseas earnings.

Example 1

Two employees each spend fifteen months working abroad (not including a complete tax year), the time abroad and in the UK being as follows:

	1st employee Days	2nd employee Days	1/6th limit exceeded 1st employee	2nd employee
Abroad	100	100		
UK	10	60		
Abroad	150	150	No (10/260)	Yes (60/310)
UK	60	10		
Abroad	130	130	No (70/450)	No (10/290)
	450	450		

A deduction of 100% is given to first employee.

Second employee will not get the 100% deduction for the first absence, nor for the second and third absences unless he can link them to a further spell of overseas duty covering 365 days in all, with the UK visit limits not being breached.

The 100% deduction also applies to earnings in a period of paid leave at the end of the employment, but if the paid leave is spent in the UK it cannot be counted as part of the 365-day qualifying period. Thus a twelve-month contract abroad with the last month of it spent on leave in the UK would not qualify, whereas if the leave were spent abroad, or the contract was a thirteen-month contract with the last month as UK leave, it would qualify (provided that the 62-day and 1/6th rules were satisfied).

The 100% deduction is given where possible through the PAYE system, but where this is not possible a refund of income tax will be made following an assessment or, from 1996/97, self-assessment.

Travelling and board and lodging expenses (TA 1988, ss 193, 194)

For an employee resident and ordinarily resident in the UK, the costs of travelling from and to the UK when taking up and ceasing an employment wholly abroad are allowed as a deduction from earnings, and also the costs of travelling between a UK employment and a foreign employment and between foreign employments. The costs of any number of outward and return journeys whilst serving abroad are also allowed so long as the expense is met by the employer (thus offsetting the benefits charge on the expense). If the employer pays or reimburses the cost of board and lodging abroad, the amount paid or reimbursed is also offset by an equivalent expenses allowance, but no deduction is given for board and lodging payments that an employee bears himself.

If an absence lasts for 60 days or more (not necessarily in one tax year) an employee can claim a deduction for the travelling expenses of two outward and two return journeys per person in any tax year for his wife and children (under 18 at the start of the journey) to visit him, but only where the travelling expenses are paid or reimbursed by the employer (so that the deduction offsets the benefits charge on the expenses) and not where the employee bears them himself.

You can only offset a benefits charge on travelling and/or board and lodging expenses met by your employer if the expense is borne by the employer directly or you pay the expense yourself and are reimbursed. A round sum expenses allowance falls outside either provision, and care must be taken that the expenses are paid in a way that entitles you to the deduction.

Earned income from self-employment abroad (TA 1988, ss 80, 81, 110A, 112, 391; FA 1995, ss 124, 125)

Where a business is carried on wholly abroad, the expenses of travelling to and from it are allowed in computing its profits. Expenses of travelling between two or more overseas trades are similarly allowable, provided that either the business at the place of departure or that at the destination is carried on wholly abroad. A deduction is also allowed for board and lodging expenses at any place where the trade is carried on and, where the trader's absence spans 60 days or more, for not more than two visits in any tax year by wife and children (under 18 at the start of the journey).

If a business is controlled in the UK, the profits are taxed under the rules of Schedule D, Case I or Case II even though some of the profits are earned abroad.

If a business is controlled abroad, the profits are charged under Schedule D, Case V as income from a foreign possession. If the business makes a loss, similar loss relief claims may be made as for a UK business (see chapter 25) but the loss may be relieved only against the profits from the same or any other foreign business, and against foreign pensions and 'foreign emoluments' (as defined on page 8).

A UK resident sole trader would find it virtually impossible to establish that his business was controlled abroad, so it is generally only the profits of partnerships that may be taxed under Case V instead of Case I or Case II.

If a business is controlled and carried on wholly abroad but has some UK resident partners, their profit shares are charged under Case V. The UK tax on a UK resident partner's share of the profits of a partnership resident abroad cannot be reduced or eliminated by double tax relief, even though the terms of the double tax agreement exempt the profits of the foreign partnership. If a foreign-controlled partnership carries on some business operations in the UK, profits from the UK activities are charged under Case I or Case II and the foreign activities under Case V.

The partnership provisions are being changed from 1997/98 (or from 1995/96 for partnerships that commenced on or after 6 April 1994). The changes are technical changes that do not affect the amount charged to tax. The profit shares of UK resident partners will be charged under Schedule D, Case I or Case II, both on UK profits and foreign profits, whether or not the partnership is controlled abroad. For a foreign-controlled partnership, this does not apply to a UK resident partner who is not ordinarily resident and/or not domiciled in the UK, who will be charged under Case I or II on the full amount of his share of UK profits, and under Case V on the part of his share of foreign profits that is remitted to the UK. Non-resident partners will be taxed under Case I or II on their shares of UK profits.

In order to charge residents on their worldwide profits and non-residents on their UK profits, when someone who carries on business wholly or partly abroad changes his country of residence, he is treated as ceasing one business and starting another. This does not prevent the carry-forward of any losses before the change if they cannot otherwise be relieved. This applies from 1995/96 onwards to anyone starting in business on or after 6 April 1994 and otherwise from 1997/98.

Income from overseas property (TA 1988, ss 65(2A)(2B), 65A; FA 1995, s 41)

If you buy investment property abroad, rents are income from a foreign possession and are charged under Schedule D, Case V (see page 556). Foreign rental income is calculated in a similar way to UK rental income (see chapter 32), but the special rules for furnished holiday lettings (see page 451) do not apply.

The rules for calculating UK rental income were changed from 1995/96, and rents and expenses for all let properties in the UK are aggregated and treated as the profits of a business. If there is an overall loss, it is carried forward to set against the letting profits of later years (see chapter 32). The same rules are to apply to foreign rental income from 1997/98, with the set-off of losses against total letting income applying from 1998/99. The profit or loss is still calculated separately for each property for 1995/96 and 1996/97. Relief for interest on borrowings to buy or improve foreign property could not previously be claimed, but may be included in allowable expenses from 1995/96 onwards.

See page 557 for the way in which Schedule D, Case V rental profits are taxed on the changeover from the previous year basis to the current year basis of assessment.

If you are a UK resident but are not UK domiciled, or are not ordinarily resident in the UK, you remain chargeable on rental income only when it is remitted to the UK (see page 557).

Other sources of foreign income (TA 1988, s 584; FA 1996, Sch 20 para 33)

For UK citizens who are resident and ordinarily resident in the UK, other sources of foreign income, such as dividends and interest, are charged on the full amount arising, with no percentage deduction available. There are provisions to treat income that is locked into a foreign country, and not capable of being extracted, as not arising until it is free to be brought to the UK.

Where the income is not received through a paying or collecting agent (see page 556) and thus does not have tax deducted at source, the way in which income is brought into account is being changed from the previous year basis to the current year basis, as explained on page 557.

Leaving and returning to the UK

If you go to live abroad, you should obtain from and send back to your tax office a form P85 (Residence or employment abroad).

In the tax year when you leave the UK to take up permanent or long-term residence abroad, you are treated as non-resident from the date of departure and get a full year's personal allowances against your income for the part of the year prior to your departure. See page 566 for the provisions exempting certain income of non-UK residents from tax.

If you are abroad for some period that includes a complete tax year and then become UK resident again, intervening visits not having exceeded 183 days in any tax year and not having averaged 91 days or more a year, you are treated as resident for income tax from the date of arrival, with a full year's allowances on your income for the remainder of the year (concession A11). If you have been away for at least 36 months, capital gains in excess of the annual exemption are charged to tax only if they arise after your return (subject to certain anti-avoidance provisions). If you have been away for less than 36 months you will be charged on all gains in excess of the exemption in the tax year you return, whether they arise before or after your arrival.

If you accompany a spouse who goes abroad to work full-time but do not work full-time yourself, your liability for the tax years in which you leave and return will be based on the time spent in the UK in each year, in the same way as for your employed spouse, providing your absence spans a complete tax year and subject to the same rules for intervening UK visits (concession A78).

Inheritance tax will continue to be chargeable so long as you remain or are regarded as UK domiciled (see chapter 5).

Non-residents — tax position and personal allowances
(TA 1988, s 278; FA 1995, s 128; FA 1996, s 145)

Non-residents cannot normally claim UK personal allowances, but allowances may be claimed by non-residents who are UK, Commonwealth or Republic of Ireland citizens or, from 6 April 1996, EEA nationals (which covers European Union countries plus Iceland, Liechtenstein and Norway), or are resident in the Isle of Man or the Channel Islands, or certain other categories. A claim for allowances may also be provided for by the terms of a double tax agreement. Where allowances are available, they are given in full against the UK income, regardless of the level of the overseas income.

Non-residents are exempt from tax on government stocks (see page 566) and may be exempt on other sources of income under a double tax agreement. Tax is not usually deducted from investment income other than property income (see page 566), or from social security benefits (see page 565), although such income is not actually exempt from tax. The *maximum* tax payable by a non-resident is the tax, if any, deducted from such income plus the tax on any other taxable income, calculated as if personal allowances were not available. If a claim is made for personal allowances, all non-exempt income is taken into account. This may limit or eliminate the benefit from making a claim.

Example 2

In 1996/97 a non-resident British citizen who is a single person has untaxed income from UK banks and building societies amounting to £1,000 and a State pension of £3,000. No tax will be payable.

If the non-resident also had rental income of £2,000, from which tax of £480 was deducted, his maximum liability would be tax on that income as if it were his only UK income. The income would then be within the lower rate band and tax at 20% would be £400, so that £80 would be repayable. He could not benefit from a claim for personal allowance, because his untaxed income of £4,000 would have to be taken into account in such a claim and that income exceeds the allowance of £3,765.

If in addition to the rental income the untaxed income had been only £3,000, the position would be:

	£
Total income	5,000
Personal allowance	3,765
	1,235
Tax at 20%	247
Tax deducted at source	480
Tax repayable	233

Husband and wife

As stated on page 552, the residence and ordinary residence status of a husband and wife is determined independently. If a wife remains in the UK while her husband is working abroad for a period which spans a tax year, she will be taxed as a UK resident on her UK and foreign income, and her husband will normally be exempt as a non-resident from UK tax on income arising outside the UK and will be able where appropriate (see above) to claim personal allowances as a non-resident against his UK income.

If a non-resident husband is entitled to personal allowances but his UK income is insufficient to absorb the married couple's allowance, he may transfer the surplus to his wife providing she is entitled to allowances either as a resident or a qualifying non-resident.

Earned income of visitors to the UK and non-residents (TA 1988, ss 18, 19, 192, 195)

Income from employment

The treatment of a visitor's earnings depends on the length of his visit. A visitor to the UK who does not remain long enough to be classed as resident is nonetheless liable to UK tax on UK earnings (although sometimes he may be exempt under the provisions of a double tax treaty — see page 569). Non-residents cannot normally claim UK personal allowances (except as described above).

Expenses of travel and of visits by wives and children are allowed (thus offsetting the benefits assessment) in the same way as described above (on page 560) for a UK resident working abroad. This only applies, however, where the employee was either not resident in the UK in either of the two tax years before the tax year of his arrival in the UK, or was not in the UK at any time during the two years immediately preceding his arrival. Where this condition is satisfied, the expenses are allowed for a period of five years beginning with the date of arrival in the UK to perform the duties of the employment.

If a visitor is classed as resident but not ordinarily resident, he is still liable only on UK earnings unless he has earnings from abroad which he remits to the UK, in which case he will be taxed as well on the full amount remitted. It is important for visitors to keep records (for example, separate bank accounts for capital and for different sources of income) to enable them to demonstrate whether or not remittances out of foreign earnings have taken place.

Once a visitor has been in the UK long enough to be classed as ordinarily resident (or where he is ordinarily resident from the outset because of the length of his proposed stay — see page 553) he is charged to tax in the same way as a UK citizen.

Income from a UK business

Non-residents who carry on business in the UK are charged to tax on the UK business profits in the same way as UK residents, the charge being under Schedule D, Case I for trades and under Schedule D, Case II for professions or vocations. From 1996/97 tax due on the profits will be self-assessed and paid by the non-resident or, where the business is carried on through a branch or agency, by the branch or agent.

State pensions and other taxable social security benefits, occupational and personal pensions

Non-residents receive State pensions and other relevant social security benefits in full, and tax is not charged on them (but see page 563 in relation to tax repayment claims). As far as occupational and personal pensions paid to non-residents are concerned, such pensions are chargeable to UK tax unless (as will usually be the case) they are exempt under a double taxation agreement. Tax is deducted from such pensions under PAYE where the payer has been instructed to do so by the tax office. In this event, the code number may take personal allowances into account.

Non-resident entertainers and sportsmen (TA 1988, ss 555–558)

Basic rate tax may be deducted at source from the UK earnings of non-resident entertainers and sportsmen. Royalty payments received from the sale of records are excluded (as they are already exempt under many double taxation agreements).

Tax need not be deducted where the person making the payment does not expect to pay more than a total of £1,000 to the individual in question during that tax year. Where tax is deducted, the Revenue may agree a rate below the basic rate. The earnings will be charged to tax on a current year basis and the tax deducted will be set against the final tax liability for the year, or repaid to the extent that it exceeds that liability.

The rules are administered by a specialist department of the Revenue.

Rental income of non-resident landlords (TA 1988, s 42A; FA 1995, s 40; SI 1995/2902)

Where UK property is let by a non-resident, the rental income from all let properties is treated as being from a single Schedule A business, as outlined in chapter 32. This applies whether the non-resident landlord is an individual, trustees or a company, except that it does not apply to the rental income of a UK branch of a non-resident company (see page 573).

From 6 April 1996, a UK agent handling let property for a non-resident landlord, or the tenant where there is no such agent, must notify the

Revenue's Financial Intermediaries and Claims Office (FICO). The agent or tenant must then deduct basic rate tax from the property income (net of allowable expenses paid by the agent or tenant), and pay it over to the Revenue within 30 days after the end of each calendar quarter. The agent or tenant must give the non-resident an annual certificate showing the tax deducted by 5 July following the tax year and must also send in a return to the Revenue by the same date. Tenants paying rent of £100 a week or less do not have to deduct tax unless told to do so by FICO. The non-resident landlord will be required to pay any balance of tax due (or claim a refund) when completing his tax return and self-assessment. Tax does not have to be deducted at source if the agent or tenant receives written notice to that effect from FICO. A landlord may apply to FICO to receive his rental income in full providing his UK tax affairs are up to date, or he has never had any UK tax obligations, or he does not expect to be liable to UK tax. He must undertake to complete tax returns if required and pay any tax due on time.

Treatment of other income, capital gains and gifts for visitors to the UK and non-residents (TCGA 1992, ss 2, 10, 12, 25; FA 1995, s 128)

Non-residents have no liability to UK tax on foreign income. If they are not ordinarily resident in the UK they are also exempt from tax in respect of interest on various government securities. The interest on such tax-exempt securities is paid without deduction of tax if a claim is made to that effect. Bank and building society interest, although not exempt from tax, is also paid without deduction of tax to those who provide the bank or building society with a declaration that they are not ordinarily resident in the UK. From 1996/97, non-residents will not be liable to pay tax on investment income other than rents, except to the extent that tax is deducted at source. Non-residents will therefore escape tax altogether on interest received in full as indicated above, and will not have to self-assess, unless they have other taxable income and are claiming a repayment. In calculating how much tax is repayable, however, any UK income that is not exempt from tax may have to be taken into account (see page 563). (The UK tax liability of someone who is non-resident for only *part* of a tax year — see page 553 — is calculated by reference to *all* taxable income of the year and the treatment indicated above does not apply.)

As far as bank accounts are concerned, if you replace your UK bank and building society accounts with foreign accounts, the interest will be free of UK tax while you are non-resident, and relief under a non-resident's personal allowances claim will not be reduced. Closing foreign accounts before you return will prevent any of the foreign interest being subject to UK tax. Non-residents who receive interest on Eurobonds via a unit trust may be able to receive it free of UK tax.

If you have a personal equity plan (see page 536), you will not lose your tax exemption on the plan when you become non-resident but you cannot contribute further or take out a new plan.

You do not escape liability to capital gains tax unless you are both not resident and not ordinarily resident in the UK. Even then, if you carry on a trade, profession or vocation in the UK through a branch or agency, you are charged to capital gains tax on the disposal of assets in the UK used for the business or by the branch or agency.

If you cease to carry on the UK branch or agency, you will be treated as if you had disposed of all the assets, and charged to capital gains tax accordingly. If, while continuing to carry on the branch or agency, you remove any of the assets from the UK, you will be treated as if you had disposed of those assets.

If you are in the UK long enough to be classed as resident, you will be liable to income tax on foreign as well as UK sources of income. If, however, you are non-UK domiciled, or you are not ordinarily resident in the UK, you will only be liable on foreign income if you remit it to the UK. You may therefore think it appropriate to invest abroad and leave the income there. An alternative for those of foreign domicile who are resident and ordinarily resident in the UK is a personal equity plan (see page 536). (See page 564 for the position on income from employment.) As a resident, you are also liable to UK capital gains tax, but if you are non-UK domiciled you will only be liable to tax on chargeable gains arising in or remitted to the UK.

A gain on the disposal of your only or main residence is, subject to certain conditions, exempt from tax.

The treatment of income and gains may be varied by the provisions of a double tax treaty (see page 568).

The normal inheritance tax provisions apply to gifts of UK assets (see chapter 5).

Social security and national insurance contributions

If you leave the UK for permanent or semi-permanent residence abroad, your liability to pay national insurance contributions normally ceases when you leave, unless you work abroad for an employer who has a place of business in the UK, in which case Class 1 contributions continue for the first 52 weeks. It may be to your advantage to pay voluntary contributions. If you are working temporarily abroad, or moving from one foreign location to another, the DSS may require Class 1 contributions to continue to be paid. The position is different if you go to a country with which the UK has a reciprocal social security agreement, when home country liability may sometimes continue for several years. The position is also different if you go to a country in the European Economic Area (i.e. the European Union plus Iceland, Liechtenstein and Norway), when you are liable in the country of employment from the outset, except for a short-term visit of up to 12 months (possibly extended to 24 months, or even longer), during which you will remain liable in the UK. If you work in more than one EEA country, but continue to be habitually resident in the UK, UK liability can continue.

If you leave the UK and are self-employed abroad, you are not normally *required* to pay Class 2 contributions but you may be *entitled* to pay them in some circumstances to maintain your contribution record. Again, the position is subject to variation if you work in the EEA or in a country with which the UK has a reciprocal social security agreement. A self-employed person who is not resident in the UK in a tax year is not liable to pay Class 4 contributions.

Child benefit is not normally payable unless both parent and child are UK resident, but it continues during a temporary absence of up to 8 weeks, and may be paid for longer in some circumstances.

Visitors to the UK and new permanent residents who are employees are normally not liable to pay Class 1 national insurance contributions for the first 12 months. This does not apply to someone coming from a European Economic Area country or a country with which the UK has a reciprocal social security agreement, who will either be liable to UK contributions from the outset or remain liable under his home country's rules. Where an employee is liable, the employer will be liable to pay employer's secondary contributions. This applies to all overseas employers, subject to special rules for European Economic Area countries and countries with which the UK has a reciprocal social security agreement.

People coming to the UK who are self-employed are only *required* to pay Class 2 contributions if they are ordinarily resident in the UK, or have been resident in the UK for 26 or more weeks out of the last 52. They are *entitled* to pay Class 2 contributions if they are *present* in the UK for the relevant contribution week. Again, the general rules are varied for EEA countries and countries with which the UK has a reciprocal social security agreement. Class 4 contributions are payable where relevant unless the person is not resident in the UK for the tax year concerned.

The detailed provisions are complex, so whether you are leaving or coming to the UK, it is advisable to contact the local social security office to establish your own liability to make contributions and your benefits position.

As far as State pension is concerned, if you emigrate, you are normally entitled to a pension based on the contributions you have made, but it is frozen at the rate payable when you leave the UK or when you first become entitled to it if later. This may be varied by the provisions of reciprocal social security agreements. Again, the position needs to be checked with your social security office.

Double taxation relief for individuals (TA 1988, ss 788–791, 804; TCGA 1992, s 277; FA 1994, s 217, Sch 20 paras 10–13; FA 1995, s 122)

Where the same income and gains are liable to tax in more than one country, relief for the double tax is given either under the provisions of a double tax agreement with the country concerned or unilaterally.

UK residents with foreign income and gains

Where there is a double tax agreement, it may provide for certain income and gains to be wholly exempt. If not, they are charged to UK tax, but a credit is given against the UK tax for the lower of the overseas tax liability and the UK tax liability.

Sometimes the agreements provide for a UK paying or collecting agent to adjust the UK tax he deducts to take account of the foreign tax (see page 556), so that for example the deduction on a foreign dividend may be 15% overseas withholding tax and 5% UK tax, making 20% in all. Where the overseas company pays dividends with tax credits, as in the UK, the tax credits are not eligible for double tax relief unless specifically provided for by the double tax agreement, so the amount paid is charged to UK tax.

Where there is no double tax agreement, you may claim unilateral relief against the UK tax of the lower of the UK tax and the overseas tax. If double tax relief is not claimed, the income or gain, net of the overseas tax suffered, is charged to UK tax but this would rarely be advantageous.

Adjustments to the double tax relief are made in the opening and closing years when the same profits are charged more than once, or when profits escape tax. This will continue under the current year basis of assessment. Additional tax credit relief will be given for overlap profits, and the additional relief will be recovered as and when overlap relief is given. For businesses in existence at 5 April 1994, special rules apply to the transitional year, 1996/97. Foreign tax will be averaged on the same basis as profits to establish the amount of double tax relief. Where double tax relief is not claimed, the foreign tax will be deducted from profits before they are averaged.

Non-residents with UK income and gains (TA 1988, ss 232, 233)

Income or gains may be exempt from UK tax under a double tax agreement.

Sometimes a double tax agreement may provide for income that is not exempt from UK tax to be charged at a reduced rate, for example interest may be taxed at only 10%. A non-resident will frequently be entitled to the tax credit on a dividend, and will be liable to tax at only 15% of the tax-credit inclusive amount, being entitled to a repayment accordingly (for example in the year to 5 April 1997 a dividend of £80 may be treated as income of £100, on which the tax payable would be £15, giving a repayment of £5). Where a non-resident's dividends are paid to UK nominees, the company may be authorised by the Revenue to increase the dividend payment to the nominees by the amount the shareholder would otherwise be entitled to have repaid, recovering the extra amount paid to the shareholder by crediting it against the ACT the company has to account for. (So, in the above example the company would pay £85, with a tax credit of £15. The company would get a credit for the extra £5 against its ACT liability.)

Non-residents who claim UK personal allowances (see page 563) are entitled to dividend tax credits whether or not they are entitled to them under a double tax agreement. If no claim for allowances is made, and there is no entitlement to a credit under a double tax agreement, a non-resident is liable to UK tax on the amount of the dividend plus the credit, but only to the extent of the excess, if any, of higher rate tax over the lower rate.

UK companies with interests abroad (TA 1988, ss 765–767, 788–795, 797, 799; TCGA 1992, s 140; FA 1996, Sch 14 para 42)

If a UK resident company has interests abroad, the company is liable to corporation tax on income received, before deduction of foreign taxes, the income being included either under Schedule D, Case I (profits of foreign branch or agency), Case III (foreign loans) or Case V (foreign possessions, which would include foreign let property and foreign subsidiaries), and also on any capital gains on the disposal of foreign assets. Interest on any borrowing to acquire foreign property would usually be deducted in the same way as for UK property (see page 449).

If a UK resident company carries on business abroad through a branch or agency, it is usually charged under Schedule D, Case I on all the profits of the branch or agency, unless exceptionally the trade is carried on wholly abroad, in which case the charge would be under Case V. Where business is carried on through a foreign subsidiary, the UK company's liability would arise only on amounts received from the subsidiary by way of interest or dividends, which would be charged under Schedule D, Case III or Case V.

If an overseas branch is converted into a subsidiary, Treasury consent is required unless the branch is in a European Economic Area country (defined on page 573) — but in that event the transaction may need to be reported to the Treasury. Stock has to be valued at open market value on the transfer, and there are balancing adjustments for capital allowances. Capital gains on assets held at the time of transfer may usually be deferred until the parent company disposes of its shares in the subsidiary. Alternative reliefs are available where the subsidiary is resident in another EU country (see page 574).

Double tax relief is available in respect of the foreign tax suffered on both income and gains.

Normally, only direct foreign taxes are taken into account for double tax relief but if a UK company receives dividends from a foreign company in which it owns 10% or more of the voting power, underlying taxes on the profits out of which the dividends are paid are taken into account as well. In this case the amount included in UK profits is the dividend plus both the direct and underlying foreign taxes.

Double tax relief is given either unilaterally or under the provisions of a double tax agreement.

The relief on overseas income cannot exceed the UK corporation tax payable on the overseas income, after all deductions other than advance corporation tax. It is, however, provided that in deciding how much corporation tax is attributable to the overseas income, any available deductions may broadly be set against any source of profits in the most beneficial way. The main point to bear in mind on interest relating to the trade is that it should be set against UK trading profits in priority to foreign trading profits. As far as non-trading interest is concerned, if there is a non-trading deficit for which relief is claimed against total profits (see heading (a) on page 368), the deficit must be set against the same profits for both loss relief and double tax relief. Any non-trading deficit brought forward (under heading (d) on page 368) must be regarded for double tax relief as reducing non-trading profits. ACT may be set against corporation tax on both income and gains. The set-off of ACT against any source of profits can never exceed the maximum, i.e. 20% for the year to 31 March 1997.

Double tax relief in respect of foreign tax paid on chargeable gains is limited to the UK corporation tax payable thereon.

If double tax relief is restricted because it exceeds the UK tax, the unrelieved foreign tax is wasted and cannot be carried forward or back.

Foreign income dividends (FIDs) (TA 1988, ss 246A–246Y; FA 1994, s 138 and Sch 16)

Companies with substantial overseas operations frequently have large amounts of unrelieved ACT which there is no prospect of being able to offset in the foreseeable future. UK resident companies are able to elect (not later than the date of payment) to treat particular dividend payments as 'foreign income dividends' (FIDs). ACT is payable by the company on the FIDs, but the shareholders do not receive tax credits. The FIDs are treated as being net of 20% tax, so that higher rate taxpayers have to pay a further 20%. Non-taxpayers, on the other hand, cannot claim repayment. The fact that the dividend is a FID carrying a notional tax credit which is not repayable is stated on the dividend voucher.

FIDs paid and received are not franked payments and franked investment income (and cannot be treated as group income in a 51% group — see page 40). ACT is payable on an excess of FIDs paid over FIDs received on the same cumulative basis as for franked payments (see chapter 3), and the net ACT paid for the year on the FIDs is set as far as possible against the mainstream tax liability. If the FIDs received in the year should exceed the FIDs paid, the surplus is carried forward to the next year (FIDs received not being chargeable to corporation tax). FIDs are entered in a separate section of the CT61 quarterly return form.

Example 3

			£
Company's profits for year to 31 March 1997 are:			
UK trading profits before interest			950,000
Foreign trading profits £600,000 less overseas tax			
of £192,000			408,000
UK chargeable gains			30,000

Debenture interest payable for the year was £80,000 and the company paid a dividend in October 1996 giving rise to ACT of £240,000.

Computation of double tax relief:

	Case I UK profits	Foreign profits	Total
Trading profits before interest	950,000	600,000	1,550,000
Less debenture interest payable	(80,000)		(80,000)
Case I	870,000	600,000	1,470,000
Chargeable gains	30,000		30,000
Profits chargeable to corporation tax	900,000	600,000	1,500,000
Corporation tax @ 33%	297,000	198,000	495,000
Less double tax relief		(192,000)	(192,000)
	297,000	6,000	303,000
Less ACT:			
Against UK profits (maximum)	(180,000)		(180,000)
Against foreign profits (maximum set-off £120,000 but restricted to balance of tax payable)		(6,000)	(6,000)
Final mainstream tax payable	£117,000	—	£117,000

Surplus ACT to be carried back or forward
as the case may be (£240,000 – £186,000)   £54,000

If the company had elected to pay the dividend as a foreign income dividend, and could show that the dividend was paid out of foreign profits, the surplus ACT would be repaid.

At a later date, providing the company can show that the FIDs were matched with distributable foreign profits of the current or previous year, or a later year, a claim may be made (usually in the corporation tax return) for any surplus ACT relating to the FIDs to be repaid. Special rules apply to groups, and certain 80% foreign-owned companies are able to pay FIDs without paying ACT.

See example 3 on page 572.

Controlled foreign companies and dual resident companies

Complicated provisions outside the scope of this book enable the Revenue to direct in certain circumstances that tax be charged on a UK company in respect of profits of a foreign company in which the UK company has a 10% stake or more. They are outlined very briefly on page 607. There are also anti-avoidance provisions in relation to dual resident companies, which are also outlined on page 607.

European Economic Interest Groupings (TA 1988, s 510A)

A European Economic Interest Grouping (EEIG) is a new form of business entity that may be set up by enterprises of states in the European Economic Area (i.e the European Union plus Iceland, Liechtenstein and Norway) for activities such as packing, processing, marketing or research.

The EEIG's profits are taxable and losses allowable only in the hands of the members. The EEIG cannot be formed to make profits for itself. Any trade or profession carried on by the members is treated as carried on in partnership, with the normal rules of income tax (except those relating to joint assessment of individual partners), corporation tax and capital gains tax applying.

The 'fiscal transparency' of the EEIG will not apply to provisions other than charging tax on income and gains, so that an EEIG registered in the UK will be required to collect and account for tax on interest, etc. and under PAYE.

Non-resident companies with interests in the UK (TA 1988, ss 6, 11, 43, 100, 343; TCGA 1992, ss 25, 172)

If a non-resident company carries on business in the UK through a branch or agency, it is liable to corporation tax on the trading income from the branch, income from property or rights held by the branch and capital gains on the disposal of assets situated in the UK used for the trade or by the branch or agency. The company will be liable to income tax on other UK sources of income not connected with the branch or agency in the same way as companies not operating through a branch or agency (see below).

If the UK business ceases, or the assets are removed from the UK, the company is treated as if it had disposed of the assets, and gains are charged to tax accordingly. If, however, the branch is converted into a UK subsidiary, a claim may be made for the assets to be transferred from the parent to the subsidiary on a no gain/no loss basis. The subsidiary may also take over stock at cost, and be treated for losses and capital allowances as if there had been no change.

If a non-resident company does not carry on business in the UK through a branch or agency, it is not liable to corporation tax but is liable to income tax on UK sources of income, e.g. under Schedule A on rental income from UK property. The charging provisions for rental income are the same as those for individuals (see page 565). A gain on the disposal of such a let property would not be charged to tax.

UK subsidiaries of foreign companies (TA 1988, ss 14, 231, 238)

A UK resident subsidiary of a foreign company is liable to corporation tax in the same way as any other resident company, and an ACT liability arises on the payment of dividends. An overseas parent is not normally entitled to a tax credit on the dividend, although some double tax treaties provide for a limited credit.

Company ceasing to be resident (TA 1988, ss 765–767; TCGA 1992, ss 185–187)

A company incorporated in the UK cannot now cease to be resident in the UK, no matter where the business is carried on (see page 553), unless it becomes unincorporated by a private Act of Parliament, or it is treated as non-resident under the provisions of a double tax treaty (see page 554). If a foreign-registered company that is resident in the UK ceases to be so resident, it is charged to tax as if it had disposed of all its assets at that time, unless they are retained in a UK branch or agency. The tax charge is postponed if the company is a 75% subsidiary of a UK resident company and the two companies so elect within two years. The parent company is then charged to tax on the net gains on the deemed disposal as and when the subsidiary disposes of the assets, or ceases to be a subsidiary.

Transfer pricing (TA 1988, ss 770, 773)

Non-arm's length transactions between associated bodies where one is and one is not resident in the UK have to be adjusted for tax purposes to the normal arm's length price. See page 575 re disputes between member States of the European Union.

European Union

Corporation tax provisions (TCGA 1992, ss 140A–140D)

A claim may be made for the transfer of all or part of a UK trade between companies resident in different European Union States, in exchange for shares or securities, to be treated as a no gain/no loss disposal for capital gains purposes provided certain conditions are satisfied. There are similar provisions to prevent a capital gains charge, or allow a tax credit for any tax paid, on the transfer of a non-UK trade between companies resident in different European Union States.

The Arbitration Convention of 23 July 1990, which came into force from 1 January 1995, provides for a mechanism for resolving transfer pricing disputes within the European Union.

Value added tax

The VAT treatment of transactions between European Union countries is outlined on page 105. Customs and Excise publish a series of Information Sheets on detailed aspects of the Single Market provisions and also provide information in their 'Single Market Report' and 'Customs News'.

If a trader suffers VAT in another EU State on goods or services bought and used there (say while participating in a trade fair), it cannot be treated as input VAT in the UK, but it may be recoverable from the other EU State. Details are in C & E Notice 723.

Foreign exchange and financial instruments transactions (FA 1993, ss 125–170 and Schs 15–18; FA 1994, ss 147–177 and Sch 18; FA 1996, s 101 and Sch 14 paras 67–79)

For UK resident companies, the treatment of profits and losses arising from exchange rate fluctuations changed for accounting periods beginning on or after 23 March 1995, the broad outline of the new provisions being as follows. Foreign exchange gains and losses on monetary assets and liabilities (such as cash, bank deposits and debts), and on forward contracts to buy or sell currency, are taxed as income or allowed as deductions as they accrue. Monetary assets in foreign currency are no longer subject to capital gains tax. Exchange differences on monetary items are taken into account as they accrue. Unrealised gains above certain limits on long-term capital items may be partly deferred. Trading profits before capital allowances may, subject to conditions, be calculated in foreign currencies. Exchange differences on borrowing that 'matches' a non-monetary asset are deferred until the asset is disposed of, and then dealt with under the capital gains tax rules.

New provisions for the taxation treatment of financial instruments for managing interest rate and currency risk were introduced with effect from the same date as the foreign exchange provisions. These provisions have now been supplemented and in some respects superseded by the new rules for dealing with a company's 'loan relationships' (see page 27). The rules for bringing into account foreign exchange gains and losses and gains and losses on financial instruments are the same as those for a company's loan relationships. Gains and losses that relate to the trade are taken into account in arriving at the trading result. Non-trading gains and losses under all three headings are merged and dealt with under the provisions on pages 27 and 368.

As far as VAT is concerned, Customs take the view that foreign exchange transactions are outside the scope of VAT. A case on the point is being taken to the High Court.

Trusts (TCGA 1992, ss 13(10), 69–73, 80–98, 168 and Sch 5)

A trust is treated as not resident and not ordinarily resident in the UK if the general administration of the trust is carried on abroad and a majority of the trustees are not resident and not ordinarily resident in the UK. Special provisions apply to prevent trusts obtaining tax advantages through becoming non-resident.

Exit charge when trust becomes non-resident

Where a trust becomes non-resident, all the trust assets (except any that remain within the scope of UK tax, for example assets that continue to be used in a UK trade) are treated as disposed of and reacquired at market value, and gains are charged to tax. The charge is at the settlor's rate if he has a present or future right to the income or property of the trust (see page 583). Rollover relief on replacement of business assets cannot be claimed if the new assets are acquired after the trust becomes non-resident and are outside the UK tax charge. These provisions also apply to dual resident trusts that are exempt from UK tax on gains because of a double tax treaty.

Charge on settlor

Where a settlor who is UK domiciled and ordinarily resident has an interest in a non-resident trust (or a dual resident trust outside the UK capital gains charge), gains of the trust are charged on the settlor (the settlor having the right to recover the tax from the trustees). A settlor is treated as having an interest in a trust if his wife, children or their spouses have an interest, or an interest is held by a company controlled by him and/or them. These provisions apply to trusts created on or after 19 March 1991 and to settlements existing at that date if funds are subsequently added or the beneficiaries are changed.

Charge on beneficiaries

Where gains are not charged on a settlor as indicated above, UK domiciled beneficiaries are charged to capital gains tax on their share of the gains of a non-resident trust if they receive capital payments from the trustees when they are resident in the UK. The tax on a capital payment to a beneficiary is increased by a supplementary charge if gains are not distributed to the beneficiaries in the tax year in which they are made or the following year. The charge runs from 1 December in the tax year following that in which the trustees' gains arose to 1 December in the tax year after that in which the gain is distributed to the beneficiary. The charge is at an annual rate of 10% of the tax on the capital payment, with a maximum of six years, giving an overall maximum possible rate of 60% × 40% = 24%, in addition to the capital gains tax of up to 40% already payable.

Council tax

Even though you spend time abroad, you will be liable to pay council tax on property you own in the UK if it is still your only or main residence. If it is not your home, but it is the only or main home of someone else, that person will be liable (see page 112). If property owned by a non-resident is not anyone's only or main home, the owner is liable to pay 50% of the tax.

Tax points

● Watch the timing of overseas work periods. Breaching the UK visit limits for long absences will deny you the deduction of 100% of overseas earnings in calculating your tax bill.

● If you plan to obtain the 100% deduction for employment abroad or to have a period of non-UK residence, the situation may be changed by factors outside your control. Consider taking out insurance to cover the risk of extra tax liabilities through early return.

● Even though earnings abroad are covered by the 100% deduction, they still qualify as relevant earnings for pension purposes and could support a pension premium in the next six years.

● Try to arrange for your employer to meet the cost of overseas board and lodging, so that the taxable benefit can then be offset by an expenses claim; otherwise, in addition to having to bear the cost yourself, you will get no tax relief on it.

● If you are resident, ordinarily resident and domiciled in the UK, you have to pay tax on all your income wherever in the world it arises. You don't escape income tax by investing in offshore roll-up funds — see page 608.

● If you are charged on the amount of income or gains you remit to the UK, keep funds abroad separate where possible, supported by detailed records, so that you can demonstrate, where appropriate, that remittances do not represent either chargeable gains or income.

● The Revenue produce useful booklets IR 138 for those living or retiring abroad, IR 139 for those with income from abroad and IR 140 for non-resident landlords, their agents and tenants.

● If you are entitled to the capital gains advantages of a settlement with non-resident trustees that was created before 19 March 1991, take care that present transactions or arrangements do not prejudice those advantages. Whilst there is a detailed Revenue Statement of Practice (SP 5/92), the provisions are very complicated, and specialist advice is essential.

577

42
Trusts and estates

Background

A trust, sometimes called a settlement, arises when someone transfers assets to trustees who hold them and the income from them for the benefit of one or more persons.

A trust can be created in lifetime, or on death by a will or under the intestacy rules where a person does not leave a will (sometimes referred to as a statutory trust). Where the trust comes into being on death, the personal representatives must first complete the administration of the estate. They need to deal with the deceased's tax position for the year of death and also their own tax position as personal representatives until the administration of the estate is completed. Under self-assessment, the normal time limit for enquiring into a tax return is twelve months from the due date for the return (see page 123). To minimise delays in winding up estates and trusts, and distributing estate or trust property, the Revenue have announced that they will, on request, issue tax returns before the end of the tax year of death, or of winding up an estate or trust, and will give early confirmation if they do not intend to enquire into the return.

The overseas aspect of trusts is dealt with on page 576.

Administration of an estate

Personal representatives deal with the estate of a deceased either under the terms of the will or according to the rules of intestacy where there is no will. (For the way an intestate person's estate is distributed see page 482.) Income tax is payable on the income of the deceased up to the date of death, with a full year's allowances, any unused married couple's allowance of a husband being transferable to the wife if the personal representatives notify the Revenue. (See pages 464, 465 for the position on death where married couple's allowance has been transferred to the wife.) If the deceased had capital gains in excess of the annual exemption in the tax year of his death, capital gains tax will also be payable. If there are capital losses in the year of death, they may be carried back to set against gains of the three previous tax years, latest first (ignoring any gains already covered by the annual exemption), and tax will be repaid accordingly (but from 1996/97 interest on the repayment will run from the payment date for the tax year of death — see page 119). Inheritance tax will be payable on the estate if the transfers in the seven years before death which were either chargeable or potentially exempt, together with the estate at death, exceed the threshold (currently £200,000). See page 135 for the provisions under which an inheritance tax account does not have to be submitted for small estates. Property left to a surviving spouse on death is not counted in the taxable estate. The value of business and agricultural property can be eliminated in some circumstances. The way in which the tax is calculated is dealt with in chapter 5. The administration period during which the personal representatives deal with the collection of assets and payment of liabilities and the distribution of the estate may last some months or even years if the estate is complex.

Income during the administration period (TA 1988, ss 695–701; FA 1995, ss 75, 76 and Sch 18; FA 1996, Sch 6 para 17)

From 6 April 1996, the personal representatives are liable to income tax at the lower rate of 20% on savings income and at the basic rate of 24% on other income. Before 6 April 1996, the 20% rate applied only to dividends. Personal representatives are not liable to higher rate tax, nor can they claim personal allowances. The income will be distributed to the beneficiaries entitled to it either because they are entitled absolutely to the assets or because, while the assets remain in trust, they are entitled to the income (known as a life interest or an interest in possession). Any payments to a beneficiary on account of income during the administration period are net of lower rate tax or basic rate tax according to the income they represent, the gross equivalent being included in the beneficiary's taxable income at that time. Payments are treated as being out of non-savings income in priority to savings income, the total income having first been apportioned between beneficiaries on a just and reasonable basis. When the administration period is completed and the final amount of income due to each beneficiary ascertained, the beneficiary is treated as having received the balance due to him in the tax year in which the administration is completed (or, for someone with a life tenancy whose interest ceased earlier, say because of his death, in the tax year when the interest ceased). The amount due will be grossed up at the lower rate or basic rate according to the income it represents. On a written request from the beneficiaries, the personal representatives must supply them with details of payments made and the rate of tax on the payments.

Capital gains during the administration period (TCGA 1992, ss 3(7), 62)

No capital gains tax arises on the transfer of assets to legatees, who acquire them at market value at the date of death. Assets that pass to the personal representatives are also acquired by them at market value at the date of death. Any gains arising on a disposal by the personal representatives are calculated by reference to their sales proceeds less the value at death as increased by the indexation allowance. The annual exemption, currently £6,300, is available against gains by the personal representatives in the tax year of death and the next two years, but not thereafter. Gains in excess of the exempt limit are charged at 24% (from 6 April 1996, previously 25%). If any losses arise, they may only be set against gains of the personal representatives. They cannot be transferred to beneficiaries.

End of administration period

The administration period will end either when the whole estate is finally distributed if no trust has been created, or when the residue of the estate after payment of debts and legacies is transferred to a trust fund. The trustees and personal representatives are usually, but not necessarily, the same persons. There is no chargeable gain on personal representatives when they transfer assets to beneficiaries or trustees, the assets transferred being regarded as acquired at market value at the date of death.

Tax liability on setting up a trust (IHTA 1984, s 200; TA 1988, ss 660A–660G; TCGA 1992, ss 165, 260 and Sch 4; FA 1995, s 74 and Sch 17)

The deceased's estate will be charged to inheritance tax where appropriate before property is transferred to a trust created by his will.

Lifetime transfers to trusts for the disabled, to accumulation and maintenance trusts for the settlor's children, or to trusts in which someone is entitled to the income (known as an 'interest in possession') are potentially exempt from inheritance tax and will only be taken into account if the settlor dies within seven years. For trusts created in lifetime in which no-one has a *right* to the income (known as 'discretionary trusts') the settlor is liable to inheritance tax at one-half of the scale rate on the property transferred to the trust, except to the extent that the transfer is within the nil threshold. The transfer has to be grossed up if the settlor also pays the tax (see chapter 5). If the settlor dies within seven years, tax is recalculated using the full rate and scale applicable at the date of death.

It is possible for the settlor to settle sums on himself and/or his wife. (An outright gift to a spouse with no strings attached does not count as a settlement.) The transfer into the trust does not in these circumstances have to be reckoned for inheritance tax since the settlor or his wife is still enjoying the benefit of the capital. Any income in the trust is taxed on the settlor, or his wife after his death. If assets chargeable to capital gains tax are transferred into the trust, the transfer is a chargeable disposal at open market value. The calculated gains may, however, be covered by reliefs or the annual exemption. Any gains subsequently made by the trustees are charged to capital gains tax at the settlor's rate (see page 583).

On the transfer of any chargeable assets into trust between 6 April 1981 and 13 March 1989, gifts holdover relief was available, under which the settlor could avoid paying capital gains tax by electing for the gain to be held over and regarded as reducing the trustees' base acquisition cost. The same applied to assets transferred by the trustees to beneficiaries in circumstances when a chargeable gain would otherwise have arisen. This is only possible for transfers on or after 14 March 1989 if they are qualifying business assets (see page 60) or the assets are transferred into discretionary trusts (other than accumulation and maintenance trusts).

Where gifts holdover relief has been claimed, the effect is to increase the chargeable gain when the donee disposes of the asset. Where, however, the holdover occurred between 6 April 1981 and 31 March 1982, the heldover gain escapes tax because of the uplifting of values for capital gains tax on that day, and the donee's acquisition cost is not reduced. If the holdover occurred after 31 March 1982 and before 6 April 1988, and the relevant asset was acquired before 31 March 1982, the reduction in the donee's acquisition cost is halved when calculating tax on the disposal of the asset.

As far as income tax is concerned, the settlor will continue to be liable for income tax on the trust income if he or his spouse has retained an interest in the settlement or where the settlement transfers income but not capital. 'Spouse' does not include a future, former or separated spouse or the settlor's widow or widower. Further, even though a settlement is of capital in which the settlor does not retain an interest, if income of the settlement is paid to or for the benefit of an unmarried child of the settlor who is under 18, it is treated as the settlor's income, subject to the exceptions on page 463 (see also pages 582, 587). The settlor is entitled to recover the tax paid by him from the trustees, or from the person who received the income.

Types of trust

There are basically four types of trust:

(a) 'bare' trusts, where the trustee is effectively a nominee for the beneficiary;
(b) trusts with an interest in possession, i.e. where someone has a right for the time being to receive the income of the trust, often called a life tenant (although the interest may in fact end during lifetime, for example when a widow is only entitled to the income until she remarries);
(c) discretionary trusts, in which no-one has a right to the income; and
(d) accumulation and maintenance trusts, under which income is, broadly, accumulated for minor children until they reach a specified age.

Tax position of trustees

The tax position of the trustees under the various trusts is outlined below. Where tax is payable by the trustees, the normal payment dates apply. Under self-assessment from 1996/97, the trustees are required to complete tax returns and self-assess the trust income and gains in the same way as individuals, and are required to make provisional income tax payments half-yearly on 31 January and 31 July, based on the previous year's net income tax, and a balancing payment including any capital gains tax on the following 31 January due date for submission of the tax return. For discretionary trusts liable at the 34% rate (see page 586), the extra tax above that deducted at source has been payable for years up to 1995/96 on 1 December following the tax year. Such tax will now be included in the provisional half-yearly payments for continuing sources of income.

Bare trusts

A bare trust is one in which the beneficiary has an absolute right to the property and income, but the trustees are the legal owners and hold the property effectively as nominee. The transfer to the bare trust is a potentially exempt transfer for inheritance tax, becoming completely exempt if the donor survives the seven-year period.

The tax position of the trust depends on the beneficiary's circumstances rather than the trustee's, so that the beneficiary's income tax personal allowances and lower rate bands are available, and also capital gains tax reliefs and exemptions on the disposal of chargeable assets.

This still applies even if such a trust is made by a parent in favour of a child (and the parent could be the trustee), providing the income is not actually paid to or for the benefit of the child while the child is unmarried and under 18. If it is, the income would then be treated as the parent's under the provisions on page 581. The child cannot be prevented from having the property put into his own legal ownership at age 18.

A bare trust could simply be a bank or building society account in the settlor's name as trustee for the beneficiary, and in that event the trust income would not be depleted by administration expenses.

Trusts with an interest in possession

Income tax

Where there is an interest in possession, one or more beneficiaries has a right to the trust income.

The trustees are charged to tax on income other than savings income at 24%, the rate on savings income being 20% from 6 April 1996. The tax deducted from savings income (or credited on dividends) thus covers the liability. Trustees are not liable to higher rate tax. Income is calculated in the same way as for an individual. There are, however, no deductions for personal allowances. There is no relief for expenses of managing the trust, which are therefore paid out of the after-tax income. They are treated as paid out of savings income in priority to other income (TA 1988, s 689B; FA 1996, Sch 6 para 16).

The beneficiaries entitled to the income are personally liable to income tax on it, whether they draw the income or leave it in the trust fund (except where the settlor has retained an interest and the tax is payable by him). They are entitled to a credit for the tax paid by the trustees.

Example 1

Trust's income comprises rents of £3,200 gross, £2,432 net after tax of £768. The trust expenses are £152. The beneficiary will receive £2,280, which is equivalent to gross income of £3,000. If he is a basic rate taxpayer he will have no further liability and will retain the £2,280. If he is not liable to tax he will reclaim tax of £720, and if he is a higher rate payer he will have an additional liability of 16% of £3,000, i.e. £480.

If instead the trust's net income comprised rents of £1,216 after tax of £384, and cash dividends of £1,216 with tax credits of £304, the trust expenses would reduce the dividend income to £1,064, with a tax credit of £266. The beneficiary would still receive £2,280, but the gross income would be £2,930. A basic rate taxpayer would retain the £2,280. A non-taxpaying beneficiary would be able to reclaim only £650. A higher rate payer would have to pay 16% of £1,600 = £256 plus 20% of £1,330 = £266, giving a total of £522.

The need to pay expenses out of the taxed income of the trust may be minimised if specific income can be paid direct to the beneficiary, for example, by a mandate to a company to pay dividends direct, with a consequent saving in administration expenses.

Capital gains tax (TCGA 1992, ss 71–74, 77–79, 165 and Schs 1, 7; FA 1995, Sch 17 paras 27–29)

If the settlor transfers chargeable assets to the trust, he will be liable to capital gains tax, unless the gifts holdover relief is available (see page 581).

When the trustees dispose of any chargeable assets they are liable to capital gains tax at 24% (25% before 6 April 1996), subject to the special rules on page 581 for assets acquired before 31 March 1982, and subject to an annual exemption (£3,150 for 1996/97). Where there are a number of trusts created by the same settlor, the amount of £3,150 is divided equally between them, subject to a minimum exemption of £630 for each trust. Trusts for the disabled qualify for the full annual exemption of £6,300, reduced where the same settlor has created several disabled trusts, with a minimum exemption for each disabled trust of £630.

Where an individual has transferred assets to trustees, but he or his wife retains a present or future right to the income or property of the trust, any gains made by the trustees are taxed as if they were his personal gains rather than being allowed the trust's exemption and being taxed at the trust's fixed rate of 24%.

When a beneficiary becomes absolutely entitled to trust property following the death of the person entitled to the income, the trustees are regarded as disposing of the property to the beneficiary at its then market value, but no capital gains tax liability arises. Any increase in value up to that time escapes capital gains tax. A tax-free uplift for capital gains tax also occurs on property that remains in the trust after the death of the person entitled to the income. In both cases, however, where the capital gains tax cost of the property had been reduced by gifts holdover relief, there is a chargeable gain equal to the heldover amount (subject to the special rules on page 581 where gains relate wholly or partly to a period before 31 March 1982).

When a life interest terminates other than on death, for example because a widow remarries, but the property remains in trust, there is neither a chargeable gain nor any change in the base value of the property for future capital gains tax disposals by the trustees.

When, however, a beneficiary becomes absolutely entitled to trust property other than on the death of the person entitled to the income, this is regarded as a disposal at market value at that date, and capital gains tax will be payable on the increase in value, subject to relief for indexation and subject to the special rules on page 581 for assets acquired before 31 March 1982 on which gifts holdover relief had been claimed. If gifts holdover relief is still available on the property because it is a qualifying business asset (see page 60), the trustees and the beneficiary may elect for the tax liability to be deferred by treating the gain as reducing the base acquisition cost of the beneficiary.

If when a life interest ends, the property goes back to the settlor, the trustees will only be chargeable to tax to the extent that gains have been held over, and even then, the special rules on page 581 may apply. The settlor is treated as acquiring the property at its indexed cost (and as having held it on 31 March 1982 if it was settled before that date, enabling him to use 31 March 1982 value to compute a gain if appropriate). The indexation allowance incorporated into cost cannot, however, be used to create or increase a loss when the settlor disposes of the property.

If a beneficiary under a trust transfers his interest to someone else, this is not normally treated as a chargeable disposal for capital gains tax, whether he is transferring a life interest or a reversionary interest (i.e. the right to the capital of the trust when those with life interests die or give up their interests). There is a chargeable disposal if the beneficiary had bought the interest from someone else, or had acquired it by gift from someone who had bought it.

Inheritance tax (IHTA 1984, Pt III)

Someone entitled to the income for the time being from a trust fund is regarded as entitled to the underlying capital, so that he will be treated as making a chargeable transfer of the underlying capital on his death. If he ceases to be entitled to the income in lifetime, with the trust assets passing either to someone else for life, or to someone else absolutely, or to an accumulation and maintenance or disabled trust, the transfer is potentially exempt. It will only become chargeable if he dies within seven years. Although any tax is calculated by reference to his own chargeable position, it has to be paid by the trustees. The fact that trust funds are treated as belonging to the beneficiary entitled to the income prevents wealth being protected from inheritance tax through the use of trusts. It may also result in inheritance tax being paid on the income beneficiary's own estate whereas his estate would have been below the nil band if the trust funds had not been included.

Example 2

A taxpayer died on 30 September 1996, having made no transfers in lifetime other than a potentially exempt transfer of £106,000 after annual exemptions of £6,000 in June 1994. At his death, his own assets less liabilities (called his free estate) were valued at £100,000. He was also entitled to the income from trust funds, the value of which were £50,000 and to which his daughter became absolutely entitled. He was a widower, his estate being left to his son.

The inheritance tax payable on his death is:

		Gross	Tax
Lifetime transfer*		106,000	—
Free estate at death	100,000		
Trust funds at death	50,000	150,000	22,400
		£256,000	£22,400

The tax is payable as follows:

From free estate	$\dfrac{100,000}{150,000}$	× £22,400	14,933
From trust funds	$\dfrac{50,000}{150,000}$	× £22,400	7,467
			£22,400

If the trust fund had not counted as part of the chargeable estate, the inheritance tax on the estate would have been (206,000 − 200,000) = £6,000 @ 40%, i.e. £2,400.

*Although potentially exempt in lifetime, the transfer must be taken into account at death because the taxpayer died within seven years of making it.

Where there are successive charges on the trust property within five years, the tax payable on the later transfer may be reduced by quick succession relief (see chapter 5).

Since the creation of a trust fund in which someone is entitled to the income is potentially exempt from inheritance tax, and will only attract tax if the settlor dies within seven years, such trusts provide an efficient means of inheritance tax planning and family provision. By the creation of the trust you have transferred funds without giving the transferee absolute control over them. Any growth in the value of the assets will be within the trust fund and not in your personal estate. There is no tax charge if the beneficiary entitled to the income receives a capital sum from the fund, since he is regarded as being entitled to the capital anyway. Tax may be payable if the income beneficiary continues to hold his interest until death, because the funds will be treated as part of his estate. If the interest comes to an end in his lifetime, other than by being transferred to a discretionary trust, potential exemption will again be available.

Discretionary trusts

Income tax (TA 1988, ss 686, 687, 689B, 832; FA 1996, Sch 6 para 16)

Where trustees have discretionary power over the distribution of income and no-one is entitled to it as of right, the income tax treatment is the same as that for trusts with an interest in possession, except that the trustees are liable to tax at 34% instead of 24% (35% and 25% before 6 April 1996). They are, however, entitled to deduct their expenses in arriving at the amount chargeable at the 34% rate. Expenses are set against savings income in priority to other income, so that the part of the trust's income used to pay expenses will bear tax either at 20% if it is savings income or 24% if it is other income. If the trust has any exempt income, either because the trustees are not resident or are treated as being non-resident under a double tax treaty, the allowable expenses are proportionately restricted. The trustees are not chargeable if the income is treated as the settlor's income (see page 581). In that event the settlor may recover from them (or from beneficiaries who receive the income) the tax he pays.

From 1996/97, the amount due at the 34% rate is included in provisional half-yearly payments under self-assessment (see page 582).

Any income paid to beneficiaries (other than any that is treated as the settlor's income) is net of 34% tax. Income of £132 net is thus equivalent to income of £200 from which £68 tax has been deducted, the beneficiary being entitled to an income tax repayment if the income is less than available personal allowances.

Capital gains tax (TCGA 1992, ss 165, 260)

The settlor will be chargeable to capital gains tax on any gains on chargeable assets transferred to the trust, but the gains may be treated as reducing the trustees' acquisition cost under the gifts holdover relief provisions (see page 581).

Capital gains tax is payable on disposals of chargeable assets by the trustees, subject to the special rules on page 581 for assets acquired before 31 March 1982, and subject to the annual exemption of £3,150 for 1996/97 (or proportionate part thereof where there are associated trusts). The rate of tax is 34%, i.e. the same rate as that payable on income. When a beneficiary becomes absolutely entitled to any chargeable assets of the trust, the trustees are treated as disposing of the assets at market value at that date for capital gains tax purposes (subject to the special rules for assets acquired before 31 March 1982), but the trustees and beneficiary may jointly elect for the tax liability to be deferred by treating the gains as reducing the beneficiary's acquisition cost for capital gains tax (see page 581).

Inheritance tax (IHTA 1984, Pt III)

The inheritance tax position of discretionary trusts is complex and is to some extent dependent upon the position of the settlor. Since no-one has a right to the income, there is no-one who can be treated as entitled to the underlying capital. In order to prevent the inheritance tax avoidance this would otherwise permit, there is a charge on the trust funds every ten years. A charge also arises when funds leave the trust (called an exit charge) and when a person becomes absolutely entitled to the fund or to the income from it. The ten-year and exit charges are, however, only at 15% of the scale rate, giving a maximum rate of 6% on the current scale. This makes a discretionary trust a useful vehicle where flexibility of beneficiary is required.

Accumulation and maintenance trusts

These are a special sort of discretionary trust giving flexibility to a parent or grandparent in providing funds for the benefit of children.

Income tax (TA 1988, s 660B; FA 1995, Sch 17)

The rule that a parent remains chargeable to income tax on income from funds settled on his own unmarried children under age 18 does not apply where the capital and income are required to be held on accumulation and maintenance trusts for the benefit of the children, except to the extent that any income is paid to or for the benefit of the child (for example for education or maintenance). Payments of capital to or for the benefit of the child are also caught if the trust fund has any undistributed income. Any such income or capital payments are treated as the parent's income and taxed on him (unless, together with any other income from the parent, they do not exceed £100 in any tax year).

Since the trust is a discretionary trust, the trustees pay tax at 34% on income accumulated within the fund. When the accumulated income is transferred when the child reaches the appropriate age, it does so as capital and thus does not attract any further income tax at that time.

Capital gains tax (TCGA 1992, ss 165, 260)

The capital gains tax position of an accumulation and maintenance trust is the same as that of any other discretionary trust (see page 586) except as regards the availability of gifts relief. Since the transfer is potentially exempt from inheritance tax, gifts relief is not available when assets are transferred to the trust unless they are qualifying business assets (see page 581). There is also a gifts relief problem when assets leave the trust. There is a specific provision enabling gains on non-business assets to be held over and treated as reducing a beneficiary's capital gains tax cost where the assets are transferred out of an accumulation and maintenance trust, but this relief is not available unless the beneficiary becomes entitled to both capital and income of the trust at the same time. Where, as is often the case, the child becomes entitled to income at 18 and capital at say 25, the relief is only available on qualifying business assets.

Inheritance tax (IHTA 1984, s 71)

Accumulation and maintenance settlements receive favourable treatment for inheritance tax where one or more of the beneficiaries will become entitled to the trust property (or to the income from it) not later than age 25. To qualify for this treatment, the settlement must either terminate as an accumulation and maintenance settlement not more than 25 years after its creation (or 25 years from 15 April 1976 if later) or all the beneficiaries must have a common grandparent. If such beneficiaries do not survive, their children or widows/ widowers can stand in their shoes. 'Children' includes step-children, adopted children and illegitimate children.

The advantages of such a settlement are that the transfer into it is a potentially exempt transfer, there is no ten-yearly charge on the trust funds and no exit charges when a distribution is made to a beneficiary or when a beneficiary becomes absolutely entitled to the trust property or to the income from it. The transfer of property from the settlement to the beneficiaries is thus free of tax in these circumstances.

Position of infants

Where income is paid to beneficiaries (and is not treated as a parent's income), it is after deduction of tax at 20% if it relates to savings, or otherwise at 24%, except for discretionary trusts where the rate on both types of income is 34%. If the beneficiaries are infants, a repayment of tax will often be due because of their personal allowances. The parent or guardian can make the repayment claim, or it may be made by the beneficiary himself in respect of the previous six years on his reaching age 18.

Stamp duty

No duty is payable where a trust is created by will or where a lifetime trust is created, except for a 50p duty on the lifetime declaration of trust. There is also no duty payable when trust property is transferred to a beneficiary.

Tax points

- Providing personal representatives have done everything possible to trace potentially exempt transfers made by the deceased in the seven years before his death and disclose them to the Revenue, they will not usually be asked to pay the tax on any untraced transfers that subsequently come to light.

- Where a person entitled to trust income has unused personal allowances, it is better to arrange for income to be paid direct to him, because the income will not then be depleted by trust expenses, and he will get a higher income tax repayment where tax has been deducted.

- Your child's personal allowance can be used to cover income from funds provided by you if the funds are held on a bare trust (say in a bank or building society account in your name as trustee of the child), providing the income is not actually paid to or for the benefit of the child (see page 582). But you may see it as a disadvantage that you cannot stop the child getting the trust funds at age 18.

- Since inheritance tax is less where the value transferred is lower, it is usually beneficial to transfer assets that are growing in value earlier rather than later, giving the intended beneficiary an interest for the time being in the income through an appropriately drawn trust. A transfer to such a trust will be potentially exempt, but even if the donor dies within seven years the benefit of transferring assets when their value was lower will be retained. The supporting capital can eventually be transferred free of inheritance tax to the person enjoying the income.

  To the extent that assets transferred into or out of the trust qualify for business gifts holdover relief (see page 60), the value for capital gains tax purposes when the property was originally settled is also retained, but otherwise the capital gains tax effect must be considered.

- Where assets are put into a discretionary trust, the trustees may pay the inheritance tax rather than the settlor. If they do, and dependent upon the type of asset, the tax may be payable by instalments (see page 85). You also avoid having to treat the amount settled as its gross equivalent when calculating the tax.

- If you are entitled to trust income that you do not need and you would like some or all of the underlying capital to go to the person who will eventually be entitled to it, you could disclaim your entitlement to the income on the appropriate amount of capital. Part of the disclaimed amount would be covered by inheritance tax annual exemptions if not otherwise used and the balance would be treated as a potentially exempt transfer, so there would be no immediate tax charge. If the potentially exempt transfer was within your nil rate band, no tax would be payable even if you died within seven years (although in that event the nil rate band available on your estate at death would be correspondingly reduced). If the potentially exempt transfer was above the nil band, tax would be payable by the donee if you did not survive the seven-year period, but it would be reduced if you had survived for more than three years (see page 75).

- For capital gains tax purposes, those entitled to the assets in a deceased's estate acquire them at market value at the date of death. If assets have fallen in value since death, losses made by the personal representatives on disposal cannot be used by the beneficiaries. If, on the other hand, the assets themselves, rather than cash proceeds from their sale, are transferred to beneficiaries, losses on disposal by the beneficiaries will be their own allowable losses for capital gains purposes.

- For additional tax points on trusts, see chapter 35.

43
Charities and charitable trusts

Formation and legal status

Many new charities are set up and registered each year. In order to register a charity, it is necessary to satisfy the Charity Commissioners in England and Wales, or the Inland Revenue in Scotland and Northern Ireland, that the purposes or objects of the organisation fall entirely under one or more 'heads of charity'. These are as follows.

The relief of poverty.
The advancement of education.
The advancement of religion.
Other purposes beneficial to the community.

A charity may be a limited company with a separate legal existence independent of its members, or an unincorporated association which has no separate status so that assets must be held on its behalf by trustees.

Although charitable trusts are frequently national organisations, such as the Churches' children's organisations and bodies for medical research and care, there is nothing to prevent individuals creating and registering a charitable trust which remains under their control as trustees, so long as the 'heads of charity' are satisfied.

Tax status

Income tax and corporation tax (TA 1988, ss 505, 506; FA 1993, s 80; FA 1996, s 146)

Registered charities are exempt from tax on investment income used only for charitable purposes, including that received from covenants. A charity's investment income in the form of dividends was reduced from 6 April 1993 because the accompanying tax credits became only 1/4 of the dividend instead of 1/3, significantly reducing the amount of income tax repayable to the charity. For a limited period charities may make a claim, within two years after the end of their accounting period, for an additional payment from the Revenue, equal to the following fraction of the cash dividends:

1993/94   1/15th
1994/95   1/20th
1995/96   1/30th
1996/97   1/60th

A cash dividend of £600 in 1996/97 would therefore have a repayable tax credit of £150 plus an additional payment of £10, giving £160.

Trading profits are exempt where the trading is in the course of actually carrying out the charity's primary purpose. This includes trading that is mainly carried on by the beneficiaries of the charity. By concession C4, the profits of fundraising events such as bazaars, jumble sales, etc., by the charities or by voluntary organisations are exempt providing the conditions set out in the concession are satisfied.

Trading by the charity that is not within the exemption is often carried out by a separate limited company. Although the profits will be liable to tax, they may be covenanted to the charity, so that the charity can reclaim the tax deducted and accounted for to the Revenue by the company (see page 595).

If a charity deposits money with a bank or building society, the bank or building society will pay the interest in full without deducting income tax.

Capital gains tax (TCGA 1992, s 256)

A charity is not liable to capital gains tax on gains arising on the disposal of assets where the gains are applied for charitable purposes.

Value added tax (VATA 1994, Sch 8 Groups 4, 12 and 15)

Where a charity makes taxable supplies it must register for VAT subject to the normal rules relating to exempt supplies and taxable turnover (see chapter 7). If a charity has a number of branches which are virtually autonomous, each branch having control over its own financial and other affairs, each branch will be regarded as a separate entity for VAT purposes and will be required to register only if its taxable supplies exceed £47,000.

Where a charity supplies goods or services consistently below cost for the relief of distressed persons, for example meals on wheels, such supplies are not regarded as being made in the course of business and hence are not liable to VAT. Sales of donated goods at a charity shop are zero-rated. Where, however, the charity sells used goods on behalf of others and charges a commission, VAT is chargeable on the commission but not on the actual sale proceeds.

Although newspaper, broadcast, etc. advertising is normally standard-rated, it is zero-rated where it is for the charity's fundraising or for publicising the charity.

As far as buildings are concerned, zero-rating does not apply to new buildings bought by charities or to services provided in the construction of buildings for charities, unless the charity uses the building solely for charitable purposes (which means otherwise than in the course of a business), or as a village hall, or to provide social or recreational facilities for a local community. Any other use strictly falls foul of these provisions (for example allowing someone to rent a room for a children's party), but Customs and Excise have indicated that business use can be ignored where it is likely to be less than 10% of the total time that the building is normally available. Even if zero-rating applies, it does not apply to the services of architects and surveyors.

When buildings are rented, landlords have the option to charge VAT on rents except for buildings or parts of buildings used for charitable purposes (but the exception does not cover the charity's offices). The landlord is entitled to add VAT to existing rents unless the agreement specifically prevents him from doing so. In that event, the rent would have to be treated as VAT inclusive until such time as the landlord has a right under the agreement to increase it.

Customs & Excise have leaflets (701/1/95 and 700/22/89) on the subject of charities, which are available from local VAT offices.

Stamp duty (FA 1982, s 129)

No stamp duty is payable on documents transferring assets to charities (including leases).

National insurance

Charities receive no special treatment. Employers' national insurance is dealt with in chapter 13.

Business rates

There is both mandatory and discretionary relief from business rates on premises occupied by a registered charity and used for charitable purposes. 'Charitable purposes' includes shops used for the sale of goods donated to the charity. The mandatory relief is 80% and discretionary relief can increase this to 100%, so that no rates are payable. Discretionary relief up to 100% may be awarded by local authorities to various non-profit-making organisations such as schools and colleges, societies concerned with literature and the arts, and recreational clubs and societies.

Giving to charity

Fundraising events

Where voluntary organisations have fundraising trading events for charities, the profits are exempt under concession C4 providing the conditions set out in the concession are satisfied.

Covenanting

A covenant is a legally binding transfer of income from one person to another. It signifies an enforceable obligation to make the payment, thus distinguishing it from a voluntary payment, and can be used to transfer income in a tax efficient way to charities, because the payer hands over an amount net of basic rate tax, and obtains tax relief on the payment, while the charity is entitled to repayment of the tax deducted on making a repayment claim to the Revenue. Covenants have to be signed in the presence of a witness.

Charity covenants need only be capable of exceeding three years, so that the most popular term is four years. Provided the covenant is *capable* of exceeding the stipulated period, it is immaterial whether it in fact does so. The covenant must, however, be irrevocable during the stipulated period. 'Escape clauses', allowing the covenantor to terminate the covenant in certain circumstances, will usually make it invalid.

Charities usually have printed covenant forms available for intending donors.

Covenants by individuals (TA 1988, ss 347A, 660A(9); FA 1989, s 59; FA 1995, s 74 and Sch 17)

Relief is normally given to the payer at his top rate of tax. The payer deducts and retains basic rate income tax when he makes the covenanted payments. An annual certificate R185 showing the amount of the covenanted payment and the tax deducted is given to the charity unless the Revenue agree to dispense with it.

The extra relief due to a higher rate taxpayer will be given in charging tax on his income or by repayment. If the payer is not liable to income tax, or is liable only at the lower rate of 20%, he should strictly hand over the appropriate part of the tax deducted to the Revenue, since to the extent that he has not been charged at the basic rate of tax, he is not entitled to retain that part of the tax relief. In practice, the Revenue will not usually seek to collect the tax, but where a tax repayment is being claimed, the repayment will be restricted to cover the amount due because of the charitable payment.

The ability to recover tax deducted from covenanted income substantially boosts charities' funds. Since relief is normally given to the donor at his highest rate of tax on an unlimited amount of charity covenants, the higher rate taxpayer may be persuaded to increase his gross covenanted sum, thus making a larger contribution to the charity. See example 1.

Example 1

Taxpayer is prepared to contribute £1,200 per annum to a charity.

	Donor liable to tax at 24% £	Donor liable to tax at 40% £
Total income received by charity	1,580	2,000
Less tax deducted and repaid to charity	380	480
Net payment by donor	1,200	1,520
Higher rate relief to donor @ 16%	—	320
Net cost to donor	1,200	1,200

Charities cannot reclaim tax on covenanted amounts that represent membership subscriptions, except to the extent that the subscription gives the right of free or cheap entry to view the charity's property. Relief will not be available if the subscription covers other benefits.

Covenants by limited companies (TA 1988, ss 338, 339)

Companies deduct basic rate income tax when making a covenanted payment, accounting to the Revenue for the tax deducted. The gross amount of the covenanted payment is then treated as a charge on the profits of the company in calculating corporation tax payable. The after-tax cost to the company in the year to 31 March 1997 may be either 67%, 76% or 64.75% depending on whether the company is paying tax at 33%, 24% or the marginal small companies rate of 35.25%. The cost may indeed be 100% if the company has no taxable profits, because in that case loss relief cannot be claimed for covenanted payments (except within a group of companies by way of group relief).

Deposited covenants

Both individuals and companies can give a charity the benefit of an immediate lump sum while retaining the tax advantages of covenants by means of a 'deposited covenant'. There are in effect two transactions:

(i) An interest-free loan repayable in four equal instalments.
(ii) A deed of covenant for four annual payments, the net amount of each covenanted payment being equal to one-quarter of the loan.

The loans must not be made before the payer makes the deed of covenant.

The annual loan repayments cover the amount due under the covenant.

The charity benefits because it has the use of the money at the outset, then reclaiming tax each year on the covenanted payments. For gifts of £250 net or more (or of any amount if made by non-close companies) the provisions outlined below will give the same tax effect without the delay in obtaining tax relief.

'Gift aid' for single gifts by individuals (FA 1990, s 25; FA 1993, s 67)

Where an individual makes a single gift to a charity of £250 or more, the payment may be treated in the same way as a charitable covenant, i.e. basic rate income tax is regarded as having been deducted and higher rate relief is given where appropriate. The individual gives the charity a certificate (R190 (SD)) to enable the charity to get the tax back. The basic rate tax may have to be accounted for to the Revenue if the donor is not entitled to keep the tax relief.

Non-covenanted donations by limited companies (TA 1988, ss 339, 339A; FA 1993, s 67)

Both close and non-close companies (see chapter 3) may claim to treat one-off donations to a charity as a charge against profits, deducting and accounting to the Revenue for tax at the basic rate, which can then be recovered by the charity (the company supplying the charity with a certificate (form R240(SD)) for this purpose). For close companies, this relief is only available where the gift after deducting income tax is at least £250. There is no minimum for a non-close company.

Payroll deduction scheme — Give As You Earn (TA 1988, ss 86A, 202; FA 1993, s 69; FA 1996, s 109)

Employees can authorise participating employers to deduct up to £1,200 per annum (£900 per annum before 6 April 1996) from their earnings before tax, for passing on to charities chosen by the employee, through charity agencies with which the employer has made an arrangement. The employee thus receives full tax relief for the contributions made. If the agency runs the scheme for the employer, voluntary payments to the agency by the employer to cover running costs are allowed against the employer's taxable profits.

Capital gains tax (TCGA 1992, s 257)

Gifts of chargeable assets to charities are exempt from capital gains tax, so neither chargeable gain nor allowable loss will arise. Alternatively, the asset can be sold and the proceeds given to the charity. If a loss would arise, selling the asset would establish the allowable loss and the cash could then be given to the charity, either under the 'gift aid' provisions or, if the cash gift is less than £250, by way of deposited covenant (see above). Even if the sale of the asset would result in a chargeable gain, a tax saving compared with giving the asset would still be made if the charity was given the balance of the cash after payment of the capital gains tax, provided that the net gift was at least £250, because tax would be saved under gift aid on the amount of the gift. (The same saving could be made on a smaller gift by way of deposited covenant, but there would be a cash flow disadvantage both to the charity and to a higher rate taxpayer, who would only get the extra tax saving year by year rather than in the year the gift was made.) See example 2.

Example 2

Chargeable asset would realise £3,000 net of expenses, and the gain would be £500. Assume taxpayer has a marginal tax rate of 40% and has used his annual exemption.

If asset is given to charity

Charity receives value of £3,000 (adjusted for expenses). Donor's tax position not affected.

If asset is sold and net proceeds given to charity under gift aid

Tax on gain is £500 @ 40% = £200, so net proceeds are £2,800. This represents a gift of £3,684 from which tax of £884 has been deducted, which the charity can reclaim. The donor is entitled to higher rate relief, less basic rate already retained, so he will save tax of £3,684 @ 16% = £589. Both the charity and the donor are better off than if the asset had been given.

Had the donor been a basic rate taxpayer, he would make no extra tax saving but the charity would still receive a larger sum.

Inheritance tax (IHTA 1984, ss 23, 58, 70, 76)

All gifts to charity are exempt whether made in lifetime, on death or out of a discretionary trust.

Where the charity is a discretionary trust, inheritance tax will not be payable by the trustees unless property leaving the trust is used for a non-charitable purpose.

Employees seconded to charities (TA 1988, s 86)

The salaries of employees temporarily seconded to charities, local education authorities or other approved educational bodies may be deducted as a business expense even though, because of the secondment, the salaries are not paid wholly and exclusively for the purposes of the trade.

Intermediary charities

Individuals and companies may want to give regularly to several charities, but may not want to commit themselves to a four-year covenant to any one of them. Apart from making one-off payments under the 'gift aid' provisions (see page 596), there are two ways of achieving this and still retaining the tax advantages. The simplest way is to make payments to an intermediary organisation such as the Charities Aid Foundation, either by covenant or as a gift aid payment. You can tell the organisation which particular charities you want to benefit. Alternatively, and especially where the size of the covenant is more significant, it is possible for individuals or companies to set up their own intermediary charity. A simple charitable trust whose objects include all the four charitable heads (see page 591) can be set up relatively easily although it is essential to have proper professional advice. Additionally, for small amounts, the payroll deduction scheme may enable the recipient charity to be varied.

Abuse of charity tax reliefs (TA 1988, ss 505, 506 and Sch 20)

A charity's tax relief may be restricted if it uses its funds for non-charitable purposes, or makes payments to overseas bodies without taking reasonable steps to ensure that they are used for charitable purposes, or makes certain loans or investments for tax avoidance rather than for the benefit of the charity. Where a charity receives a grant from another charity, the grant is chargeable to tax, but will be exempt if used for charitable purposes. Covenanted payments by a company to its parent charity must be paid net of tax, and that tax must be accounted for to the Revenue, although the tax will be recoverable by the parent charity if the parent satisfies the conditions for exemption.

Tax points

● If you set up your own charitable trust, the trustees must not profit from their position or allow their duties and responsibilities to conflict with their personal interests. You can, however, appoint a professional trustee, such as a solicitor or accountant, and an appropriate charging clause in the trust deed will enable his fees to be paid.

● If you are a higher rate taxpayer and make a deposited covenant, the relief at the higher rate is not given all at once but only as each annual payment is made by taking it from the loan. For a gift under the gift aid provisions, higher rate relief is given in the year in which the gift is made.

- Deeds of covenant from individuals do not have to be sent with a charity's claim for the refund of tax deducted from its income, but they must be kept for inspection by the Revenue.

- The Revenue will check that covenanted payments have actually been received by the charity. Charities receiving regular amounts in cash (notably church collections) must have a system that demonstrates that the covenanted amounts have been received.

- For the paying company to get relief from corporation tax for an accounting period on a covenanted payment, the payment must be made in that accounting period. Where a charity has a fund-raising subsidiary company that has covenanted its entire trading profit to the charity, the exact amount of that profit will not be known until after the end of the accounting period. The company will often make a payment to the charity during its accounting period that is more than the likely profit, recovering the overpayment from the charity later. The company will have accounted to the Revenue for the income tax deducted from the payment. If the Revenue has made an excessive tax repayment to a charity because of this, then unless it is a significant amount they are usually prepared to set it off against later repayments.

- A covenant is a legally binding obligation, and if it is not paid, the charity is entitled to take appropriate action for recovery. But where the covenantor's circumstances change, so that he has difficulty in meeting his obligations, the charity will not usually wish to pursue the right to payment, and is not obliged to do so.

  If a covenanted payment is not made, the covenantor cannot be called upon to account for the tax he would have deducted if he had made the payment, nor can the charity make a repayment claim.

- To get income tax relief for one-off gifts to charity under gift aid, you have to make a cash gift of at least £250 (treated as a gross amount of £329). For smaller gifts, you must still covenant for the minimum four-year term in order for the charity to get the tax benefit.

- If you have covenanted to a charity, you must be a taxpayer for at least as much tax as the amount you have deducted from the covenant. Tax paid by your spouse does not count. If you are caught by this, the charity will usually allow the covenant to lapse and your spouse can make a new covenant to replace it.

- 'Charity affinity cards', i.e. credit cards on which some of the money you spend goes to a charity, will not give the charity a tax liability if the money is channelled through a trading subsidiary that covenants its income to the charity. For VAT purposes, Customs and Excise has agreed that one-fifth of the income will usually be treated as liable to VAT as income from promotional activities and the remaining four-fifths will not attract VAT.

44
Subcontractors in the construction industry

Tax deduction scheme (TA 1988, ss 559–567; FA 1995, s 139 and Sch 27; FA 1996, s 178; SI 1993/743)

Changes are to be made to the subcontractors tax deduction scheme from a date to be fixed, not earlier than 1 August 1998. The proposed changes are outlined on page 601. The existing rules described below will continue to apply in the meantime.

Under the construction industry tax deduction scheme, a contractor must deduct and pay over to the Collector each month tax at a prescribed rate from any labour payment made to a subcontractor, unless that person produces a valid 'exemption certificate' (form 714), when payment can be made gross. The prescribed rate is 25% for payments up to 30 June 1996 and 24% thereafter. These rules apply whether the subcontractor is an individual, a partnership or a company. Interest is charged on underpaid tax in the same way as for PAYE (see page 165). Contractors may pay the Collector quarterly rather than monthly if they expect their average payments of PAYE, national insurance contributions and subcontractor deductions to be less than £600 a month.

Any person carrying on a business that includes construction operations is a contractor, and also any person whose expenditure on construction operations averages more than £250,000 per annum over three years.

The rules for obtaining an 'exemption certificate' are rigorous, but basically the Inspector of Taxes to whom an application is addressed must be satisfied that an individual applicant

(a) is working in the UK in the construction industry,
(b) is trading from identifiable premises,
(c) is keeping proper records to enable accounts to be prepared,
(d) has a continuous period of working in the UK of three years in the six years immediately prior to the application (but a six-month period of unemployment within the three-year qualifying period may be ignored),
(e) has a bank account through which the business is substantially conducted, and

(f) has paid all tax and national insurance due and has kept his tax affairs satisfactorily up-to-date.

Exemption certificates have up to now been issued for a standard three-year period. Conditions for certificates under the new rules will be more rigorous, so all certificates issued from January 1995 until early 1998 will show an expiry date of 31 July 1998.

A special certificate (form 714S) is available which allows payments of up to £150 per week to be made gross to individuals who may not satisfy condition (d) above because of their age, i.e. students leaving school, college or higher education, and to certain other individual applicants providing the Revenue with a bank guarantee in a standard form prescribed by the Revenue. The amount of the guarantee is £2,500 for each year in which the special certificate is valid.

Individuals who do not themselves satisfy the conditions cannot hide behind a limited company which has a clean taxation record. The legislation enables the Revenue to look behind the company to its shareholders and officers in determining whether a certificate should be issued.

There is a right of appeal against a Revenue refusal to issue a certificate.

Where a subcontractor holds a certificate, he supplies the contractor with a voucher (715) for every payment received (except where the subcontractor is a company holding exemption certificate 714C).

Where a subcontractor does not hold a certificate and tax is deducted from the labour content of payments to him, the payer must issue a certificate of earnings and tax deducted (form SC60). Form SC60 is also required for payments in excess of £150 to someone holding form 714S. The subcontractor is entitled to this certificate at the end of each of his contracts for his main contractor, and also at each 5 April for a contract that straddles that date. The earnings are brought into the self-employed accounts of the subcontractor, and the tax deducted becomes a payment on account of the tax due. The deduction of tax by the contractor does not absolve the subcontractor from preparing accounts and submitting returns, and if his liability is greater than the tax deducted there is the possibility of interest and penalties if he has not complied with time limits for submission of returns and payment of tax.

Proposed changes

Changes to the scheme were introduced in the 1995 Finance Act, to come into force on or after 1 August 1998. To qualify for a certificate, an applicant will have to have complied promptly with his tax obligations for the previous three years, and will not be able simply to get up to date before applying. Even if they meet all other criteria, subcontractors will need to have a turnover in excess of a prescribed level to be entitled to gross payment, which will limit the scheme to larger businesses. Those without certificates will have tax deducted at a lower rate than the basic rate, to take account of tax rates and allowances. The school leaver's certificate 714S will be discontinued. It will no longer be necessary for an applicant to have been employed or self-employed for a three-year qualifying period, but evidence will be required of periods of unemployment, full-time education or residence abroad. The procedure for 715 vouchers and SC60s will be standardised, and one voucher or SC60 may cover all payments under a contract within a quarterly period (or shorter period to or from the subcontractor's accounting date). Tax vouchers under the scheme will be similar to credit card vouchers, with copies sent to the Revenue. Larger payers with appropriate computer systems will be able to provide information in non-paper form. The threshold for treating those outside the construction industry as contractors will be raised from £250,000 to £1,000,000.

It has been decided that, under the revised scheme, subcontractors without exemption certificates will be required to have registration cards carrying their name, photograph, tax reference, and probably their national insurance number. This will assist in the deduction arrangements, and will enable subcontractors to obtain quicker repayments.

Provisional half-yearly payments on account of tax liabilities under the self-assessment rules should not be required if the subcontractor's income arises mainly in the building industry, as his tax deductions will be credited automatically to his account with the Revenue.

Employed or self-employed?

The fact that someone holds a subcontractor's exemption certificate does not mean that he is self-employed in any work he undertakes. The Revenue and the DSS have issued a special version of their combined leaflet IR148/CA69 'Are your workers employed or self-employed?' for contractors in the construction industry, which outlines the factors to be taken into account.

Tax points

- Since basic rate tax is presently deducted from the full labour content of a payment to a subcontractor, an overpayment will normally arise because of the expenses of the trade and the personal allowances and 20% tax rate band available. This can only be obtained by submitting accounts and returns.

- The definition of the construction industry is wide. Contractors who should have applied the scheme, but have not, may find themselves accountable for the tax which should have been deducted plus interest. Fringe trades should check the legislation to see if they are included.

- If you hold an exemption certificate you will have given your main contractor a receipt from the book supplied by the Revenue (715 voucher), giving details of his payments to you. Make sure that your annual trading accounts can be reconciled to those receipts.

- If you have an exemption certificate or are seeking one, it is imperative that you file your tax returns and business accounts promptly, since you may otherwise be disadvantaged when you apply for the renewal of your existing certificate or the issue of one for the first time, and without the certificate, the contractors for whom you work will have no alternative but to deduct the appropriate amount of tax.

- Although a subcontractor without an exemption certificate is not in the long run disadvantaged because any tax deducted from him is taken into account in what further tax he has to pay or what may be repaid to him, there is a short term cash-flow disadvantage which often discourages someone who is unemployed from taking up self-employment because condition (d) on page 600 cannot be satisfied. Whilst this is unfortunate, there is usually nothing you can do about it. This condition will no longer apply when the new rules are introduced on or after 1 August 1998, but see next tax point.

- Although it will no longer be necessary to have a three-year employed/self-employed qualifying period to be eligible for an exemption certificate under the new rules to be introduced on or after 1 August 1998, you will have to provide evidence that your turnover is likely to reach a prescribed level. This will make the scheme unavailable to a large number of people. On the other hand, the rate at which tax will be deducted if you don't qualify will be broadly equal to the average rate of tax and Class 4 NIC paid by subcontractors, rather than the full basic rate.

- Exemption certificates under the existing rules will expire before the new rules start, so that existing holders will have to meet the new requirements.

- Contractors should be sure that the terms under which workers operate bring them within the self-employed category if they are to treat them as subcontractors. If workers are wrongly classified, the contractor could be held liable for the PAYE tax that should have been deducted, plus employers' and employees' national insurance contributions, and possibly penalties as well.

45
Main anti-avoidance provisions

Background

In addition to a wide range of specific anti-avoidance measures, the Revenue's powers to counter what they see as unacceptable ways of avoiding tax have been significantly strengthened by various court decisions. Schemes which include steps inserted purely for tax avoidance are almost certain to prove unsuccessful, although bona fide commercial arrangements will usually be effective provided that they do not breach any of the specific provisions.

The legislation relating to tax avoidance, and its interpretation in the courts, is necessarily complex, and what follows is only a brief indication. In addition to these specific provisions, much recent legislation granting reliefs has anti-avoidance measures within it, e.g. demergers, companies purchasing their own shares and the enterprise investment scheme. (These reliefs are dealt with in chapter 29.) There are also specific provisions penalising transactions that are aimed at artificially increasing the amounts that escape tax on the introduction of self-assessment (see page 293). Most anti-avoidance legislation enables the Revenue to obtain information from third parties.

A significant part of the legislation is intended to prevent what is really income being taxed as a capital gain. Despite capital gains now being taxed at income tax rates, the distinction between income and capital remains important (e.g. for capital gains tax retirement relief, exchange of shares when a company is taken over, etc.). On the other hand, income can be sheltered by, for example, a purchase of property in an enterprise zone, whereas a capital gain cannot, so that in certain circumstances, a capital gain may be less attractive than income, thereby turning some of the anti-avoidance legislation to the advantage of the taxpayer.

Stripping income from securities (TA 1988, ss 703–709)

Where in consequence of a transaction in securities a person has obtained a tax advantage, then unless he shows that the transaction was for bona fide commercial reasons or in the course of making or managing investments, and that none of the transactions had as their main object, or one of their main objects, the realising of a tax advantage, that tax advantage may be nullified.

These provisions have been used particularly where elaborate schemes have been devised with the aim of extracting the undistributed profits of companies in a capital form. In view of the far reaching implications there is an appropriate clearance procedure which it is wise to follow wherever shares are being sold in closely controlled companies with significant distributable reserves.

The Revenue are also using either these provisions or the general 'series of transactions with a tax-avoidance motive' approach to attack schemes under which a group parent company seeks to avoid paying ACT that it will be unable to recover in the short term by arranging to receive dividends with tax credits attached, either from a newly-acquired subsidiary with the facility to carry back ACT or from an existing subsidiary with such a facility. Specific provisions have now been introduced to block the carry-back of ACT in newly-acquired subsidiaries (see page 606). The Revenue gave their views on when they may seek to use Section 703 in their November 1992 Tax Bulletin.

Avoiding income on securities (TA 1988, ss 729–738)

Someone who habitually times their sales of securities so that income is not received but is reflected in a capital surplus on sale may be treated as having received the income that has accrued on a day-to-day basis, and be charged to tax at the excess of higher rate tax over the basic rate. These provisions only apply to equities and preference shares, because interest is in any event treated as accruing on a day-to-day basis where other securities are sold, whether the sales have been habitual or not, under the provisions of the accrued income scheme — see page 497. There are provisions to ensure that the legislation does not inhibit the properly controlled operation of the financial markets.

There are also provisions preventing the purchase and sale of securities being used to create tax allowable trading losses or to enable tax-exempt persons to claim repayments.

Securities issued at a discount (FA 1996, Sch 13)

For private investors, special provisions apply to securities issued at a 'deep' discount. These are outlined on page 533. The provisions no longer apply to companies from 1 April 1996 because new rules have been introduced dealing with all of a company's 'loan relationships' (see page 27).

Change in ownership of a company

Trading losses and surplus ACT (TA 1988, ss 245, 245A, 245B, 768, 768A, 769; FA 1993, s 81)

Carry-forward of trading losses and surplus ACT is prevented where within a period of three years there is both a change in ownership of a company and a major change in the nature or conduct of its trade. The rules also apply where ownership changes after activities have sunk to a low level and before any significant revival. Similar provisions apply to prevent trading losses and surplus ACT of an accounting period ending *after* the change of ownership being carried back to an accounting period beginning *before* the change.

To prevent a company circumventing these rules by surrendering ACT to a subsidiary before the surrendering company's trade changes, the subsidiary cannot carry the surrendered ACT forward if a major change in the trade of the parent company occurs within the six years commencing three years before the change of ownership of the parent company.

A further restriction prevents a company buying a company with unrelieved ACT and transferring to it assets that are about to be sold at a capital gain. ACT on distributions made before the company is purchased cannot be set against tax on gains on assets transferred to the company on a no gain/no loss basis if they are disposed of within three years after the change of ownership. This provision is not linked to any major change in the business of either company.

The Revenue have issued a Statement of Practice (SP 10/91) giving their interpretation of a 'major change in the nature or conduct of a trade'.

Capital loss buying (TCGA 1992, s 177A and Sch 7A; FA 1993, s 88 and Sch 8; FA 1994, ss 93(8)–(10), 94)

Very detailed and complex provisions have been introduced to counter the practice in groups of companies of avoiding tax on capital gains by acquiring a company with capital losses and using the inter-group no gain/no loss rules to transfer assets to the purchased company before disposing of them outside the group. The provisions broadly restrict relief for unused losses brought forward at the time the company joins the group, and also for later losses on the disposal of assets owned by the company at that time, to gains on assets owned by the company before it joined the group, or acquired later (other than from a group company) for use in a pre-existing trade.

Schemes to avoid corporation tax liabilities (TA 1988, ss 767A, 767B; FA 1994, s 135)

There are provisions to counteract schemes under which a company's trading assets are transferred to another group company prior to the sale of the first company and the new owners strip the company of the remaining cash assets, leaving the company unable to pay its corporation tax. Corporation tax liabilities arising before the sale of a company may in prescribed circumstances be collected from the previous owners.

Sale of subsidiaries (TA 1988, Sch 18; TCGA 1992, ss 31–33, 170)

There are provisions to prevent companies reducing or eliminating capital gains by reducing the value of a subsidiary before its sale. Where unrealised gains are distributed by a subsidiary to its parent company as group income (on which no ACT has to be accounted for) prior to the sale of the subsidiary, the parent company is treated as if it had received additional consideration of an equivalent amount.

There are also provisions to prevent companies retaining a subsidiary within a group for capital gains purposes by means of issuing special types of shares, while selling commercial control of the company.

Dual resident companies (TA 1988, s 404; TCGA 1992, ss 139, 160, 171, 175, 188; FA 1994, ss 249–251)

Where an investment company is resident both in the UK and in another country, that company cannot surrender losses, charges, etc. under the group relief provisions (see page 40). Such companies are also unable to take advantage of the various capital allowances provisions that would normally prevent transfers to them being treated as being at open market value.

Where a company is treated as resident in another country rather than in the UK under a 'tie-breaker' clause in a double tax agreement, it is treated from 30 November 1993 as non-resident for UK tax purposes, even if it was incorporated in the UK. A company caught by this change will not, however, be treated as disposing of its assets for capital gains purposes under the provisions outlined on page 574 if they were exempt under the double tax agreement. If they were not, payment of tax will be deferred until the company actually disposes of the assets, or until 30 November 1999 if earlier.

Controlled foreign companies (TA 1988, ss 747–756 and Schs 24–26; FA 1993, s 119; FA 1994, s 134; FA 1996, s 182 and Sch 36)

Complicated legislation enables the Revenue to direct that a UK resident company be charged to tax in respect of the profits of a foreign company if the foreign company is under overall UK control, and pays tax in its country of residence at less than three-quarters of the amount that a UK resident company would pay, where the UK company and associates have at least a 10% stake in the foreign company. No Revenue direction will be made if the foreign company satisfies one or more of certain tests as to acceptable distribution policy, exempt activities, public quotation or motive, or if its profits for a twelve-month period were less than £20,000. The acceptable level of distributions was previously 50% of accounting profits, but for accounting periods commencing on or after 28 November 1995 it is 90% of taxable profits net of capital gains and foreign tax. A clearance procedure is available to non-trading controlled foreign companies.

Offshore funds (TA 1988, ss 757–764 and Schs 27, 28; FA 1989, s 140; FA 1995, s 134; FA 1996, Sch 10 paras 4, 7)

Gains on disposals of material interests in offshore funds by persons resident or ordinarily resident in the UK attract an income tax charge under Schedule D, Case VI instead of a capital gains tax charge, unless the offshore fund operates a full distribution policy (broadly 85% of its income). The income tax charge also arises on interests held at the taxpayer's death.

Where an investor switches from one class of investments to another, the switches are treated as disposals, and attract an income tax charge under Schedule D, Case VI or, where the fund operates a full distribution policy, a capital gains tax charge.

Transfer of assets abroad (TA 1988, ss 739–745)

The purpose of this legislation is to prevent a UK resident individual avoiding UK tax by transferring income-producing property abroad in circumstances which enable him to benefit from the property either immediately or in the future, such as a transfer to trustees of a foreign settlement made by him, of which he is a beneficiary.

Sales at artificial prices (TA 1988, ss 770–773)

Where any sales take place between persons connected with each other, including partnerships and companies, at a price other than open market value, then, if the Revenue so direct, the sale price of the one and purchase price of the other must be adjusted to the open market value for tax purposes. This is mainly directed at transfer pricing between the UK and overseas and does not apply where both parties are trading within the UK and the amount paid is a taxable receipt of one and allowable expense of the other. If the price is excessive, however, the payer may have difficulty proving that the expenditure is 'wholly and exclusively' for the purposes of the trade. (See also page 274 re sale of stock when a trade ceases.)

Transactions between associated dealing and non-dealing companies (TA 1988, s 774)

This section prevents abuse through transfer of assets by denying relief to one company where no taxable profit arises in the other.

Disguising income from personal activities as capital (TA 1988, s 775)

This prevents those with high personal earning potential, such as entertainers, contracting their services to a company in which they hold the shares and thereby turning income into capital by later selling the shares at a price reflecting the personal earnings.

Artificial transactions in land (TA 1988, ss 776–778)

The aim of this provision is 'to prevent the avoidance of income tax by persons connected with land or the development of land'. It enables land transactions to be taxed as trading or other income instead of as a capital gain.

Sale and lease-back of land (TA 1988, ss 779, 780)

Where land is sold and leased back, the deduction allowed for rent is limited to a commercial rent. A sale at an excessive price (subject to capital gains tax) cannot therefore be compensated by an excessive rent payment allowable for income tax.

Further, if a short lease (less than 50 years) is sold and leased back for 15 years or less, part of the sale price is treated as income, that part being $(16-n)/15$ where n is the term of the new lease.

Leases other than land (TA 1988, ss 781–785)

Capital gains may in certain circumstances be treated as income, and rent payable is limited to a commercial rent.

Individuals carrying on leasing trades (TA 1988, s 384; CAA 1990, s 42)

Losses arising from capital allowances in a leasing trade may only be set against non-leasing income if the loss arose in a trade to which the individual devotes substantially the whole of his time and which has been carried on for a continuous period of six months.

Where assets are leased outside the UK, the writing-down allowance is reduced from the normal 25% to 10%. There are also limitations placed on the nature of the lease.

Relief for interest (TA 1988, ss 786, 787)

There are provisions to block the artificial creation of allowable interest and to prevent tax relief being obtained on interest that would not otherwise qualify for tax relief by means of various devices such as converting the interest into an annuity.

Other measures

There are also measures to counter avoidance in the following circumstances.

Companies leaving a group and taking out a chargeable asset acquired intra-group on a no loss/no gain basis within the previous six years (TCGA 1992, ss 178–181; FA 1993, s 89; FA 1995, s 49).

Claiming group relief for losses when arrangements exist where a company may leave the group (TA 1988, s 410).

Timing a company's entry to or exit from a group so that a time-apportioned split of the accounting period does not give a fair result in arriving at the set-off of profits/trading losses within the group under the group relief provisions (TA 1988, s 409).

Transfers of plant and machinery between associated persons in order to obtain capital allowances (CAA 1990, s 75).

Losses arising from depreciatory transactions, e.g. dividend-stripping (TCGA 1992, ss 176, 177).

Loss relief arising from dealings in commodity futures (TA 1988, s 399).

Value passing out of shares, which could have been avoided by a controlling shareholder (TCGA 1992, s 30).

Individuals realising capital gains abroad through a non-resident close company (TCGA 1992, s 13; FA 1996, s 174).

Transferring relief for partnership losses which would otherwise relate to a partner who is a company (TA 1988, s 116).

Annual payments for non-taxable consideration (TA 1988, s 125).

Transfer of chargeable assets on which holdover relief for capital gains tax is obtained into dual resident trusts (TCGA 1992, s 169).

Loans to participators in closely controlled companies (see chapter 12).

Abuse of life assurance reliefs and exemptions (see chapter 40).

Non-resident trusts (see chapter 41).

Residence of companies (see chapter 41).

Deemed disposal of assets at time of ceasing to be a UK resident company (see chapter 41).

Deemed disposal of assets when a non-resident carrying on business through a UK branch or agency removes assets from the UK, or ceases to carry on the branch or agency (see chapter 41).

Transferring income from parents to minor children (see chapters 33 and 42).

Subject index

This index lists the main subject matter referred to in the text. It does not include matters of general application (such as payment dates or bases of assessment) for which reference should be made to the Contents list at the front of the book for the chapter on the appropriate tax.

Page numbers in **bold type** indicate a chapter, or a substantial part thereof, dealing with the subject matter in question. Again, reference may be made to the Contents list for main headings within such chapters.

Reference should be made also to the 'Tax points' at the end of a chapter where appropriate.

Notes

TAXATION PUBLICATIONS

Tax Reference Annuals –

Tolley's Income Tax 1996-97 £37.95

Tolley's Corporation Tax 1996-97 £34.95

Tolley's Capital Gains Tax 1996-97 £34.95

Tolley's Inheritance Tax 1996-97 £29.95

Tolley's Value Added Tax 1996-97 £33.95

Tolley's National Insurance Contributions 1996-97 £39.95

Looseleafs

Manual of Accounting £95.00 approx

Accountancy Litigation Support £120.00 approx

Form and Content of Financial Statements £45.00

Charities Manual £99.50

Tax on Transactions £95.00 approx

VAT on Construction Land and Property £45.00

Tax Periodicals

Audit Briefing £79 p.a.

Tolley's Practical Tax £123 p.a.

Taxation £112 p.a.

Tolley's National Insurance Brief £135 p.a.

Tax Sources

Tolley's Tax Tables 1997-98 £13.95 approx

Tolley's Tax Data 1996-97 £17.95

Tolley's Tax Cases 1995 £35.95

Tolley's Tax Office Directory 1997 £11.95 approx

Tax Planning

Tolley's Tax Planning 1996-97 £74.50 (2 volumes)

Tolley's Estate Planning 1996-97 £39.95

Tolley's Tax Planning for Family Companies £34.95

General Tax Guides

Financial Management Handbook £49.95 approx

Share Valuation £44.95 approx

Professional Partnership Handbook £35.95

Tolley's Guide to Self-Assessment for the Self-Employed £18.95

Tolley's Guide to Self-Assessment for Employers and Employees £18.95

Tolley's Accounting Principles for Tax Purposes £42.95 approx

Tolley's Self-Assessment £39.95

Tolley's Tax Guide 1996-97 £24.95 (pre-pub offer)

Specialist Tax Guides

Tolley's Taxation of Lloyds Underwriters £59.95 approx

Treasury Management Handbook £85.00 approx

Tax Indemnities and Warranties £75.00 approx

Fund Raising for Charity £35.95

Taxation of Securities and Financial Instruments £49.95

Double Taxation Relief £39.95 approx

Tolley's Taxation in Corporate Insolvency £39.95

Tolley's Taxation of Foreign Exchange Gains and Losses £49.95 (pre-pub offer)

Tolley's Property Taxes 1996-97 £39.95 approx

Tolley's Stamp Duties and Stamp Duty Reserve Tax £33.95

Tolley's Purchase and Sale of a Private Company's Shares £39.95 approx

Tolley's UK Taxation of Trusts £41.95 approx

Business Tax

Tolley's Tax on Business Profits (Formerly Taxation of Trades and Professions) £49.95 approx

Tolley's Capital Allowances 1996-97 £33.95

Tolley's Roll-over, Hold-over and Retirement Reliefs £42.95

Tolley's Partnership Taxation £36.95

Employee Taxation

Tolley's Taxation of Employments £34.95

Value Added Tax

Tolley's VAT Planning 1996-97 £39.95

Tolley's Practical VAT (Newsletter) £113 p.a.

Tolley's VAT Cases 1996 £64.50

Tolley's VAT and Duties Appeals £29.95

Tax Computations

Tolley's Tax Computations 1996-97 £38.95

Tolley's Taxwise I 1996-97 £27.95

Tolley's Taxwise II 1996-97 £26.95

Overseas Tax

Tolley's International Tax Planning (2 volumes) £99.50

Tolley's Tax Havens £54.50

Tolley's Taxation of Offshore Trusts and Funds £65.00 approx

Tolley's Taxation in the Republic of Ireland 1996-97 £32.95

Tolley's Taxation in the Channel Islands and Isle of Man 1996-97 £32.95

Client and Adviser Guides

Client and Adviser Guide: Hotels £34.95

Client and Adviser Guide: Housing Associations £34.95

Client and Adviser Guide: Charities £34.95

FREE

to all purchasers of Tolley's Tax Guide 1996-97

Tax Bulletin

This valuable 12 page publication (Available in early 1997) includes highlights of the 1997 Finance Bill and a useful year end tax planner which identifies those financial areas which should be reviewed before the end of the fiscal year and restructured, if necessary, in order to minimise tax liabilities.

How to order

To order your free Tax Bulletin and other Tolley Tax books (See previous page for details), simply complete the order form below and post today, FREEPOST, at the address shown. We look forward to hearing from you.

ORDER FORM   COMPLETE AND RETURN TODAY

To: Tolley Publishing Company Ltd., FREEPOST, Tolley House, 2 Addiscombe Road, Croydon, Surrey CR9 5WZ
or call Customer Services Department on 0181-686 9141

Delivery: Thank you for your order – your copy(ies) will be despatched to you as a matter of urgency upon publication.

Tolley Tax books
Please list the titles that you require on the form below:

Title	No. of copies	Price	Amount £
		Total £	

SIGNATURE _____ Date _____

Surname _____ Initials _____ Title (Mr, Mrs, Miss, Ms) _____

Job Title _____ Telephone _____

Full Name of Firm *(if applicable)* _____

Address _____

_____ Postcode _____

Type of Organisation/Business _____
Number of Employees A ☐ 1-5 B ☐ 6-50 C ☐ 51-200 D ☐ 201-1000 E ☐ 1000+

Registered No.729731 England   VAT Registered No.243 3583 67

Tolley

Please tick to request further information	
Tolley Catalogue 1995-96	☐
Details of Tolley Conferences	☐
Details of Practice Development Services	☐

Please tick

FREE Tax Bulletin
Please send me my FREE Tax Bulletin including the highlights of the 1997 Finance Bill ☐

Choice of payment method:

Cheque enclosed £_____

Please make cheques payable to:
Tolley Publishing Company Ltd.

Please debit Tolley/Access/Visa† Account No.

[   ]

† *Please delete as necessary*

Expiry Date

[/   ]
Month Year

Please enter name and address of cardholder

Name _____

Address _____

_____

_____ Postcode _____

Please enter Tolley Account number if applicable

[   ]